Strategic Compensation

FIFTH EDITION

STRATEGIC COMPENSATION

A Human Resource Management Approach

Joseph J. Martocchio

University of Illinois at Urbana-Champaign

PEARSON

Prentice
Hall

Upper Saddle River, New Jersey 07458

Library of Congress Cataloging-in-Publication Data

Martocchio, Joseph J.
    Strategic compensation : a human resource management approach/Joseph J.
Martocchio.—5th ed.
        p. cm.
    ISBN-13: 978-0-13-600744-9 (hbk.)
    ISBN-10: 0-13-600744-9 (hbk.)
    1. Compensation management.   I. Title.
    HF5549.5.C67M284 2009
    658.3'22—dc22

                                                                        2007050115

Editor-in-Chief: David Parker
Product Development Manager: Ashley Santora
Editorial Assistant: Elizabeth Davis
Marketing Manager: Nikki Jones
Marketing Assistant: Ian Gold
Senior Managing Editor, Production: Judy Leale
Associate Managing Editor, Production: Suzanne DeWorken
Production Project Manager: Carol Samet
Permissions Coordinator: Charles Morris
Senior Operations Specialist: Arnold Vila
Cover Design: Bruce Kenselaar
Cover Illustration/Photo: Colin Anderson/Blend Images/Getty Images, Inc.
Composition: Integra
Full-Service Project Management: Thistle Hill Publishing Services, LLC
Printer/Binder: Hamilton
Typeface: 10/12 Times Ten Roman

Credits and acknowledgments borrowed from other sources and reproduced, with permission, in this textbook appear on appropriate page within the text.

Pearson Education LTD.
Pearson Education Singapore, Pte. Ltd
Pearson Education, Canada, Ltd
Pearson Education—Japan

Pearson Education Australia PTY, Limited
Pearson Education North Asia Ltd
Pearson Educación de Mexico, S.A. de C.V.
Pearson Education Malaysia, Pte. Ltd.

10 9 8 7 6 5 4
ISBN-13: 978-0-13-600744-9
ISBN-10:   0-13-600744-9

To my mother Rose.
Who taught me that anything is possible when you
work hard and smart enough for it.

Brief Contents

Contents

Preface

Companies' success in the marketplace is as much a function of the way business practitioners manage employees as it is a function of companies' structures and financial resources. Compensating employees represents a critical human resource management practice: Without sound compensation systems, companies cannot attract and retain the best-qualified employees.

Compensation systems can promote companies' competitive advantage when they are properly aligned with strategic goals. Compensation practices can also undermine competitive advantage when they are designed and implemented haphazardly. The title of this book—*Strategic Compensation: A Human Resource Management Approach*—reflects the importance of employees as key elements of strategic compensation programs.

The purpose of this book is to provide knowledge of the art and science of compensation practice and its role in promoting companies' competitive advantage. Students will be best prepared to assume the roles of competent compensation professionals if they possess a grounded understanding of compensation practices and the environments in which business professionals plan, implement, and evaluate compensation systems. Thus, we examine the context of compensation practice, the criteria used to compensate employees, compensation system design issues, employee benefits, challenges of compensating key strategic employee groups, and pay and benefits around the world.

ABOUT THIS BOOK

This book contains 16 chapters, lending itself well to courses offered as 10-week quarters or 15-week semesters. The chapters are organized in six parts:

- Part I: Setting the Stage for Strategic Compensation
- Part II: Bases for Pay
- Part III: Designing Compensation Systems
- Part IV: Employee Benefits
- Part V: Compensation Challenges for Strategic Employee Groups
- Part VI: Compensation Issues Around the World

Course instructors on a 10-week schedule might consider spending about 2 weeks on each part. Instructors on a 15-week schedule might consider spending about 1 week on each chapter. Compressed 8-week schedules can accommodate 2 chapters per week.

Each chapter contains a chapter outline, learning objectives, key terms, and discussion questions. In addition, each chapter includes two features that we are putting in the hands of course instructors for this edition. The "Stretching the Dollar" and "Flip Side of the Coin" features describe challenges facing compensation professionals. These features are described in the "New to the Fifth Edition" section.

This textbook is well-suited to a variety of students, including undergraduate and master's degree students. In addition, the book was prepared for use by all business students, regardless of their majors. Both human resource management majors and other majors (e.g., accounting, finance, general management, international management, marketing, and organizational behavior) will benefit equally well from *Strategic Compensation*. After all, virtually every manager, regardless of functional area, will be involved in making compensation decisions. Practitioners beginning work in compensation or current professionals will find *Strategic Compensation* a useful reference.

NEW TO THE FIFTH EDITION

Two all-new chapters are included, raising the number of chapters to 16 altogether since the previous edition of this book:

- Chapter 12 is devoted exclusively to employer-sponsored health insurance programs and retirement plans because of the widespread attention companies are giving them as costly features of the employee benefits program. For example, we are witnessing a shift from defined benefit pension plans to defined contribution retirement plans. In addition, the Supreme Court has addressed the vexing question about whether cash balance plans are discriminatory. In the health care arena, we are dealing with a drive toward consumer-driven health care that shifts more of the financial burden from employers to employees.

- Chapter 16 is devoted to surveying compensation and benefits practices in a variety of countries around the world. In past editions, we devoted an entire chapter to expatriate pay, and still do in this edition (Chapter 15); however, as more U.S. companies outsource business to other countries, it is essential that they have knowledge of the minimum legal requirements for setting pay and benefits.

Of course, the other fifth edition chapters have been thoroughly revised to describe current issues facing compensation professionals.

AVAILABLE TEACHING AND LEARNING AIDS

The teaching and learning accessories are designed to promote a positive experience for both instructors and students. University of Illinois doctoral candidate Niti Pandey developed the Instructor's Manual and Test Item File that accompanies *Strategic Compensation*. In addition, David Barcelona and I prepared an experiential case simulation (available from Prentice Hall at *www.prenhall.com/martocchio*) titled *Building Strategic Compensation Systems* to accompany this textbook. This simulation will allow students to develop a strategic compensation plan in four stages, and to apply core knowledge about compensation systems explained in the *Strategic Compensation* textbook.

Instructor's Resource Center

At *www.prenhall.com/irc*, instructors can access a variety of print, digital, and presentation resources available with this text in downloadable format. Registration is simple and gives you immediate access to new titles and new editions. As a registered faculty member, you can download resource files and receive immediate access and instructions for installing course management content on your campus server.

If you ever need assistance, our dedicated technical support team is ready to help with the media supplements that accompany this text. Visit *www.247. prenhall.com* for answers to frequently asked questions and toll-free user support phone numbers.

The following supplements are available to adopting instructors (for detailed descriptions, please visit *www.prenhall.com/irc*:)

- **Instructor's Resource Center (IRC) on CD-ROM**—ISBN: 0-13-600104-1
- **Printed Instructor's Manual and Test Item File**—ISBN: 0-13-600099-1
- **TestGen Test Generating Software**—Available at the IRC online.
- **PowerPoint Slides**—Available at the IRC (online or on CD-ROM).

Companion Website

This text's Companion Website at *www.prenhall.com/martocchio* contains valuable resources for students, including access to a student version of the PowerPoint package an online Study Guide, and access to the experiential case simulation titled, *Building Strategic Compensation Systems.*

Accompanying Experiential Case

Building Strategic Compensation Systems will allow students to work in small compensation consulting teams charged with the responsibility for developing a compensation plan for a company named e-sonic. The project is divided into four sections, which correspond to fundamental goals of compensation practitioners as described in chapters in this textbook:

> *StrategicAnalysis:* Chapters 1 through 3
> *Section 1:* Chapter 7
> *Section 2:* Chapter 8
> *Section 3:* Chapters 4 through 6, 9, and 10 through 12

The development of a strategic analysis guides all decisions made regarding students' compensation systems throughout the project. The strategic analysis reveals firm-specific challenges, objectives, and initiatives that allow students to align the goals of a compensation system effectively with that of their company strategy.

Section I introduces students to the specification of internally consistent job structures. Through writing job descriptions, the development of job structures, and both the development and implementation of a point evaluation method to quantify job differences objectively, students build the framework for internal equity.

Section II shifts students' focus outside of their firm to understand its relationship with the external marketplace. Students will use market survey data to compare pay rates of positions inside the firm with those in the marketplace to establish the foundations of market-competitive pay. The analysis of market data also leads students to the determination of appropriate pay-policy mixes for each of their job structures.

Finally, in Section III, students will recognize the contributions of individual employees through the creation of a merit-pay system, and put their plan into action by paying employees within their firm. Hypothetical pay discrepancies are introduced to each student group for resolution within the parameters of their designed compensation system. They are tasked with many of the difficult decisions that compensation professionals face on a daily basis.

The Strategic Analysis section and Sections 1 through 3 may each be completed in 2 to 3 weeks, which fits well with semester-long courses. Instructors whose courses include a variety of additional activities or span only 7 to 10 weeks may have students complete only three of the four sections in either configuration (Strategic Analysis and Sections 1 and 2, or Sections 1 through 3). The instructor may have student groups prepare written reports or oral presentations to the class. Report outlines are included in the instructor's and student's casebook versions.

There are both an **Instructor's Manual** (available in print and on the IRC) and **Student Manual** that accompany Building Strategic Compensation Systems. The Student Manual can be value-packed at a reduced price with new copies of this text. Please contact your Pearson Sales Rep for more information on this.

CourseSmart eTextbooks Online

Developed for students looking to save money on required or recommended textbooks, CourseSmart eTextbooks Online saves students money compared to the suggested list price of the print text. Students simply select their eText by title or author and purchase immediate access to the content for the duration of the course using any major credit card. With a CourseSmart eText, students can search for specific keywords or page numbers, make notes online, print out reading assignments that incorporate lecture notes, and bookmark important passages for later review. For more information, or to purchase a CourseSmart eTextbook, visit *www.coursesmart.com.*

FEEDBACK

The authors and the product team would appreciate hearing from you! Let us know what you think about this textbook by writing to college_marketing@prenhall.com. Please include "Feedback about Martocchio 5e" in the subject line.

For any questions related to this product, please contact our customer service department online at *www.247.prenhall.com.*

ACKNOWLEDGMENTS

Many individuals made valuable contributions to the first three editions. I am indebted to the reviewers who provided thoughtful remarks on chapter drafts during the development of this textbook:

Martha Andrews, Florida State University

Eric Austin, Alltel Co. (University of Central Arkansas)

Cam Caldwell, Washington State University

Shawn Carraher, Indiana University–Gary

Robert Figler, University of Akron

Daniel Hoyt, Arkansas State University

Deborah Knapp, Cleveland State University

Maria Kraimer, Melbourne University

LaVelle Mills, West Texas A&M University

Lyle Schoenfeldt, Appalachian State University

Steve Thomas, Southwest Missouri State University

As in past editions, I thank Margaret Chaplan and Katie Dorsey. Margaret Chaplan, a labor librarian, provided invaluable assistance by sharing her wealth of knowledge. Katie Dorsey, a library clerk, also offered excellent reference assistance.

At Prentice Hall, I thank the following individuals for their guidance and expertise: David Parker, Ashley Santora, and Nikki Jones. Many other professionals worked behind the scenes in the design, marketing, and production of this edition. I thank each and every one of those individuals for their contributions.

Joseph J. Martocchio

CHAPTER I

Strategic Compensation
A Component of Human Resource Systems

Chapter Outline

- Exploring and Defining the Compensation Context
  What Is Compensation?
  Core Compensation
  Employee Benefits

- A Historical Perspective on Compensation: The Road Toward Strategic Compensation

- Strategic versus Tactical Decisions
  Competitive Strategy Choices
  Tactical Decisions That Support the Firm's Strategy

- Compensation Professionals' Goals
  How HR Professionals Fit into the Corporate Hierarchy
  How the Compensation Function Fits into HR Departments
  The Compensation Department's Main Goals

- Stakeholders of the Compensation System

- Summary

- Key Terms

- Discussion Questions

- Exercises

- Endnotes

Learning Objectives

In this chapter, you will learn

1. Basic compensation concepts and the context of compensation practice

2. A historical perspective on compensation—from an administrative function to a strategic function

3. The difference between strategic and tactical compensation

4. Compensation professionals' goals within a human resource department

5. How compensation professionals relate to various stakeholders

For most of the twentieth century, the predecessor to contemporary human resource management practices was initially referred to as manpower planning or personnel management. In the earlier part of that century, manpower planning often focused on the effective deployment of employees in factories to achieve the highest manufacturing output per employee per unit of time. For instance, management sought to increase the number of handmade garments per hour.

Extensive government regulation involving payroll taxes, minimum wage laws, and antidiscrimination laws later gave rise to the personnel management function. Legal compliance necessitated that personnel management take on the role of an administrative, support function to maintain compliance with the myriad details of the laws (i.e., determining what equal work is and the prevailing wage in specific localities). Since the 1970s, there has been widespread recognition that managing employees or human resources can contribute to company success. Administrative efficiency of the personnel functions (i.e., recruiting, performance appraisal, compensating employees) certainly contributes indirectly to company success through cost control.

In recent years, researchers and HR practitioners have worked steadily to quantify the impact of managing human resources on business success in terms of such outcomes as innovation, higher sales, product quality, exemplary customer service, and so forth. Some have described the evolving HR professional's role from compliance (policing) to consultation with a carpenter's eye toward quality HR system design. Designing HR practices with business outcomes in mind is a necessary first step, and compensation plays an important role in contributing to successful business outcomes:

> The number one factor that will restrict a company's growth in the next decade is its inability to attract and retain employees. While many people perceive this statement as a given, the compensation profession has not responded. Human resources executives report that only about half of their companies' rewards strategies are linked to business or people strategies. This has powerful implications for compensation professionals, who need to rethink their roles in organizations. Management needs them to apply their expertise in a way that helps run business.
>
> Most compensation processes are geared to control managers rather than facilitate their success. Examples of control are top-down salary and merit budgets, job evaluation schemes, salary grades, salary increase matrices, and limitations governing short- and long-term variable plans. Intended to help managers run their businesses, these processes constrain managers, as shown when they regularly push the bounds of "acceptable" practice. If HR management and business management are true partners, leaders need to be provided with tools, not rules.
>
> In the New Economy, rules need to be replaced by tools that help managers run business. The consultant's new role is that of a master compensation carpenter, who designs and teaches. To implement the role of master carpenter, compensation professionals need to:
>
> - Skillfully and creatively apply the fundamentals of their trade to build management tools that fit within the context of their businesses
> - Teach managers how to use those management tools to unleash the potential within their workforce to drive the business forward in quantum leaps
> - Let go, viewing their roles as process facilitators, not owners

The transformation from compensation consultant to master compensation carpenter requires three things:

- *A solid foundation in a company's business environment, strategy, and organizational structure, processes, and culture should exist.* One must marry that expertise with the competency to know how to design that plan according to the needs of a particular business. That deeper understanding only comes from thoroughly knowing the nuances of a company and industry, and being able to apply the sound technical knowledge.

- *A manager's toolbox should contain the tools required to run the business.* A set of tools should be created that is appropriate for the environment and allows managers to do the right thing in each unique situation. Historically, managers have been given only one tool to deal with a variety of situations across the bulk of populations—merit pay. This is akin to the master carpenter giving an apprentice a hammer and then trying to teach him to build something: Everything the apprentice looks at appears to be a nail. As a master carpenter, compensation professionals are expert builders.

- *Managers should be taught how to use each tool.* Any carpenter can build, but the master carpenter teaches. More importantly, the master carpenter teaches both the right use and application for each tool, knowing that, although he has many tools available to him, he only applies a tool appropriate for a specific time, place or situation.[1]

EXPLORING AND DEFINING THE COMPENSATION CONTEXT

The compensation function does not operate in isolation. To the contrary, it is just one component of a company's human resource system. In addition, compensation professionals interact with members of various constituencies, including union representatives and top executives. We will explore these ideas in more detail after we have introduced some fundamental compensation concepts.

What Is Compensation?

Compensation represents both the intrinsic and extrinsic rewards employees receive for performing their jobs. Together, both intrinsic and extrinsic compensation describes a company's total compensation system. This system of practices is depicted in Figure 1-1. **Intrinsic compensation** reflects employees' psychological mind-sets that result from performing their jobs. **Extrinsic compensation** includes both monetary and nonmonetary rewards. Organizational development professionals promote intrinsic compensation through effective job design. Compensation professionals are responsible for extrinsic compensation. Although extrinsic compensation is the focus of this book, we will take a moment briefly to explore the intrinsic compensation concept.

Intrinsic Compensation

Intrinsic compensation represents employees' critical psychological states that result from performing their jobs. **Job characteristics theory** describes these critical psychological states. According to this job theory, employees experience enhanced psychological states (that is, intrinsic compensation) when their jobs rate high on five core job dimensions: skill variety, task identity, task significance, autonomy, and feedback.[2] Jobs that lack these core characteristics do not provide much intrinsic

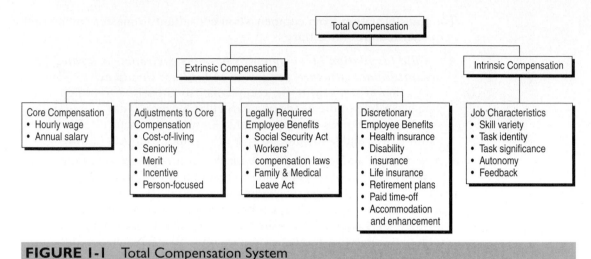

FIGURE 1-1 Total Compensation System

compensation. Figure 1-2 illustrates the influence of core job characteristics on intrinsic compensation and subsequent benefits to employers.

- Skill variety is the degree to which the job requires the person to perform different tasks and involves different skills, abilities, and talents.
- Task identity is the degree to which a job enables a person to complete an entire job from start to finish.
- Task significance is the degree to which the job has an impact on the lives or work of other people.
- Autonomy is the amount of freedom, independence, and discretion the employee enjoys in determining how to perform the job.
- Feedback is the degree to which the job or employer provides the employee with clear and direct information about job outcomes and performance.

FIGURE 1-2 The Influence of Core Job Characteristics of Intrinsic Compensation and Subsequent Benefits to Employers

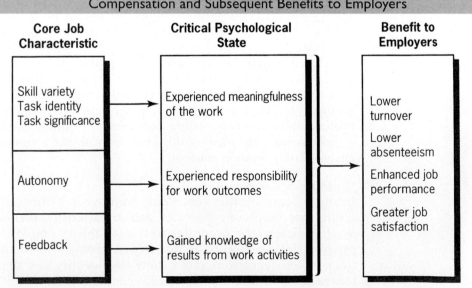

What are some examples of these critical psychological states, or intrinsic compensation? According to job characteristics theory, jobs that demand skill variety, task identity, and task significance enable employees to experience meaningfulness of work (i.e., cancer researchers). Jobs that provide autonomy lead to experienced responsibility for outcomes of work (i.e., farmers). Jobs that convey feedback enhance employees' knowledge of the actual results of their work activities, or how well they have performed (i.e, automobile salespeople). Employers ultimately hope to benefit from increased job performance, lower absenteeism, and higher employee satisfaction.

How do these characteristics translate into practice? Consider the problem of turnover of information technology employees. In general, company demand for these employees outpaces supply. Over time, base salaries and bonuses have risen dramatically to promote the recruitment and retention of the very best, but turnover continues to be a problem. Indeed, many companies believe that intrinsic compensation complements traditional pay and that the use of intrinsic compensation may help to reduce excessive turnover. Examples include new technologies, learning and training opportunities, and challenging technical environments.

Principles of intrinsic compensation also provide the basis for nonmonetary recognition awards. The importance of nonmonetary recognition programs has increased for a variety of reasons, including the smaller pay increase budgets relative to the lucrative years in the 1990s.

Extrinsic Compensation

Extrinsic compensation includes both monetary and nonmonetary rewards. Compensation professionals establish monetary compensation programs to reward employees according to their job performance levels or for learning job-related knowledge or skills. As we will discuss shortly, monetary compensation represents **core compensation**. Nonmonetary rewards include protection programs (i.e., medical insurance), paid time off (i.e, vacations), and services (i.e., day care assistance). Most compensation professionals refer to nonmonetary rewards as **employee benefits**.

Core Compensation

There are seven types of monetary, or core, compensation. The elements of base pay adjustments are listed in Table 1-1.

Base Pay

Employees receive **base pay**, or money, for performing their jobs (Chapter 8). Base pay is recurring; that is, employees continue to receive base pay as long as they remain in their jobs. Companies disburse base pay to employees in one of two forms: **hourly pay** or **wage**, or as **salary**. Employees earn hourly pay for each hour worked. They earn salaries

---

TABLE 1-1 Elements of Core Compensation

Base Pay
- Hourly pay
- Annual salary

How Base Pay Is Adjusted over Time
- Cost-of-living adjustments
- Seniority pay
- Merit pay
- Incentive pay
- Person-focused pay: pay-for-knowledge and skill-based pay

for performing their jobs, regardless of the actual number of hours worked. Companies measure salary on an annual basis. The Fair Labor Standards Act (Chapter 3) established criteria for determining whether employees should be paid hourly or by salary.

Companies typically set base pay amounts for jobs according to the level of skill, effort, and responsibility required to perform the jobs and the severity of the working conditions. Compensation professionals refer to skill, effort, responsibility, and working conditions factors as **compensable factors** because they influence pay level (Chapters 3 and 7). Courts of law use these four compensable factors to determine whether jobs are equal per the Equal Pay Act of 1963. According to the Equal Pay Act, it is against the law to pay women less than men for performing equal work. Compensation professionals use these compensable factors to help meet three pressing challenges, which we will introduce later in this chapter: internal consistency (Chapter 7), market competitiveness (Chapter 8), and recognition of individual contributions (Chapter 9).

Over time, employers adjust employees' base pay to recognize increases in the cost of living, differences in employees' performance, or differences in employees' acquisition of job-related knowledge and skills. We will discuss these core compensation elements next.

Cost-of-Living Adjustments (COLAs)

Cost-of-living adjustments (COLAs) represent periodic base pay increases that are founded on changes in prices as indexed by the consumer price index (CPI). COLAs enable workers to maintain their purchasing power and standard of living by adjusting base pay for inflation. COLAs are most common among workers represented by unions. Union leaders fought hard for these improvements to maintain their members' loyalty and support. Many employers use the CPI to adjust base pay levels for newly hired employees.

Seniority Pay

Seniority pay systems reward employees with periodic additions to base pay according to employees' length of service in performing their jobs (Chapter 4). These pay plans assume that employees become more valuable to companies with time and that valued employees will leave if they do not have a clear idea that their wages will progress over time. This rationale comes from **human capital theory**,[3] which states that employees' knowledge and skills generate productive capital known as **human capital**. Employees can develop such knowledge and skills from formal education and training, including on-the-job experience. Over time, employees presumably refine existing skills or acquire new ones that enable them to work more productively. Seniority pay rewards employees for acquiring and refining their skills as indexed by length (years) of employment.

Merit Pay

Merit pay programs assume that employees' compensation over time should be determined, at least in part, by differences in job performance (Chapter 4). Employees earn permanent increases to base pay according to their performance. Merit pay rewards excellent effort or results, motivates future performance, and helps employers retain valued employees.

Incentive Pay

Incentive pay or **variable pay** rewards employees for partially or completely attaining a predetermined work objective. Incentive pay is defined as compensation (other than base wages or salaries) that fluctuates according to employees' attainment of some standard based on a preestablished formula, individual or group goals, or company earnings (Chapter 5).

Pay-for-Knowledge Plans and Skill-Based Pay

Pay-for-knowledge plans reward managerial, service, or professional workers for successfully learning specific curricula (Chapter 6). **Skill-based pay**, used mostly for employees who perform physical work, increases these workers' pay as they master new skills (Chapter 6). Both skill- and knowledge-based pay programs reward employees for the range, depth, and types of skills or knowledge they are capable of applying productively to their jobs. This feature distinguishes pay-for-knowledge plans from merit pay, which rewards employees' job performance. Said another way, pay-for-knowledge programs reward employees for their potential to make meaningful contributions on the job.

Employee Benefits

Earlier, we noted that employee benefits represent nonmonetary rewards. Employee benefits include any variety of programs that provide paid time off, employee services, and protection programs. Companies offer many benefits on a discretionary basis. We refer to these as **discretionary benefits** (Chapters 10 and 11). In addition, the U.S. government requires most employers to provide particular sets of benefits to employees. We refer to these as **legally required benefits** (Chapter 12). Different forces led to the rise of legally required and discretionary employee benefits, which we discuss shortly.

Discretionary Benefits

The first signs of contemporary discretionary employee benefits were evident in the late 1800s when large companies such as American Express offered pension plans to employees. Most of the development in employee benefits practice for the next few decades resulted from government legislation, as previously noted. Discretionary benefits offerings became more prominent in the 1940s and 1950s due in large part to federal government restrictions placed on increasing wage levels. Employee benefits were not subject to those restrictions.

Discretionary benefits fall into three broad categories: protection programs, paid time off, and services (Chapter 11). Protection programs provide family benefits, promote health, and guard against income loss caused by such catastrophic factors as unemployment, disability, or serious illness. Not surprisingly, **paid time off** provides employees with pay for time when they are not working (i.e., vacation). **Services** provide such enhancements as tuition reimbursement and day care assistance to employees and their families.

Employers typically spend substantial amounts to pay employees and provide benefits. Table 1-2 lists the major legally required and discretionary benefits and the typical expenses incurred by employers to offer these benefits as of March 2007.[4] This table also includes the cost of wages and salaries. The costs are expressed on an hourly basis per employee. For example, in March 2007, employers characteristically spent $27.82 per employee per hour worked.

Legally Required Benefits

Legally required benefits historically provided a form of social insurance. Prompted largely by the rapid growth of industrialization in the United States during the late nineteenth and early twentieth centuries as well as the Great Depression of the 1930s, initial social insurance programs were designed to minimize the possibility of destitution for individuals who were unemployed or became severely injured while working. In addition, social insurance programs aimed to stabilize the well-being of dependent family members of injured or unemployed individuals. Further, early social insurance programs were designed to enable retirees to maintain subsistence income levels.

TABLE 1-2 Employer Costs per Hour Worked for Employee Compensation and Costs as a Percent of Total Compensation: Civilian Workers, by Major Occupational Groups, March 2007

Compensation component	All workers[1]		Management, professional, and related		Sales and office		Service	
	Cost	Percent	Cost	Percent	Cost	Percent	Cost	Percent
Total compensation............................	$27.82	100.0	$46.42	100.0	$21.01	100.0	$15.51	100.0
Wages and salaries..........................	19.47	70.0	32.89	70.9	14.93	71.1	10.95	70.6
Total benefits.................................	8.35	30.0	13.53	29.1	6.08	28.9	4.56	29.4
Paid leave....................................	1.96	7.0	3.73	8.0	1.41	6.7	.91	5.9
Vacation..............................	.92	3.3	1.70	3.7	.67	3.2	.43	2.8
Holiday................................	.64	2.3	1.20	2.6	.47	2.2	.28	1.8
Sick....................................	.30	1.1	.62	1.3	.21	1.0	.15	1.0
Other...................................	.10	.4	.21	.5	.06	.3	.05	.3
Supplemental pay..........................	.70	2.5	1.11	2.4	.48	2.3	.28	1.8
Overtime and premium[2]..............	.25	.9	.16	.3	.14	.7	.16	1.0
Shift differentials.......................	.07	.2	.11	.2	.02	.1	.06	.4
Nonproduction bonuses...............	.38	1.4	.85	1.8	.32	1.5	.07	.4
Insurance......................................	2.33	8.4	3.47	7.5	1.88	8.9	1.32	8.5
Life..	.05	.2	.08	.2	.03	.2	.02	.1
Health..	2.19	7.9	3.23	7.0	1.78	8.5	1.27	8.2
Short-term disability....................	.05	.2	.07	.2	.03	.2	.02	.1
Long-term disability....................	.04	.1	.08	.2	.03	.1	(3)	(4)
Retirement and savings..................	1.16	4.2	2.14	4.6	.65	3.1	.62	4.0
Defined benefit..........................	.71	2.6	1.29	2.8	.29	1.4	.50	3.2
Defined contribution...................	.45	1.6	.85	1.8	.35	1.7	.12	.8
Legally required benefits.................	2.21	7.9	3.07	6.6	1.66	7.9	1.43	9.2
Social Security and Medicare........	1.56	5.6	2.52	5.4	1.24	5.9	.88	5.7
Social Security[5].......................	1.24	4.5	1.98	4.3	1.00	4.7	.70	4.5
Medicare.................................	.32	1.1	.54	1.2	.24	1.2	.18	1.1
Federal unemployment insurance..	.03	.1	.02	[6]	.03	.2	.03	.2
State unemployment insurance.....	.14	.5	.14	.3	.14	.7	.12	.8
Workers' compensation...............	.48	1.7	.39	.8	.25	1.2	.39	2.5

[1] Includes workers in the private nonfarm economy excluding households and the public sector excluding the federal government.
[2] Includes premium pay for work in addition to the regular work schedule (i.e., overtime, weekends, and holidays).
[3] Cost per hour worked is $0.01 or less.
[4] Less than .05 percent.
[5] Comprises the Old-Age, Survivors, and Disability Insurance (OASDI) program.

Source: U.S. Department of Labor (June 21, 2007). Employer costs for employee compensation, March 2007 (USDL: 07–0877) [online]. Available: *www.bls.gov/ect/htm,* accessed June 25, 2007.

These intents of legally required benefits remain intact today. The U.S. government has established programs to protect individuals from such catastrophic events as disability and unemployment. Legally required benefits are **protection programs** that attempt to promote worker safety and health, maintain the influx of family income, and assist families in crisis. The key legally required benefits are mandated by the Social Security Act of 1935, various state workers' compensation laws, and the Family and Medical Leave Act of 1993. All provide protection programs to employees and their dependents (Chapter 12).

A HISTORICAL PERSPECTIVE ON COMPENSATION: THE ROAD TOWARD STRATEGIC COMPENSATION

Agriculture and small family craft businesses were the bases for the U.S. economy before the 1900s. The turn of the twentieth century marked the beginning of the Industrial Revolution in the United States. During the Industrial Revolution, the economy's transition from agrarian and craft businesses to large-scale manufacturing began. Individuals were increasingly becoming employees of large factories instead of self-employed farmers or small-business owners. This shift from the agricultural sector to the industrial sector promoted the beginnings of the field of human resources management.[5]

The factory system gave rise to divisions of labor based on differences in worker skill, effort, and responsibilities. The growth in the size of the workplace necessitated practices to guide such activities as hiring, training, setting wages, handling grievances, and terminating employment. At the time, practitioners referred to these activities as personnel administration, which is the predecessor of modern human resource management.

The early personnel (and compensation) function emphasized labor cost control and management control over labor. Many employers instituted so-called **scientific management practices** to control labor costs, as well as welfare practices to maintain control over labor. Scientific management practices gave rise to individual incentive pay systems. Welfare practices represent the forerunner of modern discretionary employee benefits practices.

Scientific management practices promoted labor cost control by replacing inefficient production methods with efficient production methods. Factory owners used time-and-motion studies and job analysis to meet that objective. **Time-and-motion studies** analyzed the time it took employees to complete their jobs. These studies literally focused on employees' movements and the identification of the most efficient steps to complete jobs in the least amount of time.[6] Job analysis is a systematic process for gathering, documenting, and analyzing information in order to describe jobs. At the time, employers used job analysis to classify the most efficient ways to perform jobs.

How did scientific management methods influence compensation practices? Scientific management methods gave rise to the use of piecework plans (Chapter 5). Under piecework plans, an employee's compensation depends on the number of units she or he produces over a given period. Specifically, these plans reward employees on the basis of their individual hourly production against an objective output standard, determined by the pace at which manufacturing equipment operates. For each hour, workers receive piecework incentives for every item produced over the designated production standard.

There were also developments in the area of employee benefits during World War II. **Welfare practices** were generous endeavors undertaken by some employers, motivated in part to minimize employees' desire for union representation, to promote good management and to enhance worker productivity. Welfare practices were "anything for the comfort and improvement, intellectual or social, of the employees, over and above wages paid, which is not a necessity of the industry nor required by law."[7] Companies' welfare practices varied. For example, some employers offered such facilities as libraries and recreational areas; others offered financial assistance for education, home purchases, and home improvements. In addition, employer sponsorship of medical insurance coverage became common. The use of welfare practices created the need to administer them. Welfare secretaries served as an intermediary between the company and its employees, and they were essentially predecessors of human resource (HR) professionals.[8]

In the 1960s, the U.S. government instituted major legislation aimed at protecting individual rights to fair treatment in the workplace. Most often, fair treatment means making employment-related decisions according to job performance—for example, awarding higher merit pay increases to the better performers.

Federal laws led to the bureaucratization of compensation practice. Personnel and compensation administrators took the lead in developing and implementing employment practices that upheld the myriad federal employment laws. These professionals also maintained records, creating documentation in the event of legal challenges to employment practices. In short, compensation professionals were largely administrators who reacted to government regulation.

Personnel administration was transformed from a purely administrative function to a competitive resource in many companies during the 1980s as technology transformed the workplace and pressures from global competitors intensified. Since the early 1980s, compensation professionals have designed and implemented compensation programs that contribute to companies' competitive advantage by motivating employees to excel, learn new knowledge and skills, and to take on a sense of ownership in the company.[9]

Competitive advantage describes a company's success. **Competitive advantage** refers specifically to a company's ability to maintain market share and profitability over a sustained period of several years. Employers began to recognize that employees are key resources necessary for a company's success, particularly in changing business environments characterized by rapid technological change and intense business competition from foreign countries. Employers' recognition that employees represent an important resource led to the view of employees as human resources. In line with this view, companies design human resource management practices to promote competitive advantage.

As technology leads to the automation of more tasks, employers combine jobs and confer broader responsibilities on workers. For example, the technology of advanced automated manufacturing, such as that used in the automobile industry, began doing the jobs of people, including the laborer, the materials handler, the operator-assembler, and the maintenance person. A single employee now performs all of these tasks in a position called "manufacturing technician." The expanding range of tasks and responsibilities in this job demands higher levels of reading, writing, and computation skills than did the jobs that it replaced, which required strong eye–hand coordination. Most employees must possess higher levels of reading skills than before because they must be able to read the operating and troubleshooting manuals (when problems arise) of automated manufacturing equipment that is based on computer technology. Manufacturing equipment previously had a relatively simple design, based on such easily understood mechanical principles as pulleys, and it was easy to operate.

Increased global competition has forced companies in the United States to become more productive. More than ever, companies must now provide their employees with leading-edge skills and encourage them to apply their skills proficiently to sustain a competitive advantage. Evidence suggests that workers in other countries are more skilled and able to work more productively than U.S. employees.[10] In addition, companies, particularly in Japan, adopted lean manufacturing and process development techniques that enabled workers to contribute to products of outstanding quality.

Compensation practices contribute to competitive advantage by developing more productive and highly skilled workforces. Well-designed merit pay programs reinforce excellent performance by awarding pay raises commensurate with performance attainments. The use of incentive pay practices is instrumental in changing the prevalent entitlement mentality U.S. workers have toward pay and in containing compensation costs by awarding one-time increases to base pay once work objectives have been attained.

Pay-for-knowledge and skill-based pay programs are key to giving employees the necessary knowledge and skills to use new workplace technology effectively. Management can use discretionary benefit offerings to promote particular employee behaviors that have strategic value. For example, employees who take advantage of tuition reimbursement programs are more likely to contribute to the strategic imperatives of product or service differentiation and cost-reduction objectives.

Moving to the realm of executive compensation (Chapter 13) becomes quite interesting because the rules for establishing compensation and benefits for employees are cast aside for a set of unique rules that creates tremendous wealth for executives. In addition, the pay-for-performance ethic that we stress for nonexecutive employees becomes debated among shareholders of companies, employees, labor unions, and the government.

Compensation professionals face additional challenges as defining who is an employee becomes complex and, as a result, who is responsible for compensating and providing benefits for nonemployees. These nonemployees are members of the growing contingent workforce in the United States. As we will learn in Chapter 14, there are multiple types of contingent workers and the compensation and benefits issues vary with these various contingent worker classifications.

It is not surprising that the globalization of business often requires that employees be sent from their home countries (e.g., a U.S. citizen working for Microsoft) as expatriates to manage business activities throughout the world. As we will see in Chapter 15, compensation professionals must learn about the techniques for compensating expatriate employees. In addition, as U.S. companies expand their operations to the far reaches of the world, it is essential that they become familiar with the laws and norms that define compensation and benefits practices in those countries. We will review the compensation and benefits issues around the globe in Chapter 16.

STRATEGIC VERSUS TACTICAL DECISIONS

Business professionals make two kinds of decisions—strategic decisions and tactical decisions. **Strategic decisions** guide the activities of companies in the market; **tactical decisions** support the fulfillment of strategic decisions. Business professionals apply these decisions to companies' functions, including manufacturing, engineering, research and development, management information systems, HR, and marketing. For example, HR professionals make strategic compensation decisions and tactical compensation decisions. Figure 1-3 shows the relationship between strategic decisions and tactical decisions.

Strategic management entails a series of judgments, under uncertainty, that companies direct toward achieving specific goals.[11] Companies base strategy formulation on environmental scanning activities (as described later in this chapter). Discerning threats and opportunities is the main focus of environmental scanning. Strategic management is an inexact process because companies distinguish between threats and opportunities based on interpretation. A threat suggests a negative situation in which loss is likely and over which an individual has relatively little control. An opportunity implies a positive situation in which gain is likely and over which an individual has a fair amount of control.[12]

For instance, Mercedes-Benz, a manufacturer of luxury automobiles, stepped outside its typical product offerings by introducing the C230, a well-equipped hatchback model in the $25,000 to $30,000 price range. Most new well-equipped Mercedes vehicles retail well above the $40,000 level and are bought by affluent individuals who are

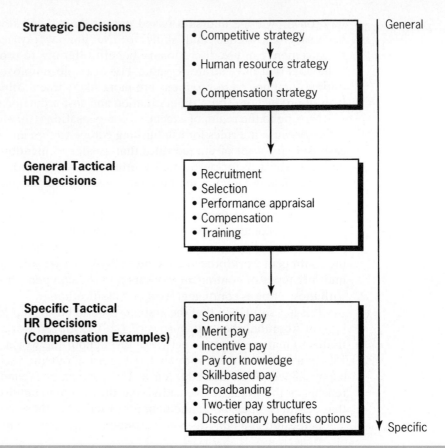

Strategic Decisions

- Competitive strategy
- Human resource strategy
- Compensation strategy

General

**General Tactical
HR Decisions**

- Recruitment
- Selection
- Performance appraisal
- Compensation
- Training

**Specific Tactical
HR Decisions
(Compensation Examples)**

- Seniority pay
- Merit pay
- Incentive pay
- Pay for knowledge
- Skill-based pay
- Broadbanding
- Two-tier pay structures
- Discretionary benefits options

Specific

FIGURE 1-3   Relationship between Strategic and Tactical Decisions

into their forties and beyond. The new Mercedes offering is geared toward extending its market base to car buyers in their twenties and thirties who typically cannot afford the Mercedes price tag. Given so many fine car alternatives, Mercedes hopes to build loyalty among a younger following of car buyers with the idea that loyal Mercedes owners will continue to buy Mercedes in the future. Table 1-3 illustrates additional threats and opportunities.

Tactical decisions support the fulfillment of strategic decisions, which we discuss shortly. We will look at Eli Lilly's Web site to illustrate these practices in the following paragraphs.

Strategic planning supports business objectives. Companies' executives communicate business objectives in competitive strategy statements. **Competitive strategy** refers to the planned use of company resources—technology, capital, and human—to promote and sustain competitive advantage. The time horizon for strategic decisions may span two or more years. Lilly's competitive strategy:

> Eli Lilly and Company is a leading, innovation-driven corporation committed to developing a growing portfolio of best-in-class and first-in-class pharmaceutical products that help people live longer, healthier and more active lives. Lilly products treat depression, schizophrenia, attention-deficit hyperactivity disorder, diabetes, osteoporosis and many other conditions. We are committed to providing answers that matter—through medicines and information—for some of the world's most urgent medical needs.[13]

TABLE 1-3 Threats and Opportunities in Sample Industries

Sporting Goods

Growth in the $150 billion global sporting goods industry is slowing down following years of moderate growth. Much of the industry's slowdown can be attributed to the decline of children's participation in sports. Many children instead choose to watch television or videos, surf the Internet, and play video games.

Wireless Communications Services

Wireless services are on the rise as e-mail capabilities and Internet access are becoming increasingly mobile. This industry currently has provided services that deliver voice and data over cellular telephones, pagers, and handheld computers. There is a rapid trend toward personalizing these services to appeal to users of smaller devices. Growth in subscriptions to mobile phone service is accelerating quickly in large part due to these trends in service options and decreasing prices. In addition, moving from analog networks to digital networks has contributed to rises in subscriptions because digital networks provide higher quality service(i.e., better sound quality and data services).

Apparel, Shoes, and Accessories

Sales increased for some retailers as signs of economic slowdown became apparent, but not for others. Many consumers have quickly changed their focus from such upscale retail stores as Federated Department Stores, the May Department Store Company, and Dillard's to discount retail stores, including Wal-Mart and Target. In response to these trends, many upscale stores have reduced the number of name brands, which are often associated with hefty designer fees. Instead, these stores are carrying high-quality private-label brands that come at a lower cost than name brands.

   Many apparel, shoe, and accessory manufacturers have made efforts to sell goods to retail stores at lower costs. One of the main strategies has entailed opening production facilities in foreign countries where labor costs are lower and closing domestic production facilities. Weaker labor laws in Mexico and Southeast Asia permit employers to pay workers at substantially lower rates than in U.S. facilities.

Restaurant Industry

The restaurant industry distinguishes between two kinds of restaurants: full service and fast food. Full-service restaurants include family restaurants (e.g., Advantica's Denny's), dinner houses (e.g., Darden Restaurants' Red Lobster), and grill or buffet types of eateries (c.g., Metromedia's Ponderosa). The fast-food sector includes sandwich shops, Mexican food, and pizza (e.g., Burger King, KFC, McDonald's, Pizza Hut, and Taco Bell). The sluggish economy has resulted in slower sales in full-service restaurants. Some of the people who have cut back on their visits to full-service restaurants have opted for less expensive fast food. Both types of restaurants are facing a labor shortage because the supply of workers age 16 to 24 has been declining. This age group represents the primary population of restaurant employees. Restaurants have attempted to maintain staffing by recruiting retirees, a growing segment of the population.

Human resource executives collaborate with other company executives to develop human resource strategies. **Human resource strategies** specify the use of multiple HR practices. These statements are consistent with a company's competitive strategy. At Lilly:

> No matter where you are in your career, you ask questions. As a new college graduate, you wonder what kind of opportunities you'll have and how your education can help you make an impact in your first job. As an experienced professional, you want to know how your contributions will positively impact the patient and how you can make a difference by providing the answers that matter. If you're in sales, you might ask where you can go to do more, get more, and be more.
>
>   At Lilly, we have the answers.
>
>   We'll provide the insight to build a fulfilling career with a company that impacts lives every day by delivering solutions to some of the world's toughest health care issues. Our commitment to meeting the needs of our patients is at the forefront of everything we do and a shared goal among our team members.

We've laid the foundation for continued success with a rich pipeline of best-in-class, first-in-class pharmaceutical products, and a collaborative culture that supports people in reaching their greatest potential. You'll work alongside and learn from a team of top professionals whose diverse perspectives and experiences enable us to provide our patients with the medicines they need to lead longer, healthier lives.[14]

Compensation and benefits executives work with the lead HR executive and the company's chief budget officer to prepare total compensation strategies. Total compensation strategies describe the use of compensation and benefits practices that support both human resource strategies and competitive strategies.

With flextime, employees can work with their management to vary their work schedules in a way that meets both personal and business needs. Full-time employees who "flex" arrive at work between 6:00 and 9 A.M. and leave work after a full day, between 3 and 6:00 P.M. Employees in manufacturing areas may have opportunities for shift-trading and other flexible options.

As part of this effort, Lilly provides its employees with numerous programs and options, which may vary according to job and location. These include flexible work options; on-site child care; parenting resources; maternity and dependent care leave; adoption assistance; nursing mother stations; health and dental benefits; health and wellness programs; and on-site conveniences, such as a credit union, a dry cleaner, a convenience store and ready-to-serve hot meals; and special events.

Competitive Strategy Choices

Lowest-Cost Strategy

The **cost leadership** or **lowest-cost strategy** focuses on gaining competitive advantage by being the lowest-cost producer of a product or service within the marketplace, while selling the product or service at a price advantage relative to the industry average. Lowest-cost strategies require aggressive construction of efficient-scale facilities and vigorous pursuit of cost minimization in such areas as operations, marketing, and HR.

Southwest Airlines is an excellent illustration of an organization that pursues a lowest-cost strategy because its management successfully reduced operations costs. At least two noteworthy decisions have contributed to Southwest's goals. First, Southwest's training and aircraft maintenance costs are lower than similar competitors' costs because the airline uses only Boeing 737 aircraft. Southwest enjoys substantial cost savings because it does not need to buy different curricula for training flight attendants, mechanics, and pilots to learn about procedures specific to different aircraft makes (e.g., Boeing and McDonnell-Douglas) and models (e.g., Boeing 737 and Boeing 777). Second, Southwest passengers may sit anywhere they like as long as they get there first, and the airline uses ticketless travel (a practice now known as the e-ticket that virtually all U.S. airlines typically use). These choices greatly reduce administrative costs.

Differentiation Strategy

Companies adopt **differentiation strategies** to develop products or services that are unique from those of its competitors. Differentiation strategy can take many forms, including design or brand image, technology, features, customer service, and price. Differentiation strategies lead to competitive advantage through building brand loyalty among devoted consumers. Brand-loyal consumers are less sensitive to price increases, which enables companies to invest in research and development initiatives to further differentiate themselves from competing companies.

The Iams Company, a cat and dog food manufacturer, successfully pursues a differentiation strategy based on brand image and price premiums. The company offers two separate dog food lines—Iams, a super-premium line that is nutritionally well-balanced for dogs and uses high-quality ingredients, and Eukanuba, an ultra-premium line that contains more chicken and vital nutrients than the Iams line, as well as OmegaCOAT Nutritional Science (fatty acids), which promotes shiny and healthy coats. Together, Iams and Eukanuba appeal to a substantial set of dog owners. The Iams Company distinguishes Eukanuba from Iams by claiming that Eukanuba is "What healthy pets are made of." The Eukanuba slogan is the company's basis for brand image.

In addition to brand image the Iams Company also differentiates its Eukanuba line by charging a price premium. This price premium has enabled the Iams Company to be an innovator in canine nutrition by investing heavily in product research and development. Eukanuba offers several formulas to meet the needs of small, medium, and large breeds of dogs according to life stage, activity level, and particular health conditions.

Tactical Decisions That Support the Firm's Strategy

Human resource tactics and practices in other functional areas support a company's competitive strategy. Functional area capabilities include manufacturing, engineering, research and development, management information systems, HR, and marketing. Compensation and HR professionals can orchestrate human resource and other functional tactics to promote competitive strategy. In addition, HR practices support competitive advantage through energizing employees to perform the jobs for which they were hired.

Tactics in Other Functional Areas

Companies must determine which functional capabilities are most crucial to maintaining a competitive advantage. For example, rapid advances in medical science are moving toward less-invasive surgical procedures that require special surgical instruments. One noteworthy example is arthroscopic surgery. Arthroscopes enable surgeons to perform knee and shoulder surgeries without invasive surgical openings. A competitive advantage in this industry depends largely on researching, developing, and manufacturing leading-edge surgical instruments for these new, less-invasive surgical procedures.

Employee Roles Associated with Competitive Strategies

Common wisdom and experience tell us that HR professionals must decide which employee roles are instrumental to the attainment of competitive strategies. Knowledge of these required roles should enable HR professionals to implement HR tactics that encourage their enactment of these roles. Of course, compensation professionals are responsible for designing and implementing compensation tactics that elicit strategy-consistent employee roles.

For the lowest-cost strategy, the imperative is to reduce output costs per employee. The desired employee roles for attaining a lowest-cost strategy include repetitive and predictable behaviors, a relatively short-term focus, primarily autonomous or individual activity, high concern for quantity of output, and a primary concern for results.

The key employees' roles for differentiation strategies include highly creative behavior, a relatively long-term focus, cooperative and interdependent behavior, and a greater degree of risk taking. Compared with lowest-cost strategies, successful attainment of differentiation strategies depends on employee creativity, openness to novel work approaches, and willingness to take risks. In addition, differentiation strategies require longer time frames to provide sufficient opportunity to yield the benefits of these behaviors.

COMPENSATION PROFESSIONALS' GOALS

Understanding compensation professionals' goals requires knowing the role of HR within companies and specific HR practices, particularly how HR professionals fit into the corporate hierarchy and how the compensation function fits into HR departments.

How HR Professionals Fit into the Corporate Hierarchy

Line function and staff function broadly describe all employee functions. **Line employees** are directly involved in producing companies' goods or delivering their services. Assembler, production worker, and salesperson are examples of line jobs. **Staff employees'** functions support the line functions. Human resource professionals and accountants are examples of staff employees. Human resource professionals are staff employees because they offer a wide variety of support services for line employees. In a nutshell, HR professionals promote the effective use of all employees in companies. Effective use means attaining work objectives that fit with the overall mission of the company. According to Jay Hannah, BancFirst Corp. executive vice president of financial services, "The HR department is the source and keeper of critical information, which is key in today's workplace. With the information they provide, we in turn can build and design strategies to hire and retain the best workforce possible. And this may sound clichéd, but it's very true—the real competitive advantage is our company's human resources."[15]

Human resource professionals design and implement a variety of HR practices that advance this objective. In addition to compensation, HR practices include:

- Recruitment
- Selection
- Performance appraisal
- Training
- Career development
- Labor–management relations
- Employment termination
- Managing HR within the context of legislation

Most company structures include an HR department. Traditionally, HR departments were thought of as an administrative or support function for the company because the financial or market value of HR was not as readily apparent as sales, manufacturing, or marketing functions. Some practitioners and researchers are suspect about the future of internal HR functions.

How the Compensation Function Fits into HR Departments

Human resource practices do not operate in isolation. Every HR practice is related to others in different ways. For example, Microsoft Corporation publicly acknowledges the relationships between compensation and other HR practices:

> We've said this for years, and it's still as true as it ever was: our employees are our greatest asset. And as such, we believe in making a long-term investment in you. That includes your financial well-being and your progress within our

company. In this section you'll find three areas of discussion—covering career development, compensation and investment programs—designed to help you better understand the concerted effort we make to ensure your experience at Microsoft is future-focused and enriching from day one.[16]

Let's consider additional relationships between compensation and each of the HR practices.

Compensation, Recruitment, and Selection

Job candidates choose to work for particular companies for a number of reasons, including career advancement opportunities, training, the company's reputation for being a "good" place to work, location, and compensation. Companies try to spark job candidates' interest by communicating the positive features of the core compensation and employee benefits programs. As we will discuss in Chapter 8, companies use compensation to compete for the very best candidates. In addition, companies may offer such inducements as one-time signing bonuses to entice high-quality applicants. It is not uncommon for signing bonuses to amount to as much as 20 percent of starting annual salaries. Signing bonuses are useful when the supply of qualified candidates falls short of companies' needs for these candidates.

The next three sections will address performance appraisal, training, and career development. Before discussing these issues, however, let's look at how Microsoft explicitly acknowledges the relationship between compensation and these HR practices:

> Once a year, you'll have the opportunity to take the long view on your performance and, with your manager, assess the value of your work and plan for your next move at Microsoft. This is done through a process called "reviews," and it provides a forum for you to evaluate your work and progress against measurable objectives you've previously identified and agreed upon with your manager. Your manager will also independently evaluate your work—again, in the context of those previously identified objectives and with regard to your role and team. You'll then meet with your manager to review your previous year's work and to set new goals to challenge you, expand your abilities, and grow your career in the coming year. It's also during this review process that merit bonuses and salary increases are determined, as they are generally reflective of your contribution in the context of your team and group at Microsoft.
>
> To complement this review, you will have a discussion with your manager halfway through the year to discuss your career objectives and planning. This is a time to review your personal goals in a formal setting, make changes as needed and carve your 3–5 year career path. At this time, strategic educational planning will also be implemented.
>
> Achieve your goals and measure your success. Depending on how you've moved toward accomplishing and surpassing the personal goals that you've set for yourself, we're ready to express our appreciation. We expect you to move forward on your career path and we're always ready to inspire your next step.
>
> *Base pay.* Our salaries are competitive within the industry, and specifics will be provided if we reach an offer stage with you.
>
> *Bonus awards.* Employees are eligible for a cash bonus award that may be determined during their formal review as described above. Bonus awards are based on the ability to meet specific personal performance goals that have

been outlined and accessed periodically by both the employee and the employee's manager.

Merit increases. Employees may be considered for merit increases during their formal review as described above. Merit increases are based on skill, experience, contribution and performance on your own personal goals.

Stock option grants. Microsoft believes employees who become shareholders have an even bigger interest in working hard to help the company succeed. Microsoft's stock option program recognizes employee contribution and potential, and it provides a long-term incentive for future performance and contribution. Stock option grants may be awarded on a discretionary basis to employees at their time of hiring and/or annually.[17]

Compensation and Performance Appraisal

Accurate performance appraisals are integral to effective merit pay programs. For merit pay programs to succeed, employees must know that their efforts toward meeting production quotas or quality standards will lead to pay raises. Job requirements must be realistic, and employees must be prepared to meet job goals with respect to their skills and abilities. Moreover, employees must perceive a strong relationship between attaining performance standards and receiving pay increases. Merit pay systems require specific performance appraisal approaches. Administering successful merit pay programs depends as much on sound performance appraisal practices as it does on the compensation professional's skill in designing and implementing such plans.

Compensation and Training

Successful pay-for-knowledge plans depend on a company's ability to develop and implement systematic training programs. When training is well designed, employees should be able to learn the skills needed to increase their pay, as well as the skills necessary to teach and coach other employees at lower skill levels. Companies implementing pay-for-knowledge plans typically increase the amount of classroom and on-the-job training. Pay-for-knowledge systems make training necessary rather than optional. Companies that adopt pay-for-knowledge systems must accordingly ensure that all employees have equal access to the training needed to acquire higher-level skills.

Compensation and Career Development

Most employees expect to experience career development within their present companies. Employees' careers develop in two different ways. First, some employees change the focus of their work—for example, from supervisor of payroll clerks to supervisor of inventory clerks. This change represents a lateral move across the company's hierarchy. Second, others maintain their focus and assume greater responsibilities. This change illustrates advancement upward through the company's hierarchy. Advancing from payroll clerk to manager of payroll administration is an example of moving upward through a company's hierarchy. Employees' compensation changes to reflect career development.

Compensation and Labor–Management Relations

Collective bargaining agreements describe the terms of employment (e.g., pay, work hours) reached between management and the union. Compensation is a key topic. Unions have fought hard for general pay increases and regular COLAs to promote their members' standard of living. In Chapter 3, we will review the role of unions in compensation, and in Chapter 4, we indicate that unions have traditionally bargained for seniority pay systems in negotiations with management. More recently, unions have been willing to incorporate particular incentive pay systems. For example, unions appear to be receptive to behavioral encouragement plans because improving worker safety and minimizing absenteeism serve the best interests of both employees and employers.

Compensation and Employment Termination

Employment termination takes place when an employee's agreement to perform work is terminated. Employment terminations are either involuntary or voluntary. The HR department plays a central role in managing involuntary employment terminations. Companies initiate involuntary terminations for a variety of reasons, including poor job performance, insubordination, violation of work rules, reduced business activity due to sluggish economic conditions, and plant closings. Discharge represents involuntary termination for poor job performance, insubordination, or gross violation of work rules. Involuntary layoff describes termination under sluggish economic conditions or because of plant closings. In the case of involuntary layoffs, HR professionals typically provide outplacement counseling to help employees find work elsewhere. Companies may choose to award **severance pay**, which usually amounts to several months' pay following involuntary termination and, in some cases, continued coverage under the employer's medical insurance plan. Employees often rely on severance pay to meet financial obligations while they search for employment. In the past, companies commonly offered a year or more of severance pay. Severance benefits today tend to be less generous. For example, as part of Delta Airlines' 2005 closure of its Boston reservation center, the company offered only six weeks of severance pay regardless of seniority with the company.

Employees initiate voluntary terminations, most often to work for other companies or to retire. In the case of retirement, companies sponsor pension programs. **Pension programs** provide income to individuals throughout their retirement. Companies sometimes use **early retirement programs** to reduce workforce size and trim compensation expenditures. Early retirement programs contain incentives designed to encourage highly paid employees with substantial seniority to retire earlier than they had planned. These incentives expedite senior employees' retirement eligibility and increase their retirement income. In addition, some companies continue retirees' medical benefits.

Compensation and Legislation

Employment laws establish bounds of both acceptable employment practices and employee rights. Federal laws that apply to compensation practices are grouped according to four themes:

- Income continuity, safety, and work hours
- Pay discrimination
- Accommodating of disabilities and family needs
- Prevailing wage laws

Table 1-4 lists for each theme the major laws that influence compensation practice.

The federal government enacted income continuity, safety, and work hours laws (e.g., the Fair Labor Standards Act of 1938) to stabilize individuals' incomes when they became unemployed because of poor business conditions or workplace injuries, as well as to set pay minimums and work-hour limits for children. The civil rights movement of the 1960s led to the passage of key legislation (e.g., the Equal Pay Act of 1963 and the Civil Rights Act of 1964) designed to protect designated classes of employees and to

TABLE 1-4   Laws That Influence Compensation

Income Continuity, Safety, and Work Hours
Minimum wage laws—Fair Labor Standards Act of 1938
   Minimum wage
   Overtime provisions
     Portal-to-Portal Act of 1947
     Equal Pay Act of 1963
   Child labor provisions
Work Hours and Safety Standards Act of 1962
McNamara–O'Hara Service Contract Act of 1965

Pay Discrimination
Equal Pay Act of 1963
Civil Rights Act of 1964, Title VII
Bennett Amendment (1964)
Executive Order 11246 (1965)
Age Discrimination in Employment Act of 1967 (amended in 1978, 1986, 1990)
Executive Order 11141 (1964)
Civil Rights Act of 1991

Accommodating Disabilities and Family Needs
Pregnancy Discrimination Act of 1978
Americans with Disabilities Act of 1990
Family and Medical Leave Act of 1993

Prevailing Wage Laws
Davis–Bacon Act of 1931
Walsh–Healey Public Contracts Act of 1936

uphold their individual rights against discriminatory employment decisions, including matters of pay. Congress enacted legislation (e.g., the Pregnancy Discrimination Act of 1978, the Americans with Disabilities Act of 1990, and the Family and Medical Leave Act of 1993) to accommodate employees with disabilities and pressing family needs. Prevailing wage laws (e.g., the Davis–Bacon Act of 1931) set minimum wage rates for companies that provide paid services—such as building maintenance—to the U.S. government.

The Compensation Department's Main Goals

Compensation professionals promote effective compensation systems by meeting three important goals: internal consistency, market competitiveness, and recognition of individual contributions.

Internal Consistency

Internally consistent compensation systems clearly define the relative value of each job among all jobs within a company. This ordered set of jobs represents the job structure or hierarchy. Companies rely on a simple, yet fundamental, principle for building internally consistent compensation systems: Employees in jobs that require greater qualifications, more responsibilities, and more complex job duties should be paid more than employees whose jobs require lesser qualifications, fewer responsibilities, and less-complex job duties. Internally consistent job structures formally recognize differences in job characteristics, which therefore enable compensation managers to set pay accordingly.

Compensation professionals use job analysis and job evaluation to achieve internal consistency. **Job analysis** is a systematic process for gathering, documenting, and analyzing information in order to describe jobs. Job analyses describe content or job duties, worker requirements, and sometimes the job context or working conditions.

Compensation professionals use **job evaluation** systematically to recognize differences in the relative worth among a set of jobs and to establish pay differentials accordingly. Whereas job analysis is almost purely descriptive, job evaluation partly reflects the values and priorities that management places on various positions. Based on job content differences (i.e., job analysis results) and the firm's priorities, managers establish pay differentials for virtually all positions within the company.

Market Competitiveness

Market-competitive pay systems play a significant role in attracting and retaining the most qualified employees. Compensation professionals build market-competitive compensation systems based on the results of strategic analyses (Chapter 2) and compensation surveys.

A **strategic analysis** entails an examination of a company's external market context and internal factors. Examples of external market context are the industry profile, information about competitors, and long-term growth prospects. Internal factors encompass the company's financial condition and functional capabilities—for example, marketing and human resources. Strategic analyses permit business professionals to see where they stand in the market based on external and internal factors.

Compensation surveys collect and then analyze competitors' compensation data. Compensation surveys traditionally focused on competitors' wage and salary practices. Now, employee benefits are also a target of surveys because benefits are a key element of market-competitive pay systems. Compensation surveys are important because they enable compensation professionals to obtain realistic views of competitors' pay practices. In the absence of compensation survey data, compensation professionals would have to use guesswork to build market-competitive compensation systems.

Recognizing Individual Contributions

Pay structures represent pay rate differences for jobs of unequal worth and the framework for recognizing differences in employee contributions. No two employees possess identical credentials or perform the same jobs equally well. Companies recognize these differences by paying individuals according to their credentials, knowledge, or job performance. When completed, pay structures should define the boundaries for recognizing employee contributions. Well-designed structures should promote the retention of valued employees.

Pay grades and pay ranges are structural features of pay structures. **Pay grades** group jobs for pay policy application. Human resource professionals typically group jobs into pay grades based on similar compensable factors and value. These criteria are not precise. In fact, no single formula determines what is sufficiently similar in terms of content and value to warrant grouping into a pay grade. **Pay ranges** build upon pay grades. Pay ranges include minimum, maximum, and midpoint pay rates. The minimum and maximum values denote the acceptable lower and upper bounds of pay for the jobs in particular pay grades. The midpoint pay value is the halfway mark between the minimum and maximum pay rates.

STAKEHOLDERS OF THE COMPENSATION SYSTEM

The HR department provides services to stakeholders within and outside the company. These include:

- Employees
- Line managers
- Executives
- Unions
- U.S. government

The success of HR departments depends on how well they serve various stakeholders. "Each constituency [stakeholder] has its own set of expectations regarding the personnel department's activities; each holds its own standards for effective performance; each applies its own standards for assessing the extent to which the department's activities meets its expectations; and each attempts to prescribe preferred goals for the subunit or presents constraints to its sphere of discretion. Multiple stakeholders often compete directly or indirectly for the attention and priority of the personnel department."[18] Our focus is on some of the ways compensation professionals serve these stakeholders.

Employees

As we discussed earlier, successful pay-for-knowledge programs depend on a company's ability to develop and implement systematic training programs. Compensation professionals must educate employees about their training options and how successful training will lead to increased pay and advancement opportunities within the company. These professionals should not assume that employees will necessarily recognize these opportunities unless they are clearly communicated. Written memos and informational meetings conducted by compensation professionals and HR representatives are effective communication media.

Discretionary benefits provide protection programs, paid time off, and services. As compensation professionals plan and manage employee benefits programs, they should keep these functions in mind. There is probably no single company that expects its employee benefits program to meet all these objectives. Compensation professionals as representatives of company management, along with union representatives, must therefore determine which objectives are the most important for their particular workforce.

Line Managers

Compensation professionals use their expert knowledge of the laws that influence pay and benefits practices to help line managers make sound compensation judgments. For example, the Equal Pay Act of 1963 (discussed in Chapter 3) prohibits sex discrimination in pay for employees performing equal work, so compensation professionals should advise line managers to pay the same hourly pay rate or annual salary for men and women hired to perform the same job.

Line managers turn to compensation professionals for advice about appropriate pay rates for jobs. Compensation professionals oversee the use of job evaluation to establish pay differentials among jobs within a company. In addition, they train line managers how to evaluate jobs properly.

Executives

Compensation professionals serve company executives by developing and managing sound compensation systems. Executives look to them to ensure that the design and implementation of pay and benefits practices comply with pertinent legislation. Violation of these laws can lead to substantial monetary penalties to companies. Executives also depend on compensation professionals' expertise to design pay and benefits systems that will attract and retain the best-qualified employees. As we will discuss in Chapter 2, employees play a major role in a company's success.

Unions

As noted earlier, collective bargaining agreements describe the terms of employment reached between management and the union. Compensation professionals are responsible for administering the pay and benefits policies specified in collective bargaining agreements. They mainly ensure that employees receive COLAs and seniority pay increases on a timely basis.

U.S. Government

The U.S. government requires that companies comply with all employment legislation. Compensation professionals apply their expertise regarding pertinent legislation to design legally sound pay and benefits practices. In addition, since the passage of the Civil Rights Act of 1991, compensation professionals have applied their expertise to demonstrate that alleged discriminatory pay practices are a business necessity. As we will discuss in Chapter 3, compensation professionals possess the burden of proof to demonstrate that alleged discriminatory pay practices are not discriminatory.

SUMMARY

This chapter introduced basic compensation concepts and the context of compensation practice. We distinguished between intrinsic and extrinsic compensation, noting that our focus is on extrinsic compensation. Next, we reviewed the evolution of compensation from an administrative function to a strategic function, as well as the strategic role of compensation in attaining competitive advantage. We then looked at how HR professionals fit in the corporate hierarchy and how compensation professionals fit into HR departments. Specifically, we learned that compensation professionals focus on internal and external pay differentials among jobs, as well as on creating pay structures that recognize employees for their particular contributions. Finally, we concluded with how compensation professionals relate to a company's various stakeholders.

Students of compensation should keep the following in mind: Compensation systems are changing. Change creates many exciting challenges for those who wish to work as compensation professionals. This book highlights those challenges.

KEY TERMS

- intrinsic compensation, 3
- extrinsic compensation, 3
- job characteristics theory, 3
- core compensation, 5
- employee benefits, 5
- base pay, 5
- hourly pay, 5
- wage, 5
- salary, 5
- compensable factors, 6

- cost-of-living adjustments (COLAs), 6
- seniority pay, 6
- human capital theory, 6
- human capital, 6
- merit pay, 6
- incentive pay, 6
- variable pay, 6
- pay-for-knowledge, 7
- skill-based pay, 7

- discretionary benefits, 7
- legally required benefits, 7
- protection programs, 8
- paid time off, 7
- services, 7
- scientific management practices, 9
- time-and-motion studies, 9
- welfare practices, 9
- competitive advantage, 10

DISCUSSION QUESTIONS

1. Define compensation.
2. Presumably, five core job characteristics promote intrinsic compensation. Give examples of jobs that you believe rate highly on these core job characteristics. Explain your answer.
3. Identify two companies—one that you believe pursues a lowest-cost strategy and another that pursues a differentiation strategy. Relying on personal knowledge, company annual reports, or articles in newspapers and business periodicals, discuss these companies' competitive strategies.
4. Describe your reaction to the following statement: Compensation has no bearing on a company's performance.
5. Are the three main goals of compensation departments equally important, or do you believe that they differ in importance? Give your rationale.

EXERCISES

Compensation Online

For Students

Exercise 1: Find relevant journal articles

Use your school library's online catalog or Web sites to locate articles pertaining to compensation and competitive strategy. Find and read several of the articles to get a feel for topics that are currently important in these areas. If you were asked to write a short paper on the topic of most interest to you, what topic would you choose? Why?

Exercise 2: Use an Internet search engine

Each search engine allows its users to narrow their searches in order to better locate the sites for which they are looking.

Go to the Yahoo! search engine at *www.yahoo.com*

Type the words *strategic compensation*, and click on the search button. How many sites were found? Click on a couple of the sites. How could you use the information on these sites to demonstrate knowledge and understanding to a job interviewer?

Exercise 3: Conduct an advanced search

Go back to the Yahoo! homepage and click on the advanced search link (located next to the search button). Type in *strategic compensation* again in the "exact phrase" box. Click on the search button. How did the results change from the regular search? Now, go back to the advanced search page and select "more options." Select English language, show pages only from the United States, and show pages updated in the last three months. How did the changes affect the search results?

Using a different search engine, go to the same Web site or find a related site. Compare and contrast the two search engines for ease of accessibility and amount of information available.

For Professionals

Exercise 1: Search for government documents

Your budget for securing compensation information is limited. A colleague points you to a free resource: the federal government. Search government sites for the

Bureau of Labor Statistics and the Department of Labor for documents regarding human resources. Also use Yahoo! to search for "federal government" or "federal laws." Visit several of the sites listed. What are some of the key topics covered on these sites?

Exercise 2: Review a company Web page

Assume you are a compensation professional in some industry of interest to you. You have been assigned the task of finding out as much as you can about your competitors' strategies. Using Yahoo!, find the homepages of a few of your competitors. These sites will have links about employment and investor information. Click these links. Using the information from these sites as well as information from Chapter 1, try to estimate each company's competitive strategy.

Use a different search engine (e.g., Google) and search for the same companies. Compare and contrast the two search engines for ease of accessibility and the amount of information available.

Exercise 3: Review a compensation Web site

Your company is seeking to develop a new compensation system, and you are in charge of finding a compensation consulting firm. Use the Internet to identify firms. Research what resources and services each consulting firm offers.

ENDNOTES

1. Quotation excerpted from Todd M. Manas, CCP, Arthur Andersen LLP, *Workspan,* September 2001, Vol. 44, No. 9.
2. Hackman, J. R., & Oldham, G. R. (1976). Motivation through the design of work: Test of a theory. *Organizational Behavior and Human Performance, 16*, pp. 250–279.
3. Becker, G. (1976). *Human Capital.* New York: National Bureau of Economic Research.
4. U.S. Department of Labor (June 21, 2007). Employer costs for employee compensation, March 2007 (USDL: 07–0877) [online]. Available: *www.bls.gov/ect/htm,* accessed June 25, 2007.
5. Baron, J. N., Dobbin, F., & Jennings, P. D. (1986). War and peace: The evolution of modern personnel administration in U.S. industry. *American Journal of Sociology, 92,* pp. 350–383.
6. Person, H. S. (1929). The new attitude toward management. In H. S. Person (Ed.), *Scientific Management in American Industry.* New York: Harper & Brothers.
7. U.S. Bureau of Labor Statistics. (1919). Welfare work for employees in industrial establishments in the United States. *Bulletin #250,* pp. 119–123.
8. Eilbirt, H. (1959). The development of personnel management in the United States. *Business History Review, 33,* pp. 345–364.
9. Pfeffer, J. (1995). Producing sustainable competitive advantage through the effective management of people. *Academy of Management Executives, 9,* pp. 55–69.
10. Carnevale, A. P., & Johnston, J. W. (1989). *Training in America: Strategies for the Nation.* Alexandria, VA: National Center on Education and the Economy and the American Society for Training and Development.
11. Lengnick-Hall, C. A., & Lengnick-Hall, M. L. (1990). *Interactive Human Resource Management and Strategic Planning.* New York: Quorum Books.
12. Dutton, J. E., & Jackson, S. E. (1987). The categorization of strategic issues by decision makers and its links to organizational action. *Academy of Management Review, 12,* pp. 76–90.
13. Lilly's competitive strategy statement [online]. Available: *www.lilly.com/about/overview/do.html,* accessed June 27, 2007.
14. Ibid.
15. Quotation excerpted from Leonard, B. (2002) Straight talk: Executives sound off on why they think HR professionals lost strategic ground, and what they can do to earn a place "at the table." *HRMagazine,* January, Vol. 9 (1) [online] *www.shrm.org,* accessed April 1, 2005.
16. Microsoft's statement on employee enrichment [online]. Available: *www.microsoft.com/mba/benefits/default.asp,* accessed April 1, 2007.
17. Microsoft's statement on employee enrichment [online]. Available: *www.microsoft.com/mba/benefits/default.asp,* accessed April 1, 2007.
18. Tsui, A. S. (1984). Personnel department effectiveness: A tripartite approach. *Industrial Relations, 23,* p. 187.

CHAPTER 2

Strategic Compensation in Action
Strategic Analysis and Contextual Factors

Chapter Outline

- Strategic Analysis
    External Market Environment
    Labor Market Assessment
    Internal Capabilities

- Factors That Influence Companies' Competitive Strategies
  and Compensation Practices
    National Culture
    Organizational Culture
    Organizational and Product Life Cycles

- Summary

- Key Terms

- Discussion Questions

- Exercises

- Endnotes

Learning Objectives

In this chapter, you will learn about

1. Strategic analysis factors

2. Industry classification: North American Industry Classification System (NAICS)

3. External market aspects of strategic analysis

4. Internal capabilities dimensions of strategic analysis

5. Factors that influence companies' competitive strategies and compensation practices

Compensation professionals should be knowledgeable about their company's competitive situation. Such knowledge enables them to guide the development and implementation of strategic compensation practices (i.e., compensation practices for promoting competitive advantage). A strategic analysis represents an important step toward attaining competitive advantage.

A **strategic analysis** entails an examination of a company's external market context and internal factors. Examples of external market factors include industry profile, information about competitors, and long-term growth prospects. Internal factors encompass financial condition and functional capabilities (e.g., marketing and human resources). Strategic analyses permit business professionals to see where they stand in the market based on external and internal factors. Companies with strong potential to increase sales levels tend to have a better standing than companies with weak potential to maintain or increase sales. Companies with a strong standing should be able to devote more financial resources to fund compensation programs than weaker companies. Compensation professionals should also be familiar with several factors that influence a company's choice of competitive strategies and compensation tactics, including national culture, organizational culture, and organizational and product (or service) life cycle.

STRATEGIC ANALYSIS

We will illustrate a strategic analysis for a hypothetical company named Fly-You-There. Fly-You-There operates in the scheduled passenger air transportation industry. The airline offers no-frills commercial flights along the West Coast, including several cities throughout California, Oregon, Washington, and Alaska. The company, located in San Francisco, is pursuing a lowest cost strategy. Its goal is to be the number one or two commercial airline in its markets by the year 2010. Key to Fly-You-There's success are operating efficiencies as measured through average cost per passenger, passenger safety, and on-time arrivals and departures.

The company was founded in 1982. Its workforce and enplanements grew slowly, but steadily, until the economic slowdown that began in the year 2000 and intensified after the September 11 terrorist attacks in 2001. During these years, Fly-You-There has maintained a union-free workforce. The airline compensated its pilots, flight attendants, and ground crew about 5 percent higher than its competitors' average pay and benefits while maintaining profitability. Although many people have returned to commercial flights, enplanements are still below normal levels prior to the economic slowdown. As a result, Fly-You-There cannot afford to maintain its market lead in pay and compensation.

Barbara Viera has just joined Fly-You-There as the compensation director. Before joining Fly-You-There, Barbara served as a successful compensation manager for one of its main competitors. Based on her experience, Barbara's first task is to prepare an overview of the competitiveness of Fly-You-There's compensation program. She must then recommend compensation policies to Fly-You-There's CEO.

Strategic analyses begin with the identification of a company's industry classification because companies compete with one another for customers' business. For example, Verizon Wireless and Sprint PCS compete against each other for consumers who want wireless telephone service. The **North American Industry Classification System Manual** classifies industries based on the **North American Industry Classification System (NAICS)**. NAICS codes represent keys to pertinent information for strategic analyses. As we'll see shortly, the U.S. federal government publishes different bulletins that contain information about industry and employment outlooks based on the NAICS. These bulletins permit compensation professionals and top managers to answer such questions as, "Will consumer demand increase for regional air service on the West Coast over the next 5 years?" "Are there sufficient numbers of well-trained commercial airline pilots?" and "What do commercial airline pilots typically earn?"

The NAICS provides an excellent starting point because it enables companies to identify direct product or service market competitors. The NAICS is the classification system for industries used in all federal government economic statistics. Many private-sector companies also rely on the NAICS to conduct strategic analyses. The federal government publishes NAICS codes in the North American Industry Classification System Manual.[1] It created the NAICS in cooperation with the Canadian and Mexican governments to cover the entire field of economic activities common to all three countries. NAICS uses a hierarchical structure to classify establishments from the broadest level to the most detailed level using the following format:

Sector	2-digit	Sectors represent the highest level of aggregation. There are 20 sectors in NAICS representing broad levels of aggregation.
Subsector	3-digit	Subsectors represent the next, more detailed level of aggregation in NAICS. There are 100 subsectors in NAICS.
Industry group	4-digit	Industry groups are more detailed than subsectors. There are 317 industry groups in NAICS.
NAICS industry	5-digit	NAICS industries are the level that, in most cases, represents the lowest level of three country comparability. There are 725 five-digit industries in NAICS.
National industry	6-digit	National industries are the most detailed level of NAICS. These industries represent the national level detail necessary for economic statistics in an industry classification. There are 1,179 U.S. industries in NAICS United States, 2002.

Table 2-1 lists these 20 sectors. Fly-You-There falls in the Transportation and Warehousing sector.

The NAICS generally uses five-digit classification codes that are common to the United States, Canada, and Mexico. In many instances, you will find six-digit NAICS codes that represent U.S. industries. The sixth digit represents specialized industries that are unique to the United States. Figure 2-1 shows the elements of NAICS codes and a sample—713120. The first two digits represent the **sector**, which is the broadest classification of economic activities (based on the list presented in Table 2-1). The numbers 71 denote the arts, entertainment, and recreation sector. The first three digits stand for the **subsector**, classifying broad sectors into particular subsets of the arts, entertainment, and recreation sector. The numbers 713 represent the amusement, gambling, and recreation subsector. The first four digits represent the **industry group**. The numbers 7131 stand for amusement and theme parks. The five-digit code stands for the **industry**. The numbers 71312 represent video game arcades (nongambling). **National industries** are the most detailed level of NAICS with six digits. These industries represent the national level detail necessary for economic statistics in an industry classification. The numbers 71310 refers to casinos, except hotel casinos. This industry comprises establishments primarily engaged in operating gambling facilities

TABLE 2-1   NAICS Sectors

Code	NAICS Sectors
11	Agriculture, Forestry, Fishing, and Hunting
21	Mining, Quarrying, and Oil and Gas Extraction
22	Utilities
23	Construction
31–33	Manufacturing
42	Wholesale Trade
44–45	Retail Trade
48–49	Transportation and Warehousing
51	Information
52	Finance and Insurance
53	Real Estate and Rental and Leasing
54	Professional, Scientific, and Technical Services
55	Management of Companies and Enterprises
56	Administrative and Support and Waste Management and Remediation Services
61	Education Services
62	Health Care and Social Assistance
71	Arts, Entertainment, and Recreation
72	Accommodation and Food Services
81	Other Services (except Public Administration)
92	Public Administration

Source: http://www.census.gov/epcd/www/naicsect.htm

that offer table wagering games along with such other gambling activities as slot machines and sports betting. These establishments often provide food and beverage services. Floating casinos (i.e., gambling cruises, riverboat casinos) are included in this industry.

Fly-You-There's NAICS code is 48111. The digits 48 represent the sector Transportation and Warehousing. Companies in this sector engage in some of the following activities:

- Air transportation (passenger and cargo)
- Rail transportation
- Water transportation
- Truck transportation

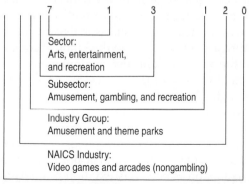

FIGURE 2-1   NAICS Code Elements

The digits 481 stand for Air Transportation subsector, including two industry groups (four-digit classifications):

- Scheduled air transportation (4811), including such commercial passenger airlines as American Airlines, Delta Airlines, Northwest Airlines, and United Airlines
- Nonscheduled air transportation (4812), including commercially chartered airplanes and aerial sightseeing tours

Fly-You-There's industry group is scheduled air transportation (4811), and this NAICS industry group contains two NAICS industries (five-digit classifications):

- Scheduled passenger air transportation (48111)
- Scheduled freight air transportation (48112)

Fly-You-There's NAICS industry code is 48111, which is scheduled passenger air transportation. Companies in this industry primarily engage in providing air transportation of passengers and/or cargo over regular routes and on regular schedules. Companies in this industry operate flights even if they are partially loaded. Scheduled air passenger carriers, including commuter and helicopter carriers (except scenic and sightseeing), fall in this industry.

External Market Environment

Compensation professionals, top management, and consultants examine five elements of the external environment as they conduct strategic analyses.

- Industry profile
- Competition
- Foreign demand
- Industry's long-term prospects
- Labor market assessment

Several sources provide detailed information about external markets. Government sources are available at no cost. These sources include the U.S. Bureau of Labor Statistics (*www.bls.gov*), the U.S. Census Bureau's (*www.census.gov*) annual publication titled *Statistical Abstract of the United States*, and the U.S. Department of Commerce (*www.commerce.gov*). Private companies also provide excellent information about external markets, but they generally charge a fee. Some of these sources include *Business Week* (*www.businessweek.com*), Hoovers (*www.hoovers.com*), and the *Wall Street Journal* (*www.wsj.com*).

Industry Profile

Industry profiles describe such basic industry characteristics as sales volume, the impact of relevant government regulation on competitive strategies, and the impact of recent technological advancements on business activity. Compensation professionals use industry profile information to determine the kinds of compensation practices they should recommend to top management. For example, pay-for-knowledge programs may be appropriate if employees must learn to use new technology. In the case of sales stagnation, companies might choose to use incentive pay plans geared toward rewarding employees for contributing to increased sales activity.

The U.S. airline industry has experienced marked changes since the year 2000. Fewer airlines serve markets because of mergers and acquisitions. For example, United Airlines has acquired Continental Airlines, and American Airlines has acquired Trans World Airlines. Fewer competitors and consolidation of many air routes have made it easier for airlines to increase airfares somewhat because consumers face limited flight alternatives; however, the widespread economic recession since the year 2000, the uncertainties about passenger safety due to the September 11 attacks, and record-high fuel costs have weakened the airline industry. The general economic recession has led companies to reduce business travel in their quest to limit expenditures. Widespread layoffs and worries about job security cut into leisure travel. Not surprisingly, terrorists' downing of four commercial airline flights on September 11 raised fears about the safety of air travel, in large part because of gaps in airport security. Airlines reduced capacity by as much as 20 percent. That means, on average, that one of every five flights was eliminated.

Competition

Companies take stock of competitors' business activities to help position themselves in the market. Companies can distinguish themselves from the competition in different ways (e.g., top-notch customer service or state-of-the-art products), and they can achieve lowest-cost objectives in various ways (e.g., reducing advertising expenditures versus minimizing staffing levels). Compensation professionals play a role by recommending pay systems (Chapters 4, 5, and 6) and setting pay levels (Chapter 8) that support differentiation or lowest-cost objectives.

Fly-You-There competes mainly with companies in the passenger airline business that serve markets along the West Coast and in Alaska. Jet Blue, Southwest Airlines, and Song Airways are among Fly-You-There's competitors. Fly-You-There must carefully establish a competitive strategy that distinguishes itself from these competitors. For example, Fly-You-There may introduce no-frills service in markets where only a few, high-priced competitors operate. In practice, compensation professionals would give careful consideration to the specific factors that make their competitors successful and to how compensation practices can be used to create competitive advantage for their own company.

Foreign Demand

Most companies are interested in foreign demand for their products or services because such demand is an indicator of additional sales revenue potential. Compensation professionals factor in this impact of foreign demand when making their pay policy recommendations. In general, compensation professionals may feel that higher base pay rates or incentive awards are warranted in the presence of higher foreign demand. In addition, the anticipated level of demand over time is important. Compensation professionals are unlikely to alter pay policy recommendations for short-term increases (or decreases, for that matter) in foreign demand.

Foreign demand does not apply to Fly-You-There simply because the airline operates exclusively as a regional carrier within the United States. Foreign demand, however, is pertinent to U.S. airlines that serve cities outside the United States. For example, U.S. airlines face stiff competition from such airlines as KLM and Lufthansa that regularly add air service from large U.S. cities to destinations outside the United States.

Industry's Long-Term Prospects

Long-term prospects set the backdrop for strategic planning because these prospects are indicators of companies' futures. Companies establish strategic plans that fit with their industries' long-term prospects. For example, the cost of paper used in book printing has increased dramatically in recent years. Publishing companies will contain costs in other areas to limit substantial price increases because consumers will probably not purchase as many books if book prices increase commensurably with paper costs. In this type of situation, compensation professionals employed by publishing companies are apt to recommend pay policies that contribute to cost-containment objectives. At the same time, many publishers are providing access to publications through secured computer networks on the Internet, which protects them somewhat from increasing paper costs.

Long-term prospects for companies in the U.S. airline industry are unclear. Future success will turn on such factors as general national economic health, greater comfort with air transportation, and fuel costs. Of course, sluggish economic conditions, insecurities about flying safely, and higher fuel costs will curb the industry's success.

Labor Market Assessment

General Considerations

Labor market assessments represent key activities. Companies should carefully assess the labor market to determine the availability of qualified employees. In the future, many industries such as health care will find staffing more challenging. According to the U.S. Bureau of Labor Statistics, over the 2002–12 decade, total employment is projected to increase by 21.3 million jobs, or 15 percent. Over the previous decade (1992–2002), total employment grew by 20.7 million jobs, but at a slightly faster rate, 17 percent.[2]

These labor force trends have direct implications for compensation practice. In general, there will be more competition among companies for fewer qualified individuals. Higher demand for labor relative to labor supply should lead to higher wages. Companies will have to increase wages to entice the best individuals to choose employment in their companies rather than their competitors' companies. The greater prevalence of older employees also should increase typical wage levels. As we will discuss in Chapter 4, older workers will probably have higher wages than younger workers. The prevalence of older workers relative to younger workers should translate into higher compensation costs to companies.[3]

The civilian labor force is projected to increase by 17.4 million over the 2002–12 decade, reaching 162.3 million by 2012. This 12 percent increase is greater than the 11.3-percent increase over the previous decade, 1992–2002, when the labor force grew by 14.4 million. Changes in the demographic composition of the labor force are expected because of changes both in the composition of the population and in the rates of labor force participation across demographic groups.

The projected growth of the labor force will be affected by the aging of the baby-boom generation—persons born between 1946 and 1964. In 2012, baby boomers will be 48 to 66 years old. The number of workers in this age group is expected to increase significantly over the 2002–12 decade. The labor force will continue to age, with the number of workers in the 55-and-older group projected to grow by 49.3 percent, four times the 12 percent growth projected for the overall labor force. In 2012, youths—those between the ages of 16 and 24—will constitute 15 percent of the labor force, and prime-age workers—those between the ages of 25 and 54—will make up 66 percent of the labor force. The share of the 55-and-older age group will increase from 14.3 percent to 19.1 percent of the labor force.

The labor force participation rates of women in nearly all age groups are projected to increase. The number of women in the labor force is projected to grow by 14.3 percent, faster than the 10 percent growth projected for men. As a result, women's share of the labor force is expected to increase by 1 percent, from 46.5 percent in 2002 to 47.5 percent by 2012. In contrast, men's share is projected to decline by 1 percent—from 53.5 percent to 52.5 percent over the 2002–12 decade.

By 2012, the Hispanic labor force is expected to reach 23.8 million, due to faster population growth resulting from a younger population, higher fertility rates, and increased immigration levels. Despite relatively slow growth, white non-Hispanics will remain the largest group, composing 66 percent of the labor force. Asians will continue to be the fastest growing of the four labor force groups.

Occupation-Specific Considerations

Companies should keep tabs on the occupational mix of their workforces and the relative importance of these occupations to maintaining competitive advantage. Compensation levels generally increase with the strategic importance of jobs to companies' strategic values and, as mentioned previously, the relative supply of labor.

For illustrative purposes, let's consider the labor market status of commercial airline pilots. Every airline naturally needs pilots to operate aircraft to ensure the safety of passengers. An excellent starting point is the Bureau of Labor Statistics *Occupational Outlook Handbook*. This handbook contains pertinent information for conducting effective strategic analyses:

- Qualifications and training
- Job outlook
- Typical earnings range

First, information about qualifications and training helps companies focus recruitment efforts on individuals with the necessary qualifications. Pilots who are paid to transport passengers or cargo must possess a commercial pilot's license with an instrument rating. The Federal Aviation Administration (FAA) issues this license and rating to a pilot based on sufficient flight experience in designated conditions, good health and vision, and written and flight tests to demonstrate acceptable knowledge and skills. In addition, candidates for positions with airlines must have an airline transport pilot's license. Earning this license entails at least 1,500 hours of flying experience, including night and instrument experience, and successful completion of additional written and flight tests. Furthermore, applicants must possess advanced ratings that certify their competence to fly particular kinds of aircraft based on job requirements. For example, pilots assigned to fly Boeing 747 aircraft must have demonstrated competence to fly this type of plane before they may be compensated to transport passengers in Boeing 747s. Finally, some airlines may require applicants to pass tests of judgment under stress conditions.

Second, the BLS job outlook provides companies an indication of job prospects. Three scenarios describe possible job outlooks: retrenchment, status quo, and growth. Retrenchment means that fewer jobs will be available for a designated period. Status quo suggests that the present level of job opportunities will remain constant for a designated period. Under the growth scenario, job opportunities will be higher than present levels for a designated period. The BLS predicts that airline pilots will face growth at least until 2012, with an expected increase of 18.5 from 2002 employment levels.[4]

Third, the typical earnings range helps companies establish competitive pay levels. Companies would find it difficult to attract well-qualified candidates if they set pay levels and benefits too low. In addition, paying and setting benefits well above the market may present a cost burden to companies. According to the BLS:

Earnings of aircraft pilots and flight engineers vary greatly depending on whether they work as airline or commercial pilots. Earnings of airline pilots are among the highest in the nation, and depend on factors such as the type, size, and maximum speed of the plane and the number of hours and miles flown. For example, pilots who fly jet aircraft usually earn higher salaries than do pilots who fly turboprops. Airline pilots and flight engineers may earn extra pay for night and international flights. In 2002, median annual earnings of airline pilots, copilots, and flight engineers were $109,580. The lowest 10 percent earned less than $55,800. More than 25 percent earned over $145,000. Median annual earnings of commercial pilots were $47,970 in 2002. The middle 50 percent earned between $33,830 and $70,140. The lowest 10 percent earned less than $26,100, and the highest 10 percent earned more than $101,460.

Airline pilots usually are eligible for life and health insurance plans financed by the airlines. They also receive retirement benefits and, if they fail the FAA physical examination at some point in their careers, they get disability payments. In addition, pilots receive an expense allowance, or "per diem," for every day they are away from home. Some airlines also provide allowances to pilots for purchasing and cleaning their uniforms. As an additional benefit, pilots and their immediate families usually are entitled to free or reduced-fare transportation on their own and other airlines.

More than half of all aircraft pilots are members of unions. Most of the pilots who fly for the major airlines are members of the Airline Pilots Association, International, but those employed by one major airline are members of the Allied Pilots Association. Some flight engineers are members of the Flight Engineers' International Association.[5]

In sum, labor market assessments are key elements of strategic analyses. Based on our analysis of Fly-You-There's situation, their compensation professionals should include a labor market assessment of pilots. Pilots, therefore, are obviously key to airline operations.

Internal Capabilities

Compensation professionals, top management, and consultants should examine three internal capabilities as part of strategic analyses:

- Functional capabilities
- Human resource capabilities
- Financial condition

Functional Capabilities

Companies must determine which functional capabilities are most crucial to maintaining competitive advantage. Functional capabilities include manufacturing, engineering, research and development, operations, management information systems, human resources (HR), and marketing. Competition among airlines necessitates that Fly-You-There maintains such strong functional capabilities as marketing and operations to spread the word that the airline offers competitive fares and regular on-time arrivals and departures.

Research and development is not a critical function for all companies. For example, companies such as PepsiCo rely on marketing savvy to remain competitive. Many consumers of diet soft drinks complain that their taste is not as appealing as regular soft drinks that contain sugar. PepsiCo's introduction of the Pepsi One diet soft drink represents the corporation's attempt to increase sales and market share by identifying with diet soft drink consumers who want a taste that more closely resembles sugared soft drinks.

Human Resources Capabilities

State-of-the-art research equipment, manufacturing systems, and efficient marketing distribution systems do not provide competitive advantage unless staffed with knowledgeable and productive employees. Pay-for-performance and pay-for-knowledge programs promote productive and knowledgeable employees. Merit pay programs reinforce prior excellent job performance with permanent base pay increases. Incentive pay programs reward employees for attaining predetermined performance standards. Employees generally know in advance that rewards increase with higher performance attainments, as well as how much they will earn for achieving particular performance goals. Companies design pay-for-knowledge programs to reward self-improvement, and these programs are essential when technology advances rapidly.

Financial Condition

A company's **financial condition** is a key consideration for top management officials and HR professionals. Financial condition has implications for a company's ability to compete. Sound financial conditions enable companies to meet operating and capital requirements; poor financial conditions prevent companies from adequately meeting operating and capital requirements.

Operating requirements encompass all HR programs. Top management limits funding increases for compensation programs when financial conditions are poor. As a result, employees' salaries stagnate, and job offers to potential employees will probably not be competitive. Salary stagnation leads to turnover, particularly among highly qualified employees, because they will have higher-paying job opportunities elsewhere. **Capital requirements** include automated manufacturing technology and office and plant facilities. Companies that pursue differentiation strategies require state-of-the-art instruments and work facilities to conduct leading-edge research. Lowest-cost companies need efficient equipment that keeps costs per unit as low as possible.

FACTORS THAT INFLUENCE COMPANIES' COMPETITIVE STRATEGIES AND COMPENSATION PRACTICES

Several factors influence a company's choice of competitive strategies and compensation tactics. These include national culture, organizational culture, and organizational and product (or service) life cycle. Table 2-2 lists the particular dimensions of these influences on competitive strategy and compensation tactics.

National Culture

National culture refers to the set of shared norms and beliefs among individuals within national boundaries who are indigenous to that area. National culture has increasingly become an important consideration in strategic compensation and influences the effectiveness of various forms of pay as motivators of proficient employee behavior. The U.S. managers responsible for managing compensation programs abroad may find that cultural differences reduce the effectiveness of U.S. compensation practices. This problem is particularly troublesome, given the rise in U.S. companies' presence in such foreign countries as India, the Philippines, Mexico, and the People's Republic of China. Foreign offices or plants of multinational corporations tend to employ local nationals who may not understand U.S. culture. In the People's Republic of China, native Chinese who work for U.S.–Chinese joint venture companies are not accustomed to performance-based pay because the Communist influence in China led to need-based pay programs.

TABLE 2-2 Influences on Competitive Strategy

National Culture

- Power distance
- Individualism–collectivism
- Uncertainty avoidance
- Masculinity–femininity

Organizational Culture

- Traditional organizational hierarchy
- Flatter organizational structures
- Team orientation

Organizational and Product Life Cycle

- Growth
- Maturity
- Decline

Compensation experts maintain that understanding the normative expectations of different national cultures should promote competitive advantage.[6] Thus, it is important to be familiar with differences in national culture and to understand how those differences may influence the effectiveness of alternative pay programs. Geert Hofstede, a renowned researcher of national cultures, categorizes national cultures among four dimensions: power distance, individualism–collectivism, uncertainty avoidance, and masculinity–femininity.[7] Although Hofstede developed this categorization more than 25 years ago, it is still relevant today. This categorization of variations in national culture facilitates a discussion of how they may affect compensation tactics.

Power distance is the extent to which people accept a hierarchical system or power structure in companies. Status differentials between employees and employers are typical in high power distance cultures. Cultures that highly value power distance are likely to have compensation strategies that reinforce status differentials among employees, perhaps using visible rewards that project power. For example, Venezuela, the Philippines, and Arab nations rate high on power distance, according to Hofstede. Where power distance is not a dominant value, compensation strategies probably should endorse egalitarian compensation tactics as well as participatory pay programs. Australia, Sweden, and the Netherlands rate lower on power distance.

Individualism–collectivism is the extent to which individuals value personal independence or group membership. Individualist cultures value personal goals, independence, and privacy. Collectivist cultures favor social cohesiveness and loyalty to such groups as co-workers and families. Individualist cultures adopt compensation strategies that reward individual performance, as well as acquisition of skill or knowledge. In collectivist societies, employers reward employees on the basis of group performance and individual seniority to recognize the importance of employees' affiliations with groups. We will shortly contrast U.S. and Japanese cultures, which exemplify individualism and collectivism, respectively.

Uncertainty avoidance represents the method by which society deals with risk and instability for its members. Fear of random events, value of stability and routines, and risk aversion are hallmarks of high uncertainty avoidance. Italy and Greece are examples of countries that rate high on uncertainty avoidance. On the other hand, welcoming random events, valuing challenge, and seeking risk characterize low uncertainty avoidance. Where uncertainty avoidance is high, employers probably use bureaucratic pay policies, emphasize fixed pay as more important than variable pay, and bestow little discretion to supervisors in distributing pay. Where uncertainty avoidance is low, employers probably use incentive pay programs and grant supervisors extensive latitude in pay allocation. Singapore and Denmark rate low on uncertainty avoidance.

Masculinity–femininity refers to whether masculine or feminine values are dominant in society. "Masculinity" favors material possessions. "Femininity" encourages caring and nurturing behavior. The compensation strategies of masculine cultures are likely to contain pay policies that allow for inequities by gender, as well as paternalistic benefits for women in the form of paid maternity leave and day care. Mexico and Germany possess masculine national cultures. In contrast, the compensation strategies of feminine cultures may encourage job evaluation regardless of gender composition, as well as offer perquisites on bases other than gender. Finland and Norway possess feminine national cultures.

In sum, national culture is a complex phenomenon that is related to differences in compensation practices. Hofstede provides a useful framework for describing the dimensions of national culture. Next, we contrast the national cultures of the United States and Japan to illustrate the influence of national culture on compensation practices. The individualism–collectivism dimension characterizes the differences between U.S. and Japanese culture. Cultural norms should be evident as we review compensation and benefits practices in selected countries around the world.

U.S. Culture

The U.S. culture is a good example of individualism and emphasizes instrumentality. Employees strive for high levels of performance when they believe that better performance leads to better pay. Money derives importance from what it can buy, the sense of security it creates, its perception as a sign of achievement, and its definition of personal relationships. Although team-based compensation programs are becoming increasingly popular in U.S. companies, the predominant compensation practices in U.S. companies reward individual performance (i.e., merit pay and incentive pay) or individuals' acquisition of job-relevant knowledge or skills (i.e., pay-for-knowledge and skill-based pay). Moreover, U.S. companies that adopt team-based programs offer them as a supplement rather than as an alternative to individual-based compensation practices.

Japanese Culture

Japan's national culture is collectivist. Influenced by the Zen, Confucian, and Samurai traditions, the predominant values of Japanese culture are social cooperation and responsibility, acceptance of reality, and perseverance. People hold dear their membership in groups. Duty to group needs prevails over each individual's needs and personal feelings. Failure to meet group needs results in personal shame because society disapproves of individuals who do not hold group interests in high esteem.

These principles apply to all aspects of Japanese life, including employment. Traditionally, employers have highly valued employees' affiliations, and they have taken personal interest in employees' personal lives as well as their work lives. The value placed on group membership leads employers to care about the well-being of their employees' families because families are important groups in Japan. Employers generally award base pay to meet families' needs as well as according to seniority to honor affiliation as employees.

Compared with North Americans, the Japanese are more likely to produce at high levels because of the values that they embrace rather than because of what is in it for them.[8] This contrast holds implications for compensation tactics in these two countries. Compensation professionals traditionally designed U.S. compensation systems to reward individual performance. The time orientation also tends to be short-term—typically one year or less.[9] In Japan, compensation professionals design pay systems to reward employees' loyalty and to meet the personal needs of the individual because Japanese employers value employees' affiliation with their companies. Japanese compensation systems focus on the long term, changing as employees' needs change throughout their work lives.

Organizational Culture

Organizational culture is an organization's system of shared values and beliefs that produce norms of behavior. These values are apparent in companies' organizational and work structures. Organizational culture also influences HR systems designs, including compensation.

Traditional Hierarchy

The traditional design of U.S. companies emphasizes efficiency, decision making by managers, and dissemination of information from the top of the company to lower levels. Figure 2-2 illustrates a traditional organizational hierarchy. The company's executive vice president is the intermediary for the company's chief executive officer and

FIGURE 2-2 Traditional Organizational Structure

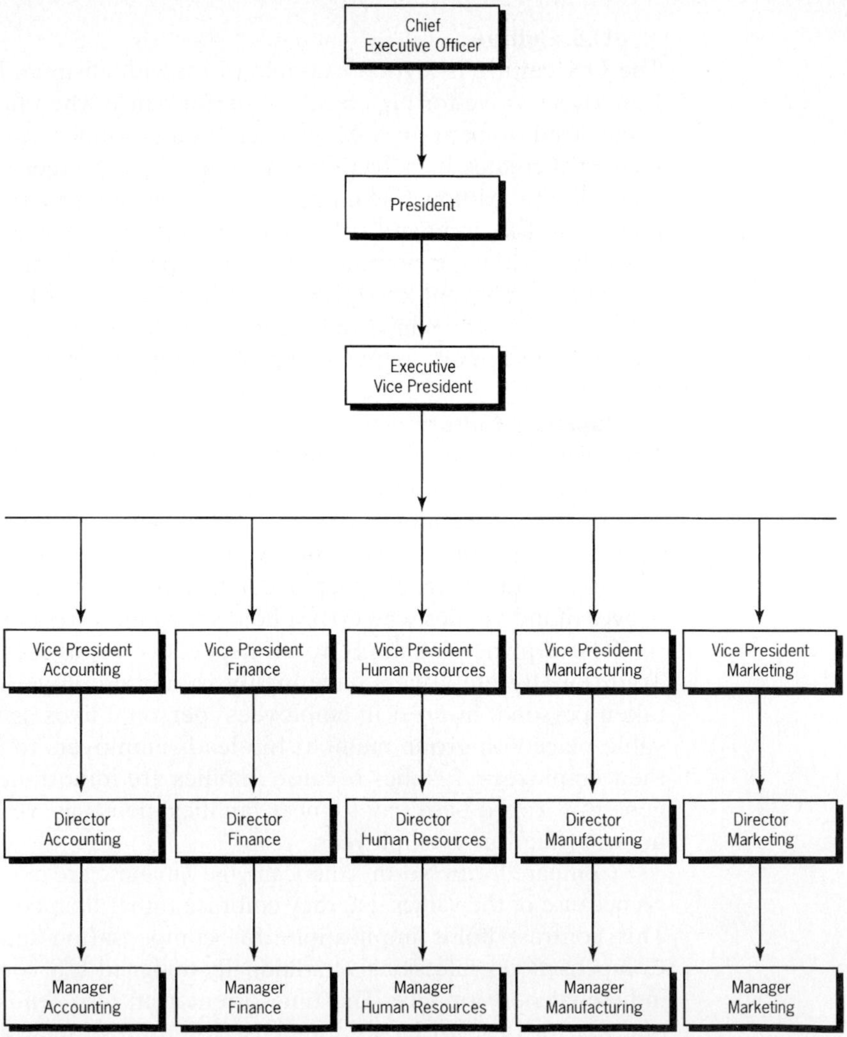

the vice presidents of the functional areas. Within the functional areas, the decision making flows downward from the vice presidents to managers of specialties within the functions.

For example, a company's top executives recognize the need to motivate employees to learn new skills associated with changing workplace technology. As discussed in Chapter 1, systematic training programs and pay-for-knowledge programs go hand in hand. Thus, the executive vice president communicates the strategic imperative for developing a pay-for-knowledge program to the vice presidents of training and compensation. These vice presidents in turn charge their directors and managers with the responsibility of developing such programs. The managers identify the major design considerations of pay-for-knowledge programs (Chapter 9). Table 2-3 lists these main considerations.

Seniority pay (Chapter 4) and such pay-for-performance programs as merit pay (Chapter 4) fit best with traditional hierarchical structures. Seniority pay programs create hierarchies based on length of time in a job. Under seniority systems, employees performing the same jobs may receive markedly different pay. Likewise, merit pay programs create hierarchies: The use of narrower pay grades (i.e., pay grades that contain relatively few jobs) tends to promote hierarchy. As we discussed in Chapter 1, pay grades group jobs for pay policy application, and pay ranges indicate acceptable minimum, midpoint, and maximum pay rates for each pay grade. In addition, we discussed that compensation professionals group jobs into pay grades based on such compensable factors as skill, effort, responsibility, and working conditions. In general, minimum, midpoint, and maximum pay rates increase as the level of compensable factors (e.g., greater skill) increases.

Flattening the Organization

Although traditional hierarchical organizational structures are still prevalent, many companies' structures are flattening, or becoming less bureaucratic.[10] Many companies have recognized the need to move to an adaptive, high-involvement organizational structure. In the adaptive organizational structure, employees are in a constant state of learning and performance improvement.[11] Employees are free to move wherever they are needed in the company. Employees, managers, vendors, customers, and suppliers work together to improve service quality and to create new products and services. Line employees are trained in multiple jobs, communicate directly with suppliers and customers, and interact frequently with engineers, quality experts, and employees from other functions.

TABLE 2-3 Designing Pay-for-Knowledge Programs

Establishing Skill Blocks

- Skill type
- Number of skills
- Grouping of skills

Transition Matters

- Skills assessment
- Aligning pay with the knowledge structure
- Access to training

Training and Certification

- In-house or outsourcing training
- Certification and recertification

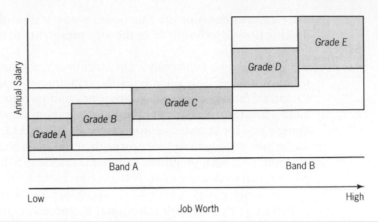

FIGURE 2-3   Broadbanding Structure and Its Relationship to Traditional Pay Grades and Ranges

Broadbanding (Chapter 9) represents the increasing organizational trend toward flatter, less hierarchical corporate structures that emphasize teamwork over individual contributions alone. Broadbanding uses only a few large salary ranges, spanning levels within the organization previously covered by several pay grades. Thus, HR professionals place jobs that were separated by one or more pay grades in old pay structures into the same band under broadbanding systems, minimizing hierarchical differences among jobs. Figure 2-3 illustrates the broadbanding concept.

Team Orientation

Employers in the United States are increasingly using teams to get work done. Two main changes in the business environment have led to this development. First, in the 1980s, the rise in the number of Japanese companies conducting business in the United States was dramatic. The team approach to work is a common feature of Japanese companies. Second, team-based job design promotes innovation in the workplace. Whirlpool Corporation uses teams to manufacture appliances, and Saturn uses teams to manufacture automobiles.

Companies need to change individualistic compensation practices so that groups are rewarded for their collaborative behavior. Accordingly, team-based pay plans should emphasize cooperation between and within teams, compensate employees for additional responsibilities they often must assume in their roles as members of a team, and encourage team members to attain predetermined objectives for the team.

Team-based organizational structures encourage team members to learn new skills and assume broader responsibility than is expected of them under traditional pay structures that are geared toward individuals. Employees who work in teams must initiate plans for achieving their team's production goals. A pay plan for teams usually emphasizes cooperation, rewarding its members for the additional responsibilities they must take on and for the skills and knowledge they must acquire. Chapter 5 addresses the design of team incentive pay plans. Chapter 6 will show how skill-based pay plans and knowledge-based pay can address these additional responsibilities.

Organizational and Product Life Cycles

Many business professionals set competitive strategies on the basis of organizational and product life cycles. **Organizational and product life cycles** describe the evolution of companies and products in terms of human life cycle stages. Much as people are born, grow, mature, decline, and die, so do companies, products, and services. Business priorities, including HR, vary with life cycle stages. In particular, life cycle stages influence the choice of competitive strategies and such specific HR strategies as compensation.

Growth Phase

Differentiation strategies are most appropriate for companies in the growth phase. In competitive markets, newcomers must distinguish themselves from the established competitors in ways that appeal to prospective consumers and clients. Failure to do so will create competitive disadvantages. After all, why purchase a product or service from a new, unknown company when you can get exactly the same thing from a well-known company?

Companies that provide services on the Internet are growth companies. The Internet is a single network that connects millions of computers around the world. The number of computers connected to the Internet has grown exponentially. Likewise, the amount of information on the Internet has grown exponentially. There does not appear to be a foreseeable slowdown in the expansion of the Internet. Lycos and Google are examples of growth companies that provide services on the Internet. These companies offer "search engines" that enable individuals to systematically locate, identify, and edit material on the Internet on the basis of key words and concepts. Research and development is a key focus because these companies continually develop new software to increase their search capabilities.

Growth companies experience cash demands to finance capital expansion projects (e.g., new buildings, manufacturing equipment, or enhanced telecommunications services). These companies also strive to employ the best-qualified employees for key positions. Getting the most talented executives and professional employees often requires exorbitant expenditures on compensation, discounting labor cost containment strategies. As a result, growth companies tend to emphasize market-competitive pay systems over internally consistent pay systems.

Not all core compensation tactics are appropriate for growth companies. Long-term incentive programs with annual or longer goals for professionals and executives are suitable. Rewarding engineers' innovations in product design requires a long-term orientation: It takes an extended amount of time to move through the series of steps required to bring the innovation to the marketplace (i.e., patent approval, manufacturing, and market distribution). The incentives that executives receive are based on long-term horizons because their success is matched against the endurance of their companies over time (Chapter 13). Lucrative long-term incentive awards may be able to maintain key employees' commitment to growth objectives over time.

Core compensation tactics for staff (e.g., compensation specialist) and lower-level line employees (e.g., first-line supervisors) typically consist of base pay periodically increased with modest merit awards. Base pay levels are usually consistent with external market pay rates. Although these employees are not directly responsible for company growth, they do contribute by offering consistency in the product manufacturing or service delivery processes. In some cases, growth companies may set base pay levels somewhat below external market rates to maximize cash flow for research and development (R&D) activities or marketing campaigns. As we will discuss in Chapter 9, setting base pay too low may make it difficult for companies to recruit and retain well-qualified employees.

Growth companies tend to keep discretionary benefits offerings to a minimum. As we will discuss in Chapter 11, discretionary benefits represent a significant fiscal cost to companies. In March 2007, U.S. companies spent an average of $12,771 per employee annually to provide discretionary benefits.[12] Such discretionary benefits accounted for approximately one third of employers' total payroll costs (i.e., the sum of core compensation and all fringe compensation costs). For too many years, companies have awarded benefits to employees regardless of employee's performance or the cost impact of these benefits on company performance. Growth companies cannot afford expenditures that do not contribute directly to growth objectives.

Maturity

Lowest-cost strategies are most appropriate for mature companies. Products and services have fully evolved within the constraints of technology. Mature companies strive to maintain or gain market share. Efficient operations are paramount to striking a balance between cost containment and offering the best possible quality products or services.

Southwest Airlines is an example of a mature company that successfully pursues a lowest-cost strategy. Several features of Southwest's operations account for its success as a low-cost, yet safe and reliable airline. Southwest does not offer as many nonstop flight arrangements as do its competitors. For example, flying from New Orleans to Indianapolis may require three separate flights—New Orleans to Houston, Houston to St. Louis, and St. Louis to Indianapolis. By offering shorter flights, Southwest can more easily fill its planes, thereby increasing cost efficiency. Southwest also saves money by using an open seating policy on its flights. This open seating policy frees up reservationists' time for booking additional reservations. Finally, Southwest Airlines manages costs by not offering full meal services on its flights.

Mature companies usually have large, well-developed internal labor markets. Internal labor markets are pools of skills and abilities from among a company's current workforce. As companies mature, employees presumably become more skilled and able to make greater contributions to the attainment of companies' goals. Management can capitalize on internal labor markets through the implementation of career development programs. Current excellent performers may receive promotions, leaving mainly entry-level job openings available to external candidates.

As we will discuss in Chapter 6, pay-for-knowledge and skill-based pay programs are suitable for companies that pursue lowest-cost strategies. Both programs are instrumental in developing internal labor markets. In the short run, pay-for-knowledge and skill-based pay programs may undermine the imperatives of lowest-cost strategies because of the associated training costs; however, productivity enhancements and increased flexibility should far outweigh the short-run costs.

Other core compensation programs may be appropriate for lowest-cost strategies as well. Base pay rates logically should be set below the market average to contain costs; however, compensation professionals must recommend pay rates that strike a balance between efficiency man-dates and the need to retain valued employees. Setting base pay to meet market averages often strikes this balance when this tactic is augmented with incentive pay. Lowest-cost strategies demand reduced output costs per employee. As we discussed in Chapter 1, incentive pay fluctuates according to employees' attainment of some standard based on a preestablished formula, individual or group goals, or company earnings. Merit pay systems are most appropriate only when the following two conditions are met: (1) Pay increases are commensurate with employee productivity, and (2) employees maintain productivity long after receiving permanent increments to base pay.

Decline

Companies in decline experience diminishing markets and, subsequently, poor business performance. Several factors can result in decline, including limited financial resources and changes in consumer preferences. Business leaders can respond to decline in either of two ways. They can allow decline to continue until the business is no longer profitable, or they can make substantial changes that reverse decline. A company's response to decline determines whether lowest-cost or differentiation strategies are most appropriate.

Differentiation strategies become the focus when companies choose to redirect activities toward distinguishing themselves from the competition by modifying existing products or services in some creative way or by developing new products or services. American Express Corporation differentiated itself in response to the declining market for its charge cards. Changes in preferences have led consumers to choose credit cards over charge cards. These changes created problems for American Express, which is well known for charge cards. Charge card agreements require cardholders to pay balances in full, typically on a monthly basis. Credit cards are based on revolving debt. Credit card holders have the option to pay balances in full, typically on a monthly basis, without paying interest charges. On the other hand, credit card holders may pay only a small percentage (usually 5 percent or less) of their debt every month, but pay interest on remaining balances to the credit card companies. Credit card purchases are consistent with the trend in U.S. consumer purchasing patterns toward spending now and paying much later. The American Express Company lost considerable market share and revenue because of this trend in consumer purchasing patterns. In response to these changing consumer preferences, the American Express Company began offering a variety of credit cards to suit various consumer preferences for repayment options (e,g., repayment over extended periods, repayment in full some months later) and rewards programs (e.g., airline frequent flyer miles, discounts on shopping).

Lowest-cost strategies are most appropriate when companies allow decline to continue to business closure. The era of small, family-owned furniture stores is coming to an end as large discount furniture stores take hold. This trend is the result of two factors. First, small, family-owned furniture stores generally charge substantial price premiums (anywhere from 200 percent to 300 percent more than the manufacturers' suggested prices). Large discount stores usually price furniture well below manufacturers' suggested rates—anywhere from 30 percent to 80 percent. Second, showroom space is quite limited in family-owned stores relative to the large discount stores. As a result, the family-owned businesses display far less furniture, giving the consumer fewer options from which to choose. These factors make it virtually impossible for family-owned furniture stores to compete. Many of these small businesses choose to go out of business. Upon making this decision, these businesses adopt lowest-cost strategies in which they offer deep discounts to sell remaining inventories as quickly as possible. Although profit margins are lower under these circumstances, business owners are more likely sooner to minimize losses by eliminating such overhead expenses as rent, utilities, insurance, and compensation.

SUMMARY

This chapter reviewed strategic compensation in action. We discussed the importance of strategic analysis in identifying competitive forces facing companies. Strategic analyses enable compensation professionals to better understand the internal and external contexts of their companies, giving them a better sense of how much they can afford to compensate employees. We then discussed factors that influence competitive strategies and compensation practices: national culture, organizational culture, and organizational and product life cycle. As competition increases, compensation professionals must move into action by skillfully choosing compensation practices to promote the attainment of competitive advantage.

KEY TERMS

- strategic analysis, 27
- North American Industry Classification System Manual, 27
- North American Industry Classification System (NAICS), 27
- sector, 28
- subsector, 28

- industry group, 28
- industry, 28
- national industry, 28
- industry profiles, 30
- labor market assessments, 32
- financial condition, 35
- operating requirements, 35
- capital requirements, 35

- national culture, 35
- power distance, 36
- individualism–collectivism, 36
- uncertainty avoidance, 36
- masculinity–femininity, 37
- organizational and product life cycles, 40

DISCUSSION QUESTIONS

1. Discuss what strategic compensation means to you.
2. Describe the purpose of the NAICS.
3. Earlier, we referred to a few of Fly-You-There's competitors. Go to the Web sites of three competitors and summarize similarities and differences between two competitors' business objectives.
4. Describe why a company's long-term prospects are an important consideration to compensation professionals.
5. National culture is a more important influence on compensation systems than organizational culture. Discuss whether you agree or disagree with this statement.
6. Identify three products or services with which you are familiar. Discuss whether these are in growth, maturity, or decline stages.

EXERCISES

Compensation Online

For Students

Exercise 1: Find relevant journal articles

Use your school library's online catalog to locate articles pertaining to competitive strategies, organizational cultures, and organizational life cycles. Find and read several current articles in these areas. As a student who will be looking for employment in the near future, what sort of culture will you look for in prospective employers?

Exercise 2: Review a research site

An assignment requires you to analyze a certain industry with which you are not familiar. Using the Yahoo! search engine, type in "NAICS" and click on the search button. Find the NAICS homepage. Read over their homepage to understand what information is available in the NAICS manual.

Using a different search engine, go to the same Web site or find a related site. Compare and contrast the two search engines for ease of accessibility and amount of information available.

Exercise 3: Research a government document

Go to the NAICS Web site, click on the New Code System link, which is located on the left side of the homepage. Review the information on this page. Write a brief description of how this information will affect you in your career.

For Professionals

Exercise 1: Research trade magazines and newsletters

You have just begun working for a company in an industry that is entirely new to you. Use a search engine to find examples of trade magazines and newsletters of any industry you are interested in. Read about different aspects of the industry environment, and try to think how you might use this information if you were working in this industry.

Exercise 2: Examine industry profiles

Your company is set to overhaul policies and operations, including pay. You must get your department started on some basic industry analysis. Search for "industry profile" and use the resulting sites to learn characteristics of different industries. How will things like nature of business, number of competitors, and industry regulation affect you in your HR career?

Exercise 3: Analyze an organization's Web page

You have been asked to sit in on a meeting with representatives of the World Trade Organization. You naturally want to be as prepared as you can. Using the Google search engine, type in "World Trade Organization" and click on the search button. Under the Web sites listing, click on the World Trade Organization (WTO) link. Read over the page and click on a couple of the links to see what information is available.

Using a different search engine, go to the same Web site or find a related site. Compare and contrast the two search engines for ease of accessibility and amount of information available.

What does the WTO do? What interactions might you have with the WTO when you begin your career? Think about working in a few different industries and how much the WTO would be involved with each.

ENDNOTES

1. U.S. Office of Management and Budget. (2007). *North American industry classification system manual.* [online]. Available: *www.nits.gov/naics*, accessed June 29, 2007.
2. U.S. Department of Labor. (2004). *BLS releases 2002–12 employment projections* (USDL 04–148). Washington, DC: Author.
3. Ibid.
4. U.S. Department of Labor. (2004). *Occupational projections and training data* (Bulletin 2572). Washington, DC: Government Printing Office.
5. Ibid.
6. Gòmez-Mejía, L. R., & Welbourne, T. (1991). Compensation strategies in a global context. *Human Resource Planning, 14*, pp. 29–41.
7. Hofstede, G. (1980). *Culture's Consequences.* Newbury Park, CA: Sage.
8. Muczyk, J. P., & Hastings, R. E. (1985). In defense of enlightened hardball management. *Business Horizons,* July–August, pp. 23–29.
9. Heneman, R. L., & Werner, J. M. (2005). *Merit Pay: Linking Pay to Performance in a Changing World.* Greenwich, CT: Information Age Publishers.
10. Barney, J., & Hesterly, W. (2006). *Strategic Management and Competitive Advantage: Concepts and Cases.* Upper Saddle River, NJ: Prentice Hall.
11. Ibid.
12. U.S. Bureau of Labor Statistics. (2007). *Employer costs for employee compensation—March 2007* [online]. Available: *www.bls.gov/ncs/ect/home.htm*, accessed June 30, 2007.

CHAPTER 3

Contextual Influences on Compensation Practice

Chapter Outline

- Compensation and the Social Good
    Employees' Goals
    Employers' Goals
    Government's Goals

- Employment Laws That Influence Compensation Tactics
    Income Continuity, Safety, and Work Hours
    Pay Discrimination
    Accommodating Disabilities and Family Needs
    Prevailing Wage Laws

- Laws that Guide Discretionary Employee Benefits
    Internal Revenue Code (IRC)
    Employee Retirement Income Security Act of 1974 (ERISA)
    Consolidated Omnibus Budget Reconciliation Act of 1985 (COBRA)
    Health Insurance Portability and Accountability Act of 1996 (HIPAA)
    Pension Protection Act of 2006

- Contextual Influences on the Federal Government as an Employer

- Labor Unions as Contextual Influences

- Market Influences

- Summary

- Key Terms

- Discussion Questions

- Exercises

- Endnotes

Learning Objectives

In this chapter, you will learn about

1. Compensation and the social good

2. Various laws that influence private sector companies' and labor unions' compensation practices

3. Contextual influences on the federal government's compensation practices

4. Labor unions' influence on companies' compensation practices

5. Market factors' impact on companies' compensation practices

As competition increased in the textile industry, the original concern of the mill owners for their employees gave way to stricter controls that had nothing to do with the well-being of the workers. Employers reduced wages, lengthened hours, and intensified work. For a workday ranging from 11½ to 13 hours, making up an average week of 75 hours, the women operatives were generally earning less than $1.50 a week (exclusive of board) by the late 1840s, and they were being compelled to tend four looms, whereas they had only taken care of two in the 1830s. [The manager] ordered them [the female textile workers] to come before breakfast. "I regard my work-people just as I regard my machinery. So long as they can do my work for what I choose to pay them, I keep them, getting out of them all I can."[1]

Anne Brown, the claims department manager of a small insurance company, said to Bill Smith, the human resource (HR) manager, "I'm sick and tired of having clerks who just don't work out. The quality of their work is not very good nor are they reliable—they are frequently absent or late. They are limiting my ability to maintain timely and accurate claims processing." Bill replied, "You get no argument from me. It's been nearly impossible to recruit top quality clerks ever since ABC Automobile Parts Company established a manufacturing facility across town. After all, ABC's clerks earn nearly 40 percent more than our clerks."

The previous quotations illustrate three major contextual influences on companies' compensation practices. The first quotation captures the inherent conflict between employers and employees—employers' profit maximization objectives and employees' desire for equitable and fair treatment. This conflict gave rise to the first two contextual influences that we will review in this chapter—federal protective legislation and labor unions.

The second quotation represents a third contextual influence, market forces. In particular, this quotation illustrates a potential consequence of interindustry compensation differentials—the inability to recruit top quality employees. We will address these differentials later in the chapter.

COMPENSATION AND THE SOCIAL GOOD

The social good refers to a booming economy, low levels of unemployment, progressive wages and benefits, and safe and healthful working conditions. Compensation promotes the social good by enabling citizens actively to participate as consumers in the economy. Conflicting goals among employees, employers, and the government, however, can threaten the social good. Figure 3-1 illustrates the relationships among employees', employers', and the government's goals.[2] The overlapping areas represent the mutual goals between any two or all three groups. The nonoverlapping areas represent unique goals that can undermine the social good.

Employees, employers, and the government do share some common goals. Each group wants a booming economy. Employers' profits and the demand for their products and services tend to be high within booming economies. Employees prosper because unemployment is low and consumers tend to have confidence in the future, which leads to higher spending. Higher income tax revenues enable the government to fund programs (e.g., national defense) and government employees' compensation packages.

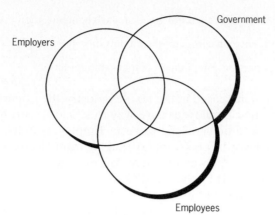

FIGURE 3-1 Employers', Employees', and Government's Goals

Employees' Goals

Employees' fundamental goals are to attain high wages, comprehensive benefits, safe and healthful work conditions, and job security. Prior to the 1930s, employees did not possess the right to negotiate with their employers over terms and conditions of employment. As a result, many workers were subjected to poor working conditions, low pay, and excessive work hours.[3] as illustrated by the first opening quotation. Unemployment was an employee's main alternative to enduring these conditions. Employment legislation and labor unions now protect workers' rights and status. Employer abuses are much less prevalent than they were before the passage of legislation and the rise of labor unions. Nevertheless, employers still maintain the fundamental profit maximization objective, which necessitates legal and labor union interventions.

Employers' Goals

The employers depicted in Figure 3-1 are private sector companies. Private sector employers strive to increase profits, market share, and returns on investment. These employers expect workers to be as productive as possible and to produce the highest quality of products and services. The majority of U.S. civilian employees work under this objective. In May 2007, about 85 percent of all U.S. civilian employees worked for private sector businesses, and the remaining 15 percent worked for the government (municipal, state, or federal).[4]

Government's Goals

The government's ultimate goal is to promote the social good without extensive involvement in private sector employers' operations. It must operate as both an employer and consumer to achieve the social good. In 2007, the government employed 15 percent—about 22 million employees—of all U.S. civilian employees to ensure national security and legal compliance.[5]

In addition, the government is both a buyer and consumer of the products and services that private sector companies produce. In 2007, the federal government's expenditures were expected to exceed $2.7 trillion.[6] The government uses energy to run its buildings, and it engages in contracts with private sector companies for a multitude of goods and services (e.g., building construction and multimillion dollar defense systems). The vast total of the government's expenditures were for nondefense purposes. The federal government awarded contracts to private sector companies that totaled $453 billion.

EMPLOYMENT LAWS THAT INFLUENCE COMPENSATION TACTICS

Employment laws are essential to maintain a balance of power; in the case of compensation practice, helping to ensure that pursuit of goals by any one group does not undermine others' goals, particularly those with the least amount of power—employees. In a nutshell:

> The freedom to contract is crucial to freedom of the market; an employee may choose to work or not to work for a given employer, and an employer may choose to hire or not to hire a given applicant. As a result, the employment relationship is regulated in some important ways. Congress tries to avoid telling employers how to manage their employees. . . . However, Congress has passed employment-related laws when it believes that the employee is not on equal footing with the employer. For example, Congress has passed laws that require employers to pay minimum wages and to refrain from using certain criteria, such as race or gender, in arriving at specific employment decisions. These laws reflect the reality that employers stand in a position of power in the employment relationship. Legal protections granted to employees seek to make the power relationship between employer and employee one that is fair and equitable.[7]

The **federal constitution** forms the basis for employment laws. The following four amendments of the Constitution are most applicable:

> **Article I, Section 8.** "The Congress shall have Power . . . to regulate Commerce with foreign Nations, and among the several States, and with the Indian Tribes. . . ."
> **First Amendment.** "Congress shall make no law respecting an establishment of religion, or prohibiting the free exercise thereof; or abridging the freedom of speech, or of the press; or the right of the people peaceably to assemble, and to petition the Government for a redress of grievances."
> **Fifth Amendment.** "No person shall . . . be deprived of life, liberty, or property, without due process of law. . . ."
> **Fourteenth Amendment, Section 1.** ". . . No State shall make or enforce any law which shall abridge the privileges or immunities of citizens of the United States, nor shall any State deprive any person of life, liberty, or property without due process of law; nor deny any person within its jurisdiction the equal protection of the laws."

Government in the United States is organized at three levels roughly defined by geographic scope:

- Federal
- State
- Local

A single **federal government** oversees the entire United States and its territories. The vast majority of laws that influence compensation were established at the federal level. Next, individual **state governments** enact and enforce laws that pertain exclusively to their respective regions (e.g., Illinois and Michigan). Most noteworthy are differences in state minimum wage laws, which we will discuss shortly. Finally, **local governments** enact and enforce laws that are most pertinent to smaller geographic regions (e.g., Champaign County in Illinois and the city of Los Angeles). Many of the federal laws have counterparts in state and local legislation. State and local legislation may be concurrent with federal law or may exist in the absence of similar federal legislation. Federal law prevails wherever state or local laws are inconsistent with federal legislation.

The federal government has three branches:

- Legislative branch
- Executive branch
- Judicial branch

Congress creates and passes laws within the **legislative branch**. The **executive branch** enforces the laws of various quasi-legislative and judicial agencies. The President of the United States possesses the authority to establish **executive orders** that influence the operation of the federal government and companies that are engaged in business relationships with the federal government. The **judicial branch** is responsible for interpreting the laws. The U.S. Supreme Court, which consists of nine life-appointed justices, is the forum for these interpretations.

Federal laws that apply to compensation practices are grouped according to key themes:

- Income continuity, safety, and work hours
- Pay discrimination
- Accommodating disabilities and family needs
- Prevailing wage laws

Income Continuity, Safety, and Work Hours

Three factors led to the passage of income continuity, safety, and work hours legislation. The first factor was the **Great Depression**, the move from family businesses to large factories, and divisions of labor within factories. During the Great Depression, which took place in the 1930s, scores of businesses failed, and many workers became chronically unemployed. Government enacted key legislation designed to stabilize the income of an individual who became unemployed because of poor business conditions or workplace injuries. The **Social Security Act of 1935 (Title IX)** provided temporary income to workers who became unemployed through no fault of their own. **Workers' compensation** programs granted income to workers who were unable to work because of injuries sustained on the job. Supporting workers during these misfortunes promoted the well-being of the economy: These income provisions enabled the unemployed to participate in the economy as consumers of essential goods and services. We will defer a more detailed discussion of the Social Security Act of 1935 and workers' compensation laws until Chapter 12 because these laws represent legally required employee benefits.

Second, the main U.S. economic activities prior to the twentieth century were agriculture and small family businesses that were organized along craft lines. Workers began to move from their farms and small family businesses to capitalists' factories for employment. The character of work changed dramatically with the move of workers to factories. An individual's status changed from owner to employee. This status change meant that individuals lost control over their earnings and working conditions.

Third, the factory system also created divisions of labor characterized by differences in skills and responsibilities. Some workers received training, whereas others did not. This contributed greatly to differences in skills and responsibilities. Workers with higher skills and responsibilities did not necessarily earn higher wages than workers with fewer skills and responsibilities. Paying some workers more than others only increased costs, which is something factory owners avoided whenever possible.

In sum, factory workers received very low wages, and the working conditions were often unsafe. Factory workers received low wages and worked in unsafe conditions because factory owners sought to maximize profits. Offering workers high wages and providing safe working conditions would have cut into factory owners' profits. These conditions led to the passage of the **Fair Labor Standards Act of 1938 (FLSA)**. The FLSA addresses major abuses that intensified during the Great Depression and the transition from agricultural to industrial enterprises. These include substandard pay, excessive work hours, and the employment of children in oppressive working conditions.

Fair Labor Standards Act of 1938

The FLSA addresses three broad issues:

- Minimum wage
- Overtime pay
- Child labor provisions

The U.S. Department of Labor enforces the FLSA.

Minimum Wage The purpose of the minimum wage provision is to ensure a minimally acceptable standard of living for workers. The original minimum wage was 25 cents per hour. Since the act's passage in 1938, the federal government has raised the minimum wage several times. The previous minimum wage increase, to $5.15 per hour, was signed into law in August of 1996. In 2007, Congress passed an increase in the federal minimum wage from $5.15 to $7.25 that will be implemented in three increments through 2009. The change from 25 cents per hour to the current $5.15 per hour represents a 1,960 percent minimum wage increase! Most minimum wage earners unfortunately struggle to sustain a minimally acceptable standard of living because the costs of goods and services have increased at a much greater rate.

The increase in cost of living relative to the increase in minimum wage is devastating when we consider the federal government's annual poverty threshold. The poverty guidelines, issued each year by the U.S. Department of Health and Human Services, represent the minimum annual earnings used by the federal government to determine financial eligibility for certain programs. An individual who earns the minimum wage has an annual income totaling $10,712 ($5.15 per hour × 40 hours per week × 52 weeks). The annual poverty threshold in 2007 for a household of two individuals was $13,690, according to the *Federal Register* (Vol. 72, No. 15, pp. 3147–3148). In 2007, assuming a single parent earns the minimum wage to care for a dependent child; this person's minimum wage income fell below the poverty threshold by nearly $3,000. The picture for individuals with additional dependents is much worse. Let's consider an individual who supports a spouse and two dependent children. This individual's minimum wage income ($10,712) fell below the 2007 poverty threshold (e.g., $17,170) by more than $6,000.

The picture is actually bleaker when we consider the difference between nominal dollars and real dollars. Nominal dollars refer to the face value of money. The nominal value of a $10 bill is 10 dollars; the nominal value of a quarter is 25 cents. Real dollars, on the other hand, represent the purchasing power of money. Over time, increases in the costs of goods and services, or inflation, diminish the value of nominal dollars. Let's consider the nominal and real values of the minimum wage over time.

Let's look at an example of the nominal and real differences between the minimum wage of $3.80 in 1990 and the minimum wage of $5.15 in April 2007. The nominal increase in minimum wage was $1.35, or 36 percent. At first glance, it appears that purchasing power increased by 36 percent over this 12-year period. This conclusion would be correct if the prices of goods and services did not increase between 1990 and April 2007; however, the cost of living increased dramatically during this period. In April 2007, a dollar, on average, purchased only 42 percent as much as it could in 1990. Said another way, the purchasing power of the dollar (or the value of the real dollar) eroded by about 58 percent between 1990 and April 2007. The level of erosion (58 percent) exceeded the level of nominal increase (36 percent). Thus, purchasing power of the minimum wage fell between 1990 and April 2007.

Approximately 30 states have minimum wage laws that currently specify higher minimum wage rates than the FLSA. This number will decrease substantially with the passage of the new federal minimum wage level, which is greater than most state-mandated minimum wage rates. It is not likely that many states will quickly move to increase minimum wages above the new federal level because of pressure from businesses that raising the rate too high will cut into profits. Business owners are concerned that workers with pay above the minimum wage will expect pay increases to maintain the spread between their earnings and the recently implemented federal minimum rate.

Specific FLSA exemptions permit employers to pay some workers less than the minimum wage. Students employed in retail or service businesses, on farms, or in institutions of higher education may be paid less than the minimum wage with the consent of the Department of Labor. With explicit permission from the Department of Labor, employers can pay less than the minimum wage for trainee positions or to prevent a reduction in the employment of mentally or physically disabled individuals. Table 3-1 lists the six factors that define trainees.

Overtime Provisions   The FLSA requires employers to pay workers at a rate equal to time and one-half for all hours worked in excess of 40 hours within a 7-day period. For example, a worker's regular hourly rate is $10 for working 40 hours or less within a 7-day period. The FLSA requires the employer to pay this employee $15 per hour for each additional hour worked beyond the regular 40 hours within this 7-day period.

There are some general exceptions to this rule: Negotiated overtime pay rates contained within collective bargaining agreements prevail over the one and one-half time rule. In health care facilities, a base work period is 80 hours during 14 consecutive days rather than 40 hours during 7 consecutive days. Workers in health facilities receive overtime base pay for each hour worked over 80 within a 14-day period. At first glance, the guidelines for calculating overtime pay appear to be relatively straightforward; however, calculating overtime pay in practice is more complex. The overtime provisions and basic exceptions are based on employees' working set hours during fixed work periods; however, many employees work irregular hours that fluctuate from week to week as is the case with contingent workers (Chapter 14). A Supreme Court

---

TABLE 3-1   Six Defining Factors of a Trainee for the FLSA

- The training, even though it includes actual operation of the employers' facilities, is similar to that which would be provided in a vocational school.
- The training is for the benefit of the trainee.
- The trainee works under closer supervision and does not displace regular employees.
- The employer providing the training gains no immediate advantage from the trainees' activities; on occasion, the employer's operation may in fact be hindered.
- The trainee is not guaranteed a job at the completion of the training.
- The employer and the trainee understand that the employer is not obligated to pay wages during the training period.

SOURCE: J. E. Kalet, Primer on Wage and Hour Laws (Washington, DC: Bureau of National Affairs, 1987).

ruling (***Walling v. A. H. Belo Corp.***)[8] requires employers to guarantee fixed weekly pay when the following conditions prevail:

- The employer typically cannot determine the number of hours employees will work each week, and
- The workweek period fluctuates both above and below 40 hours per week.

Overtime work becomes necessary when employees cannot meet higher than normal workloads during the standard workweek. Overtime pay is often typically more cost effective than hiring additional permanent employees: Companies pay a fixed amount to provide employees' fringe benefits. In other words, benefits costs generally do not increase with the number of hours worked. Overtime practices increase wage costs; however, hiring additional permanent workers leads to higher total wage and fixed fringe benefits costs. Awarding existing employees overtime pay also is less expensive than hiring temporary workers. Temporary workers may be less productive in the short run because they are not familiar with specific company work procedures.

The overtime provision does not apply to all jobs. Executive, administrative, learned professional, creative professional, computer workers and outside sales employees are generally **exempt** from the FLSA overtime and minimum wage provisions. Table 3-2 describes the definition of these job categories. Most other jobs are **nonexempt**. Nonexempt jobs are subject to the FLSA overtime pay provision.

Classifying jobs as either exempt or nonexempt is not always clear-cut. In ***Aaron v. City of Wichita, Kansas***,[9] the city contended that its fire chiefs were exempt as executives under the FLSA because they spent more than 80 percent of their work hours managing the fire department. The fire chiefs maintained that they should not be exempt from the FLSA because they did not possess the authority to hire, fire, authorize shift trades, give pay raises, or make policy decisions. The court offered several criteria to determine whether these fire chiefs were exempt employees, including:

- Relative importance of management as opposed to other duties
- Frequency with which they exercised discretionary powers
- Relative freedom from supervision
- Relationship between their salaries and wages paid to other employees for similar nonexempt workers

TABLE 3-2 FLSA Exemption Criteria

Executive	Management of the enterprise or a recognized department or subdivision.
Administrative	Performing office or nonmanual work directly related to the management or general business operations of the employer or employer's customers.
Learned Professional	Performing office or nonmanual work requiring knowledge of an advanced type in a field of science or learning, customarily acquired by a prolonged course of specialized intellectual instruction, but which also may be acquired by such alternative means as an equivalent combination of intellectual instruction and work experience.
Creative Professional	Performing work requiring invention, imagination, originality, or talent in a recognized field of artistic or creative endeavor.
Computer	Employed as a computer systems analyst, computer programmer, software engineer or other similarly skilled worker in the computer field.
Outside Sales	Making sales or obtaining orders or contracts for services or for future use of facilities for which a consideration will be paid by the client or customer. Customarily and regularly engaged a way from the employer's place or places of business.

Note: No minimum salary requirement.

SOURCE: U.S. Department of Labor (2007). Wage and Hour Division Web site [online]. Available: *www.dol.gov/esa/whd*, accessed June 1, 2007.

Based on these criteria, the court determined that the City of Wichita improperly exempted fire chiefs from the FLSA overtime pay provisions.

Determining whether jobs are exempt from the FLSA overtime pay provision has become even more complex since the U.S. Department of Labor introduced revised guidelines known as the **FairPay Rules** in August 2004. An employee was previously considered exempt under the FLSA overtime pay provisions if an employee earned more than the minimum wage and exercised independent judgment when working (see Table 3-2). Under the new FairPay rules, workers earning less than $23,660 per year—or $455 per week—are guaranteed overtime protection. The U.S. Department of Labor provides extensive information regarding the new FairPay Rules, including instructional videos and a "frequently asked questions" section (*www.dol.gov*).

The federal government broadened the scope of the FLSA twice since 1938 through the passage of two acts:

- Portal-to-Portal Act of 1947
- Equal Pay Act of 1963

The **Portal-to-Portal Act of 1947** defines the term *hours worked* that appears in the FLSA. Table 3-3 lists the compensable activities that precede and follow the primary work activities. For example, time spent by state correctional officers caring for police dogs at home is compensable under the FLSA (***Andres v. DuBois***).[10] The care of dogs, including feeding, grooming, and walking, is indispensable to maintaining dogs as a critical law enforcement tool, it is part of officers' principal activities, and it benefits the corrections department; however, this court ruled that time spent by state correction canine handlers transporting dogs between home and correctional facilities is not compensable under FLSA.

The **Equal Pay Act of 1963** prohibits sex discrimination in pay for employees performing equal work. We will discuss the Equal Pay Act of 1963 later in this chapter.

Child Labor Provisions   The FLSA child labor provisions protect children from being overworked, working in potentially hazardous settings, and having their education jeopardized due to excessive work hours. The restrictions vary by age:

- Children under age 14 usually cannot be employed.
- Children ages 14 and 15 may work in safe occupations outside school hours if their work does not exceed 3 hours on a school day (18 hours per week while school is in session). When school is not in session, as in the summer, children cannot work more than 40 hours per week.
- Children ages 16 and 17 do not have hourly restrictions; however, they cannot work in hazardous jobs (e.g., the use of heavy industrial equipment or exposure to harmful substances).

TABLE 3-3   Compensable Factors That Precede and Follow Primary Work Activities

- The time spent on the activity was for the employer's benefit.
- The employer controlled the amount of time spent.
- The time involved is categorized as "suffered and permitted," meaning that the employer knew the employee was working on incidental tasks either before or after the scheduled tour of duty.
- The time spent was requested by the employer.
- The time spent is an integral part of the employee's principal duties.
- The employer has a union contract with employees providing such compensation, or, as a matter of custom or practice, the employer has compensated the activities in the past.

Work Hours and Safety Standards Act of 1962

Coverage extends to all laborers and mechanics who are employed by contractors who meet the following criterion: Federal loans or grants fund part or all the contracts. The act requires that contractors pay employees one and one-half times their regular hourly rate for each hour worked in excess of 40 hours per week.

McNamara–O'Hara Service Contract Act of 1965

The **McNamara–O'Hara Service Contract Act of 1965** applies to all contractors who employ service workers. The term *contractor* refers to companies doing business with the United States. For this act, service employees work in recognized trades or crafts other than skilled mechanical or manual jobs. Plumbers and electricians are recognized trades workers. The act contains two main provisions. First, all contractors must pay at least the minimum wage as specified in the FLSA. Second, contractors holding contracts with the federal government that exceed $2,500 in value must pay the local prevailing wages. In addition, contractors must offer fringe compensation equal to the local prevailing benefits.

Pay Discrimination

The civil rights movement of the 1960s led to the passage of key legislation designed to protect designated classes of employees and to uphold their rights individually against discriminatory employment decisions. Some of these laws, such as the **Civil Rights Act of 1964**, apply to all employment-related decisions (i.e., recruitment, selection, performance appraisal, compensation, and termination). Other laws, such as the Equal Pay Act of 1963, apply specifically to compensation practices. These laws limit employers' authority over employment decisions.

Equal Pay Act of 1963

Congress enacted the Equal Pay Act of 1963 to remedy a serious problem of employment discrimination in private industry: "Many segments of American industry [have] been based on an ancient but outmoded belief that a man, because of his role in society, should be paid more than a woman even though his duties are the same."[11] The Equal Pay Act of 1963 is based on a simple principle. Men and women should receive equal pay for performing equal work.

The Equal Employment Opportunity Commission (EEOC) enforces the Equal Pay Act of 1963. The EEOC possesses the authority to investigate and reconcile charges of illegal discrimination. The act applies to all employers and labor organizations. In particular,

> No employer . . . shall discriminate within any establishment in which such employees are employed, between employees on the basis of sex by paying wages to employees in such establishment at a rate less than the rate at which he pays wages to employees of the opposite sex . . . for equal work on jobs the performance of which requires equal skill, effort, and responsibility, and which are performed under similar working conditions. . . . [29 USC 206, Section 6, paragraph (d)]

The Equal Pay Act of 1963 pertains explicitly to jobs of equal worth. Companies assign pay rates to jobs according to the skill, effort, responsibility, and working conditions required. Skill, effort, responsibility, and working conditions represent **compensable factors**. The U.S. Department of Labor's definitions of these compensable factors are listed in Table 3-4.

How do we judge whether jobs are equal? The case ***EEOC v. Madison Community Unit School District No. 12***[12] sheds light on this important issue. The school district

Factor	Definition
Skill	Experience, training, education, and ability as measured by the performance requirements of a job
Effort	The amount of mental or physical effort expended in the performance of a job
Responsibility	The degree of accountability required in the performance of a job
Working conditions	The physical surroundings and hazards of a job, including dimensions such as inside versus outside work, heat, cold, and poor ventilation

TABLE 3-4 U.S. Department of Labor Definitions of Compensable Factors

SOURCE: U.S. Department of Labor, *Equal pay for equal work under the Fair Labor Standards Act* (Washington, DC: U.S. Government Printing Office, December 31, 1971).

paid female athletic coaches of girls' sports teams less than it paid male athletic coaches of boys' teams. The judge concluded:

> The jobs that are compared must be in some sense the same to count as "equal work" under the Equal Pay Act of 1963; and here we come to the main difficulty in applying the Act; whether two jobs are the same depends on how fine a system of job classification the courts will accept. If coaching an athletic team in the Madison, Illinois, school system is considered a single job rather than a [collection] of jobs, the school district violated the Equal Pay Act prima facie by paying female holders of this job less than male holders. . . . If on the other hand coaching the girls' tennis team is considered a different job from coaching the boys' tennis team, and if coaching the girls' volleyball or basketball team is considered a different job (or jobs) from coaching the boys' soccer team, there is no prima facie violation. So the question is how narrow a definition of job the courts should be using in deciding whether the Equal Pay Act is applicable. We can get some guidance from the language of the Act. The act requires that the jobs compared have "similar working conditions," not the same working conditions. This implies that some comparison of different jobs is possible . . . since the working conditions need not be "equal," the jobs need not be completely identical. . . . Above the lowest rank of employee, every employee has a somewhat different job from every other one, even if the two employees being compared are in the same department. So, if "equal work" and "equal skill, effort, and responsibility" were taken literally, the Act would have a minute domain. . . .

The courts have thus had to steer a narrow course. The cases do not require an absolute identity between the jobs, but do require substantial identity.

Pay differentials for equal work are not always illegal. Pay differentials between men and women who are performing equal work are acceptable where

> . . . such payment is made pursuant to (i) a seniority system; (ii) merit system; (iii) a system which measures earnings by quantity or quality of production; or (iv) a differential based on any other factor other than sex: Provided, that an employer who is paying a wage rate differential . . . shall not . . . reduce the wage rate of any employee. [29 USC 206, Section 6, paragraph (d)]

As an aside, comparable worth is an ongoing debate in American society that differs from the issues addressed in the Equal Pay Act of 1963. The debate centers on the pervasive pay differentials between men and women who perform comparable, but not equal, work.[13] In a nutshell, jobs held predominantly by women are paid at substantially lower rates than jobs held predominantly by men that require comparable skill, effort, responsibility, and working conditions. Researchers have compared female-dominated jobs with male-dominated jobs:

- Nurses to tree trimmers
- Clerical workers to parking lot attendants
- Clerk typists to delivery van drivers

These comparisons show that the jobs require comparable skill, effort, responsibility, and working conditions; however, on average the female-dominated jobs received substantially lower compensation than did male-dominated jobs. **Comparable worth** advocates maintain that employers should pay employees holding predominantly female jobs the same as employees holding predominantly male jobs if these jobs require comparable skills, effort, responsibility, and working conditions.

Civil Rights Act of 1964

The Civil Rights Act of 1964 is a comprehensive piece of legislation. **Title VII** of the Civil Rights Act is the most pertinent to compensation. Legislators designed Title VII to promote equal employment opportunities for underrepresented minorities. According to Title VII:

> It shall be an unlawful employment practice for an employer—(1) to fail or refuse to hire or to discharge any individual, or otherwise to discriminate against any individual with respect to his compensation, terms, conditions, or privileges of employment, because of such individual's race, color, religion, sex, or national origin; or (2) to limit, segregate, or classify his employees or applicants for employment in any way which would deprive or tend to deprive any individual of employment opportunities or otherwise adversely affect his status as an employee, because of such individual's race, color, religion, sex, or national origin. (42 USC 2000e-2, Section 703)

The courts have distinguished between two types of discrimination covered by Title VII: disparate treatment and disparate impact. **Disparate treatment** represents intentional discrimination, occurring whenever employers intentionally treat some workers less favorably than others because of their race, color, sex, national origin, or religion. Applying different standards to determine pay increases for blacks and whites may result in disparate treatment. For example, awarding pay increases to blacks according to seniority and to whites based on performance may lead to disparate treatment, particularly if blacks have significantly less seniority than whites.

Disparate impact represents unintentional discrimination. It occurs whenever an employer applies an employment practice to all employees, but the practice leads to unequal treatment of protected employee groups. Awarding pay increases to male and female production workers according to seniority could lead to disparate impact if females had less seniority, on average, than men.

Title VII protects employees who work for all private sector employers, local, state and federal governments, and educational institutions that employ 15 or more individuals. Title VII also applies to private and public employment agencies, labor organizations, and joint labor management committees controlling apprenticeship and training.

It is becoming more difficult to sue employers for pay discrimination under Title VII. Title VII imposes a statute of limitation period, typically 180 days, after which employees may file claims of illegal discrimination against employers. The U.S. Supreme Court has rendered a very strict interpretation as to when the statute of limitations period begins for women to sue their employers for discrimination in pay. In *Ledbetter v. Goodyear Tire & Rubber Co.,*[14] a female employee named Ledbetter sued Goodyear Tire & Rubber Co. after she learned that some male employees with the same job had been paid substantially more than her over a period of several years. Ledbetter claimed that the statute of limitation period began when each discriminatory pay decision was made and communicated to her. She argued that multiple pay decisions were made over the years each time Goodyear endorsed each paycheck, making each paycheck a separate act of illegal pay discrimination. The Supreme Court rejected Ledbetter's allegation that each paycheck (following the initial paycheck when the pay disparity first existed) represented an intentionally discriminatory act by the employer. Instead, any act of discrimination occurred each time pay raise decisions were made. In Ledbetter's case, the court argued that any discriminatory decisions literally occurred years prior to raising her concerns with the EEOC. The later effects of past discrimination do not restart the clock for filing an EEOC charge, making Ledbetter's claim an untimely one. Not all of the judges agreed with this ruling, noting that given pay secrecy policies in most companies many employees would have no idea within 180 days that they had received a lower raise than others. In addition, an initial disparity in pay may be small, leading a woman or minority group member not to make waves in order to try to succeed.

Bennett Amendment

This provision is an amendment to Title VII. The **Bennett Amendment** allows employees to charge employers with Title VII violations regarding pay only when the employer has violated the Equal Pay Act of 1963. The Bennett Amendment is necessary because lawmakers could not agree on the answers to the following questions:

- Does Title VII incorporate both the Equal Pay Act of 1963's equal pay standard and the four defenses for unequal work [(i) a seniority system; (ii) merit system; (iii) a system which measures earnings by quantity or quality of production; or (iv) a differential based on any other factor other than sex]?
- Does Title VII include only the four exceptions to the Equal Pay Act of 1963 standard?

Some lawmakers believed that Title VII incorporates the equal pay standard (i.e., answering yes to the first question and no to the second question); however, other lawmakers believed that Title VII did not incorporate the equal pay standard (i.e., answering *no* to the first question and *yes* to the second question). If Title VII did not incorporate the equal pay standard, then employees could raise charges of illegal discrimination (on the basis of race, religion, color, sex, or national origin) for unequal jobs.

Executive Order 11246

This executive order extends Title VII standards to contractors holding government contracts worth more than $10,000 per year. In addition, **Executive Order 11246** imposes additional requirements on contractors with government contracts worth more than $50,000 per year and 50 or more employees. These contractors must develop written plans each year (i.e., **affirmative action** plans). In affirmative action plans contractors specify goals and practices that they will use to avoid or reduce Title VII discrimination over time.

Age Discrimination in Employment Act of 1967 (as Amended in 1978, 1986, 1990)

Congress passed the **Age Discrimination in Employment Act of 1967 (ADEA)** to protect workers age 40 and older from illegal discrimination. This act provides protection to a large segment of the U.S. population known as the **baby boom generation** or "baby boomers." The baby boom generation was born roughly between 1946 and 1964 and represented a swell in the American population. Some members of the baby boom generation reached age 40 in 1986, and the youngest of them are now over age 40.

A large segment of the population will probably continue to work beyond age 65, which is the "traditional" retirement age, because many fear that Social Security retirement income (Chapter 12) will not provide adequate support. The U.S. Census Bureau predicts that individuals aged 65 and over will increase from about 25 million in 2001 (12.4 percent of the population) to about 77 million (20.3 percent of the population) by 2050.[15] Thus, the ADEA should be extremely relevant for some time to come.

The ADEA established guidelines prohibiting age-related discrimination in employment. Its purpose is "to promote the employment of older persons based on their ability rather than age, to prohibit arbitrary age discrimination in employment, and to help employers and workers find ways of meeting problems arising from the impact of age on employment." The ADEA specifies that it is unlawful for an employer:

(1) to fail or refuse to hire or to discharge any individual or otherwise discriminate against any individual with respect to his compensation, terms, conditions, or privileges of employment, because of such individual's age; (2) to limit, segregate or classify his employees in any way which would deprive or tend to deprive any individual of employment opportunities or otherwise adversely affect his status as an employee, because of such individual's age; or (3) to reduce the wage rate of any employee in order to comply with this act. (29 USC 623, Section 4)

The ADEA applies to employee benefits practices as well:

[A]ny employer must provide that any employee aged 65 or older, and any employee's spouse aged 65 or older, shall be entitled to coverage under any group health plan offered to such employees under the same conditions as any employee, and the spouse of such employee, under age 65. [29 USC 623, Section 4, paragraph (g)(1)]

The ADEA also sets limits on the development and implementation of employers' "early retirement" practices, which many companies use to reduce workforce sizes. Most early retirement programs are offered to employees who are at least 55 years of age. These early retirement programs are permissible when companies offer them to employees on a voluntary basis. Forcing early retirement upon older workers represents age discrimination (***EEOC v. Chrysler***).[16]

Employee layoffs may create the context for alleging discrimination, which is now especially relevant. It is not uncommon to read about layoffs at companies on a daily basis in newspapers. For example, three Circuit City employees laid off as part of a restructuring measure to save costs have alleged that the employer's decision violates California law prohibiting age discrimination. Circuit City announced that it would lay off nearly 3,500 employees who are paid above the typical salary range for comparable jobs in other companies. Also, the company indicated that it would replace the highly paid workers with lower-paid new hires. The three workers, ranging in age from 57 to 66, believe that protected older workers are being unfairly targeted (compared with younger workers) because they earn substantially more than younger new full- or part-time hires.

The **Older Workers Benefit Protection Act (OWBPA)**—the 1990 amendment to the ADEA—placed additional restrictions on employer benefits practices. Under particular circumstances, employers can require older employees to pay more for health care insurance than younger employees. This practice is permissible when older workers collectively do not make proportionately larger contributions than the younger workers. For instance, let's assume that Company A has 3,000 employees, and 25 percent (750 employees) are age 40 or older, whereas 75 percent (2,250 employees) are age 39 or younger. Let's also assume that the annual employee contributions total $120,000 for Company A's workforce. Finally, an analysis of these contributions reveals that the older workers paid $84,000, accounting for 70 percent of these contributions (70% × $120,000). The younger workers paid $36,000, accounting for only 30 percent (30% × $120,000). The older workers paid disproportionately more than the younger workers.

- Older workers: 25 percent of the workforce paid 70 percent of the total contributions.
- Younger workers: 75 percent of the workforce paid 30 percent of the total contributions.

In addition, employers can legally reduce life insurance coverage for older workers only if the cost for providing insurance to them is significantly greater than the cost for younger workers. Furthermore, the OWBPA enacts the **equal benefit or equal cost principle**: Employers must offer benefits to older workers that are equal to or more than the benefits given to younger workers with one exception: The OWBPA does not require employers to provide equal or greater benefits to older workers when the costs to do so are greater than for younger workers.

Finally, employers may make across-the-board cuts in benefits to save costs. Employers similarly can negotiate changes in a collective bargaining agreement to restrict retiree health benefits to individuals age 50 or older, even though this change eliminates benefits for some ADEA-protected workers who could have received health benefits at retirement.[17]

The ADEA covers private employers with 20 or more employees, labor unions with 25 or more members, and employment agencies. The EEOC enforces this act.

Executive Order 11141

This executive order extends ADEA coverage to federal contractors.

Civil Rights Act of 1991

Congress enacted the **Civil Rights Act of 1991** to overturn several Supreme Court rulings. The reversal of **Atonio v. Wards Cove Packing Co**. is perhaps the most noteworthy.[18] The Supreme Court ruled that plaintiffs (employees) must indicate which employment practice created disparate impact and demonstrate how the employment practice created disparate impact. Since the passage of the Civil Rights Act of 1991, employers must show that the challenged employment practice is a business necessity. Thus, the Civil Rights Act of 1991 shifted the burden of proof from employees to employers.

Two additional sections of the Civil Rights Act of 1991 apply to compensation practice. The first feature pertains to seniority systems. As we will discuss in Chapter 4, public sector employers make employment decisions based on employees' seniority. For example, public sector employers award more vacation days to employees with higher seniority than to employees with lower seniority. The Civil Rights Act of 1991 overturned the Supreme Court's decision in **Lorance v. AT&T Technologies**,[19] which allowed employees to challenge the use of seniority systems only within 180 days from the system's implementation date. Employees may now file suits claiming discrimination either when the system is implemented or whenever the system negatively affects them.

A second development addresses the geographic scope of federal job discrimination. Prior to the Civil Rights Act of 1991, the U.S. Supreme Court (**Boureslan v. Aramco**)[20] ruled that federal job discrimination laws do not apply to U.S. citizens working for U.S. companies in foreign countries. Since the act's passage, U.S. citizens working overseas may file suit against U.S. businesses for discriminatory employment practices.

The Civil Rights Act of 1991 provides coverage to the same groups protected under the Civil Rights Act of 1964. The 1991 act also extends coverage to Senate employees and political appointees of the federal government's executive branch. The EEOC enforces the Civil Rights Act of 1991. Since the passage of the 1991 act, the EEOC helps employers avoid discriminatory employment practices through the Technical Assistance Training Institute.

Accommodating Disabilities and Family Needs

Congress enacted the Pregnancy Discrimination Act of 1978, the Americans with Disabilities Act of 1990, and the Family and Medical Leave Act of 1993 to accommodate employees with disabilities and pressing family needs. These laws protect a significant number of employees: In 2000, approximately 68 percent of employed women were responsible for children under the age of 18. The preamble to the Americans with Disabilities Act states that it covers 43 million Americans. Many employees will benefit from the Family and Medical Leave Act if they need substantial time away from work to care for newborns or elderly family members. Two trends explain this need. First, many elderly and seriously ill parents of the employed baby boom generation depend on their children. Second, both husbands and wives work full-time jobs now more than ever before, necessitating extended leave to care for newborns or for children who become ill.

Pregnancy Discrimination Act of 1978

The **Pregnancy Discrimination Act of 1978 (PDA)** is an amendment to Title VII of the Civil Rights Act of 1964. The PDA prohibits disparate impact discrimination against pregnant women for all employment practices. Employers must not treat pregnancy less favorably than other medical conditions covered under employee benefits plans. In addition, employers must treat pregnancy and childbirth the same way they treat other causes of disability. Furthermore, the PDA protects the rights of women who take leave for pregnancy-related reasons. The protected rights include:

- Credit for previous service
- Accrued retirement benefits
- Accumulated seniority

Americans with Disabilities Act of 1990

The **Americans with Disabilities Act of 1990 (ADA)** prohibits discrimination against individuals with mental or physical disabilities within and outside employment settings, including public services and transportation, public accommodations, and employment. It applies to all employers with 15 or more employees, and the EEOC is the enforcement agency. In employment contexts, the ADA:

> [P]rohibits covered employers from discriminating against a "qualified individual with a disability" in regard to job applications, hiring, advancement, discharge, compensation, training or other terms, conditions, or privileges of employment. Employers are required to make "reasonable accommodations" to the known physical or mental limitations of an otherwise qualified individual with a disability unless to do so would impose an "undue hardship."[21]

Title I of the ADA requires that employers provide "reasonable accommodation" to disabled employees. Reasonable accommodation may include such efforts as making existing facilities readily accessible, job restructuring, and modifying work schedules. Every "qualified individual with a disability" is entitled to reasonable accommodation. A qualified individual with a disability, however, must be able to perform the "essential functions" of the job in question. Essential functions are those job duties that are critical to the job.

Let's apply these principles to an example. Producing printed memoranda is a key activity of a clerical worker's job. Most employees manually keyboard the information by using a word processing program to generate written text. In this case, the essential function is producing memoranda using word processing software; however, manual input represents only one method to enter information. Information input based on a voice recognition input device is an alternative method for entering information. If a clerk develops crippling arthritis, the ADA may require that the employer make reasonable accommodation by providing him with a voice-recognition input device.

Family and Medical Leave Act of 1993

The **Family and Medical Leave Act of 1993 (FMLA)** aimed to provide employees with job protection in cases of family or medical emergency. The basic thrust of the act is guaranteed leave, and a key element of that guarantee is the right of the employee to return to either the position he or she left when the leave began, or to an equivalent position with the same benefits, pay, and other terms and conditions of employment. We will discuss this act in greater detail in Chapter 12 because compensation professionals treat such leave as a legally required benefit.

Prevailing Wage Laws

Davis–Bacon Act of 1931

The **Davis–Bacon Act of 1931** establishes employment standards for construction contractors holding federal government contracts valued at more than $2,000. Covered contracts include highway building, dredging, demolition, and cleaning, as well as painting and decorating public buildings. This act applies to laborers and mechanics who are employed on-site. Contractors must pay wages at least equal to the prevailing wage in the local area. The U.S. Secretary of Labor determines prevailing wage rates based on compensation surveys of different areas. In this context, "local" area refers to the general location where work is performed. Cities and counties represent local areas. The "prevailing wage" is the typical hourly wage paid to more than 50 percent of all laborers and mechanics employed in the local area. The act also requires that contractors offer fringe benefits that are equal in scope and value to fringe compensation that prevails in the local area.

Walsh–Healey Public Contracts Act of 1936

This act covers contractors and manufacturers who sell supplies, materials, and equipment to the federal government. Its coverage is more extensive than is the Davis–Bacon Act. The **Walsh–Healey Public Contracts Act of 1936** applies to both construction and nonconstruction activities. In addition, this act covers all of the contractors' employees except office, supervisory, custodial, and maintenance workers who do any work in preparation for the performance of the contract. The minimum contract amount that qualifies for coverage is $10,000 rather than the $2,000 amount under the Davis–Bacon Act of 1931.

The Walsh–Healey Act of 1936 mandates that contractors with federal contracts meet guidelines regarding wages and hours, child labor, convict labor, and hazardous working conditions. Contractors must observe the minimum wage and overtime provisions of the FLSA. In addition, this act prohibits the employment of individuals younger than 16, as well as convicted criminals. Furthermore, this act prohibits contractors from exposing workers to any conditions that violate the **Occupational Safety and Health Act of 1970.** This act was passed to assure safe and healthful working conditions for working men and women by authorizing enforcement of the standards under the act.

LAWS THAT GUIDE DISCRETIONARY EMPLOYEE BENEFITS

Many laws guide discretionary employee benefits practices. Here we review only the major laws on this topic:the Internal Revenue Code (IRC), the Employee Retirement Income Security Act of 1974 (ERISA), the Consolidated Omnibus Budget Reconciliation Act of 1985 (COBRA), the Health Insurance Portability and Accountability Act of 1996, the Pension Protection Act of 2006, key antidiscrimination laws, and the Fair Labor Standards Act.

Internal Revenue Code

The **Internal Revenue Code (IRC)** is the set of regulations pertaining to taxation in the United States (e.g., sales tax, company [employer] income tax, individual [employee] income tax, property tax). Taxes represent the main source of revenue to fund federal, state, and local government programs. The Internal Revenue Service (IRS) is the government agency that develops and implements the IRC, and levies penalties against companies and individuals who violate the IRC. Since 1916, the federal government has encouraged employers to provide retirement benefits to employees with tax breaks or deductions. In other words, the government allowed employers to exclude retirement plan payments from their income subject to taxation. This "break" reduced the amount of a company's required tax payments. In general, the larger the contributions to retirement plans, the greater the reduction in the amount of taxes owed to the government.

The IRC contains multiple regulations for legally required and discretionary benefits. For example, the **Federal Insurance Contributions Act (FICA)**[22] taxes employees and employers to finance the Social Security Old-Age, Survivor and Disability Insurance Program (OASDI). Unemployment insurance benefits are financed by federal and, sometimes, state taxes levied on employers. Federal tax is levied on employers under the **Federal Unemployment Tax Act (FUTA)**.[23]

Since the inception of the IRC, the federal government also contains incentives for employers who offer discretionary benefits and for employees as recipients of these benefits. An employee may deduct the cost of benefits from annual income, thereby reducing tax liability. Employers may also deduct the cost of benefits from their annual income as a business or trade expense when the cost is an ordinary and necessary expense of the company's trade or business. For example, the costs of electricity for a factory and the purchase of raw materials to manufacture products are ordinary and necessary expenses. Payroll costs and benefits costs also qualify as ordinary and necessary business expenses. Without pay and benefits, companies would not be able to recruit and retain competent employees who are crucial for business operations. In addition, companies can deduct these costs only during the current tax period. So, the benefits costs incurred during 2008 may be deducted only for the 2008 tax year.

The tax deductibility of benefits costs also requires that employers meet additional requirements set forth by the Employee Retirement Income Security Act of 1974. Benefits qualify for tax deductibility when they meet nondiscrimination rules. **Nondiscrimination rules** prohibit employers from giving preferential treatment to key employees and highly compensated employees, for example, by contributing 10 percent of annual salary to their retirement accounts, but only 5 percent to other employees. The

IRS defines the meanings of these employee groups. The term **key employee** means any employee who at any time during the year is:

- A 5 percent owner of the employer,
- A 1 percent owner of the employer having an annual compensation from the employer of more than $150,000, or
- An officer of the employer having an annual compensation greater than $145,000 in 2007 (indexed for inflation in increments of $5,000 beginning in 2003).

U.S. Treasury Regulations define the term *officer* used in this definition of key employees:[24]

> Generally, the term officer means an administrative executive who is in regular and continued service. The term officer implies continuity of service and excludes those employed for a special and single transaction. An employee who merely has the title of an officer but not the authority of an officer is not considered an officer for purposes of the key employee test. Similarly, an employee who does not have the title of an officer but has the authority of an officer is an officer for purposes of the key employee test. In the case of one or more employers treated as a single employer under sections 414(b), (c), or (m), whether or not an individual is an officer shall be determined based upon his responsibilities with respect to the employer or employers for which he is directly employed, and not with respect to the controlled group of corporations, employers under common control or affiliated service group.

A partner of a partnership will not be treated as an officer for purposes of the key employee test merely because he or she owns a capital or profits interest in the partnership, exercises voting rights as a partner, and may, for limited purposes, be authorized and does in fact act as an agent of the partnership.

The IRS defines a **highly compensated employee** as one of the following during the current or preceding year:

- A 5 percent owner at any time during the year or the preceding year.
- For the preceding year had compensation from the employer in excess of $100,000 in 2007.
- If the employer elects the application of this clause for a plan year, was in the top-paid group of employees for the preceding year.

Employee Retirement Income Security Act of 1974 (ERISA)

ERISA was established to regulate the implementation of various employee benefits programs, including medical, life, and disability programs, as well as pension programs. The essence of ERISA is protection of employee benefits rights.

ERISA addresses matters of employers' reporting and disclosure duties, funding of benefits, the fiduciary responsibilities for these plans, and vesting rights. Companies must provide their employees with straightforward descriptions of their employee benefit plans, updates when substantive changes to the plan are implemented, annual synopses on the financing and operation of the plans, and advance notification if the company intends to terminate the benefits plan. The funding requirement mandates that companies meet strict guidelines to ensure having sufficient funds when employees reach retirement. Similarly, the fiduciary responsibilities require that companies not engage in transactions with parties having interests adverse to those of the recipients of the plan and not deal with the income or assets of the employee benefits plan in the company's own interests.

Vesting refers to an employee's acquisition of nonforfeitable rights to an employer's contributions to fund pension benefits. Employees often must be 100 percent vested between 3 and 6 years of service, depending on the vesting schedule. One hundred percent vested means that an employee cannot lose the pension benefits even if the employee leaves the job before retirement; employees are entitled to every dollar contributed on their behalf by the employer.

There are two minimum criteria for eligibility under ERISA. First, employees must be allowed to participate in a pension plan after they reach age 21. Second, employees must have completed 1 year of service based on at least 1,000 hours of work. There is no maximum age limit for eligibility.

Since the passage of ERISA, there have been a number of amendments to this act. The impetus for these amendments has been the ever-changing laws relating to the tax treatment of employees' contributions to pension plans. For example, the tax laws offer employees the opportunity to deduct a limited amount of their gross income (i.e., income before any federal, state, or local taxes are assessed) for investment in a pension plan. Such deductions reduce the taxable gross pay amount on which taxes are assessed, thereby clearly lowering employees' tax burdens. The amendments are quite complex and technical, requiring familiarity with the IRC. The key amendments include the Tax Equity and Fiscal Responsibility Act of 1982, Deficit Reduction Act of 1984, the Tax Reform Act of 1986, and the Economic Growth and Tax Relief Reconciliation Act of 2001.

Consolidated Omnibus Budget Reconciliation Act of 1985 (COBRA)

The **Consolidated Omnibus Budget Reconciliation Act of 1985 (COBRA)** was enacted to provide employees with the opportunity to continue receiving their employer-sponsored medical care insurance temporarily under their employer's plan if their coverage otherwise would cease because of termination, layoff, or other change in employment status. COBRA applies to a wide variety of employers, with exemptions available only for companies that normally employ fewer than 20 workers, church plans, and plans maintained by the U.S. government.

Under COBRA, individuals may continue their coverage, as well as coverage for their spouses and dependents, for up to 18 months. Coverage may extend for up to 36 months for spouses and dependents facing a loss of employer-provided coverage because of an employee's death, a divorce or legal separation, or certain other qualifying events, which include employee termination, retirement, and layoff. Table 3-5 displays the maximum continuation period for particular qualifying events.

Companies are permitted to charge COBRA beneficiaries a premium for continuation coverage of up to 102 percent of the cost of the coverage to the plan. The 2 percent markup reflects a charge for administering COBRA. Employers that violate the COBRA requirements are subject to an excise tax per affected employee for each day that the violation continues. In addition, plan administrators who fail to provide required COBRA notices to employees may be personally liable for a civil penalty for each day the notice is not provided.

Continuation of Coverage Under COBRA

The following information applies to health, vision, and dental coverage only. For information on life insurance when employment terminates, refer to Chapter 10 for other areas that describe life coverage.

COBRA was signed into law on April 7, 1986, as P.L. 99-272. Under COBRA, the employer must provide covered members and their dependents who would lose coverage under the plan the option to continue coverage. The mandate is restricted to certain conditions under which coverage is lost, and the election to continue must be made within a specified election period. COBRA went into effect for members and their dependents on July 1, 1986.

A. COBRA Requirements

Qualifying Events	Maximum Continuation Period
Member	
a. Termination of employment for any reason, including termination of disability benefits and layoff, except for gross misconduct	18 months.
b. Loss of eligibility due to reduction in work hours.	18 months
c. Determination by the Social Security Administration (SSA) of disability that existed at time of qualifying event.	29 months
Dependent	
a. Member's termination of employment as stated above.	18 months
b. Member's loss of eligibility due to reduction in work hours.	18 months
c. Member's death, divorce, or legal separation.	
1. spouse or ex-spouse, under age 55	36 months
2. spouse or ex-spouse age 55 or older	The date spouse or ex-spouse becomes entitled to Medicare
d. Member's Medicare entitlement. (Under certain conditions, this could be 36 months.)	18 months
e. Ceases to satisfy plan's eligibility requirements for dependent status.	36 months
f. Determination by the SSA of disability that existed at time of qualifying event. Must have been covered under member's insurance at time of qualifying event.	29 months

If you are covered under COBRA and have been determined to be disabled by the federal SSA, you may be eligible to extend your coverage time from 18 months to 29. You must submit a copy of the SSA determination to the state's COBRA Administrator within 60 days of the date of the SSA determination letter and before the end of the original 18-month COBRA coverage period. Failure to notify the administrator and submit the required documentation within the 60-day period will disqualify you for the extension.

To be eligible for the extension of time, members must have been determined by the SSA to be disabled at the time of the event that qualified them for COBRA. Dependents must have been determined by the SSA to be disabled at the time of the event that qualified the member for COBRA and that dependent must have been covered by the member for insurance at that time.

Health Insurance Portability and Accountability Act of 1996 (HIPAA)

This act contains four main provisions. The first provision is intended to guarantee that employees and their dependents that leave their employer's group health plan will have ready access to coverage under a subsequent employer's health plan, regardless of their health or claims experience. The second provision sets limits on the length of time that health plans and health insurance issuers may impose preexisting conditions, and identify conditions to which no preexisting condition may apply. The third provision counts periods of continuous coverage under another form of comprehensive health coverage toward a preexisting condition limit. The fourth provision protects the transfer, disclosure, and use of health care information.

Pension Protection Act of 2006

The Pension Protection Act is designed to strengthen protections for employees' company-sponsored retirement plans in at least two ways. The first consideration refers to defined benefit plans and the second refers to defined contribution plans. First, this law should strengthen the financial condition of the Pension Benefit Guaranty Corporation (PBGC) by requiring that private sector companies that underfund their defined benefit plans pay substantially higher premiums (that is, cost to provide insurance protection) to insure retirement benefits. After all, experience tells us there is a greater likelihood that the PBGC has had to take over highly underfunded defined benefit plans. The increase in underfunded plans poses a greater risk to the financial solvency of the PBGC. In other words, think of the PBGC as an automobile insurance company and young drivers with automobile insurance as companies with underfunded defined benefit plans. An automobile insurance company charges higher premiums to drivers under age 25 because years of data show that young drivers are more likely to get into multiple serious accidents than older drivers. After getting into a car accident, a person files a claim to the insurance company to pay for the costs of repairs. Of course, repair costs for serious accidents will be much more expensive than for minor accidents. So, insurance companies charge higher premiums to these drivers because they are more likely to file claims. Higher premiums will make it easier for insurance companies to stay financially solvent because they anticipated such claims. The Pension Protection Act law also aims to sure up the PBGC financial condition by making it more difficult for companies to skip making premium payments. Finally, this new law raises the amount that employers can contribute to pension funding with tax advantages, creating an additional incentive to adequately fund pension plans.

Second, the Pension Protection Act makes it easier for employees to participate in such employer-sponsored defined contribution plans as 401(k) plans. Millions of workers who are eligible to participate in their employers' defined contribution plans do not contribute to them. There are a variety of reasons why employees choose not to participate; however, a prominent reason is that most individuals feel they do not have sufficient knowledge about how to choose investment options (e.g., a high-risk mutual fund versus a fixed rate annuity) that will help them earn sufficient money for retirement. In addition, once employees make the decision to participate in these plans and have been making regular contributions, they are not likely to stop. With these issues in mind, the Pension Protection Act enables companies to enroll their employees automatically in defined contribution plans and provides greater access to professional advice about investing for retirement. In addition, this Act requires that companies give multiple investment options to allow employees to select how much risk they are willing to bear. As an aside, risky investments usually have the potential for substantial gains or losses in value. Less risky investments usually have the potential for lower gains or losses. Some companies previously limited investment opportunities to company stock, which exposes employees to substantial investment risk.

CONTEXTUAL INFLUENCES ON THE FEDERAL GOVERNMENT AS AN EMPLOYER

As we discussed previously, federal government employees do not receive protection under Title VII, ADEA, and the Equal Pay Act of 1963. Shortly after the passage of these acts during the 1960s, the President of the United States and Congress enacted

TABLE 3-5   Executive Orders and Laws Enacted to Protect Federal Government Employees
• **Executive Order 11478** prohibits employment discrimination on the basis of race, color, religion, sex, national origin, handicap, and age (401 *FEP Manual* 4061).
• **Executive Order 11935** prohibits employment of nonresidents in U.S. civil service jobs (401 *FEP Manual* 4121).
• **The Rehabilitation Act** mandates that federal government agencies take affirmative action in providing jobs for individuals with disabilities (401 *FEP Manual* 325).
• The **Vietnam Era Veterans Readjustment Assistance Act** applies the principles of the Rehabilitation Act to veterans with disabilities and veterans of the Vietnam War (401 *FEP Manual* 379).
• The **Government Employee Rights Act of 1991** protects U.S. Senate employees from employment discrimination on the basis of race, color, religion, sex, national origin, age, and disability (401 *FEP Manual* 851).
• The **Family and Medical Leave Act of 1993** grants civil service employees, U.S. Senate employees, and U.S. House of Representatives employees a maximum of 12 weeks unpaid leave in any 12-month period to care for a newborn or a seriously ill family member (401 *FEP Manual* 891).

executive orders and laws to prohibit job discrimination and promote equal opportunity in the federal government. These executive orders and laws apply to employees who work within:

- Military service (civilian employees only)
- Executive agencies
- Postal service
- Library of Congress
- Judicial and legislative branches

Table 3-5 contains a summary of these key executive orders and laws. We already discussed the FMLA because it also applies to private sector employers.

LABOR UNIONS AS CONTEXTUAL INFLUENCES

Since the passage of the **National Labor Relations Act of 1935 (NLRA)**, the federal government requires employers to enter into good-faith negotiations with workers over the terms of employment. Workers join unions to influence employment-related decisions, especially when they are dissatisfied with job security, wages, benefits, and supervisory practices.

Since the 1950s, the percentage of U.S. civilian workers in both the public and private sectors represented by unions has declined steadily. In 2006, the percentage of U.S. civilian workers in both the public and private sectors represented by unions declined steadily to a 12.0 percent representation since 1983 when the representation rate was 20.1 percent.[25] The unionization rate of government workers was 36.2 percent, compared with 7.4 percent among private sector employees in 2006. As we will discuss shortly, union representation will probably continue to decline in the future. This decline may be attributed to the reduced influence of unions. We will present reasons for this conclusion later in this section. Nevertheless, 12.0 percent of the U.S. civilian workforce stands for a large number of workers—approximately 15 million.

National Labor Relations Act of 1935

The purpose of this act was to remove barriers to free commerce and to restore equality of bargaining power between employees and employers. Employers denied workers the rights to bargain collectively with them on such issues as wages, work hours, and working conditions. Employees consequently experienced poor working conditions, substandard wage rates, and excessive work hours. Section 1 of the NLRA declares the policy of the United States to protect commerce:

> . . . by encouraging the practice and procedure of collective bargaining and by protecting the exercise by workers of full freedom of association, self-organization, and designation of representatives of their own choosing for the purpose of negotiating the terms and conditions of employment. . . .

Sections 8(a)(5), 8(d), and 9(a) are key provisions of this act. Section 8(a)(5) provides that it is an unfair labor practice for an employer ". . . to refuse to bargain collectively with the representatives of his employees subject to the provisions of Section 9(a)."

Section 8(d) defines the phrase "to bargain collectively" as the "performance of the mutual obligation of the employer and the representative of the employees to meet at reasonable times and confer in good faith with respect to wages, hours, and other terms and conditions of employment. . . ."

Section 9(a) declares:

> Representatives designated or selected for the purposes of collective bargaining by the majority of employees in a unit appropriate for such purposes, shall be the exclusive representatives of all the employees in such unit for the purposes of collective bargaining in respect to rates of pay, wages, hours of employment, or other conditions of employment. . . .

The National Labor Relations Board (NLRB) oversees the enforcement of the NLRA. The president of the United States appoints members to the NLRB for five-year terms.

Compensation Issues in Collective Bargaining

Union and management negotiations usually center on pay raises and fringe benefits. Unions fought hard for general pay increases and regular cost-of-living adjustments (COLAs). COLAs represent automatic pay increases that are based on changes in prices, as indexed by the consumer price index (CPI). COLAs enable workers to maintain their standards of living by adjusting wages for inflation. Union leaders fought hard for these improvements to maintain the memberships' loyalty and support.

Unions generally secured high wages for their members through the early 1980s. In fact, it was not uncommon for union members to earn as much as 30 percent more than their nonunion counterparts. Unions also improved members' employee benefits. The establishment of sound retirement income programs was most noteworthy.

Unions' gains also influenced nonunion companies' compensation practices. Many nonunion companies offered similar compensation to their employees. This phenomenon is known as a **spillover effect** because management of nonunion firms generally offered higher wages and benefits to reduce the chance that employees would seek union representation.[26]

Unions' influence has declined since the 1980s for three key reasons. First, union companies demonstrated consistently lower profits than nonunion companies.[27] As a result, management has been more reluctant to agree on large pay increases, which represent costs that lead to lower profits. Second, drastic employment cuts have taken place in various industries, including the highly unionized commercial airline, automobile, and steel industries.[28] In the case of automobiles and steel, technological advances and foreign competition have contributed to declines in those industries. Automated work processes in both the automobile and steel industries made many workers' skills obsolete. Moreover, Japanese automobile manufacturers produced higher-quality vehicles than did U.S. automobile manufacturers. Although these vehicles were more expensive, U.S. consumers were willing to pay higher prices in exchange for better quality. U.S. automakers argued that as much as $2,000 of the price of a car helped cover the costs of union workers' excellent health care insurance coverage. Workforces in Japanese automakers are not unionized, which allows them to devote more resources to quality improvement. Fourth, U.S. companies laid off droves of union workers in favor of employing nonunion workers in countries outside the U.S. at substantially lower pay rates.

As a result of the changing business landscape, unions tempered their stance in negotiations with management. Many unions focused more heavily on promoting job security than securing large pay increases. This is known as **concessionary bargaining**. Available data indicates that annual negotiated pay raises declined steadily after 1980. During the 1980s, concessions were most prevalent in small companies, in high-wage companies, and in companies with a small percentage of employees covered by unions. We've more recently begun witnessing some employee groups giving substantially larger concessions to management than ever before. For instance, the union that represents the pilots of Delta Air Lines agreed to substantial cuts in base pay and in future retirement income to help the company avoid dissolution. Substantial cuts like these were not prevalent during the 1980s and would not have been tolerated previously by the unions; however, the dire financial conditions of companies have led unions to give in to such demands in order to keep their members employed with the hope of regaining some of the lost pay and benefits in the future when companies' financial condition improves.

As the revision of this book was being prepared, it was anticipated that the United Auto Workers will make two concessions in their negotiations for a new collective bargaining agreement with the Big Three U.S. automakers (i.e., Chrysler, Ford, and General Motors) to help improve the financial condition of these ailing corporations. First, the union may agree to manage the health care coverage costs of workers rather than leave it to the responsibility of these companies. If this concession were to be made, U.S. automakers would possess substantially more money to invest in quality development to be competitive with rival Japanese automakers. This concession would require the automakers to make a substantial one-time contribution to a health care fund that would be managed by the unions. In addition, workers would be expected to contribute substantially more each month for their health care coverage. The companies are currently responsible for ensuring that union workers receive health care coverage no matter how expensive per their current collective bargaining agreement.

The second concession pertains to retirement plans. Union workers currently participate in defined benefit pension plans. It is possible that the union will agree to have newly hired workers participate in a defined contributions plan instead of the long-standing defined benefit plan. As we will discuss in Chapter 11, companies establish retirement or pension plans following one of two design configurations: a defined benefit plan or a defined contribution plan. The configuration determines such outcomes as whether retirement income is fixed by a formula or depends on the performance of such investment vehicles as company stock, company profits, mutual funds, or bonds. With **defined benefit plans**, retirees receive guaranteed payments for the duration of their lives, but represent a substantial cost burden to companies that must ensure adequate funding to support retirees for longer periods based on rises in life expectancy. From the union's and employee's perspectives, **defined contribution plans** are much riskier than defined benefit plans because the amount and duration of retirement income depends mainly on the performance of investments. Shifting the risk from the employer to the employee is at the heart of concessionary bargaining and, as we have seen, is not something unions would have considered in previous years.

MARKET INFLUENCES

In competitive labor markets, companies attempt to attract and retain the best individuals for employment partly by offering lucrative wage and benefits packages. Some companies unfortunately were unable to compete on the basis of wage and benefits, as illustrated in the second opening quotation. Indeed, there are differences in wages across industries. These differences are known as **interindustry wage or compensation differentials**. Table 3-6 displays the average weekly earnings in various industries for selected years between 1990 and 2007. Construction and mining establishments paid the highest wages throughout this period; retail trade and service companies paid the lowest wages.

Interindustry differentials can be attributed to a number of factors, including the industry's product market, the degree of capital intensity, the profitability of the industry, unionization, and gender mix of the workforce.[29] Companies that operate in product markets where there is relatively little competition from other companies tend to pay higher wages because these companies exhibit substantial profits. This phenomenon can be attributed to such factors as higher barriers to entry into the product market and an insignificant influence of foreign competition. Government regulation and extremely expensive equipment represent entry barriers. The U.S. defense industry and the public utilities industry have high entry barriers and no threats from foreign competitors.

Capital intensity (i.e., the extent to which companies' operations is based on the use of large-scale equipment) also explains pay differentials between industries. The amount of average pay varies with the degree of capital intensity. On average, capital-intensive industries (e.g., manufacturing) pay more than industries that are less capital intensive (e.g., service industries). Capital intensive businesses require highly capable employees who have the aptitude to learn how to use complex technology. Service industries are not capital intensive, and most have the reputation of paying low wages. The operation of service industries depends almost exclusively on employees with relatively common skills rather than on employees with specialized skills to operate such physical equipment as casting machines or robotics.

Furthermore, companies in profitable industries tend to pay higher compensation, on average, than companies in less profitable industries. Employees in profitable industries

TABLE 3-6   Average Weekly Earnings by Industry Group, Selected Years 1990 through 2007[a]

Industry	1990	1995	1998	2002	2005	2007
Mining	$603	$684	$744	$756	$800	$946
Construction	$526	$587	$629	$711	$750	$794
Manufacturing	$442	$515	$557	$618	$673	$707
Finance, insurance, real estate	$357	$442	$512	$586	$642	$695
Services	$319	$369	$420	$488	$526	$545
Retail trade	$194	$221	$310	$360	$377	$380

[a] 2007 figures for March.

SOURCE: U.S. Bureau of Labor Statistics. *Employment Situation.* [online] *www.bls.gov/ces/cesbtabs.htm.* Accessed July 5, 2007.

presumably receive higher pay because their skills and abilities contribute to companies' success and are more productive; however, as more companies have failed to meet financial goals over the past few years, they have struggled with how best to pay for performance.

Following our recent discussion of unionization, highly unionized industries tend to pay higher wages, on average, than do nonunion industries. At the same time, most highly unionized industries (e.g., manufacturing, construction, mining) are capital intensive, requiring employees with the aptitude to learn and use complex production technology.

Following our earlier discussion of comparable worth, industries that employ substantially larger percentages of women than men tend to pay less. According to comparable worth proponents, women's work is undervalued relative to men's work in society. At the same time, most female-dominated industries appear in the service sector in such functions as in retail (e.g., store clerks) and education (e.g., primary school teachers).

Most recently, U.S. companies' practices of outsourcing jobs to people from other countries have had a significant impact on compensation in the United States. Companies typically establish operations in other countries where labor costs are substantially lower than they are in the United States, and fewer laws restrict companies' wage setting. Companies traditionally outsourced factory (blue collar) jobs to Mexico and Southeast Asian countries. U.S. companies are increasingly outsourcing professional (white collar) jobs to India because the wage levels in India are only about one fifth as much as in the United States for information technology and financial services workers. U.S. companies often may have the best of both worlds because they pay much less to hire (often) individuals in India who were trained in prestigious U.S. universities.

SUMMARY

This chapter provided a discussion of the various contextual influences on compensation practice. These include laws, labor unions, and market forces. These contextual influences pose significant challenges for compensation professionals. Aspiring compensation professionals must be familiar with the current contextual influences and anticipate impending ones. For example, most companies must adjust in order to accommodate workers with disabilities.

KEY TERMS

- federal constitution, 49
- federal government, 49
- state governments, 49
- local governments, 49
- legislative branch, 50
- executive branch, 50
- executive orders, 50
- judicial branch, 50
- Great Depression, 50
- Social Security Act of 1935 (Title IX), 50
- workers' compensation, 50
- Fair Labor Standards Act of 1938 (FLSA), 51
- *Walling v. A. H. Belo Corp.,* 53
- exempt, 53
- nonexempt, 53
- *Aaron v. City of Wichita, Kansas,* 53

- FairPay Rules, 54
- Portal-to-Portal Act of 1947, 54
- *Andres v. DuBois,* 54
- Equal Pay Act of 1963, 54
- McNamara–O'Hara Service Contract Act of 1965, 55
- Civil Rights Act of 1964, 55
- compensable factors, 55
- *EEOC v. Madison Community Unit School District No. 12,* 55
- comparable worth, 57
- Title VII, 57
- disparate treatment, 57
- disparate impact, 57
- Bennett Amendment, 58
- Executive Order 11246, 58
- affirmative action, 58

- Age Discrimination in Employment Act of 1967 (ADEA), 58
- baby boom generation, 58
- *EEOC v. Chrysler,* 59
- Older-Workers Benefit Protection Act (OWBPA), 59
- equal benefit or equal cost principle, 60
- Civil Rights Act of 1991, 60
- *Atonio v. Wards Cove Packing Co.,* 60
- *Lorance v. AT&T Technologies,* 60
- *Boureslan v. Aramco,* 60
- Pregnancy Discrimination Act of 1978 (PDA), 61
- Americans with Disabilities Act of 1990 (ADA), 61

DISCUSSION QUESTIONS

1. Identify the contextual influence that you believe will pose the greatest challenge to companies' competitiveness, and identify the contextual influence that will pose the least challenge to companies' competitiveness. Explain your rationale.
2. Should the government raise the minimum wage? Explain your answer.
3. Do unions make it difficult for companies to attain competitive advantage? Explain your answer.
4. Select one of the contextual influences presented in this chapter. Identify a company that has dealt with this influence, and conduct some research on the company's experience. Be prepared to present a summary of the company's experience in class.
5. Some people argue that there is too much government intervention, while others say there is not enough. Based on the presentation of laws in this chapter, do you think there is too little or too much government intervention? Explain your answer.

EXERCISES

Compensation Online

For Students

Exercise 1: Find relevant journal articles

One of your classes will hold a debate next week. You have been given the topic of affirmative action. Your opponent will argue that affirmative action is reverse discrimination and infringes upon the right of the company to select the best person for each job. You will have to convince the rest of the class otherwise. Search your library's online catalog for affirmative action and read up to prepare for the debate.

Exercise 2: Review a government document

Imagine that you must write a short history on workplace legislation. Using Yahoo!, search for Title VII. Find the text and read over Sec. 2000e1–4. What is this section about? Using a different search engine, go to the same Web site or find a related site. Compare and contrast the two search engines for ease of accessibility and amount of information available.

Exercise 3: Review an organization's Web site

Your class will be performing a mock negotiation next week, and you will play the role of union representation. To best prepare for the project, use Yahoo! and search for AFL-CIO. Go to the AFL-CIO official site. Read through the information on the site. Write a brief abstract on the topics covered in this chapter from the perspective of organized labor.

For professionals

Exercise 1: Research a compliance with federal law

You are a human resources consultant, and one of your clients, concerned about legal issues, has asked you to review their policies for compliance. Using the search engine of your choice, search for FMLA. Visit a few of the sites and determine what compliance is and what common mistakes are made in this area.

Exercise 2: Research compliance services

Your own company has not had any legal problems but would like to review current policies and practices. You have been asked to find a consultation firm to aid in the process. From the Yahoo! homepage, click the Business & Economy link, then the Business to Business link, and then Consulting and Human Resources. From here, find a few firms that fit the needs of the project and compare their services.

Exercise 3: Review professional references

As an HR consultant, an issue has arisen for which you do not have an immediate answer. Using at least two search engines, search for "human resources law." Review some of the sites and determine which sites would be most helpful as quick references and simple-to-use guides in day-to-day practice.

ENDNOTES

1. Dulles, F. R., & Dubofsky, M. (1984). *Labor in America: A History* (4th ed.). Arlington Heights, IL: Harlon Davidson Inc., p. 72.

2. Dunlop, J. T. (1993). *Industrial Relations Systems* (Rev. ed.). Boston: Harvard Business School Press.

3. Dulles, F. R., & Dubofsky, M. (1984). *Labor in America: A History* (4th ed.). Arlington Heights, IL: Harlon Davidson Inc., p. 72.

4. U.S. Bureau of Labor Statistics (2007). *Employment situation: May 2007* (USDL 07–793) [online]. Available: *stats.bls.gov/newsrels.htm,* accessed June 5, 2007.

5. Ibid.

6. U.S. Office of Management and Budget (2007). *Historical Tables: Budget of the United States, 2007.* Washington, DC: Author.

7. Bennett-Alexander, D. D., & Hartman, L. P. (2007). *Employment Law for Business,* 5th ed. Burr Ridge, IL: McGraw-Hill/Irwin, p. 3.

8. *Walling v. A.H. Belo Corp.,* 316 U.S. 624 1942, 2 WH Cases 39 (1942).

9. *Aaron v. City of Wichita, Kansas,* 54 F. 3d 652 (10th Cir. 1995), 2 WH Cases 2d 1159 (1995).

10. *Andres v. DuBois,* 888 F. Supp. 213 (D.C. Mass 1995), 2 WH Cases 2d 1297 (1995).

11. S. Rep. No. 176, 88th Congress, 1st Session, 1 (1963).

12. *EEOC v. Madison Community Unit School District No. 12,* 818 F. 2d 577 (7th Cir. 1987).

13. Anker, R. (1998). *Gender and Jobs: Sex Segregation of Occupations in the World.* Washington, DC: International Labor Organization.

14. *Ledbetter v. Goodyear Tire & Rubber Co.,* No. 05–1074, (U.S. Supreme Court, May 29, 2007).

15. U.S. Department of Commerce (2004–2005). *Statistical Abstracts of the United States* (124th ed.), U.S. Department of Census (May 2001). Profile of general demographic statistics, Table DP–1 [online]. Available: *www.census.gov,* accessed June 5, 2007.

16. *EEOC v. Chrysler Corp.,* 652 F. Supp. 1523 (D.C. Ohio 1987), 45 FEP Cases 513.

17. *General Dynamics Land Systems Inc. v. Cline,* No. 09–1080 (U.S. Feb. 24, 2004) 93 FEP.

18. *Atonio v. Wards Cove Packing Co.,* 490 U.S. 642, 49 FEP Cases 1519 (1989).

19. *Lorance v. AT&T Technologies,* 49 FEP Cases 1656 (1989).

20. *Boureslan v. Aramco,* 499 U.S. 244, 55 FEP Cases 449 (1991).

21. Bureau of National Affairs (1990). Americans with Disabilities Act of 1990: Text and analysis. *Labor Relations Reporter, 134 (3).* Washington, DC: Author.

22. U.S. Bureau of Labor Statistics. (2007). *Union members in 2006* (USDOL 07–113) [online]. Available: *stats.bls.gov/newsrels.htm,* accessed June 5, 2007.

23. U.S. Bureau of Labor Statistics (2007). *Employment situation: May 2007* (USDL 07–793) [online]. Available: *stats.bls.gov/newsrels.htm,* accessed June 5, 2007.

24. Ibid.

25. Ibid.

26. Solnick, L. (1985). The effect of the blue collar unions on white collar wages and benefits. *Industrial and Labor Relations Review,* 38, pp. 23–35.

27. Blanchflower, D. G., & Freeman, R. B. (1992). Unionism in the United States and other advanced OFCD countries. *Industrial Relations,* 31, pp. 56–79.

28. Kochan, T. R., Katz, H. C., & McKersie, R. B. (1994). *The Transformation of American Industrial Relations.* Ithaca, NY: ILR Press.

29. Osburn, J. (2000). Interindustry wage differentials: patterns and possible sources. *Monthly Labor Review, February,* pp. 34–46; Krueger, A. B., & Summers, L. H. (1987). Reflections on inter-industry wage structure. In K. Lang & J. S. Leonard (Eds.), *Unemployment and the Structure of the Labor Market* (pp. 14–17). New York: Basil Blackwell.

CHAPTER 4

Traditional Bases for Pay
Seniority and Merit

Chapter Outline

- Seniority and Longevity Pay
  - Historical Overview
  - Who Participates?
  - Effectiveness of Seniority Pay Systems
  - Design of Seniority Pay and Longevity Pay Plans
  - Advantages of Seniority Pay
  - Fitting Seniority Pay with Competitive Strategies

- Merit Pay
  - Who Participates?
  - Exploring the Elements of Merit Pay

- Performance Appraisal
  - Types of Performance Appraisal Plans
  - Exploring the Performance Appraisal Process

- Strengthening the Pay-for-Performance Link
  - Link Performance Appraisals to Business Goals
  - Analyze Jobs
  - Communicate
  - Establish Effective Appraisals
  - Empower Employees
  - Differentiate among Performers

- Possible Limitations of Merit Pay Programs
  - Failure to Differentiate among Performers
  - Poor Performance Measures
  - Supervisors' Biased Ratings of Employee Job Performance
  - Lack of Open Communication between Management and Employees
  - Undesirable Social Structures
  - Factors Other Than Merit
  - Undesirable Competition
  - Little Motivational Value

- Linking Merit Pay with Competitive Strategy
  - Lowest-Cost Competitive Strategy
  - Differentiation Competitive Strategy

- Summary

- Key Terms
- Discussion Questions
- Exercises
- Endnotes

Learning Objectives

In this chapter, you will learn about

1. The traditional U.S. business practice of setting employees' base pay on their seniority or longevity with the company

2. The fit of seniority pay practices with the two competitive strategies—lowest cost and differentiation

3. The traditional U.S. business practice of setting employees' base pay on their merit

4. The role of performance appraisal in the merit pay process

5. Ways to strengthen the pay-for-performance link

6. Some possible limitations of merit pay programs

7. How merit pay programs fit with the two competitive strategies—lowest cost and differentiation

For decades, companies have awarded raises to base pay according to employees' seniority or job performance. Many companies, such as IBM, tended to pay employees according to performance, but the system became one of entitlements (i.e., employees expected pay raises regardless of performance). Changes in the global marketplace forced many companies to reconsider their approach to employee compensation. Fierce global competition requires that employees perform their jobs better than ever before to enable companies to offer the best possible product and services at the lowest cost. As a solution, many companies use compensation programs that emphasize rewards according to performance attainment.

In this chapter, we will consider the traditional seniority and longevity approaches to compensating employees. We will then turn our attention to merit pay, which is a widely used form of performance-based pay in U.S. companies. In Chapter 5, we will take up a variety of incentive programs that reward pay for performance.

SENIORITY AND LONGEVITY PAY

Seniority pay and **longevity pay** systems reward employees with periodic additions to base pay according to employees' length of service in performing their jobs. These pay plans assume that employees become more valuable to companies with time, and that valued employees will leave if they do not have a clear idea that their salaries will progress over time.[1] This rationale comes from **human capital theory**,[2] which states that employees' knowledge and skills generate productive capital known as **human capital**. Employees can develop such knowledge and skills from formal education and training, including on-the-job experience. Over time, employees presumably refine existing skills or acquire new ones that enable them to work more productively. Thus, seniority pay rewards employees for acquiring and refining their skills as indexed by seniority.

Before we begin a discussion of seniority and longevity pay (and merit pay, for that matter), it is important to answer the question, "What is base pay?" because it is the foundation on which these adjustments to base pay are built. Although we defined base pay briefly in Chapter 1, the concept and practice is more extensive.

Historical Overview

A quick look back into U.S. labor relations history can shed light on the adoption of seniority pay in many companies. President Franklin D. Roosevelt advocated policies designed to improve workers' economic status in response to the severely depressed economic conditions that had started in 1929. Congress instituted the National Labor Relations Act (NLRA) in 1935 to protect workers' rights, predicated on a fundamental, but limited, conflict of interest between workers and employers. President Roosevelt and other leaders felt that companies needed to be regulated to establish an appropriate balance of power between the parties. The NLRA established a collective bargaining system nationwide to accommodate employers' and employees' partially conflicting and partially shared goals.

Collective bargaining led to **job control unionism**,[3] in which collective bargaining units negotiate formal contracts with employees and provide quasi-judicial grievance procedures to adjudicate disputes between union members and employers. Union shops establish workers' rights and obligations and participate in describing and delineating jobs. In unionized workplaces, terms of collective bargaining agreements may determine the specific type of seniority system used, and seniority tends to be the deciding factor in nearly all job scheduling, transfer, layoff, compensation, and promotion decisions. Moreover, seniority may become a principal criterion for selecting one employee over another for transfer or promotion. Table 4-1 illustrates the rules for a seniority pay program contained in a collective bargaining agreement between the Board of Trustees of the University of Illinois and Local 698 of The American Federation of State, County, and Municipal Employees, AFL-CIO. It shows the actual rates for job classification and seniority level.

Employees shall be paid a rate equal to 80 percent of the full base rate of the job classification and shall advance to the full base rate as follows:

Number of months worked	Percentage of full base rate
9	85
18	90
27	95
36	100

TABLE 4-1 Hourly Wage Rates by Seniority Level

Classification Title	Start	13 Months	25 Months	37 Months	49 Months
Staff Nurse I	$19.07	$20.19	$21.31	$22.40	$23.49
Nursing Assistant	$ 9.94	$10.17	$10.53	$10.83	$11.01
Medical Assistant	$14.65	$15.40	$16.13	$16.92	$17.83
Medical Technologist	$17.66	$18.90	$20.13	$21.38	$22.60

SOURCE: Agreement between the Board of Trustees of the University of Illinois and Local 698 of The American Federation of State, County, and Municipal Employees, AFL-CIO.

Political pressures probably drive the prevalence of public sector seniority pay. Seniority-based pay systems essentially provide automatic pay increases. Performance assessments tend to be subjective rather than objective (e.g., production data including dollar volume of sales and units produced, and human resource data including accidents and absenteeism) because accurate job performance measurements are very difficult to obtain. In contrast, employees' seniority is easily indexed (i.e., time on the job is a relatively straightforward and concrete concept). Implementing such a system that specifies the amount of pay raise an employee will receive according to his or her seniority is automatic. Politically, "automatic" pay adjustments protect public sector employees from the quirks of election-year politics.[4] In addition, the federal, state, and local governments can avoid direct responsibility for pay raises so employees can receive fair pay without political objections.

Who Participates?

Today, most unionized private sector and public sector organizations continue to base salary on seniority or length of employee service. The total number of unionized employees in both sectors is quite large. In 2006, the percentage of U.S. civilian workers in both the public and private sectors represented by unions had declined steadily to a 12.0 percent representation since 1983, when the representation rate was 20.1 percent.[5] The unionization rate of government workers was 36.2 percent, compared with 7.4 percent among private-sector employees in 2006. Members of union bargaining units whose contracts include seniority provisions, usually rank-and-file as well as clerical workers, receive automatic raises based on the number of years they have been with the company. In the public sector (i.e., municipal, state, and federal government organizations) most administrative, professional, and even managerial employees receive such automatic pay raises.

Effectiveness of Seniority Pay Systems

Virtually no systematic research has demonstrated these pay plans' effectiveness, nor is there any documentation regarding their prevalence. Seniority or longevity pay plans are likely to disappear from for-profit companies in increasingly competitive markets. Such external influences as increased global competition, rapid technological advancement, and skill deficits of new and current members of the workforce necessitate a strategic orientation toward compensation. These influences will probably force companies to establish compensation tactics that reward their employees for learning job-relevant knowledge and skills and for making tangible contributions toward companies' quests for competitive advantage. Seniority pay meets neither goal.

Public sector organizations had until the 1990s faced less pressure to change these systems because they exist to serve the public rather than make profits. For example, the Internal Revenue Service (IRS) is responsible for collecting taxes from U.S. citizens. Paying taxes to the federal government is an obligation of virtually all U.S. citizens. The amount of taxes each citizen pays is based on established tax codes. The IRS is not in the business of finding new customers to pay taxes. It does not compete against any other businesses for taxpayers.

The federal government, however, has now raised questions about the effectiveness of its seniority pay system for white-collar workers—the General Schedule—which we will discuss shortly. Questions about the effectiveness of its seniority pay system are based on how the world of work has dramatically changed since the system's inception in 1949.

Design of Seniority Pay and Longevity Pay Plans

Although seniority pay and longevity pay are similar, there are some important distinctions between them. The object of seniority pay is to reward job tenure or

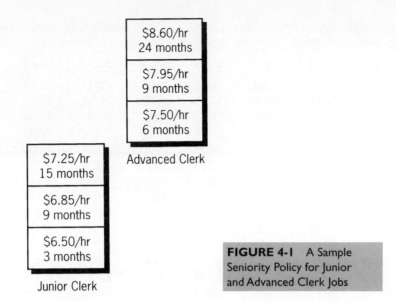

$8.60/hr
24 months

$7.95/hr
9 months

$7.50/hr
6 months

Advanced Clerk

$7.25/hr
15 months

$6.85/hr
9 months

$6.50/hr
3 months

Junior Clerk

FIGURE 4-1   A Sample Seniority Policy for Junior and Advanced Clerk Jobs

employees' time as members of a company explicitly through permanent increases to base salary. Employees begin their employment at the starting pay rate established for the particular jobs. At specified time intervals, which can be as short as 3 months and as long as 3 years, employees receive designated pay increases. These pay increases are permanent additions to current pay levels. Over time, employees will reach the maximum pay rate for their jobs. Companies expect that most employees will earn promotions into higher paying jobs that have seniority pay schedules. Figure 4-1 illustrates a seniority pay policy for a junior clerk job and an advanced clerk job. Pay rates are associated with seniority. When employees reach the top pay rate for the junior clerk position, they are presumably qualified to assume the duties of the advanced clerk position.

Longevity pay rewards employees who have reached pay grade maximums and who are not likely to move into higher grades. State and local governments often use longevity pay as an incentive to reduce employee turnover and to reward employees for continuous years of service. Longevity pay may take the form of a percentage of base pay, a flat dollar amount, or a special step increase based on the number of years the employee has spent with the organization.[6]

Federal employees are subject to longevity pay via the **General Schedule (GS)**, which is shown in Table 4-2. The General Schedule classifies federal government jobs into 15 classifications (GS-1 through GS-15) based on such factors as skill, education, and experience levels. In addition, jobs that require high levels of specialized education (e.g., a physicist), influence public policy significantly (e.g., law judges), or require executive decision making are classified in separate categories: Senior Level (SL), Scientific & Professional (SP) positions, and the Senior Executive Service (SES). The government typically increases all pay amounts annually to adjust for inflation.

Employees are eligible for 10 within-grade step pay increases. At present, it takes employees 18 years to progress from Step 1 to Step 10. The waiting periods within steps are:

- Steps 1–3: 1 year
- Steps 4–6: 2 years
- Steps 7–9: 3 years

TABLE 4-2 Salary Table 2007-GS, General Schedule Incorporating a 1.70% General Increase Effective January 2007. Annual Rates by Grade and Step

Grade	Step 1	Step 2	Step 3	Step 4	Step 5	Step 6	Step 7	Step 8	Step 9	Step 10
1	16630	17185	17739	18289	18842	19167	19713	20264	20286	20798
2	18698	19142	19761	20286	20512	21115	21718	22321	22924	23527
3	20401	21081	21761	22441	23121	23801	24481	25161	25841	26521
4	22902	23665	24428	25191	25954	26717	27480	28243	29006	29769
5	25623	26477	27331	28185	29039	29893	30747	31601	32455	33309
6	28562	29514	30466	31418	32370	33322	34274	35226	36178	37130
7	31740	32798	33856	34914	35972	37030	38088	39146	40204	41262
8	35151	36323	37495	38667	39839	41011	42183	43355	44527	45699
9	38824	40118	41412	42706	44000	45294	46588	47882	49176	50470
10	42755	44180	45605	47030	48455	49880	51305	52730	54155	55580
11	46974	48540	50106	51672	53238	54804	56370	57936	59502	61068
12	56301	58178	60055	61932	63809	65686	67563	69440	71317	73194
13	66951	69183	71415	73647	75879	78111	80343	82575	84807	87039
14	79115	81752	84389	87026	89663	92300	94937	97574	100211	102848
15	93063	96165	99267	102369	105471	108573	111675	114777	117879	120981

SOURCE: U.S. Office of Personnel Management [online]. Available: *www.opm.gov,* accessed June 5, 2007.

The aging of the baby boom generation may make companies' use of seniority or longevity infeasible. Most individuals in the baby boom generation are currently in the workforce, and only a small segment of them are presently approaching retirement age. Companies that use seniority plans are likely to find the costs burdensome.

Advantages of Seniority Pay

Seniority pay offers a number of advantages to both employees and employers. Employees are likely to perceive they are treated fairly because they earn pay increases according to seniority, which is an objective standard. Seniority stands in contrast to subjective standards based on supervisory judgment. The inherent objectivity of seniority pay systems should lead to greater cooperation among co-workers.

Seniority pay offers two key advantages to employers. First, seniority pay facilitates the administration of pay programs. Pay increase amounts are set in advance, and employers award raises according to a pay schedule, much like the federal government's GS. A second advantage is that employers are less likely to offend some employees by showing favoritism to others because seniority is an objective basis for making awards. The absence of favoritism should enable supervisors and managers effectively to motivate employees to perform their jobs.

Fitting Seniority Pay with Competitive Strategies

Seniority pay does not fit well with the imperatives of competitive strategies because employees can count on receiving the same pay raises for average and exemplary performance, and this fact represents the greatest disadvantage of seniority pay systems. Employees who make significant contributions in the workplace receive the same pay increases as co-workers who make modest contributions. In addition, employees receive pay raises without regard to whether companies are meeting their differentiation or cost goals. Employees clearly do not have any incentives actively to improve their skills or to take risks on the job because they receive pay raises regardless of any initiative they show.

So, in light of increased external pressures on companies to promote productivity and product quality, will seniority or longevity pay be gradually phased out? With the exception of companies that are shielded from competitive pressures (e.g., public utilities) it is likely that companies that intend to remain competitive will set aside seniority pay practices. Although seniority pay plans reflect employees' increased worth, they measure such contributions indirectly rather than based on tangible contributions or the successful acquisition of job-related knowledge or skills. Now more than ever, companies need to be accountable to shareholders, which will require direct measurement of employee job performance.

To illustrate the incompatibility of seniority pay structures with the attainment of competitive strategy further, Toyota, a manufacturer of automobiles, abandoned its seniority-based wage system for a performance-based pay system. Traditional Japanese companies defined *seniority* as employee age. Despite Toyota's worldwide reputation as a manufacturer of high-quality automobiles, company management continually adopts employment practices that encourage even better-quality products. Performance-based pay fits with Toyota's mission.

MERIT PAY

Merit pay programs assume that employees' compensation over time should be determined, at least in part, by differences in job performance.[7] Employees earn permanent merit increases based on their performance. The increases reward excellent effort or results, motivate future performance, and help employers retain valued employees. Merit increases are usually expressed as a percentage of hourly wages for nonexempt employees and as a percentage of annual salaries for exempt employees. In 2006, employees earned average merit increases of about 4.0 percent with the same rate anticipated for 2007.[8]

Who Participates?

Merit pay is one of the most commonly used compensation methods in the United States. Various small-scale surveys of no more than a few thousand companies,[9] conducted by compensation consulting firms and professional associations, demonstrate that merit pay plans are firmly entrenched within U.S. business. Its popularity may result from the fact that merit pay fits well with U.S. cultural ideals that reward individual achievement.[10] Merit pay programs occur most often in the private "for-profit" sector of the economy rather than in such public sector organizations as local and state governments.[11]

Exploring the Elements of Merit Pay

Managers rely on objective as well as subjective performance indicators to determine whether an employee will receive a merit increase and the amount of increase warranted. As a rule, supervisors give merit increases to employees based on subjective appraisal of employees' performance.[12] Supervisors periodically review individual employee performance to evaluate how well each worker is accomplishing assigned duties relative to established standards and goals. Thus, as we will discuss later in this chapter, accurate performance appraisals are key to effective merit pay programs.

For merit pay programs to succeed, employees must know that their efforts in meeting production quotas or quality standards will lead to pay raises. Job requirements must be realistic, and employees must have the skills and abilities to meet job goals. Moreover, employees must perceive a strong relationship between attaining performance standards and receiving pay increases.

Furthermore, companies that use merit programs must ensure that the funds needed to fulfill these promises to compensate employees are available. For now, we assume that adequate funding for merit pay programs is in place. We will address the ramifications of insufficient budgets for funding merit pay programs in Chapter 9.

Finally, companies should make adjustments to base pay according to changes in the cost of living or inflation before awarding merit pay raises. Merit pay raises should always reward employee performance rather than represent adjustments for inflation. Inflation represents rises in the cost of consumer goods and services (e,g., food and health care) that boost the overall cost of living. Over time, inflation erodes the purchasing power of the dollar. You've no doubt heard the comment, "It's harder to stretch a dollar these days." Employees are concerned about how well merit increases raise purchasing power. Compensation professionals attempt to minimize negative inflationary effects by making permanent increases to base pay known as cost-of-living adjustments. For now, let's assume that inflation is not an issue. (As an aside, this principle also applies to seniority pay. Pay increases should reflect additional seniority after making specific adjustments for inflation.)

Although fairly common, merit pay systems are not appropriate for all companies. Compensation professionals should consider two factors—commitment from top management and the design of jobs—before endorsing the use of merit pay systems. Top management must be willing to reward employees' job performances with meaningful pay differentials that match employee performance differentials. Companies ideally should grant sufficiently large pay increases to reward employees for exemplary job performance and to encourage similar expectations about future good work.

The amount of a merit pay increase should reflect prior job performance levels and motivate employees toward striving for exemplary performance. The pay raise amount should be meaningful to employees. The concept of **"just-meaningful pay increase"** refers to the minimum pay increase that employees will see as making a meaningful change in compensation.[13] The basic premise of this concept is that a trivial pay increase for average or better employees is not likely to reinforce their performance or to motivate enhanced future performance. We will take up the specifics of the just-meaningful pay increase concept in Chapter 9.

In addition to top management's commitment to merit pay programs, HR professionals must design jobs explicitly enough that employees' performance can be measured accurately. Merit programs are most appropriate when employees have control over their performances and when conditions outside employees' control do not substantially affect their performance. Conditions beyond employees' control that are likely to limit job performance vary by the type of job. For sales professionals, recessionary economic spells generally lead consumers to limit spending on new purchases because they anticipate the possibility of layoffs. Sales professionals certainly do not create recessionary periods, nor can they allay consumers' fears about the future. For production workers, regular equipment breakdowns will lead to lower output.

Furthermore, there must be explicit performance standards that specify the procedures or outcomes against which employees' job performance can be clearly evaluated. At Pratt & Whitney, HR professionals and employees worked together to rewrite job descriptions. The purpose was to define and put into writing the major duties of a job and to specify written performance standards for each duty to ensure that the job requirements provided a useful measurement standard for evaluation. The main performance standards included such factors as quality, quantity, and timeliness of work.

Table 4-3 displays a job description for a manager for an anti-money laundering compliance officer at JPMorgan Chase. The duties describe the activities the jobholder performs, prior experience, and necessary skills to perform this job at an acceptable level. For instance, a successful candidate must demonstrate an understanding of how money laundering occurs.

TABLE 4-3 Anti-Money Laundering Compliance Officer

Description

JPMorgan Chase is a leading global financial services firm with assets of $1.1 trillion and operations in more than 50 countries. The firm is a leader in investment banking, financial services for consumers and businesses, financial transaction processing, asset and wealth management, and private equity. The firm serves millions of consumers under the JPMorgan, Chase, and Bank One brands in the United States and many of the world's most prominent corporate, institutional and government clients.

If you're interested in working in an environment where leadership, excellence, integrity and diversity are among the core principles, then explore the opportunities at JPMorgan Chase. Furthermore information about careers at JPMorgan Chase can be found on their Web site: *www.jpmorganchase.com*.

International Financial Services (IFS) is responsible for conducting periodic reviews of account activity for certain designated high-risk clients in order to comply with the spirit and letter of the Bank Secrecy Act as well as the U.S. Patriot Act. The primary responsibilities of the AML/KYC Analyst are:

Duties

Conduct periodic reviews of designated high-risk client account activity

Using information obtained from the account activity review, existing Know Your Customer/Client (KYC) information and additional research performed by the Analyst to determine if the activity occurring is potentially suspicious/unusual

Prepare referrals to BSA monitoring areas for SAR filing when appropriate

Maintain various database systems to track designated high-risk client information

Produce reports and MIS as needed by management

Work closely with other compliance officers, risk managers and sales staff

Qualifications

Strong working knowledge of AML laws and regulations

Strong understanding of how money laundering occurs and understanding of what "suspicious activity" is and is not

Able to use Microsoft Office (Excel, Word and Access) to obtain information, produce reports and MIS as needed, and update existing databases with new information

At least (1) year experience dealing with client transaction processing

The candidate should hold a 4-year bachelors degree, at a minimum.

Have strong communication skills (verbal and written)

Have strong interpersonal skills

Be able to work well in a goal-oriented, production environment

Job profile

Job category: Consumer/Retail and Middle Market
Locations: US–NY–New York
Organization: Office of the General Counsel
Schedule: Full-time
Job Type: Standard
Shift: Day Job
Travel: Yes, 25 percent of the time

SOURCE: *www.jpmorganchase.com*, accessed April 5, 2005.

PERFORMANCE APPRAISAL

Effective performance appraisals drive effective merit pay programs. Merit pay systems require specific performance appraisal approaches, as noted previously. Administering successful merit pay programs depends as much on supervisors' appraisal approaches as it does on the professionals' skills in designing and implementing such plans.

Types of Performance Appraisal Plans

Performance appraisal methods fall into four broad categories:

- Trait systems
- Comparison systems
- Behavioral systems
- Goal-oriented systems

The four kinds of performance appraisal methods are next described in order.

Trait Systems

Trait systems ask raters to evaluate each employee's traits or characteristics (e.g., quality of work, quantity of work, appearance, dependability, cooperation, initiative, judgment, leadership responsibility, decision-making ability, or creativity). Appraisals are typically scored using descriptors ranging from unsatisfactory to outstanding. Table 4-4 contains an illustration of a trait method of performance appraisal.

Trait systems are easy to construct, use, and apply to a wide range of jobs. They are also easy to quantify for merit pay purposes. Trait systems are increasingly becoming common in companies that focus on the quality of interactions with customers. For example, Leon Leonwood Bean, founder of L. L. Bean, made customer service the foundation of his business from its beginning in 1912. Bean referred to the necessity of positive customer service as one of the business's golden rules: Sell good merchandise at a reasonable profit, treat your customers like human beings, and they will always come back for more.[14]

The trait approach does have limitations. First, trait systems are highly subjective[15] because they are based on the assumption that every supervisor's perception of a given trait is the same. For example, the trait "quality of work" may be defined by one supervisor as "the extent to which an employee's performance is free of errors." To another

TABLE 4-4   A Trait-Oriented Performance Appraisal Rating Form

| *Employee's Name:* | | *Employee's Position:* | | |
| *Supervisor's Name:* | | *Review Period:* | | |

Instructions: For each trait below, circle the phrase that best represents the employee.

1. Diligence

a. outstanding	b. above average	c. average	d. below average	e. poor

2. Cooperation with others

a. outstanding	b. above average	c. average	d. below average	e. poor

3. Communication skills

a. outstanding	b. above average	c. average	d. below average	e. poor

4. Leadership

a. outstanding	b. above average	c. average	d. below average	e. poor

5. Decisiveness

a. outstanding	b. above average	c. average	d. below average	e. poor

supervisor, quality of work might mean "the extent to which an employee's performance is thorough." Human resource professionals and supervisors can avoid this problem by working together in advance to specify the definition of traits clearly.

Another drawback is that systems rate individuals on subjective personality factors rather than objective job performance data. Essentially, trait assessment focuses attention on employees rather than on job performances. Employees may simply become defensive rather than trying to understand the role that the particular trait plays in shaping their job performance and then taking corrective actions.

Comparison Systems

Comparison systems evaluate a given employee's performance against the performance of other employees. Employees are ranked from the best performer to the poorest performer. In simplest form, supervisors rank each employee and establish a performance hierarchy such that the employee with the best performance receives the highest ranking. Employees may be ranked on overall performance or on various traits.

An alternative approach, called a **forced distribution** performance appraisal, assigns employees to groups that represent the entire range of performance. For example, three categories that might be used are best performers, moderate performers, and poor performers. A forced distribution approach, in which the rater must place a specific number of employees into each of the performance groups, can be used with this method. Table 4-5 displays a forced distribution rating form for an animal keeper job with five performance categories.

Many companies use forced distribution approaches to minimize the tendency for supervisors to rate most employees as excellent performers. This tendency usually arises out of supervisors' self-promotion motives. Supervisors often provide positive performance ratings to most of their employees because they do not want to alienate them. After all, their performance as supervisors depends largely on how well their employees perform their jobs.

Forced distribution approaches have drawbacks. The forced distribution approach can distort ratings because employee performance may not fall into these predetermined

---

TABLE 4-5 A Forced Distribution Performance Appraisal Rating Form

Instructions: You are required to rate the performance for the previous 3 months of the 15 workers employed as animal keepers to conform with the following performance distribution:

- *15 percent* of the animal keepers will be rated as having exhibited poor performance.
- *20 percent* of the animal keepers will be rated as having exhibited below average performance.
- *35 percent* of the animal keepers will be rated as having exhibited average performance.
- *20 percent* of the animal keepers will be rated as having exhibited above average performance.
- *10 percent* of the animal keepers will be rated as having exhibited superior performance.

Use the following guidelines for rating performance. On the basis of the five duties listed in the job description for animal keeper, the employee's performance is characterized as:

- *Poor* if the incumbent performs only one of the duties well.
- *Below average* if the incumbent performs only two of the duties well.
- *Average* if the incumbent performs only three of the duties well.
- *Above average* if the incumbent performs only four of the duties well.
- *Superior* if the incumbent performs all five of the duties well.

distributions. Let's assume that a supervisor must use the following forced distribution to rate her employees' performance:

- 15 percent well below average
- 25 percent below average
- 40 percent average
- 15 percent above average
- 5 percent well above average

This distribution is problematic to the extent that the actual distribution of employee performance is substantially different from this forced distribution. If 35 percent of the employees' performance were either above average or well above average, then the supervisor would be required to underrate the performance of 15 percent of the employees. Based on this forced distribution, the supervisor can rate only 20 percent of the employees as having demonstrated above average or well above average job performance. Management–employee relationships ultimately suffer because workers feel that ratings are dictated by unreal models rather than by individual performance.

A third comparative technique for ranking employees establishes **paired comparisons.** Supervisors compare each employee to every other employee, identifying the better performer in each pair. Table 4-6 displays a paired comparison form. Following the comparison, the employees are ranked according to the number of times they were identified as being the better performer. In this example, Allen Jones is the best performer because he was identified most often as the better performer, followed by Bob Brown (identified twice as the better performer) and Mary Green (identified once as the better performer).

Comparative methods are best suited for small groups of employees who perform the same or similar jobs. They are cumbersome for large groups of employees or for employees who perform different jobs. For example, it would be difficult to judge whether a production worker's performance is better than a secretary's performance because the jobs are substantively different. The assessment of a production worker's performance is based on the number of units he or she produces during each work shift; a secretary's performance is based on the accuracy with which he or she types memos and letters.

As do trait systems, comparison approaches have limitations. They tend to encourage subjective judgments, which increase the chance for rater errors and biases. In addition, small differences in performance between employees may become exaggerated by using such a method if supervisors feel compelled to distinguish among levels of employee performance.

Behavioral Systems

Behavioral systems rate employees on the extent to which they display successful job performance behaviors. In contrast to trait and comparison methods, behavioral methods

---

TABLE 4-6 A Paired Comparison Performance Appraisal Rating Form

Instructions: Please indicate by placing an X which employee of each pair has performed most effectively during the past year.

__X__	Bob Brown		__X__	Mary Green
_____	Mary Green		_____	Jim Smith
__X__	Bob Brown		_____	Mary Green
_____	Jim Smith		__X__	Allen Jones
_____	Bob Brown		_____	Jim Smith
__X__	Allen Jones		__X__	Allen Jones

rate objective job behaviors. When correctly developed and applied, behavioral models provide results that are relatively free of rater errors and biases. The three main types of behavioral systems are the critical incident technique (CIT), behaviorally anchored rating scales (BARS), and behavioral observation scales (BOS).

The **critical incident technique (CIT)**[16] requires job incumbents and their supervisors to identify performance incidents (e.g., on-the-job behaviors and behavioral outcomes) that distinguish successful performances from unsuccessful ones. The supervisor then observes the employees and records their performance on these critical job aspects. Supervisors usually rate employees on how often they display the behaviors described in each critical incident. Table 4-7 illustrates a CIT form for an animal keeper job. Two statements represent examples of ineffective job performance (numbers 2 and 3), and two statements represent examples of effective job performance (numbers 1 and 4).

The CIT tends to be useful because this procedure requires extensive documentation that identifies successful and unsuccessful job performance behaviors by both the employee and the supervisor. The CIT's strength, however, is also its weakness: Implementation of the CIT demands continuous and close observation of the employee. Supervisors may find the record keeping to be overly burdensome.

Behaviorally anchored rating scales (BARS)[17] are based on the critical incident technique, and these scales are developed in the same fashion with one exception. For the CIT, a critical incident would be written as "the incumbent completed the task in a timely fashion." For the BARS format, this incident would be written as "the incumbent is expected to complete the task in a timely fashion." The designers of BARS write the incidents as expectations to emphasize the fact that the employee does not have to demonstrate the exact behavior that is used as an anchor in order to be rated at that level. Because a complete array of behaviors that characterize a particular job would take many pages of description, it is not feasible to place examples of all job behaviors on the scale. Experts therefore list only those behaviors that they believe are most representative of the job the employee must perform. A typical job might have 8 to 10 dimensions under BARS, each with a separate rating scale. Table 4-8 contains an illustration of a BARS for one dimension of an animal keeper job (i.e., cleaning animal enclosures and removing refuse from the public walkways). The scale reflects

---

TABLE 4-7 A Critical Incidents Performance Appraisal Rating Form

Instructions: For each description of work behavior below, circle the number that best describes how frequently the employee engages in that behavior.

1. The incumbent removes manure and unconsumed food from the animal enclosures.

1	2	3	4	5
Never	Almost never	Sometimes	Fairly often	Very often

2. The incumbent haphazardly measures the feed items when placing them in the animal enclosures.

1	2	3	4	5
Never	Almost never	Sometimes	Fairly often	Very often

3. The incumbent leaves refuse dropped by visitors on and around the public walkways.

1	2	3	4	5
Never	Almost never	Sometimes	Fairly often	Very often

4. The incumbent skillfully identifies instances of abnormal behavior among the animals, which represent signs of illness.

1	2	3	4	5
Never	Almost never	Sometimes	Fairly often	Very often

TABLE 4-8   A Behaviorally Anchored Rating Scale

Instructions: On the scale below, from 7 to 1, circle the number that best describes how
frequently the employee engages in that behavior.

7 The incumbent could be expected to clean the animal enclosures thoroughly and remove
| refuse from the public walkways as often as needed.

6
|

5 The incumbent could be expected to clean the animal enclosures thoroughly and remove
| refuse from the public walkways twice daily.

4
|

3 The incumbent could be expected to clean the animal enclosures and remove refuse from
| the public walkways in a haphazard fashion twice daily.

2
|

1 The incumbent could be expected rarely to clean the animal enclosures or remove refuse
   from the public walkways.

the range of performance on the job dimension from ineffective performance (1) to
effective performance (7).

As with all performance appraisal techniques, BARS has its advantages and disadvantages.[18] Among the various performance appraisal techniques, BARS is the most
defensible in court because it is based on actual observable job behaviors. In addition,
BARS encourages all raters to make evaluations in the same way. Perhaps the main
disadvantage of BARS is the difficulty of developing and maintaining the volume of
data necessary to make it effective. The BARS method requires companies to maintain
distinct appraisal documents for each job. As jobs change over time, the documentation must be updated for each job.

Another kind of behavior system, a **behavioral observation scale (BOS)**,[19] displays
illustrations of positive incidents (or behaviors) of job performance for various job
dimensions. The evaluator rates the employee on each behavior according to the
extent to which the employee performs in a manner consistent with each behavioral
description. Scores from each job dimension are averaged to provide an overall rating
of performance. BOS is developed in the same way as a BARS instrument, except that
it incorporates only positive performance behaviors. The BOS method tends to be
difficult and time-consuming to develop and maintain. Moreover, to assure accurate
appraisal, raters must be able to observe employees closely and regularly. Observing
employees on a regular basis may not be feasible where supervisors are responsible for
several people.

Goal-Oriented Systems

Management by objectives (MBO)[20] could be the most effective performance
appraisal technique because supervisors and employees determine objectives for
employees to meet during the rating period and employees appraise how well they
have achieved their objectives. Management by objectives is used mainly for managerial and professional employees and typically evaluates employees' progress toward
strategic planning objectives.

Employees and supervisors together determine particular objectives tied to corporate strategies. Employees are expected to attain these objectives during the rating
period. At the end of the rating period, the employee writes a report explaining his or
her progress toward accomplishing the objectives, and the employee's supervisor

appraises the employee's performance based on accomplishment of the objectives. Despite the importance of managerial employees to company success, it is often difficult to establish appropriate performance goals because many companies simply do not fully describe the scope of these positions. Management by objectives can promote effective communication between employees and their supervisors. On the downside, management by objectives is time-consuming and requires a constant flow of information between employees and employers. Moreover, its focus is only on the attainment of particular goals, often to the exclusion of other important outcomes. This drawback is known as a "results at any cost" mentality.[21] The role of automobile sales professionals historically was literally limited to making sales. Once these professionals and customers agreed on the price of a car, the sales professionals' work with customers was completed. Automobile salespeople today remain in contact with clients for as long as several months following the completion of the sale. The purpose is to ensure customer satisfaction and build loyalty to the product and dealership by addressing questions about the vehicle's features and reminding clients about scheduled service checks.

Goal-oriented systems are often a component of broader development programs that help employees achieve career goals. ExxonMobil blends goal-oriented systems with performance discussions between managers and employees in the HR function:

> When you join ExxonMobil, your career path in Human Resources is marked by assignments of increasing responsibility. You will progress from analyst to supervisory and management positions. This is facilitated by our strong commitment to mentoring and coaching.
>
> The Human Resources function at ExxonMobil is integrated into our many different businesses. In addition to gaining valuable functional experience, you will also have an understanding of how HR is integrated into our various companies and operations around the world.[22]

Exploring the Performance Appraisal Process

Performance appraisals represent a company's way of telling employees what is expected of them in their jobs and how well they are meeting those expectations. Performance appraisals typically require supervisors to monitor employees' performance, complete performance appraisal forms about the employees, and hold discussions with employees about their performance. Companies that use merit pay plans must assess employee job performance, which serves as a basis for awarding merit pay raises. Awarding merit pay increases on factors other than job performance, except for four exceptions (i.e., a seniority system, merit system, quality or quantity of production, and any factor besides sex), could lead some employees to level charges of illegal pay discrimination against the employer based on the Equal Pay Act of 1963.

One such violation of the Equal Pay Act involved two female employees of Cascade Wood Components Company, which remanufactures lumber products.[23] The job in question was the sawyer job; a sawyer is responsible for cutting the best-grade wood segments that will be manufactured into the highest-grade lumber. Cascade awarded pay increases to male sawyers before awarding pay increases to more experienced female sawyers. The court found Cascade in violation of the Equal Pay Act because the higher pay raises awarded to the male sawyers could not be accounted for by commensurate differences in job performance, seniority, a merit system that measures earnings by quantity or quality of production, or any factor other than sex.

Chapter 3 emphasized how U.S. civil rights laws protect employees from illegal discrimination based on age, race, color, religion, sex, national origin, or qualified disability. Because negative performance appraisals can affect an individual's employment status and such related decisions as pay levels and increases, promotions, and discharges, appraisals must be based on job-related factors and not on any discriminatory factors.

Legislation and court decisions have subjected performance appraisals to close scrutiny. In ***Brito v. Zia Company***, the court found that the Zia Company violated Title VII when a disproportionate number of protected class individuals were laid off on the basis of low performance appraisal scores. Zia's action was a violation of Title VII because the use of the performance appraisal system in determining layoffs was indeed an employment test. In addition, the court ruled that the Zia Company had not demonstrated that its performance appraisal instrument was valid. In other words, the appraisal did not assess any job-related criteria based on quality or quantity of work.[24]

Four Activities to Promote Nondiscriminatory Performance Appraisal Practices
Since the *Brito v. Zia Company* decision, court opinions and compensation experts suggest the following four points to ensure nondiscriminatory performance appraisal practices and to protect firms using merit pay systems if legal issues arise.[25] Nondiscriminatory performance appraisal systems are key to effective merit pay systems because they accurately measure job performance.

1. **Conduct job analyses to ascertain characteristics necessary for successful job performance.**
   Companies must first establish definitions of the jobs and then discover what employee behaviors are necessary to perform the jobs. Job analysis is essential for the development of content-valid performance appraisal systems. Content validity displays connections between the measurable factors upon which the employee is being appraised and the job itself. For example, customer service associates' performance might be judged on the basis of courtesy and knowledge of the company's products or services, and these measures would be content-valid dimensions. Both measures are representative of and relative to the job. On the other hand, knowledge of the company's financial accounting practices would not be a content-valid criterion of customer service associates' performance.

   Human resource and compensation experts must review performance appraisal tools regularly to ensure that the tools adequately reflect the key behaviors necessary for effective job performance. Jobholders, supervisors, and clients can often give the most relevant input to determine whether a performance appraisal system contains dimensions that relate to a particular job.

2. **Incorporate these characteristics into a rating instrument.**
   Although the professional literature recommends rating instruments that are tied to specific job behaviors (e.g., behaviorally anchored rating scales), the courts routinely accept such less-sophisticated approaches as simple graphic rating scales and trait ranges. Regardless of the method, HR departments should provide all supervisors and raters with written definitive standards.

   The examples given earlier about the animal keeper job indicate that effective performance appraisal instruments are based on explicitly written job duties conveyed in the job description.

3. **Train supervisors to use the rating instrument properly.**
   Raters need to know how to apply performance appraisal standards when they make judgments. The uniform application of standards is extremely important. In addition, evaluators should be aware of common rater errors, which will be discussed later in this chapter.

4. **Several cases demonstrate that formal appeal mechanisms and review of ratings by upper-level personnel help make performance appraisal processes more accurate and effective.**

Allowing employees to voice their concerns over ratings they believe to be inaccurate or unjust opens a dialogue between employees and their supervisors that may shed light on the performance appraisal outcomes. Employees may be able to point out instances of their performances that may have been overlooked in the appraisal process or explain particular extreme instances as the result of extraordinary circumstances. For example, an ill parent in need of regular attention is the reason for an employee's absence rather than an employee's deliberate breach of work responsibilities because the employee chose to relax at the beach.

Sources of Performance Appraisal Information

Information for performance appraisal can be ascertained from five sources:

- Employee (i.e., the individual whose job performance is being appraised)
- Employee's supervisor
- Employee's co-workers
- Employee's supervisees
- Employee's customers or clients

More than one source can provide performance appraisal information. Although supervisory input is the most common source of performance appraisal information, companies are increasingly calling on as many sources of information as possible to gain a more complete picture of employee job performance. Performance appraisal systems that rely on many appropriate sources of information are known as **360-degree performance appraisals**.

Companies are increasingly relying on the 360-degree performance appraisal methods to reduce the costs of recruiting and hiring new employees. This method helps companies develop a more complete understanding of current employee performance by formulating a judgment on input from multiple sources. Companies often feel more confident about promoting employees from within when multiple sources of information support positive performance judgments.

Three criteria should be used to judge the appropriateness of the information source.[26] First, the evaluators should be aware of the objectives of the employee's job. Second, the evaluators should frequently have occasion to observe the employee on the job. Third, the evaluators should be capable of determining whether the employee's performance is satisfactory.

The use of 360-degree performance appraisals is on the rise in U.S. businesses. Three main factors account for this trend. First, as companies downsize, the organizational structures are becoming less hierarchical. As a result, managers and supervisors are increasingly responsible for more workers. With responsibility for more employees, it has become difficult for managers and supervisors to provide sufficient attention to each employee throughout the appraisal period.

Second, the use of 360-degree performance appraisal methods is consistent with the increased prevalence of work teams in companies. At Whirlpool Corporation, members of semiautonomous work teams communicate their work goals to the entire team. At the end of the designated appraisal period, team members judge others' performances based on the prior statement of work goals.

Third, companies are placing greater emphasis on customer satisfaction as competition for a limited set of customers increases. Companies presently turn to customers as a source of performance appraisal information. For example, it is common for restaurants, furniture stores, moving companies, and automobile manufacturers to ask customers to complete short surveys designed to measure how well they were satisfied with various aspects of their interactions. Volkswagen of America uses the services of a

TABLE 4-9 Sample Customer Satisfaction Survey

Before and During Your Move:	*Yes*	*No*
1. Did our moving consultant help with packing and moving day suggestions?	☐	☐
2. Were we on time?	☐	☐
3. Was our packing service satisfactory?	☐	☐
4. Were our moving personnel courteous?	☐	☐
5. Did your possessions arrive in good condition?	☐	☐
6. Would you recommend us to your friends?	☐	☐

Why did you choose us?

☐ Reputation   ☐ Contacted by salesperson
☐ Have used before   ☐ Recommended by friends
☐ Selected by employer   ☐ Recommended by employer
☐ Contacted by telemarketer   ☐ Other: _____

How can we better serve you?

_____

_____

_____

_____

professional survey company to call VW car owners to rate their experiences with VW dealer service departments. Table 4-9 illustrates a major moving company's customer satisfaction survey, which it mails to customers after a move.

Errors in the Performance Appraisal Process

Almost all raters make **rating errors**. Rating errors reflect differences between human judgment processes versus objective, accurate assessments uncolored by bias, prejudice, or other subjective, extraneous influences.[27] Rating errors occur because raters must always make subjective judgments. Human resource departments can help raters to minimize errors by carefully choosing rating systems and to recognize and avoid common errors. Major types of rater errors include:[28]

- Bias errors
- Contrast errors
- Errors of central tendency
- Errors of leniency or strictness

Bias Errors

Bias errors happen when the rater evaluates the employee based on a personal negative or positive opinion of the employee rather than on the employee's actual performance. Four ways supervisors may bias evaluation results are first-impression effects, positive and negative halo effects, similar-to-me effects, and illegal discriminatory biases.

A manager biased by a **first-impression effect** might make an initial favorable or unfavorable judgment about an employee and then ignore or distort the employee's actual performance based on this impression. For instance, a manager expects that a newly hired graduate of a prestigious Ivy League university will be an exemplary performer. After one year on the job, this employee fails to meet many of the work objectives; nevertheless, the manager rates the job performance more highly because of the initial impression.

A **positive halo effect** or **negative halo effect** occurs when a rater generalizes an employee's good or bad behavior on one aspect of the job to all aspects of the job. A secretary with offensive interpersonal skills is a proficient user of various computer software programs and an outstanding typist. The secretary's supervisor receives frequent complaints from other employees and customers. At performance appraisal time, the supervisor gives this employee an overall negative performance rating.

A **similar-to-me effect** refers to the tendency on the part of raters to judge favorably employees whom they perceive as similar to themselves. Supervisors biased by this effect rate more favorably employees who have attitudes, values, backgrounds, or interests similar to theirs. For example, employees whose children attend the same elementary school as their manager's children receive higher performance appraisal ratings than do employees who do not have children. "Similar-to-me" errors or biases easily can lead to charges of **illegal discriminatory bias**, wherein a supervisor rates members of his or her race, gender, nationality, or religion more favorably than members of other classes.

Contrast Errors

Supervisors make **contrast errors** when they compare an employee with other employees rather than to specific, explicit performance standards. Such comparisons qualify as errors because other employees are required to perform only at minimum acceptable standards. Employees performing at minimally acceptable levels should receive satisfactory ratings, even if every other employee doing the job is performing at outstanding or above-average levels.

Errors of Central Tendency

When supervisors rate all employees as average or close to average, they commit **errors of central tendency**. Such errors are most often committed when raters are forced to justify only extreme behavior (i.e., high or low ratings) with written explanations; therefore, HR professionals should require justification for ratings at every level of the scale and not just at the extremes.

Errors of Leniency or Strictness

Raters sometimes place every employee at the high or low end of the scale, regardless of actual performance. With a **leniency error**, managers tend to appraise employees' performance more highly than they really rate compared with objective criteria. Over time, if supervisors commit positive errors, their employees will expect higher-than-deserved pay rates.

On the other hand, **strictness errors** occur when a supervisor rates an employee's performance lower than it would be if compared against objective criteria. If supervisors make this error over time, employees may receive smaller pay raises than deserved, lower their effort, and perform poorly. In effect, this error erodes employees' beliefs that effort varies positively with performance and that performance influences the amount of pay raises.

STRENGTHENING THE PAY-FOR-PERFORMANCE LINK

Companies who don't consider these possible limitations ultimately weaken the relationship between pay and performance. Human resource managers can employ a number of approaches to strengthen the link between pay and job performance.

Link Performance Appraisals to Business Goals

The standards by which employee performance is judged should be linked to a company's competitive strategy or strategies. For example, each member of a product development team that is charged with the responsibility of marketing a new product might be given merit increases if certain sales goals are reached.

Analyze Jobs

Job analysis (Chapter 7) is vital to companies that wish to establish **internally consistent compensation systems**. As discussed earlier, job descriptions (Chapter 7)—a product of job analyses—can be used by supervisors to create objective performance measures. Job descriptions note the duties, requirements, and relative importance of a job within the company. Supervisors appraising performances can match employees' performances to these criteria. This approach may help reduce supervisors' arbitrary decisions about merit increases by clarifying the standards against which employees' performances are judged.

Communicate

For merit pay programs to succeed, employees must clearly understand what they need to do to receive merit increases and what the rewards for their performances will be. Open communication helps an employee develop reasonable expectations and encourages them to trust the system and those who operate it. Figure 4-2 illustrates worksheets both supervisors and employers may use to establish performance expectations.

Establish Effective Appraisals

During performance appraisal meetings with employees, supervisors should discuss goals for future performance and employee career plans. When performance deficiencies are evident, the supervisor and employee should work together to identify possible causes and develop an action plan to remedy these deficiencies. The performance standards listed within job descriptions should serve as the guides for establishing performance targets. For example, a company's job description for a secretary specifies that the job incumbent must be able to use one word processing software package proficiently. The supervisor should clearly explain what software usage proficiency means. Proficiency may refer to the ability to operate certain features of the software well, including the mail merge utility, the table generator, and the various outlining utilities, or proficiency may refer to the ability to operate all features of the software well.

Empower Employees

Because formal performance appraisals are conducted periodically—maybe only once per year—supervisors must empower their employees to make performance self-appraisals between formal sessions.[29] Moreover, supervisors need to take on a coach's role to empower their workers.[30] As coaches, supervisors must ensure that employees have access to the resources necessary to perform their jobs. Supervisors-as-coaches should also help employees interpret and respond to work problems as they develop. Empowering employees in this fashion should lead to more self-corrective actions rather than reactive courses of action to supervisory feedback and only to the criticisms addressed in performance appraisal meetings.

Differentiate among Performers

Merit increases should consist of meaningful increments. If employees do not see significant distinctions between top performers and poor performers, top performers may become frustrated and reduce their levels of performance. When companies' merit increases don't clearly reflect differences in actual job performances, they may need to provide alternative rewards (e.g., employee benefits—additional vacation days or higher discounts on the company's product or service—can complement merit pay increases).

FIGURE 4-2 Supervisor's and Employee's Performance Planning Worksheets

Supervisor's Performance Planning Worksheet

To be filled out by supervisor

Name of Employee: **Date:**

Employee Title: **Department:**

1. List what you consider to be the primary job duties or assignments at this time (list in order of priority):

2. Describe contributions, achievements, or improvements made by the employee during the past appraisal period:

3. Describe any specific change, improvements, or goals desired for the employee's performance in the next appraisal period:

4. Describe the coaching, training, or development activities you would support in pursuit of improved performance, employee growth, learning, and/or career development:

——————————————— ———— ——————————————— ————
Employee   Date   Supervisor   Date

Employee's Performance Planning Worksheet

To be filled out by employee

Name of Employee: **Date:**

Employee Title: **Department:**

1. List what you consider to be your primary job duties or assignments at this time (list in order of priority):

2. Describe contributions or achievements that indicate your success at improving your performance or exceeding job requirements during the past appraisal period:

3. Describe any specific changes or improvements you want to make in your performance in the next appraisal period. Describe obstacles to getting your job done and suggest possible solutions:

4. Describe the coaching, training, or development activities that would help you pursue improved performance, job growth, learning, and/or career development:

——————————————— ————
Employee Signature   Date

———— (Initial) I have been given the opportunity to fill this out and choose not to do so.

POSSIBLE LIMITATIONS OF MERIT PAY PROGRAMS

Despite the popularity of merit pay systems, these programs are not without potential limitations, which may lessen their credibility with employees. If employees do not believe in a merit pay program, the pay system will not bring about the expected motivational impacts. Supervisors, HR managers, and compensation professionals must address the following eight potential problems with merit pay programs.

Failure to Differentiate among Performers

Employees may receive merit increases even if their performance does not warrant them because supervisors want to avoid creating animosity among employees. Poor performers, therefore, may receive the same pay increase as exemplary performers, and poor performers may come to view merit pay increases as entitlements. Superior performers consequently may question the value of striving for excellent performance.

Poor Performance Measures

Accurate and comprehensive performance measures that capture the entire scope of an employee's job are essential to successful merit pay programs. In most companies, employees' job performances tend to be assessed subjectively, based on their supervisors' judgments. As discussed, merit pay programs rely on supervisors' subjective assessments of employees' prior job performances. Developing performance measures for every single job unfortunately is both difficult and expensive.

Supervisors' Biased Ratings of Employee Job Performance

As we discussed earlier, supervisors are subject to a number of errors when they make subjective assessments of employees' job performances. These errors often undermine the credibility of the performance evaluation process. Performance evaluation processes that lack credibility do little to create the perception among employees that pay reflects performance.

Lack of Open Communication between Management and Employees

If managers cannot communicate effectively with employees, employees will not trust the performance appraisal processes. Trust is difficult to build when decisions are kept secret and employees have no influence on pay decisions. Thus, merit pay decision systems can cause conflict between management and employees. If mistrust characterizes the relationship, then performance appraisals will mean little to employees and could even lead to accusations of bias. In an environment of secrecy, employees lack the information necessary to determine if pay actually is linked to job performance.

Undesirable Social Structures

We acknowledged that relative pay grades can reflect status differentials within a company: Employees with lucrative salaries are usually granted higher status than lower-paid employees. Permanent merit increases may rigidify the relative pay status of employees over time.[31] Table 4-10 shows the permanence of the relative pay difference between two distinct jobs that each receive a 5 percent merit increase each year. Even though both employees performed well and received "equal" merit increases in percentage terms, the actual salary differentials prevail each year. Thus, where pay level is an indicator of status, permanent merit increases may reinforce an undesirable social structure. Lower-paid employees may resent never being able to catch up.

TABLE 4–10 The Impact of Equal Pay Raise Percentage Amounts for Distinct Salaries

At the end of 2005, Anne Brown earned $50,000 per year as a systems analyst and John Williams earned $35,000 per year as an administrative assistant. Each received a 5 percent pay increase every year until the year 2010.

	Anne Brown	*John Williams*
2006	$52,500	$36,750
2007	$55,125	$38,587
2008	$57,881	$40,516
2009	$60,775	$42,542
2010	$63,814	$44,669

Factors Other Than Merit

Merit increases may be based on factors other than merit, which will clearly reduce the emphasis on job performance. For example, supervisors may subconsciously use their employees' ages or seniority as bases for awarding merit increases. Studies show that the extent to which supervisors like the employees for whom they are responsible determines the size of pay raises in a merit pay program.[32] In addition, company politics assumes that the value of an employee's contributions depends on the agenda, or goals, of the supervisor[33] rather than on the objective impact of an employee's contributions to a rationally determined work goal. For instance, an accounting manager wishes to employ accounting methods other than top management's accounting methods. She believes that she can gain top management support by demonstrating that the accounting staff agrees with her position. The accounting manager may give generally positive performance evaluations, regardless of demonstrated performance, to those who endorse her accounting methods.

Undesirable Competition

Because merit pay programs focus fundamentally on individual employees, these programs do little to integrate workforce members.[34] With limited budgets for merit increases, employees must compete for a larger share of this limited amount. Competition among employees is counterproductive if teamwork is essential for successfully completing projects. Thus, merit increases are best suited for jobs where the employee works independently (e.g., clerical positions), and many professional positions from job families (e.g., accounting).

Little Motivational Value

Notwithstanding their intended purpose, merit pay programs may not positively influence employee motivation. Employers and employees may differ in what they see as "large enough" merit increases really to motivate positive worker behavior. For example, increases diminish after deducting income taxes and contributions to Social Security, and differences in employees' monthly paychecks may be negligible.

LINKING MERIT PAY WITH COMPETITIVE STRATEGY

As you will recall, in Chapter 2 we reviewed a framework for establishing a basis for selecting particular compensation tactics to match a company's competitive strategy. How do merit systems fit with the two fundamental competitive strategies (i.e., lowest cost and differentiation)? Merit pay systems, when properly applied, ultimately can contribute to meeting the goals of lowest-cost and differentiation strategies; however, the rationale for the appropriateness of merit pay systems differs according to the imperatives of the lowest-cost and differentiation competitive strategies.

Lowest-Cost Competitive Strategy

Lowest-cost strategies require firms to reduce output costs per employee. Merit pay systems are most appropriate only when the following two conditions are met: (1) Pay increases are commensurate with employee productivity, and (2) employees maintain productivity levels over time. Factors outside companies' control ultimately may from time to time lead to lower employee productivity. Personal illness and a shortage of raw materials for production are examples of factors that undermine employee productivity. Companies that typically experience such slowdowns are likely to find that merit pay systems run counter to cost-containment goals.

Differentiation Competitive Strategy

A differentiation strategy requires creative, open-minded, risk-taking employees. Compared with lowest-cost strategies, companies that pursue differentiation strategies must take a longer-term focus to attain their preestablished objectives. Merit pay has the potential to promote creativity and risk taking by linking pay with innovative job accomplishments; however, objectives that are tied to creativity and risk taking must be established on a regular basis for merit pay to be effective under differentiation strategies. Granting merit pay raises for past performance would be tantamount to rewarding employees long after the impact of their past performance has subsided.

SUMMARY

This chapter provided a discussion of the seniority pay and merit pay concepts. Companies should move away from rewarding employees solely on the basis of seniority and toward rewarding employees for measurable accomplishments. To be successful, merit pay programs must be founded on well-designed performance appraisal systems that accurately measure performance. In addition, rewards commensurate with past performance should be rewarded. Perhaps the greatest challenge for companies is to ensure that employees are given the opportunity to perform at exemplary levels.

KEY TERMS

- seniority pay, 76
- longevity pay, 76
- human capital theory, 76
- human capital, 76
- job control unionism, 77
- General Schedule (GS), 79
- merit pay programs, 81
- just-meaningful pay increase, 82
- trait systems, 84
- comparison systems, 85
- forced distribution, 85
- paired comparisons, 86

- behavioral systems, 86
- critical incident technique (CIT), 87
- behaviorally anchored rating scales (BARS), 87
- behavioral observation scale (BOS), 88
- management by objectives (MBO), 88
- *Brito v. Zia Company,* 90
- 360-degree performance appraisal methods, 91
- rating errors, 92

- bias errors, 92
- first-impression effect, 92
- positive halo effect, 92
- negative halo effect, 92
- similar-to-me effect, 93
- illegal discriminatory bias, 93
- contrast errors, 93
- errors of central tendency, 93
- leniency error, 93
- strictness errors, 93
- internally consistent compensation systems, 94

DISCUSSION QUESTIONS

1. Human capital theory has been advanced as a rationale underlying seniority pay. Identify two individuals you know who have performed the same job for at least 2 years. Ask them to describe the changes in knowledge and skills they experienced from the time they assumed their jobs to the present. Discuss your findings with the class.
2. Subjective performance evaluations are subject to several rater errors, which makes objective measures seem a better alternative. Discuss when subjective performance evaluations might be better (or more feasible) than objective ratings.
3. Consider a summer job that you have held. Write a detailed job description for that job. Then, develop a behaviorally anchored rating scale (BARS) that can be used to evaluate an individual who performs that job in the future.
4. This chapter indicates that merit pay plans appear to be the most common form of compensation in the United States. Although widely used, these systems are not suitable for all kinds of jobs. Based on your knowledge of merit pay systems, identify at least three jobs for which merit pay is inappropriate. Be sure to provide your rationale given the information in this chapter.
5. Select three distinct jobs of your choice (i.e., a clerical job, a technical job, and a professional job). For each job, identify what you believe is the most appropriate performance appraisal method. Based on your choices, sketch a performance appraisal instrument. Discuss the rationale for your choice of performance appraisal methods.

EXERCISES

Compensation Online

For Students

Exercise 1: Search for relevant journal articles

Search article databases for seniority and merit pay. Using the information you find through your search and the information in Chapter 4, write a short explanation of the pros and cons of each system, which you would advocate, and why.

Exercise 2: Search for government salary schedules

Using Yahoo!, go to the federal government's General Schedule by clicking on the advance search link, typing in "general schedule," selecting the *exact phrase match*, and clicking on the *search* button. Scroll down to the *General Schedule Classification System* link and click on it. Read over the page and then click on the *Classification Standards* (located at the bottom of the page under Related Topics). Review the page and click on a couple of the links. Write a brief description about the contents of this site, describing what information it contains and how valuable you think this site might be for you as a student.

Exercise 3: Research employment discrimination laws

Using the search engine of your choice, search for Equal Pay Act of 1963. Find articles or government Web sites, and gather information on how this law has been interpreted over the years and what sorts of cases have been most common. Write a short timeline of how the Equal Pay Act and related cases have changed over the life of the Act.

For Professionals

Exercise 1: Research an organizational Web site

Using Yahoo!, click on the *advanced search* button. Type "Institute of Management and Administration" in the window, click on the exact phrase match and the Web site options, and then click on the *search* link. Read over its homepage (*www.ioma.com*). Review the page and then click on some of the topics. Do you think this site might be of value to you as a professional? Describe the features of the IOMA organization that you would find most helpful.

Exercise 2: Search for a union's Web sites

Certain Web resources are sometimes not what you need. For instance, you would like specifically to find only current events and recent issues pertaining to the United Auto

Workers. Using Yahoo!, click on the *advanced search* button and type in "United Auto Workers." Select the exact phrase match and Web sites options, and click on the *search* button. Click on each of the *Categories, Web Pages*, and *News and Stories* buttons and review the information available on each one. What did you find when you clicked on each button? When would you use one button rather than the other? Find a site that pertains to the UAW and collective bargaining. Describe the relevant information for a human resource professional.

Exercise 3: Research different performance management practices

The vice president of HR has expressed dissatisfaction with your company's current performance management system. Search for performance appraisal and/or performance *management*. Find consulting firms that specialize in these areas. Compare and contrast the services offered by each firm. How would you determine the reputability of each firm?

ENDNOTES

1. Cayer, N. J. (1975). Public Personnel Administration in the United States. New York: St. Martin Press.
2. Becker, G. (1975). *Human Capital*. New York: St. Martin Press.
3. Kochan, T. R., Katz, H. C., & McKersie, R. B. (1994). *The Transformation of American Industrial Relations*. Ithaca, NY: ILR Press.
4. Cayer, N. J. (1975). *Public Personnel Administration in the United States*. New York: St. Martin Press.
5. U.S. Bureau of Labor Statistics. (2007). *Union members in 2006* (USDOL 07–113) [online]. Available: *stats.bls.gov/newsrels.htm,* accessed June 5, 2007.
6. Kernel, R. C., & Moorage, K. S. (1990). Longevity pay in the States: Echo from the past or sound of the future? *Public Personnel Management, 19*, pp. 191–200.
7. Peck, C. (1984). *Pay and performance: The interaction of compensation and performance appraisal* (Research Bulletin No. 155). New York: The Conference Board.
8. WorldatWork (2007). *Average Merit/Salary Increase 4% in 2006* [online]. Available: *worldatwork.org,* accessed June 5, 2007.
9. Ibid.
10. Heneman, R. L., & Werner, J. M. (2005). *Merit Pay: Linking Pay to Performance in a Changing World*. Greenwich, CT: Information Age Publishers.
11. Ibid.
12. Latham, G. P., & Wexley, K. N. (1982). *Increasing Productivity through Performance Appraisal*. Reading, MA: Addison-Wesley.
13. Krefting, L. A., & Mahoney, T. A. (1977). Determining the size of a meaningful pay increase. *Industrial Relations, 16*, pp. 83–93.
14. Bean, Leon Leonwood. *Today's commitment to customer values: L. L. Bean's golden rule* [online]. Available: *www.llbean.com,* accessed: March 8, 2005.
15. Bernardin, H. J., & Beatty, R. W. (1984). *Performance Appraisal: Assessing Human Behavior at Work*. Boston: Kent.
16. Fivars, G. (1975). The critical incident technique: A bibliography. *JSAS Catalog of Selected Documents in Psychology, 5*, p. 210.
17. Smith, P., & Kendall, L. M. (1963). Retranslation of expectation: An approach to the construction of unambiguous anchors for rating scales. *Journal of Applied Psychology, 47*, pp. 149–155.
18. Latham, G. P., & Wexley, K. N. (1982). *Increasing Productivity through Performance Appraisal*. Reading, MA: Addison-Wesley.
19. Latham, G. P., & Wexley, K. N. (1977). Behavioral observation scales for performance appraisal purposes. *Personnel Psychology, 30*, pp. 255–268.
20. Bernardin, H. J., & Beatty, R. W. (1984). *Performance Appraisal: Assessing Human Behavior at Work*. Boston: Kent.
21. Ibid.
22. Excerpt from ExxonMobil's Web site: *Your career: The opportunities* [online]. Available: *www.exxonmobil.com,* accessed April 5, 2005.
23. *Coe v. Cascade Wood Components*, 48 FEP Cases 664 (W.D. OR. 1988).
24. *Brito v. Zia Company*, 478 F2d 1200, CA 10 (1973).
25. Barrett, G. V., & Kernan, M. C. (1987). Performance appraisal and terminations: A review of court decisions since *Brito v. Zia Company* with implication for personnel practices. *Personnel Psychology, 40*, pp. 489–503.
26. Latham, G. P., & Wexley, K. N. (1982). *Increasing Productivity through Performance Appraisal*, Reading, MA: Addison-Wesley.
27. Blum, M. L., & Naylor, J. C. (1968). *Industrial Psychology: Its Theoretical and Social Foundations*. New York: Harper & Row.
28. Bernardin, H. J., & Beatty, R. W. (1984). *Performance Appraisal: Assessing Human Behavior at Work*. Boston: Kent.

29. Noe, R. A. (2005). Employee training (3rd edition). Burr Ridge, IL: McGraw-Hill.

30. Evered, R. D., & Selman, J. C. (1989). Coaching and the art of management. *Organizational Dynamics, 18*, pp. 16–33.

31. Haire, M., Ghiselli, E. E., & Gordon, M. E. (1967). A psychological study of pay. *Journal of Applied Psychology Monograph, 51* (Whole No. 636).

32. Cardy, R. L., & Dobbins, G. H. (1986). Affect and appraisal: Liking as an integral dimension in evaluating performance. *Journal of Applied Psychology, 71*, 672–678.

33. Murphy, K. R., & Cleveland, J. N. (1991). *Performance Appraisal: An Organizational Perspective*. Boston: Allyn & Bacon.

34. Lawler, E. E., III, & Cohen, S. G. (1992). Designing a pay system for teams. *American Compensation Association Journal*, 1, pp. 6–19.

CHAPTER 5

Incentive Pay

Chapter Outline

■ Discussion Questions

■ Exercises

■ Endnotes

Learning Objectives

In this chapter, you will learn about

1. How incentive pay and traditional pay systems differ

2. Plans that reward individual behavior

3. A variety of plans that reward group behavior

4. The most broadly used corporate-wide incentive programs—profit sharing and employee stock option plans

5. Considerations for designing incentive pay plans

6. How individual, group, and gain sharing incentive plans contribute to differentiation and lowest-cost competitive strategies

As we will discuss momentarily, incentive pay places some portion of employee compensation at risk. When employees, groups of employees, or entire companies fail to meet preestablished performance standards (e.g., annual sales), they forfeit some or all of their compensation. Expert incentive pay consultants argue that a critical element of successful incentive pay plans is the provision of regular, honest communication to employees. We will explore this issue and several others related to effective incentive pay design.

EXPLORING INCENTIVE PAY

Incentive pay or **variable pay** rewards employees for partially or completely attaining a predetermined work objective. Incentive or variable pay is defined as compensation, other than base wages or salaries, that fluctuates according to employees' attainment of some standard, such as a preestablished formula, individual or group goals, or company earnings.[1]

Effective incentive pay systems are based on three assumptions:[2]

• Individual employees and work teams differ in how much they contribute to the company, both in what they do as well as in how well they do it.

• The company's overall performance depends to a large degree on the performance of individuals and groups within the company.

• To attract, retain, and motivate high performers and to be fair to all employees, a company needs to reward employees on the basis of their relative performance.

Much like seniority and merit pay approaches, incentive pay augments employees' base pay, but incentive pay appears as one-time payments. Employees usually receive a combination of recurring base pay and incentive pay, with base pay representing the greater portion of core compensation. More employees are presently eligible for incentive pay than ever before, as companies seek to control costs and motivate personnel continually to strive for exemplary performance. Companies increasingly recognize the importance of applying incentive pay programs to various kinds of employees as well, including production workers, technical employees, and service workers.

Some companies use incentive pay extensively. Lincoln Electric Company, a manufacturer of welding machines and motors, is renowned for its use of incentive pay plans. At Lincoln Electric, production employees receive recurring base pay as well as incentive pay. The company determines incentive pay awards according to five performance criteria: quality, output, dependability, cooperation, and ideas.

Companies generally institute incentive pay programs to control payroll costs or to motivate employee productivity. Companies can control costs by replacing annual merit or seniority increases or fixed salaries with incentive plans that award pay raises only when the company enjoys an offsetting rise in productivity, profits, or some other measure of business success. Well-developed incentive programs base pay on performance, so employees control their own compensation levels. Companies can choose incentives to further business objectives. For example, the management of H. Lee Moffitt Cancer Center and Research Institute at the University of South Florida continually strives to improve patient care as well as control costs. Moffitt's incentives are usually tied to net income or operating surplus, quality of care measures, patient satisfaction scores, and operating efficiencies. Princess Cruise Lines is another company that relies heavily on incentive pay to remain competitive. One goal of Princess Cruise Lines is to provide passengers with excellent service (e.g., food, entertainment, and shore excursions) in the hope that they will select Princess Cruise Lines for their next vacation instead of a competing cruise line (e.g., Carnival Cruises). Princess Cruise Lines offers regular incentives to the crews of each ship based on the overall level of customer satisfaction.

CONTRASTING INCENTIVE PAY WITH TRADITIONAL PAY

In traditional pay plans, employees receive compensation based on a fixed hourly pay rate or annual salary. Annual raises are linked to such factors as seniority and past performance. Some companies use incentive pay programs that replace all or a portion of base pay in order to control payroll expenditures and to link pay to performance. Companies use incentive pay programs in varying degrees for different kinds of positions. Some compensation programs consist of both traditional base pay and incentive pay, whereas other programs, usually for sales jobs, offer only incentive pay, in which case all pay is at risk.[3]

Traditional core compensation generally includes an annual salary or hourly wage that is increased periodically on a seniority or merit basis. Companies usually base pay rates on the importance they place on each job within their corporate structure and on the "going rate" that each job commands in similar companies. For example, Lincoln Electric determines the importance of the jobs within its job structure based on job evaluation techniques. The five criteria on which Lincoln evaluates jobs are skill, responsibility, mental aptitude, physical application, and working conditions. Lincoln Electric next surveys the pay rates of competitors, and it uses these data to set base pay rates.

As we discussed in Chapter 4, employees under traditional pay structures earn raises according to their length of service in the organization and to supervisors' subjective appraisals of employees' job performance. Again, both merit pay raises and seniority pay raises are permanent increases to base pay. Annual merit pay increase amounts usually total no more than a small percentage of base pay (i.e., 2 to 6 percent is presently not uncommon), but the dollar impact represents a significant cost to employers over time. Table 5-1 shows the contrast in rate of compensation increase between a traditional merit compensation plan and an incentive plan.

TABLE 5-1 Permanent Annual Merit Increases versus Incentive Awards: A Comparison

(At the end of 2007, John Smith earned an annual salary of $35,000.)

		Cost of Increase (Total Current Salary—2007 Annual Salary)		Total Salary Under:	
Year	Increase Amount	Permanent Merit Increase	Incentive Award	Permanent Merit Increase (% Increase × Previous Annual Salary)	Incentive Award (% Increase × 2007 Annual Salary)
2008	3%	$1,050	$1,050	$36,050	$36,050
2009	5%	$2,853	$1,750	$37,853	$36,750
2010	4%	$4,367	$1,400	$39,367	$36,400
2011	7%	$7,122	$2,450	$42,122	$37,450
2012	6%	$9,649	$2,100	$44,649	$37,100
2013	5%	$11,881	$1,750	$46,881	$36,750
2014	3%	$13,287	$1,050	$48,287	$36,050
2015	6%	$16,185	$2,100	$51,185	$37,100
2016	8%	$20,279	$2,800	$55,279	$37,800
2017	7%	$24,148	$2,450	$59,148	$37,450

Companies use incentive pay to reward individual employees, teams of employees, or whole companies based on their performance. Incentive pay plans are not limited solely to production or nonsupervisory workers. Many incentive plans apply to such categories of employees as sales professionals, managers, and executives. Management typically relies on business objectives to determine incentive pay levels. At Taco Bell, restaurant managers receive biannual bonuses based on the attainment of three objectives:

- Target profit levels
- Quality of customer service based on an independent assessment by a market research company
- Store sales

Management then communicates these planned incentive levels and performance goals to restaurant managers. Although merit pay performance standards aim to be measurable and objective, incentive levels tend to be based on even more objective criteria, such as quantity of items an employee produces per production period or market indicators of a company's performance (e.g., an increase in market share for the fiscal year). Moreover, supervisors communicate the incentive award amounts in advance that correspond to objective performance levels. On the other hand, supervisors generally do not communicate the merit award amounts until after they offer subjective assessments of employees' performance.

Incentive pay plans can be broadly classified into three categories:

- **Individual incentive plans.**   These plans reward employees whose work is performed independently. Some companies have piecework plans, typically for their production employees. Under piecework plans, an employee's compensation depends on the number of units she or he produces over a given period.
- **Group incentive plans.**   These plans promote supportive, collaborative behavior among employees. Group incentives work well in manufacturing and service delivery environments that rely on interdependent teams. In gain sharing

TABLE 5-2   Typical Performance Measures for Individual, Group, and Companywide Incentive Plans
Individual Incentive Plans
Quantity of work output
Quality of work output
Monthly sales
Work safety record
Work attendance
Group Incentive Plans
Customer satisfaction
Labor cost savings (base pay, overtime pay, benefits)
Materials cost savings
Reduction in accidents
Services cost savings (e.g., utilities)
Companywide Incentive Plans
Company profits
Cost containment
Market share
Sales revenue

programs, group improvements in productivity, cost savings, or product quality are shared by employees within the group.

- **Companywide plans.**   These plans tie employee compensation to a company's performance over a short time frame, usually from a 3-month period to a 5-year period.

Table 5-2 lists common performance measures used in individual, group, and companywide incentive plans.

INDIVIDUAL INCENTIVES

Individual incentive pay plans are most appropriate under three conditions. First, employees' performance can be measured objectively. Examples of objective performance measures include:

- Number of units produced—an automobile parts production worker's completion of a turn signal lighting assembly
- Sales amount—a Mary Kay Cosmetics sales professional's monthly sales revenue
- Reduction in error rate—a word processor's reduction in typing errors

Second, individual incentive plans are appropriate when employees have sufficient control over work outcomes. Factors such as frequent equipment breakdowns and delays in receipt of raw materials limit employees' ability to control their performance levels. Employees are not likely to be diligent when they encounter interference: Chances are good that employees who previously experienced interference will expect to encounter interference in the future. Employees' resistance threatens profits because companies will find it difficult to motivate people to work hard when problem factors are not present.

Third, individual incentive plans are appropriate when they do not create a level of unhealthy competition among workers that ultimately leads to poor quality. For example, a company may create unhealthy competition when it limits the number of incentive awards to only 10 percent of the employees who have demonstrated the highest levels of performance. If the company judges performance according to volume, then employees may sacrifice quality as they compete against each other to outmatch quantity. In addition, under an incentive plan that rewards quantity of output, those employees who meet or exceed the highest standard established by their employer may be subject to intimidation by workers whose work falls below the standard.[4] Unions may use these intimidation tactics to prevent plan standards from being raised.

Defining Individual Incentives

Individual incentive plans reward employees for meeting such work-related performance standards as quality, productivity, customer satisfaction, safety, or attendance. Any one of these standards by itself or in combination may be used. A company ultimately should employ the standards that represent work that an employee actually performs. For instance, take the case of telemarketers. Customer satisfaction and sales volume measures indicate telemarketers' performance. Tardiness would not be as relevant unless absenteeism was a general management problem.

Managers should also choose factors that are within the individual employee's control when they create individual performance standards. Furthermore, employees must know about standards and potential awards before the performance period starts. When designed and implemented well, individual incentive plans reward employees based on results for which they are directly responsible. The end result should be that excellent performers receive higher incentive awards than poor performers.

Types of Individual Incentive Plans

There are four common types of individual incentive plans:

- Piecework plans
- Management incentive plans
- Behavioral encouragement plans
- Referral plans

Piecework Plans

Companies generally use one of two **piecework plans**.[5] The first, which is typically found in manufacturing settings, rewards employees based on their individual hourly production against an objective output standard and is determined by the pace at which manufacturing equipment operates. For each hour, workers receive piecework incentives for every item produced over the designated production standard. Workers also receive a guaranteed hourly pay rate regardless of whether they meet the designated production standard. Table 5-3 illustrates the calculation of a piecework incentive.

Companies use piecework plans when the time to produce a unit is relatively short, usually less than 15 minutes, and the cycle repeats continuously. Piecework plans are usually found in such manufacturing industries as textiles and apparel.

Quality is also an important consideration. Companies do not reward employees for producing defective products. In the apparel industry, manufacturers attempt to minimize defect rates because they cannot sell defective clothing for the same price as nondefective clothing. Selling defective clothing at a lower price reduces company profits.

The second type of piecework incentive plan establishes individual performance standards that include both objective and subjective criteria. Units produced represent an objective standard. Overall work quality is a subjective criterion that is based on supervisors' interpretations and judgments. For example, supervisors may judge

TABLE 5-3   Calculation of a Piecework Award for a Garment Worker

Piecework standard: 15 stitched garments per hour

Hourly base pay rate awarded to employees when the standard is not met: $4.50 per hour. That is, workers receive $4.50 per hour worked regardless of whether they meet the piecework standard of 15 stitched garments per hour.

Piecework incentive award: $0.75 per garment stitched per hour above the piecework standard

	Guaranteed Hourly Base Pay	*Piecework Award (No. of Garments Stitched Above the Piecework Standard × Piecework Incentive Award)*	*Total Hourly Earnings*
First hour	$4.50	10 garments × $0.75/garment = $7.50	$12.00
Second hour	$4.50	Fewer than 15 stitched garments, thus piecework award equals $0	$4.50

customer service representatives' performances to be higher when sales professionals emphasize the benefits of purchasing extended product warranties than when sales professionals merely mention the availability and price of extended product warranties.

Economists argue that there are two advantages to companies of using piecework plans in manufacturing settings known as the **incentive effect** and **sorting effect**.[6] The incentive effect refers to a worker's willingness to work diligently to produce more quality output than simply attending work without putting in the effort. To put this simply, employees earn much less under the piecework system than they would under a standard hourly pay system. Whereas employees are certainly expected to perform without an incentive (piecerate), research shows that incentives often are associated with higher employee performance. The sorting effect addresses an employee's choice to stay versus leave their employer for another job, presumably one without an incentive pay contingency. Specifically, a hard-working, highly skilled employee is likely to choose to remain employed under an incentive system because both diligence and skill presumably contribute to higher quantity and quality of output; thus, higher pay.

Management Incentive Plans

Management incentive plans award bonuses to managers when they meet or exceed objectives based on sales, profit, production, or other measures for their division, department, or unit. Management incentive plans differ from piecework plans in that piecework plans base rewards on the attainment of one specific objective and management incentive plans often require multiple complex objectives. For example, management incentive plans reward managers for increasing market share or reducing their budgets without compromising the quality and quantity of output. The best-known management incentive plan is management by objectives (MBO).[7] In Chapter 4, MBO was presented as an outcome-oriented performance appraisal technique for merit pay systems. When MBO is used as part of merit pay systems, superiors make subjective assessments of managers' performances, and they use these assessments to determine permanent merit pay increases. When used as part of incentive programs, superiors communicate the amount of incentive pay managers will receive based on the attainment of specific goals.

Behavioral Encouragement Plans

Under **behavioral encouragement plans**, employees receive payments for specific behavioral accomplishments (e.g., good attendance or safety records). For example, companies usually award monetary bonuses to employees who have exemplary attendance records for a specified period. When behavioral encouragement plans are

TABLE 5-4 A Sample Behavioral Encouragement Plan That Rewards Employee Attendance

At the end of each 3-month period, employees with exemplary attendance records will receive monetary incentive awards according to the following schedule. Note that the number of days absent does not refer to such company-approved absences as vacation, personal illness, jury duty, bereavement leave, military duty, scheduled holidays, and educational leave.

Number of Days Absent	*Monetary Incentive Award*
0 days (perfect attendance)	$250
1 day	$200
2 days	$100
3 days	$50
4 days	$25

applied to safety records, workers earn awards for lower personal injury or accident rates associated with the improper use of heavy equipment or hazardous chemicals. Table 5-4 contains an illustration of a sample behavioral encouragement plan that rewards employees for excellent attendance. Employees can earn $250 for perfect attendance during a 3-month period. With perfect attendance for an entire year, employees can earn $1,000.

Referral Plans

Companies commonly rely on referral bonuses to enhance recruitment of highly qualified employees. Employees may receive monetary bonuses under **referral plans** for referring new customers or recruiting successful job applicants. In the case of recruitment, employees can earn bonuses for making successful referrals for job openings. For example, there has been a tremendous shortage of nurses for the past several years. Because of the shortage, hospitals offer sign-on bonuses of up to $15,000 to recruit nurses and referral bonuses of up to $5,000. A successful referral usually means that companies award bonuses only if hired referrals remain employed with the company in good standing beyond a designated period, often at least 30 days. Referral plans rely on the idea that current employees' familiarity with company culture should enable them to identify viable candidates for job openings more efficiently than employment agencies could because agents are probably less familiar with client companies' cultures. Employees are likely to make only those referrals they truly believe are worthwhile because their personal reputations are at stake.

Advantages of Individual Incentive Pay Programs

There are three key advantages of individual incentive pay plans. First, individual incentive plans can promote the relationship between pay and performance. As discussed in Chapter 1, employees in the United States are motivated primarily by earning money. Employees strive for excellence when they expect to earn incentive awards commensurate with their job performance.

Second, individual incentive plans promote an equitable distribution of compensation within companies (i.e., the amount employees earn depends upon their job performance). The better they perform, the more they earn. Equitable pay ultimately enables companies to retain the best performers. Paying better performers more money sends a signal that the company appropriately values positive job performance.

A third advantage of individual incentive plans is their compatibility with such individualistic cultures as the United States. Because U.S. employees are socialized to make individual contributions and be recognized for them, the national culture of the United States probably enhances the motivational value of individual incentive programs.

Disadvantages of Individual Incentive Pay Programs

Although individual incentive plans can prove effective in certain settings, these programs also have serious limitations. Supervisors, human resource (HR) managers, and compensation professionals should know about three potential problems with individual incentive plans.

Individual incentive plans possess the potential to promote inflexibility. Because supervisors determine employee performance levels, workers under individual incentive plans become dependent on supervisors for setting work goals. If employees become highly proficient performers, they are not likely to increase their performance beyond their reward compensation. For example, let's assume that management defines the maximum incentive award as $500 per month, which is awarded to employees whose productivity rates 15 percent above the performance standard. Employees who produce more than 15 percent above the production standard will not receive additional incentive pay beyond the $500. With this design, employees would not be motivated to improve their performance.

With merit pay systems, supervisors must develop and maintain comprehensive performance measures to properly grant incentive awards. Individual incentive programs pose measurement problems when management implements improved work methods or equipment. When such changes occur, it will take some time for employees to become proficient performers. Thus, it will be difficult for companies to determine equitable incentive awards, which may lead to employees' resistance to the new methods.

A third limitation of individual incentive plans is that they may encourage undesirable workplace behavior when these plans reward only one or a subset of dimensions that constitute employees' total job performance. Let's assume that an incentive plan rewards employees for quantity of output. If employees' jobs address such various dimensions as quantity of output, quality, and customer satisfaction, employees may focus on the one dimension—in this case, quantity of output—that leads to incentive pay, and thereby neglect the other dimensions.

GROUP INCENTIVES

U.S. employers are increasingly using teams to get work done. Two main changes in the business environment have led to an increased use of teams in the workplace.[8] First, in the 1980s, many Japanese companies began conducting business in the United States, particularly in the automobile industry. A common feature of Japanese companies was the use of teams, which contributed to superior product quality. Second, team-based job design promotes innovation in the workplace.[9] At Rubbermaid, a manufacturer of such plastic household products as snap-together furniture and storage boxes, product innovation has become the rule since the implementation of project teams. Team members represent various cross-functional areas, including research and development (R&D), marketing, finance, and manufacturing. Rubbermaid attributes the rush on innovation to the cross-fertilization of ideas that has resulted from the work of these diverse teams.

Companies that use work teams need to change individualistic compensation practices so that groups are rewarded for their behavior together.[10] Team-based pay plans should accordingly emphasize cooperation between and within teams, compensate employees for additional responsibilities they often must assume in their roles as members of a team, and encourage team members to attain predetermined objectives for the team.[11] Merit, seniority, or individual incentives do not encourage team behaviors and may potentially limit team effectiveness. Experts suggest that traditional pay programs will undermine the ability of teams to function effectively.[12] Both merit- and seniority-based pay emphasize hierarchy among employees, which is incompatible with the very concept of a team.

Team-based organizational structures encourage team members to learn new skills and assume broader responsibility than is expected of them under traditional pay structures that are geared toward individuals. Rather than following specific orders from a supervisor, employees who work in teams must initiate plans for achieving their team's production. A pay plan for teams usually emphasizes cooperation and rewards its members for the additional responsibilities they must take on, as well as the skills and knowledge they must acquire. Chapter 6 will show how skill- and knowledge-based pay plans can address these additional responsibilities.

Defining Group Incentives

Group incentive programs reward employees for their collective performance, rather than for each employee's individual performance. Group incentive programs are most effective when all group members have some impact on achieving the goal, even though individual contributions might not be equal. Boeing utilizes a team-based approach to manufacture its model 777 jumbo jet. More than 200 cross-functional teams contribute to the construction of each jet, and the contribution of each individual is clearly not equal. Installing such interior trim features as upholstery is not nearly as essential to the airworthiness of each jet as are the jobs of ensuring the aerodynamic integrity of each aircraft.

Well-designed group incentive plans ultimately reinforce teamwork, cultivate loyalty to the company, and increase productivity. For instance, at General Motors's Saturn division, each team is responsible for managing itself. As a result, each team manages its own budget and determines whom to hire. The renowned quality of Saturn automobiles has been attributed to the effective utilization of teams.

Types of Group Incentive Plans

Companies use two major types of group incentive plans:

- *Team-based or small-group incentive plans.*   A small group of employees shares a financial reward when a specific objective is met.
- *Gain sharing plans.*   A group of employees, generally a department or work unit, is rewarded for productivity gains.

Team-Based or Small-Group Incentive Plans

Team-based incentives are similar to individual incentives with one exception. Each group member receives a financial reward for the attainment of a group goal. The timely completion of a market survey report depends on the collaborative efforts of several individual employees. For example, some group members design the survey; another set collects the survey data; and a third set analyzes the data and writes the report. It is the timely completion of the market survey report, not the completion of any one of the jobs that are required to produce it, that determines whether group members will receive incentive pay.

There are many kinds of team incentive programs. Most companies define these programs based on the type of team:[13]

Work (process) teams refer to organizational units that perform the work of the organization on an ongoing basis. Membership is relatively permanent, and members work full time in the team. Customer service teams and assembly teams on production lines represent excellent examples of work teams. Work teams are effective when individuals are cross-trained to perform team members' work when they are absent. The goal is to maintain consistency in performance quality (e.g., addressing customer concerns promptly even when one or more team members are absent) and output (e.g., in the case of assembly teams). Team members ultimately engage in performance sharing rather than focusing exclusively on one set of tasks. The knowledge and skillsets required to contribute effectively to the work of a process team can be acquired with the assistance of person-focused pay, which we discuss in Chapter 6.

Project teams consist of a group of people assigned to complete a one-time project. Members usually have well-defined roles and may work on specific phases of the project, either full-time or in addition to other work responsibilities of the team. Project teams usually work across such functions as engineering, product development, and marketing to ensure that the final product meets company specifications in terms of cost, quality, and responsiveness to market demands (e.g., Toyota's hybrid vehicles). Many individuals collaborated to ensure the production of cars that rely less on fossil fuels, demonstrate excellent gas mileage, and offer the same driving experience that people have come to expect of gasoline-powered automobiles.

Parallel teams, or **task forces**, include employees assigned to work on a specific task in addition to normal work duties. The modifier *parallel* indicates that an employee works on the team task while continuing to work on normal duties. Also, parallel teams or task forces operate on a temporary basis until its work culminates in a recommendation to top management. Task forces are used to evaluate existing systems and processes, to select new technology, and to improve existing products. People often serve on a voluntary basis or are appointed; in many cases, they are not compensated specifically for extra work or outcome of extra work.

Teams or groups may ultimately receive incentive pay based on such criteria as customer satisfaction (i.e., customer service quality), safety records, quality, and production records. Although these criteria apply to other categories of incentive programs as well (individual, companywide, and group plans), companies allocate awards to each worker based on the group's attainment of predetermined performance standards.

Human resource managers must devise methods for allocating incentives to team members. Although the team-based reward is generated by the performance of the team, the incentive payments are typically distributed to members of the team individually. Human resource experts allocate rewards in one of three ways:

- Equal incentive payments to all team members
- Differential incentive payments to team members based on their contribution to the team's performance
- Differential payments determined by a ratio of each team member's base pay to the total base pay of the group

The first method—the equal incentives payment approach—reinforces cooperation among team members except when team members perceive differences in members' contributions or performance. The second method—the differential incentive payments approach—distributes rewards based to some extent on individual performance. Differential approaches obviously can hinder cooperative behavior. Some employees may focus on their own performance rather than on the group's performance because they wish to maximize their income. As a compromise, companies may base part of the incentive on individual performance, with the remainder based on the team's performance. The third disbursement method—differential payments by ratio of base pay—rewards each group member in proportion to her or his base pay. This approach assumes that employees with higher base pay contribute more to the company, and so should be rewarded in accord with that worth.

Gain Sharing Plans

Gain sharing describes group incentive systems that provide participating employees with an incentive payment based on improved company performance for increased productivity, increased customer satisfaction, lower costs, or better safety records.[14] Gain sharing was developed so that all employees could benefit financially from productivity improvements resulting from the suggestion system. In addition to serving as a compensation tool, most gain sharing reflects a management philosophy that emphasizes employee involvement. The use of gain sharing is most appropriate where workplace technology does not constrain productivity improvements. For example, assembly line workers' abilities to improve productivity may be limited. Increasing the speed of the conveyor belts may compromise workers' safety.

Most gain sharing programs have three components:[15]

- Leadership philosophy
- Employee involvement systems
- Bonus

The first component—leadership philosophy—refers to a cooperative organizational climate that promotes high levels of trust, open communication, and participation. The second component—employee involvement systems—drives organizational productivity improvements. Employee involvement systems use broadly based suggestion systems. Anyone can make suggestions to a committee made up of both hourly and management employees who oversee the suggestion implementation. This involvement system also may include other innovative employee involvement practices (e.g., problem-solving task forces).

The bonus is the third component of a gain sharing plan. A company awards gain sharing bonuses when its actual productivity exceeds its targeted productivity level. The gain sharing bonuses are usually based on a formula that measures productivity that employees perceive as fair and the employer believes will result in improvements in company performance. Employees typically receive gain sharing bonuses on a monthly basis. Most bonuses range between 5 and 10 percent of an employee's base annual pay. A noteworthy exception to this norm is AmeriSteel. On average, AmeriSteel's gain sharing plan pays out between 35 and 45 percent of base pay.

Although many accounts of gain sharing use can be found in the practitioner and scholarly literature, no one has completed a comprehensive, soundly designed investigation of the effectiveness of gain sharing programs.[16] Meanwhile, gain sharing programs' success has been attributed to company cultures that support cooperation among employees.[17] Some gain sharing attempts have failed. Such organizational, external environment, and financial information factors as poor communications within and across departments, highly competitive product markets, and variable corporate profits over time can inhibit effective gain sharing programs.[18] Poor communications will stifle the creativity needed to improve the efficiency of work processes when employees focus exclusively on their own work. Highly competitive product markets often require companies to make frequent changes to their production methods, as in the automobile industry, where such changes occur each year with the introduction of new models. When companies make frequent or sudden changes, employees must have time to learn the new processes well before they can offer productive suggestions. Companies that experience variable profits from year to year most likely do not use gain sharing because management sets aside as much excess cash as possible in reserve for periods when profits are down and excess cash is scarce.

The Scanlon, Rucker, and Improshare gain sharing plans are the most common forms used in companies, and they were also the first types of gain sharing plans developed and used by employers. These plans were adopted wholesale in the early days of gain sharing. Employers today generally modify one of these traditional plans to meet their needs or adopt hybrid plans.

The Scanlon Plan

Joseph Scanlon first developed the gain sharing concept in 1935 as an employee involvement system without a pay element. The hallmark of the **Scanlon Plan** is its emphasis on employee involvement. Scanlon believed that employees will exercise self-direction and self-control if they are committed to company objectives and that employees will accept and seek out responsibility if given the opportunity.[19] Current Scanlon plans include monetary rewards to employees for productivity improvements. Scanlon plans assume that companies will be able to offer higher pay to workers, generate increased profits for stockholders, and lower prices for consumers. The Scanlon plan is a generic term referring to any gain sharing plan that has characteristics common to the original gain sharing plan devised by Scanlon. Scanlon plans have the following three components:[20]

- An emphasis on teamwork to reduce costs, assisted by management-supplied information on production concerns
- Suggestion systems that route cost-saving ideas from the workforce through a labor–management committee that evaluates and acts on accepted suggestions
- A monetary reward based on productivity improvements to encourage employee involvement

Scanlon plan employee involvement systems include a formal suggestion program structured at two levels. Production-level committees, usually including a department foreman or supervisor and at least one elected worker, communicate the suggestion program and its reward features to workers. Production committee members encourage and assist workers in making suggestions and formally record suggestions for consideration. Production committees may also reject suggestions that are not feasible, but they must provide a written explanation of the reasons for the rejection to the worker who made the suggestion. Providing the written rationale under this circumstance is key to helping employees understand why the suggestions are not feasible and, thus, workers are not discouraged from making suggestions in the future. After employees' suggestions have been fully implemented, they typically receive bonuses on a monthly basis.

The production committee forwards appropriate suggestions to a companywide screening committee, which also includes worker representatives. This committee reviews suggestions referred by the production committees, serves as a communications link between management and employees, and reviews the company's performance each month.

Actual gain sharing formulas are designed to suit the individual needs of the company.[21] Formulas are usually based on the ratio between labor costs and **sales value of production (SVOP)**.[22] The SVOP is the sum of sales revenue plus the value of goods in inventory.

Smaller Scanlon ratios indicate that labor costs are lower relative to SVOP. Companies definitely strive for lower ratios, as Table 5-5 illustrates. In addition, Table 5-5 shows the calculation for a bonus distribution under a Scanlon plan.

TABLE 5-5 Illustration of a Scanlon Plan

For the past 3 years, the labor costs of XYZ Manufacturing Company have averaged $44,000,000 per year. During the same 3-year period, the sales value of XYZ's production (SVOP) averaged $83,000,000 per year. (As an aside, of the $83,000,000, $65,000,000 represents sales revenue, and $18,000,000 represents the value of goods held in inventory.) The Scanlon ratio for XYZ Manufacturing Company is:

$$\$44,000,000/\$83,000,000 = 0.53$$

The ratio of 0.53 is the base line. Any benefits that result from an improvement (e.g., an improvement in production methods that results in a reduction in labor costs, are shared with workers. In other words, when improvements lead to a Scanlon ratio that is lower than the standard of 0.53, employees will receive gain sharing bonuses.

The operating information for XYZ Manufacturing Company for March 2003 was as follows:

Total labor costs	$3,100,000
SVOP	$7,200,000

The Scanlon ratio, based on March 2003 information was

$$\frac{\$3,100,000}{\$7,200,000} = 0.43$$

The Scanlon ratio for March 2003 was less than the standard of 0.53, which was based on historical data. In order for there to be a payout, labor costs for March 2003 must be less than $3,816,000 (i.e., 0.53 × $7,200,000); $3,816,000 represents allowable labor costs for March 2003 based on the Scanlon standard established for XYZ Manufacturing.

In summary, the allowable labor costs for March 2003 were $3,816,000. The actual labor costs were $3,100,000. Thus, the savings $716,000 ($3,816,000 – $3,100,000) is available for distribution as a bonus.

The Rucker Plan

Similar to Scanlon's plan, the **Rucker Plan** was developed by Allan W. Rucker in 1933. Both the Scanlon and Rucker plans emphasize employee involvement and provide monetary incentives to encourage employee participation. The main difference lies in the formula used to measure productivity. Rucker plans use a **value-added formula** to measure productivity. Value added is the difference between the value of the sales price of a product and the value of materials purchased to make the product. The following example illustrates the concept of value added based on the sequence of events that eventually lead to selling bread to consumers. These events include growing the wheat, milling the wheat, adding the wheat to other ingredients to make bread, and selling the bread to consumers.

First, a farmer grows the wheat and sells it to a miller; the added value is the difference in the income the farmer receives for the wheat and the costs incurred for seed, fertilizer, fuel, and other supplies. The miller, in turn, buys the wheat from the farmer, mills it, and then sells it to a bakery. The difference in the cost of buying the wheat and the price it is sold for to the baker is the amount of "value" the miller "adds" in the milling processes. The same process is repeated by the baker, as the flour that was milled by the miller is mixed with other ingredients, baked, and sold as bread either to the consumer or to a retailer who in turn sells it to the consumer. The baker "adds value" by blending in the other ingredients to the flour and baking the bread. If the bread is sold to the consumer through a retailer, then the retailer also "adds value" by buying the bread from the bakery, transporting it to a store convenient for the consumer, displaying the bread, and selling it. The total of all the added values from each step along the way equals the total contribution to the overall economy from the chain of events.[23]

The following ratio is used to determine whether bonuses will be awarded under a Rucker plan:

$$\frac{\text{Value added}}{\text{Total employment costs}}$$

In contrast to the Scanlon ratio, companies prefer a larger Rucker ratio. A larger Rucker ratio indicates that the value added is greater than total employment costs. Table 5-6 illustrates the calculation for bonus distribution under the Rucker plan.

Invented by Mitchell Fein in 1973, **Improshare**—Improved Productivity through Sharing—measures productivity physically rather than in terms of dollar savings like those used in the Scanlon and Rucker plans. These programs aim to produce more products with fewer labor hours. Under Improshare, the emphasis is on providing employees with an incentive to finish products.

The Improshare bonus is based on a **labor hour ratio formula**. A standard is determined by analyzing historical accounting data to find the number of labor hours needed to complete a product. Productivity is then measured as a ratio of standard labor hours and actual labor hours. Unlike the Rucker and Scanlon plans, employee participation is not a feature, and workers receive bonuses on a weekly basis.

Improshare plans feature a **buy-back provision**. Under this provision, a maximum productivity improvement payout level is placed on productivity gains. Any bonus money that is generated because of improvements above the maximum is placed in a reserve. If productivity improves to the point where the maximum is repeatedly exceeded, the firm buys back the amount of the productivity improvement over the maximum with a one-time payment to employees. This payment usually is equal to the amount in the reserve. The company then is permitted to adjust the standards so that a new ceiling can be set at a higher level of productivity. In unionized settings, management's discretion may be challenged by unions when union leadership believes that

---

TABLE 5-6   Illustration of a Rucker Plan

Last year, ABC Manufacturing Company generated net sales of $7,500,000. The company paid $3,200,000 for materials, $250,000 for sundry supplies, and $225,000 for such services as liability insurance, basic maintenance, and utilities. On the basis of these data, value added was $3,825,000 (i.e., net sales − costs of materials, supplies, and services rendered). For this example: $7,500,000 − ($3,200,000 + $250,000 + $225,000).

For the same year, total employment costs were $2,400,000, which includes hourly wages for nonexempt workers, annual salaries for exempt employees, payroll taxes, and all benefit costs. Based on the Rucker formula, the ratio of value added to total employment costs was 1.59. This ratio means that if there are to be bonuses, each dollar attributed to employment costs must be accompanied by creating at least $1.59 of value added.

The operating information for ABC Manufacturing Company for the month July 2003 was as follows:

Value added	$670,000
Total employment costs	$625,000

The Rucker ratio, based on July 2000 information, was:

$$\frac{\$670,000}{\$625,000} = 1.07$$

The Rucker ratio for July 2003 is less than the standard of 1.59, which was based on historical data. In order for there to be a payout, value added for July 2003 must be more than the standard, which would be $1,065,300 (1.59 × $670,000). However, based on the Rucker ratio obtained for July 2003 (1.07), value added was only $716,900. Employees of ABC Manufacturing, therefore, will not receive any gain sharing bonuses for July 2003 performance.

TABLE 5-7 Scanlon, Rucker, and Improshare Plans: A Comparison of Key Features

Feature	Scanlon	Rucker	Improshare
Program goal	Productivity improvement	Productivity improvement	Productivity improvement
Basis for savings	Labor costs	Labor costs plus raw materials costs plus services costs (e.g., utilities)	Completing work at or sooner than production standard
Employee involvement	Required	Required	NA
Type of employee involvement	Screening and production committees	Screening and production committees	NA
Bonus payout frequency	Monthly	Monthly	Weekly

management is simply trying to exploit workers by making it more difficult for them to receive bonuses.

In summary, the Scanlon, Rucker, and Improshare plans are among the best-known kinds of gain sharing programs that are used by companies. Although the principle underlying these different plans is the same (i.e., a group incentive system that provides all or most employees a bonus payment based on improved company performance) they each rest on slightly different assumptions. Table 5-7 details a comparison of these three plans.

One final point about gain sharing plans warrants attention. We reviewed the most common types of gain sharing plans used in the United States. Companies are increasingly combining typical gain sharing plans with other approaches to boost productivity and cost savings to an even greater degree than ever before. Exhibit 5-2 describes the combination of gain sharing and Six Sigma process improvement techniques.

Advantages of Group Incentives

The use of group incentive plans has two advantages for companies. First, companies can more easily develop performance measures for group incentive plans than they can for individual incentive plans. There are obviously fewer groups in a company than individuals. Thus, companies generally use fewer resources (e.g., staff time) to develop performance measures. In addition, judging the quality of the final product makes the most sense because companies must deliver high-quality products to maintain competitiveness. During the late 1970s and early 1980s, U.S. automobile manufacturers (especially Chrysler Corporation) lost substantial market share to foreign automobile manufacturers (e.g., Honda and Toyota) because foreign automakers marketed automobiles of substantially higher quality than U.S. automakers. The trend did not change until U.S. automakers manufactured high-quality vehicles, which they began to market in the late 1980s.

Greater group cohesion is the second advantage associated with group incentive plans.[24] Cohesive groups usually work more effectively toward achieving common goals than do individual group members focusing on the specific tasks for which they are responsible. Working collaboratively is undoubtedly in group members' best interests in order to maximize their incentive awards.

Disadvantages of Group Incentives

The main disadvantage of group incentive compensation is employee turnover. Companies' implementation of group incentive programs may lead to turnover because of the **free-rider effect**. Some employees may make fewer contributions to the group goals because they possess lower ability, skills, or experience than other group members. In some groups, members may deliberately choose to put forth less effort, particularly when each group member receives the same incentive compensation regardless of individual contributions to the group goals. In any case, the free-rider effect initially leads to feelings of inequity among those who make the greatest contributions to the attainment of the group goal. Over time, members who make the greatest contributions are likely to leave.

Group members may feel uncomfortable with the fact that other members' performance influences their compensation level. Exemplary performers are more likely to feel this way when other group members are not contributing equally to the attainment of group goals. The lower performance of a few group members may lead to lower earnings for all members of the group. Discomfort with group incentive plans is likely to be heightened where incentive compensation represents the lion's share of core compensation.

COMPANYWIDE INCENTIVES

The use of companywide incentive plans can be traced to the nineteenth century. Companies instituted profit sharing programs to ease workers' dissatisfaction with low pay and to change their beliefs that company management paid workers substandard wages while earning substantial profits. Quite simply, management believed that workers would be less likely to challenge managerial practices if they received a share of company profits.

Defining Companywide Incentives

Companywide incentive plans reward employees when the company exceeds minimum acceptable performance standards (e.g., profits or the overall value of the company based on its stock price). As competitive pressures on companies increased, management sought methods to improve employee productivity. Companies presently use companywide incentive programs to motivate employees to work harder for increased profits or increased company value to owners. Advocates of companywide incentive plans believe that well-designed programs make workers' and owners' goals more compatible as workers strive toward increasing company profits or value.

Types of Companywide Incentive Plans

Companies use two major types of companywide incentive plans:

- *Profit sharing plans.* Employees earn a financial reward when their company's profit objective is met.
- *Employee stock option plans.* Companies grant employees the right to purchase shares of company stock.

Profit Sharing Plans

Profit sharing plans pay a portion of company profits to employees, separate from base pay, cost-of-living adjustments, or permanent merit pay increases. Two basic kinds of profit sharing plans are used widely today. First, **current profit sharing** plans award cash to employees, typically on a quarterly or annual basis. Second, **deferred profit sharing** plans place cash awards in trust accounts for employees. These trusts are set aside on employees' behalf as a source of retirement income. Apart from the time horizon, these plans differ with regard to taxation. Current profit sharing plans provide cash to employees as part of their regular core compensation; thus, these payments are subject to IRS taxation when they are earned. Deferred profit sharing plans are not taxed until the employee begins to make withdrawals during retirement. Premature withdrawal of funds that were secured under a deferred compensation plan is subject to stiff tax penalties (up to 20 percent). The IRS established this penalty to discourage employees from making premature withdrawals. Some companies offer deferred compensation as one kind of retirement program. We will discuss deferred profit sharing plans in Chapter 11. The focus here will be on current profit sharing plans because employees receive cash compensation as a reward for on-the-job performance.

Calculating Profit Sharing Awards

Human resource professionals determine the pool of profit sharing money with any of three possible formulas. A fixed first-dollar-of-profits formula uses a specific percentage of either pretax or posttax annual profits, contingent upon the successful attainment of a company goal. For instance, a company might establish that the profit sharing fund will equal 7 percent of corporate profits; however, payment is contingent on a specified reduction in scrap rates.

Second, companies may use a graduated first-dollar-of-profits formula instead of a fixed percentage. For example, a company may choose to share 3 percent of the first $8 million of profits and 6 percent of the profits in excess of that level. Graduated formulas motivate employees to strive for extraordinary profit targets by sharing even more of the incremental gain.

Third, profitability threshold formulas fund profit sharing pools only if profits exceed a predetermined minimum level but fall below some established maximum level. Companies establish minimums to guarantee a return to shareholders before they distribute profits to employees. They establish maximums because they attribute any profits beyond this level to factors other than employee productivity or creativity (e.g., technological innovation).

After management selects a funding formula for the profit sharing pool, they must consider how to distribute pool money among employees. Companies usually make distributions in one of three ways: equal payments to all employees, proportional payments to employees based on annual salary, and proportional payments to employees based on their contribution to profits. Equal payments to all employees reflect a belief that all employees should share equally in the company's gain in order to promote cooperation among employees; however, employee contributions to profits probably vary. Most employers accordingly divide the profit sharing pool among employees based on a differential basis.

Companies may disburse profits based on proportional payments to employees based on their annual salaries. As we will detail in Chapters 7 and 8, salary levels vary based on both internal and external factors; in general, the higher the salary, the more work the company assigns to a job. Higher-paying jobs presumably indicate more potential to influence a company's competitive position. For any given job, pay will differ according to performance or seniority. Chapter 4 notes that higher performance levels and seniority result in greater worth.

Still another approach is to disburse profits as proportional payments to employees based on their contribution to profits. Some companies measure employee contributions to profit based on job performance; however, this approach is not very feasible because it is difficult to isolate each employee's contributions to profits. For example, how does a secretary's performance (based on answering telephones, greeting visitors, and typing memos) directly contribute to company performance?

Companies can treat profit sharing distributions either as compensation awarded in addition to an employee's base pay or as "pay at risk." In the former case, base pay is set at externally competitive levels, which makes any profit sharing tantamount to a bonus. In the latter case, base pay is set below the average for competing employers, which creates a sense of risk. Employees' earnings for a given period may thus be relatively meager or relatively sizable, compared with what they could earn elsewhere.

Advantages of Profit Sharing Plans

The use of a profit sharing plan has two main advantages, one for employees and the other for companies. When properly designed, profit sharing plans enable employees to share in companies' fortunes. As employees benefit from profit sharing plans, they will be more likely to work productively to promote profits. The upshot of enhanced employee productivity obviously is greater profits for companies that use profit sharing plans.

Companies that use profit sharing programs gain greater financial flexibility. As we discussed, monetary payouts to employees vary with profit levels. During economic downturns, payout levels are significantly lower than they are during economic boom periods. This feature of profit sharing plans enables companies to use limited cash reserves where needed (e.g., for R&D) activities.

Disadvantages of Profit Sharing Plans

There are two main disadvantages associated with profit sharing plans. The first one directly affects employees; the second affects companies. Profit sharing plans may undermine the economic security of employees, particularly if profit sharing represents a sizable portion of direct compensation. Because company profits vary from year to year, so do employees' earnings. Thus, employees will find it difficult to predict their earnings, which will affect their saving and buying behavior. If there is significant variability in earnings, a company's excellent performers are likely to leave for employment with competitors. The turnover of excellent performers certainly represents a significant disadvantage to companies.

Employers also find profit sharing programs to be problematic under certain conditions. Profit sharing plans may fail to motivate employees because they do not see a direct link between their efforts and corporate profits. Hourly employees in particular may have trouble seeing this connection because their efforts appear to be several steps removed from the company's performance. For instance, an assembly line worker who installs interior trim (e.g., carpeting and seats) to automobiles may not find any connection between his or her efforts and the level of company profits because interior trim represents just one of many steps in the production of automobiles.

Employee Stock Option Plans

Under **employee stock option plans**, companies grant employees the right to purchase shares of company stock. **Company stock** represents total equity of a company. **Company stock shares** represent equity segments of equal value. Equity interest increases positively with the number of stock shares. **Stock options** describe an employee's right to purchase company stock. Employees do not actually own stock until they exercise the stock option rights. This is done by purchasing stock at a designated price after a company-chosen time period lapses, usually no more than 5 years. Employee stock options provide an incentive to work productively, with the expectation that collective employee productivity will increase the value of company stock over time. Employees earn monetary compensation when they sell the stock at a higher price than they originally paid for it.

Employee stock option plans represent just one type of general stock compensation plan. Two other basic kinds of stock plans are widely used today. First, **employee stock ownership plans (ESOPs)** place company stock in trust accounts for employees. The purpose of ESOPs is similar to deferred profit sharing because these trusts are set aside on employees' behalf as a source of retirement income, and these awards provide favorable treatment to employees. Discussion of ESOPs is deferred to Chapter 11. Second, **stock compensation plans** represent an important type of deferred compensation for executives. **Deferred compensation** is supposed to create a sense of ownership, aligning the interests of the executive with those of the owners or shareholders of the company over the long term. There are several kinds of stock compensation plans for executives. Discussion of these types of plans is set aside for Chapter 13.

DESIGNING INCENTIVE PAY PROGRAMS

When designing an incentive pay plan, HR professionals and line managers should consider five key factors:

- Whether the plan should be based on group or individual employee performance
- The level of risk employees will be willing to accept in their overall compensation package
- Whether incentive pay should replace or complement traditional pay
- The criteria by which performance should be judged
- The time horizon for goals—long-term, short-term, or a combination of both

Group versus Individual Incentives

Companies considering various design alternatives should choose a design that fits the structure of the company. Group incentive programs are most suitable where the nature of the work is interdependent and the contributions of individual employees are difficult to measure. In such situations, companies require cooperative behavior among their employees. Companies may be able to encourage team behavior by linking compensation to the achievement of department or division goals and eliminating from the pay determination process such factors that are outside the group's control as the late delivery of raw materials by an independent vendor.

On the other hand, individual incentive plans reward employees for meeting or surpassing such predetermined individual goals as production or sales quotas. As with group incentive programs, the attainment of individual goals should be well within the control of the employees. Moreover, goals for individual incentive programs should be based on independent work rather than interdependent work. For example, it would be appropriate to base an employee's incentive on typing accuracy because the work can be performed independently and there are few external constraints on an employee's ability to complete such work. At the group level, it would be reasonable to provide incentives to the individual members of a sales team. In the case of computer hardware and networks, the sale and implementation of these products involve a team of marketing professionals and technical experts who depend on the others' expertise to identify the appropriate configuration of hardware and networking equipment (i.e., meeting the client's needs) and to install the equipment in the client's company successfully.

Level of Risk

Careful consideration should be given to the level of risk employees are willing to accept. As mentioned previously, incentive pay may complement base salary or may be used in place of all or a portion of base salary. The level of risk clearly increases as incentive pay represents a greater proportion of total core compensation. The level of risk tends to be greater among higher-level employees than among those who are at the lower levels of a company's job structure. It is reasonable to infer that the attainment of a first-line supervisor's goal of maintaining a packing department's level of productivity above a predetermined level is less risky than the achievement of a sales manager's goal of increasing market share by 10 percent in a market where the competition is already quite stiff. Apart from an employee's rank, the level of risk chosen should depend on the extent to which employees control the attainment of the desired goal. The adoption of incentive pay programs makes the most sense when participants have a reasonable degree of control over the attainment of the plan's goals. Incentive programs logically are bound to fail when the goals are simply out of reach because they are too difficult or because extraneous factors are hampering employees' efforts to meet goals.

Complementing or Replacing Base Pay

When complementing base pay, a company awards incentive pay in addition to an employee's base pay and benefits. On the other hand, companies may reduce base pay by placing the reduced portion at risk in an incentive plan. For instance, if a company grants its employees 10 percent raises each year, the company could, instead, grant its employees a 4 percent cost-of-living increase and use the remaining 6 percent as incentive by awarding none of it to below-average performers, only half of it to employees whose performance is average, and the entire 6 percent to employees whose performance is above average. In this scenario, the 6 percent that was expected by the employees to become part of their base pay is no longer a guarantee because that potential salary has been placed at risk. By introducing risk into the pay program, employees have the potential to earn more than the 6 percent because poor performers will receive less, leaving more to be distributed to exemplary performers.

Companies in such cyclical industries as retail sales could benefit by including an incentive component in the core compensation programs they offer to employees. During slow business periods, the use of regular merit pay programs that add permanent increments to base pay can create budget problems. If incentive pay were used instead of permanent merit raises, then the level of expenditure on compensation would vary with levels of business activity. In effect, the use of incentive pay can lower payroll costs during lean periods and enhance the level of rewards when business activity picks up.

Performance Criteria

As seen in the discussion of performance appraisal in Chapter 4, the measures used to appraise employee performance obviously should be quantifiable and accessible. For incentive pay programs, common measures of employee performance are company profits, sales revenue, and number of units produced by a business unit. The measures chosen preferably should relate to the company's competitive strategy. For instance, if a company is attempting to enhance quality, its incentive plan would probably reward employees on the basis of customer satisfaction with quality.

In reality, more than one performance measure may be relevant. In such instances, a company is likely to employ all of the measures as a basis for awarding incentives. The weighting scheme would reflect the relative importance of each performance criterion to the company's competitive strategy [e.g., company performance (10 percent), unit performance (40 percent), and individual performance (50 percent), incorporating all of the organizational levels]. An employee clearly would receive an incentive even if company or departmental performance was poor. In effect, the relative weights are indicative of the degree of risk to an employee that is inherent in these plans. Compared with the previous example, the following plan would be quite risky: 50 percent company performance, 35 percent departmental performance, and 15 percent individual performance. Employees' earnings would depend mainly on company and departmental performance over which they possess less control than they do over their own performance.

Time Horizon: Short Term versus Long Term

A key feature of incentive pay plans is the time orientation. There are no definitive standards to distinguish between short term and long term. A general rule of thumb is that short-term goals generally can be achieved in 5 years or less, and that long-term goals may require even longer.

In general, incentives for lower-level employees tend to be based on short-term goals that are within the control of such employees. For example, production workers' performance is judged on periods as short as 1 hour. On the other hand, incentive programs for professionals and executives have a long-term orientation. For instance, rewarding an engineer's innovation in product design requires a long-term orientation because it takes an extended amount of time to move through the series of steps required to bring the innovation to the marketplace (i.e., patent approval, manufacturing, and market distribution). The incentives that executives receive are based on a long-term horizon because their success is matched against the endurance of a company over time.

LINKING INCENTIVE PAY WITH COMPETITIVE STRATEGY

As you will recall, in Chapter 2 we reviewed a framework for establishing a basis for selecting particular compensation tactics to match a company's competitive strategy. How do incentive pay systems fit with the two fundamental competitive strategies—lowest cost and differentiation? Incentive pay systems, when properly applied, can ultimately contribute to meeting companies' goals of lowest-cost and differentiation strategies; however, the rationale for the appropriateness of incentive pay systems differs according to the imperatives of these strategies.

Lowest-Cost Competitive Strategy

Lowest-cost strategies demand reduced output costs per employee. In general, incentive pay appears to be suited to meeting this productivity focus, as we have shown in this chapter, by companies that are pursuing a lowest-cost strategy. The suitability of specific incentive pay programs merits comment.

Individual incentive programs such as piecework systems connect core compensation costs to employee productivity. From a company's perspective, a well-designed piecework system aligns its expenditure on compensation with the level of employee output. Piecework plans are especially effective when they motivate employees to keep up with the demand for companies' products. When employees' output matches market demand, then the company will cover its expenditure on incentive compensation and generate a profit.

Behavioral encouragement plans provide effective incentives for companies pursuing a lowest-cost strategy if these companies suffer excessive absenteeism or poor safety records. Absenteeism poses direct fiscal costs to employers and disrupts workflow that can lead to compromises in production or service delivery. Poor safety records cost employers stiff monetary penalties that arise from violations of the Occupational Safety and Health Act. In addition, employers are liable for on-the-job accidents and carry workers' compensation insurance (Chapter 12). The cost of workers' compensation insurance increases dramatically for companies with poor safety records.

Among the group incentives, gain sharing programs are appropriate for companies that pursue a lowest-cost strategy. Simply put, employee involvement facilitates productivity enhancements. Such improvements result from more efficient ways to conduct work and enhanced employee motivation that comes from greater participation in workplace matters.

Current profit sharing plans are probably the least likely form of incentive to support lowest-cost strategies. As mentioned earlier in this chapter, profit sharing can be an ineffective incentive when employees do not perceive links between their work contributions and company profits. When profit share awards do not motivate employees, then their productivity is unlikely to be influenced, and this money will be "wasted" from the company's standpoint.

Differentiation Competitive Strategy

Differentiation strategies mandate creativity, novel ways of approaching work, and risk taking. Compared with lowest-cost strategies, companies that pursue differentiation strategies hold a longer-term focus with regard to the attainment of preestablished objectives. Among the incentives that we reviewed earlier, team-based incentives and gain sharing are clearly the most appropriate for companies pursuing differentiation strategies. By their very nature, team-based incentives and gain sharing programs promote interaction among co-workers and some degree of autonomy to devise the "best" way to achieve the objectives set by management.

Piecework plans and current profit sharing plans provide inappropriate incentives if a company wishes to promote differentiation. Piecework plans focus on increasing employees' productivity on their existing jobs rather than encouraging employees to offer creative ideas that may lead to product or service differentiation. As before, profit sharing plans may be ineffective where employees see no link between job performance and profits.

SUMMARY

This chapter provided a discussion of the incentive pay concept—how incentive pay differs from traditional bases for pay such as seniority pay and merit pay; varieties of individual, group, and companywide incentives; issues about designing incentive pay programs; and its fit with competitive strategy. Companies should seriously consider adopting incentive pay programs when the conditions for using incentive pay programs are appropriate. Perhaps one of the greatest challenges for companies is to ensure that employees perceive a connection between job performance and the rewards they receive. Another challenge is for companies to balance the level of risk employees will bear, particularly given the fact that U.S. employees are accustomed to receiving base pay and regular permanent increases according to seniority or merit pay systems.

KEY TERMS

- incentive pay, 103
- variable pay, 103
- piecework plans, 107
- sorting effect, 108
- management incentive plans, 108
- behavioral encouragement plans, 108
- referral plans, 109
- group incentive programs, 111
- team-based incentives, 111
- work (process) teams, 111
- product teams, 112

- parallel teams, or task forces, 112
- gain sharing, 113
- Scanlon Plan, 114
- sales value of production (SVOP), 114
- Rucker Plan, 115
- value-added formula, 115
- Improshare, 116
- labor hour ratio formula, 116
- buy-back provision, 116
- free-rider effect, 118
- profit sharing plans, 118

- current profit sharing, 118
- deferred profit sharing, 118
- employee stock option plans, 120
- company stock, 120
- company stock shares, 120
- stock options, 120
- employee stock ownership plans (ESOPs), 120
- stock compensation plans, 120
- deferred compensation, 120

DISCUSSION QUESTIONS

1. Indicate whether you agree or disagree with the following statement: "Individual incentive plans are less preferable than group incentives and companywide incentives." Explain your answer.
2. There is currently a tendency among business professionals to endorse the use of incentive pay plans. Identify two jobs for which individual incentive pay is appropriate

and two jobs for which individual incentive pay is inappropriate. Be sure to include your justification.

3. Critics of profit sharing plans maintain that these plans do not motivate employees to perform at higher levels. Under what conditions are profit sharing plans not likely to motivate employees?

4. Unlike individual incentive programs, group and companywide incentive programs reward individuals based on group (e.g., cost savings in a department) and companywide (e.g., profits) performance standards, respectively. Under group and companywide incentive programs, it is possible for poor performers to benefit without making substantial contributions to group or company goals. What can companies do to ensure that poor performers do not benefit?

5. Opponents of incentive pay programs argue that these programs manipulate employees more than seniority and merit pay programs. Discuss your views of this statement.

EXERCISES

Compensation Online

For Students

Exercise 1: Find relevant journal articles

Use your school's online catalog to search for articles on incentive pay. Compare what you learned about merit pay in Chapter 4 with what you find out about incentive pay. What are the main differences between these two systems, and what type of behavior is each likely to reward?

Exercise 2: Search for stock prices

One of your classes deals at length with stock as compensation. You have been assigned the project of finding and tracking 10 stock prices over the course of the semester. Use three search engines: Yahoo!, Lycos, and one of your choice. Using one search engine at a time, type in "stock prices," and click on the *search* button. Look up the New York Stock Exchange symbol for AT&T, and then search for the information available on AT&T. Click on the various buttons available and review the information each button presents. What is the NYSE symbol for AT&T? How did each search engine differ in the way they presented the information? Did you prefer one search engine over another? As a human resource professional, how could this type of search benefit you?

Exercise 3: Research the Scanlon Plan

One of your professors announces that there will be significant extra credit to the top five short essays on the Scanlon Plan. Essays will be judged solely on demonstrated understanding of how the Scanlon Plan came about and how it works. Using Yahoo!, type "Scanlon Plan" into the search window, and click on the *search* link. Click on a site that concerns the history of the plan. Did you learn anything about the Scanlon Plan that you did not already know? Do you think this site might be of use to you in other classes or in your profession?

Using a different search engine, go to the same Web site or find a related site. Compare and contrast the two search engines for ease of accessibility and amount of information available.

For Professionals

Exercise 1: Research performance management issues

You have been asked to return to your alma mater and speak to current students about performance management issues. To make the most of this experience for yourself and the students, conduct an advanced search for "performance management," and focus particularly on news and articles. Read up on the current trends and thinking on the subject of performance management.

Exercise 2: Research employee stock ownership plans

Your company is about to extend its ESOP to a broader group of employees. You have been asked to work with colleagues from the finance department to develop a proper system. To bring yourself up to speed and start off on the right foot with your co-workers, you want to update your understanding of ESOP. Search for "employee stock ownership plans" and look at everything from consulting services to news articles.

Exercise 3: Research a company's Web site

Using the search engine of your choice, research both the Motorola and Sprint Web pages for information concerning the compensation and benefits they offer. Which site did you find most informative? When you become a human resource professional, would you suggest your company promote its compensation and benefits packages like Motorola's or Sprint's? Why?

ENDNOTES

1. Peck, C. (1993). *Variable pay: Nontraditional programs for motivation and reward.* New York: The Conference Board.
2. Gómez-Mejía, L. R., & Balkin, D. R., (1992). *Compensation, Organizational Strategy and Firm Performance.* Cincinnati, OH: South-Western.
3. Schuster, J. R., & Zingheim, P. K. (1992). *The New Pay: Linking Employee and Organizational Performance.* New York: Lexington Books.
4. Dulles, F. R., & Dubofsky, M. (1984). *Labor in America: A History* (4th ed.). Arlington Heights, IL: Harlan Davidson.
5. Peck, C. (1993). Variable pay: Nontraditional programs for motivation and reward. New York: The Conference Board.
6. Lazear, E. P. (1998). *Personnel Economics for Managers.* New York: John Wiley and Sons.
7. Drucker, P. (1954). *The Practice of Management.* New York: Harper.
8. Jackson, S. E. (1992). Team composition in organizational settings: Issues in managing an increasingly diverse work force. In S. Worchel, W. Wood, & J. A. Simpson (Eds.), *Group Process and Productivity* (pp. 138–173). Newbury Park, CA: Sage.
9. Kanter, R. M. (1988). When a thousand flowers bloom: Structural, collective, and social conditions for innovation in organizations. In B. M. Staw & L. L. Cummings (Eds.), *Research in Organizational Behavior* (vol. 10, pp. 169–211). Greenwich, CT: JAI.
10. Worchel, S., Wood, W., & Simpson, J. A. (Eds.). (1992). *Group Process and Productivity.* Newbury Park, CA: Sage.
11. Kanin-Lovers, J., & Cameron, M. (1993). Team-based reward systems. *Journal of Compensation and Benefits,* January–February, pp. 55–60.
12. Schuster, J. R., & Zingheim, P. K. (1993). Building pay environments to facilitate high-performance teams. *ACA Journal, 2,* pp. 40–51.
13. Greene, R. J. (2007). Team incentives. In D. Scott (Ed.). *Incentive Pay: Creating a Competitive Advantage.* Phoenix, AZ: WorldatWork Press.
14. Belcher, J. G., Jr. (1994). Gain sharing and variable pay: The state of the art. *Compensation & Benefits Review,* May–June, pp. 50–60.
15. Doyle, R. J. (1983). *Gain Sharing and Productivity.* New York: American Management Association.
16. Peck, C. (1993). *Variable pay: Nontraditional programs for motivation and reward.* New York: The Conference Board.
17. Milkovich, G. T., & Newman, J. M. (1993). *Compensation* (4th ed.). Homewood, IL: Irwin.
18. Ross, T. (1990). Why gain sharing sometimes fails. In B. Graham-Moore & T. Ross (Eds.), *Gain Sharing: Plans for Improving Performance* (pp. 100–115). Washington, DC: Bureau of National Affairs.
19. Lesiur, F. G. (Ed.). (1958). *The Scanlon Plan: A Frontier in Labor–Management Cooperation.* Cambridge, MA: MIT Press.
20. Bullock, R. J., & Lawler, E. E., III. (1984). Gain sharing: A few questions and fewer answers. *Human Resource Management, 23,* pp. 18–20.
21. Smith, B. T. (1986). The Scanlon Plan revisited: A way to a competitive tomorrow. *Production Engineering, 33,* pp. 28–31.
22. Geare, A. J. (1976). Productivity from Scanlon type plans. *Academy of Management Review, 1,* pp. 99–108.
23. Myers, D. W. (1989). *Compensation Management.* Chicago: Commerce Clearing House.
24. Lawler, E. E., III, & Cohen, S. G. (1992). Designing a pay system for teams. *American Compensation Association Journal, 1,* pp. 6–19.

CHAPTER 6

Person-Focused Pay

Chapter Outline

■ Defining Competency-Based Pay, Pay-for-Knowledge, and Skill-Based Pay
    What Is a "Competency"?

■ Usage of Pay-for-Knowledge Pay Programs

■ Reasons to Adopt Pay-for-Knowledge Pay Programs
    Technological Innovation
    Increased Global Competition

■ Varieties of Pay-for-Knowledge Pay Programs

■ Contrasting Person-Focused Pay with Job-Based Pay

■ Advantages of Pay-for-Knowledge Pay Programs
    Advantages to Employees
    Advantages to Employers

■ Disadvantages of Pay-for-Knowledge Pay Programs

■ Linking Pay-for-Knowledge Pay with Competitive Strategy
    Lowest-Cost Competitive Strategy
    Differentiation Competitive Strategy

■ Summary

■ Key Terms

■ Discussion Questions

■ Exercises

■ Endnotes

Learning Objectives

In this chapter, you will learn about

1. Differing opinions on the meaning of competency-based pay

2. Traditional person-focused pay plans, pay-for-knowledge pay, and skill-based
   pay programs

3. Reasons that companies adopt pay-for-knowledge pay and skill-based pay programs

4. Pay-for-knowledge pay and skill-based pay variations

5. Contrasts between person-focused pay systems and incentive pay or merit pay concepts

6. Advantages and disadvantages of using pay-for-knowledge pay plans and skill-based pay plans

7. How pay-for-knowledge pay plans and skill-based pay plans fit with differentiation and lowest-cost competitive strategies

In Chapters 4 and 5, we discussed compensation systems that reward employees for performance. Since the 1980s, strong competitive pressures and technological changes often have swiftly left employees with obsolete knowledge and skills. In the health care industry, for example, patient financial specialists have faced many challenges. Patient financial specialists, typically employed in hospitals, clinics, and doctors' offices, ensure that insurance providers pay claims on behalf of insured patients. The increasing variety of different types of "insurance" (e.g., indemnity plans, HMOs, and PPOs, all of which we discuss in Chapter 11) rendered many patient financial services employees outdated in their knowledge and skills. In addition, the ongoing developments in diagnostic testing and treatments have added volumes to what these specialists must know. This chapter will review person-focused pay practices and the many challenges companies face when considering person-focused pay approaches.

DEFINING COMPETENCY-BASED PAY, PAY-FOR-KNOWLEDGE, AND SKILL-BASED PAY

Person-focused pay plans generally reward employees for acquiring job-related competencies, knowledge, or skills rather than for demonstrating successful job performance. **Competency-based pay** often refers to two basic types of person-focused pay programs: pay-for-knowledge and skill-based pay. These competency-based pay programs sometimes incorporate a combination of both types of person-focused pay systems, which reward employees for successfully acquiring new job-related knowledge or skills. There are other times when companies combine competency-based pay programs with traditional merit pay programs by awarding pay raises to employees according to how well they demonstrate competencies.

Pay-for-knowledge plans reward managerial, service, or professional workers for successfully learning specific curricula. The Federal Express Corporation pay-for-knowledge program rewards its customer service employees who learn how to calculate delivery rates and how to document packages for shipment from the United States to various foreign countries.[1] **Skill-based pay**, a term used mostly for employees who do physical work, increases these workers' pay as they master new skills. For example, both unions and contractors who employ carpenters use skill-based pay plans. Carpenters earn additional pay as they master more advanced woodworking skills (e.g., cabinet-making).

Both skill- and knowledge-based pay programs reward employees for the range, depth, and types of skills or knowledge they are capable of applying productively to their jobs. This feature distinguishes pay-for-knowledge plans from merit pay, which rewards employees' job performance. Said another way, pay-for-knowledge programs reward employees for their potential to make meaningful contributions on the job.

In this chapter, we use the term *pay-for-knowledge* to refer to both pay-for-knowledge and skill-based pay programs. Although we noted differences between the two earlier, the basic principles underlying these programs are similar.

Human resource (HR) professionals can design pay-for-knowledge plans to reward employees for acquiring new horizontal skills, vertical skills, or a greater depth of knowledge or skills. Employees can earn rewards for developing skills in one or more of these dimensions based on the kind of skills the company wants to foster. **Horizontal skills** (or **horizontal knowledge**) refer to similar skills or knowledge. For example, clerical employees of a retail store might be trained to perform several kinds of record-keeping tasks. They may maintain employee attendance records, schedule salespeople's work shifts, and monitor the use of office supplies (e.g., paper clips and toner cartridges for laser printers) for reordering. Although focused on different aspects of a store's operations, all three of these tasks are based on employees' fundamental knowledge of record keeping.

Vertical skills (or **vertical knowledge**) are those skills traditionally considered supervisory (e.g., scheduling, coordinating, training, and leading others). These types of supervisory skills are often emphasized in pay-for-knowledge pay plans designed for self-managed work teams because team members often need to learn how to manage one another.[2] Such work teams, which can be referred to as self-regulating work groups, autonomous work groups, or semiautonomous work groups, typically bring employees together from various functional areas to plan, design, and complete one product or service. At Chrysler Corporation, teams of skilled employees from a variety of functions (e.g., marketing, finance, engineering, and purchasing) redesign and manufacture Chrysler vehicle models. One of the most recent innovations resulting from this team approach is the redesigned Jeep Grand Cherokee, a popular sport utility vehicle. Its popularity can be attributed to the ingenuity of the work teams. These teams capitalized on the unique talents—both knowledge and skills—of different employees who together produced a reasonably priced sport utility vehicle with features (e.g., four-wheel drive, leather seats) that met market demand.

Depth of skills (or **depth of knowledge**) refers to the level of specialization or expertise an employee brings to a particular job. Some pay-for-knowledge pay plans reward employees for increasing their depth of skills or knowledge. Human resource professionals may choose to specialize in managing a particular aspect of the HR function (e.g., compensation, benefits administration, training evaluation, or new employee orientation). To be considered a compensation specialist, HR professionals must develop depth of knowledge by taking courses offered by WorldatWork on job evaluation, salary survey analysis, principles of pay-for-knowledge pay system design, merit pay system design, and incentive pay system design, among others. The more compensation topics HR professionals master, the greater their depth of knowledge about compensation.

What Is a "Competency"?

Many HR professionals and other functional managers (e.g., marketing) comment on the importance of paying employees based on competencies. There unfortunately seem to be as many definitions of competencies as there are professionals' calls for competency-based pay. Many HR professionals typically refer to competencies as uniquely combined characteristics of the person, including personality, attitudes, knowledge, skills, and behaviors that enable an employee to fulfill job requirements well. Others simply use the terms *knowledge* and *skills* as synonyms for competencies. Competency-based pay programs apply to technical, managerial, service, or professionals employees (e.g., HR manager, marketing director) for whom it is difficult to define job performance according to observable or concrete behaviors. For instance, an animal keeper can be observed removing debris from enclosed animal habitats. On the other hand, a

---

TABLE 6-1   A Description of GE's Human Resource Leadership Program

The Human Resources Leadership Program (HRLP) is GE's premier entry-level training program for high-potential individuals seeking an accelerated career in human resources. HRLP is the cornerstone in the development of future HR leaders at GE. The program consists of three 8- to 12-month rotational assignments at a GE business combined with training. HRLP candidates attend four developmental seminars, are provided a self-study program in basic financial skills, and are exposed to GE leaders through both formal and informal mentoring and networking opportunities.

The HRLP provides formal training in advanced human resources:

- Techniques and business concepts, as well as hands-on field experience.
- Three challenging and in-depth 8-month rotations assignments.
- Broad-based skills developed via hands-on experiences in two HR assignments plus a third in a cross-functional assignment outside of HR such as finance, quality, or business development.
- Assignments are held at major GE locations, satellite plants, and field offices. Wherever the program leads, GE's supportive environment and free flow of information encourages people to take risks and stretch their capabilities.
- Formal classroom training in advanced HR techniques and business concepts.
- Extensive contact with peers and senior level business leaders from around the world.
- Program seminars provide exposure to key GE business initiatives and the opportunity to interact with senior-level business leaders from around the world.
- The HRLP graduates emerge prepared to plan and implement the strategic initiatives that enable GE to build and maintain its diverse, global teams.
- The people involved in the program become a support network throughout a GE career.

SOURCE: *www.GE.com,* accessed June 5, 2007.

---

compensation director may be responsible for overseeing the ongoing development and implementation of an effective compensation system.

Core competencies are often derived from the overall strategic statements of companies. For example, General Electric (GE) emphasizes three strategic goals for corporate growth: Globalization, Product Services, and Six Sigma (quality improvement). GE's top management relies on four core competencies to drive business success, which they call the four "E's": high Energy, the ability to Energize others, Edge (i.e., the ability to make tough calls), and Execute (i.e., the ability to turn vision into results).

Core competencies are very general, as you can see from the previous example. Companies often offer training to help employees develop particular competency sets (e.g., technical skills, knowledge of the business) or to become more aware of competencies they already possess (e.g., leadership). GE offers a comprehensive training program to entry-level HR professionals. Table 6-1 describes the purpose of GE's training program and particular statements regarding competency sets they expect participants to acquire as successful business professionals.

USAGE OF PAY-FOR-KNOWLEDGE PAY PROGRAMS

A wide variety of employers have established pay-for-knowledge pay programs;[3] however, no systematic survey research documents the actual number. Companies of various sizes use pay-for-knowledge pay programs. More than half of the companies known to be using this kind of pay system employ between 150 and 2,000 employees. The absence of detailed evaluative data makes it impossible to conclude whether size is related to the success of these programs.

These programs are most commonly found in continuous process settings (e.g., manufacturing companies that use assembly lines where one employee's job depends on the work of at least one other employee). At Bell Sports, a manufacturer of motorcycle safety helmets, the assembly process includes applying enamel to the helmets and attaching visors to the helmets. Both tasks clearly require different sets of skills. Applying enamel requires the ability to use automated sprayers. This skill specifically demands that workers possess strong literacy skills so that they can interpret read-outs from the sprayers that suggest possible problems. Attaching visors to the helmets requires proficient motor skills that involve eye–hand coordination. When employees learn how to perform different jobs, they can cover for absent co-workers. In the event of absenteeism or turnover, Bell Sports benefits from having cross-trained employees because it is more capable of meeting its production schedules.

Pay-for-knowledge pay programs that emphasize vertical skills work well at manufacturing companies that organize work flow around high-performance work teams in which employees are expected to learn both functional and managerial tasks (e.g., work scheduling, budgeting, and quality control). This means that groups of employees work together to assemble entire products such as cellular telephones (Motorola) and furniture (Steelcase, a manufacturer of office furniture), and each team member learns how to perform the jobs of other team members.

Companies increasingly recognize the importance of using person-focused pay. Pay-for-knowledge pay programs have been adopted most widely in service and manufacturing industries. Companies have more recently been striving to adopt pay-for-knowledge pay programs for professional employees. Pay-for-knowledge pay programs also represent a prevalent basis for pay among clerical and skilled trade employees (e.g., carpenters and electricians).

REASONS TO ADOPT PAY-FOR-KNOWLEDGE PAY PROGRAMS

Pay-for-knowledge pay programs represent important innovations in the compensation field. Pay-for-knowledge pay systems imply that employees must move away from viewing pay as an entitlement. Instead, these systems treat compensation as a reward earned for acquiring and implementing job-relevant knowledge and skills. Advocates of pay-for-knowledge pay programs offer two key reasons that firms seeking competitive advantage should adopt this form of compensation: technological innovation and increased global competition.[4]

Technological Innovation

In an age of technological innovation in which robots, telecommunications, artificial intelligence, software, and lasers perform routine tasks, some skills have become obsolete.[5] Jobs therefore require new and different worker skills. The skills needed by automobile mechanics, for instance, have changed dramatically. Competent automobile mechanics previously were adept at manually assembling and disassembling carburetors. Since then, electronic fuel injection systems, which are regulated by onboard computers, have replaced carburetors, necessitating that auto mechanics possess different kinds of skills. Auto mechanics specifically must now be able to use computerized diagnostic systems to assess the functioning of fuel injectors.

As technology leads to the automation of more tasks, employers combine jobs and confer broader responsibilities on workers. For example, the technology of advanced automated manufacturing (e.g., in the automobile industry) has required some employees to begin doing the jobs of other employees, including the laborer, the materials handler, the operator-assembler, and the maintenance person. A single employee now performs all of these tasks in a position called "manufacturing technician." The expanding range of tasks and responsibilities in this job demands higher levels of reading, writing, and computation skills than did its predecessor, which required strong eye–hand coordination. Most employees must possess better reading skills than before because they must be able to read the operating manuals and, when problems arise, the troubleshooting manuals of automated manufacturing equipment based on computer technology. The design of manufacturing equipment previously was relatively simple and easy to operate, based on such simple mechanical principles as pulleys.

These technological changes have fostered increased autonomy and team-oriented workplaces, which also demand different job-related skills than employees needed previously.[6] The manufacturing technician's job is generally more autonomous than was its predecessor. Thus, technicians must be able to manage themselves and their time.

Employers now rely on working teams' technical and interpersonal skills to drive efficiency and improve quality. Today's consumers often expect customized products and applications, and employees must have sufficient technical skill to tailor products and services to customers' needs, as well as the interpersonal skills necessary to determine client needs and handle customer service.[7] Telephone service providers such as AT&T and Verizon seek competitive advantage by serving clients' present needs as well as by anticipating possible changes in customers' service needs. Lower costs of cellular phone service, with the inclusion of domestic long-distance service, create an even stronger imperative for land-line service providers to be as responsive as possible to market needs and preferences. As a result, these companies offer programs to provide clients the most favorable long-distance telephone rates based on their particular calling patterns. To be successful, these companies must have customer service associates who maintain current knowledge of these programs as well as the skills needed to match service plans to clients' long-distance service requirements.

Increased Global Competition

Increased global competition has forced companies in the United States to become more productive. Now more than ever, to sustain competitive advantage, companies must provide their employees with leading-edge skills and encourage employees to apply their skills proficiently. Evidence clearly shows that the foreign workers are better skilled and able to work more productively than U.S. employees in at least two ways.

First, employers in both the European Common Market and some Pacific Rim economies emphasize learning. In both cases, employers use classes and instruction as proactive tools for responding to strategic change. In Ireland, the private sector offers graduate employment programs to employees in such skill areas as science, marketing, and technology.[8] An example of a marketing skill is the application of inferential statistics to a market analysis. Marketing professionals use inferential statistics to draw conclusions about whether the level of satisfaction with Brand A athletic shoes among a small sample of Brand A athletic shoe owners represents the level of satisfaction among every person who has purchased Brand A athletic shoes.

Second, both Western European and some Pacific Rim cultures provide better academic preparation and continuing workplace instruction for the non–college-bound portions of their workforces. Although the United States is well regarded for the quality of education its colleges and universities provide to such skilled professionals as engineers, the Europeans are much better at educating the "vocational" segment of their workforces. Western European workplaces emphasize applied rather than theoretical instruction for vocational employees. The European apprenticeship structure mixes academic and applied learning both in "high schools" and in continuing education for employees.

To establish and maintain competitive advantage, companies should carefully consider pay-for-knowledge pay systems. As discussed earlier, many companies already compensate employees on this basis because they have discovered the advantages of such plans. Of course, as companies consider adopting these pay systems, they must tailor compensation programs to the particular kinds of skills they wish to foster. Human resource professionals can guide employee development through a variety of pay-for-knowledge pay systems.

Companies strive to market the highest quality of products and services in the face of increased global competition and the availability of new technology.

VARIETIES OF PAY-FOR-KNOWLEDGE PAY PROGRAMS

A **stair-step model** actually resembles a flight of stairs, much like the arrangement illustrated in Figure 6-1 for an assembly technician. The steps represent jobs from a particular job family that differs in terms of complexity. Jobs that require more skills are more complex than jobs with fewer skills. For example, an Assembly Technician 1 job

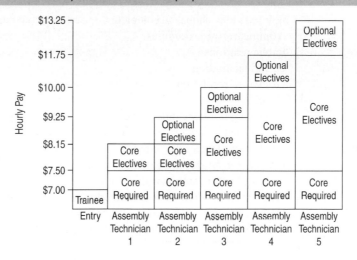

FIGURE 6-1   A Stair-Step Model at ABC Company

Core Required

Employees must complete all three workshops.

1. Orientation Workshop: The goal of this workshop is to familiarize employees with ABC's pay schedule, offerings of employee benefits, work hours, holiday and vacation policies, and grievance procedures.

2. Safety Workshop: The goal of this workshop is to educate employees about the procedures for ensuring the health and safety of themselves and co-workers while using and being around the machinery.

3. Quality Workshop: The goal of this workshop is to acquaint employees with ABC's procedures for maintaining quality standards for parts assembly.

(Continued)

FIGURE 6-1 Continued

Core Electives

Employees must complete all core elective courses for the designated job before they assume the commensurate duties and responsibilities.

Assembly Technician 1:	a. Line restocking
	b. Pallet breakdown
Assembly Technician 2:	a. Core electives for Assembly Technician 1
	b. Burr removal
	c. Line jockey
Assembly Technician 3:	a. Core electives for Assembly Technician 2
	b. Major assembly
	c. Soldering
Assembly Technician 4:	a. Core electives for Assembly Technician 3
	b. Acid bath
	c. Final inspection
Assembly Technician 5:	a. Core electives for Assembly Technician 4
	b. Equipment calibration
	c. Training

Optional Electives

Employees may choose to complete up to two optional electives at each step.

Administrative procedures
Public relations
Group facilitation
Grievance resolution
Training
Marketing fundamentals (basic)
Marketing fundamentals (intermediate)
Finance fundamentals (basic)
Finance fundamentals (intermediate)
Accounting fundamentals (basic)
Accounting fundamentals (intermediate)
Human resource management fundamentals (basic)
Human resource management fundamentals (intermediate)

requires employees to possess two skills: line restocking and pallet breakdown. An Assembly Technician 3 job requires employees to possess six skills: line restocking, pallet breakdown, burr removal, line jockey, major assembly, and soldering. In terms of the stairs, higher steps represent jobs that require more skills than lower steps. Compensation specialists develop separate stair-step models for individual job families (e.g., clerks or accountants). Thus, a company may have more than one stair-step model, each corresponding to a particular job family such as accounting, finance, or clerical. No stair-step model should include both clerical workers and skilled trade workers (e.g., carpenters, electricians, and plumbers).

How do employees earn increases in hourly pay based on a stair-step model? Using the model in Figure 6-1, Howard Jones wants to become an assembly technician. ABC Manufacturing Company hires Howard as an assembly technician trainee at $7.00 per hour. Howard starts by completing three core workshops designed for

Assembly Technician 1: a company orientation, a safety workshop and a quality workshop. After successfully completing all three courses, based on earning greater than the minimum scores on tests for each subject, he receives a $0.50 per hour pay increase, making his total hourly pay $7.50. In addition, Howard completes the core electives designated for his Assembly Technician 1 job: He learns how to restock lines and break down pallets. Upon successfully completing both courses, he receives a $0.65 per hour pay raise, making his total hourly pay $8.15, and earning him the Assembly Technician 1 title. Howard may continue to learn more skills for an assembly technician by completing the curriculum for the Assembly 2 level. If he chooses so thereafter, Howard can complete the curricula to move to level 3.

Training courses may be offered in-house by the company, at a local vocational school, or at a local community college or four-year university. Companies usually offer specialized courses in-house for skills that pertain to highly specialized work or to work that bears on a company's competitive advantage. Federal Express sponsors customer service training internally because the skills and knowledge required to be an effective Federal Express customer service employee distinguish its service from other express mail companies, including United Parcel Service (UPS). For more common skills or skills that do not have an effect on competitive advantage, companies typically arrange to have their employees take training courses offered by such external agents as community colleges. Most companies require clerical employees to be able to use word processing programs effectively. Thus, companies commonly sponsor their employees' training in word processing at local community colleges.

The **skill blocks model** also applies to jobs from within the same job family. Just as in the stair-step model, employees progress to increasingly complex jobs; however, in a skill blocks program, skills do not necessarily build on each other. Thus, an employee may progress two or more steps, earning the pay that corresponds with each step. Although similar, the stair-step model and the skill blocks model differ in an important way. The stair-step model addresses the development of knowledge or skills depth. In particular, Howard Jones could develop his skills depth as an assembly technician by taking the five separate curricula. With the successful completion of each curriculum, Howard will enhance the depth of his skills as an assembly technician. As we will see shortly, the skill blocks model emphasizes both horizontal and vertical skills.

As shown in Figure 6-2, Pro Company hired Bobby Smith as a Clerk 1 because her employment tests demonstrated her proficiency in the skills and knowledge that she needs for this level job. These required skills correspond to Clerk 1 core requirements (i.e., filing, typing, and possessing a working knowledge of one word processing program). Moreover, Bobby knows transcription and shorthand, which are Level 1 core electives. During employee orientation for new clerical hires, an HR representative explained the pay-for-knowledge pay program available to this employee group. In particular, Bobby knows that she can advance to any level in the clerical pay structure by successfully completing the corresponding curriculum. To make her goal of becoming a Clerk 4, Bobby simply needs to complete the Level 4 curriculum. She need not take the curricula for the Clerk 2 and Clerk 3 jobs. Taking the Clerk 2, 3, or 4 curricula will enhance Bobby's horizontal skills. The Clerk 3 curriculum provides the knowledge required to successfully manage different types of ledgers. Taking the Clerk 5 curriculum will increase Bobby's vertical skills, including project scheduling and assigning personnel to projects.

A **job-point accrual model** encourages employees to develop skills and learn to perform jobs from different job families. A company would benefit if its employees were proficient in a small subset of jobs. Employees are generally not free to learn as many jobs as they would like. Companies limit the number of jobs employees are

FIGURE 6-2 A Skill Blocks Model at Pro Company

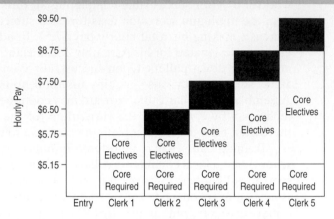

Core Required

All employees must be proficient in all of the following skills or take the necessary courses that are offered by Pro Company in order to become proficient.

Principles of filing

Typing skill, 40 words per minute minimum speed

Working knowledge of one word processing program such as Word or WordPerfect

Core Electives

Employees must complete all core elective courses for the designated job before they assume the commensurate duties and responsibilities.

Clerk 1:	a. Transcription
	b. Shorthand
Clerk 2:	a. Maintaining office supplies inventory
	b. Ordering office supplies from local vendor
Clerk 3:	a. Accounts receivable ledgers
	b. Accounts payable ledgers
	c. Working knowledge of one spreadsheet program, for example, Lotus 1-2-3 or Excel
Clerk 4:	a. Payroll records
	b. Maintaining records of sick pay usage, vacation usage, and performance bonus awards based on company policy
Clerk 5:	a. Project scheduling
	b. Assigning personnel to projects

Optional Electives

Employees may choose to complete up to two optional electives at each step.

Public relations (basic, intermediate, advanced)

Supervisory skills

Resolving minor employee conflicts

Effective written communication skills (basic, intermediate, advanced)

Effective oral communication skills (basic, intermediate, advanced)

allowed to learn in order to avoid having them become "jacks of all trades." Job-point accrual methods create organizational flexibility and promote company goals by assigning a relatively greater number of points to skills that address key company concerns (e.g., customer relations). The more points employees accrue, the higher their core compensation level will be.

For example, let's assume that ZIP-MAIL is a new company that competes in express mail delivery service against established firms in the business (i.e., Federal Express and UPS). ZIP-MAIL couriers must meet their delivery promise of 7:30 A.M., which is at least a half-hour earlier than some of the competitors. They must also convey a professional image and establish rapport with corporate clients to encourage individuals and representatives from client companies to choose ZIP-MAIL over other competitors. In other words, customer relations skills are essential to ZIP-MAIL's success. ZIP-MAIL stands to benefit from a pay-for-knowledge pay program, particularly one that follows the job-point accrual model. Under this system, employees who successfully complete customer relations training courses would earn more points than they'd earn by taking other kinds of training offered by ZIP-MAIL, creating an incentive for employees to learn customer relations skills over other kinds of skills.

Although the job-point accrual model and the cross-departmental model are similar, the intended purposes of these programs differ. The job-point accrual model encourages employees to learn skills and acquire knowledge that bear directly on companies' attainment of competitive advantage, as in the case of ZIP-MAIL. **Cross-departmental models** promote staffing flexibility by training employees in one department with critical skills they would need to perform effectively in other departments. If the shipping department experienced a temporary staffing shortage, a production department supervisor who has been trained in distribution methods can be "lent" to the shipping department. The cross-departmental model can help production environments manage sporadic, short-term staffing shortages. Such cross-training can also help companies meet seasonal fluctuations in demand for their products or services.

The holiday shopping rush represents an excellent context in which a company can benefit from cross-departmental training systems. Retail business activity varies widely, with enhanced volume during the holiday shopping season during the fall months. Business activity tends to subside dramatically. Let's consider a company that manufactures and distributes custom-made shoes. For weeks prior to the holidays, employees in the production department are working rapidly to complete all the telephone gift orders that must be shipped before Chanukah and Christmas day. Within a few days of the holidays, the company is likely to receive fewer orders because purchasers of custom-made shoes recognize that they need to place orders well in advance of the date they expect to receive their shoes. As orders drop off, many workers in both sales and production will be less busy than workers in the distribution department. Under the cross-departmental pay-for-knowledge pay system, sales and production department workers will be rewarded for learning how to package shoes properly and how to complete express mail invoices so that they can assist the shipping department during its peak activity periods.

CONTRASTING PERSON-FOCUSED PAY WITH JOB-BASED PAY

Companies institute job-based pay plans or person-focused pay plans based on very different fundamental principles and goals. Table 6-2 lists the key differences between these two pay programs. **Job-based pay** compensates employees for jobs they currently perform. Human resource professionals establish a minimum and maximum acceptable amount of pay for each job. In the case of merit pay, managers evaluate employees based on how well they fulfilled their designated roles as specified by their job

TABLE 6-2 Person-Focused and Job-Based Pay: A Comparison

Feature	Skill-Based	Job-Based
Pay level determination	Market basis for skill valuation	Market basis for job valuation
Base pay	Awarded on how much an employee knows or on skill level	Awarded on the value of compensable factors
Base pay increases	Awarded on an employee's gain in knowledge or skills	Awarded on attaining a job-defined goal or
Job promotion	Awarded on an employee's skills base and proficiency on past work	Awarded on exceeding job performance standards
Key advantage to employees	Job variety and enrichment	Perform work and receive pay for a defined job
Key advantage to employers	Work scheduling flexibility	Easy pay system Administration

descriptions and periodic objectives. Managers then award a permanent merit addition to base pay, based on employee performance.

With incentive pay, managers award one-time additions to base pay. Pay raise amounts are based on the attainment of work goals, which managers communicate to employees in advance. Consider the executives of Acme Manufacturing Company, who are dissatisfied with their level of defective disk drives for computers, which is significantly higher than that of their competitor, Do-Rite Manufacturing Company. Acme's monthly defect rate is 6,500 disk drives per employee, whereas Do-Rite's monthly defect rate is significantly less at 3,000 disk drives per employee. Acme executives decided to implement an incentive system to encourage employees to make fewer defective disk drives, with the ultimate goal of having a lower defect rate than Do-Rite. At the end of every month, Acme employees receive a monetary award based on their defect rate for that month. Table 6-3 displays the incentive plan for Acme. As you can see, employees earn a larger incentive award as the defect rate decreases.

TABLE 6-3 Acme's Incentive Plan for Reductions in Monthly Defect Rates

Acme's goal is to achieve a monthly defect rate of 3,000 disk drives per employee to match Do-Rite's (the competition's) per employee defect rate. Employees whose monthly defect rates falls below 3,000 disk drives will receive an incentive award that is commensurate with the following schedule.

Reduction in Error Rate	Monthly Incentive Award
91–100%	$500
81–90%	$450
71–80%	$400
61–70%	$350
51–60%	$300
41–50%	$250
31–40%	$200
21–30%	$150
11–20%	$100
1–10%	$ 50

TABLE 6-4 Job Description for a Toll Collector

Collects toll charged for use of bridges, highways, or tunnels by motor vehicles, or fare for vehicle and passengers on ferryboats. Collects money and gives customer change. Accepts toll and fare tickets previously purchased. At end of shift balances cash and records money and tickets received. May sell round-trip booklets. May be designated according to place of employment as Toll-Bridge Attendant (government service), or type of fare as Vehicle-Fare Collector (motor trans.; water trans.). May admit passengers through turnstile and be designated Turnstile Collector (water trans.).

SOURCE: Reprinted from *Dictionary of Occupational Titles*, Vol. 1, 4th ed. (Washington, DC: U.S. Government Printing Office, 1991).

Person-focused pay compensates employees for developing the flexibility and skills to perform a number of jobs effectively. Moreover, these programs reward employees on their potential to make positive contributions to the workplace based on their successful acquisition of work-related skills or knowledge. Job-based pay plans reward employees for the work they have done as specified in their job descriptions or periodic goals (i.e., how well they have fulfilled their potential to make positive contributions in the workplace).

Finally, job-based pay programs apply to an organizationwide context because employees earn base pay rates for the jobs they perform. (We will address how management establishes these pay rates in Chapter 8.) Pay-for-knowledge pay plans apply in more limited contexts because not all jobs can be assessed based on skill or knowledge. Table 6-4 describes the duties that toll booth operators perform. This position would clearly not be appropriate in a pay-for-knowledge pay system because the job is narrowly defined and the skills are very basic. Toll booth operators probably master the required skills and knowledge soon after assuming their responsibilities.

ADVANTAGES OF PAY-FOR-KNOWLEDGE PAY PROGRAMS

Although no large-scale studies have clearly demonstrated these benefits, case studies suggest that employees and companies enjoy advantages from pay-for-knowledge pay programs. Well-designed pay-for-knowledge pay systems, which will be discussed in Chapter 9, can provide employees and employers with distinct advantages over traditional pay systems.

Advantages to Employees

Employees usually like pay-for-knowledge pay systems for the following two reasons. First, they can provide employees with both job enrichment and job security. Job enrichment refers to a job design approach that creates more intrinsically motivating and interesting work environments. Companies can enrich jobs by combining narrowly designed tasks so that an employee is responsible for producing an entire product or service.[9]

According to job characteristics theory, employees are more motivated to perform jobs that contain a high degree of core characteristics, such as:[10]

1. *Skill variety.* The degree to which the job requires the person to do different tasks and involves the use of different skills, abilities, and talents.
2. *Task identity.* The degree to which a job enables a person to complete an entire job from start to finish.

3. *Autonomy.*   The amount of freedom, independence, and discretion the employee enjoys in determining how to do the job.
4. *Feedback.*   The degree to which the job or employer provides the employee with clear and direct information about job outcomes and performance.

At Volvo's Uddevalla manufacturing facility in Sweden, teams of 7 to 10 hourly workers produce entire vehicles rather than focusing solely on certain aspects such as installing a drivetrain assembly or attaching upholstery to a car's interior.[11] Contributing to all aspects of manufacturing automobiles expands the horizontal dimensions (skill variety) of workers' jobs. In some cases, an employer empowers teams to manage themselves and the work they do. These managing duties, including controlling schedules, dividing up tasks, learning multiple jobs, and training one another, represent the vertical dimensions (autonomy) of work. Pay-for-knowledge pay programs can help companies design such intrinsically motivating jobs, especially with regard to skill variety and autonomy. Both pay-for-knowledge pay programs and job enrichment programs expand both horizontal and vertical work dimensions.

So far, evidence does suggest that pay-for-knowledge pay plans lead to increased employee commitment, enhanced work motivation, and improved employee satisfaction.[12] These results are probably due to the fact that well-designed pay-for-knowledge pay plans promote skill variety and autonomy. Some experts attribute these positive outcomes of pay-for-knowledge pay programs to the fact that employees can increase their skills and be paid for it.[13]

The second advantage for employees is that, because pay-for-knowledge pay programs create more flexible workers, these programs can actually represent better job security for employees. Rather than being laid off during periods of low product demand, employees can perform a variety of jobs that draw upon the skills they have attained through pay-for-knowledge pay programs. During periods of slow sales, many companies conduct inventories of their products. Customer service employees who have learned inventory accounting techniques are less likely to be laid off during periods of low sales than are customer service employees who have not learned inventory techniques. Furthermore, employees who update their skills will also be more attractive applicants to other employers. Clerical employees who become proficient in the use of Windows-based computer software will very definitely have more employment opportunities available to them than clerical employees who have resisted learning these programs. Likewise, HR professionals who become familiar with the constraints placed on compensation practice by recent laws (Civil Rights Act of 1991 and the Americans with Disabilities Act) will probably have more employment opportunities available to them than will HR professionals who choose not to become familiar with these pertinent laws.

Advantages to Employers

Employers like pay-for-knowledge pay systems because, when properly designed and implemented, these programs can lead to enhanced job performance, reduced staffing, and greater flexibility. First, pay-for-knowledge pay programs can influence both the quantity and the quality of an employee's work. Employees who participate in a pay-for-knowledge pay program often exhibit higher productivity levels because employees who know more about an entire process may also be able to identify production shortcuts that result in increased productivity. For example, electrical wiring in an automobile runs along the vehicle's interior beneath the seats and carpeting. Members of auto assembly teams familiar with all aspects of the automobile manufacturing process could potentially identify and fix problems with the wiring before the seats and carpeting are installed. If such problems were identified after the seats and carpeting were installed, completion of the vehicle would be delayed, and fewer automobiles could be counted as finished.

Product or service quality should also gain from these programs. As employees learn more about the entire production process, the quality of both the product and its delivery often improve. Schott Transformers, a supplier of magnetic components and power systems to the computer and telecommunications industries, instituted a pay-for-knowledge pay program and experienced a significant increase in the quality of their service as measured by customer satisfaction surveys.[14] Such customer satisfaction increases usually follow a company's implementation of self-directed work teams in which employees develop both horizontal and vertical skills. If employees feel responsible for entire products, they take more care to ensure that customers are satisfied.

Second, companies that use pay-for-knowledge pay systems can usually rely on leaner staffing because multiskilled employees are better able to cover for unexpected absenteeism, family or medical leave, and training sessions that take individual employees away from their work. The successful operation of a restaurant depends on coordinated efforts from buspersons, waitstaff, chefs, and other food preparers. When one or two buspeople are absent, the restaurant will not be able to serve its reservations customers on time. If employees are cross-trained in a number of jobs, fewer employees will have to be on hand to provide backup for absent buspeople.

Third, pay-for-knowledge pay systems provide companies with greater flexibility in meeting staffing demands at any particular time. Quite simply, because participants in pay-for-knowledge pay plans have acquired a variety of skills, they can perform a wider range of tasks. This kind of staffing flexibility helps companies when unexpected changes in demand occur. After a tornado devastated a densely populated area in Illinois, the municipal water supply was not fit for drinking because areawide power outages disabled the pumps that purify the water. As a result, residents living in the affected areas rushed to grocery stores to purchase bottled water. Because this sudden demand exceeded the normal inventories of bottled water in grocery stores, such wholesale distributors as SuperValu had to respond quickly by moving bottled water inventories from their warehouses to the retail grocery stores.

DISADVANTAGES OF PAY-FOR-KNOWLEDGE PAY PROGRAMS

Although pay-for-knowledge pay programs present many advantages, they have the following three limitations. First, employers feel that the main drawback of pay-for-knowledge pay systems is that hourly labor costs, training costs, and overhead costs can all increase. Hourly labor costs often increase because greater skills should translate into higher pay levels for the majority of workers. Because training is an integral component of pay-for-knowledge pay systems, training costs are generally higher than they are at companies with job-based pay programs. These costs can be especially high during initial start-up periods as HR professionals attempt to standardize employee backgrounds. This process begins with assessing the skills levels of employees. Federal Express tests its employees twice per year.[15] The company pays for 4 hours of study time and 2 hours of actual test time, which are bound to be quite expensive.

Second, pay-for-knowledge pay systems may not mesh well with existing incentive pay systems.[16] When both pay-for-knowledge and incentive pay systems are in operation, employees may not want to learn new skills when the pay increase associated with learning a new skill is less than an incentive award employees could earn based on skills they already possess. Employees often place greater emphasis on maximizing rewards in the short term rather than preparing themselves to maximize the level of rewards over time, which can be facilitated through pay-for-knowledge pay programs.

An assembly line worker chooses to focus on his or her work because he or she receives monetary incentives for meeting weekly production goals set by management rather than taking skills training in inventory control for which he or she will earn additional pay upon successful completion of the training. In the short term, this worker is earning a relatively large sum of money; in the long term, however, he or she may be jeopardizing earnings potential and job security. In the future, the company may experience reduced demand for its product, which would eliminate the incentive program. During such times, the company may also place production workers in other jobs (e.g., in the warehouse) until the demand for the product returns to normal. Without the skills required to work in the warehouse, this employee may be targeted for a layoff or a reduced work schedule, clearly leading to lower personal earnings.

Third, effective person-focused pay programs depend, in large part, on well-designed training programs. There is a lot at stake: Person-focused pay systems include costly training programs, and these systems award pay raises to employees who successfully complete training. These programs also require that employers bear the price of base pay and benefits while employees attend training during regular work hours. Finally, companies must wait patiently before realizing a return on investment for training. Several months may pass before employees apply newly learned knowledge and skills to their jobs. After all, practice makes perfect, and training programs cannot anticipate all the circumstances employees face when performing their jobs.

LINKING PAY-FOR-KNOWLEDGE PAY WITH COMPETITIVE STRATEGY

As you will recall, in Chapter 2 we reviewed a framework for establishing a basis for selecting particular compensation tactics to match a company's competitive strategy. How do pay-for-knowledge pay systems fit with the two fundamental competitive strategies—lowest cost and differentiation? Pay-for-knowledge pay systems, when properly applied, can ultimately contribute to meeting the goals of lowest-cost and differentiation strategies; however, the rationale for the appropriateness of pay-for-knowledge pay systems differs according to the imperatives of the lowest-cost and differentiation competitive strategies.

Lowest-Cost Competitive Strategy

Lowest-cost strategies require firms to reduce output costs per employee. Pay-for-knowledge pay systems are appropriate when the training employees receive enables them to work more productively on the job with fewer errors. Pay-for-knowledge pay plans may seem to contradict the lowest-cost imperative because of several factors in the short term. The cost of providing training, downtime while employees are participating in training, and inefficiencies that may result back on the job while employees work on mastering new skills can easily increase costs in the short term. Recall that Federal Express tests its employees twice per year.[17] Because the company pays for study time and actual test time, the lowest-cost strategy is expensive.

A longer-term perspective, however, may well lead to the conclusion that pay-for-knowledge pay programs support the lowest-cost imperative. Over time, productivity enhancements and increased flexibility should far outweigh the short-run costs if a company ultimately provides exemplary service to its customers. For example, Federal Express is renowned for its worldwide express delivery service because of its remarkable track record in consistently meeting delivery promises in a timely fashion for a reasonable price. Much of Federal Express's success can be attributed to its knowledgeable customer service employees. These individuals play a key role in determining how best to manage the delivery of packages across time zones and through international customs checkpoints.

Differentiation Competitive Strategy

A differentiation strategy requires creative, open-minded, risk-taking employees. Compared with lowest-cost strategies, companies that pursue differentiation strategies must take a longer-term focus to attain their preestablished objectives. Pay-for-knowledge compensation is appropriate when employees are organized into teams that possess some degree of autonomy over how work will be performed. Employers that pursue differentiation strategies often rely on employees' technical and interpersonal skills in working teams to drive efficiency, quality improvements, and new applications for existing products and services. As discussed earlier, at Chrysler, teams of skilled employees from a variety of functions (i.e., marketing, finance, engineering, and purchasing) redesign and manufacture Chrysler vehicle models. One innovation that resulted from this team approach is the redesigned Jeep Grand Cherokee, whose popularity can be attributed to the ingenuity of the work teams. Such "cutting-edge" companies often focus on new technology that employees must learn—a goal consistent with pay-for-knowledge pay programs.

New technology also allows customization of products, which requires employees with sufficient technical skills and imagination to tailor products and services to customers' needs, as well as the interpersonal skills necessary to provide good customer service. Northern Telecom is clearly an exemplar of a telecommunications company that continually provides differentiated service to its customers—both technically and interpersonally—because of its investment in pay-for-knowledge pay compensation programs.

SUMMARY

This chapter discussed pay-for-knowledge, reasons companies should adopt pay-for-knowledge pay programs, varieties of pay-for-knowledge pay programs, how pay-for-knowledge pay relates to merit pay and incentive pay programs, advantages as well as disadvantages of pay-for-knowledge pay programs, and the fit of these programs with competitive strategy. Companies should seriously consider adopting pay-for-knowledge pay programs in order to keep up with technological innovation and to compete internationally. Perhaps the greatest challenge for companies is to ensure that employees are given the opportunity to apply newly learned skills in productive ways.

KEY TERMS

- person-focused pay plans, 128
- competency-based pay, 128
- pay-for-knowledge, 128
- skill-based pay, 128
- horizontal skills, 129
- horizontal knowledge, 129
- vertical skills, 129
- vertical knowledge, 129
- depth of skills, 129
- depth of knowledge, 129
- stair-step model, 133
- skills blocks model, 135
- job-point accrual model, 135
- cross-departmental models, 137
- job-based pay, 137

DISCUSSION QUESTIONS

1. "Pay-for-knowledge pay plans are least preferable compared with individual incentive pay programs" (Chapter 5). Indicate whether you agree or disagree with this statement. Detail your arguments to support your position.

2. Pay-for-knowledge pay is becoming more prevalent in companies; however, pay-for-knowledge pay programs are not always an appropriate basis for compensation. Discuss the conditions under which incentive pay (Chapter 5) is more appropriate than pay-for-knowledge pay programs. Be sure to include your justification.

3. Name at least three jobs that have been influenced by such technological advances as robotics, word processing software, fax machines, and electronic mail. Describe the jobs prior to the technological advances and explain how these jobs have changed or will change because of the technological advances. For each job, list the new skills that you feel are relevant for pay-for-knowledge pay programs.

4. Discuss your reaction to the following statement: "Companies should not provide training to employees because it is the responsibility of individuals to possess the necessary knowledge and skills prior to becoming employed."

5. As discussed in the chapter, pay-for-knowledge pay programs are not suitable for all kinds of jobs. Based on your understanding of pay-for-knowledge pay concepts, identify at least three jobs for which this basis for pay is inappropriate. Be sure to provide your rationale, given the information in this chapter.

EXERCISES

Compensation Online

For Students

Exercise 1: Find relevant journal articles

Search your school's online catalog for pay-for-knowledge plans. Select two or three of these topics and describe how each works to reward the employee and/or benefit the employer.

Exercise 2: Research a relevant topic on pay systems

Your professor wants you to find examples of the topics covered in Chapter 6 in practice. Using the advanced search link in Yahoo!, use the "an exact phrase match" option for Web sites pertaining to "person-focused pay" and/or "performance appraisal." Select and review at least two of the sites. Compare and contrast the information on the two sites. What circumstances do you think affected the decision to use these different pay systems?

Exercise 3: Research the use of training

Visit company Web sites and look for the kind of training or career development they offer. Are there any companies with noteworthy or innovative training programs? Write a review of the one or two that you find most interesting.

For Professionals

Exercise 1: Review union Web sites

You work in human resources for a small manufacturer. There is talk of an organizing campaign, and you want to be prepared for any questions that might come up. One of the main issues is that workers find the training and development program at the company to be lacking. This is the issue for which you wish to be best prepared. Search different unions' Web sites for articles or stances on training and development. What sorts of things do unions value, and what do they view as significant drawbacks?

Exercise 2: Research training and development services

Some firms provide in-house training programs; some companies choose to outsource them. From Yahoo!, click Business and Economy > Business to Business > Consulting >

Human Resources. Look for firms that provide training services. Write a short memo to the Director of Human Resources on the benefits and drawbacks to using these services as opposed to developing the training programs from within the company.

Exercise 3: Research relevant news

As a practicing professional, it is important to keep up with issues. Conduct an advanced search on Yahoo! for "pay for performance." Concentrate on the news section. Read through some articles and identify any major trends or stories that may have implications for HR professionals.

ENDNOTES

1. Filipowski, D. (1992). How Federal Express makes your package its most important. *Personnel Journal, 71*, pp. 40–46.

2. Bureau of National Affairs (2002). Skill-based pay. *BNA's Library on Compensation & Benefits CD* [CD-ROM]. Washington, DC: Author.

3. Jenkins, G. D., Jr., Ledford, G. E., Jr., Gupta, N., & Doty, D. H. (1992). *Skill-Based Pay: Practices, Payoffs, Pitfalls, and Prescriptions*. Scottsdale, AZ: American Compensation Association.

4. Schuster, J. R., & Zingheim, P. K. (1992). *The New Pay: Linking Employee and Organizational Performance*. New York: Lexington Books.

5. American Society for Training and Development (1989). *Training America: Learning to Work for the 21st Century*. Alexandria, VA: Author.

6. Doeringer, P. B. (1991). *Turbulence in the American Workplace*. New York: Oxford University Press.

7. Manz, C. C., & Sims H. P., Jr. (1993). *Business without Bosses: How Self-Managing Work Teams Are Building High Performance Companies*. New York: John Wiley & Sons.

8. Carnevale, A. P., & Johnston, J. W. (1989). *Training in America: Strategies for the Nation*. Alexandria, VA: National Center on Education and the Economy and the American Society for Training and Development.

9. Lawler, E. E. (1986). *High Involvement Management*. San Francisco: Jossey-Bass.

10. Nadler, D. A., Hackman, J. R., & Lawler, E. E. (1979). *Managing Organizational Behavior*. Boston: Little, Brown.

11. Carrell, M. R., Elbert, N. F., & Hatfield, R. D. (1995). *Human Resource Management: Global Strategies for Managing a Diverse Workforce* (5th ed.). Upper Saddle River, NJ: Prentice Hall.

12. Gupta, N., Schweizer, T. P., & Jenkins, G. D., Jr. (1987). Pay-for-knowledge compensation plans: Hypotheses and survey results. *Monthly Labor Review, 110*, pp. 40–43.

13. Caudron, S. (1993). Master the compensation maze. *Personnel Journal, 72*, pp. 64a–64o.

14. Schilder, J. (1992). Work teams boost productivity. *Personnel Journal, 72*, pp. 64–71.

15. Filipowski, D. (1992). How Federal Express makes your package its most important. *Personnel Journal, 71*, pp. 40–46.

16. Jenkins, G. D., Jr., & Gupta, N. (1985). The payoffs of paying for knowledge. *National Productivity Review, 4*, pp. 121–130.

17. Filipowski, D. (1992). How Federal Express makes your package its most important. *Personnel Journal, 71*, pp. 40–46.

CHAPTER 7

Building Internally Consistent Compensation Systems

Chapter Outline

- Internal Consistency

- Job Analysis
    Steps in the Job Analysis Process
    Legal Considerations for Job Analysis
    Job Analysis Techniques
    U.S. Department of Labor's Occupational Information Network (O*NET)

- Job Evaluation
    Compensable Factors
    The Job Evaluation Process

- Job Evaluation Techniques
    The Point Method
    Alternative Job-Content Evaluation Approaches
    Alternatives to Job Evaluation

- Internally Consistent Compensation Systems and Competitive Strategy

- Summary

- Key Terms

- Discussion Questions

- Exercises

- Endnotes

Learning Objectives

In this chapter, you will learn about

1. The importance of building internally consistent compensation systems

2. The process of job analysis

3. Job descriptions

4. O*NET

5. The process of job evaluation

6. A variety of job evaluation techniques

7. Alternatives to job evaluation

8. Internally consistent compensation systems and competitive strategy

Job descriptions serve as a cornerstone in the development of internally consistent compensation systems as well as performance standards in performance evaluation systems. Nevertheless, human resources (HR) professionals have debated over the usefulness of job descriptions. Opponents often say that job descriptions simply are not realistic depictions of what many employees actually do each day. Nevertheless, as we will see shortly, job descriptions serve as the cornerstone for determining the relative worth of jobs.

INTERNAL CONSISTENCY

Internally consistent compensation systems clearly define the relative value of each job among all jobs within a company. This ordered set of jobs represents the job structure or hierarchy. Companies rely on a simple yet fundamental principle for building internally consistent compensation systems: Jobs that require higher qualifications, more responsibilities, and more complex job duties should be paid more than jobs that require lower qualifications, fewer responsibilities, and less complex job duties. Internally consistent job structures formally recognize differences in job characteristics that enable compensation managers to set pay accordingly. Figure 7-1 illustrates an internally consistent job structure for employee benefits professionals. As Figure 7-1 indicates, a benefits manager should earn substantially more than a benefits counselor I. Benefits managers have far greater responsibility for ensuring effective benefits practices than does the entry-level counselor. The difference in average pay rates between benefits counselor II and benefits counselor I jobs should be far less than the difference in average pay rates between benefits manager and benefits counselor I jobs because the differences in responsibility between benefits counselor II and benefits counselor I are far less than the differences between benefits manager and benefits counselor I.

Compensation experts and HR professionals create internally consistent job structures through two processes—job analysis followed by job evaluation. **Job analysis** is almost purely a descriptive procedure; job evaluation reflects value judgments. Effective job analysis identifies and defines **job content**. Job content describes job duties and tasks as well as such pertinent factors as the skill and effort (i.e., compensable factors) needed to perform the job adequately.

Human resource specialists lead the job analysis process. As we will discuss shortly, they solicit the involvement of employees and supervisors, who offer their perspectives on the nature of the jobs being analyzed. Based on this information, HR specialists write job descriptions that describe the job duties and minimum qualifications required of individuals to perform their jobs effectively.

Job evaluation is key for casting internally consistent compensation systems as strategic tools. Compensation professionals use job evaluation to establish pay differentials among employees within a company. The descriptive job analysis results directly aid compensation professionals in their pay-setting decisions by quantifying the key similarities and differences between jobs based on job content identified in the job analysis process.

Exhibit 7-1 makes a positive case for the importance of conducting job analysis and job evaluation in organizations. In particular, by taking a proactive approach, compensation professionals are in a better position to contribute to company effectiveness.

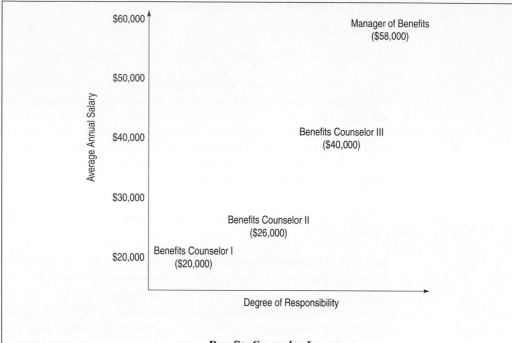

Benefits Counselor I

Provides basic counseling services to employees and assistance to higher-level personnel in more complex benefits activities. Works under general supervision of higher-level counselors or other personnel.

Benefits Counselor II

Provides skilled counseling services to employees concerning specialized benefits programs or complex areas of other programs. Also completes special projects or carries out assigned phases of the benefits counseling service operations. Works under general supervision from Benefits Counselor III or other personnel.

Benefits Counselor III

Coordinates the daily activities of an employee benefits counseling service and supervises its staff. Works under direction from higher-level personnel.

Manager of Benefits

Responsible for managing the entire benefits function from evaluating benefits programs to ensuring that Benefits Counselors are adequately trained. Reports to the Director of Compensation and Benefits.

FIGURE 7-1   Internally Consistent Compensation Structure

JOB ANALYSIS

Competent compensation professionals are familiar with job analysis concepts, the process of conducting job analysis, and fundamental job analysis techniques. Job analysis is a systematic process for gathering, documenting, and analyzing information in order to describe jobs. Job analyses describe content or job duties, worker requirements, and, sometimes, the job context or working conditions.

Job content refers to the actual activities that employees must perform on the job. Job content descriptions may be broad, general statements of job activities or detailed descriptions of duties and tasks performed on the job. Greeting clients is common to receptionist jobs. The job activity of greeting clients represents a broad statement. Describing the particular activities associated with greeting clients (e.g., saying "hello," asking the clients' names, using the telephone to notify the employees of their clients' arrivals, and offering beverages) represents a detailed statement.

Worker requirements represent the minimum qualifications and skills that people must have to perform a particular job. Such requirements usually include education, experience, licenses, permits, and specific abilities and skills such as typing, drafting, or editing. For example, the minimum educational qualification for a lead research scientist in a jet propulsion laboratory is a Ph.D. in physics.

Working conditions are the social context or physical environment where work will be performed. For instance, social context is a key factor for jobs in the hospitality industry. Hospitality industry managers emphasize the importance of employees' interactions with guests. Hotel registration desk clerks should convey an air of enthusiasm toward guests and be willing to accommodate each guest's specific requests for a nonsmoking room or an early check-in time.

Physical environments vary along several dimensions, based on the level of noise and possible exposure to hazardous factors, including hazardous chemicals. Work equipment also defines the character of the physical environment. Nuclear power plant employees work in rather hazardous physical environments because of possible exposure to dangerous radiation levels. Accountants perform their jobs in relatively safe working environments because office buildings must meet local building safety standards.

Steps in the Job Analysis Process

The job analysis process has five main activities:

- Determine a job analysis program.
- Select and train analysts.
- Direct job analyst orientation.
- Conduct the study: Data collection methods and sources of data.
- Summarize the results: Writing job descriptions.

Determine a Job Analysis Program

A company must decide between using an established system or developing its own system tailored to specific requirements. Both established and custom job analysis programs vary in the method of gathering data. The most typical methods for collecting job analysis information are questionnaires, interviews, observation, and participation. Administrative costs often represent a major consideration in selecting a job analysis method.

Select and Train Analysts

Job analysts generally must be able to collect job-related information through various methods, relate to a wide variety of employees, analyze the information, and write clearly and succinctly. A task force of representatives from throughout the company ideally conducts the analysis, and HR staff members coordinate it. Although some companies rely on HR professionals to coordinate and conduct job analysis, many use teams to represent varying perspectives on work because virtually all employees interact with co-workers and supervisors.

Before the task force embarks on a job analysis, members need to be taught about the basic assumptions of the model and the procedures they must follow. The training should include discussions of the study's objectives, how the information will be used, methodology overviews, and discussions and demonstrations of the information-gathering techniques. Analysts also should be trained to minimize the chance that they will conduct ineffective job analyses. For example, analysts should involve as many job incumbents as possible within the constraints of staff time to have representative samples of job incumbents' perceptions.

Finally, job analysts must be familiar with the structure of pertinent job data. Job analysis data are configured in levels, hierarchically from specific bits of information to progressively broader categories that include the prior specific pieces. Table 7-1 defines representative analysis levels and lists examples of each one. The most specific information is a job element, and the broadest element is an occupation.

The U.S. Office of Management and Budget published The Standard Occupational Classification System (SOC), which identifies 23 **major occupational groups**. The SOC system replaces the government's longstanding *The Dictionary of Occupational Titles* (published in 1938 and subsequently revised in 1949, 1964, 1977, and 1991). Table 7-2 lists the 23 major occupational groups based on the 2000 edition. A revision to update the SOC was begun in 2005. It will be completed in 2008 for use starting in 2010, and it will be available on the U.S. Bureau of Labor Statistics Web site (*www.bls.gov/soc/*). One of the main goals of revision will be to overcome the limitations of the 2000 edition.

These occupational group concepts are relevant for making compensation decisions, but the current version of the SOC has limited use because of its focus on

---

TABLE 7-1   Units of Analysis in the Job Analysis Process

1. An element is the smallest step into which it is practical to subdivide any work activity without analyzing separate motions, movements, and mental processes involved. Connecting a flash drive into a USB port is an example of a job element.

2. A task is one or more elements and is one of the distinct activities that constitute logical and necessary steps in the performance of work by the worker. A task is created whenever human effort, physical or mental, is exerted to accomplish a specific purpose. Keyboarding text into memo format represents a job task.

3. A position is a collection of tasks constituting the total work assignment of a single worker. There are as many positions as there are workers. John Smith's position in the company is clerk typist. His tasks, which include keyboarding text into memo format, running a spell check on the text, and printing the text on company letterhead, combine to represent John Smith's position.

4. A job is a group of positions within a company that are identical with respect to their major or significant tasks and sufficiently alike to justify their being covered by a single analysis. There may be one or many persons employed in the same job. For example, Bob Arnold, John Smith, and Jason Colbert are clerk typists. With minor variations, they essentially perform the same tasks.

5. A job family is a group of two or more jobs that call for either similar worker characteristics or similar work tasks. File clerk, clerk typist, and administrative clerk represent a clerical job family because each job mainly requires employees to perform clerical tasks.

6. An occupation is a group of jobs, found at more than one establishment, in which a common set of tasks are performed or are related in terms of similar objectives, methodologies, materials, products, worker actions, or worker characteristics. File clerk, clerk typist, administrative clerk, staff secretary, and administrative secretary represent an office support occupation. Compensation analyst, training and development specialist, recruiter, and benefits counselor represent jobs from the human resources management occupation.

SOURCE: U.S. Department of Labor. (1991). *The Revised Handbook for Analyzing Jobs*. Washington, DC: U.S. Government Printing Office, 1991.

TABLE 7-2 Major Occupational Groups of the Standard
Occupational Classification

- Management occupations
- Business and financial operations occupations
- Computer and mathematical occupations
- Architecture and engineering occupations
- Life, physical, and social science occupations
- Community and social services occupations
- Legal occupations
- Education, training, and library occupations
- Arts, design, entertainment, sports, and media occupations
- Healthcare practitioners and technical occupations
- Healthcare support occupations
- Protective service occupations
- Food preparation and serving related occupations
- Building and grounds cleaning and maintenance occupations
- Personal care and service occupations
- Sales and related occupations
- Office and administrative support occupations
- Farming, fishing, and forestry occupations
- Construction and extraction occupations
- Installation, maintenance, and repair occupations
- Production occupations
- Transportation and material moving occupations
- Military specific occupations

SOURCE: U.S. Bureau of Labor Statistics. (1999). *Revising the Standard
Occupational Classification System* [Report 929]. Washington, DC: U.S.
Government Printing Office.

broad occupations. Considering the units of analysis may ultimately influence compensation professionals' judgments about whether work is dissimilar or similar. Human resource manager, purchasing manager, and payroll clerk are dissimilar jobs because employees in these jobs perform different duties; however, HR manager and purchasing manager are similar at the occupational level because they fall under the management occupation. In addition, HR manager and payroll clerk are quite different at the occupational level because HR manager is classified as a management occupation, whereas payroll clerk falls under the office and administrative support occupation. The revised SOC is expected to include detailed information about jobs, allowing compensation professionals to make more precise comparisons for pay setting purposes.

Direct Job Analyst Orientation
Before analysts start specific job analysis techniques, they must analyze the context in which employees perform their work to better understand influencing factors. In addition, analysts should obtain and review such internal information as organizational charts, listings of job titles, classifications of each position to be analyzed, job incumbent names and pay rates, and any instructional booklets or handbooks for operating equipment. Job analysts may also find pertinent job information in such external sources as *The Standard Occupational Classification System*, trade associations, professional societies, and trade unions.

Conduct the Study: Data Collection Methods and Sources of Data

Once analysts have gathered and made sense of these preliminary data, they can begin gathering and recording information for each job in the company. Analysts should carefully choose the method of data collection and the sources of data. The most common methods are questionnaires and observation. Questionnaires direct job incumbents' and supervisors' descriptions of the incumbents' work through a series of questions and statements, for example:

- Describe the task you perform most frequently.
- How often do you perform this task?
- List any licenses, permits, or certifications required to perform duties assigned to your position.
- List any equipment, machines, or tools you normally operate as part of your position's duties.
- Does your job require any contacts with other department personnel, other departments, outside companies, or agencies? If yes, please describe.
- Does your job require supervisory responsibilities? If yes, for which jobs and for how many employees?

Observation requires job analysts to record perceptions they form while watching employees perform their jobs.

The most common sources of job analysis data are job incumbents, supervisors, and the job analysts. Job incumbents should provide the most extensive and detailed information about how they perform job duties. Experienced job incumbents will probably offer the most details and insights. Supervisors also should provide extensive and detailed information, but with a different focus. Supervisors specifically are most familiar with the interrelationships among jobs within their departments. They are probably in the best position to describe how employees performing different jobs interact. Job analysts also should involve as many job incumbents and supervisors as possible because employees with the same job titles may have different experiences.

For example, parts assembler John Smith reports that a higher level of manual dexterity is required than parts assembler Barbara Bleen reports. Parts assembler supervisor Jan Johnson indicates that assemblers interact several times a day to help each other solve unexpected problems, and supervisor Bill Black reports no interaction among parts assemblers. Including as many job incumbents and supervisors as possible will provide a truer assessment of the parts assembler job duties.

Of course, job analysts represent a source of information. In the case of observation, job analysts write descriptions. When using questionnaires, job analysts often ask follow-up questions to clarify job incumbents' and supervisors' answers. In either case, job analysts' HR expertise should guide the selection of pertinent follow-up questions.

Companies ultimately strive to conduct job analyses that lead to reliable and valid job evaluation results. A **reliable job analysis** yields consistent results under similar conditions. For example, let's assume that two job analysts independently observe John Smith perform his job as a retail store manager. The method is reliable if the two analysts reach similar conclusions about the duties that constitute the retail store manager job. Although important, reliable job analysis methods are not enough. Job analyses also must be valid.

A **valid job analysis** method accurately assesses each job's duties. Neither researchers nor practitioners unfortunately can demonstrate whether job analysis results are definitively accurate. At present, the "best" approach to producing valid job descriptions requires that results among multiple sources of job data (i.e., job incumbents, analysts, supervisors, customers) and multiple methods (i.e., interview, questionnaire, observation) converge.[1]

Reliable and valid job analysis methods are essential to building internally consistent compensation systems. The factors that describe a particular job should indeed reflect the actual work. Failure to match accurately compensable factors with the work employees perform may result in either inadequate or excessive pay rates. Both cases are detrimental to the company. Inadequate pay may lead to dysfunctional turnover (i.e., the departure of high-quality employees). Excessive pay represents a cost burden to the company that can ultimately undermine its competitive position. Moreover, basing pay on factors that do not relate to job duties leaves a company vulnerable to allegations of illegal discrimination.

What can compensation professionals do to increase the likelihood that they will use reliable and valid job analysis methods? Whenever time and budgetary constraints permit, job analysts should use more than one data collection method, and they should collect data from more than one source. Including multiple data collection methods and sources minimizes the inherent biases associated with any particular one. For example, job incumbents may view their work as having greater impact on the effectiveness of the company than does the incumbents' supervisor. Observation techniques do not readily indicate why an employee performs a task in a specific way, but the interview method provides analysts with an opportunity to make probing inquiries.

Summarize the Results: Writing Job Descriptions

Job descriptions summarize a job's purpose and list its tasks, duties, and responsibilities, as well as the skills, knowledge, and abilities necessary to perform the job at a minimum level. Effective job descriptions generally explain:

- What the employee must do to perform the job
- How the employee performs the job
- Why the employee performs the job in terms of its contribution to the functioning of the company
- Supervisory responsibilities, if any
- Contacts (and purpose of these contacts) with other employees inside or outside the company
- The skills, knowledge, and abilities the employee should have or must have to perform the job duties
- The physical and social conditions under which the employee must perform the job

Job descriptions usually contain four sections:

- Job title
- Job summary
- Job duties
- Worker specifications

Table 7-3 contains a job description for a training and development specialist.

Job titles indicate the name of each job within a company's job structure. In Table 7-3, the job title is training and development specialist. The **job summary** statement concisely summarizes the job with two to four descriptive statements. This section usually indicates whether the job incumbent receives supervision and by whom. The training and development specialist works under general supervision from higher-level training and development professionals or other designated administrators.

The **job duties** section describes the major work activities and, if pertinent, supervisory responsibilities. For instance, the training and development specialist evaluates training needs of employees and departments by conducting personal interviews, questionnaires, and statistical studies.

TABLE 7-3 Job Description: Training and Development Specialist

Job Summary

Training and development specialists perform training and development activities for supervisors, managers, and staff to improve efficiency, effectiveness, and productivity. They work under general supervision from higher-level training and development professionals.

Job Duties

A training and development specialist typically:

1. Recommends, plans, and implements training seminars and workshops for administrators and supervisors, and evaluates program effectiveness.
2. Evaluates training needs of employees and departments by conducting personal interviews, questionnaires, and statistical studies.
3. Researches, writes, and develops instructional materials for career, staff, and supervisor workshops and seminars.
4. Counsels supervisors and employees on policies and rules.
5. Performs related duties as assigned.

Worker Specifications

1. Any one or any combination of the following types of preparation:
   a. credit for college training leading to a major or concentration in education or other fields closely related to training and development (such as human resource management or vocational education).

   —or—

   b. two years of work experience as a professional staff member in a human resource management department.
2. Two years of professional work experience in the training and development area in addition to the training and experience required in item 1, above.

The **Worker Specifications** section lists the education, skills, abilities, knowledge, and other qualifications individuals must possess to perform the job adequately. **Education** refers to formal training. Minimum educational levels can be a high school diploma or a general equivalency diploma (GED) through such advanced levels as masters' or doctoral degrees.

The **Equal Employment Opportunity Commission (EEOC)** guidelines distinguish among the terms knowledge, skill, and ability. **Skill** refers to an observable competence to perform a learned psychomotor act. Typing 50 words per minute is an example of a psychomotor act. Typing requires knowledge of the keyboard layout and manual dexterity. According to the EEOC, **ability** refers to a present competence to perform an observable behavior or a behavior that results in an observable product. For example, possessing the competence to mediate a dispute between labor and management successfully reflects ability. **Knowledge** refers to a body of information applied directly to the performance of a function. Companies measure knowledge with tests, or they infer that employees have knowledge based on formal education completed. For instance, compensation professionals should know about the Fair Labor Standards Act's overtime pay requirements.

Legal Considerations for Job Analysis

The government does not require companies to conduct job analysis; however, conducting job analyses increases the chance that employment decisions are based solely on pertinent job requirements. Under the Equal Pay Act (Chapter 3), companies must justify pay differences between men and women who perform equal work. Different job titles do not suffice as justification. Instead, companies must demonstrate substantive differences in job functions. Job analysis helps HR professionals discern whether substantive differences between

TABLE 7-4 EEOC Interpretive Guidelines for Essential Job Functions under the Americans with Disabilities Act

- The reason the position exists is to perform the function.
- The function is essential or possibly essential. If other employees are available to perform the function, the function probably is not essential.
- A high degree of expertise or skill is required to perform the function.
- The function is probably essential; and
- Whether a particular job function is essential is a determination that must be made on a case-by-case basis and should be addressed during job analysis. Any job functions that are not essential are determined to be marginal. Marginal job functions could be traded to another position or not done at all.

SOURCE: From the text of the Americans with Disabilities Act, *Federal Register* 35734 (July 26, 1991).

job functions exist. Job analysis is also useful for determining whether a job is exempt or nonexempt under the Fair Labor Standards Act (FLSA). As we discussed in Chapter 3, failure to pay nonexempt employees an overtime hourly pay rate violates the FLSA.

Companies may perform job analysis to see if they comply with the Americans with Disabilities Act (ADA), also discussed in Chapter 3. As long as disabled applicants can perform the essential functions of a job with reasonable accommodation, companies must not discriminate against these applicants by paying them less than other employees performing the same job. Human resource professionals use job analysis to define essential job functions systematically. Companies may consult the EEOC's interpretive guidelines to determine whether a job function is essential. Table 7-4 lists these guidelines.

Legal compliance has been exacerbated by the increasing abundance of job titles in private sector companies. Exhibit 7-2 describes the substantial legal challenges compensation professionals face due to the increase in job titles. This feature also recommends approaches to avoid legal violations.

Job Analysis Techniques

Human resource professionals can either choose from a variety of established job analysis techniques or custom design them. Most companies generally choose to use established job analysis techniques because the costs of custom-made job analysis techniques often outweigh the benefits. Besides, many of the established job analysis techniques apply to a wide variety of jobs, and both researchers and practitioners have already tested and refined them.

Choosing one established plan over another depends on two considerations: applicability and cost. Some job analysis techniques apply only to particular job families (e.g., managerial jobs), but others can be applied more broadly. In addition, some methods are proprietary, yet others are available to the public at no charge. Private consultants or consulting firms charge substantial fees to companies that use their methods, but the U.S. Department of Labor does not charge fees to use its job analysis method. Next, we will review the U.S. Department of Labor's **Occupational Information Network** (O*NET).

U.S. Department of Labor's Occupational Information Network (O*NET)

The U.S. Department of Labor's Employment and Training Administration spearheaded the development of O*NET during the 1990s to replace its previous methods of analyzing and describing jobs (*Revised Handbook for Analyzing Jobs*[2] and *The Dictionary of Occupational Titles*).[3] O*NET is a database, and it was created for two reasons. First, it is designed to describe jobs in the relatively new service sector of the economy (e.g., wireless telecommunications). Second, O*NET more accurately describes jobs that evolved as the result of technological advances (e.g., software and hardware engineers).

O*NET is comprehensive because it incorporates information about both jobs and workers. The O*NET **Content Model** lists six categories of job and worker information. Job information contains the components that relate to the actual work activities of a job (i.e., information that HR professionals should include in the summary and duties sections of job descriptions). Worker information represents characteristics of employees that contribute to successful job performance. Figure 7-2 shows the six categories of the O*NET content model. According to the creators of O*NET, the Content Model was developed using research on job and organizational analysis. It embodies a view that reflects the character of occupations (via job-oriented descriptors) and people (via worker-oriented descriptors). The Content Model also allows occupational information to be applied across jobs, sectors, or industries (cross-occupational descriptors) and within occupations (occupational-specific descriptors). A description of each content area follows.

Experience Requirements

Experience requirements include:

- Experience and training
- Licensing

Experience and training information describes specific preparation required for entry into a job plus past work experience contributing to qualifications for an occupation. **Licensing** information describes licenses, certificates, or registrations that are used to

FIGURE 7-2   O*Net Content Model

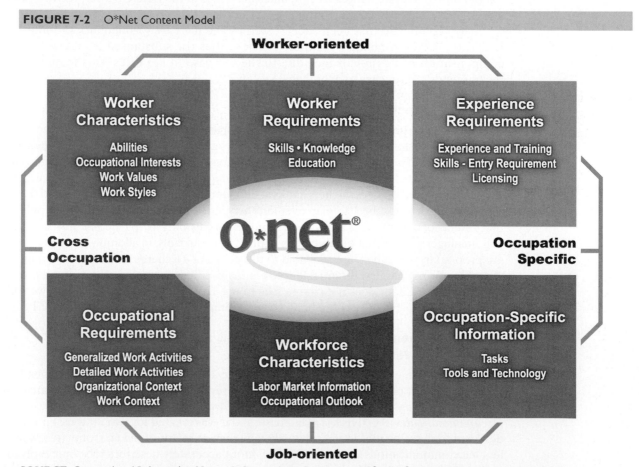

SOURCE: Occupational Information Network Consortium. Content model [online] *www.onetcenter.org/content.html.*

TABLE 7-5 O*NET Content Model: Experience Requirements

Experience Requirements

- Experience and training
  1. Related work experience
  2. On-site or in-plant training
  3. On-the-job training
  4. Apprenticeship
- Licensing
  - License, certificate, or registration required
  - Education, training, examination or other requirements for license, certificate, or registration
    1. Post-secondary degree
    2. Graduate degree
    3. On-the-job training
    4. Examination
    5. Character references
  - Additional education and training
  - Organization and agency requirements
    1. Legal requirement
    2. Employer requirement
    3. Union, guild, or professional association requirement

SOURCE: Occupational Information Network Consortium. Content model [online] *www.onetcenter.org/content.html.*

identify levels of skill and required for entry and advancement in an occupation, pre-ferred education or training, and required apprenticeships will be documented by this part of the model. Table 7-5 lists the specific experience requirements.

Occupation Requirements
Occupation requirements include:

- Generalized work activities
- Organizational context
- Work context

The occupation requirements domain includes information about typical activities required across occupations. Identifying generalized work activities (GWAs) and detailed work activities (DWAs) summarizes the broad and more specific types of job behaviors and tasks that may be performed within multiple occupations. Using this framework makes it possible to use a single set of descriptors to describe many occupa-tions. Contextual variables such as the physical, social, or structural context of work that may impose specific demands on the worker or activities are also included in this section.

Generalized work activities information describes general types of job behaviors occurring on multiple jobs. **Organizational context** information indicates the characteris-tics of the organization that influence how people do their work. **Work context** informa-tion describes physical and social factors that influence the nature of work. Table 7-6 lists examples of particular occupational requirements.

Occupation-Specific Requirement
Occupation-specific requirements detail a comprehensive set of elements that apply to a single occupation or a narrowly defined job family. These particular requirements are occupational skills, knowledge, tasks, duties, machines, tools, and equipment. This domain parallels other Content Model domains because it includes requirements such

TABLE 7-6 O*NET Content Model: Sample Occupation Requirements

- Generalized work activities
  - Information input
    - Looking for and receiving job-related information
    - Identifying/evaluating job-relevant information
  - Mental processes
    - Information/data processing
    - Reasoning/decision making
  - Work output
    - Performing physical and manual work activities
    - Performing complex/technical activities
  - Interacting with others
    - Communicating/interacting
    - Coordinating/developing/managing/advising others
- Organizational context
  - Structural characteristics
    - Organizational structure
      - Decision-making system
        - Decentralization and employee empowerment
        - Individual versus team structure
      - Job characteristics
        - Skill variety
        - Task significance
        - Task identity
        - Autonomy
        - Feedback
  - Human resources systems and practices
    - Recruitment and selection
      - Recruitment operations
      - Reward system
        - Basis of compensation
          - Which of the following is part of your compensation package?
          1. Profit sharing
          2. Gain sharing
          3. Knowledge/skill-based pay
          4. Pay based on your individual performance
          5. Pay based on the performance of your team
          6. Pay based on customer satisfaction
          7. Pay based on job tenure/seniority
          8. Pay based on job attributes
          9. None of the above
        - Benefits
          - Which of the following is part of your benefits?
          1. Stock ownership in the organization
          2. Retirement plan
          3. Major medical insurance
          4. Life insurance
          5. Disability insurance
          6. Flexible working hours
          7. Daycare
          8. Paid leave
          9. None of the above

TABLE 7-6 (*cont.*)

- Social processes
  - Goals
    - Individual goal characteristics
    - Goal feedback
  - Roles
    - Role conflict
    - Role negotiability
    - Role overload
  - Culture
    - Organizational value
      - How important are each of the following?
        1. Taking chances; going out on a limb
        2. Fairness; justice
        3. Precision; paying attention to even the smallest details
  - Supervisor role
- Work context
  - Interpersonal relationships
    - Communication
    - Role relationships
      - Job interactions
    - Responsibility for others
    - Conflictual contact
  - Physical work conditions
    - Work setting
    - Environmental conditions
    - Job hazards
    - Body positioning
    - Work attire
  - Structural job characteristics
    - Criticality of position
    - Routine versus challenging work
    - Level of competition
    - Pace and scheduling

SOURCE: Occupational Information Network Consortium. Content model [online] *www.onetcenter.org/content.html*.

as work-related knowledge, skills, and tasks in addition to the machines, equipment, tools, software, and information technology workers may use in their workplace.

Workforce characteristics

Workforce characteristics refer to variables that define and describe the general characteristics of occupations that may influence occupational requirements. Organizations do not exist in isolation. They must operate within a broader social and economic structure. To be useful, an occupational classification system must incorporate global contextual characteristics. O*NET provides this information by linking descriptive occupational information to statistical labor market information. This includes compensation and wage data, employment outlook, and industry size information. Much of this information is collected outside of the O*NET program's immediate scope. Collaborative efforts with such organizations as the Bureau of Labor Statistics, the Department of Commerce, the Department of Defense, Career One

Stop, the U.S. Bureau of the Census, and the Employment and Training Administration facilitate these labor market information linkages. These characteristics include:

- Labor Market Information
- Occupational Outlook

Labor market information describes current labor force characteristics of occupations. Occupational outlook describes future labor force characteristics of occupations. We discussed issues of labor market information and occupation outlook in Chapter 2 and will address wage information in Chapter 8.

Worker Characteristics

Worker characteristics information includes:

- Abilities
- Interests
- Work styles

Abilities are enduring attributes of the individual that influence performance. **Interests** describe preferences for work environments and outcomes. **Work styles** are personal characteristics that describe important interpersonal and work style requirements in jobs and occupations. Table 7-7 lists the particular abilities, interests, and work styles.

TABLE 7-7 O*NET Content Model: Worker Characteristics

- Abilities
  - Cognitive abilities
    - Verbal abilities
      1. Oral comprehension
      2. Written comprehension
      3. Oral expression
      4. Written expression
    - Idea generation and reasoning abilities
      1. Fluency of ideas
      2. Originality
      3. Problem sensitivity
      4. Deductive reasoning
      5. Inductive reasoning
      6. Information ordering
      7. Category flexibility
    - Quantitative abilities
      1. Mathematical reasoning
      2. Number facility
    - Memory
      1. Memorization
    - Perceptual abilities
      1. Speed of closure
      2. Flexibility of closure
      3. Perceptual speed
    - Spatial abilities
      1. Spatial orientation
      2. Visualization
    - Attentiveness
      1. Selective attention
      2. Time sharing

TABLE 7-7 *(cont.)*

- Psychomotor abilities
  - Fine manipulative abilities
    1. Arm–hand steadiness
    2. Manual dexterity
    3. Finger dexterity
  - Control movement abilities
    1. Control precision
    2. Multilimb coordination
    3. Response orientation
    4. Rate control
  - Reaction time and speed abilities
    1. Reaction time
    2. Wrist–finger dexterity
    3. Speed of limb movement
- Physical abilities
  - Physical strength abilities
    1. Static strength
    2. Explosive strength
    3. Dynamic strength
    4. Trunk strength
  - Endurance
    1. Stamina
  - Flexibility, balance, and coordination
    1. Extent flexibility
    2. Dynamic flexibility
    3. Gross body coordination
    4. Gross body equilibrium
- Sensory abilities
  - Visual abilities
    1. Ncar vision
    2. Far vision
    3. Visual color discrimination
    4. Night vision
    5. Peripheral vision
    6. Depth perception
    7. Glare sensitivity
  - Auditory and speech abilities
    1. Hearing sensitivity
    2. Auditory attention
    3. Sound localization
    4. Speech recognition
    5. Speech clarity
- Interests
  - Holland occupational classification
    1. Realistic
    2. Investigative
    3. Artistic
    4. Social
    5. Enterprising
    6. Conventional
  - Occupational values
    - Achievement

(continued)

TABLE 7-7   *(cont.)*

    1. Ability utilization
    2. Achievement
- Comfort
    1. Activity
    2. Independence
    3. Variety
    4. Compensation
    5. Security
    6. Working conditions
- Status
    1. Advancement
    2. Recognition
    3. Authority
    4. Social values
- Altruism
    1. Co-workers
    2. Social service
    3. Moral values
- Safety
    1. Company policies and practices
    2. Supervision, human relations
    3. Supervision, technical
- Autonomy
    1. Creativity
    2. Responsibility
    3. Autonomy
- Work Styles
  - Achievement orientation
    1. Achievement/effort
    2. Persistence
    3. Initiative
  - Social influence
    1. Energy
    2. Leadership orientation
  - Interpersonal orientation
    1. Cooperation
    2. Concern for others
    3. Social orientation
  - Adjustment
    1. Self-control
    2. Stress tolerance
    3. Adaptability/flexibility
  - Conscientiousness
    1. Dependability
    2. Attention to detail
    3. Integrity
  - Independence
  - Practical intelligence
    1. Innovation
    2. Analytical thinking

SOURCE: Occupational Information Network Consortium. Content model [online]
www.onetcenter.org/content.html.

Worker Requirements

Worker requirements include:

- Basic skills
- Cross-functional skills
- Knowledge
- Education

Worker requirements represent developed or acquired attributes of an individual that may be related to work performance such as work-related knowledge and skill. Knowledge represents the acquisition of facts and principles about a domain of information. Experience lays the foundation for establishing procedures to work with given knowledge. These procedures are more commonly known as skills. Skills may be divided further into basic skills and cross-functional skills. Basic skills (e.g., reading) facilitate the acquisition of new knowledge. Cross-functional skills (e.g., problem solving) extend across several domains of activities.

Basic skills information describes developed capacities that facilitate learning or the more rapid acquisition of knowledge. **Cross-functional skills** information indicates developed capacities that facilitate performance of activities that occur across jobs. Knowledge information describes organized sets of principles and facts applying in general domains. Education information details prior educational experience required to perform in a job. Table 7-8 lists the particular basic skills, cross-functional skills, knowledge, and educational requirements.

Using O*NET

Human resource professionals use O*NET by consulting the **O*NET User's Guide** as well as the most current **O*NET database**.[4] They may find the latest O*NET information on the U.S. Department of Labor Employment and Training Administration's Web site (*http://online.onetcenter.org*).

TABLE 7-8 O*NET Content Model—Worker Requirements

- Basic Skills
  - Content
    1. Reading comprehension
    2. Active listening
    3. Writing
    4. Speaking
    5. Mathematics
    6. Science
  - Process
    1. Critical thinking
    2. Active learning
    3. Learning strategies
    4. Monitoring
- Cross-functional skills
  - Social skills
    1. Social perceptiveness
    2. Coordination
    3. Persuasion
    4. Negotiation
    5. Instructing
    6. Service orientation

(continued)

TABLE 7-8 (*cont.*)

- Complex problem-solving skills
  1. Problem identification
  2. Information gathering
  3. Information organization
  4. Synthesis/reorganization
  5. Idea generation
  6. Idea evaluation
  7. Implementation planning
  8. Solution appraisal
- Technical skills
  1. Operations analysis
  2. Technology design
  3. Equipment selection
  4. Installation
  5. Programming
  6. Testing
  7. Operation monitoring
  8. Operation and control
  9. Product inspection
  10. Equipment maintenance
  11. Troubleshooting
  12. Repairing
- Systems skills
  1. Visioning
  2. Systems perception
  3. Identification of downstream consequences
  4. Identification of key causes
  5. Judgment and decision making
  6. Systems evaluation
- Resource management skills
  1. Time management
  2. Management of financial resources
  3. Management of material resources
  4. Management of personal resources
- Knowledge—organized sets of principles and facts applying in general domains
  - Business and management
    1. Administration and management
    2. Clerical
    3. Economics and accounting
    4. Sales and marketing
    5. Customer and personal service
    6. Personnel and human resources
  - Manufacturing and production
    1. Production and processing
    2. Food production
  - Engineering and technology
    1. Computers and electronics
    2. Engineering and technology
    3. Design
    4. Building and construction
    5. Mechanical

TABLE 7-8 *(cont.)*

- Mathematics and science
  1. Mathematics
  2. Physics
  3. Chemistry
  4. Biology
  5. Psychology
  6. Sociology and anthropology
  7. Geography
- Health services
  1. Medicine and dentistry
  2. Therapy and counseling
- Education and training
  1. Education and training
- Arts and humanities
  1. English language
  2. Foreign language
  3. Fine arts
  4. History and archeology
  5. Philosophy and theology
- Law and public safety
  1. Public safety and security
  2. Law, government, and jurisprudence
- Communications
  1. Telecommunications
  2. Communications and media
- Transportation
  1. Transportation
- Education
  - Level of education
    1. Less than a high school diploma
    2. High school diploma (or high school equivalency)
    3. Post-secondary certificate
    4. Some college courses
    5. Associate's degree (or other 2-year degree)
    6. Bachelor's degree
    7. Post-baccalaureate certificate
    8. Master's degree
    9. Post-master's certificate
    10. First professional degree
    11. Doctoral degree
    12. Post-doctoral certificate
  - Instructional program required
  - Level of education in specific subject
    1. Technical vocational
    2. Business vocational
    3. English/language arts
    4. Oral communication
    5. Languages
    6. Basic math
    7. Advanced math
    8. Physical science
    9. Computer science

(continued)

TABLE 7-8 *(cont.)*

- Level of education in specific subject (*cont.*)
  - 10. Biological science
  - 11. Applied science
  - 12. Social science
  - 13. Arts
  - 14. Humanities
  - 15. Physical education

SOURCE: Occupational Information Network Consortium. Content model [online] *www.onetcenter.org/content.html.*

JOB EVALUATION

Compensation professionals use **job evaluation** to systematically recognize differences in the relative worth among a set of jobs and establish pay differentials accordingly. Whereas job analysis is almost purely descriptive, job evaluation partly reflects the values and priorities that management places on various positions. Based on job content and the firm's priorities, managers establish pay differentials for virtually all positions within the company.

Compensable Factors

Compensation professionals generally base job evaluations on **compensable factors**, which are the salient job characteristics by which companies establish relative pay rates. Most companies consider skill, effort, responsibility, and working conditions, which were derived from the Equal Pay Act. These four dimensions help managers determine whether dissimilar jobs are "equal."

Skill, effort, responsibility, and working conditions are **universal compensable factors** because virtually every job contains these four factors. How, then, can meaningful distinctions regarding the value of jobs be made with such broad factors? Many companies break these general factors into more specific factors. For example, responsibility required could be further classified as responsibility for financial matters and responsibility for personnel matters.

Most jobs today can be described broadly in terms of knowledge, skills, and abilities given the evolution of jobs that require greater cognitive skills and mental (versus physical) effort. A working conditions compensable factor is most helpful when a company expects a substantial difference in working conditions for similar jobs. For example, a company may employ geologists, some of whom are required to work in the field where possible dangers are greater, and other geologists to work within the safe confines of a laboratory.

In any event, compensation professionals should choose compensable factors based on two considerations. First, factors must be job-related. The factors that describe a particular job should indeed reflect the actual work that is performed: Failure to match compensable factors accurately with the actual work may result in either inadequate or excessive pay rates. Both cases are detrimental to the company because inadequate pay may lead to dysfunctional turnover.

Second, compensation professionals should select compensable factors that further a company's strategies. For example, companies that value product differentiation probably consider innovation to be an important compensable factor for research scientist and marketing manager jobs. Companies that distinguish themselves through high-quality customer relations are likely to place great value on such compensable factors as product knowledge and interpersonal skills. Lowest-cost strategies may emphasize different kinds of compensable factors (e.g., efficiency and timeliness).

The Job Evaluation Process

The job evaluation process entails six steps:

- Determining single versus multiple job evaluation techniques
- Choosing the job evaluation committee
- Training employees to conduct job evaluations
- Documenting the job evaluation plan
- Communicating with employees
- Setting up the appeals process

Determining Single Versus Multiple Job Evaluation Techniques

Compensation professionals must determine whether a single job evaluation technique is sufficiently broad to assess a diverse set of jobs. In particular, the decision is prompted by such questions as, "Can we use the same compensable factors to evaluate a forklift operator's job and the plant manager's job?" If the answer is *yes*, then a single job evaluation technique is appropriate. If not, then more than one job evaluation approach should be employed. It is not reasonable to expect that a single job evaluation technique, based on one set of compensable factors, can adequately assess diverse sets of jobs (i.e., operative, clerical, administrative, managerial, professional, technical, and executive). A carpenter's job is clearly distinct from a certified public accountant's position because manual dexterity is an important compensable factor that describes carpentry work and is not nearly as central to an accounting position.

Choosing the Job Evaluation Committee

Human resource professionals help put together a committee of rank-and-file employees, supervisors, managers, and, if relevant, union representatives to design, oversee, and evaluate job evaluation results. The functions, duties, responsibilities, and authority of job evaluation committees vary considerably from company to company. In general, committees simply review job descriptions and analyses, and then evaluate jobs. Larger companies with a multitude of jobs often establish separate committees to evaluate particular job classifications such as nonexempt, exempt, managerial, and executive jobs. The immense number of jobs in large companies would otherwise preclude committee members from performing their regular duties.

Job evaluation is an important determinant of a job's worth within many companies. All employees, regardless of their functions, wish to be compensated and valued for their efforts. All employees strive for a reasonable pay-effort bargain (i.e., a compensation level consistent with their contributions). Managers strive to balance employee motivation with cost control because they have limited resources for operating their departments. Union representatives strive to ensure that members enjoy a good standard of living. Therefore, unions try to prevent the undervaluation of jobs.

Job evaluation committees help ensure commitment from employees throughout companies. They also provide a checks-and-balances system. Job evaluation procedures are not scientifically accurate because these evaluation decisions are based on ordinary human judgment. Therefore, a consensus of several employees helps to minimize the biases of individual job evaluators.

Training Employees to Conduct Job Evaluations

Individuals should understand the process objectives. In addition to knowing company objectives, evaluators also should practice using the chosen job evaluation criteria before applying them to actual jobs. Similar to job analysis procedures, evaluators should base their decisions on sound job- and business-related rationales to ensure legal compliance.

Documenting the Job Evaluation Plan

Documenting the job evaluation plan is useful for legal and training purposes. From an employer's perspective, a well-documented evaluation plan clearly specifies job- and business-related criteria against which jobs are evaluated. Well-documented plans can allow employees to understand clearly how their jobs were evaluated and the outcome of the process. In addition, well-documented plans provide guidelines for clarifying ambiguities in the event of employee appeals or legal challenges.

Communicating with Employees

Job evaluation results matter personally to all employees. Companies must formally communicate with employees throughout the job analysis and evaluation processes to ensure employees' understanding and acceptance of the job evaluation process and results. Information sessions and memoranda are useful media. Employers should share basic information, and employees should be given the opportunity to respond to what they believe are either unsatisfactory procedures or inaccurate outcomes of the job evaluation process.

Setting Up the Appeals Process

Companies should set up appeals procedures that permit reviews on a case-by-case basis to provide a check on the process through reexamination. Such appeals reduce charges of illegal discrimination that would be more likely to occur if employees were not given a voice. Compensation professionals usually review employees' appeals. Companies increasingly process appeals through committees made up of compensation professionals and a representative sample of employees and supervisors. Grievants are more likely to judge appeals decisions as fair if committees are involved: Committee decisions should reflect the varied perspectives of participants rather than the judgment of one individual.

JOB EVALUATION TECHNIQUES

Compensation professionals categorize job evaluation methods as either market-based evaluation or job-content evaluation techniques. **Market-based evaluation** plans use market data to determine differences in job worth. Many companies choose market-based evaluation methods because they wish to assign job pay rates that are neither too low nor too high relative to the market. Setting pay rates too low will make it difficult to recruit talented candidates, whereas setting pay rates too high will result in an excessive cost burden for the employer. Compensation professionals rely on compensation surveys to determine prevailing pay rates of jobs in the relevant labor market. We will address that issue in Chapter 8.

Job-content evaluation plans emphasize the company's internal value system by establishing a hierarchy of internal job worth based on each job's role in company strategy. Compensation professionals review preliminary structures for consistency with market pay rates on a representative sample of jobs known as benchmark jobs. Compensation professionals ultimately must balance external market considerations with internal consistency objectives. In practice, compensation professionals judge the adequacy of pay differentials by comparing both market rates and pay differences among jobs within their companies. They consult with the top HR official and chief financial officer when discrepancies arise, particularly if company pay rates are generally lower than the market rates. Upon careful consideration of the company's financial resources and the strategic value of the jobs in question, these executives decide whether to adjust internal pay rates for jobs with below-market pay rates.

Neither market-based nor job-content evaluation approaches alone enable compensation professionals to balance internal and external considerations. Most companies therefore rely on both approaches. The point method is the most popular job-content method because it gives compensation professionals better control over balancing internal and market considerations. Chapter 8 fully addresses how compensation professionals combine point method results with market approaches; however, a brief overview will follow our discussion of the point method in this chapter.

The Point Method

The **point method** is a job-content valuation technique that uses quantitative methodology. Quantitative methods assign numerical values to compensable factors that describe jobs, and these values are summed as an indicator of the overall value for the job. The relative worth of jobs is established by the magnitude of the overall numerical value for the jobs.

The point method evaluates jobs by comparing compensable factors. Each factor is defined and assigned a range of points based on the factor's relative value to the company. Compensable factors are weighted to represent the relative importance of each factor to the job. Job evaluation committees follow seven steps to complete the point method.

Step 1: Select Benchmark Jobs

Point method job evaluations use **benchmark jobs** to develop factors and their definitions to select jobs to represent the entire range of jobs in the company. Benchmark jobs, found outside the company, provide reference points against which jobs within the company are judged. Table 7-9 lists the characteristics of benchmark jobs.[5]

Step 2: Choose Compensable Factors Based on Benchmark Jobs

Managers must define compensable factors that adequately represent the scope of jobs slated for evaluation. Each benchmark job should be described by those factors that help distinguish it from the value of all other jobs. In addition to the "universal" factors (e.g., skill, effort, responsibility, and working conditions) additional factors may be developed to the extent that they are job- and business-related.

Compensable factor categories may be broken down further into specific related factors or subfactors. For example, skill may include job knowledge, education, mental ability, physical ability, accuracy, and dexterity. Effort may include factors relating to both physical and mental exertion. Responsibility may include considerations related to fiscal, material, or personnel responsibilities. Working conditions may be unpleasant because of extreme temperatures or possible exposure to hazardous chemicals.

TABLE 7-9 Characteristics of Benchmark Jobs

1. The contents are well-known, relatively stable over time, and agreed upon by the employees involved.
2. The jobs are common across a number of different employers.
3. The jobs represent the entire range of jobs that are being evaluated within a company.
4. The jobs are generally accepted in the labor market for the purposes of setting pay levels.

SOURCE: Milkovich, G. T., & Newman, J. M. (1996). *Compensation* (5th ed.) Homewood, IL: Irwin.

The number of compensable factors should companies use varies. Compensation professionals should select as many compensable factors as are needed to describe the range of benchmark jobs adequately.

Step 3: Define Factor Degrees

Although compensable factors describe the range of benchmark jobs, individual jobs vary in scope and content. Evaluators must therefore divide each factor into a sufficient number of degrees to identify the level of a factor present in each job. To clarify this idea of factor degrees, it is helpful to think about a paint sample that can be found in any home improvement store. Specifying a color such as gray is not straightforward because there are various shades of gray. Likewise, a compensable factor is similar to a color. For example, the compensable factor *writing ability* can be described in degrees (shades of color) ranging from the ability to write simple sentences to the ability to write paragraphs of complex information.

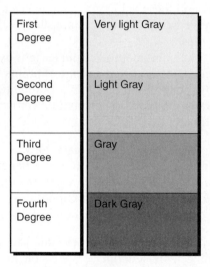

First Degree	Very light Gray
Second Degree	Light Gray
Third Degree	Gray
Fourth Degree	Dark Gray

Table 7-10 illustrates a factor definition for writing ability and its degree statements. Degree definitions should set forth and limit the meaning of each degree so that evaluators can uniformly interpret job descriptions. It is generally helpful to include a few actual work examples as anchors.

The number of degrees will vary based on the comprehensiveness of the plan. For example, if the plan covers only a limited segment of jobs (e.g., clerical employees), fewer degrees will be required than if the plan covered every group of employees. Take education as an example. Only two degrees may be necessary to describe the educational requirements for clerical jobs (i.e., high school diploma or equivalent and an associate's degree). More than two degrees would be required to describe adequately the educational requirements for administrative, production, managerial, and professional jobs (i.e., high school diploma or equivalent, associate's degree, bachelor's degree, master's degree, and doctorate). Most analyses anchor minimum and maximum degrees, with specific jobs representing these points.

Step 4: Determine the Weight of Each Factor

Weighting compensable factors represents the importance of the factor to the overall value of the job. The weights of compensable factors are usually expressed as percentages. Weighting is often done by management or by a job evaluation committee's decision. All of the factors are ranked according to their relative importance, and final weights are assigned after discussion and consensus. For example, let's

TABLE 7-10 Writing Ability: Factor Definition and Degree Statements

Definition	Capacity to communicate with others in written form.
First Degree	Print simple phrases and sentences, using normal work order and present and past tenses.
Sample Anchor	Prints shipping labels for packages, indicating the destination and the contents of the packages.
Second Degree	Write compound and complex sentences, using proper end punctuation and adjectives and adverbs.
Sample Anchor	Fills requisitions, work orders, or requests for materials, tools, or other stock items.
Third Degree	Write reports and essays with proper format, punctuation, spelling, and grammar, using all parts of speech.
Sample Anchor	Types letters, reports, or straight-copy materials from rough draft or corrected copy.
Fourth Degree	Prepare business letters, expositions, summaries, and reports using prescribed format and conforming to all rules of punctuation, grammar, diction, and style.
Sample Anchor	Composes letters in reply to correspondence concerning such items as request for merchandise, damage claims, credit information, delinquent accounts, or to request information.
Fifth Degree	Write manuals or speeches.
Sample Anchor	Writes service manuals and related technical publications concerned with installation, operation, and maintenance of electronic, electrical, mechanical, and other equipment.

assume the relative importance of skill, effort, responsibility, and working conditions to ABC Manufacturing Corporation:

- Skill is the most highly valued compensable factor, weighted at 60 percent.
- Responsibility is the next most important factor, weighted at 25 percent.
- Effort is weighted at 10 percent.
- The working conditions factor is least important, weighted at 5 percent.

Step 5: Determine Point Values for Each Compensable Factor

Compensation professionals set point values for each compensable factor in three stages. First, they must establish the maximum possible point values for the complete set of compensable factors. This total number is arbitrary, but it represents the possible maximum value jobs can possess. As a rule of thumb, the total point value for a set of compensable factors should be determined by a simple formula (i.e., the number of compensable factors times 250). ABC Manufacturing sets 1,000 (4 compensable factors × 250) as the possible maximum number of points.

Second, the maximum possible point value for each compensable factor is based on total weight as described in Step 4. Again, for ABC Manufacturing, skill equals 60 percent, responsibility equals 25 percent, effort equals 10 percent, and working conditions equals 5 percent:

- The maximum possible total points for skills equal 600 points (60% × 1,000 points).
- The maximum possible total points for responsibility equal 250 points (25% × 1,000 points).
- The maximum possible total points for effort equal 100 points (10% × 1,000 points).
- The maximum possible total points for working conditions equal 50 points (5% × 1,000 points).

Third, compensation professionals distribute these points across degree statements within each compensable factor. The point progression by degrees from the lowest to the highest point value advances arithmetically (i.e., a scale of even incremental values). This characteristic is essential for conducting regression analysis (i.e., a statistical analysis method that we will address in Chapter 8 in the discussion of integrating internal job structures—based on job evaluation points—with external pay rates for benchmark jobs).

How do compensation professionals assign point values to each degree? Let's illustrate this procedure by example, using the skill compensable factor. Let's also assume that the skill factor has five degree statements. Degree 1 represents the most basic skill level, and degree 5 represents the most advanced skill level. The increment from one degree to the next highest is 120 points (600 point maximum/5 degree statements).

- Degree 1 = 120 points (120 points × 1)
- Degree 2 = 240 points (120 points × 2)
- Degree 3 = 360 points (120 points × 3)
- Degree 4 = 480 points (120 points × 4)
- Degree 5 = 600 points (120 points × 5)

Step 6: Verify Factor Degrees and Point Values

Committee members should independently calculate the point values for a random sample of jobs. Table 7-11 shows a Sample Job Evaluation Worksheet. After calculating the point values for this sample, committee members should review the point totals for each job. Committee members give careful consideration to whether the hierarchy of jobs makes sense in the context of the company's strategic plan, as well as to the inherent content of the jobs. For instance, sales jobs should rank relatively high on the job hierarchy within a sales-oriented company such as the pharmaceuticals industry. Research scientist jobs ought to rank relatively high for a company that pursues a differentiation strategy. Messenger jobs should not rank more highly than claims analyst jobs in an insurance

TABLE 7-11   Sample Job Evaluation Worksheet

Job Title: _____

Evaluation Date: _____

Name of Evaluator: _____

Compensable Factor	Degree 1	2	3	4	5	Total
Skill						
Mental skill	60	120	180	240	(300)	300
Manual skill	60	(120)	180	240	300	120
Effort						
Mental effort	10	20	30	40	(50)	50
Physical effort	10	20	(30)	40	50	30
Responsibility						
Supervisory	25	50	(75)	100	125	75
Department budgeting	(25)	50	75	100	125	25
Working conditions						
Hazards	10	20	30	(40)	50	40
Total job value						640

company. In short, where peculiarities are apparent, committee members reconsider compensable factor definitions, weights, and actual ratings of the benchmark jobs.

Step 7: Evaluate All Jobs

Committee members evaluate all jobs in the company once the evaluation system has been tested and refined. Each job then is evaluated by determining which degree definition best fits the job and by assigning the corresponding point factors. All points are totaled for each job, and all jobs are ranked according to their point values.

Balancing Internal and Market Considerations Using the Point Method

How do compensation professionals balance internal and market considerations with point method results? They convert point values into the market value of jobs through regression analysis, a statistical technique. As we will discuss in Chapter 8, regression analysis enables compensation professionals to set base pay rates in line with market rates for benchmark or representative jobs. Companies identify market pay rates through compensation surveys. Of course, a company's value structure for jobs based on the point method will probably differ somewhat from the market pay rates for similar jobs. Regression analysis indicates base pay rates that minimize the differences between the company's point method results and the market pay rates.

Alternative Job-Content Evaluation Approaches

Most other job-content approaches use qualitative methods. Qualitative methods evaluate entire jobs and typically compare jobs with each other or some general criteria. These criteria are usually vague (e.g., importance of jobs to departmental effectiveness). The prevalent kinds of qualitative job evaluation techniques include:

- Simple ranking plans
- Paired comparisons
- Alternation ranking
- Classification plans

Simple Ranking Plans

Simple ranking plans order all jobs from lowest to highest according to a single criterion (e.g., job complexity or the centrality of the job to the company's competitive strategy). This approach considers each job in its entirety, usually in small companies that have relatively few employees. In large companies that classify many jobs, members of job evaluation committees independently rank jobs on a departmental basis. Different rankings will likely result. When this occurs, job evaluation committees discuss the differences in rankings and choose one set of rankings by consensus.

Paired Comparison and Alternation Ranking

Two common variations of the ranking plan are paired comparison and alternation ranking. The **paired comparison** technique is useful if there are many jobs to rate, usually more than 20. Job evaluation committees generate every possible pair of jobs. For each pair, committee members assign a point to the job with the highest value, whereas the lowest-value job does not receive a point. After evaluating each pair, the evaluator sums the points for each job. Jobs with higher points are more valuable than are jobs with fewer points. The job with the most points is ranked the highest; the job with the fewest points is ranked the lowest.

The **alternation ranking** method orders jobs by extremes. Yet again, committee members judge the relative value of jobs according to a single criterion (e.g., job complexity or the centrality of the job to the company's competitive strategy). This ranking process begins by determining which job is the most valuable, followed by determining which job is the least valuable. Committee members then judge the next most valuable job and the next least valuable job. This process continues until all jobs have been evaluated.

Despite the simplicity of ranking plans, they exhibit three limitations. First, ranking results rely on purely subjective data; the process lacks objective standards, guidelines, and principles that would aid in resolving differences of opinion among committee members. Companies usually do not fully define their ranking criteria. For example, the criterion job complexity can be defined as level of education or as number of distinct tasks that the workers must perform daily.

Second, ranking methods use neither job analyses nor job descriptions, which makes this method difficult to defend legally. Committee members rely on their own impressions of the jobs.

Third, ranking approaches do not incorporate objective scales that indicate how different in value one job is from another. For instance, let's assume that a committee decides on the following ranking for training and development professionals (listed from most valuable to least valuable):

- Director of training and development
- Manager of training and development
- Senior training and development specialist
- Training and development specialist
- Training and development assistant

Rankings do not offer standards for compensation professionals to facilitate answering such questions as, "Is the director of training and development job worth four times as much as the training and development assistant job?" Compensation professionals' inability to answer such questions makes it difficult to establish pay levels according to job content differences.

Classification Plans

Companies use **classification plans** to place jobs into categories based on compensable factors. Public sector organizations (e.g., civil service systems), use classification systems most prevalently. The federal government's classification system is a well-known example. As we discussed in Chapter 4, the General Schedule classifies federal government jobs into 15 classifications (GS-1 through GS-15) based on such factors as skill, education, and experience levels. In addition, jobs that require high levels of specialized education (e.g., a physicist), significantly influence public policy (e.g., law judges), or require executive decision making are classified in separate categories: Senior Level (SL) positions, Scientific & Professional (SP) positions, and the Senior Executive Service (SES).

The GS classification system enables the federal government to set pay rates for thousands of unique jobs based on 18 classes. Pay administration is relatively simple because pay rates depend on GS level and the employees' relevant work seniority, as we discussed in Chapter 4. The most noteworthy disadvantage is the absence of regular procedures for rewarding exceptional performance, which, ultimately, discourages employees from working as productively as possible.

Alternatives to Job Evaluation

Compensation professionals assign pay rates to jobs in numerous ways other than through the job evaluation process as previously defined. These alternate methods include reliance on market pay rates, pay incentives, individual rates, and collective bargaining. Many companies determine the value of jobs by paying the average rate in the external labor market. The procedures for assessing market rates are addressed fully in Chapter 8.

In addition to the market pay rate, pay incentives may also be the basis for establishing the core compensation for jobs. As we discussed extensively in Chapter 5, incentives tie part or all of an employee's core compensation to the attainment of a predetermined performance objective. Next, both core and fringe compensation may be determined through negotiations between an individual and an employer. The employer typically uses the market rate as a basis for negotiations, agreeing to higher pay if the supply of talented individuals is scarce and the individual in question has an established track record of performance. Finally, when unions are present, pay rates are established through the collective bargaining process, which we already considered in Chapter 3.

INTERNALLY CONSISTENT COMPENSATION SYSTEMS AND COMPETITIVE STRATEGY

To this point, we have examined the principles of internally consistent compensation systems and the rationale for building them. Moreover, we reviewed the key processes (i.e., job analysis and job evaluation) that lead to internally consistent compensation systems. Although we made the case for building internally consistent pay systems, these systems do have some limitations.

Internally consistent pay systems may reduce a company's flexibility to respond to changes in competitors' pay practices because job analysis leads to structured job descriptions and job structures. In addition, job evaluation establishes the relative worth of jobs within the company. Responding to the competition may require employees to engage in duties that extend beyond what's written in their job descriptions whenever competitive pressures demand. In the process, the definitions of jobs become more fluid, which makes equity assessments more difficult.

Another potential limitation of internally consistent compensation structures is the resultant bureaucracy. Companies that establish job hierarchies tend to create narrowly defined jobs that lead to greater numbers of jobs and staffing levels.[6] Such structures promote heavy compensation burdens. Employees' core compensation depends on the jobs they perform, how well they perform their jobs, or the skills they possess. Employee benefits (Chapters 10, 11, and 12), however, represent fixed costs that typically do not vary with employees' job performance, or their skills.

SUMMARY

This chapter discussed internally consistent pay systems and described two important tools HR and compensation professionals use to build them (i.e., job analysis and job evaluation). Job analysis represents a descriptive process that enables HR professionals systematically to describe job duties, worker specifications, and job context. Compensation professionals use job evaluation to assess the relative worth of jobs within companies. Job analysis and job evaluation are an art because they require the HR and compensation professionals' sound judgments. We discussed the strategic role that job analysis and job evaluation play in companies' quests for competitive advantage; however, we also pointed out some of the shortcomings of these approaches. Compensation professionals must carefully weigh the possible benefits and consequences of these methods in attaining competitive advantage.

KEY TERMS

- internally consistent compensation systems, 147
- job analysis, 147
- job content, 147
- job evaluation, 147
- worker requirements, 149
- working conditions, 149
- major occupational groups, 150
- reliable job analysis, 152
- valid job analysis, 152
- job descriptions, 153
- job titles, 153
- job summary, 153
- job duties, 153
- worker specification, 154
- education, 154

- Equal Employment Opportunity Commission, 154
- skill, 154
- ability, 154
- knowledge, 154
- Occupational Information Network, 155
- Content Model, 156
- experience and training, 156
- licensing, 156
- occupation requirements, 157
- generalized work activities, 157
- organizational context, 157
- work context, 157
- occupation-specific requirements, 157
- worker characteristics, 160
- abilities, 160

- interests, 160
- work styles, 160
- basic skills, 163
- cross-functional skills, 163
- O*NET User's Guide, 163
- O*NET database, 163
- job evaluation, 166
- compensable factors, 166
- universal compensable factors, 166
- market-based evaluation, 168
- job-content evaluation, 168
- point method, 169
- benchmark jobs, 169
- simple ranking plans, 173
- paired comparison, 173
- alternation ranking, 173
- classification plans, 174

DISCUSSION QUESTIONS

1. Discuss the differences between job analysis and job evaluation. How do these practices help establish internally consistent job structures?
2. Conduct a job analysis of a person you know, and write a complete job description (no longer than one page) according to the principles described in this chapter. In class, be prepared to discuss the method you used for conducting the job analysis and some of the challenges you encountered.
3. This chapter provides rationale for conducting job analysis, and it indicates some of the limitations. Take a stand for or against the use of job analysis, and provide convincing arguments for your position.
4. Respond to the statement "Building an internally consistent job structure is burdensome to companies. Instead, it is best to simply define and evaluate the worth of jobs by surveying the market."
5. Do you consider job evaluation to be an art or a science? Please explain.

EXERCISES

Compensation Online

For Students

Exercise 1: Find relevant journal articles

Your professor has asked you to write an essay explaining why internal consistency is important from the company standpoint. Use your school library's online catalog to locate articles pertaining to job evaluation and job analysis. Find and read several current articles in these areas.

Exercise 2: Research online job search sites

As a student, you are no doubt currently looking for a job, or will be soon. This exercise will be useful in that regard, and it will also help you understand one of the topics covered in this chapter. Part of Chapter 7 focuses on job descriptions. One way to determine how businesses view the responsibility it assigns to its employees is to examine how they choose to describe a position when they recruit to fill it. Go onto a job search site such as Monster at *www.monster.com*. Review the descriptions companies provide for the openings they have, and answer the following questions: How thorough are the descriptions? How would you change the descriptions if you had to write them? Do you get a sense of how much the companies value the positions by reading the descriptions? Are the companies clear about the minimal qualifications they want the applicants to have?

Exercise 3: Calculate geographic pay differences

As a job seeker, the following exercise will help you understand what to expect and what you can ask for when it comes time to determine your salary. One of the major variables to consider is the cost of living differences between cities, which are, in part, based on their geographic location. Using these different Web sites, calculate geographic differences in pay for the same two cities.

www.homefair.com (Select the Salary Calculator)

www.datamasters.com (Select Salary/Cost-of-Living Data)

cgi.money.cnn.com/tools/costofliving/costofliving.html (CNNMoney)

www.bestplaces.net (Cost-of-Living)

You can also use a search engine and search for "salary calculator" or "salary calculator cost of living." Are the numbers the same for each Web site? Why or why not? Take the validity of each Web site into consideration.

For Professionals

Exercise 1: Keep informed on current events related to human resources

As an HR professional, it is important to keep abreast of current issues and developments. One site that will allow you to do this is the Web site for the Society for Industrial and Organizational Psychology (SIOP). Click on its Web address, *www.siop.org*.

Click on SIOP Search and type in "job analysis." How many resources were available? Choose one, and write a brief abstract on the article.

Exercise 2: Research job evaluation methods

Conduct an advanced search for "job evaluation." Look for Web pages that allow you to look at and even fill out sample questionnaires or analysis forms. Put yourself in the place of an HR professional in a specific company. How would you adapt the questionnaire based on the material contained in this chapter?

Exercise 3: Write a job description

Conduct an advanced search for "job descriptions." Visit some of the resulting Web sites and view sample job descriptions. Identify the kind of information that is important, and then think of your current job or one you would like to hold as your career develops. Write a job description for yourself based on the samples you viewed on the Internet.

ENDNOTES

1. Harvey, R. J. (1991). Job analysis. In M. D. Dunnette & L. M. Hough (Eds.), *Handbook of Industrial and Organizational Psychology* (vol. 2). Palo Alto, CA: Consulting Psychologists Press.
2. U.S. Department of Labor (1991). *The Revised Handbook for Analyzing Jobs.* Washington, DC: Government Printing Office.
3. U.S. Department of Labor (1991). *The Dictionary of Occupational Titles.* Washington, DC: Government Printing Office.
4. U.S. Department of Labor, Employment and Training Administration (2007). *O*NET.* Washington, DC: Government Printing Office [online]. Available: *www.doleta.gov,* accessed June 10, 2007.
5. Milkovich, G. T., & Newman, J. M. (1996). *Compensation* (5th ed.). Homewood, IL: Richard D. Irwin.
6. Lawler, E. E., III. (1986). What's wrong with point-factor job evaluation? *Compensation and Benefits Review*, 18, pp. 20–28.

CHAPTER 8

Building Market-Competitive Compensation Systems

Chapter Outline

- Market-Competitive Pay Systems: The Basic Building Blocks

- Compensation Surveys
    Preliminary Considerations
    Using Published Compensation Survey Data
    Compensation Surveys: Strategic Considerations
    Compensation Survey Data

- Integrating Internal Job Structures with External Market Pay Rates

- Compensation Policies and Strategic Mandates

- Summary

- Key Terms

- Discussion Questions

- Exercises

- Endnotes

Learning Objectives

In this chapter, you will learn about

1. Market-competitive compensation systems

2. Compensation surveys

3. Statistical analysis of compensation surveys

4. Integrating the internal job structure with external market pay rates

5. Compensation policies and strategic mandates

ompanies rely on compensation surveys as a benchmark for setting pay and benefits to recruit highly qualified applicants and to retain valued employees. The number of salary surveys has risen with the popularity of the Internet. The end-of-chapter appendix contains an excellent example of a salary survey that is administered each year by WorldatWork.

MARKET-COMPETITIVE PAY SYSTEMS: THE BASIC BUILDING BLOCKS

Market-competitive pay systems represent companies' compensation policies that fit the imperatives of competitive advantage. Market-competitive pay systems play a significant role in attracting and retaining the most qualified employees. Well-designed pay systems should promote companies' attainment of competitive strategies. Paying more than necessary can undermine lowest-cost strategies: Excessive pay levels represent an undue burden. In addition, excessive pay restricts companies' abilities to invest in other important strategic activities (e.g., research and development, training) because money is a limited resource. Companies that pursue differentiation strategies must strike a balance between offering sufficiently high salaries to attract and retain talented candidates and providing sufficient resources to enable them to be productively creative.

Compensation professionals create market-competitive pay systems based on four activities:

- Conducting strategic analyses
- Assessing competitors' pay practices with compensation surveys
- Integrating the internal job structure with external market pay rates
- Determining compensation policies

First, a **strategic analysis** entails an examination of a company's external market context and internal factors. Examples of external market factors include industry profile, information about competitors, and long-term growth prospects. Internal factors encompass financial condition and functional capabilities (e.g., marketing and human resources). Refer to Chapter 2 for a detailed description of the components of strategic analysis.

Second, **compensation surveys** involve the collection and subsequent analysis of competitors' compensation data. Compensation surveys traditionally focused on competitors' wage and salary practices. Employee benefits have more recently also become a target of surveys because benefits are a key element of market-competitive pay systems. Compensation surveys are important because they enable compensation professionals to obtain realistic views of competitors' pay practices. In the absence of compensation survey data, compensation professionals would have to use guesswork to try to build market-competitive compensation systems, and making too many wrong guesses could lead to noncompetitive compensation systems that undermine competitive advantage.

Third, compensation professionals integrate the internal job structure (Chapter 7) with the external market pay rates identified through compensation surveys. This integration results in pay rates that reflect both the company's and the external market's valuations of jobs. Most often, compensation professionals rely on regression analysis, a statistical method, to achieve this integration.

Finally, compensation professionals recommend pay policies that fit with their companies' standing and competitive strategies. As we discuss later in this chapter, compensation professionals must strike a balance between managing costs and attracting and retaining the best-qualified employees. Top management ultimately makes compensation policy decisions after careful consideration of compensation professionals' interpretation of the data.

COMPENSATION SURVEYS

The second step compensation professionals undertake to assure external competitiveness is to consult or develop compensation surveys. Compensation surveys contain data about competing companies' compensation practices.

Preliminary Considerations

There are two important preliminary considerations compensation professionals take under advisement before investing time and money into compensation surveys:

- What companies hope to gain from compensation surveys
- Custom development versus use of an existing compensation survey

What Companies Hope to Gain from Compensation Surveys

Clarifying what companies hope to gain from compensation surveys is critical to developing effective compensation systems. Compensation professionals usually want to learn about competitors' compensation practices and something about employees' preferences for alternative forms of compensation due to economic changes. Staying abreast of new developments in market surveys will enable compensation professionals to get the most out of surveys. Information to be learned about competitors' compensation offerings includes base pay levels, incentive award structures, and both the mix and levels of discretionary benefits. Mix can be described as the percentage of employer compensation costs applied to compensation and benefits. For example, health insurance coverage accounts for 40 percent of total dollars spent on employee benefits. Levels refer to amounts actually or potentially paid to employees or beneficiaries. For instance, the average annual pay for day care workers is $16,000, and life insurance benefits are subject to a maximum payout of $250,000.

Compensation professionals wish to make sound decisions about pay levels based on what the competition pays its employees. Sound pay decisions promote companies' efforts to sustain competitive advantage, and poor pay decisions compromise competitive advantage. Compensation surveys enable compensation professionals to make sound judgments about how much to pay employees. Offering too little will limit a company's ability to recruit and retain high-quality employees. Paying well above the competition represents opportunity costs. Financial resources are limited. Companies therefore cannot afford to spend money on everything they wish. Excessive pay represents an opportunity cost because it is money companies could have spent on other important matters.

Compensation professionals must also take into account employees' preferences for alternative forms of compensation amid changes in the economic and social climates. For instance:

> In another study measuring employees' commitment and motivation on the job, employees were less satisfied with every aspect of compensation than they had been in previous years, from overall pay to the pay system itself. This was true even though raises have consistently ranged from 3.7 percent to 4 percent

for the last several years, according to Jim Kochanski, a senior vice president at Sibson Consulting, which undertook the study.

"There's a huge drop in satisfaction with their pay increases even if their pay increases were the same as they've been," Mr. Kochanski said. The differences are not all that surprising if you take the long view. For the last decade or more, many employers have shown a willingness to scale back their work force if it makes strategic sense.

At the same time, as they have faced steep increases in the cost of health care, many have responded by scaling back what they provide or by asking employees to pay for more themselves. And accounting rule changes have made it more costly to offer options to lots of employees.

Many employers are now putting more emphasis on other benefits, like flex-time options and enhanced career development, that are often enormously popular with certain segments of the work force, like younger workers with children.

But for large numbers of employees, who have perhaps lived through layoffs and sharp cuts in benefits, those kinds of goodies are less attractive than cash. Sure enough, while employers in the Watson Wyatt survey believed that the biggest reasons that top-performing employees changed jobs were career development and promotion opportunities, top-performing employees themselves said the biggest reason for moving would be pay.

If the labor market had more slack, the disconnect between employer and employee might not affect much beyond employee morale. But in a tight market for highly skilled workers, the effect can be very different.

For employers who want to head off major defections, the advice often given in "Can This Marriage . . ." applies: communication is vital. Surveys can reveal a wealth of information about what benefits workers want most. So can solid analyses of work force demographics: younger employers are more likely to care about benefits like child care subsidies and generous leave policies, while older workers might focus almost solely on health and retirement benefits.

Scana, a gas and electric utility based in Columbia, S.C., is one company that has studied the demographics of its work force. Roughly half of its employees will be eligible to retire in the next 5 to 10 years, said Chris McSwain, director of compensation and benefits, so he plans to use benefits to attract and retain workers and to make the transition as smooth as possible.[1]

Custom Development versus Use of an Existing Compensation Survey

Managers must decide whether to develop their own survey instruments and administer them or rely on the results of surveys conducted by others. In theory, customized surveys are preferable because the survey taker can tailor the questions the survey asks and select respondent companies to provide the most useful and informative data. Custom survey development should enable employers to monitor the quality of the survey developers' methodologies.

In practice, companies choose not to develop and implement their own surveys for three reasons. First, most companies lack employees qualified to undertake this task. Developing and implementing valid surveys requires specialized knowledge and expertise in sound questionnaire design, sampling methods, and statistical methods.

Second, rival companies are understandably reluctant to surrender information about their compensation packages to competitors because compensation systems are instrumental to competitive advantage issues. If companies are willing to cooperate, the information may be incomplete or inaccurate. For example, rival companies may choose to report the salaries for their lowest-paid accountants instead of the typical salary levels. Such information may lead the surveying company to set accountants' salaries much lower than if they had accurate, complete information about typical salary levels. Setting accountants' salaries too low may hinder recruitment efforts. Thus, custom development is potentially risky.

Third, custom survey development can be costly. Although cost figures are not readily available, it is reasonable to conclude that most companies use published survey data to minimize such costs as staff salaries and benefits (i.e., for those involved in developing a compensation survey as well as analyzing and interpreting the data), telephone and mail charges (i.e., depending upon the data collection method), and computers for data analyses.

Using Published Compensation Survey Data

Companies usually rely on existing compensation surveys rather than creating their own. Using published compensation survey data starts with two important considerations:

- Survey focus: core or employee benefits
- Sources of published survey data

Survey Focus: Core or Employee Benefits

Human resource professionals should decide whether to obtain survey information about base pay, employee benefits, or both. Companies historically competed for employees mainly on the basis of base pay. Many companies offered similar, substantial benefits packages to employees without regard to the costs. Companies typically did not use benefits offerings to compete for the best employees.

Times have changed. Benefits costs are now extremely high, which has led to greater variability in benefits offerings among companies. As of March 2007, companies spent an average $12,771 per employee annually to provide discretionary benefits.[2] Discretionary benefits account for as much as 25 percent of employers' total payroll costs (i.e., the sum of core compensation and all employee benefits costs). That is a huge cost to employers, but one that cannot be avoided; benefits have become a basis for attracting and retaining the best employees, particularly as noted earlier in this chapter. As a result, employers are likely to use compensation surveys to obtain information about competitors' base pay and benefits practices so that they can compete effectively for the best candidates.

Sources of Published Compensation Surveys

Companies can obtain published survey data from various sources (e.g., professional associations, industry associations, consulting firms, and the federal government). Professional and industry associations survey members' salaries, compile the information in summary form, and disseminate the results to members. The survey data tend to be accurate because participants—as well as association members—benefit from the survey results. In addition, membership fees often entitle members to survey information at no additional cost.

For example, the Society for Industrial and Organizational Psychology's (SIOP) primary membership includes college and university faculty members and practitioners who specialize in such HR management-related fields as selection, training, performance appraisal, and career development. SIOP periodically provides members' salary information based on gender, age, employment status (i.e., part-time versus full-time), years since earning degree, and geographic region according to metropolitan area (e.g., Boston, San Francisco/San Jose, and Washington, DC). Employers use the survey results to judge whether they are paying employees too much or too little relative to the market and to determine how much to pay new hires. Employees use the survey results to judge the adequacy of job offers and to ask their deans for pay raises when their salaries fall below the market rates.

Professional associations that specialize in the field of compensation often conduct surveys that focus on broader types of employees and employers. WorldatWork collects comprehensive data on an annual basis. The end-of-chapter appendix shows WorldatWork's 2007/2008 Total Salary Increase Budget Survey. As you will see, some of the survey topics include salary structures, promotions, and attraction and retention incentive practices.

Consulting firms are another source of compensation survey information. Some firms specialize on particular occupations (e.g., engineers) or industries (e.g., financial services); other firms do not. Examples of consulting firms that provide compensation services include:

- Buck Consultants (*www.buckconsultants.com*)
- Frederic W. Cook & Company (*www.fwcook.com*)
- The Hay Associates (*www.haygroup.com*)
- Hewitt Associates (*www.hewitt.com*)
- Pearl Meyer & Partners (*www.pearlmeyer.com*)
- Towers Perrin (*www.towersperrin.com*)
- William M. Mercer (*www.mercerhr.com*)
- Watson Wyatt (*www.watsonwyatt.com*)

You will find useful updates about compensation and benefits on these firms' Internet sites. Clients may have two choices. First, consulting firms may provide survey data from recently completed surveys. Second, these firms may literally conduct surveys from scratch exclusively for a client's use. In most cases, the first option is less expensive to companies than the second option; however, the quality of the second option may be superior because the survey was custom-designed to answer a client's specific compensation questions.

The federal government is an invaluable source of compensation survey information. The U.S. Bureau of Labor Statistics (BLS) provides free salary surveys to the public. Highly qualified survey takers and statisticians are responsible for producing these surveys. Many factors contributed to the implementation of BLS pay and benefits surveys. The government began collecting compensation data in the 1890s to assess the effects of tariff legislation on wages and prices. The government's survey programs have been rooted in competitive concerns ever since.

The BLS presently conducts various surveys that provide the following types of information (the survey names are listed in parentheses):

- Wages (National Compensation Survey)
- Compensation cost trends (Employment Cost Index; Employer Costs for Employee Compensation)
- Benefits (National Compensation Survey)

The following summary of these programs was excerpted from the public domain BLS Web site (*www.bls.gov*). Survey data are available to the public on the Web site. There are no fees associated with accessing information from this Web site.

Wages   The **National Compensation Survey (NCS)** makes it easy to find information on occupational wages paid in or near your area. The data available include:

- Average hourly wages for 800 occupations in more than 80 metropolitan and nonmetropolitan localities
- Weekly and annual earnings and hours for full-time workers
- Earnings by work level that permit wage comparisons across occupational groups
- Data presented at three levels: localities, broad regions, and the nation
- Workers as a total (all workers) and broken out by private industry and state and local government
- Wage data by industry, occupational group, full-time and part-time status, union and nonunion status, establishment size, time and incentive status, and job level

Compensation Cost Trends   The Employment Cost Index (ECI) is a quarterly measure of changes in labor costs. It is one of the principal economic indicators used by the Federal Reserve Bank. Some of its main features are that it:

- Shows changes in wages and salaries and benefit costs, as well as changes in total compensation
- Presents data as a total for all workers and separately for private industry and for state and local government workers
- Reports compensation changes by industry, occupational group, union and nonunion status, region, and metropolitan/nonmetropolitan status
- Provides seasonally adjusted and unadjusted data
- Presents historical data on changes in labor costs
- Uses fixed weights to control for shifts among occupations and industries

  Why was the Employment Cost Index developed?

- The ECI was developed in the mid-1970s in response to the rapid acceleration of both wages and prices at that time.
- Monetary and fiscal policymakers needed a more accurate measure of the actual changes in employers' labor costs.
- The ECI was first published for the third quarter, September through December, of 1975.
- It was initially very limited, covering only wage and salary changes in private industry.
- Benefits and total compensation series were added in 1981.

The Employer Costs for Employee Compensation (ECEC) program is an annual survey that shows employers' average hourly cost for total compensation and its components. As its key features it:

- Shows compensation costs as a total and broken out by (1) wages and salaries; (2) total benefit costs; (3) separate benefit costs for broad benefit categories such as paid leave, supplemental pay, insurance, retirement and savings, legally required benefits, and other benefits; or (4) separate benefit costs for such detailed benefits as paid holidays, health insurance, defined benefit pension, and workers' compensation
- Provides cost data in dollar amounts and as percentages of compensation

- Breaks out data on civilian workers into estimates for white-collar, blue-collar, and service groups or state and local government workers into estimates for white-collar workers, service occupations, and service industries
- Reports compensation costs by major occupation, industry, region, union and nonunion status, establishment size, and full- or part-time status
- Uses current weights to reflect today's labor force composition

Benefits The National Compensation Survey (NCS) covers the incidence and detailed provisions of selected employee benefit plans in small private establishments, medium and large private establishments, and state and local governments. The data are presented as the percentage of employees who have access to or participate in certain benefits or as average benefit provisions (e.g., the average number of paid holidays provided to employees each year).

Estimates are published by:

- Broad occupational groups
- Full- and part-time status of employees
- Union and nonunion status
- Workers with average wages less than $15 per hour and $15 per hour or higher
- Goods-producing and service-providing industries
- Establishments with fewer than 100 workers and 100 workers or more
- Broad geographic regions and industry sectors

The NCS provides incidence and extensive provisions data for two major benefit areas:

- Health insurance
- Retirement (both defined benefit and defined contribution components)

With the exception of broad incidence data, which were produced by major region, all of the NCS benefits data were national. They were presented for three broad occupational groupings: professional, technical, and related; clerical and sales; and blue-collar and service employees. Broad incidence data were also available by goods- and service-producing, union affiliation, and full- and part-time status.

For the next several years, all private industry establishments, regardless of size, will be studied each year. Data on both private industry establishments and state and local government workers will eventually be produced every year. Incidence and key provisions for all benefits plans, as well as detailed plan provisions for health care and retirement plans, will be studied each year; the plan is to make these data available by additional occupational and industry detail categories.

Benefits data will be added by such establishment and employee characteristics as:

- Establishment size
- Industry group
- Profit versus nonprofit status
- Time versus incentive status

The same detailed benefits data that are produced for the nation are also to be produced for the ten largest metropolitan areas and for nine census divisions. The NCS also conducts special studies in new benefit trends:

- Stock options
- Child care resource and referral services

Compensation Surveys: Strategic Considerations

Two essential strategic considerations are:

- Defining the relevant labor market
- Choosing benchmark jobs

Defining the Relevant Labor Market

Relevant labor markets represent the fields of potentially qualified candidates for particular jobs. Companies collect compensation survey data from the appropriate relevant labor markets. Relevant labor markets are defined on the basis of occupational classification, geography, and product or service market competitors.

Occupational classification refers to a group of two or more jobs that are based on similar work characteristics (e.g., blue- versus white-collar work), duties (e.g., work mainly with people or with machines), and responsibilities (e.g., supervision of other employees). The U.S. Bureau of Labor Statistics publishes the *Occupational Classification System Manual,* which helps business professionals and government economists make proper occupational matches for collecting compensation data. In fact, the NCS survey program is based on nine major occupational groupings described in the manual with detailed information about specific occupations:

- Professional, technical, and related occupations
- Executive, administrative, and managerial occupations
- Sales occupations
- Administrative support occupations, including clerical
- Precision production, craft, and repair occupations
- Machine operators, assemblers, and inspectors
- Transportation and material-moving occupations
- Handlers, equipment cleaners, helpers, and laborers
- Service occupations, except private household

This manual is available on the BLS Web site (*www.bls.gov/ncs/ocs/ocsm/commain.htm*).

Companies that plan to hire accountants and auditors should consider data about accountants and auditors only, rather than individuals from such other job families as engineers. After all, the worker characteristics and work tasks are clearly different: Accountants and auditors prepare, analyze, and verify financial reports and taxes, as well as monitor information systems that furnish this information to managers in business, industrial, and government organizations. Engineers apply the theories and principles of science and mathematics to the economical solution of practical technical problems. For example, civil engineers design, plan, and supervise the construction of buildings, highways, and rapid transit systems.

Companies search over a wider geographical area for candidates for jobs that require specialized skills or skills that are low in supply relative to the demand. For instance, hospitals are likely to search nationwide for neurosurgeons because their specialized skills are scarce. Companies are likely to limit searches for clerical employees to more confined local areas because clerical employees' skills are relatively common, and their supply tends to be higher relative to companies' demand for them. An insurance company based in Hartford, Connecticut, restricts its search for clerical employees to the Hartford area.

Companies use product or service market competitors to define the relevant labor market when industry-specific knowledge is a key worker qualification and competition for market share is keen. For example, such long-distance telephone companies as

AT&T probably prefer to lure marketing managers away from industry competitors rather than from such unrelated industries as snack foods or medical and surgical supplies. Knowledge about customer preferences in snack foods has little to do with customers' preferences for long-distance telephone service.

Occupational classification, geographic scope, and product or service market competitors are not necessarily independent dimensions. For example, a company uses product or service market competitors as the basis for defining the relevant labor market for product managers; however, this dimension overlaps with geographic scope because competitor companies are located throughout the country (e.g., Boston, San Francisco, Dallas, and Miami).

With many professional, technical, and management positions, all three factors (i.e., job family, geographic scope, and companies that compete on the basis of product or service) can be applicable. For more information about relevant labor markets for various occupations, employers can consult professional and industrial associations and consulting firms.

Choosing Benchmark Jobs

As we discussed in Chapter 7, benchmark jobs are key to conducting effective job evaluations. They also play an important role in compensation surveys. Human resource professionals determine the pay levels for jobs based on typical market pay rates for similar jobs. In other words, HR professionals rely on benchmark jobs as reference points for setting pay levels. As we discussed in Chapter 7, benchmark jobs have four characteristics:[3]

- The contents are well-known, relatively stable over time, and agreed upon by the employees involved.
- The jobs are common across a number of different employers.
- The jobs represent the entire range of jobs that are being evaluated within a company.
- The jobs are generally accepted in the labor market for the purposes of setting pay levels.

Why are benchmark jobs necessary? Human resource professionals ideally would match each job within their companies to jobs contained in compensation surveys; however, in reality, one-to-one matches are not feasible for two reasons. First, large companies may have hundreds of unique jobs, making one-to-one matches tedious, time-consuming, and expensive because of the salary and benefits paid to staff members responsible for making these matches. Second, it is highly unlikely that HR professionals will find perfect or close matches between each of a company's jobs and jobs contained in the compensation surveys: Companies adapt job duties and scope to fit their particular situations. In other words, jobs with identical titles may differ somewhat in the degrees of compensable factors. Perfect matches are the exception rather than the rule. For example, Company A's secretary I job may require only a high school education or GED equivalent. Company B's secretary I job may require an associate's degree in office administration.

Companies can make corrections for differences between their jobs and external benchmark jobs. These corrections are based on subjective judgment rather than on objective criteria. Job incumbents and compensation professionals should independently compare compensable factors for a company's jobs with the compensable factors for the external benchmark jobs. Table 8-1 illustrates a rating scale for this purpose. Both job incumbents and supervisors should complete this questionnaire separately to minimize rater biases (see Chapter 4, performance appraisal section). Differences in ratings can be reconciled through discussion.

The discussion about compensation surveys is focused on U.S. companies' pay rates. Compensation professionals are presently interested in surveying pay rates

TABLE 8-1 Comparing Companies' Jobs with Benchmark Jobs

Instructions to Job Incumbents: Compare elements of your job with elements of the survey benchmark job.

Instructions to Supervisors: Compare elements of your employee's job with elements of the survey benchmark job.

	Adjust Pay	
Skill (Check the statement that most applies.)		
My (employee's) job requires substantially more skill than the benchmark job	☐	+4%
My (employee's) job requires somewhat more skill than the benchmark job	☐	+2%
My (employee's) job and benchmark job require equal skill.	☐	0%
My (employee's) job requires somewhat less skill than the benchmark job	☐	−2%
My (employee's) job requires substantially less skill than the benchmark job	☐	−4%
Knowledge (Check the statement that most applies.)		
My (employee's) job requires substantially more knowledge than the benchmark job	☐	+2%
My (employee's) job requires somewhat more knowledge than the benchmark job.	☐	+1%
My (employee's) job and benchmark job require equal knowledge	☐	0%
My (employee's) job requires somewhat less knowledge than the benchmark job.	☐	−1%
My (employee's) job requires substantially less knowledge than the benchmark job.	☐	−2%
Abilities (Check the statement that most applies.)		
My (employee's) job requires substantially more abilities than the benchmark job.	☐	+4%
My (employee's) job requires somewhat more abilities than the benchmark job.	☐	+2%
My (employee's) job and benchmark job require equal abilities	☐	0%
My (employee's) job requires somewhat less abilities than the benchmark job	☐	−2%
My (employee's) job requires substantially less abilities than the benchmark job. than the benchmark job.	☐	−4%

Pay adjustment calculation: Sum the percentages for the three checked items. Possible range is from +10% to −10%.

Pay adjustment (e.g., a total of 0% means no adjustment is required; +3% indicates that the job's pay rate be increased by 3%, and −3% indicates that the job's pay rate be decreased by 3%).

in other countries because they send U.S. employees to work in foreign outposts (see Chapter 15), or hire foreign nationals to work in their own country for U.S. companies (e.g., IBM hires people from the Indian continent to serve in call centers).

Compensation Survey Data

Compensation professionals should be aware of three compensation survey data characteristics. First, compensation surveys contain immense amounts of information. A perusal of every datum point would be mind-boggling even to the most mathematically inclined individuals. In addition, there is bound to be wide variation in pay rates across companies, making it difficult to build market-competitive pay systems. Thus, compensation professionals should use statistics to describe large sets of data efficiently. Second, compensation survey data are outdated because there is a lag between when the data were collected and when employers implement the compensation plan based on the survey data. Third, compensation professionals must use statistical analyses to integrate their internal job structures (based on job evaluation points; see Chapter 7) with the external market based on the survey data. We will discuss this matter in detail later in this chapter.

Table 8-2 contains sample salary information collected from a salary survey of 35 accounting jobs according to seniority. Accountant I incumbents possess less than 2 years of accounting work experience. Accountant II incumbents have 2 to less

TABLE 8-2	Raw Compensation Survey Data for Accountants in Atlanta, Georgia	
Company	*Job Title*	*2005 Annual Salary*
A	Accountant I	$33,000
A	Accountant I	34,500
A	Accountant II	36,000
A	Accountant III	43,500
B	Accountant I	33,000
B	Accountant I	33,000
B	Accountant I	36,000
B	Accountant II	37,500
B	Accountant II	36,000
B	Accountant II	37,500
B	Accountant III	45,000
B	Accountant III	43,500
C	Accountant I	34,500
C	Accountant II	37,500
C	Accountant III	43,500
D	Accountant I	36,000
D	Accountant I	36,000
D	Accountant III	55,000
E	Accountant I	33,000
E	Accountant I	33,000
E	Accountant I	34,500
E	Accountant II	36,000
E	Accountant II	36,000
E	Accountant II	37,500
E	Accountant III	45,000
F	Accountant I	34,500
F	Accountant II	37,500
F	Accountant III	45,000
F	Accountant III	45,000
F	Accountant III	43,500
G	Accountant I	34,500
G	Accountant I	33,000
G	Accountant II	37,500
G	Accountant II	37,500
G	Accountant III	43,500

TABLE 8-3   Frequency Table for Accountants

Salary Interval	Number of Salaries from Survey
$30,000–$35,000	11
$35,001–$40,000	14
$40,000–$45,000	9
$45,0001+	1

than 4 years of accounting work experience. Accountant III incumbents possess 4 to 6 years of work experience as accountants. Seven companies (A–G) from Atlanta participated in the survey, and most have more than one incumbent at each level. Company B has three accountant I incumbents, three accountant II incumbents, and two accountant III incumbents.

As a starting point, let's begin with basic tabulation of the survey data. Basic tabulation helps organize data, promotes decision makers' familiarization with the data, and reveals possible extreme observations (i.e., outliers). Table 8-3 displays a frequency table, and Figure 8-1 displays a histogram. Both indicate the number of job incumbents whose salaries fall within the specified intervals. For example, 11 accountants' annual salaries range between $30,000 and $35,000. Only one job incumbent falls in the $45,001 and above interval, which suggests the possibility of an outlier. We'll discuss the importance of outliers shortly.

Using the Appropriate Statistics to Summarize Survey Data
Two properties describe numerical data sets:

- Central tendency
- Variation

FIGURE 8-1   Histogram of Survey Data for Accountants

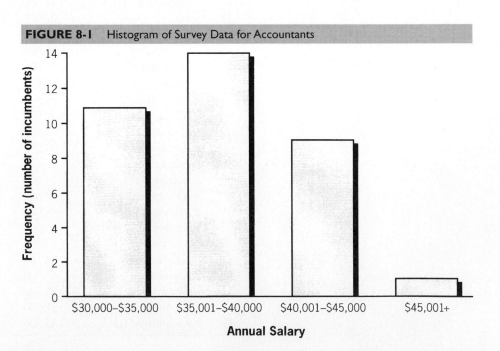

Central tendency represents the fact that a set of data clusters or centers around a central point. Central tendency is a number that represents the typical numerical value in the data set. What is the typical annual salary for accountants in our data set? Two types of central tendency measures are pertinent to compensation—arithmetic mean (often called mean or average) and median.

We calculate the **mean** annual salary for accountants by adding all the annual salaries in our data set and then dividing the total by the number of annual salaries in the data set. The sum of the salaries in our example is $1,337,500 based on 35 salaries. Thus, the mean equals $38,214.29 (i.e., $1,337,500 divided by 35). In this example, the mean informs compensation professionals about the "typical" salary or going market rate for the group of accountants I, II, and III. Compensation professionals often use the mean as a reference point to judge whether employees' compensation is below or above the market.

We use every data point to calculate the mean. As a result, one or more outliers can lead to a distorted representation of the typical value. The mean understates the "true" typical value when there is one or more extremely small value, and it overstates the "true" typical value when there is one or more extremely large value. The mean's shortcoming has implications for compensation professionals.

Understated mean salaries may cause employers to set starting salaries too low to attract the best-qualified job candidates. Overstated mean salaries probably promote recruitment efforts because employers may set starting salaries higher than necessary, a condition that creates a cost burden to companies.

The **median** is the middle value in an ordered sequence of numerical data. If there is an odd number of data points, the median literally is the middle observation. Our data set contains an odd number of observations. The median is $36,000. Table 8-4 illustrates the calculation of the median.

If there is an even number of data points, the median is the mean of the values corresponding to the two middle numbers. Let's assume that we have four salaries, ordered from the smallest value to the highest value: $25,000, $28,000, $29,500, and $33,000. The median is $28,750. The median does not create distorted representations like the mean because its calculation is independent of the magnitude of each value.

Variation is the second property used to describe data sets. **Variation** represents the amount of spread or dispersion in a set of data. Compensation professionals find three measures of dispersion to be useful (i.e., standard deviation, quartile, and percentile).

Standard deviation refers to the mean distance of each salary figure from the mean (i.e., how larger observations fluctuate above the mean and how smaller observations fluctuate below the mean). Table 8-5 demonstrates the calculation of the standard deviation for our data set.

The standard deviation equals $5,074.86. Compensation professionals find standard deviation to be useful for two reasons. First, as we noted previously, compensation professionals often use the mean as a reference point to judge whether employees' compensations are below or above the market. The standard deviation indicates whether an individual salary's departure below or above the mean is "typical" for the market. For example, Irwin Katz's annual salary is $27,500. His salary falls substantially below the typical average salary: The difference between the mean salary and Katz's salary is $10,714.29 ($38,214.29 − $27,500). This difference is much greater than the typical departure from the mean because the standard deviation is just $5,074.86.

Second, the standard deviation indicates the range for the majority of salaries. The majority of salaries falls between $33,139.43 ($38,214.29 − $5,074.86) and $43,289.15

TABLE 8-4   Calculation of the Median for Accountant Survey Data

The salary data are arranged in ascending order. The median is $(n + 1)/2$, where n equals the number of salaries. The median is item 18 ($[35 + 1]/2$). Thus, the median value is $36,000.

1. $33,000
2. $33,000
3. $33,000
4. $33,000
5. $33,000
6. $33,000
7. $34,500
8. $34,500
9. $34,500
10. $34,500
11. $34,500
12. $36,000
13. $36,000
14. $36,000
15. $36,000
16. $36,000
17. $36,000
18. $36,000   ←—— median
19. $37,500
20. $37,500
21. $37,500
22. $37,500
23. $37,500
24. $37,500
25. $37,500
26. $43,500
27. $43,500
28. $43,500
29. $43,500
30. $43,500
31. $45,000
32. $45,000
33. $45,000
34. $45,000
35. $55,000

($38,214.29 + $5,074.86). Remember, $38,214.29 is the mean, and $5,074.86 is the standard deviation. Compensation professionals can use this range to judge whether their company's salary ranges are similar to the market's salary ranges. A company's salary ranges are not typical of the market if most fall below or above the market range. A company will probably find it difficult to retain good employees when most salaries fall below the typical market range.

TABLE 8-5 Calculation of the Standard Deviation (S.D.) for Accountant Survey Data

$$\sqrt{\sum^n X_i^2 - nM^2}$$

...vations.

...e square of the mean for the

$...38,214.92)^2$

...rsion by indicating the percentage of ... illustrates the use of quartiles and ...ompensation professionals to describe ...se pay amount—based on four group- ...,25 percent of the salary figures are less ... is $36,000. Fifty percent of the salary ... third quartile is $43,500. Seventy-five ...equal to $43,500. The fourth quartile is ...figures are less than or equal to $55,000. ...g from the first percentile to the one ...enth percentile equals $33,000, and the

...nt standard deviations by indicating the ...below particular figures. Compensation ...quartiles can enhance their insights into the ...ompensation professionals want to know the percentage of ... rticular salary level or less. If $33,000 represents the tenth percentile for ... its' annual salaries, then only 10 percent earn $33,000 or less. Compensation professionals are less likely to recommend similar pay for new accountant hires. Although paying at this level represents a cost savings, companies are likely to experience retention problems because 90 percent of accountants earn more than $33,000.

It is important to keep in mind that statistics of a given type (e.g., central tendency) provide consistent information for a given set of data. As we discussed, the mean and median are measures of central tendency. The mean and median are often different for a given set of data points. When the distribution of data is skewed to the left (i.e., there is a higher frequency of larger values than smaller values), the mean will be less than the median. On the other hand, when the distribution of data is skewed to the right (i.e., there is a lower frequency of larger values than smaller values), the mean will be greater than the median.

TABLE 8-6	Percentile and Quartile Ranks for Accountant Survey Data

$33,000
$33,000
$33,000 ⟵——— 10th percentile
$33,000
$33,000
$33,000
$34,500
$34,500
$34,500 ⟵——— 1st quartile
$34,500
$34,500
$36,000
$36,000
$36,000
$36,000
$36,000
$36,000
$36,000 ⟵——— 2nd quartile
$37,500   (also 50th percentile)
$37,500
$37,500
$37,500
$37,500
$37,500
$37,500
$43,500
$43,500
$43,500 ⟵——— 3rd quartile
$43,500
$43,500
$45,000
$45,000 ⟵——— 90th percentile
$45,000
$45,000
$55,000 ⟵——— 4th quartile

Let's look at an example. The mean hourly wage rate for production workers in Company A is $8.72. The union in Company A is demanding that management grant pay raises to production workers because the mean hourly pay rate for production workers in Company B is higher—$9.02. The mean value for Company B is based on the following survey of its production workers:

Hourly Wage Rates of Production Workers
$8.15, $8.39, $8.51, $8.55, $8.60, $10.25, $10.72

Company A's management is unwilling to raise production workers' pay: Company A's production workers earn a higher mean hourly wage ($8.72) than the median hourly wage rate of Company B's production workers ($8.55).

Updating the Survey Data

Companies establish pay structures for future periods. Let's assume that a compensation professional wants to develop a pay structure for the period June 1, 2007, through May 31, 2008. For this illustration, it is now April 2007 when the compensation professional is establishing this plan. The salary survey data were obtained in April 2007 and these figures represent 2006 annual pay averages. These data will be 6 and 18 months old at the pay plan's implementation (on June 1, 2007) and end (May 31, 2008), respectively. Compensation professionals typically use historical salary data to build market-competitive pay systems because it is impossible to obtain actual salary data for the *future* compensation plan period (6/1/2007–5/31/2008) in April 2007 when the plan is being developed. Companies therefore update survey data with simple techniques to correct for such lags (see Table 8-8 as an example). This process updates the salary survey data for the start and end of the plan year (i.e., in this example, June 1, 2007, and May 31, 2008, respectively). As shown in Table 8-8, footnote 3, we estimated the cost-of-living increase based on the previous year's actual increase.

Several factors play an important role in updating. The most influential factors are economic forecasts and changes in the costs of consumer goods and services. Employers generally award small permanent pay increases (e.g., 3 to 4 percent) when the economic forecast is pessimistic. Pessimistic forecasts suggest the possibility of recession or higher unemployment levels. Thus, employers are less willing to commit substantial amounts to fund pay increases because they may not be able to afford them. Employers typically award higher permanent pay increases when the economic forecast is optimistic. Optimistic forecasts imply enhanced business activity or lower unemployment levels. Management discretion dictates actual pay increase amounts.

Changes in the cost of living tend to make survey data obsolete fairly quickly. Over time, the average cost of goods and services increases. Companies therefore update salary survey data with the **Consumer Price Index (CPI)**, the most commonly used method for tracking cost changes throughout the United States. The BLS reports the CPI in the *CPI Detailed Report* every month. Each January issue provides annual averages for the prior year. Current and historical CPI data are also available on the BLS Web site (*www.bls.gov*). Table 8-7 describes some basic facts about the CPI and how to interpret it. Table 8-8 details the procedure for updating salary survey data with the CPI.

INTEGRATING INTERNAL JOB STRUCTURES WITH EXTERNAL MARKET PAY RATES

In Chapter 7, we discussed that compensation professionals use job evaluation methods to establish internally consistent job structures. In other words, companies value jobs that possess higher degrees of compensable factors (e.g., 10 years of relevant work experience) than jobs with fewer degrees of compensable factors (e.g., one year of relevant work experience). These valuation differences ultimately should correspond to pay differences based on compensation survey data.

Earlier, we indicated that paying well below or well above the typical market rate for jobs can create a competitive disadvantage for companies. Thus, it is important that companies set pay rates by using market pay rates as reference points. To this end, we use **regression analysis**, which is a statistical analysis technique. Regression analyses

TABLE 8-7 The Consumer Price Index: Basic Facts and Interpretation Issues

Basic Facts

The CPI indexes monthly price changes of goods and services that people buy for day-to-day living. The index is based on a representative sample of goods and services, because obtaining information about all goods and services would not be feasible. The BLS gathers price information from thousands of retail and service establishments (e.g., gasoline stations, grocery stores, and department stores). Thousands of landlords provide information about rental costs, and thousands of home owners give cost information pertaining to home ownership.

The CPI represents the average of the price changes for the representative sample of goods and services within each of the following areas:

- Urban United States
- 4 regions
- 4 class sizes based on the number of residents
- 27 local metropolitan statistical areas

The BLS publishes CPI for two population groups: a CPI for All Urban Consumers (CPI-U) and the CPI for Urban Wage Earners and Clerical Workers (CPI-W). The CPI-U represents the spending habits of 80 percent of the population of the United States. The CPI-U covers wage earners; clerical, professional, managerial, and technical workers; short-term and self-employed workers; unemployed persons; retirees; and others not in the labor force. The CPI-W represents the spending habits of 32 percent of the population, and it applies to consumers who earn more than one-half of their income from clerical or wage occupations. The distinction between the CPI-U and CPI-W is important because the CPI-U is most representative of all consumers, whereas unions and management use the CPI-W during negotiations to establish effective cost-of-living adjustments; most unionized jobs are clerical or wage jobs rather than salaried professional, managerial, or executive jobs.

Interpreting the CPI: Percentage Changes vs. Point Changes

The span from 1982 to 1984 is the base period for the CPI-U and CPI-W, which is 100. Compensation professionals use the base period to determine the changes in prices over time. How much did consumer prices increase in Atlanta between the base period and December 31, 2001?

The *CPI Detailed Report* indicates that the 2001 CPI-U for Atlanta was 176.2. We know that the base period CPI is 100. Consumer prices in Atlanta increased 76.2 percent between 2001 and the base period. We determine price change with the formula:

$$\frac{(\text{Current CPI} - \text{Previous CPI})}{\text{Previous CPI}} \times 100\%$$

For this example:

$$\frac{(176.2 - 100)}{100} \times 100\% = 76.2\%$$

Compensation professionals are most concerned with annual CPI changes because they are updating recently collected survey data. The same formula yields price changes between periods other than the base period. How much did prices increase in Atlanta between 1999 and 2001? The CPI Detailed Report (January 2002) indicates that the 1999 annual CPI-U for Atlanta was 161.2, and we know that the 2001 annual average is 176.2.

$$\frac{(176.2 - 161.2)}{161.2} \times 100\% = 9.31\%$$

Consumer prices in Atlanta increased 9.31 percent between 1999 and 2001.

SOURCE: U.S. Bureau of Labor Statistics. (2002). *CPI Detailed Report.* Washington, DC: U.S. Government Printing Office.

TABLE 8-8 Updating Salary Survey, Using CPI-U, South U.S. Region

April 2007	*June 1, 2007*	*May 31, 2008*
Market survey data for 2006 CPI-U, 195.0	Pay plan begins CPI-U, 199.7 *Actual increase* Jan. 1, 2007 April, 2007: 2.4%[1]	Pay plan ends *Estimated increase* June 1, 2007– May 31, 2008: 1.7[3]
Dec. 2006 Survey mean: $38,000.00	April 2007 Survey mean: 38,912.00[2]	May 31, 2008, Survey mean: $39,573.50[4]

[1][(199.7 − 195.0)/195.0] × 100%.

[2]$38,000.00 + ($38,000.00 × 2.4%)

[3]Estimated based on the actual increase for the Southern region between June 2006 and April 2007 [(199.7 − 196.3)/196.3]. Note that 196.3 is the June 2006 CPI-U index reported by the BLS.

[4]$38,912.00 + ($38,912.00 × 1.7%)

enable compensation professionals to establish pay rates for a set of jobs that are consistent with typical pay rates for jobs in the external market.

We'll apply regression analysis to determine pay rates for the accountant I, accountant II, and accountant III jobs listed in Table 8-2. Before presenting the regression analysis technique, we need two sets of information: the job evaluation point totals for each accountant job based on job evaluation and the updated salary survey data. In this sample, the accountant jobs have the following job evaluation points: accountant I (100 points), accountant II (500 points), and accountant III (1,000) points.

Regression analysis enables decision makers to predict the values of one variable from another. Compensation professionals' goals are to predict salary levels for each job based on job evaluation points. Why not simply "eyeball" the list of salaries in the survey to identify the market rates? There are two reasons. First, companies pay different rates to employees who are performing the same (or very similar) jobs. Our salary survey indicates that accountant III pay rates vary between $43,500 and $55,000. "Eyeballing" the typical rate from the raw data is difficult when surveys contain large numbers of salaries.

Second, we wish to determine pay rates for a set of jobs in a particular company (i.e., accountant I, accountant II, and accountant III) based on their relative worth to typical market pay rates for the corresponding jobs contained in the salary survey. Our focus is on pricing a job structure, not pricing one job in isolation.

How does regression analysis work? Regression analysis finds the best-fitting line between two variables. Compensation professionals use job evaluation points assigned to benchmark jobs (based on the matching process discussed earlier) and the salary survey data for the benchmark jobs. They refer to the best-fitting line as the **market pay line**. The market pay line is representative of typical market pay rates relative to a company's job structure. Pay levels that correspond with the market pay line are market-competitive pay rates. Figure 8-2 displays the regression results.

The following equation models the prediction.

$$\hat{Y} = a + bX$$

$\hat{Y}$ = predicted salary

X = job evaluation points

a = the Y intercept (This is the Y value at which X = 0.)

b = the slope

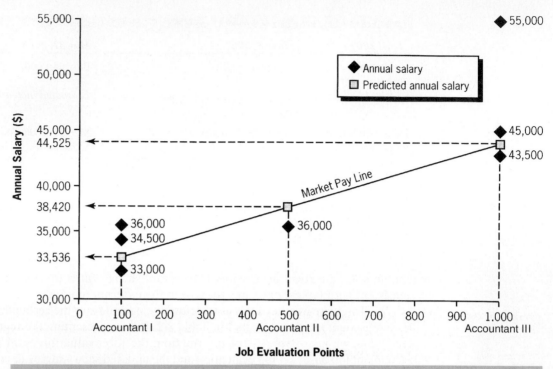

FIGURE 8-2 Regression Analysis Results for the Accountant Survey Data

The slope represents the change in Y for every one unit change in job evaluation points. In other words, the slope represents the dollar value of each job evaluation point. For example, let's assume that the slope is 26. A job consisting of 301 job evaluation points is worth $26 more than a job consisting of 300 job evaluation points.

For our data, the equation is:

$$\hat{Y} = \$32,315.66 + \$12.21X$$

Thus, this market policy line indicates the following market pay rates:

- Accountant I: $33,536.66

$$\hat{Y} = \$32,315.66 + \$12.21 \text{ (100 job evaluation points)}$$

- Accountant II: $38,420.66

$$\hat{Y} = \$32,315.66 + \$12.21 \text{ (500 job evaluation points)}$$

- Accountant III: $44,525.66

$$Y = \$32,315.66 + \$12.21 \text{ (1,000 job evaluation points)}$$

The regression analysis provides an additional important statistic known as R^2. This statistic tells us how well the variation in the company's valuation of jobs based on job evaluation points explains the variation in market pay rates from the compensation survey. The R^2 statistic can range in numerical value between zero and one. When R^2 equals zero, none (0%, that is $.0 \times 100\%$) of the variation in market pay rates can be explained by the company's job structure. When R^2 equals one, this means that all (100%) of the variation in market pay rates can be explained by the company's job structure. Just one more example—when R^2 equals .52, 52 percent (i.e., $.52 \times 100$ percent) of the variation in market pay rates can be explained by the company's job structure; .36 (36 percent) of the variation in market pay rates can be explained by the company's job structure. As you can see, we interpret R^2 in this context as the percentage variation in y values (market pay rates) that can be explained by x values (job evaluation points).

By now, you may be asking how to describe the difference between an R^2 equal to 1.0 and, for example, an R^2 equal to .71 in this situation. The difference (.29) refers to the percentage of variation in market pay rates that cannot be explained by the company's job structure. In this illustration, 29 percent of the variation is unexplained. Discrepancies often exist between the job duties of the jobs specified in the compensation survey (i.e., the benchmark jobs) and the company's job definitions.

Your HR colleagues are likely to ask you to interpret your conclusion even further because they will want to know whether the obtained R^2 value represents a small, medium, or large amount. As a rule of thumb, R^2 values between .0 and .30 represent a small amount; between .31 and .70 represent a medium amount; and between .71 and 1.0 represent a large amount.

COMPENSATION POLICIES AND STRATEGIC MANDATES

Companies can choose from three pay level policies:

- Market lead
- Market lag
- Market match

The **market lead policy** distinguishes a company from the competition by compensating employees more highly than most competitors. Leading the market denotes pay levels that place in the area above the market pay line (Figure 8-2). The **market lag policy** also distinguishes a company from the competition, but by compensating employees less than most competitors. Lagging the market indicates that pay levels fall below the market pay line (Figure 8-2). The **market match policy** most closely follows the typical market pay rates because companies pay according to the market pay line. Thus, pay rates fall along the market pay line (Figure 8-2).

The market lead policy is clearly most appropriate for companies that pursue differentiation strategies. A company may choose a market lead pay policy for its accountants because the company needs the very best accountants to promote its competitive strategy of being the top manufacturer of lightest weight surgical instruments at the lowest possible cost by 2010.

The compensation professionals and top management officials must decide how much to lead the market (e.g., 5 percent, 10 percent, 25 percent, or more). The "how much" depends on two factors. First, how much pay differential above the market is sufficient to attract and retain the most highly qualified accountants? Second, are there other funding needs for activities that promote differentiation strategies, such as research and development? Past experience and knowledge of the industry norms should provide useful information.

The market lag policy appears to fit well with lowest-cost strategies because companies realize cost savings by paying lower than the market pay line. Paying well below the market will yield short-term cost savings; however, these short-term savings will probably be offset by long-term costs. Companies that use the market lag policy may experience difficulties in recruiting and retaining highly qualified employees. Too much turnover will undercut a company's ability to operate efficiently and to market goods and services on a timely basis. Thus, companies that adopt market lag policies need to balance cost savings with productivity and quality concerns.

The market match policy represents a safe approach for companies because they generally are spending no more or less on compensation (per employee) than competitors. This pay policy does not fit with the lowest-cost strategy for obvious reasons. It does fit better with differentiation strategies. This statement appears to contradict previous ones about differentiation strategies (i.e., pay "high" salaries to attract and retain the best talent). Some companies that pursue differentiation strategies follow a market match policy to fund expensive operating or capital needs that support differentiation (e.g., research equipment and research laboratories).

A "one size fits all" approach to policy selection is inappropriate. Most companies use more than one pay policy simultaneously. For example, companies generally use market match or market lead policies for professional and managerial talent because these employees contribute most directly to a company's competitive advantages. Companies typically apply market match or market lag policies to clerical, administrative, and unskilled employees (e.g., janitorial). Companies' demands for these employees relative to supply in the relevant labor markets are low, and these employees' contributions to attainment of competitive advantage are less direct.

SUMMARY

This chapter discussed market-competitive pay systems and described compensation surveys. Compensation surveys provide "snapshots" of competitors' pay practices. Survey information provides the reference points for establishing pay level policies. Students should realize that conducting compensation surveys requires art, not science: These practices require compensation professionals' sound judgments for making recommendations that fit well with competitive strategies. Careful thought about the meaning underlying the facts and statistics is the key to successfully building market-competitive pay systems.

KEY TERMS

- market-competitive pay systems, 179
- strategic analysis, 179
- compensation surveys, 179
- National Compensation Survey (NCS), 184
- relevant labor markets, 186
- occupational classification, 186
- central tendency, 191
- mean, 191
- median, 191
- variation, 191
- standard deviation, 191
- quartiles, 193
- percentiles, 193
- Consumer Price Index (CPI), 195
- regression analysis, 195
- market pay line, 197
- market lead policy, 199
- market lag policy, 199
- market match policy, 199

DISCUSSION QUESTIONS

1. You are a compensation analyst for Worry-Not Insurance Company, which is located in Hartford, Connecticut. Define the relevant labor market for insurance claims adjusters and for data entry clerks. Describe the rationale for your definitions.
2. Can companies easily develop compensations that are both internally consistent and market competitive? What are some of the challenges to this goal?

3. Which do you believe is most important for a company's competitive advantage: internal consistency or market competitiveness? Explain your answer.

4. Refer to the regression equation presented earlier in this chapter. When b = 0, the market pay line is parallel to the x-axis (i.e., job evaluation points). Provide your interpretation.

5. Refer to Table 8-2. Cross out salaries 26 through 35. Calculate the mean and median for this reduced data set.

EXERCISES

Compensation Online

For Students

Exercise 1: Find relevant journal articles

Your professor has assigned you to write a short paper outlining why market competitiveness is an important characteristic of a pay system. Use your school library's online catalog to locate articles pertaining to strategic analysis, benchmarking, and compensation surveys. Find and read several current articles in these areas.

Exercise 2: Find your appropriate salary level

Do Web searches using the term "salary survey." Find the most up-to-date salary survey. The search engines to use are:

www.yahoo.com
www.excite.com

List three positive attributes and three possible flaws for each survey. Is one survey superior to the others, or does each survey have benefits that would be helpful under different situations?

Exercise 3: Research external factors that may affect a company's compensation packages

Scroll down to the bottom of the homepage, and click on Press Releases. Look over the titles of the releases for the last three months. Then review one from each month that you think would have a direct impact on Sprint's compensation practices. Write a brief report on why you chose the articles you did and whether you think the information will affect Sprint's compensation practices.

For Professionals

'Exercise 1: Research professional resources

Conduct Web searches using the term "U.S. Industrial Outlook." Choose three search engines (try at least one that you have not used before). Pull up the most recent year of the outlook that you can find. Based upon what you have read in this chapter, what factors are prevalent in predicting industry profiles for the year in question?

Exercise 2: Keep informed on current events related to human resources

Using Yahoo!, do an advanced search for "human resources." Stick to the News section of the search results. Read some of the articles and note what magazines, newspapers, or journals they can be found in so that you know where to look in the future.

Exercise 3: Find information regarding salary surveys

As vice president of HR, you have noticed that a lot of your company's top talent has left the firm to seek higher paychecks. To combat this, you want to make sure your pay levels are up to par with your competitors'. Conduct an advanced search for "salary surveys" again. This time, find information on how to conduct such a survey, or find organizations that provide salary surveys as a service.

ENDNOTES

1. Holland, K. (2007). Inside the mind of your employees. *New York Times* (January 28) [online]. Available: *www.nytimes.com*, accessed July 5, 2007.
2. U.S. Bureau of Labor Statistics (2007). *Employer costs for employee compensation—March 2007*

[online]. Available: *www.bls.gov/ncs/ect/home.htm*, accessed June 30, 2007.
3. Milkovich, G. T., & Newman, J. M. (1996). *Compensation* (5th ed.). Homewood, IL: Irwin.

APPENDIX: U.S. 2007–08 Salary Budget Survey

UNITED STATES

The deadline to submit the survey is April 27, 2007
Fax or mail your completed survey to:
WorldatWork Survey Team
Fax 480/483–8352 • Toll-free fax 866/816–2962
14040 N. Northsight Blvd. • Scottsdale, AZ 85260

If your organization is multi-industry or if pay practices differ across divisions, regions, business units or subsidiaries, please complete a separate questionnaire for each.

1*. Please indicate the organizational unit you are reporting data for in this survey:
- ○ Headquarters (skip to 2)
- ○ Subsidiary/group/division
- ○ Regional headquarters
- ○ Plant/branch
- ○ Independent consultant
- ○ Consulting firm
- ○ Public sector
- ○ Educational

1a*. Please describe the division, subsidiary, region, etc., that you are reporting data for in this questionnaire (i.e., Southern region, manufacturing division, etc.): _____

2*. Please indicate the industry that best describes your organization using the U.S. Census Bureau's three-digit North American Industry Classification System (NAICS) code.

3*. What region(s) are you reporting data for in this questionnaire? (Check all that apply.)

☐ Eastern United States (CT, DC, DE, MA, MD, ME, NH, NJ, NY, PA, RI, VA, VT, WV)

☐ Central United States (IA, IL, IN, KS, KY, MI, MN, MO, NE, ND, OH, SD, WI)

☐ Southern United States (AL, AR, FL, GA, LA, MS, NC, OK, SC, TN, TX)

☐ Western United States (AK, AZ, CA, CO, HI, ID, MT, NV, NM, OR, UT, WA, WY)

*Mandatory section/question

203

Base Salary Increase

4. What is your organization's current base pay compensation philosophy for each employee category?

Employee group	To pay below the market rate	To pay at the market rate	To pay above the market rate	No formal compensation philosophy
Nonexempt Hourly Nonunion				
Nonexempt Salaried				
Exempt Salaried				
Officers/Executives				

5*. What is your organization's actual base salary budget program for 2007?

*Note: Fill in "0" (zero) **only** if there is no increase planned where one is typically given. If a particular program (i.e., general increase, COLA, merit, other) is not used/applicable in your organization, please leave the field blank.*

Number of covered employees	Employee group	Number of between increases	General increase/ COLA	Merit increase	months Other increase(not promotional)	Total increase
└─┴─┴─┴─┘	Nonexempt Hourly Nonunion	└─┴─┘	└─┴─┘.└─┘%	└─┴─┘.└─┘%	└─┴─┘.└─┘%	└─┴─┘.└─┘
└─┴─┴─┴─┘	Nonexempt Salaried	└─┴─┘	└─┴─┘.└─┘%	└─┴─┘.└─┘%	└─┴─┘.└─┘%	└─┴─┘.└─┘
└─┴─┴─┴─┘	Exempt Salaried	└─┴─┘	└─┴─┘.└─┘%	└─┴─┘.└─┘%	└─┴─┘.└─┘%	└─┴─┘.└─┘
└─┴─┴─┴─┘	Officers/ Executive	└─┴─┘	└─┴─┘.└─┘%	└─┴─┘.└─┘%	└─┴─┘.└─┘%	└─┴─┘.└─┘
└─┴─┴─┴─┘	⇐TOTAL					

5a*. If you have included an increase in the "Other increase" column, what is the nature of this increase? (Check all that apply.)
☐ Accelerated increase cycle to move employee closer to midpoint (salary progression)
☐ Compression
☐ Internal equity
☐ Market adjustment/competitive adjustment
☐ Retention/critical skill adjustment
☐ Salary range adjustment
☐ Skill-based pay increase
☐ Step rate or lump-sum increase
☐ Other increase not listed above

*Mandatory section/question

6. What percentage of your organization's employees, by category, will be receiving a base salary increase (general, COLA, merit or other) in 2007? Does this represent a larger, similar or smaller percentage of employees than in 2006?

Employee group	Percent receiving increase in 2007	Percentage is larger than 2006	Percentage is similar to 2006	Percentage is smaller than 2006
Nonexempt Hourly Nonunion	└┴┘.└┘%			
Nonexempt Salaried	└┴┘.└┘%			
Exempt Salaried	└┴┘.└┘%			
Officers/Executive	└┴┘.└┘%			

7. What is the projection/estimate for the organization's base salary budget program for 2006?

   Note: Fill in "0" (zero) **only** *if there is no increase planned where one is typically given. If a particular program (i.e., general increase, COLA, merit, other) is not used/applicable in your organization, please leave the field blank.*

Employee group	Number of months between increase	General increase/ COLA	Merit increase	Other increase (not promotional)	Total increases
Nonexempt Hourly Nonunion	└┴┘	└┴┘.└┘%	└┴┘.└┘%	└┴┘.└┘%	└┴┘.└┘%
Nonexempt Salaried	└┴┘	└┴┘.└┘%	└┴┘.└┘%	└┴┘.└┘%	└┴┘.└┘%
Exempt Salaried	└┴┘	└┴┘.└┘%	└┴┘.└┘%	└┴┘.└┘%	└┴┘.└┘%
Officers/Executive	└┴┘	└┴┘.└┘%	└┴┘.└┘%	└┴┘.└┘%	└┴┘.└┘%

7a. If you have included an increase in the "Other increase" column, what is the nature of this increase? (Check all that apply.)
   ☐ Accelerated increase cycle to move employee closer to midpoint (salary progression)
   ☐ Compression
   ☐ Internal equity
   ☐ Market adjustment/competitive adjustment
   ☐ Retention/critical skill adjustment
   ☐ Salary range adjustment
   ☐ Skill-based pay increase
   ☐ Step rate or lump-sum increase
   ☐ Other increase not listed above

8. Does your organization award lump sum increases? If so, what is the average budgeted amount as a percentage of base pay?

Employee group	Do you award lump sum increases? Yes	No	If so, what is the average budgeted amount?
Nonexempt Hourly Nonunion	○	○	└┴┘.└┘%
Nonexempt Salaried	○	○	└┴┘.└┘%
Exempt Salaried	○	○	└┴┘.└┘%
Officers/Executive	○	○	└┴┘.└┘%

Salary Structures

9. If your organization uses a formal salary range structure, by what percentage did you increase the structure in 2007?

Note: Fill in "0" (zero) if there is no increase planned where one is typically given.

Employee group	2007 salary range structure change
Nonexempt Hourly Nonunion	⊔⊔.⊔%
Nonexempt Salaried	⊔⊔.⊔%
Exempt Salaried	⊔⊔.⊔%
Officers/Executive	⊔⊔.⊔%

9a. If no increase was reported (e.g., responded with a zero or blank for any of the employee categories in question 9 above), did the structure remain the same or did you make a negative adjustment?

Employee group	Number of months since last structure increase	Structure remained the same in 2007	Made a negative structure adjustment in 2007
Nonexempt Hourly Nonunion		☐	☐
Nonexempt Salaried		☐	☐
Exempt Salaried		☐	☐
Officers/Executive		☐	☐

10. By what percentage does your organization plan to increase the salary range structure for 2008?

Employee group	2008 salary range structure change
Nonexempt Hourly Nonunion	⊔⊔.⊔%
Nonexempt Salaried	⊔⊔.⊔%
Exempt Salaried	⊔⊔.⊔%
Officers/Executive	⊔⊔.⊔%

Promotions

11. Are promotional increases identifiable as a separate budget item in your organization?
   ○ Yes
   ○ No (**skip to Variable Pay section,** beginning with question 12)

11a. In 2006, what percentage of the total employee population received a promotional increase?
   ⊔⊔.⊔%

11b. In 2006, what was the average promotional increase as a percent of the promoted employee's base salary (prior to promotion)?
   ⊔⊔.⊔%

11c. What is your organization's 2007 promotional increase budget as a percent of total base salaries?
   ⊔⊔.⊔%

Variable Pay, Incentives and Bonuses

12. Does your organization currently use variable pay, including cash incentives and bonuses (excluding noncash recognition awards and all sales force incentives)?

○ Yes

○ No (**skip to 17**)

13. Which of the following variable pay awards does your organization use (excluding all sales force incentives)? (**Check all that apply.**)

○ Yes ○ No **Organization wide awards:** provided under a formal plan based on the success of the whole organization (i.e., cash profit sharing, excluding retirement plans)

○ Yes ○ No **Unit/strategic business unit awards:** provided under a formal plan based on the success of the organization/business unit (i.e., department incentive programs, manufacturing goal sharing, call center incentives)

○ Yes ○ No **Individual incentive awards:** provided under a formal plan for employees' performance in designated jobs

○ Yes ○ No **Special individual recognition awards:** given by discretion to key contributors; performance related, not for length of service (cash only)

14. For 2006, for each employee category, please indicate the following (excluding all sales force incentives):
    a) Percentage of employees eligible for variable pay
    b) Average budgeted incentive (excluding sales force incentives) as a percentage of base pay
    c) Percentage of eligible employees who actually received an award for 2006
    d) Average incentive paid (excluding sales force incentives) as a percentage of base pay

Employee group	a. Percent of employees eligible in 2006 for variable pay	b. 2006 average budgeted incentive (as a percentage of base pay)	c. Percent of employees actually paid variable pay for 2006	d. 2006 average paid incentive (as a percentage of base pay)
Nonexempt Hourly Nonunion	⎣__⎦.⎣__⎦%	⎣__⎦.⎣__⎦%	⎣__⎦.⎣__⎦%	⎣__⎦.⎣__⎦%
Nonexempt Salaried	⎣__⎦.⎣__⎦%	⎣__⎦.⎣__⎦%	⎣__⎦.⎣__⎦%	⎣__⎦.⎣__⎦%
Exempt Salaried	⎣__⎦.⎣__⎦%	⎣__⎦.⎣__⎦%	⎣__⎦.⎣__⎦%	⎣__⎦.⎣__⎦%
Officers/Executive	⎣__⎦.⎣__⎦%	⎣__⎦.⎣__⎦%	⎣__⎦.⎣__⎦%	⎣__⎦.⎣__⎦%

15. For 2007, what is the average budgeted incentive and what is your best estimate of the average paid incentive (excluding sales force incentives) as a percentage of base pay in each of the employee categories?

Employee group	2007 average budgeted incentive	2007 average paid incentive (estimate)
Nonexempt Hourly Nonunion	⎣__⎦.⎣__⎦%	⎣__⎦.⎣__⎦%
Nonexempt Salaried	⎣__⎦.⎣__⎦%	⎣__⎦.⎣__⎦%
Exempt Salaried	⎣__⎦.⎣__⎦%	⎣__⎦.⎣__⎦%
Officers/Executive	⎣__⎦.⎣__⎦%	⎣__⎦.⎣__⎦%

16. For 2008, estimate the average budgeted incentive (excluding sales force incentives) as a percentage of base pay in each of the employee categories.

Employee group	2008 average budgeted incentive
Nonexempt Hourly Nonunion	⎿⏌⎿⏌.⎿⏌%
Nonexempt Salaried	⎿⏌⎿⏌.⎿⏌%
Exempt Salaried	⎿⏌⎿⏌.⎿⏌%
Officers/Executive	⎿⏌⎿⏌.⎿⏌%

Stock/Equity-Based Compensation Programs

17. Which of the following is your organization?
    ○ Publicly traded
    ○ Privately held with stock or stocklike vehicles
    ○ Privately held, no stock (skip to 20)
    ○ Government or nonprofit (skip to 20)

18. Does your organization have stock-based incentive programs for variable compensation purposes in 2007?
    ○ Yes
    ○ No (skip to 20)

19. Please indicate which of the following stock-based incentive programs you currently offer in 2007 to each of the employee categories.

Employee group	Stock option program	Stock grant program	Phantom stock/SAR	Restricted Stock	Performance Shares
Nonexempt Hourly Nonunion					
Nonexempt Salaried					
Exempt Salaried					
Officers/Executive					

Attraction & Retention Practices

20. Which of the following has your organization used in the past 12 months to attract and retain employees? (Check all that apply.)

☐ Employee referral bonus
☐ Exempt overtime pay or time off
☐ Larger merit increase budgets
☐ Market adjustments/increase to base
☐ Paid sabbaticals
☐ Paying above market
☐ Project milestone/completion bonus

☐ Retention/stay bonus
☐ Separate salary structures
☐ Sign-on/hiring bonus
☐ Special cash bonus/group incentives salary (not organization wide)
☐ Spot bonus (individual)
☐ Stock grant programs
☐ Stock option program

21*. In what format would you prefer to receive your complimentary copy of the survey results?
○ E-mail an electronic (.pdf) copy
○ Mail a hard copy

22*. *Please provide the name of the person completing this survey and that person's contact information (You must be a WorldatWork member to participate in the 2007–08 Salary Budget Survey):

WorldatWork Member Number: | | | | | | | | |

Name: _____

Title: _____

Company: _____

Phone: _____

E-mail: _____

23*. By submitting this survey form, I understand that if mandatory (*) sections of the survey are not completed correctly, I will not be eligible as a participant to receive a complimentary copy of the survey report.
○ I understand and agree to the statement above.

If you have a question about how to complete the survey, please call WorldatWork Knowledge Services at 480/922-2092.

The deadline to submit the survey is April 27, 2007
Fax or mail your completed survey to:
WorldatWork Survey Team • Fax 480/483–8352 • Toll-free fax 866/816–2962
14040 N. Northsight Blvd. • Scottsdale, AZ 85260

---

*Mandatory section/question

CHAPTER 9

Building Pay Structures That Recognize Employee Contributions

Chapter Outline

Learning Objectives

In this chapter, you will learn about

1. Fundamental principles of pay structure design

2. Merit pay system structures

3. Sales incentive pay structures

4. Pay-for-knowledge structures

5. Pay structure variations—broadbanding and two-tier wage plans

Pay structures assign different pay rates for jobs of unequal worth and provide the framework for recognizing differences in individual employee contributions. No two employees possess identical credentials, nor do they perform the same jobs equally well. Companies recognize these differences by paying individuals according to their credentials, knowledge, or job performance. When completed, pay structures should define the boundaries for recognizing employee contributions. Employee contributions in this context correspond to the pay bases that we addressed in previous chapters (i.e., seniority, merit, incentive pay, and person-based pay). Pay structures also have strategic value. Well-designed structures should promote the retention of valued employees. Most companies support pay-for-performance systems.

In this chapter, we will address how companies structure these pay bases, with the exception of seniority, which is typically not the main basis for pay in companies. We will start out by considering the fundamental process of constructing pay structures. We will then examine the design elements of merit pay structures. Then, we will move on to specific pay structures, including merit pay, sales incentive pay, and pay-for-knowledge.

CONSTRUCTING A PAY STRUCTURE

Compensation specialists develop pay structures based on five steps:

- Deciding on how many pay structures to construct
- Determining a market pay line
- Defining pay grades
- Calculating pay ranges for each pay grade
- Evaluating the results

Step 1: Deciding on the Number of Pay Structures

Companies often establish more than one pay structure, depending on market rates and the company's job structure. Common pay structures include exempt and nonexempt structures, pay structures based on job families, and pay structures based on geography.

Exempt and Nonexempt Pay Structures

As you will recall, these categories reflect a distinction in the Fair Labor Standards Act. Exempt jobs are not subject to the overtime pay provisions of the act. Core compensation terms for these jobs are usually expressed as an annual salary. Nonexempt jobs are subject to the overtime pay provision of the act. The core compensation for these jobs is therefore expressed as an hourly pay rate. Companies establish these pay structures for administrative ease. Some broadly consistent features distinguish exempt from nonexempt jobs: Exempt jobs, by the definition of the Fair Labor Standards Act, are generally supervisory, professional, managerial, or executive jobs that contain a wide variety of duties. Nonexempt jobs are generally nonsupervisory in nature, and the duties tend to be narrowly defined.

Pay Structures Based on Job Family

Executive, managerial, professional, technical, clerical, and craft represent distinct job families. Pay structures are also defined on the basis of job family, each of which shows a distinct salary pattern in the market. For example, the Davis–Bacon Act requires contractors and subcontractors to pay wages at least equal to those prevailing in the area where work is performed. This act applies only to employers with federal or federally financed contracts worth more than $2,000 for the construction, alteration, or repair of public works or buildings. Moreover, the Davis–Bacon Act also applies only to laborers and mechanics, excluding clerical, professional, and managerial employees. Thus, companies holding federal contracts meeting these criteria have limited latitude for setting pay for certain jobs; however, the latitude for setting pay rates for other jobs is greater.

Pay Structures Based on Geography

Companies with multiple, geographically dispersed locations such as sales offices, manufacturing plants, service centers, and corporate offices may establish pay structures based on going rates in different geographic regions because local conditions may influence pay levels. The cost of living is substantially higher in the northeast region than in the south and southeast regions of the United States. For example, in 2007, a person earning $100,000 annually in Huntsville, Alabama, would have to earn about $177,000 in Boston, Massachusetts, to maintain a comparable standard of living.

Step 2: Determining a Market Pay Line

We discussed how to determine the market pay line in Chapter 8. Again, the market pay line is representative of typical market pay rates relative to a company's job structure. Pay levels that correspond with the market pay line are market-competitive pay rates. Figure 9-1 illustrates a market pay line for a series of clerical jobs. Pay rates that fall along the market pay line represent competitive pay rates based on the company's selection of a relevant labor market, and these rates promote internal consistency because they increase with the value of jobs. The clerk I job has the least complex and demanding duties, and it has fewer worker requirements than do the remaining clerk jobs (clerk II, clerk III, and chief clerk).

Step 3: Defining Pay Grades

Pay grades group jobs for pay policy application. Human resource (HR) professionals typically group jobs into pay grades based on similar compensable factors and value. These criteria are not precise. In fact, no one formula determines what is sufficiently similar in terms of content and value to warrant grouping jobs into a pay grade.

Job groupings are ultimately influenced by such other factors as management's philosophy, as discussed earlier. Wider pay grades (i.e., grades that include a relatively large number of jobs) minimize hierarchy and social distance between employees. Narrower pay grades tend to promote hierarchy and social distance. Figure 9-2 illustrates pay grade definitions, based on the jobs used in Figure 9-1.

Human resource professionals can develop pay grade widths as either "absolute" job evaluation point spreads or as percentage-based job evaluation point

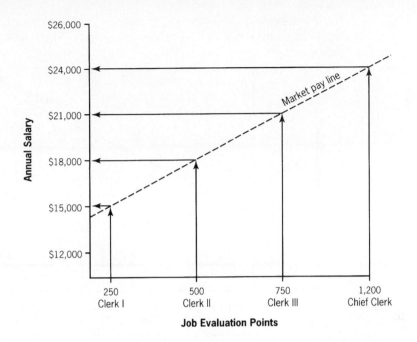

Clerk I

Employees receive training in basic office support procedures, the operation of office equipment, and the specific activities of the unit. Tasks assigned are simple and repetitive in nature and are performed in accordance with explicit instructions and clearly established guidelines. Sample duties include: files materials in established alphabetical order and prepares new file folders and affixes labels. Clerk Is must possess a high school diploma or equivalent.

Clerk II

Employees work under general supervision in support of an office. They perform routine office support tasks that require a knowledge of standard office procedures and the ability to operate a variety of office equipment. Sample duties include: prepares simple factual statements or reports involving computations such as totals or subtotals and composes memos requesting or transmitting factual information. Clerk IIs must possess a high school diploma or equivalent and 1 year work experience performing simple clerical tasks.

Clerk III

Employees work under general supervision in support of an office. They perform office support tasks requiring knowledge of general office and departmental procedures and methods and ability to operate a variety of office equipment. Sample duties include: reconciles discrepancies between unit records and those of other departments and assigns and reviews work performed by Clerks I and II. Clerk IIIs must possess a high school diploma or equivalent, 2 years work experience performing moderately complex clerical tasks, and completed coursework (five in all) in such related topics as word processing and basic accounting principles.

Chief Clerk

Employees work under direction in support of an office. They perform a wide variety of office support tasks that require the use of judgment and initiative. A knowledge of the organization, programs, practices, and procedures of the unit is central to the performance of the duties. Chief clerks must possess a high school diploma or equivalent, 4 years work experience performing moderately difficult clerical tasks, and an associate's degree in office management.

FIGURE 9-1 Pay Structure for Clerk Jobs

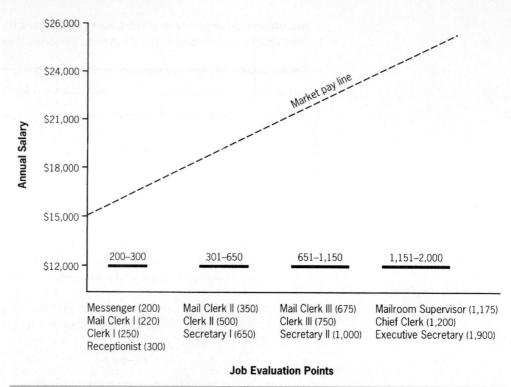

FIGURE 9-2   Pay Grade Definitions

spreads. When absolute point spreads are used, grades are based on a set number of job evaluation points for each grade. For example, a compensation professional establishes pay grades equal to 200 points each. Grade 1 includes jobs that range from 1 to 200 job evaluation points, Grade 2 contains jobs that range from 201 to 400 points, and so on.

Companies may choose to vary the "absolute" point spread by increasing the point spread as they move up the pay structure, in recognition of the broader range of skills that higher pay grades represent. For example, certified public accounting jobs require a broader range of skills (i.e., knowledge of financial accounting principles and both state and federal tax codes) than do mailroom clerk jobs. Companies often assign trainee positions to the lower, narrower pay grades because trainees generally have limited job-relevant skills. For instance, Grade 1 may contain trainee positions with job evaluation scores that range from 1 to 150, Grade 2 may contain basic jobs beyond traineeships with scores of 151 to 400, and Grade 3 may include advanced jobs with scores of 401 to 1,000.

Step 4: Calculating Pay Ranges for Each Pay Grade

Pay ranges build upon pay grades. Pay grades represent the horizontal dimension of pay structures (i.e., job evaluation points). **Pay ranges** represent the vertical dimension (pay rates). Pay ranges include midpoint, minimum, and maximum pay rates. The minimum and maximum values denote the acceptable lower and upper bounds of pay for the jobs within particular pay grades. Figure 9-3 illustrates pay ranges.

Human resource professionals establish midpoints first, followed by minimum and maximum values. The **midpoint pay value** is the halfway mark between the range minimum and maximum rates. Midpoints generally match values along the market

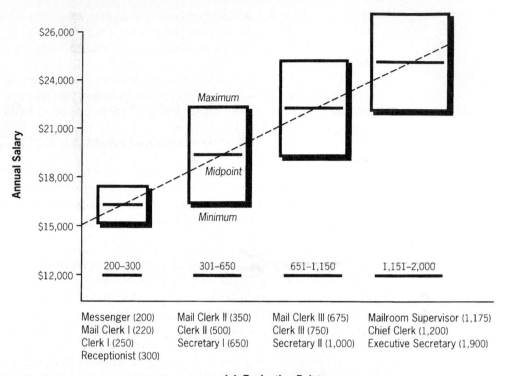

FIGURE 9-3   Pay Range Definitions

pay line, representing the competitive market rate determined by the analysis of compensation survey data. Thus, the midpoint may reflect the market average or median (Chapter 8).

A company sets the midpoints for its pay ranges according to its competitive pay policy, as discussed in Chapter 8. If the company wants to lead the market with respect to pay offerings (market lead policy), it sets the midpoint of the ranges higher than the average for similar jobs at other companies. Companies wanting to pay according to the market norm (market match policy) should set midpoints equal to the market average. Companies wanting to lag the market (market lag policy) would set the midpoints below the market average. A company's base-pay policy line graphically connects the midpoints of each pay grade.

How do compensation professionals calculate pay grade minimums and maximums? They may fashion pay grade minimums and maximums after the minimums and maximums for pay grades that their competitors have established. An alternate approach is to set the pay grade minimums and maximums on the basis of range spread. A **range spread** is the difference between the maximum and minimum pay rates of a given pay grade. It is expressed as a percentage of the difference between the minimum and maximum divided by the minimum.

Companies generally apply different range spreads across pay grades. They most commonly use progressively higher range spreads for pay grades that contain more valuable jobs in terms of the companies' criteria. Smaller range spreads characterize pay grades that contain relatively narrowly defined jobs that require simple skills with generally low responsibility. Entry-level clerical employees perform limited duties ranging from filing folders alphabetically to preparing file folders and affixing labels. These jobs presumably represent bottom-floor opportunities for employees who will probably advance to higher-level jobs as they acquire the skills needed to perform these jobs proficiently. Advanced clerical employees review and analyze forms and documents to determine the adequacy and acceptability of information.

Higher-level jobs afford employees greater promotion opportunities than entry-level jobs. Employees also tend to remain in higher pay grades longer, and the specialized skills associated with higher pay grade jobs are considered valuable. It therefore makes sense to apply larger range spreads to these pay grades. The following are typical range spreads for different kinds of positions:[1]

- 20 to 25 percent: lower-level service, production, and maintenance
- 30 to 40 percent: clerical, technical, and paraprofessional
- 40 to 50 percent: high-level professional, administrative, and middle management
- 50 percent and above: high-level managerial and executive

After deciding on range spread, compensation professionals calculate minimum and maximum rates. Figure 9-4 illustrates the calculation of minimum and maximum rates based on knowledge of the pay grade midpoint (as discussed earlier in Step 1) and the chosen range spread. Table 9-1 illustrates the impact of alternative range spread values on minimum and maximum values. This approach is typically applied when a company chooses to base the minimum and maximum rates on budgetary constraints. We will discuss budgeting issues later in this chapter.

Adjacent pay ranges usually overlap with other pay ranges so that the highest rate paid in one range is above the lowest rate of the successive pay grade. Figure 9-5 illustrates how to calculate pay range overlap. Overlapping pay ranges allow companies to promote employees to the next level without adding to their pay. Nonoverlapping pay ranges require pay increases for job promotions. Compensation professionals express overlap as a percentage. For example, the degree of overlap between pay range A and pay range B is about 33 percent.

Pay Compression

The minimum pay rate for a range usually is the lowest pay rate that the company will pay for jobs that fall within that particular pay grade. In theory, newly hired employees receive pay that is at or near the minimum. In practice, new employees often receive well above minimum pay rates, sometimes only slightly below or even higher than the pay moderately tenured employees receive. **Pay compression** occurs whenever a company's pay spread between newly hired or less qualified employees and more qualified job incumbents is small.[2]

FIGURE 9-4   Calculation of Range Spread

	Steps	
1. Identify the midpoint:	$20,000	Maximum = $23,333.33
2. Determine the range spread:	40%	
3. Calculate the minimum:		
$$\frac{midpoint}{100\% + (range\ spread/2)}$$	$$= \frac{\$20,000}{100\% + (40\%/2)}$$	Range spread = 40%
	$= \$16,666.67$	Midpoint = $20,000
4. Calculate the maximum:		
minimum + (range spread × minimum)	$= \$16,666.67 + (40\% \times \$16,666.67)$	
	$= \$23,333.33$	Minimum = $16,666.67

TABLE 9-1 The Impact of Alternative Range Spreads on Pay Range Minimum and Maximum Values, with Midpoint of $25,000

	Range Spread			
	20%	*50%*	*80%*	*120%*
Minimum:				
$\dfrac{\text{midpoint}}{100\% + (\text{range spread}/2)}$	$22,727	$20,000	$17,857	$15,625
Maximum:				
minimum + (range spread × minimum)	$27,272	$30,000	$32,143	$34,375
Difference between maximum and minimum values	$4,545	$10,000	$14,286	$18,750

Two situations result in pay compression. The first is a company's failure to raise pay range minimums and maximums. Companies that retain set range maximums over time limit increase amounts. For example, let's assume that the entry-level starting salaries for newly minted certified public accountants have increased 7 percent annually for the last 5 years. Tax-It, a small accounting firm, did not increase its pay range minimums and maximums for entry-level accountants during the same period because of lackluster profits. Nevertheless, Tax-It hired several new accountants at the prevailing market rate. Failure to pay competitive pay rates would hinder Tax-It's

FIGURE 9-5 Calculating Pay Range Overlap

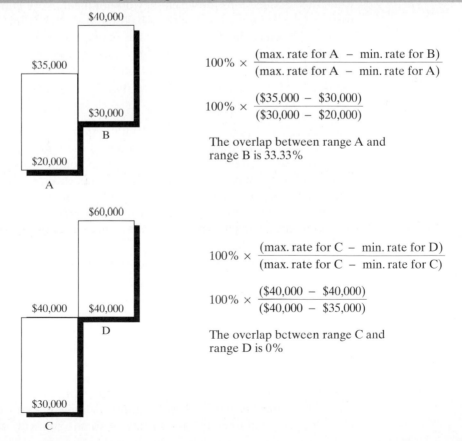

$$100\% \times \frac{(\text{max. rate for A } - \text{ min. rate for B})}{(\text{max. rate for A } - \text{ min. rate for A})}$$

$$100\% \times \frac{(\$35,000 - \$30,000)}{(\$30,000 - \$20,000)}$$

The overlap between range A and range B is 33.33%

$$100\% \times \frac{(\text{max. rate for C } - \text{ min. rate for D})}{(\text{max. rate for C } - \text{ min. rate for C})}$$

$$100\% \times \frac{(\$40,000 - \$40,000)}{(\$40,000 - \$35,000)}$$

The overlap between range C and range D is 0%

ability to recruit talented accountants. As a result, many of the Tax-It accountants with 5 or fewer years' experience have lower salaries (or slightly higher salaries at best) than newly hired accountants without work experience. The second situation that results in pay compression is a scarcity of qualified candidates for particular jobs. When the supply of such candidates falls behind a company's demand, wages for newly hired employees rise, reflecting a bidding process among companies for qualified candidates.

Pay compression can threaten companies' competitive advantage. Dysfunctional employee turnover is a likely consequence of pay compression. Dysfunctional turnover represents high-performing employees' voluntary termination of their employment. High-performing employees will probably perceive their pay as inequitable because they are receiving lower pay relative to their positive contributions (i.e., experience and demonstrated performance) than newly hired employees who are receiving similar pay.

How can companies minimize pay compression? Maximum pay rates represent the most that a company is willing to pay an individual for jobs that fall in that particular range. Maximum pay rates should be set close to the maximum paid by other companies in the labor market for similar jobs. Setting competitive maximum rates enables a company to raise pay rates for high-quality employees who may consider employment opportunities with a competitor; however, maximum rates should not exceed maximum rates offered by competitors for comparable jobs because high maximums represent costs to the company over and above what are needed to be competitive.

Green Circle Pay Rates

Employees sometimes receive below-minimum pay rates for their pay ranges, especially when they assume jobs for which they do not meet every minimum requirement in the worker specification section of the job description. Below-minimum pay range rates are known as **green circle rates**. The pay rates of employees who are paid at green circle rates should be brought within the normal pay range as quickly as possible, which requires that both employer and employee take the necessary steps to eliminate whatever deficiencies in skill or experience that warranted paying below the pay range minimum.

Red Circle Pay Rates

On occasion, companies must pay certain employees greater than maximum rates for their pay ranges. Known as **red circle rates**, these higher pay rates help retain valued employees who have lucrative job offers from competitors. On the other hand, exemplary employees may receive red circle rates for exceptional job performance, particularly when a promotion to a higher pay grade is not granted. Red circle rates also apply to employees who receive job demotions to pay grades with lower maximum rates than the employees' current pay. Companies usually reduce demoted employees' pay over time until they receive pay that is consistent with their new jobs. In this case, red circle rates allow employees a chance to adjust to pay decreases.

Step 5: Evaluating the Results

After compensation professionals establish pay structures according to the previous steps, they must evaluate the results. They must specifically analyze significant differences between the company's internal values for jobs and the market's values for the same jobs. If discrepancies are evident, the company must reconsider the internal values they have placed on jobs. If their valuation of particular jobs exceeds the market's valuation of the same jobs, they must decide whether higher-than-market pay rates will undermine attainment of competitive advantage. If a company undervalues jobs relative to the market, managers must consider whether these discrepancies will limit the company's ability to recruit and retain highly qualified individuals.

Compensation professionals must also consider each employee's pay level relative to the midpoint of the pay grade. Again, the midpoint represents a company's competitive stance relative to the market. **Compa-ratios** index the relative competitiveness of internal pay rates based on pay range midpoints. Compa-ratios are calculated as follows:

$$\frac{\text{Employee's pay rate}}{\text{Pay range midpoint}}$$

Compa-ratios are interpreted as follows: A compa-ratio of 1 means that the employee's pay rate equals the pay range midpoint. A compa-ratio less than 1 means that the employee's pay rate falls below the competitive pay rate for the job. Companies with market lag policies strive for compa-ratios of less than 1. A compa-ratio that is greater than 1 means that an employee's pay rate exceeds the competitive pay rate for the job.

Human resource professionals also can use compa-ratios to index job groups that fall within a particular pay grade. Compa-ratios specifically may be calculated to index the competitive position of a job—by averaging the pay rates for each job incumbent. Moreover, compa-ratios may be calculated for all jobs that comprise a pay grade, departments, or such functional areas as accounting.

Compa-ratios provide invaluable information about the competitiveness of companies' pay rates. Compensation professionals can use compa-ratios as diagnostic tools to judge the competitiveness of their companies' pay rates. Compa-ratios that exceed 1 tell compensation professionals that pay is highly competitive with the market. Compa-ratios that fall below 1 tell them that pay is not competitive with the market and that they should consider another course of action to increase pay over a reasonable period.

We've reviewed the elements of pay structures and the steps compensation professionals follow to construct them. Next, we will consider three popular pay structures that should be familiar to compensation professionals:

- Merit pay structure
- Sales incentive compensation structure
- Pay-for-knowledge structure

DESIGNING MERIT PAY SYSTEMS

As we noted in Chapter 4, companies that use merit pay systems must ensure that employees see definite links between pay and performance. We also reviewed the rationale for using merit pay systems, as well as the possible limitations of this kind of pay system. Establishing an effective merit pay program that recognizes employee contributions requires avoiding such pitfalls as ineffective performance appraisal methods and poor communication regarding the link between pay and performance. In addition to these considerations, managers interested in establishing a merit pay system must determine merit increase amounts, timing, and the type of merit pay increase (i.e., permanent or recurring increases versus one-time or nonrecurring additions to base pay). They must also settle on base pay levels relative to the base pay of functionally similar jobs.[3]

Merit Increase Amounts

Merit pay increases should reflect prior job performance levels and motivate employees to perform their best. As managers establish merit increase amounts, they must consider both past performance levels and they must establish rates that will motivate employees even after the impact of inflation and payroll deductions. Updating compensation survey data should account for increases in consumer prices (Chapter 8). As we noted in Chapter 4, "just-meaningful pay increases" refer to the minimum amounts employees will see as making a meaningful change in their compensation.[4] Trivial pay increases for average or better employees will not reinforce their performance or motivate them.

No precise mathematical formula determines the minimum merit increase that will positively affect performance; managers must consider three research findings.[5] First, boosting the merit increase amount will not necessarily improve productivity because research has shown diminishing marginal returns on each additional dollar allocated to merit increases.[6] In other words, each additional merit increase dollar was associated with smaller increases in production.

Second, employees' perceptions of just-meaningful differences in merit increases depend on their cost of living, their attitudes toward the job, and their expectations of rewards from the job. For employees who value pay for meeting economic necessity, a just-meaningful difference in pay increase tends to depend upon changes in the cost of living. On the other hand, for employees who value pay as a form of recognition, the size of the expected pay raise (versus cost of living) affects a just-meaningful difference.[7]

Third, for the pay increase to be considered meaningful, the employee must see the size of the increase as substantive in a relative sense as well as in an absolute sense.[8] **Equity theory** suggests that an employee must regard his or her own ratio of merit increase pay to performance as similar to the ratio for other comparably performing people in the company. In practical terms, managers should award the largest merit pay increases to employees with the best performance, and they should award the smallest increases to employees with the lowest acceptable performance. The difference between these merit increases should be approximately equal to the differences in performance.

It is also essential that compensation professionals design plans that reinforce employees' motivation to perform well, with just-meaningful pay increases and merit increase percentages that clearly distinguish among employees based on their performance; however, the best-laid plans don't always lead to the desired results. Well-designed merit pay structures (and others that we discuss shortly) will fail without adequate funding.

Compensation budgets are blueprints that describe the allocation of monetary resources to fund pay structures. Compensation professionals index budget increases that fund merit pay programs in percentage terms. For example, a 10 percent increase for next year's budget means that it will be 10 percent greater than the size of the current year's budget. This value is often an indicator of the average pay increase employees will receive. It is obvious that the greater the increase in the compensation budget, the more flexibility compensation professionals will have in developing innovative systems with substantial motivating potential.

The magnitude of the increases in compensation budgets in recent years has unfortunately been just slightly more than the average increases in cost of living. For example, the average earnings for all production or nonsupervisory employees in the United States increased only 2.8 percent in 2006, and earnings were expected to increase only 3.1 percent in 2007.[9] Although this value varies by occupation, industry, and region of the country, it does reflect a trend in the United States of stagnant growth in compensation budgets. The picture becomes less positive because the increase in cost of living for the same period was 3.1 percent.[10] This means that, on average, annual merit pay raises fell below the increase in cost of living by 0.3 percent, taking the motivational value out of pay increases.

Timing

The vast majority of companies allocate merit increases, as well as cost-of-living and other increases, annually. At present, companies typically take one of two approaches in timing these pay raises. Companies may establish a **common review date** or **common review period** so that all employees' performance are evaluated on the same date or during the same period (e.g., the month of June, which immediately follows a company's peak activity period). Best suited for smaller companies, common review dates reduce the administrative burden of the plan by concentrating staff members' efforts to limited periods.

On the other hand, companies may review employee performance and award merit increases on the **employee's anniversary date** (i.e., the day on which the employee began to work for the company). Most employees will thus have different evaluation dates. Although these staggered review dates may not monopolize supervisors' time, this approach can be administratively burdensome because reviews must be conducted regularly throughout the year.

Recurring versus Nonrecurring Merit Pay Increases

Companies have traditionally awarded merit pay increases permanently, and permanent increases are sometimes associated with some undesirable side effects (e.g., placing excessive cost burdens on the employer). In terms of costs, U.S. companies are increasingly concerned with containing costs as just one initiative in their quest to establish and sustain competitive advantage in the marketplace. Companies may advocate **nonrecurring merit increases** (i.e., lump sum bonuses), which lend themselves well to cost containment and have recently begun to gain some favor among unions, including the International Brotherhood of Electrical Workers.[11] Lump sum bonuses strengthen the pay-for-performance link and minimize costs because these increases are not permanent, and subsequent percentage increases are not based on higher base pay levels.

Present Level of Base Pay

Pay structures specify acceptable pay ranges for jobs within each pay grade. Thus, each job's base pay level should fall within the minimum and maximum rates for its respective pay grade. In addition, compensation professionals should encourage managers to offer similar base pay to new employees performing similar jobs unless employees' qualifications (i.e., education and relevant work experience) justify pay differences. This practice is consistent with the mandates of several laws (Chapter 3) (i.e., Title VII of the Civil Rights Act of 1964, the Equal Pay Act of 1963, and the Age Discrimination in Employment Act of 1967). Of course, employees' merit pay increases should vary with their performance.

Rewarding Performance: The Merit Pay Grid

Table 9-2 illustrates a typical merit pay grid that managers use to assign merit increases to employees. Managers determine pay raise amounts by two factors jointly: employees' performance ratings and the position of employees' present base pay rates within pay ranges. Pay raise amounts are expressed as percentages of base pay. For instance, let's say that two employees will each receive a 5 percent merit pay increase. One employee is paid on an hourly basis, earning $8.50 per hour, and the other is paid on an annual basis, earning $32,000. The employee whose pay is based on an hourly rate (usually nonexempt in accord with the Fair Labor Standards Act (i.e., one who must be paid overtime for time worked in excess of 40 hours per week) receives a pay raise of $0.44 per hour, increasing her hourly pay to $8.94. The employee whose pay is based on an annual rate, typically exempt from the Fair Labor Standards Act provisions, receives a pay increase of $1,600, boosting her annual pay to $33,600.

TABLE 9-2   Merit Pay Increase Grid

		Performance Rating				
		Excellent	**Above Average**	**Average**	**Below Average**	**Poor**
Q4 ⇒	$70,000					
	$65,000	5%	3%	1%	0%	0%
	$60,000					
Q3 ⇒	$55,000					
	$50,000	7%	5%	3%	0%	0%
	$45,000					
Q2 ⇒	$40,000					
	$35,000	9%	7%	6%	2%	0%
	$30,000					
Q1 ⇒	$25,000					
	$20,000	12%	10%	8%	4%	0%
	$15,000					

In Table 9-2, employees whose current annual salary falls in the second quartile of the pay range and whose performance rates an average score receive a 6 percent merit pay increase. Employees whose current annual salary falls in the first quartile of the pay range and whose job performance is excellent receive a 12 percent merit pay increase. The term *cell* (as in spreadsheet software programs such as Microsoft Excel) is used to reference the intersection of quartile ranking and performance rating. Table 9-2 contains 20 cells.

Employees' Performance Ratings

Merit pay systems use performance appraisals to determine employees' performance. Where merit pay systems are in place, an overall performance rating guides the pay raise decision. In Table 9-2, an employee receives any one of five performance ratings ranging from "Poor" to "Excellent." As you can see when we hold position in pay range constant, pay raise amounts increase with level of performance. This pattern fits well with the logic underlying pay-for-performance principles—it recognizes higher performance with greater rewards.

Employees' Positions within the Pay Range

Employees' positions within the pay range are indexed by quartile ranking, which, in Chapter 8, we described as a measure of dispersion. Again, quartiles allow compensation professionals to describe the distribution of data (i.e., in this case, hourly or annual base pay amount) based on four groupings known as quartiles. In Table 9-2, the first quartile is the point below which 25 percent of the salary data lie (and above which 75 percent of the salary data are found), which is $25,000. In this example, 25 percent of the salary figures are less than or equal to $25,000, and 75 percent of these figures are greater than $25,000. The second quartile is the point below which 50 percent of the salary data lie (and above which 50 percent of the salary figures are found), which is $40,000 for this example. The third quartile is the point below which 75 percent of the salary figures lie (and above which 25 percent of the salary figures are found), which is $55,000 for this example. The fourth quartile is the point below which all of the salary data lie, which is $70,000. The lower a person's pay falls within its designated pay grade (e.g., the first quartile versus the third quartile) the higher the percentage pay raise, all else being equal. Along those lines, the higher a person's pay within its grade, the lower the percentage pay raise, all else being equal.

Holding performance ratings constant, compensation professionals reduce merit pay increase percentages as quartile ranks increase to control employees' progression through their pay ranges. Pay grade minimums and maximums reflect both corporate criteria about the value of various groups of unlike jobs and may be dictated by budgeting. We'll look at the issue of budgeting shortly. Let's take the case of two employees whose performance ratings are identical but whose base pay places them in different quartiles of the pay grade (i.e., one in the third quartile and the other in the first quartile). If these employees were to receive the same pay raise percentage, the base pay rate for the employee in the third quartile likely would exceed the maximum pay rate for the range more quickly than would the base pay rate for the employee in the first quartile.

Merit Pay Increase Budgets

Now that we've considered the design principles for merit pay grids, we'll take a closer look at budgetary considerations. Budgets limit the merit pay increase percentages in each cell. A **merit pay increase budget** is expressed as a percentage of the sum of employees' current base pay. For instance, let's assume that a company's top financial officers and compensation professionals agree to a 5 percent merit pay increase budget. Let's also assume that the sum of all employees' current base pay is $10 million based on an employee population of 350. A 5 percent merit pay increase budget for this example equals $500,000, that is, 5 percent of the sum of all employees' current base pay totaling $10,000,000 (5% × $10,000,000). In other words, the company will distribute $500,000 to increase current base pay of its employees. As described earlier, merit pay increases awarded to individual employees will vary according to performance level and position in the pay range; however, the average of the individual pay increases must not exceed the allotted merit pay increase budget, again, $500,000 in this example. As an aside, the typical merit pay increase budget today ranges between 2 and 3 percent. This range is much lower than the average 4 percent increase in recent past years.[12]

Compensation professionals begin plans for setting the merit increase pay grid within the estimated merit increase pay budget with the following six steps:

1. Compensation professionals ask managers and supervisors to indicate the percentage of employees who they expect will fall in each of the performance categories in the performance appraisal instrument. Managers will often use the actual distribution of employees based on recent past years as an estimate for budget planning. The sample merit pay grid illustrated in Table 9 2 lists five performance categories. For illustrative purposes, let's assume the following performance distribution for employees:
    * Excellent: 10 percent
    * Above average: 20 percent
    * Average: 40 percent
    * Below average: 25 percent
    * Poor: 5 percent

2. Compensation professionals rely on position in the pay range to determine the percentage of employees whose pay falls into each pay quartile. For example, let's assume the following distribution of employees in each pay quartile:
    * Q4: 20 percent
    * Q3: 25 percent
    * Q2: 40 percent
    * Q1: 15 percent

In other words, 20 percent of employees earn pay that falls in the range from $55,000 to $70,000 (fourth quartile) in Table 9-2. Similarly, 25 percent of the employees earn pay that falls in the range from $40,000 to $55,000 (third quartile). The same rationale applies to the first and second quartiles.

3. Compensation professionals combine both sets of information to determine the percentage of employees who fall into each cell. The percentage of employees whose performance rating is excellent and whose base pay falls in the fourth quartile equals 2.0 percent (10 percent × 20 percent). The sum of the cell percentages totals 100 percent.

	Excellent	Above Average	Average	Below Average	Poor
Q4	10% × 20% = 2%	20% × 20% = 4%	40% × 20% = 8%	25% × 20% = 5%	5% × 20% = 1%
Q3	10% × 25% = 2.5%	20% × 25% = 5%	40% × 25% = 10%	25% × 25% = 6.25%	5% × 25% = 1.25%
Q2	10% × 40% = 4%	20% × 40% = 8%	40% × 40% = 16%	25% × 40% = 10%	5% × 40% = 2%
Q1	10% × 15% = 1.5%	20% × 15% = 3%	40% × 15% = 6%	25% × 15% = 3.75%	5% × 15% = 0.75%

4. Next, compensation professionals calculate the expected number of employees who fall into each cell. It is important to remember that this is the expected (versus actual) number of employees because managers provide only an estimate of employees' performance distribution. For this example, let's assume that the company employs 350 people. The number of employees whose performance rating is excellent and whose base pay falls in the fourth quartile equals 7 (350 people × 2 percent).

	Excellent	Above Average	Average	Below Average	Poor
Q4	350 × 2% = 7	350 × 4% = 14	350 × 8% = 28	350 × 5% = 17.5	350 × 1% = 3.5
Q3	350 × 2.5% = 8.75	350 × 5% = 17.5	350 × 10% = 35	350 × 6.25% = 21.875	350 × 1.25% = 4.375
Q2	350 × 4% = 14	350 × 8% = 28	350 × 16% = 56	350 × 10% = 35	350 × 2% = 7
Q1	350 × 1.5% = 5.25	350 × 3% = 10.5	350 × 6% = 21	350 × 3.75% = 13.125	350 × 0.75% = 2.625

5. Compensation professionals now distribute the merit increase budget amount ($500,000) to each cell based on the following formula:

Expected number of employees in cell × Desired pay increase for cell (%) × Current median pay level for the current quartile

We calculated the expected number of employees in each cell in the previous step. The desired pay increase amount is an estimate that we made (see Table 9-2). Compensation professionals usually specify these percentage amounts initially on pay for performance and equity considerations as described earlier (that is, holding performance constant, individuals in higher pay quartiles receive smaller percentage increases than employees in lower pay quartiles). We calculate the median values as described in Chapter 8. Let's assume for this example that the medians for each quartile are:

Q4 $65,000
Q3 $50,000
Q2 $35,000
Q1 $20,000

	Excellent	Above Average	Average	Below Average	Poor
Q4	$7 \times 5\% \times \$65,000$ $= \$22,750$	$14 \times 3\% \times \$65,000$ $= \$27,300$	$28 \times 1\% \times \$65,000$ $= \$18,200$	$17.5 \times 0\% \times \$65,000$ $= \$0$	$.5 \times 0\% \times \$65,000$ $= \$0$
Q3	$8.75 \times 7\% \times \$50,000$ $= \$30,625$	$17.5 \times 5\% \times \$50,000$ $= \$43,750$	$35 \times 3\% \times \$50,000$ $= \$52,500$	$21.875 \times 0\% \times \$50,000$ $= \$0$	$4.375 \times 0\% \times \$50,000$ $= \$0$
Q2	$14 \times 9\% \times \$35,000$ $= \$44,100$	$28 \times 7\% \times \$35,000$ $= \$68,600$	$56 \times 6\% \times \$35,000$ $= \$117,600$	$35 \times 2\% \times \$35,000$ $= \$24,500$	$7 \times 0\% \times \$35,000$ $= \$0$
Q1	$5.25 \times 12\% \times \$20,000$ $= \$12,600$	$10.5 \times 10\% \times \$20,000$ $= \$21,000$	$21 \times 7\% \times \$20,000$ $= \$29,400$	$13.125 \times 4\% \times \$20,000$ $= \$10,500$	$2.625 \times 0\% \times \$20,000$ $= \$0$

The sum of expected merit pay increases equals $523,425.

6. Compensation professionals check whether the expected merit increase total fits within the actual budgeted amount. In this example, the sum of expected increases exceeds the budgeted amount by $23,425 (i.e., $523,425 − $500,000). When the expected increase amount exceeds the budgeted amount, compensation professionals adjust the percentages in the cell with the following considerations in mind: lowering costs, recognizing performance differences, and equity.

Pay structures based on merit differ from sales compensation in at least two key ways. First, whereas sales compensation programs center on incentives that specify rewards an employee will receive for meeting a preestablished—often objective—level of performance, merit pay programs generally base an employee's reward on someone else's (most often the employee's supervisor's) subjective evaluation of the employee's past performance. Second, in most instances, a sales employee's compensation is variable to the extent that it is composed of incentives. Under a merit pay system, an employee earns a base pay appropriate for the job (as discussed earlier in this chapter) that is augmented periodically with permanent pay raises or one-time bonuses.

DESIGNING SALES INCENTIVE COMPENSATION PLANS

Compensation programs for salespeople rely on incentives.[13] Sales compensation programs can help businesses meet their objectives by aligning the financial self-interest of sales professionals with the company's marketing objectives.[14] By extension, sales compensation programs can help companies achieve strategic objectives by linking sales professionals' compensation to fulfilling customer needs or other marketing objectives (e.g., increasing market share). Thus, sales compensation plans derive their objectives more or less directly from strategic marketing objectives, which, in turn, are derived from company competitive strategy. Particular sales objectives include:[15]

- *Improve sales productivity:* more volume and profit from current investment in sales resources.

  New-customer sales volume
  New-product sales volume

New balanced product-line sales
Reduced "churn" among current customers.

- *Improve sales coverage of current customers:* Regardless of industry, customers want flexibility, customization, faster response, and personalized service. To meet these requirements, market-leading companies improve the coverage of their current customers. This often means investments in new ways to interact with customers.

Overall account volume
Greater share of the account's business
Achievement of customer objectives
More lines of business sold
Account profitability

- *Grow sales overall:* Track the percentage of sales realized from the following:

New direct customers
New distribution channels
New products

Alternative Sales Compensation Plans

Companies usually use one of five kinds of sales incentive plans. The type of plan appropriate for any given company will depend on the company's competitive strategy. The order of presentation roughly represents the degree of risk (from lowest to highest) to employees.

- Salary-only plans
- Salary-plus-bonus plans
- Salary-plus-commission plans
- Commission-plus-draw plans
- Commission-only plans

Salary-Only Plans

Under **salary-only plans**, sales professionals receive fixed base compensation, which does not vary with the level of units sold, increase in market share, or any other indicator of sales performance. From the employees' perspective, salary-only plans are relatively risk-free because they can expect a certain amount of income. From a company's perspective, salary-only plans are burdensome because the company must compensate its sales employees regardless of their achievement levels. Thus, salary-only plans do not fit well with the directive to link pay with performance through at-risk pay. Nevertheless, salary-only plans may be appropriate for such particular kinds of selling situations as:

- Sales of high-priced products and services or technical products with long lead times for sales
- Situations in which sales representatives are primarily responsible for generating demand, but other employees actually close the sales
- Situations in which it is impossible to follow sales results for each salesperson (i.e., where sales are accomplished through team efforts)
- Training and other periods when sales representatives are unlikely to make sales on their own

Salary-Plus-Bonus Plans

Salary-plus-bonus plans offer a set salary coupled with a bonus. Bonuses usually are single payments that reward employees for achievement of specific, exceptional goals.

For a real estate agent, generating in excess of $2 million in residential sales for a 1-year period may mean earning a bonus totaling several thousand dollars.

Salary-Plus-Commission Plans

Commission is a form of incentive compensation based on a percentage of the selling price of a product or service. **Salary-plus-commission plans** spread the risk of selling between the company and the sales professional. The salary component presumably enhances a company's ability to attract good employees and allows a company to direct its employees' efforts to nonselling tasks that do not lead directly to commissions (e.g., participating in further training or servicing accounts). The commission component serves as the employees' share in the gains they generated for the company.

Commission-Plus-Draw Plans

Commission-plus-draw plans award sales professionals with subsistence pay or draws—money to cover basic living expenses—yet provide them with a strong incentive to excel. This subsistence pay component is known as a **draw**. Unlike salaries, however, companies award draws as advances, which are charged against commissions that sales professionals are expected to earn.

Companies use two types of draws. **Recoverable draws** act as company loans to employees that are carried forward indefinitely until employees sell enough to repay their draws. **Nonrecoverable draws** act as salary because employees are not obligated to repay the loans if they do not sell enough. Nonrecoverable draws clearly represent risks to companies because these expenses are not repaid if employee sales performance is lackluster. Companies that adopt nonrecoverable draws may stipulate that employees cannot continue in the employment of the company if they fail to cover their draw for a specified number of months or sales periods during the year. This arrangement is quite common among car salespeople.

Commission-Only Plans

Under **commission-only plans**, salespeople derive their entire income from commissions. Three particular types of commissions warrant mention. **Straight commission** is based on a fixed percentage of the sales price of the product or service. For instance, a 10 percent commission would generate a $10 incentive for a product or service sold that is priced at $100, and $55 for a product or service sold that is priced at $550.

Graduated commissions increase percentage pay rates for progressively higher sales volume. For example, a sales professional may earn a 5 percent commission per unit for sales volume up to 100 units, 8 percent for each unit from 101 to 500 units, and 12 percent for each unit in excess of 500 sold during each sales period.

Finally, **multiple-tiered commissions** are similar to graduated commissions, but with one exception. Employees earn a higher rate of commission for all sales made in a given period if the sales level exceeds a predetermined level. For instance, employees might earn only 8 percent for each item if total sales volume falls short of 1,000 units. If total sales volume exceeds 1,000 units, however, then employees might earn a per-item commission equal to 12 percent for every item sold. Commission-only plans are well suited for situations in which:

- The salesperson has substantial influence over the sales.
- Low to moderate training or expertise is required.
- The sales cycle—the time between identifying the prospect and closing the sale—is short.

In contrast to salespeople on salary-only plans, commission-only salespeople shoulder all the risk: Employees earn nothing until they sell. Despite this risk, potential rewards are substantial, particularly with graduated and multiple-tiered commission plans.

Although commissions may fit well with cost-cutting measures, these incentives are not always the best tactic for compensating sales professionals. In fact, commission structures probably suffer from many of the same limitations of individual incentive plans that we discussed in Chapter 5 (e.g., competitive behaviors among employees). Moreover, some sales experts argue that commissions undermine employees' intrinsic motivation to sell (i.e., their genuine interest for the challenge and enjoyment that selling brings). These experts argue that once salespeople have lost that intrinsic motivation, commissions act essentially as controls to maintain sales professionals' performance levels. Said another way, such professionals may simply go through the motions in order to earn money without regard to quality and customer satisfaction.[16]

For any sales compensation plan, it is critical that companies establish realistic total sales targets and individual performance standards. Beyond reasonable limits, it is possible that sales compensation plans will backfire. Consequences of such backfire include lower employee motivation, unprofessional behavior, and compromised profits.

Sales Compensation Plans and Competitive Strategy

Sales plans with salary components are most appropriate for differentiation strategies. Under salary-based sales plans, employees can count on receiving income. By design, salary plans do not require employees to focus on attaining sales volume goals or other volume indicators (e.g., market share). Sales professionals who receive salaries can turn their attention to addressing clients' needs during the presale and servicing phases of the relationship. Salary-based sales compensation applies to the sale and servicing of such technical equipment as computer networks, including the hardware (e.g., the individual computers and network server) and the software (i.e., applications programs such as Microsoft Excel or the Windows operating system).

Commission-oriented sales compensation plans are best suited for lowest-cost strategies because compensation expenditures vary with sales revenue. As a result, only the most productive employees earn the best salaries. Commissions essentially represent rewards for "making the sale." For example, real estate sales agents' earnings depend upon two factors: number of houses sold and their selling price. New-car salespersons' earnings similarly depend on the number of cars sold and their selling price. In either situation, customers are likely to have questions and concerns following sales transactions. Many real estate sales companies employ real estate assistants at low salaries—not much more than the minimum wage—who mediate such buyers' queries of the sellers as, "What grade of rock salt is most appropriate for the water softener apparatus?" Real estate assistants are often training to be full-fledged real estate agents, and they view low pay as a necessary trade-off for learning the ropes.

Determining Fixed Pay and the Compensation Mix

Managers must balance fixed and incentive pay elements to directly affect employee motivation. The mix depends mainly on three factors:

- Influence of the salesperson on the buying decision
- Competitive pay standards within the industry
- Amount of nonsales activities required

Influence of the Salesperson on the Buying Decision

For the most part, the more influence sales professionals have on "buying" decisions, the more the compensation mix will emphasize incentive pay. Salespeople's influence varies greatly with the specific product or service marketed and the way these are sold. Many sales professionals assume an order-taker role, with little influence over purchase decisions. For example, salespeople in such large department stores as Sears have little influence over the merchandise for sale because these stores send their buyers to manufacturers to purchase lines of products that will be sold in its stores throughout the United States and beyond. Product display and promotional efforts (e.g., television or newspaper ad campaigns) are determined by store management. Although a sales clerk with a bad attitude may prevent sales from happening, these workers control very little of the marketing effort.

On the other end of the spectrum, some employees serve as consultants to the client. For instance, when a company decides to invest in computerizing its entire worldwide operations, it may approach a computer manufacturer such as IBM to purchase the necessary equipment. Given the technical complexity of computerizing a company's worldwide operations, the client would depend on IBM to translate its networking needs into the appropriate configuration of hardware and software. These IBM sales professionals ultimately influence the purchaser's decision to buy.

Competitive Pay Standards within the Industry

A company's compensation mix must be as enticing as that offered by competitors if the company wants to recruit high-quality sales professionals. Industry norms and the selling situation are among the key determinants of compensation mix. For instance, competitive standards may dictate that the company must give greater weight to either incentive or fixed pay, which we addressed earlier. Incentive (commission) pay weighs heavily in highly competitive retail industries, including furniture, home electronics, and auto sales. Salary represents a significant pay component in such high entry-barrier industries as pharmaceuticals. In the case of pharmaceuticals, barriers to entry include the U.S. Food and Drug Administration regulations on testing new products that significantly extend the time from product conception through testing to marketing for general use. Salary is an appropriate compensation choice because pharmaceutical companies face little risk of new competition.

Amount of Nonsales Activities Required

In general, the more nonsales duties salespeople have, the more their compensation package should tend toward fixed pay. Some companies and products, for instance, require extensive technical training or customer servicing activities. An excellent example is again the pharmaceuticals industry. Sales professionals employed by such companies as Bristol-Myers Squibb, Lilly, and Merck must maintain a comprehensive understanding of their products' chemical compositions, clinical uses, and contraindications.

DESIGNING PAY-FOR-KNOWLEDGE PROGRAMS

As indicated in Chapters 4 and 5, merit pay and incentive pay represent job-based approaches to compensating employees. In Chapter 6, we discussed the importance of paying for knowledge that many companies recognize. For this discussion, we use the terms *knowledge* and *skills* interchangeably, as the design features for both structures are virtually the same. In its purest form, pay-for-knowledge programs reward employees for the acquisition of job-related knowledge (or skills, in the case of skill-based pay plans). In practice, companies are concerned with how much employees' performance improves as a result of their newly acquired knowledge. Our focus in this section is on the latter.

A fundamental issue in pay-for-knowledge programs is whether investments in training provide measurable payoffs to companies. The American Society for Training and Development, a premier professional organization of training and development professionals, recently offered some insight. Based on a research study involving approximately 2,500 companies, training investments are positively related to future total stockholder return, gross profit margin, and income per employee.[17] In addition, executives within and outside the training function at IBM maintain that training programs have strategic value for companies.[18]

Establishing Skill Blocks

Skill (knowledge) blocks are sets of skills (knowledge) necessary to perform a specific job (e.g., typing skills versus analytical reasoning) or group of similar jobs (e.g., junior accounting clerk, intermediate accounting clerk, and senior accounting clerk). Table 9-3 contains an example of a knowledge block familiar to us—building market-competitive compensation systems (Chapters 2 and 8).

The number of skill blocks included in a pay-for-knowledge structure can range from two to several. Current plans average about 10 skill blocks.[19] The appropriate number of blocks depends on the variety of jobs within a company. The development of skill blocks should occur with three considerations in mind.

First, the company must develop job descriptions, which we discussed in Chapter 7. Job descriptions should be treated as blueprints for the creation of a pay-for-knowledge system. Well-crafted job descriptions should facilitate the identification of major skills, the training programs employees need to acquire horizontal and vertical skills, and accurate measures of performance.

TABLE 9-3 Knowledge Block: Building Market-Competitive Compensation Systems

I. Strategic analyses
  A. External market environment
    1. Industry profile
    2. Foreign demand
    3. Competition
    4. Long-term prospects
    5. Labor-market assessment
  B. Internal capabilities
    1. Financial condition
    2. Functional capabilities
    3. Human resource capabilities
II. Compensation surveys
  A. Using published compensation survey data
    1. Survey focus: Core or fringe compensation
    2. Sources of published compensation surveys
  B. Compensation surveys: Strategic considerations
    1. Defining relevant labor market
    2. Choosing benchmark jobs
  C. Compensation survey data: Summary, analysis, and interpretation
    1. Using the appropriate statistics to summarize survey data
      a. Central tendency
      b. Variation
    2. Updating the survey data
    3. Statistical analysis

Second, individual jobs should be organized into job families, or groups of similar jobs such as clerical, technical, and accounting. The information conveyed within a job description should enable the plan developers to identify skills that are common to all jobs in the family and skills that are unique for individual jobs in the family. Based on these groupings, all tasks necessary to perform the jobs in a job family should be listed to facilitate the identification of the skills necessary to perform the tasks.

Third, skills should be grouped into blocks. There are no hard-and-fast rules compensation professionals can follow to determine skill blocks. A general guideline is that the blocked knowledge should relate to specific job tasks and duties. Referring again to Table 9-3, knowledge about the external environment and a company's internal capabilities—two distinct sets of knowledge—together form the foundation of strategic analyses.

Transition Matters

A number of initial considerations arise in the transition from using job-based pay exclusively to using pay-for-knowledge programs as well. These issues include assessment of skills, alignment of pay with the knowledge structure, and access to training.[20]

Skills Assessment

The skills assessment issue centers on who should assess whether employees possess skills at levels that justify a pay raise, on what basis assessments should be made, and when assessments should be conducted. Gaining employee trust is critical during the transition period because employees may view new systems as threats to job security. Some combination of peer and self-assessments, as well as input from known "experts" such as supervisors, therefore might be essential. The important ingredients here are employee input and the expertise of supervisors and managers. In the case of knowledge assessment, paper-and-pencil tests are useful tools.

Having established who should conduct assessments, on what basis should assessments be made? During the transition, companies use conventional performance measures that reflect employees' proficiency in skills use, complemented by employees' self-assessments. The use of both types of data is likely to increase an employee's understanding of the new system as well as build faith in it, particularly when testimony and the more conventional performance measures converge.

A final assessment matter concerns timing. During transition phases, managers should assess employees' performance more frequently to keep employees informed of how well they are doing under the new system. In addition, more frequent assessments should reinforce the key aim of pay for knowledge (i.e., to encourage employees to learn more). Performance feedback is essential for this process.[21]

Aligning Pay with the Knowledge Structure

One of the most difficult tasks that managers face as they guide employees toward a pay-for-knowledge system is aligning pay with the knowledge structure. Upon implementation of pay for knowledge, employees' core compensation must reflect the knowledge or skills they have that the company incorporates into its pay-for-knowledge structure. If employees' actual earnings are more than the pay-for-knowledge system indicates, managers must develop a reasonable course of action so that employees can acquire skills that are commensurate with their current pay. If employees are underpaid, the company must provide pay adjustments as quickly as possible. The length of time required to make these necessary adjustments will depend on two factors: the number of such employees and the extent to which they are underpaid. With limited budgets, companies will obviously require more extended periods as either the number of underpaid employees or the pay deficit increases.

Access to Training

A final transition matter is access to training. Pay-for-knowledge systems make training necessary, rather than optional, for those employees who are motivated for self-improvement. Companies that adopt pay for knowledge must therefore ensure that all employees have equal access to the needed training for acquiring higher-level skills. They must do so both to meet the intended aim of pay-for-knowledge programs (i.e., to reward employees for enhancing their skills) and to address legal imperatives. Restricting access to training can lead to a violation of key laws (Chapter 3) (i.e., Title VII of the Civil Rights Act of 1964 and the Age Discrimination in Employment Act of 1967). Companies must also educate employees about what their training options are and how successful training will lead to increased pay and advancement opportunities within the company. In other words, employers should not assume that employees will necessarily recognize the opportunities that are available to them unless they are clearly communicated. Written memos and informational meetings conducted by HR representatives are effective communication media.

Training and Certification

Successful pay-for-knowledge programs depend on a company's ability to develop and implement systematic training programs. For many of the reasons cited in Chapter 1 (i.e., intense domestic and global competition, rapid technological advancement, and educational deficits of new workforce entrants), progressive companies in the United States have adopted a continuous learning philosophy, which, like pay for knowledge, encourages employees to take responsibility for enhancing their skills and knowledge.[22] Training clearly represents a key venue for continuous learning.

Because employees are required to learn new skills constantly, training becomes an ongoing process. Companies implementing pay for knowledge typically increase the amount of classroom and on-the-job training.[23] When training is well designed, employees should be able to learn the skills needed to increase their pay as well as the skills necessary to teach and coach other employees at lower skill levels. Accurate job descriptions are useful in determining training needs and focusing training efforts.

Employers must make necessary training available to employees so they can progress through the pay-for-knowledge system. A systematic method for ensuring adequate training coverage involves matching training programs with each skill block. Accessibility does not require that employers develop and deliver training themselves. Training that is developed and delivered by an agency not directly affiliated with the company (i.e., community college, vocational training institute, university, or private consultant) can be just as accessible when the employer integrates the offering of these other sources with its pay-for-knowledge program.

In-House or Outsourcing Training

The following criteria should be used to determine whether to develop and deliver training within the workplace or to outsource.[24]

Expertise Specialized training topics require greater expertise, and more generic topics require less expertise. Employers generally turn to in-house resources if they can draw on existing expertise. If in-house expertise is lacking, employers often seek an outside provider either to fill the need directly or to train individuals who become instructors. Employers usually rely on in-house expertise for employer- and product-specific training. Such training is governed by employer philosophies and procedures and is, therefore, not readily available in the external market.

Timeliness Employers often seek outside services if the in-house staff does not have adequate time to develop and deliver the program within the time frame requested. For example, PeopleSoft, a business applications software development company, trains its clients (e.g., Exxon-Mobil, Wal-Mart, General Motors, Ford, Citigroup, IBM, AT&T, and Verizon) on how to use the systems they install. Over time, client companies experience turnover, which often includes the departure of employees who are well trained to use installed PeopleSoft systems. To maintain effective business operations, client companies require training on demand. PeopleSoft offers training on demand to its clients through different forms of media, including the Internet and CD-ROMs.

Size of the Employee Population to Be Trained Employers typically rely on in-house resources for larger groups of employees. The major impetus behind this decision is economics. If there is a large demand for training, the program is more likely to be delivered more than once, resulting in economies of scale.

Sensitivity or Proprietary Nature of the Subject Matter Sensitive or proprietary training is defined as training used to gain a competitive advantage or training that gives access to proprietary, product, or strategic knowledge. Employers rarely issue security clearances to outside resources to provide training of this nature. If the area of the training is sensitive or proprietary, the training is likely to be done in-house regardless of the other factors just discussed.

Certification and Recertification

Certification ensures that employees possess at least a minimally acceptable level of skill proficiency upon completion of a training unit. If employees do not have an acceptable degree of skill, then the company quite simply wastes any skill-based compensation expenditure. Supervisors and co-workers, who are presumably most familiar with the intricacies of their work, usually certify workers. Certification methods can include work samples, oral questioning, and written tests. Table 9-4 illustrates an example of WorldatWork's curriculum outline for their Certified Compensation Professional (CCP) certification.

Recertification, under which employees periodically must demonstrate mastery of all the jobs they have learned or risk losing their pay rates, is necessary to maintain the workforce flexibility offered by a pay-for-knowledge plan.[25] The recertification process typically is handled by retesting employees, retraining employees, or requiring employees to occasionally perform jobs that use their previously acquired skills.

For example, the Society for Human Resource Management offers two types of professional certification: the Professional in Human Resources and the Senior Professional in Human Resources. Individuals with at least 2 years of work experience in exempt jobs (Chapter 3) earn certification when they pass a comprehensive examination of knowledge in the HR domain. Because the field of HR knowledge changes over time, individuals with certification must periodically earn continuing education credits to maintain certification. Credits are earned through a wide variety of activities, including course and/or conference attendance, membership in professional organizations, leadership with the association, teaching, speaking, writing, and projects completed on the job. This updating process is known as recertification.

TABLE 9-4 WorldatWork Training Certification: Certified Compensation Professional (CCP) and Certified Benefits Professional (CBP)

Common Core
(Required)

T1: Total Rewards Management	T2: Accounting and Finance for the Human Resources Professional	T3: Quantitative Methods

CCP
(Required)

C1: Regulatory Environments for Compensation Programs	C2: Job Analysis, Documentation, and Evaluation	C4: Base Pay Management	B1: Fundamentals of Employee Benefits Programs	B2: Retirement Plans–Design and Management	B3: Health Care and Insurance and Plans–Design and Management

CBP
(Required)

CCP
Electives (Choose three)

C5: Elements of Sales Compensation	C6: Principles of Executive Rewards	C6A: Advanced Concept in Executive Compensation	B3A: Health Care and Insurance Plans–Financial Management	B4: Strategic Benefits Planning	B5: Managing Flexible Benefits
C9: Elements of Expatriate Compensation	C11: Performance Management–Strategy, Design, and Implementation	C12: Variable Pay: Incentives, Recognition,	B9: International Benefits	T4: Strategic Communication in Total Rewards	T6: Mergers and Acquisitions: Benefits, Compensation, and Other HR Issues

CBP
Electives (Choose three)

TABLE 9-4 (cont.)

C15: Global Compensation–Strategy in Practice

C17: Market Pricing–Conducting a Competitive Analysis

T4: Strategic Communication in Total Rewards

T9: International Remuneration: An Overview of Global Rewards

T11: Fundamentals of Equity-Based Rewards

T12: Outsourcing and Managing HR Service Partners

T6: Mergers and Acquisitions: Benefits, Compensation and Other HR Issues

T9: International Remuneration: An Overview of Global Rewards

T12: Outsourcing and Managing HR Service Partners

T11: Fundamentals of Equity-based Reward

PAY STRUCTURE VARIATIONS

The principles of pay structure development reviewed previously apply to the majority of established pay structures in companies throughout the United States. Broadbanding and two-tier pay structures represent variations to those pay structure principles.

Broadbanding

The Broadbanding Concept and Its Advantages

Companies may choose **broadbanding** to consolidate existing pay grades and ranges into fewer wider pay grades and broader pay ranges. Figure 9-6 illustrates a broadbanding structure and its relationship to traditional pay grades and ranges. Broadbanding represents the organizational trend toward flatter, less hierarchical corporate structures that emphasize teamwork over individual contributions alone.[26] Some federal government agencies, including the Navy, the General Accounting Office, and the Central Intelligence Agency, began experimenting with the broadbanding concept in the 1980s to introduce greater flexibility to their pay structures. Some private sector companies began using broadbanding in the late 1980s for the same reason. General Electric's former plastics business is a noteworthy adopter of broadbanding.

Broadbanding uses only a few large salary ranges to span levels within the organization previously covered by several pay grades. Thus, HR professionals place jobs that were separated by one or more pay grades in old pay structures into the same band under broadbanding systems. For example, condensing three consecutive grades into a single broadband eliminates the hierarchical differences among the jobs evident in the original, narrower pay grade configuration. Employees holding jobs in a single broadband now have equal pay potential, unlike employees in a multiple pay grade configuration. In addition, elimination of narrow bands broadens employees' job duties and responsibilities.

Some companies establish broadbands for distinct employee groups within the organizational hierarchy (e.g., upper management, middle management, professionals, and staff). This approach reduces management layers dramatically, and it should promote quicker decision-making cycles. Other companies create broadbands on the basis of job families (e.g., clerical, technical, and administrative). Job family–based bands should give employees broader duties within their job classes. Still others may set broadbands according to functional areas, collapsing across job families. For example, a

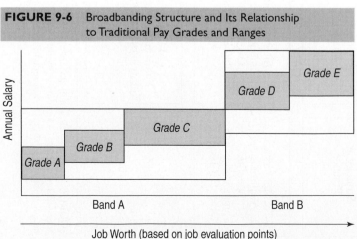

FIGURE 9-6 Broadbanding Structure and Its Relationship to Traditional Pay Grades and Ranges

Annual Salary

Grade A

Grade B

Grade C

Grade D

Grade E

Band A

Band B

Job Worth (based on job evaluation points)

broadband may be established for all HR specialists (i.e., training, compensation, recruitment, and performance appraisal). These bands should encourage employees to expand their knowledge and skills in several HR functions.

Broadbanding shifts greater responsibility to supervisors and managers for administering each employee's compensation within the confines of the broadbands. Because broadbands include a wider range of jobs than narrowly defined pay grades, supervisors have greater latitude in setting employees' pay according to the tasks and duties they perform. Under traditional pay grades, employees receive pay and pay increases based on a limited set of duties stated in their job descriptions.

Limitations of Broadbanding

Notwithstanding the benefits of broadbanding, it does possess some limitations. Broadbanding is not a cure-all for all compensation-related dysfunction within companies. For instance, broadbanding changes how compensation dollars are allocated, but not how much is allocated. Managers often think that flatter organizational structures reduce costs. To the contrary, broadbanding may lead to higher compensation expenses because managers have greater latitude in assigning pay to their employees. In fact, the federal government's limited experience showed that broadbanding structures were associated with more rapid increases in compensation costs than traditional pay structures.[27]

Broadbanding also necessitates a trade-off between the flexibility to reward employees for their unique contributions and a perception among employees that fewer promotional opportunities are available. This transition from multiple narrowly defined pay grades to fewer broadbands reduces organizational hierarchies that support job promotions. Employers and employees alike need to rethink the idea of promotions as a positive step through the job hierarchy.

Two-Tier Pay Structures

The Two-Tier Pay System Concept and Its Advantages

Two-tier pay structures reward newly hired employees less than established employees. Under the temporary basis, employees have the opportunity to progress from lower entry-level pay rates to the higher rates enjoyed by more senior employees. Permanent two-tier systems reinforce the pay-rate distinction by retaining separate pay scales: Lower-paying scales apply to newly hired employees, and current employees enjoy higher-paying scales. Although pay progresses within each scale, the maximum rates to which newly hired employees can progress are always lower than more senior employees' pay scales. Table 9-5 illustrates a typical two-tier wage structure.

Two-tier wage systems are more prevalent in unionized companies. Labor representatives have reluctantly agreed to two-tier wage plans as a cost-control measure. In exchange for reduced compensation costs, companies have promised to limit layoffs. These plans represent a departure from unions' traditional stance of single base pay rates for all employees within job classifications.

Two-tier pay structures enable companies to reward long-service employees while keeping costs down by paying lower rates to newly hired employees who do not have an established performance record within the company. As senior employees terminate their employment (i.e., taking jobs elsewhere or retiring) they are usually replaced by workers who are compensated according to the lower-paying scale.

Limitations of Two-Tier Pay Structures

A potentially serious limitation of two-tier plans is that the lower pay scale applied to newly hired workers may restrict a company's ability to recruit and retain the most highly qualified individuals. Resentment can build among employees on the lower tier toward

TABLE 9-5 Two-Tier Wage Structures

The following pay rates apply to the 2006 calendar year. Employees hired on or after January 1, 2006, will be paid according to Schedule A below. Employees hired before January 1, 2006, will be paid according to Schedule B below.

		Schedule A	
Hourly Job Classification	*Hourly Pay Rate*	*Cost-of-Living Adjustment*	*Total Hourly Pay Rate*
Shop floor laborers	$12.10	$1.36	$13.46
Assemblers	$14.05	$1.36	$15.41
Carpenters	$16.50	$1.36	$17.86
Plumbers	$16.90	$1.36	$18.26

		Schedule B	
Job Classification	*Hourly Pay Rate*	*Cost-of-Living Adjustment*	*Total Hourly Pay Rate*
Shop floor laborers	$14.10	$1.36	$15.46
Assemblers	$16.05	$1.36	$17.41
Carpenters	$18.50	$1.36	$19.86
Plumbers	$18.90	$1.36	$20.26

their counterparts on the upper tier, which may lead to lower tier employees' refusal to perform work that extends in any way beyond their job descriptions. Such resentment may lead employees on the upper tier to scale back their willingness to take on additional work to the extent that they perceive pay premiums are not sufficiently large to compensate for extra duties. In addition, opponents of two-tier wage systems contend that pay differentials cause lower employee morale. Finally, conflict between the tiers may lead to excessive turnover. When high performers leave, then the turnover is dysfunctional to the company and can have long-term implications for productivity and quality.

SUMMARY

In this chapter, we reviewed the pay structure concept as well as the building blocks needed to establish pay structures. Compensation professionals develop pay structures for the various pay bases. Pay structure development generally entails linking the internal job structure with the external market's pricing structure for jobs, knowledge, or skills. Once developed, pay structures recognize individual differences in employee contributions, and these structures represent operational plans for implementing and administering pay programs.

KEY TERMS

- pay structures, 211
- pay grades, 212
- pay ranges, 214
- midpoint pay value, 214
- range spread, 215
- pay compression, 216
- green circle rates, 218
- red circle rates, 218
- compa-ratios, 219
- equity theory, 220
- compensation budgets, 220
- common review date, 221
- common review period, 221
- employee's anniversary date, 221
- nonrecurring merit increases, 221
- merit pay increase budget, 223
- salary-only plans, 226
- salary-plus-bonus plans, 226
- commission, 227
- salary-plus-commission plans, 227
- commission-plus-draw plans, 227

DISCUSSION QUESTIONS

1. Respond to the following statement: "Pay grades limit a company's ability to achieve competitive advantage." Do you agree? Provide a rationale for your position.
2. Two employees perform the same job, and each received exemplary performance ratings. Is it fair to give one employee a smaller percentage merit increase because his pay falls within the third quartile but give a larger percentage merit increase to the other because his pay falls within the first quartile? Please explain your answer.
3. Describe some ethical dilemmas sales professionals may encounter. How can sales compensation programs be modified to minimize ethical dilemmas?
4. React to the statement: "Merit pay grids have the potential to undermine employee motivation." Please discuss your views.
5. Compression represents a serious dysfunction of pay structures. Discuss some of the major ramifications of compression. Also, discuss how companies can minimize or avoid these ramifications.

EXERCISES

Compensation Online

For Students

Exercise 1: Find relevant journal articles

Use your school library's online catalog to locate articles pertaining to job families and pay structure. Find and read several current articles in these areas. Write your best explanation of these topics, as if you had to explain it to someone else who was trying to learn.

Exercise 2: Write a short paper on pay structure design

Visit *www.hr-guide.com*. In addition, conduct an advanced Yahoo! search for "pay structures" or "pay grades." What do you find out about creating pay grades? Describe five considerations HR professionals should take into account when designing pay structures.

Exercise 3: Research compa-ratios

One of the important topics in this chapter had to do with compa-ratios. Use Yahoo! and two other search engines to find information on this topic. Which search engine did you find to be most helpful? Why?

Select one of the sites to review. Write a brief summary of the site. Did it help you understand the topic any better? Why or why not?

For Professionals

Exercise 1: Research compensation design consultants

You are working for a firm that is growing rapidly. Your current compensation administration practices were sufficient for one office and 30 employees; however, you now have offices in several cities and more than 200 employees. As the firm continues to grow, you (the HR department) need help keeping up. From Yahoo!'s Business and Economy section, search the Business to Business listing for compensation system design firms. Which ones specifically mention merit pay, incentive pay, or person-focused pay? Give examples of what they say about each topic.

Exercise 2: Research and review pay scales

Audit the pay scales of the University of Pennsylvania using their Web page, *www.hr.upenn.edu*. Click on "Compensation Salary Structure." Review the salary structure for the appropriate grade, schedule, and job type for various positions that are links at the bottom of the page. Think about the skills and responsibilities that you have had in past jobs. Based on the general level of skills and responsibilities you have had, where would your past jobs have fallen in this pay structure?

Exercise 3: Research an organization

Use Yahoo! to search for the American Payroll Association. Read about this organization and read its newsletter. How would being a part of this organization be useful to the HR professional?

ENDNOTES

1. Bureau of National Affairs (2005). *Skill-Based Pay.* BNA's Library on Compensation & Benefits on CD [CD-ROM]. Washington, DC: Author.

2. Myers, D. W. (1989). *Compensation Management.* Chicago: Commerce Clearing House.

3. Heneman, R. L. (1992). *Merit Pay: Linking Pay Increases to Performance.* Reading, MA: Addison-Wesley.

4. Krefting, L. A., & Mahoney, T. A. (1977). Determining the size of a meaningful pay increase. *Industrial Relations,* 16, pp. 83–93.

5. Heneman, R. L. (1992). *Merit pay: Linking Pay Increases to Performance.* Reading, MA: Addison-Wesley.

6. Rambo, W. W., & Pinto, J. N. (1989). Employees' perceptions of pay increases. *Journal of Occupational Psychology, 62,* pp. 135–145.

7. Krefting, L. A., Newman, J. M., & Krzystofiak, F. (1987). What is a meaningful pay increase? In D. B. Balkin, & L. R. Gómez-Mejía (Eds.), *New Perspectives on Compensation.* Upper Saddle River, NJ: Prentice Hall.

8. Heneman, R. L. (1992). *Merit Pay: Linking Pay Increases to Performance.* Reading, MA: Addison-Wesley.

9. WorldatWork (2007). The pulse of the profession: 2006–07 salary budget survey. *Workspan,* September 2006, pp. 23–26. [online]. Available: *www.worldatwork.org,* accessed June 19, 2007.

10. U.S. Bureau of Labor Statistics (2007). *Consumer Price Index* [online]. Available: *www.bls.gov/cpi,* accessed June 19, 2007.

11. Erickson, C. L. & Ichino, A. C. (1994). Lump-sum bonuses in union contracts. *Advances in Industrial and Labor Relations, 6,* pp. 183–218.

12. WorldatWork (2005). 2004 salary increases for most employees remain lower than historical average of 4% [online]. Available: *www.worldatwork.org,* accessed March 6, 2005.

13. Carey, J. F. (1992). *Complete Guide to Sales Force Compensation.* Homewood, IL: Irwin.

14. Kuhlman, D. C. (1994). Implementing business strategy through sales compensation. In W. Keenan Jr. (Ed.), *Commissions, Bonuses, & Beyond.* Chicago: Probus Publishing.

15. Colletti-Fiss, J. A., & Colletti-Fiss, M. S. (2007). Designing sales incentive plans for competitive advantage (pp. 43–56). In D. Scott (Ed.), *Incentive Pay.* Scottsdale, AZ: WorldatWork.

16. Keenan, W., Jr. (1994). The case against commissions. In W. Keenan Jr. (Ed.), *Commissions, Bonuses, & Beyond.* Chicago: Probus Publishing.

17. American Society for Training and Development (2000). *Profiting from learning: Do firms' investments in education and training pay off?* [online]. Available: *www.astd.org/virtual—community/research/ PFLWhitePaper.pdf,* accessed July 7, 2002.

18. American Society for Training and Development (2006). *C-Level perceptions of the strategic value of learning research report.* January [online]. Available: *www.astd.org/astd/research/research,* accessed June 19, 2007.

19. Bureau of National Affairs (2002). *Skill-Based Pay.* BNA's Library on Compensation & Benefits on CD [CD-ROM]. Washington, DC: Author.

20. Dewey, B. J. (1994). Changing to skill-based pay: Disarming the transition landmines. *Compensation & Benefits Review, 26,* pp. 38–43.

21. Karl, K., O'Leary-Kelly, A. M., & Martocchio, J. J. (1993). The impact of feedback and self-efficacy on performance in training. *Journal of Organizational Behavior, 14,* pp. 379–394.

22. Rosow, J., & Zager, R. (1988). *Training: The Competitive Edge.* San Francisco: Jossey-Bass.

23. Jenkins, G. D., Jr., & Gupta, N. (1985). The payoffs of paying for knowledge. *National Productivity Review, 4,* pp. 121–130.

24. Noe, R. A. (2007). *Employee Training and Development* (4th ed.). Boston: Irwin/McGraw-Hill.

25. Jenkins, G. D., Jr., Ledford, G. E., Jr., Gupta, N., & Doty, D. H. (1992). *Skill-Based Pay.* Scottsdale, AZ: American Compensation Association.

26. Risher, H. H., & Butler, R. J. (1993–94). Salary banding: An alternative salary-management concept. *ACA Journal, 2,* pp. 48–57.

27. Schay, B. W., Simons, K. C., Guerra, E., & Caldwell, J. (1992). *Broad-banding in the federal government—technical report.* Washington, DC: U.S. Office of Personnel Management.

CHAPTER 10

Discretionary Benefits

Chapter Outline

- An Overview of Discretionary Benefits
- Components of Discretionary Benefits
  Protection Programs
  Paid Time Off
  Services
- The Implications of Discretionary Benefits for Strategic Compensation
- Summary
- Key Terms
- Discussion Questions
- Exercises
- Endnotes

Learning Objectives

In this chapter, you will learn about

1. The role of discretionary benefits in strategic compensation
2. The various kinds of protection programs
3. The different types of paid time off
4. A variety of employee services
5. How discretionary benefits fit with differentiation and lowest-cost competitive strategies

Today, discretionary benefits represent a significant fiscal cost to companies. As of March 2007, companies spent an average $12,771 per employee annually to provide discretionary benefits.[1] Discretionary benefits account for as much as 25 percent of employers' total payroll costs (i.e., the sum of core compensation and all employee benefits costs).

As the term implies, "discretionary benefits" are offered at the will of company management. Unlike in well-designed pay-for-performance systems, employees view such discretionary benefits as paid vacation and holidays as an entitlement much like any of the legally required benefits that we will discuss in Chapter 12. Employers have reinforced an entitlement mentality toward benefits because they usually award discretionary benefits regardless of employee performance.

AN OVERVIEW OF DISCRETIONARY BENEFITS

Discretionary benefits fall into three broad categories: protection programs, paid time off, and services. Protection programs provide family benefits, promote health, and guard against income loss caused by such catastrophic factors as unemployment, disability, or serious illnesses. Paid time off, not surprisingly, provides employees time off with pay for such events as vacation. Services provide such enhancements as tuition reimbursement and day care assistance to employees and their families.

In the past several decades, firms have offered a tremendous number of both legally required and discretionary benefits. In Chapter 12, we will discuss how the growth in legally required benefits from a select body of federal and state legislation developed out of social welfare philosophies. Quite different from these reasons are several factors that have contributed to the rise in discretionary benefits.

Discretionary benefits originated in the 1940s and 1950s. During both World War II and the Korean War, the federal government mandated that companies not increase employees' core compensation, but it did not place restrictions on companies' employee benefits expenditures. Companies invested in expanding their offerings of discretionary benefits as an alternate to pay hikes as a motivational tool. As a result, many companies began to offer **welfare practices**. Welfare practices were "anything for the comfort and improvement, intellectual or social, of the employees, over and above wages paid, which is not a necessity of the industry nor required by law."[2] Moreover, companies offered employees welfare benefits to promote good management and to enhance worker productivity.

The opportunities to employees through welfare practices varied. For example, some employers offered libraries and recreational areas, and others provided financial assistance for education, home purchases, and home improvements. In addition, employers' sponsorships of medical insurance coverage became common.

Quite apart from the benevolence of employers, employee unions also directly contributed to the increase in employee welfare practices through the National Labor Relations Act of 1935 (NLRA), which legitimized bargaining for employee benefits. Union workers tend to participate more in benefits plans than do nonunion employees.[3] Table 10-1 illustrates some of the differences in benefits between nonunion and union employees. For example, in 2006, union workers were more likely than nonunion workers to receive health care benefits and retirement income benefits.

Unions also indirectly contributed to the rise in benefits offerings. As we discussed in Chapter 3, nonunion companies often fashion their employment practices after union companies as a tactic to minimize the chance that their employees will seek union representation[4] and may offer their employees benefits that are comparable to the benefits received by employees in union shops.

TABLE 10-I Percentage of Workers with Access to Selected Employee Benefits in Private Industry: 2006

Characteristic	Paid holidays	Paid sick leave	Paid vacation	Paid jury duty leave	Paid military leave	Family leave			Employer assistance for child care			Adoption assistance	Long-term care insurance	Flexible work place
						Paid	Unpaid	Total	Employee-assistance Plans	On-site and off-site child care	Child care resource and referral services			
Total	**77**	**57**	**77**	**69**	**48**	**7**	**81**	**14**	**40**	**5**	**15**	**10**	**11**	**4**
Worker Characteristics														
White-collar occupations	85	72	83	80	57	10	86	19	49	7	20	15	17	7
Blue-collar occupations	81	45	79	65	43	4	79	8	33	2	8	7	6	2
Service occupations	49	36	59	47	33	5	72	9	23	4	5	2	4	1
Full-time	90	68	90	77	54	9	85	16	40	6	16	12	13	5
Part-time	37	22	36	43	30	3	68	8	27	3	10	4	6	2
Union	87	59	83	83	55	6	89	18	60	7	19	14	15	2
Nonunion	75	57	77	68	47	8	80	14	37	5	14	10	11	4

SOURCE: U.S. Bureau of Labor Statistics, *Employee Benefits in Private Industry, 2006*, [online]. Available *www.bls.gov/ncs/ebs/home*, accessed July 7, 2007.

Employees came to view both legally required benefits and discretionary benefits as entitlements. Anecdotal evidence suggests that most employees still feel this way: From their perspective, company membership entitles them to employee benefits. Until recently, companies have also treated virtually all elements of employee benefits as entitlements. They have not questioned their role as social welfare mediators; however, both rising benefit costs and increased foreign competition have led companies to question this entitlement ethic. For instance, in 2007 U.S. companies typically spent more than $17,000 per employee to provide both legally required and discretionary benefits.[5]

A more recent phenomenon that gives rise to discretionary benefits is the federal government's institution of tax laws that allow companies to lower their tax liability based on the amount of money they allocate to providing employees with particular discretionary benefits. These tax laws permit companies to deduct from their pretaxable income the cost of certain benefits, thereby lowering companies' tax liabilities.

COMPONENTS OF DISCRETIONARY BENEFITS

Several benefits practices fall into the category of discretionary employee benefits. We can explore these practices by recognizing the three broad goals employers hope to achieve when offering discretionary benefits: protection, paid time off, and services to enhance work and life experiences.

Protection Programs

Income Protection Programs

Disability Insurance   Disability insurance replaces income for employees who become unable to work because of sicknesses or accidents. Employees unfortunately need this kind of protection. At all working ages, the probability of being disabled for at least 90 consecutive days is much greater than the chance of dying while working; one of every three employees will have a disability that lasts at least 90 days.[6]

Employer-sponsored or group disability insurance typically takes two forms. The first, **short-term disability insurance**, provides benefits for a limited time, usually less than 6 months. The second, **long-term disability insurance**, provides benefits for extended periods between 6 months and life. Disability criteria differ between short- and long-term plans. Short-term plans usually consider disability as an inability to perform any and every duty of the disabled person's occupation. Long-term plans use a more stringent definition, specifying disability as an inability to engage in any occupation for which the individual is qualified by reason of training, education, or experience.

Short-term disability plans classify **short-term disability** as an inability to perform the duties of one's regular job. Manifestations of short-term disability include the following temporary (short-term) conditions:

- Recovery from injuries.
- Recovery from surgery.
- Treatment of an illness requiring any hospitalization.
- Pregnancy—the Pregnancy Discrimination Act of 1978 mandates that employers treat pregnancy and childbirth the same way they treat other causes of disability (Chapter 3).

Most short-term disability plans pay employees 50 to 66.67 percent of their pretax salary on a monthly or weekly basis; however, some pay as much as 100 percent. Short-term disability plans pay benefits for a limited period, usually no more than six months (26 weeks). Many companies set a monthly maximum benefit amount, which could be less for highly paid employees.

Three additional features of short-term disability plans include the preexisting condition clause, two waiting periods, and exclusions of particular health conditions. Similar to health insurance plans, a **preexisting condition** is a mental or physical disability for which medical advice, diagnosis, care, or treatment was received during a designated period preceding the beginning of disability insurance coverage. The designated period is usually any time prior to employment and enrollment in a company's disability insurance plan. Insurance companies impose preexisting conditions to limit their liabilities for disabilities that predate an individual's coverage.

Two waiting periods include the preeligibility period and an elimination period. The **preeligibility period** spans from the initial date of hire to the time of eligibility for coverage in a disability insurance program. Once the preeligibility period has expired, an **elimination period** refers to the minimum amount of time an employee must wait after becoming disabled before disability insurance payments begin. Elimination periods exclude insignificant illnesses or injuries that limit a person's ability to work for just a few days.

Short-term disability plans often contain exclusion provisions. **Exclusion provisions** list the particular health conditions that are ineligible for coverage. Disabilities that result from self-inflicted injuries are almost always excluded. Short-term disability plans often exclude most mental illnesses or disabilities due to chemical dependencies (e.g., addictions to alcohol or illegal drugs). Employers support addicted workers through employee assistance programs, which we will discuss shortly in this chapter.

Long-term disability insurance provides a monthly benefit to employees who, due to illness or injury, are unable to work for an extended period of time. Payments of long-term disability benefits usually begin after 3 to 6 months of disability and continue until retirement or for a specified number of months. Payments generally equal a fixed percentage of predisability earnings.

Long-term disability insurance companies rely on a two-stage definition for long-term disability. **Long-term disability** initially refers to illnesses or accidents that prevent an employee from performing his or her "own occupation" over a designated period. The term *own occupation* applies to employees based on education, training, or experience. After the designated period elapses, the definition becomes more inclusive by adding the phrase, "inability to perform any occupation or to engage in any paid employment." The second-stage definition is consistent with the concept of total disability in workers' compensation programs (Chapter 12).

Long-term disability traditionally plans only covered total disabilities. Many long-term disability insurance carriers have more recently also added partial disabilities for the following reason. Including partial disabilities results in cost savings because, in most cases, totally disabled individuals avoid paid employment because they would forfeit future disability benefits. With the **partial disabilities inclusion**, long-term carriers provide supplemental benefits to cover a portion of income loss associated with part-time employment. For example, long-term disability plans become effective when part-time employment falls below a designated level expressed as a percentage of income (adjusted for cost-of-living increases) prior to the qualifying event (e.g., below 75 or 80 percent).

Full benefits usually equal 50 to 70 percent of monthly pretax salary, subject to a maximum dollar amount. As for short-term plans, the monthly maximum may be as high as $5,000. Long-term benefits are generally subject to a waiting period of anywhere from 6 months to 1 year, and usually become active only after an employee's sick leave and short-term disability benefits have been exhausted. Long-term disability insurance provides a monthly benefit to employees who, due to illness or injury, are unable to work for an extended period of time. Payments of long-term disability benefits usually begin after 3 to 6 months of disability and continue until retirement or for a specified number of months. Payments generally equal a fixed percentage of predisability earnings.

Long-term disability plans also include preexisting condition and exclusion clauses. These are similar to the provisions in short-term disability plans. Long-term plans impose two waiting periods: preeligibility period and elimination period. The preeligibility periods for short- and long-term plans are usually identical. When companies offer both plans, the elimination period expires upon the exhaustion of short-term benefits. As discussed earlier, long-term plans become effective immediately following the end of short-term benefit payments, making the elimination period virtually nonexistent. When companies offer long-term plans only, the elimination period runs between 3 and 6 months following a disability.

Both short- and long-term disability plans may duplicate disability benefits mandated by the Social Security Act and state workers' compensation laws (discussed in Chapter 12). These employer-sponsored plans generally supplement legally required benefits established by the **Employee Retirement Income Security Act of 1974**. Employer-sponsored plans do not replace disability benefits mandated by law.

Life Insurance   Employer-provided **life insurance** protects employees' families by paying a specified amount to an employee's beneficiaries upon the employee's death. Most policies pay some multiple of the employee's salary (e.g., twice the employee's annual salary). Employer-sponsored life insurance plans also frequently include accidental death and dismemberment claims, which pay additional benefits if death was the result of an accident or if the insured incurs accidental loss of a limb.

Most companies offer full-time employees life insurance. On average, companies spent $83 per nonunion employee in 2007 to provide life insurance and $145 per unionized worker.[7]

There are three kinds of life insurance: term life insurance, whole life insurance, and universal life insurance. **Term life insurance**, the most common type offered by companies, provides protection to employees' beneficiaries only during a limited period based on a specified number of years (e.g., 5 years) subject to a maximum age (e.g., 65 or 70). After that, the insurance automatically expires. Neither the employee nor his or her beneficiaries receives any benefit upon expiration. In order to continue coverage under a term life plan, an employee must renew the policy and make premium payments as long as he or she is younger than the maximum allowed age for coverage.

Whole life insurance pays an amount to the designated beneficiaries of the deceased employee, but unlike term policies, whole life plans do not terminate until payment is made to beneficiaries. As a result, whole life insurance policies are substantially more expensive than are term life policies, making the whole life insurance approach an uncommon feature of employer-sponsored insurance programs. From the employee's or his or her beneficiary's perspective, whole life insurance policies combine insurance protection with a savings (or cash accumulation plan) because a portion of the money paid to meet the policy's premium will be available in the future with a low fixed annual interest rate of usually no more than 2 or 3 percent. **Universal life insurance** provides protection to employees' beneficiaries based on the insurance feature of term life insurance and a more flexible savings or cash accumulation plan than found in whole life insurance plans.

Individuals can subscribe to life insurance on an individual basis by purchasing policies from independent insurance agents or representatives of insurance companies. On the other hand, they can subscribe to group life insurance through their employers, which has clear benefits. First, group plans allow all participants covered by the policy to benefit from coverage, and employers assume the burden of financing the plan either partly or entirely. Second, group policies permit a larger set of individuals to participate in a plan at a lower cost per person than if each person had to purchase life insurance on an individual basis.

Retirement Programs **Retirement programs**, which are often referred to as **pension plans**, provide income to employees and their beneficiaries during some or all of their retirement. Individuals may participate in more than one pension program simultaneously. It is not uncommon for employees to participate in pension plans sponsored by their companies [e.g., 401(k) plans] as well as in pension plans that they establish themselves [e.g., the individual retirement account (IRA)]. In 2007, employers' contributions to pension plans on behalf of their employees were substantial—averaging $1,809 per employee.[8]

Pension program design and implementation are quite complex, largely because of the many laws that govern their operations, particularly the Employee Retirement Income Security Act of 1974 (ERISA). We will take up a detailed treatment of retirement plan design and current issues at the forefront of a company's decision whether to offer a retirement plan and, if so, in what form, in Chapter 11.

Health Protection Programs

Health protection has captured both employees' and employers' attention for several years. From the employees' perspective, health coverage is valuable, particularly as the costs of health care have increased dramatically. Total health care expenditures rose by more than 5,000 percent from $26.9 billion in 1960. From the employer's perspective, providing health care coverage is like a two-edge sword. On one hand, the costs to extend health insurance coverage to employees is rising quickly, thereby representing a substantial cost burden. On the other hand, companies recognize that offering comprehensive health insurance protection helps recruit and retain the best-qualified individuals, and employees stand to be more productive when they can afford to (and actually do) take care of health problems that could interfere with job performance. There have been many innovations in approaches to offering health care coverage to employees. We will discuss these innovations and key issues in Chapter 11.

Paid Time Off

The second type of discretionary benefit is paid time off. This category is relatively straightforward. As the name implies, paid time off policies compensate employees when they are not performing their primary work duties. The major types of paid time off are:

- Holidays
- Vacation
- Sick leave
- Personal leave
- Jury duty
- Funeral leave
- Military leave
- Clean-up, preparation, or travel time
- Rest period "break"
- Lunch period
- Integrated paid time off policies

- Sabbatical leave
- Volunteerism

Companies offer most paid time off as a matter of custom, particularly paid holidays, vacations, and sick leave. In unionized settings, the particulars about paid time off are in the collective bargaining agreement. The paid time off practices that are most typically found in unionized settings are jury duty, funeral leave, military leave, clean-up, preparation, travel time, rest period, and lunch period.

For employees and employers, paid time-off benefits are significant. These benefits provide employees the opportunity to balance work and nonwork interests and demands. Companies stand to gain from sponsoring these benefits. Employees may legitimately take time off from scheduled work without incurring loss of pay and benefits, which should help reduce unapproved absenteeism from work. By keeping absenteeism in check, overall productivity and product or service quality should be higher. These benefits also contribute toward positive employee attitudes and commitment to the company, particularly for employees with longer lengths of service. As we will discuss shortly, the length of such paid time off as vacation can increase substantially with length of service.

The most recent comprehensive national data indicate that the majority of workers employed in private sector companies received paid time off in 2006.[9] Approximately 75 percent of employees received paid holidays and paid vacations, respectively. Substantially fewer workers received paid sick leave (57 percent) and paid military leave (48 percent). The prevalence of paid time off was greatest for white-collar workers (e.g., managers, accountants), followed by blue-collar workers (e.g., construction workers, factory workers), and service occupations (e.g., health and child care providers), respectively. The cost of paid time off benefits per hour worked amounted to $1.78, or 6.9 percent of total hourly compensation in March 2007.[10]

There have been three developments in paid time off offerings: integrated paid time off policies, sabbatical leave, and volunteerism. We will discuss each of these practices in turn, highlighting the benefits of these paid time off practices to employers.

Integrated paid time off policies or **paid time off banks** combine holiday, vacation, sick leave, and personal leave policies into a single paid time off policy. Such policies do not distinguish among reasons for absence as do specific policies. The idea is to provide individuals the freedom to schedule time off without justifying the reasons. This freedom should presumably substantially reduce the incidence of unscheduled absences that can be disruptive to the workplace because these policies require advance notice unless sudden illness is the cause (e.g., you went to sleep one evening feeling fine and then wake up the next morning on a scheduled work day with a stomach virus). Integrated paid time off policies have become an increasingly popular alternative to separate holiday, vacation, sick leave, and personal leave plans because they are more effective in controlling unscheduled absenteeism than other types of absence control policies.[11] Integrated policies also relieve the administrative burden of managing separate plans, and the necessity to process medical certifications in the case of sick leave policies.

Paid time off banks do not incorporate all types of time off with pay. Bereavement or funeral leave are stand-alone policies because the death of a friend or relative is typically an unanticipated event beyond an employee's control. Integrating funeral leave into paid time off banks would also likely create dissatisfaction among workers because it would signal that grieving for a deceased friend or relative is equivalent to a casual day off. Jury duty and witness leave, military leave, and nonproduction time are influenced by law and nonproduction time is negotiated as part of a collective bargaining agreement. Sabbatical leaves are also not included in paid time off banks because these are extended leaves provided as a reward to valued, long-service employees. **Sabbatical leaves** are paid time off for such professional activities as a research project or curriculum development. These practices are common in college and university settings and apply most often to faculty members. Universities grant sabbatical leaves to faculty members who meet minimum service requirements (e.g., 3 years of full-time service) with partial or full pay for up to an entire academic year. The service requirement is applied each time, which limits the number of leaves taken per faculty member.

Employers outside the academic world have begun offering sabbatical leaves of absence to employees to further professional development. According to the Society for Human Resource Management, approximately 11 percent of large companies offer paid sabbaticals to employees and another 29 percent offer unpaid sabbaticals.[12] Only large companies were previously known for offering employees sabbatical leaves. About 16 percent of small companies and 21 percent of midsize companies today do offer unpaid sabbaticals.

Outside academia, sabbatical leaves are usually limited to professional and managerial employees who stand to benefit from intensive training opportunities outside the company's sponsorship. Sabbatical leaves are most suitable for such employees as computer engineers whose standards of knowledge or practice are rapidly evolving. Companies establish guidelines regarding qualification, length of leave, and level of pay. An important guideline pertains to minimum length of employment following completion of a sabbatical. For example, companies require employees to remain employed for a minimum of 1 year following the sabbatical or repay part or all of one's salary received during the sabbatical. This provision is necessary to protect a company's investment and to limit moves to competitors.

As reported in the Conference Board report,[13] a survey of U.S. companies identified five different types of sabbatical leave programs:

1. *Traditional Sabbaticals.* These are leaves whose goals and objectives are very similar to those found in the academy. They are always paid leaves and employees expect to return to their same jobs at the end of the leave. Such leaves provide employees a chance to renew or retool themselves in areas related to their work.

2. *Personal Growth Leaves.* These leaves allow employees to further their education or acquire new skills or knowledge that will directly benefit them personally and subsequently be of benefit to the company.

3. *Social Service Leaves.* These are fully paid leaves during which the employee performs a significant public service either in the local community or in other areas important to the company. Such leaves enhance both the employee's personal growth as well as the company's image as a responsible corporate citizen.

4. *Extended Personal Leaves.* These are normally unpaid leaves that provide a significant break of two years or more with return to work guarantees. These leaves are commonly taken by employees with young children.

5. *Voluntary Leaves to Meet Business Needs.* These are leaves that are intended to serve the company in times of downsizing or low production in which the company offers employees extended time off in the form of unpaid leaves.

Volunteerism

Volunteerism refers to giving of one's time to support a meaningful cause. More and more companies are providing employees with paid time off to contribute to causes of their choice. From a company's standpoint, a meaningful cause is associated with the work of not-for-profit organizations such as the United Way to help improve the well-being of people. There are a multitude of meaningful causes throughout the world including improving literacy, providing comfort to terminally ill patients, serving food at shelters for individuals who cannot afford to feed themselves, serving as a mentor to children who do not have one or more parents, and spending time with elderly or disabled residents of nursing homes who may no longer have living friends or family. Companies generally do not dictate the causes for which employees would receive paid time off, except they exclude political campaign and political action groups for eligibility because of possible conflicts of interest with company shareholders and management.

Companies favor providing paid time off for volunteer work for three reasons. First, volunteer opportunities allow employees to balance work and life demands. Second, giving employees the opportunity to contribute to charitable causes on company time represents positive corporate social responsibility, enhancing the company's overall image in the public eye. Third, paid time off to volunteer is believed to help promote retention. Employees are likely to feel that the employer shares similar values, possibly boosting commitment to the company. The amount of time off ultimately varies considerably from company to company, ranging anywhere between one hour per week and, in limited cases for long-service employees, several weeks.

Services

Employee Assistance Programs

Employee assistance programs (EAPs) help employees cope with such personal problems that may impair their job performance as alcohol or drug abuse, domestic violence, the emotional impact of AIDS and other diseases, clinical depression, and eating disorders. EAPs are widely used.

Companies offer EAPs because many employees are likely to experience difficulties that interfere with job performance. Although EAP costs are substantial, the benefits seem to outweigh the costs. For example, the annual cost per employee of an EAP is approximately $50 to $60. Anecdotal evidence, however, indicates that employers' gains outweigh their out-of-pocket expenses for EAPs: savings from reduced employee turnover, absenteeism, medical costs, unemployment insurance rates, workers' compensation rates, accident costs, and disability insurance costs. Most important, the majority of employees who take advantage of EAP resources benefit; unfortunately, large-scale evaluation studies are virtually nonexistent.

Depending on the employer, EAPs provide a range of services and are organized in various ways. In some companies, EAPs are informal programs developed and run on-site by in-house staff. Other employers contract with outside firms to administer their EAPs, or they rely on a combination of their own resources and help from an outside firm.

Family Assistance Programs

Family assistance programs help employees provide elder care and child care. Elder care provides physical, emotional, or financial assistance for aging parents, spouses, or other relatives who are not fully self-sufficient because they are too frail or disabled. Child care programs focus on supervising preschool-age dependent children whose parents work outside the home. Many employees now rely on elder care programs because of their parents' increasing longevity and the growing numbers of dual-income families. Child care needs arise from the growing number of single parents and dual-career households with children.

A variety of employer programs and benefits can help employees cope with their family responsibilities. The programs range from making referrals to on-site child or elder care centers to company-sponsored day care programs, and they vary in the amount of financial and human resources needed to administer them. The least expensive and least labor-intensive programs are generally referral services. Referral services are designed to help workers identify and take advantage of available community resources, conveyed through such media as educational workshops, videos, employee newsletters and magazines, and EAPs.

Flexible scheduling and leave allows employees the leeway to take time off during work hours to care for relatives or react to emergencies. Flexible scheduling, which includes compressed work weeks (e.g., 10-hour days or 12-hour days), flextime, and job sharing, helps employees balance the demands of work and family. In addition to flexible work scheduling, some companies allow employees to extend their legally mandated leave sanctioned by the Family and Medical Leave Act (see Chapter 12). Under extended leave, employers typically continue to provide such employee benefits as insurance and promise to secure individuals comparable jobs upon their return.

Day care is another possible benefit. Some companies subsidize child or elder day care in community-based centers. Elder care programs usually provide self-help, meals, and entertainment activities for the participants. Child care programs typically offer supervision, preschool preparation, and meals. Facilities must usually maintain state or local licenses. Other companies such as Stride Rite Corporation and Fel-Pro choose to sponsor on-site day care centers, offering services that are similar to community-based centers.

Tuition Reimbursement

Companies offer **tuition reimbursement programs** to promote their employees' education. Under a tuition reimbursement program, an employer fully or partially reimburses an employee for expenses incurred for education or training. There is substantial variability in the percentage of tuition an employer reimburses. Some companies vary the percentage of tuition reimbursed according to the relevance of the course to the companies' goals or the grades employees earn.

Tuition reimbursement programs are not synonymous with pay-for-knowledge programs (Chapter 6). Instead, they fall under the category of employee benefits. Under these programs, employees choose the courses they wish to take when they want to take them. In addition, employees may enroll in courses that are not directly related to their work. As we discussed in Chapter 6, pay-for-knowledge is one kind of core compensation. Companies establish set curricula that employees take, and they generally award pay increases to employees who successfully complete courses within the curricula. Pay increases are not directly associated with tuition reimbursement programs.

Transportation Services

Some employers sponsor **transportation services** programs that help bring employees to the workplace and back home again by using more energy-efficient forms of transportation. They may sponsor public transportation or vanpools: employer-sponsored vans or buses that transport employees between their homes and the workplace.

Employers provide transit subsidies to employees working in metropolitan and suburban areas served by mass transportation (e.g., buses, subways, and trains). Companies may offer transit passes, tokens, or vouchers. Practices vary from partial subsidy to full subsidy.

Many employers must offer transportation services to comply with the law. Local and state governments increasingly request that companies reduce the number of single-passenger automobiles commuting to their workplace each day because of government mandates for cleaner air. The Clean Air Act Amendments of 1990 require employers in such large metropolitan areas as Los Angeles to comply with state and local commuter-trip reduction laws. Employers may also offer transportation services to recruit individuals who do not care to drive in rush-hour traffic. Furthermore, transportation services enable companies to offset deficits in parking space availability, particularly in congested metropolitan areas.

Employees obviously stand to benefit from these transportation services. For example, using public transportation or joining a vanpool often saves money by eliminating such commuting costs as gas, insurance, car maintenance and repairs, and parking fees. Moreover, commuting time can be quite lengthy for some employees. By leaving the driving to others, employees can use the time more productively by reading, completing paperwork, or "unwinding."

Outplacement Assistance

Some companies provide technical and emotional support through **outplacement assistance** to employees who are being laid off or terminated. They do so with a variety of career and personal programs designed to develop employees' job-hunting skills and strategies and to boost employees' self-confidence. A variety of factors leads to employee termination. Those best suited to outplacement assistance programs include:

- Layoffs due to economic hardship
- Mergers and acquisitions
- Company reorganizations
- Changes in management
- Plant closings or relocation
- Elimination of specific positions, often the result of changes in technology

Outplacement assistance provides such services as personal counseling, career assessments and evaluations, training in job search techniques, resume and cover letter preparation, interviewing techniques, and training in the use of such basic workplace technology as computers. Although beneficial to employees, of outplacement assistance programs hold possible benefits for companies as well. They can promote a positive image of the company among those being terminated, as well as their families and friends, by helping these employees prepare for employment opportunities.

Wellness Programs

In the 1980s, employers began sponsoring **wellness programs** to promote and maintain employees' physical and psychological health. Wellness programs vary in scope. They may emphasize weight loss only, or they may emphasize a range of activities such as weight loss, smoking cessation, and cardiovascular fitness. Programs may be offered on- or off-site. Although some companies invest in staffing professionals for wellness programs, others contract with such external vendors as community health agencies or private health clubs. Although wellness programs are relatively new, some evidence already indicates that these innovations can save companies money and reduce employees' needs for health care.

Smoking cessation, stress reduction, nutrition and weight loss, exercise and fitness activities, and health screening programs are the most common workplace wellness programs. Smoking cessation plans range from simple campaigns that stress the negative aspects of smoking to intensive programs directed at helping individuals to stop smoking. Many employers offer courses and treatment to help and encourage smokers to quit. Other options include offering nicotine replacement therapy (e.g., nicotine gum and patches) and self-help services. Many companies sponsor such antismoking events as the Great American Smoke-Out, during which companies distribute T-shirts, buttons, and literature that discredit smoking.

Stress management programs can help employees cope with many factors inside and outside work that contribute to stress. For instance, job conditions, health and personal problems, and personal and professional relationships can make employees anxious and therefore less productive. Symptoms of stressful workplaces include low morale, chronic absenteeism, low productivity, and high turnover rates. Employers offer stress management programs to teach workers to cope with conditions and situations that cause stress. Seminars focus on recognizing signs of stress and burnout, as well as on how to handle family- and business-related stress. Stress reduction techniques can improve quality of life inside and outside the workplace. Employers benefit from increased employee productivity, reduced absenteeism, and lower health care costs.

Weight control and nutrition programs are designed to educate employees about proper nutrition and weight loss, both of which are critical to good health. Information from the medical community has clearly indicated that excess weight and poor nutrition are significant risk factors in cardiovascular disease, diabetes, high blood pressure, and cholesterol levels. Over time, these programs should give employees better health, increased morale, and improved appearance. For employers, these programs should result in improved productivity and lower health care costs.

Companies can contribute to employees' weight control and proper nutrition by sponsoring memberships in such weight-loss programs as Weight Watchers. Sponsoring companies may also reinforce weight loss programs' positive results through support groups, intensive counseling, competitions, and other incentives. Companies sometimes actively attempt to influence employee food choices by stocking vending machines with nutritional food.

Financial Education

Some companies have added financial education to employee benefit offerings. Financial education programs provide employees with the resource for managing personal budgets and long-term savings (e.g., for retirement). Companies are increasingly including financial education as part of the benefits program. These companies reason that financial education is a relatively low-cost benefit that helps employees plan current and future (retirement) budgets.

THE IMPLICATIONS OF DISCRETIONARY BENEFITS FOR STRATEGIC COMPENSATION

Discretionary benefits, like core compensation, can contribute to a company's competitive advantage for the reasons discussed earlier (e.g., tax advantages and recruiting the best-qualified candidates). Discretionary benefits can also undermine the imperatives of strategic compensation. Companies that provide discretionary benefits to employees as entitlements are ultimately less likely to promote competitive advantage than companies that design discretionary employee benefits programs to fit the situation.

Management can use discretionary benefit offerings to promote particular employee behaviors that have strategic value. For instance, when employees take advantage of tuition reimbursement programs, they are more likely to contribute to the strategic imperatives of product or service differentiation or cost reduction. Knowledge acquired from job-relevant education may enhance the creative potential of employees, as well as their ability to suggest more cost-effective modes of work. On the other hand, ESOPs may contribute to companies' strategic imperatives by instilling a sense of ownership in employees. Having a financial stake in the company should lead employees to behave more strategically.

A company can use discretionary benefits to distinguish itself from the competition. In effect, competitive benefits programs potentially convey the message that the company is a good place to work because it invests in the well-being of its employees. Lucrative benefits programs will presumably attract a large pool of applicants that include high-quality candidates, positioning a company to hire the best possible employees.

Finally, the tax advantage afforded companies from offering particular discretionary benefits has strategic value. In effect, the tax advantage translates into cost savings to companies. These savings can be applied to promote competitive advantage. For example, companies pursuing differentiation strategies may invest these savings into research and development programs. Companies pursuing lowest-cost strategies may be in a better position to compete because these savings may enable companies to lower the prices of their products and services without cutting into profits.

SUMMARY

This chapter reviewed the role of discretionary benefits in strategic compensation and described the major kinds of discretionary benefits. At present, companies offer widely varied kinds of employee benefits practices. Companies are increasingly investing in protection programs and services that are designed to enhance the well-being of employees in a cost-efficient manner. As competition increases, placing greater pressures on cost-containment strategies, companies have already faced hard choices about the benefits they offer their employees. It is likely that this trend will continue in the foreseeable future.

KEY TERMS

- welfare practices, 242
- short-term disability insurance, 244
- long-term disability insurance, 244
- short-term disability, 244
- preexisting condition, 245
- preeligibility period, 245
- elimination period, 245
- exclusion provisions, 245
- long-term disability, 245
- partial disabilities inclusion, 245

- Employee Retirement Income Security Act of 1974, 246
- term life insurance, 246
- whole life insurance, 246
- universal life insurance, 246
- integrated paid time off policies, 248
- paid time off banks, 248
- sabbatical leaves, 249
- volunteerism, 249
- employee assistance programs (EAPs), 250

- family assistance programs, 250
- flexible scheduling and leave, 251
- day care, 251
- tuition reimbursement programs, 251
- transportation services, 251
- outplacement assistance, 252
- wellness programs, 252
- smoking cessation, 252
- stress management, 253
- weight control and nutrition programs, 253

DISCUSSION QUESTIONS

1. Many compensation professionals are faced with making choices about which discretionary benefits to drop because funds are limited, and the costs of these benefits continually increase. Assume you must make such choices. Rank order discretionary benefits, starting with the ones you would *most likely drop* to the ones you would *least likely drop*. Explain your rationale. Do such factors as the demographic composition of the workforce of the company matter? Explain.
2. Discuss your views about whether discretionary employee benefits should be an entitlement or something earned based on job performance.

3. Assume that you are an HRM professional whose responsibility is to develop a brochure for the purpose of conveying the value of your company's benefits program to potential employees. Your company has asked you to showcase the benefits program in a manner that will encourage recruits to join the company. Develop a brochure (of no more than two pages) that meets this objective. Conduct research on companies' benefits practices (in such journals as *Benefits Quarterly*) as a basis for developing your brochure.
4. Your instructor will assign you an industry. Conduct some research in order to identify the prevalent employee benefits practices for that industry. Also, what factors (e.g., technology, competition, government regulation) might influence the present practices? How will these practices change?

EXERCISES

Compensation Online

For Students

Exercise 1: Find relevant journal articles
When class discussion on discretionary benefits issues began, you immediately became intrigued and wanted to learn more. Use your school library's online catalog to locate articles pertaining to the most intriguing topic. Find and read several current articles in these areas. Be ready to explain what you learned to the other members of your class.

Exercise 2: Search for information on discretionary benefits
Using the Yahoo! search engine, click on *advanced search,* type in "discretionary benefits," select an exact phrase match search method, and click on the search link. How many sites were found? Select one of the sites that you think will provide current information about discretionary benefits. Read the information and write a brief summary on what you learned from the site, including how the information relates to what you read in the textbook.

Exercise 3: Search for information related to ERISA of 1974
The Employee Retirement Income Security Act of 1974 was briefly reviewed in this chapter. To learn more about it, conduct an advanced search for "Employee Retirement Income Security Act." Read about the Act or read the Act itself. What does Part 1 of Title 1 of ERISA require?

For Professionals

Exercise 1: Review professional resources
An issue regarding employee rights according to the Consolidated Omnibus Budget Reconciliation Act of 1985 has come across your desk. Go to *www.benefitslink.com* and click the search link. Once there, type in "COBRA." Look over the results. How can this Web site be of service in your day-to-day work as an HR professional?

Exercise 2: Review a government resource
The vice president of human resources has approached you to head up a new employee assistance initiative. She wants you to prepare a small proposal, just enough to take to the board to show them what you have in mind. Go to the U.S. Office of Personnel Management's Web site at *www.opm.gov.* Click the site index link, scroll down, and click the employee health services link. From here, look at highlighted topics such as "employee assistance" or "employee health," and review the information given to you. Describe two issues or facts from these sources that you wish to communicate to the vice president as potential benefits to the company.

Exercise 3: Review a union Web page
Unions are one of the most important parties in the work environment in regard to human resources. Visit the American Federation of State, County, and Municipal Employees Web page at *afscme.org.* Conduct a search of this site for "benefits" or some more specific topic from this chapter (e.g., "cafeteria plans"). How can this Web site help an HR professional serve both employees and shareholders?

ENDNOTES

1. U.S. Bureau of Labor Statistics (2007). *Employer costs for employee compensation—March 2007* [online]. Available: *www.bls.gov/ncs/ect/home.htm*, accessed June 30, 2007.
2. U.S. Bureau of Labor Statistics (1919). *Welfare work for employees in industrial establishments in the United States.* Bulletin # 250, pp. 119–123.
3. U.S. Department of Labor (August 2006). *National Compensation Survey: Employee benefits in private industry in the United States, March 2006* (Summary 06–05). [online]. Available: *www.bls.gov/ect/home.htm*, accessed March 5, 2007.
4. Solnick, L. (1985). The effect of the blue collar unions on white collar wages and benefits. *Industrial and Labor Relations Review, 38,* pp. 23–35.
5. U.S. Bureau of Labor Statistics (2007). *Employer costs for employee compensation—March 2007* [online]. Available: *www.bls.gov/ncs/ect/home.htm*, accessed June 30, 2007.
6. Martocchio, J. J. (2006). *Employee Benefits: A Primer for the Human Resource Professional* (2nd ed.). Burr Ridge, IL: Irwin/McGraw-Hill.
7. U.S. Bureau of Labor Statistics (2007). *Employer costs for employee compensation—March 2007* [online]. Available: *www.bls.gov/ncs/ect/home.htm*, accessed June 30, 2007.
8. U.S. Bureau of Labor Statistics (2007). *Employer costs for employee compensation—March 2007* [online]. Available: *www.bls.gov/ncs/ect/home.htm*, accessed June 30, 2007.
9. U.S. Bureau of Labor Statistics (2006). *National Compensation Survey: Employee benefits in private industry, March 2006* (USDOL 06–05). [online]. *www.bls.gov,* accessed June 29, 2007.
10. U.S. Bureau of Labor Statistics (2007). *Employer costs for employee compensation—March 2007* (USDL 07–0877). [online]. *www.bls.gov,* July 2, 2007.
11. Markowich, M. M. (2007). *Paid Time-Off Banks.* Phoenix, AZ: WorldatWork Press.
12. Society for Human Resource Management (2007). News bit. [online]. *www.shrm.org,* accessed April 10, 2007.
13. Helen Axel, H. (1992). *Redefining Corporate Sabbaticals for the 1990s,* The Conference Board Report No. 1005.

CHAPTER 11

Employer-Sponsored Retirement Plans and Health Insurance Programs

- ■ Managed Care Plans
     Health Maintenance Organizations
     Features of Health Maintenance Organizations

- ■ Preferred Provider Organizations
     Features of Provider Organizations
     Deductibles
     Coinsurance

- ■ Point-of-Service Plans

- ■ Specialized Insurance Benefits
     Prescription Drug Benefits
     Mental Health and Substance Abuse
     Features of Mental Health and Substance Abuse plans

- ■ Consumer-Driven Health Care

- ■ Summary

- ■ Key Terms

- ■ Discussion Questions

- ■ Endnotes

Learning Objectives

In this chapter, you will learn about

1. Features of defined benefit plans and defined contribution plans

2. Specific types of defined contribution plans

3. The controversy surrounding cash balance plans

4. Health insurance concepts

5. Origins of employer-sponsored health insurance programs

6. Differences between fee-for-service plans and managed care plans

7. Rationale behind consumer-driven health care plans

EXPLORING RETIREMENT PLANS

In Chapter 3 we learned that retirement or pension plans function by providing "retirement income to employees, or resulting in a deferral of income by employees for periods extending to the termination of covered employment or beyond, regardless of the method of calculating the contributions made in the plan, the method of calculating benefits under the plan, or the method of distributing benefits from the plan."[1]

The purpose of this chapter is to review the fundamentals of company-sponsored retirement plan and health care insurance design. It is essential to note that individuals may receive retirement benefits from as many as three sources. First, employer-sponsored retirement plans provide employees with income after they have met a minimum retirement age and have left the company. Second, the Social Security Old-Age, Survivor, and Disability Insurance (OASDI) program to be described in Chapter 12 provides government-mandated retirement income to employees who have made sufficient contributions through payroll taxes. Third, individuals may use their initiative to take advantage of tax regulations that have created such retirement programs as individual retirement accounts (IRAs) and Roth IRAs.

Companies establish retirement or pension plans following one of three design configurations: a defined benefit plan, a defined contribution plan, or hybrid plans that combine features of traditional defined benefit and defined contribution plans. Defined benefit plans guarantee retirement benefits specified in the plan document. This benefit usually is expressed in terms of a monthly sum equal to a percentage of a participant's preretirement pay multiplied by the number of years he or she has worked for the employer. Defined contribution plans require that employers and employees make annual contributions to separate retirement fund accounts established for each participating employee, based on a formula contained in the plan document.

In addition, tax incentives encourage companies to offer pension programs. Some of the ERISA Title I and Title II provisions set the minimum standards required to "qualify" pension plans for favorable tax treatment. Failure to meet any of the minimum standard provisions "disqualifies" pension plans for favorable tax treatment. Pension plans that meet these minimum standards are known as **qualified plans**. **Nonqualified plans** refer to pension plans that do not meet at least one of the minimum standard provisions; typically, highly paid employees benefit from participation in nonqualified plans. We will discuss qualified plans in this chapter and touch upon nonqualified plans in Chapter 13 on executive compensation.

From here, we will explore the minimum standards that distinguish qualified plans from nonqualified plans. Afterward, we will examine the features of alternative company-sponsored pension plans, including defined benefit plans, defined contribution plans, and hybrid plans.

Origins of Employer-Sponsored Retirement Benefits

Until World War II, pension plans were adopted primarily in the railroad, banking, and public utility industries. The most significant growth occurred since the favorable tax treatment of pensions was established through the passage of the Revenue Act of 1921 and government-imposed wage increase controls during World War II in the early 1940s. This led companies to adopt discretionary employee benefits plans such as pensions that were excluded from those wage increase restrictions.

The current tax treatment of qualified plans continues to provide incentives both for employers to establish plans and for employees to participate in them. In general, a contribution to a qualified plan is deductible in computing the employer's or employee's taxes based on who made the contribution. Employees pay taxes only on the amount they withdraw from the plan each year. As we discussed in Chapter 3, this preferential tax treatment is contingent on the employer's compliance with the Employee Retirement Income Security Act of 1974 (ERISA).

Trends in Retirement Plan Coverage and Costs

According to the U.S. Bureau of Labor Statistics, nearly 55 percent of workers employed in the private sector participated in at least one company-sponsored retirement plan in 1992–1993. The participation rate since then has declined slightly to approximately 50 percent in 2006; however, there has been a noticeable decrease in participation rates for defined benefit and defined contribution plans over the last 15 years. In 1992–1993, 32 percent of private sector employees participated in defined contribution plans, but slightly fewer participated in defined benefit plans. In 2006, 42 percent participated in defined contribution plans, but only 20 percent participated in defined benefit plans.

There are two important explanations for these trends in retirement plan participation. First, there has been a shift in the labor force toward different occupations and industries. There has specifically been a relative decline in employment among full-time workers, union workers, and workers in goods-producing businesses. The decline in full-time workers and increase in part-time workers has led to fewer opportunities for participation in company-sponsored retirement plans. Employers quite simply often employ part-time workers to save benefits costs. The decline in union affiliation (i.e., union members or just part of the bargaining unit) also contributes to the overall trends described earlier. In 2006, nearly 90 percent of employees affiliated with unions were eligible to participate in a retirement plan, but only about half of the nonunion workers were eligible. As we discussed in Chapter 3, unions represent workers in negotiations with management over terms of employment. The inclusion of lucrative retirement plans was among the top priorities in negotiations to maintain the support of middle-age and older workers. Finally, among employment trends, the expansion of service industries relative to somewhat stable employment in the goods-producing sector helps to explain retirement plan participation. Fewer service-oriented workers have access to defined benefit plans (19 percent versus 33 percent) although the percentage of workers with access to defined contribution plans is higher and similar in both industries (approximately 50 to 60 percent); however, actual employee participation in defined contribution plans is drastically lower in service employers than in goods-producing companies. Wages in the service-producing companies tend to be lower than they are in goods-producing companies. It is possible that service employees simply do not have enough money to set aside for retirement.

There is a second reason for changes away from participation in defined benefit plans to defined contribution plans. Defined benefit plans are quite costly to employers compared with defined contribution plans: Companies struggle to fund these plans adequately to ensure that retirees receive entitled benefits for the remainder of their lives. In addition, as discussed in Chapter 3, the Pension Benefit Guaranty Corporation (PBGC) serves as the insurer by taking over pension obligations for companies that terminate their defined benefit plans because of severe financial stress. Companies with defined benefit plans pay premiums to the PBGC to insure defined benefit plans in the event of severe financial distress. The Pension Protection Act requires that companies that are at high risk of not meeting their pension obligations pay substantially more to insure defined benefit plans, adding to the substantial cost.

QUALIFIED PLANS

Qualified plans entitle employers and employees to substantial tax benefits. Employers and employees specifically do not pay tax on their contributions within dollar limits that differ for defined benefit and defined contribution plans. In addition, the investment earnings of the trust in which plan assets are held are generally exempt from tax. Finally, participants or beneficiaries do not pay taxes on the value of retirement benefits until they receive distributions.

Minimum Standards for Qualified Plans

Qualified plans possess 13 fundamental characteristics. Table 11-1 lists these characteristics. We will review some of the more fundamental standards in this chapter.

Participation Requirements

Participation requirements include age[2] and service requirements[3] (ERISA, Title I, see the discussion in Chapter 3) for all plan designs. In general, employees must be allowed to participate in pension plans after they have reached age 21 and have completed one year of service (based on 1,000 work hours).

Coverage Requirements

Coverage requirements limit the freedom of employers to exclude employees. Qualified plans do not disproportionately favor highly compensated employees,[4] as discussed in Chapter 3.

Companies demonstrate whether plans meet the coverage requirement by maintaining a nondiscriminatory ratio of nonhighly compensated employees to highly compensated employees according to one or more tests. For example, a plan satisfies the coverage requirement for qualification status when the **ratio percentage test** shows that the percentage of nonhighly compensated employees is at least 70 percent of the percentage of highly compensated employees (as defined in Chapter 3).

Vesting Rules

Strict participation requirements apply to pension plans. Employees must specifically be allowed to participate in pension plans after they have reached age 21[5] and have completed 1 year of service (based on 1,000 work hours).[6] These hours include all paid time for performing work and paid time off (e.g., vacation, sick leave, and holidays). The 1-year requirement may be extended to 2 years if the company grants full vesting after 2 years of participation in the pension plan. In addition, companies may not exclude employees from participating in pension plans because they are too old.

As noted in Chapter 3, **vesting** refers to an employee's nonforfeitable rights to pension benefits.[7] There are two aspects of vesting. First, employees are always vested in their contributions to pension plans. Second, companies must grant full vesting rights to employer contributions on one of the following two schedules (i.e., **cliff vesting** or **6-year graduated schedule**). Cliff vesting schedules must grant employees 100 percent vesting after no more than three years of service. This schedule is known as cliff vesting because leaving one's job prior to becoming vested under this schedule

---

TABLE 11-1 Characteristics of Qualified Pension Plans

- Participation requirements
- Coverage requirements
- Vesting rules
- Accrual rules
- Nondiscrimination rules: Testing
- Key employee and top-heavy provisions
- Minimum funding standards
- Social Security integration
- Contribution and benefit limits
- Plan distribution rules
- Qualified survivor annuities
- Qualified domestic relations orders
- Plan termination rules and procedures

TABLE 11-2 Sample of a 6-Year Graduated Vesting Schedule Under ERISA

Years of Vesting Service	Nonforfeitable Percentage
2	20%
3	40
4	60
5	80
6	100

is tantamount to falling off a cliff because an employee loses all of the accrued employer contributions. On the other hand, companies may use a gradual vesting schedule. The 6-year graduated schedule allows workers to become 20 percent vested after 2 years and to vest at a rate of 20 percent each year thereafter until they are 100% vested after 6 years of service. Table 11-2 shows an example of the 6-year graduated schedule. Plans may have faster gradual schedules to 100 percent vesting in fewer than 6 years. The graduated schedule is preferable to employees who anticipate changing jobs frequently because they will earn the rights to keep part of the employer's contribution sooner. Moreover, employees recognize that layoffs are more common in today's volatile business environment and they stand to benefit by earning partial vesting rights sooner than earning full vesting rights at a later date. On the other hand, employers prefer the cliff vesting schedule recognizing that many employees tend to change jobs more frequently than ever before, allowing them to reclaim nonvested contributions for employees who leave before becoming vested.

Accrual Rules

Qualified plans are subject to minimum accrual rules based on the Internal Revenue Code (IRC) and ERISA.[8] **Accrual rules** specify the rate at which participants accumulate (or earn) benefits.

Defined benefit and defined contribution plans use different accrual rules. These will be discussed in subsequent sections of this chapter.

Nondiscrimination Rules: Testing

Nondiscrimination rules prohibit employers from discriminating in favor of highly compensated employees in contributions or benefits, availability of benefits, rights, or plan features.[9] In addition, employers may not amend pension plans so that highly compensated employees are favored.

The nondiscrimination requirement may be fulfilled in either of two ways: safe harbors or nondiscrimination testing. *Safe harbors* refer to compliance guidelines in a law or regulation. Pension plans that fall in safe harbors automatically fulfill the nondiscrimination requirement based on particular design features. Failure to fall in safe harbors requires passing at least one of two **nondiscrimination tests**. Safe harbors and nondiscrimination tests differ between defined benefit and defined contribution plans. We will review the safe harbors and nondiscrimination tests for defined benefit and defined contribution plans in the subsequent sections of this chapter.

Benefit and Contribution Limits

Benefit limits refer to the maximum annual amount an employee may receive from a qualified defined benefit plan during retirement. Contribution limits apply to defined contribution plans. Employers are limited in the amount they may contribute to an employee's defined contribution plan each year. The *Economic Growth and Tax Relief Reconciliation Act of 2001* amended IRC Section 415, mandating increases in these limits effective after December 31, 2001, and indexing them each year for inflation to keep retirement savings from falling behind increases in the cost of goods and services, thereby making retirees less dependent on Social Security retirement benefits (Chapter 12). The limits were set to expire after 2009, but the *Pension Protection Act of 2006* made the limits permanent. We will review these limits in our respective discussions of defined benefit and defined contribution plans.

Allowable Tax Deductions for Employers

Employers may take tax deductions for contributions to employee retirement plans based on three conditions. First, as you have read, retirement plans must be qualified. Second, an employer must make contributions before the due date for its federal income tax return for that year. For example, an employer received a tax deduction on contributions for 2006 when the contributions were made before April 17, 2007. Third, deductible contributions are based on designated amounts set forth by the IRC (as subsequently amended by the Economic Growth and Tax Relief Reconciliation Act of 2001 and the Pension Protection Act of 2006).

Plan Distribution Rules

Distribution refers to the payment of vested benefits to participants or beneficiaries. Distributions are payable in a variety of ways. **Lump sum distributions** are single payments of benefits. In defined contribution plans, lump sum distributions equal the vested amount (i.e., the sum of all employee and vested employer contributions, and interest on this sum). In defined benefit plans, lump sum distributions equal the equivalent of the vested accrued benefit.

A second form of distribution is the annuity. **Annuities** represent a series of payments for the life of the participant and beneficiary. Annuity contracts are usually purchased from insurance companies, which make payments according to the contract. The inherent risk of defined contribution plans has given rise to income annuities. **Income annuities** distribute income to retirees based on retirement savings paid to insurance companies in exchange for guaranteed monthly checks for life.

Plan Termination Rules and Procedures

Plan termination rules and procedures apply only to defined benefit plans. There are three types of plan terminations: standard termination, distress termination, and involuntary termination. Qualified plans must follow strict guidelines for plan terminations including sufficient notification to plan participants, notification to the PBGC, and distribution of vested benefits to participants and beneficiaries in a reasonable amount of time.

DEFINED BENEFIT PLANS

Defined benefit plans guarantee retirement benefits specified in the plan document. This benefit is usually expressed in terms of a monthly sum equal to a percentage of a participant's preretirement pay multiplied by the number of years he or she has worked for the employer. Although the benefit in these plans is fixed by a formula, the level of required employer contributions fluctuates from year to year. The level depends on the amount necessary to make certain that benefits promised will be available when participants and beneficiaries are eligible to receive them.

Benefit Formulas

Companies usually choose between two types of benefit formulas: flat benefit formulas and unit benefit formulas. The key factor distinguishing these two types of formulas is whether employees' years of service are considered. Years of service is a factor in unit benefit formulas, but not in flat benefit formulas. The IRS recognizes both formulas as appropriate calculation methods in employer-sponsored plans.

When companies introduce a defined benefit plan into an established workforce, they must decide whether to reward future performance only or to recognize past service as well. In the former case, all employees, regardless of service, are treated as new employees from the standpoint of benefits allocation.

Flat Benefit Formulas

Flat benefit formulas designate either a flat dollar amount per employee (flat amount formula) or a dollar amount based on an employee's compensation (flat percentage formula). Annual benefits are usually expressed as a percentage of final average wage or salary. The period used to calculate final average wage or salary usually equals the average amount based on the last three or four years of service.

Let's assume that in 2008 when Robert plans to retire, his final average salary in the 3-year period preceding retirement was $100,000 (based on $99,000 in 2005, $100,000 in 2006, and $101,000 in 2007). In this example, $100,000 = ($99,000 + $100,000 + $101,000)/3 years.

Also assume that the plan's designated percentage is 60 percent. Robert's annual retirement income equals $60,000 ($100,000 average annual income × 60 percent).

Flat benefit formulas often lead to resentment among employees because length of service is not a consideration. Longer-service employees expect to receive a higher percentage of final average salary during retirement than do employees who retire with substantially less service. There are two possible explanations for this expectation. First, longer-service employees feel that they have earned the right to receive a higher percentage. They argue that the combination of more years enabled them to contribute more productively to the company than employees with substantially fewer years of service. Second, the company should owe them a larger percentage in recognition of their loyalty and commitment to the company over a longer period.

Unit Benefit Formulas

Unit benefit formulas recognize length of service. Employers typically decide to contribute a specified dollar amount for each year worked by an employee. They alternatively may choose to contribute a specified percentage amount for years of service.

Annual benefits are usually based on age, years of service, and final average wages or salary. Retirement plans based on unit benefit formulas specify annual retirement benefits as a percentage of final average salary. Table 11-3 illustrates these percentages for one retirement plan based on age and years of service. Looking at this table, let's assume Mary retires at age 59 with 25 years of service. Let's also assume her final average salary is $52,500. Mary multiplies $52,500 by the annual percentage of 43.43 percent. Her annual benefit is $22,800.75 ($52,500 × 43.43 percent).

Minimum Funding Standards

As we discussed in Chapter 3, ERISA imposes strict funding requirements on qualified plans. Under defined benefit plans, employers make an annual contribution that is sufficiently large to ensure that promised benefits will be available to retirees. Actuaries periodically review several kinds of information to determine a sufficient funding level: life expectancies of employees and their designated beneficiaries, projected compensation levels, and the likelihood of employees terminating their employment before they have earned benefits. ERISA imposes the reporting of actuarial information to the IRS, which in turn submits these data to the U.S.

Department of Labor. The Department of Labor reviews the data to ensure compliance with ERISA regulations.

Benefit Limits and Tax Deductions

The IRC sets a maximum annual benefit for defined benefit plans that is equal to the lesser of $180,000 in 2007, or 100 percent of the highest average compensation for three consecutive years.[10] The limit is indexed for inflation in $5,000 increments each year beginning after 2006.[11]

TABLE 11-3   Annual Retirement Benefits Based on a Unit Benefit Formula

Years of Service	Age					
	60	59	58	57	56	55
5	...	...	...	...	...	...
6	...	...	...	...	...	...
7	...	...	...	...	...	...
8	13.36	12.56	11.76	10.96	10.15	9.35
9	15.03	14.13	13.23	12.32	11.42	10.52
10	16.70	15.70	14.70	13.69	12.69	11.69
11	18.60	17.48	16.37	15.25	14.14	13.02
12	20.50	19.27	18.04	16.81	15.58	14.35
13	22.40	21.06	19.71	18.37	17.02	15.68
14	24.30	22.84	21.38	19.93	18.47	17.01
15	26.20	24.63	23.06	21.48	19.91	18.34
16	28.10	26.41	24.73	23.04	21.36	19.67
17	30.00	28.20	26.40	24.60	22.80	21.00
18	31.90	29.99	28.07	26.16	24.24	22.33
19	33.80	31.77	29.74	27.72	25.69	23.66
20	35.70	33.56	31.42	29.27	27.13	24.99
21	37.80	35.53	33.26	31.00	28.73	26.46
22	39.90	37.51	35.11	32.72	30.32	27.93
23	42.00	39.48	36.96	34.44	31.93	29.40
24	44.10	41.45	38.81	36.16	33.52	30.87
25	46.20	43.43	40.66	37.88	35.11	32.34
26	48.30	45.40	42.50	39.61	36.71	33.81
27	50.40	47.38	44.35	41.33	38.30	35.28
28	52.50	49.35	46.20	43.05	39.90	36.75
29	54.60	51.32	48.05	44.77	41.50	38.22
30	56.70	53.30	49.90	46.49	43.09	39.69
31	59.00	55.46	51.92	48.38	44.84	41.30
32	61.30	57.62	53.94	50.27	46.59	42.91
33	63.60	59.78	55.97	52.15	48.34	44.52
34	65.90	61.95	57.99	54.04	40.08	46.13
35	68.20	68.20	68.20	68.20	68.20	68.20
36	70.50	70.50	70.50	70.50	70.50	70.50
37	72.80	72.80	72.80	72.80	72.80	72.80
38	75.10	75.00	75.00	75.00	75.00	75.00
39	77.40	75.00	75.00	75.00	75.00	75.00
40	79.70	75.00	75.00	75.00	75.00	75.00
+40	80.00	75.00	75.00	75.00	75.00	75.00

DEFINED CONTRIBUTION PLANS

Under **defined contribution plans**, employers and employees make annual contributions to separate accounts established for each participating employee, based on a formula contained in the plan document. Formulas typically call for employers to contribute a given percentage of each participant's compensation annually. Employers invest these funds on behalf of the employee, choosing from a variety of investment vehicles such as company stocks, diversified stock market funds, or federal government bond funds. Employees may be given a choice of investment vehicles based on the guidelines established by the employer. Defined contribution plans specify rules for the amount of annual contributions. Unlike defined benefit plans, these plans do not guarantee particular benefit amounts. Participants bear the risk of possible investment gain or loss. Benefit amounts depend upon several factors, including the contribution amounts, the performance of investments, and forfeitures transferred to participant accounts. **Forfeitures** come from the accounts of employees who terminated their employment prior to earning vesting rights.

Companies may choose to offer one or more specific type of defined contribution plans. Common examples of defined contribution plans include profit-sharing plans, stock bonus plans, and employee stock ownership plans. We will review each of these plans later in the chapter.

Individual Accounts

Defined contribution plans contain accounts for each employee into which contributions are made, and losses are debited or gains are credited. Contributions to each employee's account come from four possible sources. The first, employer contributions, are expressed as a percentage of an employee's wage or salary. In the case of profit-sharing plans, company profits are usually the basis for employer contributions. The second, employee contributions, are usually expressed as a percentage of the employee's wage or salary. The third, forfeitures, come from the accounts of employees who terminated their employment prior to earning vesting rights. The fourth contribution source is return on investments. In the case of negative returns (or loss), the corresponding amount is debited from employees' accounts.

Investments of Contributions

ERISA requires that a named **fiduciary** manage investments into defined contribution plans. Fiduciaries are individuals who manage employee benefit plans and pension funds. Fiduciaries also possess discretion in managing the assets of the plan, offering investment advice to employee participants, and administering the plan. Fiduciaries ultimately are responsible for minimizing the risk of loss of assets.[12]

Fiduciaries possess the authority to delegate investment responsibility to an investment manager. Under the supervision of the fiduciary, investment managers select investments based on a comparison of the risk and return potential of various investment options. Investment managers may invest assets in a variety of investment vehicles, including equities, government bonds, cash, insurance, and real estate. Investment managers usually invest assets in more than one type of investment vehicle to balance risk and return potential.

Employee Participation in Investments

Some companies may allow plan participants to choose the investment of funds in their individual accounts. It is not uncommon for large companies to offer investment alternatives through such companies as Fidelity, Vanguard, and T. Rowe Price.

Accrual Rules

The accrued benefit equals the balance in an individual's account.[13] Companies must not reduce contribution amounts based on age. They may also not set maximum age limits for discontinuing contributions.

Minimum Funding Standards

The minimum funding standard for defined contribution plans is less complex than it is for defined benefit plans. This standard is met when contributions to the individual accounts of plan participants meet the minimum amounts as specified by the plan.[14]

Contribution Limits and Tax Deductions

Employer contributions to defined contribution plans represent one factor in annual additions. **Annual addition** refers to the annual maximum allowable contribution to a participant's account in a defined contribution plan. The annual addition includes employer contributions, employee contributions, and forfeitures allocated to the participant's account.[15] In 2007, annual additions were limited to the lesser of $45,000 or 100 percent of the participant's compensation.[16]

The amount of an employer's annual deductible contribution to a participant's account depends on the type of defined contribution plan.[17] The Economic Growth and Tax Reconciliation Act of 2001 raised the allowable contribution amounts in effect before January 1, 2002. In 2005 the maximum contribution to a profit-sharing, stock bonus, or employee stock ownership plan was 25 percent of the compensation paid or accrued to participants in the plan. Section 401(k), 403(b), and 457 plans have contribution limits of $15,500 in 2007. The limit is indexed for inflation in $500 increments beginning in 2007.

TYPES OF DEFINED CONTRIBUTION PLANS

There are a variety of defined contribution plans. These include Section 401(k) plans, profit sharing, stock bonus plans, employee stock ownership plans, savings incentive match plans for employees (SIMPLEs), Section 403(b) tax-deferred annuities, and Section 457 plans. We will review each of these plans in turn.

Section 401(k) Plans

Section 401(k) plans are retirement plans named after the section of the IRC that created them. These plans, also known as cash or deferred arrangements (CODAs), permit employees to defer part of their compensation to the trust of a qualified defined contribution plan. Only private sector or tax-exempt employers are eligible to sponsor 401(k) plans.

Section 401(k) plans offer three noteworthy tax benefits. First, employees do not pay income taxes on their contributions to the plan until they withdraw funds. Second, employers deduct their contributions to the plan from taxable income. Third, investment gains are not taxed until participants receive payments.

Profit-Sharing Plans

Companies set up **profit-sharing plans** to distribute money to employees. Companies start by establishing a **profit-sharing pool** (i.e., the money earmarked for distribution to employees). Companies may also choose to fund profit-sharing plans based on gross sales revenue or some basis other than profits. Companies may also take a tax deduction for their contributions not to exceed 25 percent of the plan participants' compensation.[18]

As described in the previous section, a qualified profit-sharing plan may be the basis for a company's 401(k) plan.

Employer Contributions

Companies determine the pool of profit-sharing money by application of a formula every year or based on the discretion of their boards of directors. One of three common formulas establishes employer contributions. A **fixed first-dollar-of-profits formula** uses a specific percentage of either pretax or after-tax annual profits (alternatively, gross sales or some other basis) contingent upon the successful attainment of a company goal. For instance, a company might establish that the profit-sharing fund will equal 1 percent of corporate profits. Second, other companies use a **graduated first-dollar-of-profits formula** instead of a fixed percentage. For example, a company may choose to share 2 percent of the first $10 million of profits and 3 percent of the profits in excess of that level. Third, **profitability threshold formulas** fund profit-sharing pools only if profits exceed a predetermined minimum level, but fall below some established maximum level. Companies establish minimums to guarantee a return to shareholders before they distribute profits to employees. They establish maximums because they attribute any profits beyond this level to factors other than employee productivity or creativity (e.g., technological innovation).

Company boards of directors may use their discretion when setting contributions. This approach is somewhat risky: The IRS requires that employer contributions to qualified profit-sharing plans be made substantial and made on a recurring basis.[19] Failure to meet this criterion may require 100 percent vesting rights to all plan participants, regardless of tenure in the plan.

Allocation Formulas

After management selects a funding formula for the profit-sharing pool, they must consider how to distribute pool money among employees. Under a qualified defined contribution plan, the chosen allocation formula must not discriminate in favor of highly compensated employees. Companies usually make distributions in one of three ways: equal payments to all employees, proportional payments to employees based on annual salary, and proportional payments to employees based on their contribution to profits. **Equal payments** to all employees reflect a belief that all employees should share equally in the company's gains in order to promote cooperation among employees. Employee contributions to profits, however, probably vary. Most employers therefore divide the profit-sharing pool among employees based on a differential basis. Companies may disburse profits based on **proportional payments to employees based on their annual salary**. Higher paying jobs presumably indicate the greatest potential to influence a company's competitive position. Still, another approach is to disburse profits as **proportional payments to employees based on their contribution to profits**. Some companies measure employee contributions to profits based on job performance; however, this approach is not very feasible because it is difficult to isolate each employee's contributions to profits.

Stock Bonus Plans

As described earlier, a **stock bonus plan** may be the basis for a company's 401(k) plan. Qualified stock bonus plans and qualified profit-sharing plans are similar because both plans invest in company securities. These plans are also similar regarding nondiscrimination requirements and the deductibility of employer contributions; however, stock bonus plans reward employees with company stock (i.e., equity shares in the company). Benefits are usually paid in shares of company stock. Participants of stock bonus plans possess the right to vote as shareholders. Voting rights differ based on

TABLE 11-4 Selected Differences between Defined Benefit and Defined Contribution Plans

Characteristic	Defined Benefit Plan	Defined Contribution Plan
Benefit formula	Determines pension due at normal retirement age.	Determines amount regularly contributed to individual account.
Form of benefit expressed by formula	An annuity—a series of payments beginning at the plan's normal retirement age for the life of the participant.	A single lump sum distribution at any time.
Funding	Annual funding is based on an actuarial formula subject to strict limits set by the IRC and is not equivalent to annual increases in pension benefits.	Annual contributions and investment earnings are held in an individual account.
Investment risk/profit	Employee is guaranteed benefits regardless of investment returns on trust. Employer is responsible for ensuring sufficient funding to pay promised benefit.	Employee bears the investment risk, which can result in higher investment returns or the loss of previously accumulated pension benefits.
Insured benefit	Generally insured by PBGC.	By individual investment vehicle, if any.

SOURCE: U.S. General Accounting Office, *Cash Balance Plans: Implications for Retirement Income* (GAO/HEHS-00-207), (Washington, DC: General Accounting Office, 2000), pp. 9–10.

whether company stock is traded in public stock exchanges.[20] In the case of publicly traded stock, plan participants may vote on all issues.

Employee Stock Ownership Plans (ESOPs)

Employee stock option plans (ESOPs) may be the basis for a company's 401(k) plan, and these plans invest in company securities, making them similar to profit-sharing plans and stock bonus plans. ESOPs and profit-sharing plans differ because ESOPs usually make distributions in company stock rather than cash. ESOPs are essentially stock bonus plans that use borrowed funds to purchase stock.

ESOPs are either nonleveraged or leveraged plans.[21] In the case of **nonleveraged ESOPs**, the company contributes stock or cash to buy stock. The stock is then allocated to the accounts of participants. Nonleveraged plans are stock bonus plans. In the case of **leveraged ESOPs**, the plan administrator borrows money from a financial institution to purchase company stock. The company may use the borrowed money for different purposes, including financing of existing debt, estate planning, or financing an acquisition or divestiture. Over time, the company makes principal and interest payments to the ESOP to repay the loan. The stock purchased with the loan is placed in a suspense account until amounts equal to the employer's contributions are allocated to the individual accounts of participants.

Table 11-4 summarizes selected differences between defined benefit and defined contribution plans.

HYBRID PLANS: CASH BALANCE PLANS

Hybrid plans combine features of traditional defined benefit and defined contribution plans. We will discuss the cash balance plans, a type of hybrid plan that has stirred tremendous controversy in recent years.

Many employers have set aside traditional defined benefit pension plans for hybrid plans: Numerous accounts describe defined benefit plans as **golden handcuffs**, providing generous (golden) retirement income to workers who remain with the same employer (the handcuffs) throughout their work life. Such plans, which often base benefits on earnings in a worker's last years with the company, may provide lower benefits for those employees who work in multiple jobs throughout their lifetimes.

In January 2007, employees had worked for their current employer for an average of 3.7 years; those aged 45 to 54 had worked for their current employer an average of 7.6 years. These data suggest workers may be accumulating retirement benefits from several jobs; employers have attempted to deal with these changing needs by seeking alternative approaches to providing retirement income.

The different career plans of the younger generations have led many employers to conclude that their retirement plans were not beneficial to these younger, more mobile workers. This was not conducive to attracting potentially valuable employees that could help increase efficiency.[22]

Internal Revenue Service guidelines define **cash balance plans** as "defined benefit plans that define benefits for each employee by reference to the amount of the employee's hypothetical account balance"[23] Cash balance plans are a relatively new phenomenon compared to traditional defined benefit and defined contribution plans. Many companies have chosen to convert their defined benefit plans to cash balance plans for two key reasons. First, cash balance plans are less costly to employers than defined benefit plans. Second, they pay out benefits in a lump sum instead of a series of payments. This feature increases the portability of pension benefits from company to company. Companies are presumably in a better position to recruit more mobile workers.

Benefit Formulas

Companies establish individual accounts for employees as in defined contribution plans. They may choose from several methods of crediting contributions to cash balance plans. The most common approaches include a fixed percentage of earnings and percentages that vary by age, length of service, or earnings.

Participants receive credits expressed as a percentage of annual pay, and these credits earn interest at a designated rate. The interest rate credit is guaranteed instead of fluctuating with the performance of the investments. In addition, the amounts stated in these individual accounts are strictly hypothetical because the employer contributes money to the plan as a whole covering all employees. Complex federal rules require that employers have sufficient assets to cover the amounts expressed in every employee's hypothetical account. In defined contribution plans, on the other hand, the account balance is equal to actual assets held in trust for the participant, and the interest rate fluctuates with the performance of the investments.

Controversy Surrounding Cash Balance Plans

Two controversies have emerged. The first issue centers on favorable treatment to younger workers and unfavorable treatment to older employees. The second issue is based on the practice of converting traditional defined benefit plans to cash balance plans. We will review each of these in turn.

Age-Related Treatment

Cash balance plans are said to provide favorable treatment to younger workers and to workers who switch employers from time to time. These plans do not define benefits as a percentage of final or career average pay or as a flat dollar amount per year of service, which is the case for defined benefit plans. Defined benefit plans provide more favorable treatment to older employees because benefits accrue on an age-related basis, permitting older employees to earn benefits more quickly than younger workers.

Cash balance plans, on the other hand, award annual pay-related credits, much as defined contribution plans, with the contributions appreciating each year based on a specified interest rate.

The U.S. General Accounting Office (GAO) compared the rates of retirement benefit accrual in defined benefit plans and cash balance plans under a variety of assumptions. It concluded that cash balance plan accrual favors younger employees.[24] For example, a 25-year-old employee who is assumed to participate in a cash balance plan until retirement at age 65 accrues an incremental annuity benefit of about $1,660 at age 26, but earns a smaller incremental benefit of about $630 at age 65. Under a defined benefit plan, this same individual earns an incremental annuity benefit of $310 at age 26, but earns a higher incremental annuity benefit of about $2,440 at age 65.

The difference in accrual pattern between these plan types has led some people to question whether cash balance plans illegally discriminate on the basis of age. According to the GAO:

> Cash balance proponents define the accrued benefit as the employee's hypothetical account balance. Under this definition, cash balance plans generate a level rate of accrual for all employees regardless of age and therefore do not appear to raise issues of disparate treatment of employees based on age. Critics state that cash balance plans, as defined benefit plans under the law, must express an employee's accrued benefit as an annual benefit beginning at normal retirement age or the actuarial equivalent to a deferred annuity.[25] When cash balance plans are viewed in this way, the amount of the actuarially determined benefit is a function of the participant's age and decreases as the participant ages. Therefore, critics argue, cash balance plans violate the prohibition on age discrimination. Federal agencies are considering the issue of whether cash balance plans violate age discrimination statutes. Participants have filed a number of court cases alleging that cash balance plans are age discriminatory but no definitive decision has been reached.[26]

Converting Defined Benefit Plans to Cash Balance Plans As we discussed earlier, retirement benefits accrue at a decreasing rate in cash balance plans in contrast to an increasing rate in defined benefit plans. Converting from defined benefit plans to cash balance plans may result in older workers receiving smaller benefits. The GAO compared lump sum distributions for a traditional defined benefit plan with lump sum distributions for a cash balance plan following conversion at various ages at separation from employment.[27] Table 11-5 shows the increasing disparity in lump sum distributions for older workers after a conversion from a defined benefit plan to a cash balance plan.

Further consideration reveals that cash balance plans tend to produce the lowest annuity at retirement for the employee who was oldest at conversion. For example, the GAO study modeled benefits from a basic cash balance formula for a 35-, 45-, and 55-year-old employee with equal salary and tenure at conversion.[28] At retirement the 55-year-old employee would receive an annual annuity of $6,900 from the cash balance plan, the 45-year-old employee would receive $12,600 per year, and the 35-year-old employee about $24,000 a year. These monetary values simply represent the expected magnitude of differences.

Another problem with conversion is known as "wearaway." **Wearaway** means that some employees do not accrue benefits for a period of time following conversion, whereas others do not experience any interruption in accruing benefits. The GAO study indicated that the wearaway period at conversion is longer for older employees, and in addition, found that the wearaway period is increasingly longer for the older workers at conversion. There are two causes of wearaway. First, companies may create wearaway

TABLE 11-5   Lump Sum Distributions from a Traditional Final Average Pay Formula and a Cash Balance Formula after Conversion

Age at Separation	Final Average Pay Formula[a]	Cash Balance Formula[b]
30	$ 2,476	$ 2,476
35	7,849	13,699
40	18,684	30,358
45	39,618	54,510
50	79,096	88,926
53	117,686	116,000
55	152,611	137,322
60	288,878	204,673
65	544,153	297,625

Notes: Results are based on baseline scenario assumptions for a 30-year-old worker at conversion and show several possible ages when the worker might leave the firm. The 30-year-old worker was assigned a tenure and income value at conversion that correspond to the worker's age. Lump sum distributions paid from the traditional formula are calculated on the basis of annuity values that the formula would have produced had no conversion occurred and in accordance with IRC 417(e) regulations. Lump sum values are comparable at given ages but are not comparable across years.

[a]Based on normal retirement age annuity.

[b]Nominal account balance.

SOURCE: U.S. General Accounting Office, *Private Pensions: Implications of Conversions to Cash Balance Plans*, GAO/HEHS-00-185 (Washington, DC: General Accounting Office, 2000), pp. 22–23.

by setting a participant's hypothetical balance lower than the present value of accrued benefits under the traditional defined benefit plan. There are currently no regulations for setting opening hypothetical balances. Second, wearaway may occur because of changes in the federally mandated discount rate for determining lump sum distributions from defined benefit plans. The value of lump sum distributions increases when the discount rate falls; the value of distributions decreases when the discount rate increases.

Indeed, a variety of recent court rulings proved mixed on the issue about whether cash balance plans discriminate on the basis of age. Some courts recently concluded that these plans do not violate the Age Discrimination in Employment Act. In *Easton v. Onan Corp.*, a federal district judge ruled that pension age discrimination prohibitions do not apply to employees younger than normal retirement age.[29] The provisions were set to ensure that employees who chose to work past the normal retirement age continue to accrue pension benefits. In *Dan C. Tootle v. ARINC Inc.*, the judge ruled that a "sensible approach" to determine whether cash balance plans are discriminatory is to use a test from ERISA for defined contribution plans.[30] Plans are specifically not discriminatory as long as employer contributions are not reduced by age.

In *Cooper v. The IBM Personal Pension Plan,*[31] however, a U.S. District Court judge in southern Illinois ruled in 2003 that IBM Corporation's cash balance plan discriminated against IBM's older employees because the benefit credit provided to older employees purchased a much smaller benefit than the same benefit provided to a younger employee. The judge in the IBM case relied on ERISA-based discrimination tests for defined benefit plans as described earlier in the chapter.

Since then, language in the Pension Protection Act of 2006 tries to resolve the misunderstanding over wearaway provisions. This Act makes it illegal for employers to use wearaway provisions when converting a defined benefit plan to a cash balance plan. As a result, cash balance plan provisions must credit a participant with his or her accrued benefit under the old formula plus full credit for years of service after the adoption of the cash balance formula. The Pension Protection Act also allows employers to create new cash balance plans—or to convert existing defined benefit plans to a cash balance design—with much less fear of litigation.

Shortly after the Pension Protection Act was signed into law in August 2006, judges from the U.S. Seventh Circuit Court revisited the 2003 ruling in *Cooper v. The IBM Personal Pension Plan.* They reversed the 2003 ruling, concluding that the IBM Personal Pension Plan did not discriminate against employees on the basis of age. Older workers at IBM maintained that "Someone who leaves IBM at age 50, after 20 years of service, will have a larger annual benefit at 65 than someone whose 20 years of service conclude with retirement at age 65. The former receives 15 years' more interest than the latter." Judges in the 2006 review indicated that nothing in the ERISA language legislates against "the fact that younger workers have (statistically) more time left before retirement, and thus a greater opportunity to earn interest on each year's retirement savings. Treating the time value of money as a form of discrimination is not sensible."[32]

At the time this edition was being written, IBM made a request to the U.S. Supreme Court to hear this case in the hopes of overturning the Seventh Circuit Court's ruling. The U.S. Supreme Court declined to review the 2006 court decision in *Cooper v. The IBM Personal Pension Plan.* Nevertheless, other cases are pending in other Circuit Courts on whether cash balance plans discriminate illegally on the basis of age. No doubt, as you are reading this, it is possible that one or more have been decided, possibly endorsing or questioning whether cash balanced plans are age-biased.

DEFINING AND EXPLORING HEALTH INSURANCE PROGRAMS

Health insurance covers the costs of a variety of services that promote sound physical and mental health, including physical examinations, diagnostic testing, surgery, hospitalization, psychotherapy, dental treatments, and corrective prescription lenses for vision deficiencies. Employers usually enter into a contractual relationship with one or more insurance companies to provide health-related services for their employees and, if specified, employees' dependents. The contractual relationship, or **insurance policy**, specifies the amount of money the insurance company will pay for such particular services as physical examinations. Employers pay insurance companies a negotiated amount, or **premium**, to establish and maintain insurance policies. The term *insured* refers to employees covered by the insurance policy.

Companies can choose from three broad classes of health insurance programs in the United States, including *fee-for-service plans, managed care plans,* and *point-of-service plans. Point-of-service plans* combine features of fee-for-service and managed care plans. An emerging class of health insurance programs is based on *consumer-driven health care,* where employees play a greater role in decisions on their health care, have better access to information to make informed decisions, and share more in the costs. We discuss these types of plans later in this chapter.

It is also important to mention that health care in the United States is classified as a **multiple payer system**. In a multiple payer system, there is more than one party responsible for covering the cost of health care, including the government, employers, labor unions, employees, or individuals not currently employed (e.g., retirees, the unemployed, and employees whose employer does not pay for health care coverage). As we will discuss shortly, a variety of forces have contributed to the existence of a multiple payer health care system in the United States. A multiple payer system stands in contrast to a **single payer system** in which the government regulates the health care system and uses taxpayer dollars to fund health care such as in Canada and some other economically developed countries. Single payer systems are often referred to as **universal health care systems** because the government ensures that all of its citizens have access to quality health care regardless of ability to pay.

Origins of Health Insurance Benefits

The Great Depression of the 1930s gave rise to employer-sponsored health insurance programs. Widespread unemployment made it impossible for most individuals to afford health care. During this period, Congress proposed the Social Security Act of 1935 to address many of the social maladies caused by the adverse economic conditions, incorporating health insurance programs. President Franklin D. Roosevelt, however, opposed the inclusion of health coverage under the Social Security Act. Health insurance did not become part of the Social Security Act until an amendment to the act in 1965 established the Medicare program.

The government's choice not to offer health care benefits created opportunities for private sector companies to meet the public's need. In the 1930s hospitals controlled nonprofit companies that inspired today's Blue Cross and Blue Shield plans. At the time, Blue Cross plans allowed individuals to make monthly payments to cover the expense of possible future hospitalization. For-profit companies also formed to provide health care coverage, creating fee-for-service plans.

In the 1940s local medical associations created nonprofit Blue Shield plans, which were prepayment plans for physician services. The federal government also imposed wage freezes during World War II, which did not extend to employee benefit plans. Many employers began offering health care benefits to help compete for and retain the best employees, particularly during the labor shortage when U.S. troops were overseas fighting in World War II. In addition, employers recognized the possibility that they could promote productivity with healthier workforces. Without the assistance of employer-sponsored health insurance, employees could not afford to pay for medical services on their own. Many companies sought ways to promote productivity and morale through the implementation of welfare practices. In Chapter 1 we defined welfare practices as "anything for the comfort and improvement, intellectual or social, of the employees, over and above wages paid, which is not a necessity of the industry nor required by law."[33] Health insurance programs were among these practices.

Many companies discontinued health insurance benefits soon after the government lifted the wage freeze. The withdrawal of these and other benefits created discontent among employees, who viewed benefits as an entitlement. Legal battles ensued based on the claim that health protection was a fundamental right. In unionized companies, health insurance benefits became a mandatory subject of collective bargaining.

The 1950s were relatively uneventful years regarding employee benefits. In the 1960s the federal government amended the Social Security Act. Titles XVIII and XIX of the act established the Medicare and Medicaid programs (Chapter 12), respectively. These public programs provided access to health care services for a wide segment of the U.S. population in a relatively short period. The demand for health care services rose quickly relative to the supply of health care providers, prompting inflation in the price of health care services.

Congress enacted the Employee Retirement Income Security Act of 1974 to protect employee interests (Chapter 3). By providing financial incentives to companies, subject to becoming federally qualified, the **Health Maintenance Organization Act of 1973 (HMO Act)** promoted the use of health maintenance organizations. We will discuss the HMO Act later in the chapter.

Since the 1970s there has been substantial emphasis on managing costs, and consideration has been given to providing coverage to the uninsured (e.g., the failed national health care proposal under former President Bill Clinton). Some factors have eroded health insurance practices in companies. Unionized companies set the standards for employee benefits practices. In the 1980s unions made concessions on wages and benefits in exchange for promises of greater job security. Also, the decline in the manufacturing or goods-producing sector (e.g., automobiles, steel, mining), which was traditionally highly unionized, gave way to the typically nonunion service and information sectors of the economy (e.g., health care industry, retail trade, high-technology companies such as in software development). Furthermore, foreign competition created pressures, forcing U.S. companies to reduce costs. For example, many U.S. manufacturers moved operations to foreign countries with cheaper labor and fewer legal protections for employees (e.g., People's Republic of China, India). Notwithstanding these pressures, health insurance still is the mainstay of employee benefits programs in companies.

Health Insurance Coverage and Costs

Both employees and employers place a great deal of significance on company-sponsored health insurance benefits. Of course, company-sponsored programs provide employees with the means to afford expensive health care services. As we noted before companies stand to gain from sponsoring these benefits in at least two ways. First, a healthier workforce should experience a lower incidence of sickness absenteeism. By keeping absenteeism in check, a company's overall productivity and product or service quality should be higher. Second, health insurance offerings should help the recruitment and retention of employees. It is not surprising that a large percentage of companies include health insurance programs as a feature of employee benefits programs, extending coverage to substantial numbers of employees and their dependents. At the same time, the rampant rise in health care prices is putting substantial pressure on cost-conscious companies.

At the time of this book's publication, the most recent comprehensive national data indicate that just more than half (52 percent) of all private sector employees had access to at least one employer-sponsored health insurance program in 2006.[34] Employees' access to health insurance programs vary by their size, industry group, and union presence. A higher percentage of employees in larger companies had access to employer-sponsored health insurance than employees in smaller companies. This is also the case for employees in goods-producing companies than service-producing companies, and for union employees than nonunion employees. Table 11-6 illustrates these facts in greater detail.

Health insurance premiums are quite high, often amounting to as much as one third of annual benefits costs. In March 2006 the average monthly health insurance premium was $266.50 per employee for single coverage.[35] **Single coverage** extends benefits only to the covered employee. Family coverage is substantially higher, averaging $617.18 per employee.[36] **Family coverage** offers benefits to the covered employee and his or her family members as defined by the plan (usually, spouse and children). Since the 1980s many insurance plans have extended family coverage to unmarried heterosexual or homosexual domestic partnerships. Domestic partnership is established by providing evidence of living together, financial interdependence, and joint responsibility for each other's welfare.

Many private sector companies require employees to contribute a portion of health insurance premiums because of the considerable cost.[37] In 2006 a relatively small percentage of employees with company-sponsored health insurance coverage made no contributions (i.e., 25 percent of employees received single coverage and 13 percent received family coverage). Employee contributions represent a relatively

TABLE 11-6	Percentage of Workers with Access to Health Care, by Selected Characteristics, Private Industry			
	Medical Care	*Dental Care*	*Vision Care*	*Prescription Drug Coverage*
All employees	71	46	29	67
Worker characteristics				
White-collar occupations	77	53	32	72
Blue-collar occupations	77	46	31	73
Service occupations	45	27	19	43
Full time	85	55	34	81
Part time	22	15	11	21
Union	89	69	54	86
Nonunion	68	43	26	64
Establishment characteristics				
Goods producing	86	56	35	82
Service producing	66	43	27	62
1–99 workers	59	31	20	56
100 workers or more	84	64	40	80

SOURCE: U.S. Bureau of Labor Statistics. National Compensation Survey, March 2006 (Summary 06-05).

small percentage of the health insurance premiums. Employees with single coverage contributed nearly 23 percent and those with family coverage contributed nearly 34 percent.

Group coverage extends coverage to a group of employees and their dependents under a single master contract. Insurance providers issue master contracts to employers, professional associations, labor unions, and trust funds established to provide health insurance to designated people. These entities are known as **group policyholders**. The underwriting process is somewhat different for group policies. Group policies generally do not exclude any group member based on health status. Instead, they focus mainly on establishing the premium for the master contract, usually expressed on an annual basis. Insurance providers use experience ratings issued by actuaries to set premiums. **Experience ratings** specify the incidence, type, and financial cost of insurance claims for groups (i.e., everyone as a whole covered under a group plan). Experience ratings hold employers (and other group entities described earlier) financially accountable for past claims, establishing the basis for charging different premiums.

We will now turn our attention to long-standing and newer approaches to health insurance coverage.

FEE-FOR-SERVICE PLANS

Three long-standing forms of health insurance programs include fee-for-service plans, managed care plans, and point-of-service plans. Larger employers commonly offer employees one or more type of health insurance program. We discuss each of these in turn.

Fee-for-service plans provide protection against health care expenses in the form of a cash benefit paid to the insured or directly to the health care provider after the employee has received health care services. These plans pay benefits on a reimbursement basis. Three types of eligible health expenses are hospital expenses, surgical expenses, and physician charges. Under fee-for-service plans, policyholders (employees) may generally select any licensed physician, surgeon, or medical facility for treatment, and the insurer reimburses the policyholders after medical services are rendered.

There are two types of fee-for-service plans. The first type, **indemnity plans**, is based on a contract between the employer and an insurance company. The contract specifies the expenses that are covered and the rate. The second type, **self-funded plans**, operates in the same fashion as indemnity plans.

The main difference between insurance plans offered by independent insurance companies and self-funded insurance plans centers on how benefits provided to policyholders are financed. When companies elect indemnity plans, they establish a contract with an independent insurance company. Insurance companies pay benefits from their financial reserves, which are based on the premiums companies and employees pay to receive insurance. Companies may instead choose to self-fund employee insurance. Such companies pay benefits directly from their own assets, either current cash flow or funds set aside in advance for potential future claims. The decision to self-fund is based on financial considerations. Self-funding makes sense when a company's financial burden of covering employee medical expenses is less than the cost to subscribe to an insurance company for coverage. By not paying premiums in advance to an independent carrier, a company retains these funds for current cash flow.

Types of Medical Expense Benefits

Fee-for-service plans provide three types of medical benefits under a specified policy: hospital expense benefits, surgical expense benefits, and physician expense benefits. Companies sometimes select major medical plans to provide comprehensive medical coverage instead of limiting coverage to the three specific kinds just noted, or to supplement these specific benefits.

Hospitalization Benefits

Hospitalization benefits defray expenses associated with treatment in hospitals. Fee-for-service plans distinguish between inpatient benefits and outpatient benefits. **Inpatient benefits** cover expenses associated with overnight hospital stays; **outpatient benefits** cover expenses for treatments in hospitals not requiring overnight stays. Fee-for-service plans also describe the extent of coverage based on a schedule of benefits, usually expressed as the daily amount of the hospital stay.

Surgical Benefits

Surgical expense benefits pay for medically necessary surgical procedures but usually not for elective surgeries such as cosmetic surgery. Fee-for-service plans generally pay expenses according to a schedule of **usual, customary, and reasonable charges**. The usual, customary, and reasonable charge is defined as not more than the physician's usual charge, within the customary range of fees charged in the locality, and reasonable based on the medical circumstances. Whenever actual surgical expenses exceed the usual, customary, and reasonable level, the patient must pay the difference. Finally, such policies cover a physician's charges for services rendered in hospital on inpatient or outpatient bases as well as office visits.

Physician Benefits

Physician benefits defray the costs of physician fees associated with hospital stays or office visits. In extenuating circumstances, fee-for-service plans provide coverage for home visits. Extenuating circumstances usually refer to instances when travel to a medical facility would jeopardize a patient's life.

Features of Fee-for-Service Plans

Fee-for-service plans contain a variety of stipulations designed to control costs and to limit a covered individual's financial liability. Common fee-for-service stipulations include deductibles, coinsurance, out-of-pocket maximums, preexisting condition clauses, preadmission certification, second surgical opinions, and maximum benefits limits.

Deductible

A common feature of fee-for-service plans is the **deductible**. Over a designated period, employees must pay for services (i.e., meet a deductible) that they have to pay before insurance benefits become active. The deductible amount is modest, usually a fixed amount ranging anywhere between $100 and $500 depending on the plan. Deductible amounts may also depend on annual earnings, expressed either as a fixed amount for a range of earnings or as a percentage of income. Table 11-7 illustrates deductibles based on annual salary. The deductible feature applies to a designated period, usually a 1-year period that corresponds with the calendar year or the company's benefit plan year (see Chapter 10).

Coinsurance

Insurance plans feature coinsurance, which becomes relevant after the insured pays the annual deductible. **Coinsurance** refers to the percentage of covered expenses paid by the insured. Most indemnity plans stipulate 20 percent coinsurance. This means that the plan will pay 80 percent of covered expenses. whereas the policyholder is responsible for the difference, in this case 20 percent.

Coinsurance amounts vary according to the type of expense. Insurance plans most commonly apply no coinsurance for diagnostic testing and 20 percent for other medical services. Many insurance plans provide benefits for mental health services. Coinsurance rates for these services tend to be the highest, usually 50 percent.

Out-of-Pocket Maximum

As discussed earlier, health care costs are on the rise. Despite generous coinsurance rates, the expense amounts for which individuals are responsible can be staggering.

TABLE 11-7 Plan Year Deductibles

The benefits described in this summary represent the major areas of coverage. The plan year is July 1 through June 30 of the following year.

Plan year deductible	The plan year deductible is indexed to salary for employees. See the following table for current plan year information.
Additional deductibles	Each emergency room visit $200
	Non-PPO hospital admission $200
	Transplant deductible $100

Employee's Annual Salary (Based on each employee's annual salary as of April 1)	Member Plan Year Deductible	Family Plan Year Deductible Cap
$52,700 or less	$250	$300
$52,701–$66,000	$350	$400
$66,001 or more	$450	$550
Retiree/annuitant/survivor	$250	$300
Dependents	$200	NA

These amounts are often beyond the financial means of most individuals. Thus, most plans specify the maximum amount a policyholder must pay per calendar year or plan year, known as the **out-of-pocket maximum** provision.

The purpose of the out-of-pocket maximum provision is to protect individuals from catastrophic medical expenses or expenses associated with recurring episodes of the same illness. Out-of-pocket maximums are usually stated as a fixed dollar amount and apply to expenses beyond the deductible amount. Unmarried individuals often have an annual out-of-pocket maximum of $1,000, and family out-of-pocket maximums are as high as $3,500. For example, an insurance plan specifies a $200 deductible. An unmarried person is responsible for the first $200 of expenses plus additional expenses up to $800 per year (i.e., the out-of-pocket maximum) for a total of $1,000.

Table 11-8 shows an example of an out-of-pocket maximum as well as coinsurance rates and deductible amounts for specific services.

Preexisting Condition Clauses

A **preexisting condition** is a condition for which medical advice, diagnosis, care, or treatment was received or recommended during a designated period preceding the beginning of coverage. The designated period for preexisting conditions usually spans between 3 months and 1 year. Insurance companies impose preexisting conditions to limit their liabilities for serious medical conditions that predate an individual's coverage. As discussed in Chapter 3, the HIPPA of 1996 places restrictions on the use of preexisting condition clauses based on credits for prior coverage under a former employer's health plan.

Preadmission Certification

Many insurance plans require **preadmission certification** of medical necessity for hospitalization. Physicians specifically must receive approval from a registered nurse or medical doctor employed by an insurance company before admitting patients to the hospital on a nonemergency basis (i.e., when a patient's life is not in imminent danger). Insurance company doctors and nurses judge whether hospitalization or alternative care is necessary. In addition, they determine the length of stay appropriate for the medical condition. Precertification requirements reserve the right for insurance companies not to pay for unauthorized admissions or hospital stays that extend beyond the approved period.

Second Surgical Opinions

Second surgical opinions reduce unnecessary surgical procedures (and costs) by encouraging an individual to seek an independent opinion from another doctor.

TABLE 11-8 Deductibles and Out-of-Pocket Maximums

General Deductibles: $1,250 per individual; $2,500 per family per plan year

Professional and physician coinsurance (20%)
Physician network, where available (10%)
PPO inpatient coinsurance (10%)
Transplant deductible ($100)
Transplant inpatient and outpatient coinsurance (20%)
Standard hospital coinsurance (20%)
Standard hospital admission deductible ($200)
All emergency room deductibles ($200)
Emergency room coinsurance (20%)

Following a recommendation of surgery from a physician, many individuals are inclined to seek an independent opinion to avoid the risks associated with surgery. With second surgical opinion provisions, insurance companies cover the cost of this consultation. Some insurance companies require second surgical opinions before authorizing surgery, whereas others offer second surgical opinion consultations as an option to each individual.

Maximum Benefit Limits

Insurance companies specify **maximum benefit limits**, expressed as a dollar amount over the course of one year or over an insured's lifetime. In many cases, insurance policies specify both annual maximums and lifetime maximums. They may also choose not to set any dollar limit to benefits. Setting annual maximums provide insurance companies with greater control over total cost expenditures. A maximum lifetime benefits provision protects employers from the costs of long-term or catastrophic claims and repeating incidences of illness.

MANAGED CARE PLANS

Managed care plans emphasize cost control by limiting an employee's choice of doctors and hospitals. Three common forms of managed care are *health maintenance organizations* (HMOs), *preferred provider organizations* (PPOs), and *point-of-service* (POS) plans.

Health Maintenance Organizations

HMOs are sometimes described as providing **prepaid medical services** because fixed periodic enrollment fees cover HMO members for all medically necessary services only if the services are delivered or approved by the HMO. HMOs generally provide inpatient and outpatient care as well as services from physicians, surgeons, and other health care professionals. Most medical services are either fully covered or, in the case of some HMOs, participants are required to make nominal **copayments**. Copayments represent nominal payments an individual makes as a condition of receiving services. HMOs express copayments as fixed amounts for different services (e.g., office visits, prescription drugs, and emergency room treatment). Common copayment amounts vary between $15 and $25 for each doctor's office visit, and $10 to $50 per prescription drug. We address the reason for the wide variation in prescription drug copayment amounts later in this chapter.

Features of Health Maintenance Organizations

HMO plans share several features in common with fee-for-service plans, including out-of-pocket maximums, preexisting condition clauses, preadmission certification, second surgical opinions, and maximum benefits limits. HMOs differ from fee-for-service plans in three important ways. First, HMOs offer prepaid services, whereas fee-for-service plans operate on a reimbursement basis. Second, HMOs include the use of primary care physicians as a cost-control measure. Third, coinsurance rates are generally lower in HMO plans than in fee-for-service plans.

Table 11-9 illustrates the features of an HMO.

Primary Care Physicians

HMOs designate some of their physicians, usually general or family practitioners, as primary care physicians. HMOs assign each member to a primary care physician or require each member to choose one. **Primary care physicians** determine when

TABLE 11-9   HMO Benefits

HMO Plan Design	
Plan year maximum benefit	Unlimited
Lifetime maximum benefit	Unlimited
Hospital Services	
Inpatient hospitalization	100% after $150 copayment per admission
Alcohol and substance abuse* *(maximum number of days determined by the plan)*	100% after $150 copayment per admission
Psychiatric admission* *(maximum number of days determined by the plan)*	100% after $150 copayment per admission
Outpatient surgery	100%
Diagnostic lab & X-ray	100%
Emergency room hospital services	100% after $200 or 50% copayment, whichever is less
Professional and Other Services	
Physician visits *(including physical exams & immunizations)*	100%, $15 copayment may apply
Well baby care	100%
Psychiatric care* *(maximum number of days determined by the plan)*	100% after $20 or 20% copayment per visit
Alcohol and substance abuse care* *(Maximum number of days determined by the plan)*	100% after $20 or 20% copayment per visit
Prescription drugs restrictions may apply. Formulary Durable medical equipment	$12 copayment, generic incentive and formulary is subject to change during the plan year; 80%

*HMOs determine the maximum number of inpatient days and outpatient visits for psychiatric and alcohol/substance abuse treatment. Each plan must provide for a minimum of 10 inpatient days and 20 outpatient visits per plan year. These are in addition to detoxification benefits that include diagnosis and treatment of medical complications.

Some HMOs may provide benefit limitations on a calendar year basis.

patients need the care of specialists. HMOs use primary care physicians to control costs by significantly reducing the number of unnecessary visits to specialists. As primary care physicians, doctors perform several duties. The most important duty is perhaps to diagnose the nature and seriousness of an illness promptly and accurately, after which the primary care physician refers the patient to the appropriate specialist.

Copayments

The most common HMO copayments apply to physician office visits, hospital admissions, prescription drugs, and emergency room services. Office visits are nominal amounts, usually $10 to $15 per visit. Hospital admissions and emergency room services are higher, ranging between $50 and $150 for each occurrence. Mental health services and substance abuse treatment require copayments as well. Inpatient services require copayments that are similar in amount to those for hospital admissions for medical treatment; however, copayments for outpatient services (e.g., psychotherapy, consultation with a psychiatrist, or treatment at a substance abuse facility) are generally expressed as a fixed percentage of the fee for each visit or treatment. HMOs usually charge a copayment ranging between 15 and 25 percent.

PREFERRED PROVIDER ORGANIZATIONS

Under a **preferred provider organization (PPO)**, a select group of health care providers agrees to furnish health care services to a given population at a higher level of reimbursement than under fee-for-service plans. Physicians qualify as preferred providers by meeting quality standards, agreeing to follow cost-containment procedures implemented by the PPO, and accepting the PPOs reimbursement structure. In return, the employer, insurance company, or third-party administrator helps guarantee provider physicians minimum patient loads by furnishing employees with financial incentives to use the preferred providers.

Features of Preferred Provider Organizations

PPO plans include features that resemble fee-for-service plans or HMO plans. Features most similar to fee-for-service plans are out-of-pocket maximums and coinsurance, and those most similar to HMOs include the use of nominal copayments. Preexisting condition clauses, preadmission certification, second surgical opinions, and maximum benefits limits are similar to those in fee-for-service and HMO plans. PPOs contain deductible and coinsurance provisions that differ somewhat from other plans.

Deductibles

PPOs include deductible features. The structure and amount of deductibles under PPO plans most closely resemble practices commonly used in fee-for-service plans. Unlike fee-for-service plans, PPOs often apply different deductible amounts for services rendered within and outside the approved network. Higher deductibles are set for services rendered by nonnetwork providers to discourage participants from using services outside the network.

Coinsurance

Coinsurance is a feature of PPO plans, and its structure is most similar to fee-for-service plans. PPOs calculate coinsurance as a percentage of fees for covered services. PPOs also use two sets of coinsurance payments: The first set applies to services rendered within the network of care providers; the second to services rendered outside the network. Coinsurance rates for network services are substantially lower than they are for nonnetwork services. Coinsurance rates for network services range between 10 and 20 percent. Nonnetwork coinsurance rates run between 60 and 80 percent.

POINT-OF-SERVICE PLANS

A **point-of-service plan (POS)** combines features of fee-for-service systems and health maintenance organizations. Employees pay a nominal copayment for each visit to a designated network of physicians. In this regard, POS plans are similar to HMOs. Unlike HMOs, however, employees possess the option to receive care from health care providers outside the designated network of physicians, but they pay somewhat more for this choice. This choice feature is common to fee-for-service plans.

SPECIALIZED INSURANCE BENEFITS

Employers often use separate insurance plans to provide specific kinds of benefits. Benefits professionals refer to these plans as **carve-out plans**. Carve-out plans are set up to cover dental care, vision care, prescription drugs, mental health and substance abuse, and maternity care. Specialty HMOs or PPOs usually manage carve-out plans based on the expectation that single-specialty practices may control costs more effectively than multi-specialty medical practices. We will focus on prescription drug plans and mental health and substance abuse plans because of the rampant inflation in prescription drugs costs and the increased recognition that mental health disorders may hinder worker productivity.

Prescription Drug Plans

Prescription drug plans cover the costs of drugs. These plans apply exclusively to drugs that state or federal laws require to be dispensed by licensed pharmacists. Prescription drugs dispensed to individuals during hospitalization or treatment in long-term care facilities are not covered by prescription drug plans. Insurers specify which prescription drugs are covered, how much they will pay, and the basis for paying for drugs.

Three kinds of prescription drug programs are currently available to companies that choose to provide these benefits to employees. The first, **medical reimbursement plans**, reimburse employees for some or all of the cost of prescription drugs. These programs are usually associated with self-funded or independent indemnity plans. Similar to indemnity plans, medical reimbursement plans pay benefits after an employee has met an annual deductible for the plan. After meeting the deductible, these plans offer coinsurance, usually 80 percent of the prescription drug cost, and the participant pays the difference. Maximum annual and lifetime benefits amounts vary based on the provisions set forth in the plan.

The second kind of plan, often referred to as a **prescription card program**, operates similarly to managed care programs because it offers prepaid benefits with nominal copayments. The name arose from the common practice of pharmacies requiring the presentation of an identification card. Prescription card programs limit benefits to prescriptions filled at participating pharmacies, similar to managed care arrangements for medical treatment. Copayment amounts vary from $5 to $50 per prescription. The amount depends upon whether the prescriptions meet criteria set by the plan, including the use of generic alternatives and the categorization of prescription drugs on formularies. **Formularies** are lists of drugs proven to be clinically appropriate and cost effective. Participants pay lower copayments for prescription drugs that meet the established criteria. Prescription card programs may be associated with an independent insurer or as part of an established HMO.

The third type of plan, a **mail order prescription drug program**, dispenses expensive medications used to treat chronic health conditions such as HIV infection or such neurological disorders as Parkinson's disease. Health insurers specify whether participants must receive prescription drugs through mail order programs or locally approved pharmacies. Cost is the driving factor for this decision. Mail order programs offer a cost advantage because they purchase medications at discounted prices in large volumes. A single mail order program supplies medication to participants of many health insurance plans nationwide. Local pharmacies do not enjoy this advantage because their patronage is much smaller, limited to people who live in close proximity.

The costs of these prescription drug plans vary. Reimbursement plans tend to be most expensive because pharmacies charge full retail price. Reimbursement plans also entail substantial administrative costs because an administrator evaluates each claim, applies deductibles, and prepares an explanation of benefits. The prescription card and mail order programs are usually less expensive because insurance companies have negotiated lower prices in exchange for providing a significant volume of individuals who will need prescription medications. In addition, costs are lower because participants make copayments when they order prescriptions and the pharmacy bills the insurance company on a set interval for all the prescriptions filled during this period (e.g., every week or two weeks).

Many prescription drug plans increasingly contain two cost-control features: formularies and multiple tiers. Many plans establish formularies to manage costs. The basis for setting formularies varies from plan to plan. For example, some plans prescribe drugs that are therapeutically equivalent to more expensive drugs and they use lower levels of coinsurance or copayments to encourage usage. Other plans are more restrictive by limiting coverage only to a specified set of prescription drugs.

Multiple tiers specify copayment amounts an individual will pay for a specific prescription. Multitier prescription drug programs usually specify three tiers, from least copayment amount to highest copayment amount: generic ($5 to $10 per prescription), formulary brand name medication ($10 to $25 per prescription), and nonformulary brand name medication ($25 to full price per prescription). The idea behind multitier prescription plans is that employees will choose less-expensive and equally effective alternatives to nonformulary medications. For example, bupropion hydrochloride (used to relieve symptoms of clinical depression or to aid in smoking cessation) may be obtained as a generic of the brand name Wellbutrin, manufactured by GlaxoSmithKline.

Mental Health and Substance Abuse

Approximately 25 percent of Americans experience some form of mental illness (e.g., clinical depression) at least once during their lifetimes. Psychiatrists define mental disorder as "a behavioral or psychological syndrome or pattern . . . associated with present distress (a painful symptom) or disability (impairment in one or more important areas of functioning) or with a significantly increased risk of suffering death, pain, disability, or an important loss of freedom."[38] Nearly 20 percent develop a substance abuse problem. As a result, insurance plans provide mental health and substance abuse benefits designed to cover treatment of mental illness and chemical dependence on alcohol and legal and illegal drugs. Delivery methods include fee-for-service plans and managed care options. As we discussed in Chapter 10, employee assistance programs (EAPs) represent a portal to taking advantage of employer-sponsored mental health and substance abuse treatment options. EAPs help employees cope with personal problems that may impair their personal lives or job performance, including alcohol or drug abuse, domestic violence, the emotional impact of AIDS and other diseases, clinical depression, and eating disorders. EAPs also assist employers in helping troubled employees identify and solve problems that may be interfering with their job or personal life.

Features of Mental Health and Substance Abuse Plans

Mental health and substance abuse plans cover the costs of a variety of treatments, including prescription psychiatric drugs (e.g., antidepressant medication), psychological testing, inpatient hospital care, and outpatient care (e.g., individual or group therapy).

Mental health benefits amounts vary by the type of disorder. Psychiatrists and psychologists rely on the *Diagnostic and Statistical Manual of Mental Disorders (DSM-IV)* to diagnose mental disorders based on symptoms, and both fee-for-service and managed care plans rely on the *DSM-IV* to authorize payment of benefits. As discussed earlier, HMOs usually charge a copayment ranging between 15 and 25 percent.

From the employee's perspective, coinsurance and maximum benefits amounts are generally less generous than general health plans in three ways. First, coinsurance amounts for mental health and substance abuse benefits, expressed as a percentage of treatment cost for both indemnity and managed care plans, range between 40 and 50 percent. Second, mental health and substance abuse plans limit the annual number of outpatient visits or days of inpatient care. Third, annual and lifetime maximum benefits were set significantly lower (e.g., $1,500 and $10,000, respectively). The **Mental Health Parity Act**, however, mandated increases in annual lifetime limits for mental health plans until its current expiration date (i.e., December 31, 2007).[39]

CONSUMER-DRIVEN HEALTH CARE

Managed care plans became popular alternatives to fee-for-service plans mainly to help employers and insurance companies more effectively manage the costs of health care. As discussed, managed care plans by design imposed substantial restrictions on an employee's ability to make choices about from whom they could receive medical treatment, the gatekeeper role of primary care physicians, and the level of benefits they could receive based on designated in- and nonnetwork providers.

Despite the cost control objectives of managed care, health care costs have continued to rise dramatically over the years while also restricting employee choice. **Consumer-driven health care** refers to the objective of helping companies maintain control over costs while also enabling employees to make greater choices about health care. This approach may enable employers to lower the cost of insurance premiums by selecting plans with higher employee deductibles. The most popular consumer-driven approaches are flexible spending accounts and health reimbursement accounts. These accounts provide employees with resources to pay for medical and related expenses not covered by higher deductible insurance plans at substantially lower costs to employers.

Flexible spending accounts (FSAs) permit employees to pay for specified health care costs that are not covered by an employer's insurance plan. Prior to each plan year, employees elect the amount of pay they wish to allocate to this kind of plan. Employers then use these moneys to reimburse employees for expenses incurred during the plan year that qualify for repayment.

Qualifying expenses include an individual's out-of-pocket costs for medical treatments, products, or services related to a mental or physical defect or disease, along with certain associated costs (e.g., health insurance deductibles or transportation to get medical care); however, health, life, or long-term care insurance premiums paid for by an employer or through an employee's pretax salary reductions generally do not qualify for reimbursement under a health FSA. Other exclusions include medical expenses reimbursed through health insurance plans and the costs of purely cosmetic procedures that enhance appearance but are not related to treating a disease or defect. Over-the-counter products are qualified expenses if they are used to diagnose, treat, alleviate, or prevent a disease or ailment (e.g., blood sugar monitoring kits for diabetic patients or crutches and bandages for someone with a serious leg injury).

A significant advantage to employees is the ability to make contributions to their FSAs on a pretax basis; however, a noteworthy drawback is the "use it or lose it" provision of FSAs. FSAs require employees to estimate the amount of money they think they will need for eligible medical expenses. Of course, it is difficult to predict many medical needs and to estimate the costs of anticipated medical needs. Employees lose contributions to their FSAs when they overestimate the cost of medical needs because employers neither allow employees to carry balances nor do employers reimburse employees for balances remaining at the end of the year.

Employers bear some risk from offering FSAs to employees. The maximum amount of expenses for which an employee can be reimbursed under a dependent care FSA is $5,000 annually ($2,500 for a married taxpayer filing separately). Although there is no statutory limit on the amount of reimbursement employees can receive under a medical FSA, employers usually set a maximum limit (e.g., $3,000) to protect themselves against major losses under the **risk-of-loss rules** or **uniform coverage requirement**. Under this requirement, employers are obligated to make the full amount of benefits and coverage elected under an FSA plan available to employees from the first day the plan becomes effective, regardless of how much money an employee has actually contributed.

Let's assume an employee plans to contribute $1,500 per year to her employer's FSA plan, based on monthly contributions of $125. In this case $125 per month equals the $1,500 total annual contribution divided by 12 months per year. Continuing with this example, let's assume that this employee has a minor illness after making only three monthly contributions to the account ($375), and the medical and prescription costs to treat this minor illness are $1,275. The employer must allow this employee to withdraw $1,275 even though he or she has contributed only $375 thus far. This situation places demands on employer cash resources. In addition, if this employee were to leave the company after this 3-month period, the employer would have paid $900 out of its own funds toward this employee's treatment (i.e., $1,275 for the treatment cost less $375, this employee's contribution to the FSA).

On the other hand, employers may establish **health reimbursement accounts** (HRAs). The purpose of HRAs and FSAs are similar with two important differences. First, employers make the contributions to each employee's HRA whereas employees fund FSAs with pretax contributions deducted from their pay. Second, HRAs permit employees to carry over unused account balances from year to year, whereas employees forfeit unused FSA account balances present at the end of the year.

The idea of consumer-driven health care has most recently received substantially greater attention than before because of the Bush administration (President George W. Bush) and the Republican-led Congress, who favor greater employee involvement in their medical care and reducing the cost burden for companies to help maintain competitiveness in the global market. The **Medicare Prescription Drug, Improvement and Modernization Act of 2003**[40] added section 223 to the IRC, effective January 1, 2004, to permit eligible individuals to establish **health savings accounts** (HSAs) to help employees pay for medical expenses. In 2007, an employer, an employee, or both, may contribute as much as $2,850 annually for unmarried employees without dependent children or as much as $5,650 for married or unmarried employees with dependent children. Employers may require employees to contribute toward these limits. Employee contributions would be withheld from an employee's pay on a pretax basis. Employers offer HSAs along with a high deductible insurance policy, established for employees. **High-deductible health insurance plans** require substantial deductibles and low out-of-pocket maximums. For individual coverage, the minimum annual deductible was $1,100 with maximum out-of-pocket limits at or below $5,500 in 2007. For family coverage, the deductible was $2,200 with maximum out-of-pocket limits at or below $10,500.

HSAs offer four main advantages to employees relative to FSAs and HSAs. First, HSAs are portable, which means that the employee owns the account balance after the employment relationship ends. Second, HSAs are subject to inflation-adjusted funding limits. In 2006, total contributions from both an employer or employee to an individual's HSA could not exceed the high-deductible health plan's annual deductible or $2,850 for individual coverage ($5,650 in the case of family coverage), whichever is less. An additional $700 may be contributed for employees who are at least 55 years old, but not yet eligible for Medicare. This limit will increase annually in $100 increments until it reaches $1,000 in 2009. Third, employees may receive medical services from doctors, hospitals, and other health care providers of their choice, and they may choose the type of medical services they purchase, including such items as long-term care, eye care, and prescription drugs. FSAs and HRAs substantially limit employee choice. Fourth, HSA assets must be held in trust and cannot be subject to forfeiture (i.e., any unspent balances in the HSA can be rolled over annually and accumulate tax-free until the participant's death). There are no legal vesting requirements for FSAs and HRAs, which mean that employees do not possess the right to claim unused balances when they terminate employment.

Despite the noteworthy advantages of HSA usage to employees, relatively few employees have them as part of their benefits programs at work. According to the National Compensation Survey, only 6 percent of all private sector employees had the option to participate in an FSA in 2006, up just 1 percent from 2005.

Another concern is that users will not seek preventative or necessary care because of the cost. There could be underlying health problems in the early stages that do not affect how one feels; however, by avoiding preventive care, health issues that could have been easily treated could become serious, leading to short- or long-term disability. The cost of disability insurance will ultimately increase, adding to heavy cost burden of employee benefits plans.

SUMMARY

This chapter reviewed the fundamental concepts of company-sponsored retirement plans and company-sponsored health insurance plans. Companies must follow a set of strict guidelines in designing and implementing pension plans to qualify for favorable tax treatment. We also reviewed the main features of defined benefit, defined contribution, and hybrid plans. Following company-sponsored retirement plans, we started our review of health insurance plans with basic definitions and a perusal of the level of health insurance coverage and costs in the United States. We also studied a variety of health plans (e.g., fee-for-service plans, managed care plans, and consumer-driven health care), and discussed how these plans differ in cost control features.

KEY TERMS

- qualified plans, 259
- nonqualified plans, 259
- coverage requirements, 261
- ratio percentage test, 261
- vesting, 261
- cliff vesting, 261
- 6-year graduated schedule, 261
- accrual rules, 262
- nondiscrimination tests, 262

- distribution, 263
- lump sum distributions, 263
- annuities, 263
- income annuities, 263
- plan termination rules, 263
- defined benefit plans, 263
- flat benefit formulas, 264
- unit benefit formulas, 264
- defined contribution plans, 266

- forfeiture, 266
- fiduciary, 266
- annual addition, 267
- Section 401(k) plan, 267
- profit-sharing plans, 267
- profit-sharing pools, 267
- fixed first-dollar-of-profits formula, 268
- graduated first-dollar-of-profits formula, 268

DISCUSSION QUESTIONS

1. Are employees more likely to favor defined contribution plans over defined benefit plans? How about employers? Explain your answer.
2. Summarize the controversial issues regarding cash balance plans.
3. Discuss the basic concept of insurance. How does this concept apply to health care?
4. Describe the principles of fee-for-service plans and managed care plans. What are the similarities and differences?
5. Discuss some of the choices an employer may make to help control health care costs.

ENDNOTES

1. ERISA §3(2)(A), 29 U.S.C. §1002(2)(A).
2. Internal Revenue Code (hereafter cited I.R.C.) §§410(a)(1), 410(a)(4); Treas. Reg. §1.410(a)-3T(b); ERISA §202(a).
3. I.R.C. §410(a)(3), Treas. Reg. §1.410(a)-5, 29 C.F.R. §2530.200b-2(a), ERISA §202(a)(3).
4. I.R.C. §414(q).
5. I.R.C. §§410(a)(1), 410(a)(4); Treas. Reg. §1.410(a)-3T(b); ERISA §202(a).
6. I.R.C. §410(a)(3), Treas. Reg. §1.410(a)-5, 29 C.F.R. §2530.200b-2(a), ERISA §202(a)(3).
7. I.R.C. §§411(a)(2), 411(a)(5); Treas. Reg. §1.411(a)-3T; ERISA §203(a).
8. I.R.C. §§411(a)(7), 411(b); ERISA §§204, 3(23); Treas. Reg. §1.411(b)-1.
9. I.R.C. §401(a)(4).
10. I.R.C. §415(b).
11. I.R.C. §404(a)(1)(A)(i)–(iii).
12. §404(a)(1)(C).
13. I.R.C. §411(a)(7)(A)(ii); ERISA §204(b)(2).
14. Prop. Treas. Reg. §§1.412(b)-1(a).
15. I.R.C. §415(c)(2); Treas. Reg. §1.415–6(b)(1).
16. I.R.C. §415(c).
17. I.R.C. §§404(a)(3), 402(g).
18. I.R.C. §404(a)(3).
19. Treas. Reg. §1.401–1(b)(2).

20. I.R.C. §404(a)(3).
21. I.R.C. §§401(a), 4975(e)(7)–(8).
22. Green, L.B. (October 29, 2003). *What Is a Pension Equity Plan? Compensation and Working Conditions Online.* [Online]. *bls.gov/opub/cwc/cm20031016ar01p1.htm.* Accessed July 29, 2004.
23. 26 Code of Federal Regulations §§1.401 (a)(4)-8(c)(3)(I).
24. U.S. Department of Labor, Bureau of Labor Statistics. September 23, 2003. Questions and answers on cash balance plans. *Compensation and Working Conditions Online.* [Online]. *www.bls.gov/opub/cwc/print/cm20030917ar01p.htm.* Accessed: July 29, 2004.
25. 26 U.S.C. §411(a)(7).
26. U.S. General Accounting Office. September 2000. *Private Pensions: Implications of Conversions to Cash Balance Plans* (GAO/HEHS-00–185). Washington, DC: GAO.
27. Ibid.
28. Ibid.
29. *Eaton v. Onan Corp.,* 2000 WL 1459801 (S.D. Ind. 2000).
30. *Dan C. Tootle v. ARINC Inc.,* U.S. District Court for the District of Maryland, No. CCB-03–1086.
31. *Cooper v. The IBM Personal Pension Plan,* Civil No. 99–829-GPM (S.D. Ill. July 31, 2003).
32. *Cooper v. The IBM Personal Pension Plan,* Civil No. 05–3588, U.S. District Court of Appeals for the Seventh Circuit, August 7, 2006).
33. U.S. Bureau of Labor Statistics. 1919. Welfare Work for Employees in Industrial Establishments in the United States. *Bulletin #250,* pp. 119–23.
34. U.S. Bureau of Labor Statistics (August 2006). *National Compensation Survey: Employee Benefits in Private Industry, March 2006* (BLS 06–05). [Online]. *www.bls.gov/ncs/ebs/home.htm.* Accessed April 17, 2007.
35. Ibid.
36. Ibid.
37. Ibid.
38. American Psychiatric Association. 1994. *Diagnostic and Statistical Manual of Mental Disorders (DSM-IV).* Washington, DC: American Psychiatric Association.
39. Mental Health Parity Act, Public Law No. 104–204, August 2, 1996.
40. Public L. No. 108–173.

CHAPTER 12

Legally Required Benefits

Chapter Outline

- An Overview of Legally Required Benefits

- Components of Legally Required Benefits
  Social Security Act of 1935
  State Compulsory Disability Laws (Workers' Compensation)
  Family and Medical Leave Act of 1993

- The Implications of Legally Required Benefits for Strategic Compensation

- Designing and Planning the Benefits Program
  Determining Who Receives Coverage
  Financing
  Employee Choice
  Cost Containment
  Communication

- Summary

- Key Terms

- Discussion Questions

- Exercises

- Endnotes

Learning Objectives

In this chapter, you will learn about

1. Which employee benefits are legally required

2. The Social Security Act of 1935 and its mandated protection programs: unemployment insurance, old-age, survivor, and disability insurance (OASDI), and Medicare

3. Compulsory state disability laws (workers' compensation)

4. The Family and Medical Leave Act of 1993

5. Some of the implications for strategic compensation and possible employer approaches to managing legally required benefits

6. The considerations that go along with designing and the planning benefits program

Multiple laws require employer participation in some employee benefits programs. The Social Security programs (e.g., retirement and disability) most notably influence many people, and these are perhaps the most widely publicized legally required benefits in the United States. For years, there have been valid concerns that there will be insufficient funding to meet promised benefits. As time passes, these concerns are growing stronger. There are also ongoing political debates about how to ensure the viability of Social Security programs. President George W. Bush signed an executive order on May 2, 2001, (see Chapter 3 for a definition of executive orders) to create the new Presidential Commission to Strengthen Social Security. Politicians have debated the merits and drawbacks of various solutions to shore up the Social Security system. Under President George W. Bush's administration, the focus has been to encourage tax credits for individuals who save for retirement and to encourage more savings through employer-sponsored retirement plans. The Democrats have called for increasing the tax under the Federal Income Contributions Act to bolster the trust fund; however, it has been met with strong opposition by business leaders, particularly small businesses, which usually possess smaller profit margins. The Pension Protection Act of 2006 (discussed in Chapter 3) is expected to increase the number of people who participate in their employer-sponsored defined contribution plans by giving employers the authority to enroll new employees in the plan automatically.

AN OVERVIEW OF LEGALLY REQUIRED BENEFITS

The U.S. government established programs to protect individuals from catastrophic events such as disability and unemployment. Legally required benefits are protection programs that attempt to promote worker safety and health, maintain family income streams, and assist families in crisis. The cost of legally required benefits to employers is quite high. As of March 2007, U.S. companies spent an average $4,597 per employee annually to provide legally required benefits.[1] Human resource (HR) staffs and compensation professionals in particular must follow a variety of laws as they develop and implement programs.

Legally required benefits historically provided a form of social insurance.[2] Prompted largely by the rapid growth of industrialization in the United States in the early nineteenth century and the Great Depression of the 1930s, initial social insurance programs were designed to minimize the possibility that individuals who became unemployed or severely injured while working would become destitute. In addition, social insurance programs aimed to stabilize the well-being of dependent family members of injured or unemployed individuals. Furthermore, early social insurance programs were designed to enable retirees to maintain subsistence income levels. These intents of legally required benefits remain intact today.

Legally required benefits currently apply to virtually all U.S. companies, and they "level the playing field," so to speak. These programs are unlikely to directly lead to a competitive advantage for one company over another; however, legally required benefits may indirectly promote competitive advantage for all companies by enabling unemployed individuals, disabled employees, and their dependent family members to participate in the economy as consumers of products and services. As we discussed in Chapter 3, the government has a vested interest in promoting a vigorous economy that exhibits regular buying and selling, such that the demand for goods and services does not substantially outpace or fall below the supply of those goods and services. The key to maintaining a vigorous economy is clearly the participation of individuals as consumers of the products and services sold in the marketplace. In this chapter, it will become evident how many elements of employee benefits serve this end.

COMPONENTS OF LEGALLY REQUIRED BENEFITS

The key legally required benefits are mandated by the following laws: the Social Security Act of 1935, various state workers' compensation laws, and the Family and Medical Leave Act of 1993. All provide protection programs to employees and their dependents.

Social Security Act of 1935

Historical Background

Income discontinuity caused by the Great Depression led to the Social Security Act as a means to protect families from financial devastation in the event of unemployment. The Great Depression of the 1930s was a time when many businesses failed and masses of people became chronically unemployed. During this period, employers shifted their focus from maximizing profits simply to staying in business. Overall, ensuring the financial solvency of employees during periods of temporary unemployment and following work-related injuries promoted the well-being of the economy and contributed to some companies' ability to remain in business. These subsistence payments specifically contributed to the viability of the economy by providing temporarily unemployed or injured individuals with the means to contribute to economic activity by making purchases that result in demand for products and services.

The Social Security Act of 1935 also addresses retirement income and the health and welfare of employees and their families. Many employees could not meet their financial obligations (for example, housing expenses and food) on a daily basis, and most employees could not retire because they were unable to save enough money to support themselves in retirement. Furthermore, employees' poor financial situations left them unable to afford medical treatment for themselves and their families.

As a result of these social maladies, three programs within the act aim to relieve some of the consequences of these social problems:

- Unemployment insurance
- Old Age, Survivor, and Disability Insurance (OASDI)
- Medicare

Each of those programs will be reviewed in turn.

Unemployment Insurance

The Social Security Act founded a national federal–state unemployment insurance program for individuals who become unemployed through no fault of their own. Each state administers its own program and develops guidelines within parameters set by the federal government. States pay into a central unemployment tax fund administered by the federal government. The federal government invests these payments, and it disburses funds to states as needed. The unemployment insurance program applies to virtually all employees in the United States, with the exception of most agricultural and domestic workers (e.g., housekeepers).

Individuals must meet several criteria to qualify for unemployment benefits. Unemployment itself does not necessarily qualify a person, although these criteria vary somewhat by state. Those applying for unemployment insurance benefits must have been employed for a minimum period of time. This **base period** tends to be the first four of the last five completed calendar quarters immediately preceding the individual's benefits year. In addition, all states require sufficient previous earnings, typically $1,000 during the last four quarters combined. Other criteria are listed in Table 12-1.

TABLE 12-1 Eligibility Criteria for Unemployment Insurance Benefits

To be eligible for unemployment insurance benefits, an individual must:

1. Not have left a job voluntarily
2. Be able and available for work
3. Be actively seeking work
4. Not have refused an offer of suitable employment
5. Not be unemployed because of a labor dispute (exception in few states)
6. Not have had employment terminated because of gross violations of conduct within the workplace

---

Individuals who meet the eligibility criteria receive weekly benefits. Because the federal government places no limits on a maximum allowable amount, the benefits amount varies widely from state to state. Most states calculate the weekly benefits as a specified fraction of an employee's average wages during the highest calendar quarter of the base period.

The majority of states pay regular unemployment benefits for a maximum of 26 weeks. A 1970 amendment to this act established a permanent program of extended unemployment benefits, usually for an additional 13 weeks (totaling 39 weeks) in areas where unemployment rates run high. Another type of program that offers extended unemployment insurance benefits is the **supplemental unemployment benefit (SUB)**, which is most common in industries where employment conditions are cyclical (e.g., in the steel industry). Virtually all SUB benefits are part of collective bargaining agreements. After the September 11 attacks and the ensuing weakened U.S. economy, President George W. Bush approved a third extension of an additional 13 weeks, permitting qualified unemployed individuals to receive benefits for up to 65 weeks.

Unemployment insurance benefits are financed by federal and state taxes levied on employers under the **Federal Unemployment Tax Act (FUTA)**. State and local governments, as well as not-for-profit companies (e.g., the United Way), are generally exempt from FUTA. Alaska is currently the only state that requires employee contributions. Employer contributions amount to 6.2 percent of the first $7,000 earned by each employee (i.e., the taxable wage base). FUTA specifies $7,000 as the minimum allowable taxable wage base. Relatively few states' taxable wage base is as low as the FUTA-specified minimum (e.g., Florida, Indiana, and South Carolina). States typically set the taxable wage base according to the average wage level. In 2007, states' taxable wage base ranged from $8,000 to $35,300 in Alabama and Hawaii, respectively.

The federal government deposits 5.4 percent to the Federal Unemployment Trust Fund, which is administered by the Treasury Department. The Treasury Department invests this money in government securities, crediting the principal amount contributed by each state and investment income to an account. The federal government retains 0.8 percent to cover administrative costs and to maintain a reserve to bail out states with very low balances in their accounts.

States also impose taxes on employers to fund their unemployment insurance programs. An employer's actual tax burden varies according to an experience rating system. Every state applies different tax rates to companies, subject to statutory minimum and maximum rates. Each company's tax rate depends upon its prior experience with unemployment. A company that lays off a large percentage of employees will accordingly have a higher tax rate than will a company that lays off relatively few or none of its employees. This **experience rating system** implies that a company can manage its unemployment tax burden. In 2007, the average employer tax in all states amounted to 2.77 percent, ranging from a low of 0.78 percent in South Dakota to 5.57 percent in Pennsylvania.

Old Age, Survivor, and Disability Insurance (OASDI)

OASDI contains a number of benefits that were amended to the act following its enactment in 1935. Besides providing retirement income, the amendments include survivors' insurance (1939) and disability insurance (1965). The phrase *old age* in the title refers to retirement benefits.

Virtually all U.S. workers are eligible for protections under the OASDI and Medicare programs, except for three exempt classes. First, civilian employees of the federal government and railroad employees with at least 10 years of service are exempt from the retirement program; however, these individuals are not exempt from the Medicare program. Second, employees of state and local governments who are already covered under other retirement plans are exempt from Social Security retirement contributions unless these government organizations choose to participate in this program. Third, children under age 21 who work for a parent are exempt, except children age 18 or older who work in the parent's business.

Old Age Benefits Individuals may receive various benefit levels upon retirement, or under survivors' and disability programs, based on how much credit they have earned through eligible payroll contributions. They earn credit based on **quarters of coverage**. For example, in 2007, a worker earns credit for one quarter of coverage for each $1,000 in annual earnings on which Social Security taxes are paid. The worker gets a quarter of coverage for each quarter in which she makes $1,000 of SS-taxable income. This figure is based on the average total wages of all workers as determined by the Social Security Administration (SSA). Of course, workers may earn up to four quarters of coverage credit each year. Individuals become **fully insured** when they earn credit for 40 quarters of coverage, or 10 years of employment, and remain fully insured during their lifetime. Other eligibility criteria concerning quarters of coverage are based on more complex formulas.[3]

An individual who has become fully insured must meet additional requirements before receiving benefits under the particular programs. Under the retirement program, fully insured individuals may choose to receive benefits as early as age 62, although their benefit amounts will be permanently reduced if elected prior to age 65. Congress recently instituted changes in the minimum age for receiving full benefits. They increased the full retirement age for people born in 1938 or later because of higher life expectancies of 65-year-old individuals (i.e., 12.7 years beyond age 65 in 1940, 18.4 years in 2003). The age for collecting fully Social Security retirement benefits is gradually increasing from 60 to 67 over a 22-year period ending in 2022. The average monthly benefit for all retired workers rose 9.3 percent from $955 in 2004 to $1,049 in 2007.[4]

Survivor Benefits The SSA calculates survivors' benefits based on the insureds' employment status and the survivors' relationship to the deceased. Dependent, unmarried children of the deceased and a spouse of the deceased who is caring for a child or children may receive survivors' benefits if the deceased worker was fully insured. A widow or widower at least age 60, or a parent at least age 62 who was dependent on the deceased employee, is entitled to survivors' benefits if the deceased worker was fully insured. In May 2007, the average monthly benefit was $687 for children of disabled workers and $750 for widowed mothers and fathers.[5]

The retirement program contains incentives to encourage individuals to delay their retirement after reaching full retirement age. The Social Security Administration increases retirement benefits by a designated percent for each month worked beyond full retirement until age 70, subject to a maximum percentage increase. The percentage increase depends upon the year of birth. For example, for individuals born between 1930 and 1942, the percentage increase ranges from 4.5 percent to 7.5 percent. Individuals born after 1942 would earn an additional 8 percent.

Disability Benefits   The SSA pays benefits to seriously disabled workers and family members. In particular, Social Security pays only for total disability. Disability under Social Security is based on a person's inability to perform work done before becoming disabled and is unable to adjust to other work because of medical condition. The disability must also last or be expected to last for at least 1 year or to result in death. As we will see later in this chapter, Social Security program rules assume that working families have access to other resources to provide support during periods of short-term disabilities, including workers' compensation, short-term disability insurance (from a private insurance company), and savings and investments.

Eligibility   Disability benefits are available to disabled workers who are unable to work as a result of a serious medical or mental impairment that lasts at least 12 months. Seriously disabled workers are eligible to receive disability benefits as long as they meet two criteria. First, the worker must have accumulated at least 40 credits. Second, the worker must have earned at least 20 credits of the last 40 calendar quarters in the last 10 years ending with the year of disablement. Disability benefits are subject to a waiting period of up to 6 months. More lenient rules apply to blind individuals and younger workers. Blind workers only need 40 credits.

Younger workers need fewer quarters of coverage because they have fewer years to accumulate quarters of coverage. Workers younger than age 23 qualify with 6 credits earned in the 3-year period ending when becoming disabled. Workers ages 24 to 31 may qualify with credit for working half the time between age 21 and becoming disabled. For example, becoming disabled at age 29 requires credit for 4 years of employment (equivalent to 16 credits based on earning 4 credits per year) since the 8-year period beginning at age 21. The average monthly disability benefit in May 2007 was $978.

Medicare

The Medicare program serves nearly all U.S. citizens age 65 or older by providing insurance coverage for hospitalization, convalescent care, and major doctor bills. The Medicare program includes five separate features:

- Medicare Part A—Compulsory hospitalization insurance.
- Medicare Part B—Voluntary supplementary medical insurance.
- Medigap—Voluntary supplemental insurance to pay for services not covered in Parts A and B.
- Medicare Part C: Medicare Advantage—New choices in health care providers.
- Medicare Part D: Medicare Prescription Drug Benefit—Coverage for prescription drug medication.

Most individuals who are eligible to receive protection under Medicare may choose to receive coverage in one of two ways. A person may receive coverage under the original Medicare Plan or Medicare Advantage Plans as illustrated in Figure 12-1.

In a nutshell, the original Medicare Plan is a fee-for-service plan that is managed by the federal government. As we discussed in Chapter 11, fee-for-service plans many health care services, medical supplies, and certain prescription drugs. Participants in fee-for-service plans possess the choice to receive care from virtually any licensed health care provider or facility. On the other hand, Medicare Advantage Plans include a variety of insurance options, including health maintenance organizations, preferred provide organizations, Medicare special needs plans, and Medicare medical savings

FIGURE 12-1 Options for Receiving Medicare Benefits

Original Medicare Plan		OR	Medicare Advantage Plans like HMOs and PPOs

Original Medicare Plan

Part A (Hospital)	Part B (Medical)

Medicare provides this coverage. Part B is optional. You have your choice of doctors. Your costs may be higher than in Medicare Advantage plans.

Part D (Prescription Drug Coverage)

You can choose this coverage. Private companies approved by Medicare run these plans. Plans cover different drugs. Medically necessary drugs must be covered.

Medigap (Medicare Supplement Insurance) Policy

You can choose to buy this private coverage (or an employer/union may offer similar coverage) to fill in gaps in Part A and Part B coverage. Costs vary by policy and company.

Medicare Advantage Plans like HMOs and PPOs

Called "Part C," this option combines your Part A (Hospital) and Part B (Medical)

Private insurance companies approved by Medicare provide this coverage. Generally, you must see doctors in the plan. Your cost may be lower than in the Original Medicare Plan, and you may get extra benefits.

Part D (Prescription Drug Coverage)

Most Part C plans cover prescription drugs. If they don't you may be able to choose this coverage. Plans cover different drugs. Medically necessary drugs must be covered.

For information about
- The Original Medicare Plan, see pages 25–32.
- Medicare Advantage Plans, see pages 33–42.
- Medicare prescription drug coverage, see pages 42–56.
- Other Medicare plans, see pages 58–59.

SOURCE: U.S. Department of Health and Human Services (2007). *Medicare & You.* [online]. Available: *www.medicare.gov/Publications/Pubs/pdf/10050.pdf*. Accessed June 30, 2007.

account plans (MSA). Medicare Advantage Plans are run by private companies subject to strict regulations specified in the Medicare program. Restrictions pertain to pricing of the different plans.

Medicare Part A Coverage This compulsory hospitalization insurance covers both inpatient and outpatient hospital care and services. Social Security beneficiaries, retirees, voluntary enrollees, and disabled individuals are all entitled. Both employers and employees finance **Medicare Part A** benefits through payroll taxes of 1.45 percent on all earnings.

Examples of Part A coverage include:

- Inpatient hospital care in a semiprivate room, meals, general nursing, and other hospital supplies and services.
- Home health services limited to reasonable and essential part-time or intermittent skilled nursing care and home health aide services, and physical therapy, occupational therapy, and speech-language pathology ordered by a doctor.
- Hospice care for people with a terminal illness (that is, an illness that is expected to lead to death within 6 months), including pharmaceutical products for symptom control and pain relief, medical and support services from a Medicare-approved hospice provider, and other services not otherwise covered by Medicare (e.g., grief counseling).

- Skilled nursing facility care, including semiprivate room, meals, skilled nursing and rehabilitative services, and supplies for up to 100 days per year. Examples of skilled nursing care include physical therapy after a stroke or serious accident.
- Pints of blood administered during a Medicare approved stay in a hospital or skilled nursing facility.

In 2007, the monthly Part A premium was $410.

Medicare Part B Coverage   This voluntary supplementary medical insurance covers 80 percent of medical services and supplies after the enrolled individual pays a $110 annual deductible for services furnished under this plan. Part B helps pay for physicians' services and for some medical services and supplies not covered under Part A. Participation in Part B is voluntary and financed by monthly premiums paid jointly by the federal government and by those who enroll. Part A coverage automatically qualifies an individual to enroll in Part B coverage for a monthly premium. Starting in 2007, the monthly premium amount is based on annual income and the premium amounts will be revised annually. In 2007, monthly Part B premiums ranged from $93.50 to $161.40.

This voluntary supplementary medical insurance helps pay for medical services not covered by Part A such as doctors' services, outpatient care, clinical laboratory services (e.g., blood tests, urinalysis) and some preventive health services (e.g., cardiovascular screenings, bone mass measurement). Part B also provides ambulance services to a hospital or skilled nursing facility when transportation in any other vehicle would endanger a person's health. Part B typically covers 80 percent of medical services and supplies after the enrolled individual pays an annual deductible for services furnished under this plan. The deductible is the amount an individual pays for services before insurance benefits become active.

Medigap Insurance   **Medigap** insurance supplements Part A and Part B coverage, and is available to Medicare recipients in most states from private insurance companies for an extra fee. Most Medigap plans help cover the costs of coinsurance, copayments, and deductibles. Federal and state laws limit the sale of these plans to up to 12 different standardized choices that vary in terms of the level of protection. For example, some policies cover costs not covered by the original Medicare Plan.

Some insurers offer Medicare Select plans. **Medicare Select plans** are Medigap policies that offer lower premiums in exchange for limiting the choice of health care providers. Three states (i.e., Massachusetts, Minnesota, and Wisconsin) do not subscribe to this system for offering Medigap insurance. Separate rules apply in these states.

The Balanced Budget Act of 1997 established **Medicare+Choice**—renamed to **Medicare Advantage** in 2004 as a third Medicare program—as an alternative to the original program (Parts A & B). The Medicare Advantage program, informally referred to as Part C, provides beneficiaries the opportunity to receive health care from a variety of options, including private fee-for-service plans, managed care plans, or medical savings accounts. **Fee-for-service plans** provide protection against health care expenses in the form of cash benefits paid to the insured or directly to the health care provider after receiving health care services. These plans pay benefits on a reimbursement basis. Medicare Parts A and B are based on fee-for-service arrangements. **Managed care** plans often pay a higher level of benefits if health care is received from approved providers. Beginning in 2006, participants will have access to a wider variety of health providers.

Medicare Prescription Drug Benefit   The passage of the *Medicare Prescription Drug, Improvement and Modernization Act of 2003* (also known as the *Medicare Modernization Act of 2003* for short) instituted a prescription drug benefit for

Medicare program participants. Commonly referred to as Part D, the drug benefit was first offered in 2006. As will be noted shortly, Medicare covers 75 percent of prescription drug costs after a calendar year deductible of $250, up to $2,250. After that, expenditures up to $5,100 are not covered by Medicare. All costs are out-of-pocket. This gap in coverage is known as the "donut hole" because Medicare contributes to the payment of approved prescription medications for amounts outside the $2,250 to $5,100 range less the annual deductible. Finally, Medicare covers 95 percent of the cost of prescriptions for each dollar spent in excess of $5,100 during the calendar year. The dollar amounts were valid in 2006 and are subject to change from year to year.

Total Spent on Medication during Calendar Year	Out-of-Pocket Cost	Portion Covered by Medicare
$0–$250	Deductible is out-of-pocket	No Medicare Coverage of Costs
$250–$2,250	25% out-of-pocket	75% Covered by Medicare
$2,250–$5,100	All costs are out-of-pocket	No Medicare Coverage of Costs
more than $5,100	5% out-of-pocket	95% Covered by Medicare

Financing OASDI and Medicare Programs

Funding for OASDI and Medicare programs require equal employer and employee contributions under the **Federal Insurance Contributions Act (FICA)**.[6] FICA requires that employers pay a tax based on their payroll; employees contribute a tax based on earnings, which is withheld from each paycheck. The **Self-Employment Contributions Act (SECA)**[7] requires that self-employed individuals contribute to the OASDI and Medicare programs, but at a different tax rate. In either case, the tax rate is subject to an increase each year in order to fund OASDI programs sufficiently. In 2007 FICA required employers and employees to contribute 7.65 percent each. Self-employed individuals generally doubled that amount, or 15.3 percent in 2007. As we will discuss next this tax amount is apportioned between OASDI and Medicare programs.

OASDI Programs   The largest share of the FICA tax funds OASDI programs. In 2007, 6.20 percent of the contributions of employers and employees were set aside. Self-employed individuals contributed 12.40 percent. OASDI taxes are subject to a **taxable wage base**. Taxable wage bases limit the amount of annual wages or payroll cost per employee subject to taxation. The taxable wage base may also increase over time to account for increases in the cost of living. In 2007 the taxable wage base was $97,500 for everyone. Annual wages, payroll costs per employee, and self-employed earnings above this level were not taxed.

Medicare Programs   The **Medicare tax**, or **hospital insurance tax**, supports the Medicare Part A program. Employers, employees, and self-employed individuals contribute 1.45 percent. Self-employed individuals contribute double the amount, or 2.9 percent. The Medicare tax is not subject to a taxable wage base. All payroll amounts and wages are taxed.

According to the Social Security Administration (SSA), many people believe that the Social Security taxes they pay are held in interest-bearing accounts set aside by the federal government to meet their own future retirement income needs. To the contrary, the Social Security system represents a pay-as-you-go retirement system. In other words, Social Security taxes paid by today's workers and their employers are used to pay the benefits for today's retirees and other beneficiaries.

The Social Security Board of Trustees announced in their annual report for fiscal year 2006 that the long-range projections of the Social Security trust fund indicate that the Social Security trust fund is currently taking in more money than it pays out in retirement benefits.[8] Under the new projections, in 2017 payments made to retirement beneficiaries will begin to exceed the amount of money added to the funds based on FICA taxes. In addition, by 2040, retirement funds in the Social Security trust funds will be depleted. Finally, current projections indicate that only 74 percent of the benefits needed to pay retirees in the programs will be paid based on the expected inflow of FICA taxes from current employees. Over time, the balance in the trust fund will decrease until 2040, with an expected rapid decline after 2020.

For years, the viability of the Social Security programs has been the subject of heated debates between Democrats and Republicans across the country with no satisfactory solution. The Republican Bush administration most recently diverted more than $10 billion from the Social Security trust fund to pay for general government expenses. The Democrats criticized the Republican administration for putting the security of current and prospective Social Security benefits at risk. Debates have arisen about whether the federal government is obligated to guarantee future benefits or simply to promise benefits when economic conditions permit them.

State Compulsory Disability Laws (Workers' Compensation)

Historical Background

Workers' compensation insurance came into existence during the early decades of the twentieth century, when industrial accidents were very common and workers suffered from occupational illnesses at alarming rates.[9] The first constitutionally acceptable workers' compensation law was enacted in 1911. By 1920, all but six states had instituted workers' compensation laws.[10] State workers' compensation laws are based on the principle of liability without fault[11] (i.e., an employer is absolutely liable for providing benefits to employees that result from occupational disabilities or injuries, regardless of fault). Another key principle of workers' compensation laws is that employers should assume costs of occupational injuries and accidents. These expenses presumably represent costs of production that employers are able to recoup through setting higher prices.

Workers' compensation insurance programs, run by states individually, are designed to cover expenses incurred in employees' work-related accidents. Maritime workers within U.S. borders and federal civilian employees are covered by their own workers' compensation programs. The maritime workers' compensation program is mandated by the **Longshore and Harborworkers' Compensation Act**, and federal civilian employees receive workers' compensation protection under the **Federal Employees' Compensation Act**. Thus, workers' compensation laws cover virtually all employees in the United States, except for domestic workers, some agricultural workers, and small businesses with fewer than a dozen regular employees.[12]

Workers' Compensation Objectives and Obligations to the Public

Six basic objectives underlie workers' compensation laws:[13]

- Provide sure, prompt, and reasonable income and medical benefits to work-accident victims, or income benefits to their dependents, regardless of fault
- Provide a single remedy and reduce court delays, costs, and workloads arising out of personal injury litigation

- Relieve public and private charities of financial drains
- Eliminate payment of fees to lawyers and witnesses as well as time-consuming trials and appeals
- Encourage maximum employer interest in safety and rehabilitation through appropriate experience-rating mechanisms
- Promote frank study of causes of accidents (rather than concealment of fault), reducing preventable accidents and human suffering

Employers must fund workers' compensation programs according to state guidelines. Participation in workers' compensation programs is compulsory in 48 states and elective in New Jersey and Texas. These states generally require that employers subscribe to workers' compensation insurance through private carriers or, in some instances, through state funds. Self-insurance, another funding option allowed in the majority of states, requires companies to deposit a surety bond, enabling them to pay their own workers' claims directly.[14] Many companies select self-insurance because it gives employers more discretion in administering their own risks. Nevertheless, self-insured companies must pay their workers the same benefits as those paid by state funds or private insurance carriers.

The National Commission on State Workmen's Compensation Laws specified six primary obligations of state workers' compensation programs. This commission established these obligations to ensure prompt and just remedy for workers injured on the job.[15] Table 12-2 lists these obligations.

Claims under Workers' Compensation Programs

Employees can incur three kinds of workers' compensation claims. The first, **injury claims**, are usually defined as claims for disabilities that have resulted from such accidents as falls, injuries from equipment use, or physical strains from heavy lifting. Employees who work long hours at computer keyboards or assembly lines, performing the same task over and over again, frequently complain of numbness in the fingers and neck as well as severe wrist pain. This type of injury is known as repetitive strain injury. A recent U.S. Bureau of Labor Statistics survey reveals that repetitive strain injuries typically led an employee to miss 17 days of work.[16]

The second kind of claim, **occupational disease claims**, results from disabilities caused by ailments associated with particular industrial trades or processes. For example, black lung, a chronic respiratory disease, is a common ailment among coal miners. In older office buildings, lung disease from prolonged exposure to asbestos is

---

TABLE 12-2   Primary Obligations of State Workers' Compensation Programs

1. Take initiative in administering the law.
2. Continually review performance of the program and be willing to change procedures and to request the state legislature to make needed amendments.
3. Advise workers of their rights and obligations and assure that they receive the benefits to which they are entitled.
4. Apprise employers and insurance carriers of their rights and obligations; inform other parties in the delivery system (e.g., health care providers) of their obligations and privileges.
5. Assist in voluntary and informal resolution of disputes that are consistent with law.
6. Adjudicate claims that cannot be resolved voluntarily.

SOURCE: Nackley, J. V. (1989). *Primer on Workers' Compensation*, 2nd ed. Washington, DC: Bureau of National Affairs.

another kind of ailment. The following occupational diseases are generally covered under workers' compensation programs:

- Pneumoconioses, which are associated with exposure to dusts
- Silicosis from exposure to silica
- Asbestos poisoning
- Radiation illness

The third kind of claim, **death claims**, asks for compensation for deaths that occur in the course of employment or that are caused by compensable injuries or occupational diseases. The particular injuries and illnesses covered by workers' compensation programs vary by state.

Workers file claims to the state commission charged with administering the workers' compensation program. The names of these agencies vary by state. Examples include bureaus of workers' compensation and industrial accident boards. One state agency typically oversees the administration of the program and disburses benefits to the individuals whose claims have been deemed meritorious. Another agency within the state (e.g., the board of workers' compensation appeal) resolves conflicts that may arise (e.g., claim denials with which claimants are dissatisfied).

A total of 5 million nonfatal injuries and illnesses were reported in private industry workplaces during 2005, resulting in a rate of 4.6 cases per 100 equivalent full-time workers, according to the *Survey of Occupational Injuries and Illnesses* by the Bureau of Labor Statistics.[17] A total of 5,734 fatal work injuries were recorded in the United States in 2005.[18] The number of nonfatal and fatal injuries represents a small increase over previous years. These numbers clearly set the stage for workers' compensation claims by injured workers or families of deceased workers. Depending upon the claim, workers' compensation laws specify four kinds of benefits.

The first, medical benefits, are provided to cover the cost of treating the illness or injury. Medical fee schedules in most states specify the maximum amount paid for particular medical procedures. For example, Wisconsin would pay up to $131,000 in 2007 to cover medical treatment for an injured arm.[19] Mississippi would pay much less for the same injury (i.e., $70,288 in 2007).

The second, disability income, compensates individuals whose work-related accident or illness has at least partially limited their ability to perform the regular duties of their jobs. The amount of disability income varies by state; the norm is two thirds of the employee's average weekly wage for a predetermined period prior to the incident leading to disability. Two exceptions are Iowa and Michigan, where the weekly disability payment is calculated as 80 percent of spendable earnings.

Third, **death benefits** are awarded in two forms: burial allowances and survivors' benefits. Burial allowances reflect a fixed amount, varying by state. Maximum burial allowances range from about $3,000 to about $15,000.[20] Survivors' benefits are paid to the spouses of deceased employees and to any dependent children. The amounts vary widely by state, based on different criteria. For example, assuming no dependent children, the minimum allowable weekly payment to a spouse could be as little as $20 to as much as $500. States usually limit the duration of spousal benefits to a designated number of weeks or until remarriage, whichever comes first. Benefits for children typically equal two thirds of the deceased parent's wages each year until a designated maximum age. The maximum age increases for children in college.

The fourth benefit, rehabilitative services, covers physical and vocational rehabilitation. Claims for this benefit must usually be made within 6 months to 2 years of the accident. For instance, in Alaska, the rehabilitative benefits require the employer to pay reasonable board, lodging, and travel up to $13,300.[21]

Recent Trends in Workers' Compensation

In recent years, workers' compensation claims have risen dramatically in terms of both numbers of claims and claims amounts. The increased prevalence of repetitive strain injuries resulting from the use of keyboards has contributed to this trend. In 2007, workers' compensation cost nearly 21 percent of all legally required benefits for all civilian employees.[22] Total workers' compensation claims paid to beneficiaries exceeded $54 billion in 2003.[23]

Employers' Rights under Workers' Compensation Programs

Participation in workers' compensation programs and compliance with applicable regulations protects employers from **torts*** initiated by injured workers based on the no-fault principles of these programs; however, there are four possible exceptions to immunity from legal action:

1. An employer's intentional acts
2. Lawsuits alleging employer retaliation for filing a workers' compensation claim
3. Lawsuits against noncomplying employers
4. Lawsuits relating to "dual capacity" relationships

An Employer's Intentional Acts　　Most state courts consider intentional actions to harm employees as reasonable cause for holding an employer liable. There are two kinds of lawsuits that allege an employer's intentional acts to harm employees. The first, **deliberate and knowing torts**, entail an employer's deliberate and knowing intent to harm at least one employee. The second, **violations of an affirmative duty**, take place when an employer fails to reveal the exposure of one or more workers to harmful substances, or the employer does not disclose a medical condition typically caused by exposure. In particular, failure to notify violates an employer's affirmative duty when the illness is either correctable at the point of discovery or its progress may be stopped by removing employees from further exposure.

Retaliation against Workers Who Filed Workers' Compensation Claims　　In most states, employees possess the right to sue employers who retaliate against them for either filing a workers' compensation claim or pursuing their rights established in workers' compensation programs. Retaliation usually entails an adverse effect upon a worker's status (e.g., a demotion or pay cut) or termination of a worker's employment. Employees may initiate these lawsuits by claiming retaliatory action. Employers then possess the burden of proof to establish their actions as a legally sanctioned business necessity.

Employer Noncompliance　　Workers' compensation laws oblige employers to comply with applicable state laws. Employers begin to fulfill their obligations by purchasing insurance from state funds, private insurance carriers, or through self-insurance. Failure to carry workers' compensation insurance may lead to one or more consequences:

- Lost immunity, making violators susceptible to common-law charges (of contributory negligence or other torts)
- Monetary penalties, including fines and payment of unpaid premiums
- Criminal penalties
- Liability for the full cost of workers' compensation claims

---

*Tort laws offer remedies to individuals harmed by the unreasonable actions of others. Tort claims usually involve state law and are based on the legal premise that individuals are liable for the consequences of their conduct if it results in injury to others. Tort laws involve civil suits, which are actions brought to protect an individual's private rights.

Most states recognize two acceptable alternatives for employees to receive remedy. First, they gain the right to initiate legal action against noncompliant employers as just described. Second, most states extend workers' compensation protection to employees regardless of an employer's compliance status.

Dual Capacity   **Dual capacity** is a legal doctrine that applies to the relationship between employers and employees. A company may specifically fulfill a role for an employee that is completely different from its role as employer. Even though an employer meets its obligations under workers' compensation laws, it may be susceptible to common-law actions. An employer's immunity does not protect it from common-law actions by employees when the company also serves a dual capacity that confers duties unrelated to and independent of those imposed upon it as an employer. A Supreme Court of Pennsylvania decision offers a clear illustration of the dual capacity doctrine:

> A hospital employee who became ill while performing his job received injuries during medical treatment of the illness (by the same hospital). The hospital's role as an employer was completely unrelated to its role as a medical services provider. The court ruled that Presbyterian University Hospital fulfilled a dual capacity role as an employer and provider of medical treatment to this employee. Specifically, the court concluded that the employee's injuries were sustained because of its role as medical services provider rather than as employer—(a) the purpose of the emergency room visit was to treat the illness, (b) the immediate purpose of seeking treatment was personal, and (c) the hospital billed the employee's insurance carrier for the treatment as it would have for any patient. As a result, this employee gained the right to sue the hospital for injuries sustained during treatment because an X-ray table harness broke, causing the employee to fall onto the floor and sustain injuries.[24]

Becoming injured while using an employer's product to perform work is another instance of dual capacity. For instance, a door-to-door salesperson for Company X, a manufacturer of vacuum cleaners, becomes injured while demonstrating the use of her employer's products. A defective vacuum cleaner exploded during the demonstration, causing serious burns and the loss of her left eye. The salesperson is eligible to file a workers' compensation claim because she was injured while performing her job. She may also have the right to initiate a products liability lawsuit as the user of her employer's defective product.

Typical Employers' Defenses When Employees Challenge Immunity   As discussed earlier, employers maintain immunity from worker-initiated legal action when they are in full compliance with workers' compensation regulations. Employers lose immunity when they fail to comply. Most state courts of law usually recognize four acceptable defenses against employee lawsuits for premeditated acts. Premeditation excludes an employee's unwarrantable ignorance, bad judgment, or dishonesty. Employer defenses rely on an assertion that the causes of injuries or illnesses were unrelated to work-related activities.

- Preexisting conditions (e.g., illnesses or injuries that occurred prior to participation in an employer's workers' compensation program, except for work-related illnesses or injuries that worsen the preexisting conditions)
- Employee negligence (e.g., injuries sustained due to noncompliance with clearly communicated safety procedures)
- Employee misconduct (e.g., injuries sustained from acts of aggression against other employees)
- Safety violations by the employee

In general, employers must continue to provide workers' compensation payments even if an employee is discharged because she or he willfully violates work rules in the course of employment after sustaining an injury. For example, a Maine appeals court required that the employer restore workers' compensation payments notwithstanding an employee's intentional dishonesty:

> An injured employee began to receive workers' compensation payments for a work-related incident that led to the loss of three fingers and serious injuries to a hand, an arm, and a shoulder. After returning to work on a light-duty basis, this employee misrepresented his use of a paid sick day. In actuality, the employer learned that he missed work to participate in a golf tournament. The employer discharged this employee and terminated his workers' compensation benefits because he willfully misused the paid time-off for illness. Ultimately, the court based its decision on the irrelevance of the employee's dishonesty to the negative impact of the injuries on earnings capacity.[25]

Financing Workers' Compensation Programs

Workers' compensation laws specify the permissible methods of funding. Employers generally subscribe to workers' compensation insurance through private carriers, or, in some instances, through state funds. A third funding option, self-insurance, requires companies to deposit a surety bond, enabling them to pay their own workers' claims directly.[26] Many employers select self-insurance when available because it gives them greater discretion in administering their own risks. Nevertheless, self-insured companies must pay their workers the same benefits paid by state funds or private insurance carriers.

In most states, the insurance commissioner sets the maximum allowable workers' compensation insurance premium rates for private insurance carriers. Rates are based on each $100 of payroll. Increasingly, some states permit insurance carriers to set rates on a competitive basis.

States rely on ratemaking service organizations to set initial rates. **Ratemaking service organizations** collect data on workplace accidents and put together rating manuals. **Rating manuals** specify insurance rates based on classifications of businesses. A few states possess independent rating organizations. The remainder consults with the National Council on Compensation Insurance, a for-profit company located in Boca Raton, Florida; this organization prepares three separate manuals for state insurance agencies. Independent rating bureaus used by a few states compile manuals that correspond to the National Council's manuals.

Second-injury funds represent an important funding element of workers' compensation programs. These funds cover a portion or all of the costs of a current workers' compensation claim associated with preexisting conditions from a work-related injury during prior employment elsewhere. For instance, a current employee sustained a work-related injury to his knee while employed by Company A. A year later, he sustained a secondary injury to the same knee while working for Company B. From Company B's perspective, the injury sustained in Company A is a preexisting condition. In many cases, the cost of the second disability is compounded by the first injury (i.e., the preexisting condition). Second-injury funds cover the extra costs of the current injury due to the first injury in Company A. Coverage of preexisting conditions creates benefits for employers and qualified individuals with disabilities. Employers should be less reluctant to hire a qualified individual with a disability. Qualified individuals should have fewer barriers to employment due to the cost concerns of employers about preexisting conditions.

Employer and Employee Tax Obligations

In general, employees do not pay any income taxes on the amount of workers' compensation benefits.[27] Survivors of deceased workers do not pay any taxes on death benefits; however, three circumstances may require payment of taxes. First, employees pay taxes on their workers' compensation benefits when they return to work for light duty. Second, workers' compensation benefits are taxable when they offset (reduce) Social Security OASDI benefits. Third, employees pay taxes on workers' compensation benefits when they do not directly result from work-related illness or injury.*

Employers typically do not pay taxes on workers' compensation benefits, with one main exception: Workers' compensation benefits for nonwork-related illnesses or injuries. For this circumstance, the Federal Insurance Contributions Act (FICA) and the Federal Unemployment Tax Act (FUTA) apply. FICA requires that an employer pay a tax based on its payroll; employees contribute a tax based on earnings, which is withheld from each paycheck. FUTA requires that employers contribute 6.2 percent of the taxable wage base, currently $7,000.

Family and Medical Leave Act of 1993

The Family and Medical Leave Act (FMLA) aims to provide employees with job protection in cases of family or medical emergency. The basic thrust of the act is guaranteed leave, and a key element of that guarantee is the right of the employee to return either to the position he or she left when the leave began or to an equivalent position with the same benefits, pay, and other terms and conditions of employment. The passage of the FMLA reflects a growing recognition that many employees' parents are becoming elderly, rendering them susceptible to a serious illness or medical condition. These elderly parents are likely to require frequent (if not constant) attention for an extended period while ill, which places a burden on their adult children.

The passage of the FMLA also recognizes the increasing prevalence of two-income families and the changing roles of men regarding child care. Both partners in a marriage are now more likely to work full time and share family responsibilities, including child rearing. The number of families with two earners was 30.7 million in 2004.[28] Much like elderly parents, children can also become seriously ill, requiring parents' attention. The FMLA also enables fathers to take paternity leave to care for their newborn babies. Until the passage of the FMLA, men did not have protection comparable to what women receive under the Pregnancy Discrimination Act (Chapter 3).

Title I of the FMLA states:

> An eligible employee is entitled to 12 unpaid work weeks of leave during any 12-month period for three reasons: because of the birth or placement for adoption or foster care of a child; because of the serious health condition of a spouse, child, or parent; or because of the employee's own serious health condition. Leave may be taken for birth or placement of a child only within 12 months of that birth or placement.
>
> . . . family leave provisions apply equally to male and female employees: "A father, as well as a mother, can take family leave because of the birth or serious health condition of his child; a son as well as a daughter is eligible for leave to care for a parent."

---

*Workers' compensation benefits for nonwork-related illnesses or injuries are inconsistent with the objectives of workers' compensation programs; however, an IRS ruling (Rev. Rul. 72–191, 1972–1 CB 45) classifies these benefits as part of state workers' compensation programs.

The minimum criteria for eligibility under this act include the following: Eligible workers must be employed by a private employer or by a civilian unit of the federal government. Eligible workers must also have been employed for at least 12 months by a given employer. Finally, eligible workers have provided at least 1,250 hours of service during the 12 months prior to making a request for a leave. Employees who do not meet these criteria are excluded, as are those who work for an employer with fewer than 50 employees within a 75-mile radius of the employee's home. The FMLA does not explicitly define "hours of service." As a result, many disgruntled employees have filed lawsuits against employers' definitions of hours of service.

Employers may require employees to use paid personal, sick, or vacation leave first as part of the 12-week period. If an employee's paid leave falls short of the 12-week mandated period, then the employer must provide further leave—unpaid—to total 12 weeks. While on leave, employees retain all previously earned seniority or employment benefits, though employees do not have the right to add such benefits while on leave. Furthermore, while on leave, employees are entitled to receive health insurance benefits. Finally, employees may be entitled to receive health benefits if they do not return from leave because of a serious health condition or some other factor beyond their control.

Human resource professionals, along with department managers, should develop proactive plans that will enable companies to manage workloads of employees who take leave effectively. One approach is to cross-train workers, who will then have the knowledge and skills to cover vacant jobs while their co-workers are on leave. Pay-for-knowledge programs (Chapter 6) lend themselves well toward enabling employers to meet this objective, particularly when vacant jobs require company-specific knowledge, as in the case of customer service representatives, or highly specialized skills, as in the case of quality assurance inspectors. Companies can also staff temporarily vacant job openings with temporary workers. This approach is reasonable for jobs that do not require company-specific knowledge (e.g., the case of many clerical jobs such as filing clerks and word processor operators).

THE IMPLICATIONS OF LEGALLY REQUIRED BENEFITS FOR STRATEGIC COMPENSATION

Employee benefits are unlike most bases for monetary compensation (i.e., merit, pay-for-knowledge, and incentives). Under these programs, the amount of compensation employees receive varies with their level of contributions to the company. Instead, benefits tend to emphasize social adequacy. Under the principle of social adequacy, benefits are designed to provide subsistence income to all beneficiaries regardless of their performance in the workplace.[29] Thus, although humanitarian, legally required benefits do not directly meet the imperatives of competitive strategy. Legally required benefits, however, may contribute indirectly to competitive advantage by enabling individuals to remain participants in the economy.

Nevertheless, legally required benefits may be a hindrance to companies in the short term because these offerings require substantial employer expenditures (e.g., contributions mandated by the Social Security Act and various state workers' compensation laws). Without these mandated expenditures on compensation, companies could choose to invest these funds in direct compensation programs designed to boost productivity and product or service quality. Companies could also choose investments in research and development activities essential for product differentiation. Finally, for companies pursuing lowest-cost strategies, management could simply choose to place these funds in reserve, representing a reduction in the overall cost to conceive, develop, and deliver a product or service.

How can HR managers and other business professionals minimize the cost burden associated with legally required benefits? Let's consider this issue for both workers' compensation and unemployment insurance benefits. In the case of workers' compensation, employers can respond in two ways. The first response is to reduce the likelihood of workers' compensation claims. The implementation of workplace safety programs is one strategy for reducing workers' compensation claims. Effective safety programs include teaching safe work procedures and safety awareness to employees and supervisors. Another strategy for reducing workers' compensation claims is health promotion programs that include inspections of the workplace to identify health risks (e.g., high levels of exposure to toxic substances), and then to eliminate those risks.

The second employer response is to integrate workers' compensation benefits into the rest of the benefits program. Because of the rampant cost increases associated with workers' compensation, several state legislatures have considered integrating employer-sponsored medical insurance and workers' compensation programs. This "24-hour" coverage would specifically roll the medical component of workers' compensation into traditional employer-provided health insurance. Some companies have already experimented with 24-hour coverage. For instance, Polaroid Corporation found cost advantages associated with integrating medical insurance and workers' compensation: reduced administrative expense through integration of the coverages, better access to all employee medical records, and a decrease in litigation.[30]

Use of 24-hour coverage is not widespread for a number of reasons.[31] Many insurance companies view this approach as complicated. In addition, some companies are concerned that this coverage would cost them in unanticipated ways.

Employers also can contain their costs for unemployment insurance. As discussed earlier, the amount of tax employers contribute to providing unemployment insurance depends partly on their experience rating. Thus, employers can contain costs by systematically monitoring the reasons they terminate workers' employment and avoiding terminations that lead to unemployment insurance claims whenever possible. For example, it is not uncommon for companies to employ workers on a full-time basis when they experience increased demand for their products or services. Adding full-time workers is reasonable when companies expect that the higher demand will last for an extended period (e.g., more than 2 years); however, when demand is lower in the short term, companies usually reduce their workforce through layoffs. Unless the laid-off employees immediately find employment, they will file claims with their local employment security office for unemployment insurance. Their claims contribute to the companies' unemployment experience rating and, thus, their cost expenditures.

DESIGNING AND PLANNING THE BENEFITS PROGRAM

As noted earlier, discretionary benefits can work strategically by offering protection programs, paid time off, and services. As they plan and manage employee benefits programs, HR professionals should keep these functions in mind. There is probably no single company expects its employee benefits program to meet all these objectives. Company management, along with union representatives as appropriate, must therefore determine which objectives are the most important for a particular workforce.

Many experts argue that employee input is key to developing a "successful" program. Such input helps companies target the limited resources they have available for employee benefits to those areas that best meet employees' needs. For example, if a company's workforce includes mostly married couples who are raising young children, family assistance programs would probably be a priority. By involving employees in program development, they are most likely to accept and appreciate the benefits they receive. Companies can involve employees in the benefits determination process in such ways as surveys, interviews, and focus groups.

As they design benefit programs, HR professionals must address fundamental issues, including:

- Who receives coverage
- Whether to include retirees in the plan
- Whether to deny benefits to employees during their probationary periods
- Financing of benefits
- Degree of employee choice in determining benefits
- Cost containment
- Communication

Employers can ascertain key information from employees that can be useful in designing these programs. Table 12-3 lists examples of the kinds of information employers may want from their employees. The areas of input emphasize employees' beliefs about other employers' benefits offerings and employees' thoughts about the value of the benefits they receive.

Determining Who Receives Coverage

Companies decide whether to extend benefits coverage to full-time and part-time employees or to full-time employees only. The trend is toward offering part-time employees no benefits.

Deciding Whether to Include Retirees in the Plan

This decision centers on whether to extend medical insurance coverage to employees beyond the COBRA-mandated coverage period, as discussed earlier. Offering medical coverage to retirees benefits them in obvious ways because employers usually finance these benefits either wholly or partly, enabling many retirees on limited earnings to receive adequate medical protection. Extending medical insurance coverage to retirees also until recently benefited employers: The money they spent to extend coverage to retirees was tax deductible. Starting in 1997, however, employers' contributions to extend medical coverage to retirees are no longer tax deductible, which means that such expenses will reduce company earnings in the short-term. As a result, fewer employers are expected to finance medical insurance coverage for retirees in the future.

TABLE 12-3   Types of Employee Input for Designing Benefits Programs

Ask employees:

- What they know about existing benefits
- What they perceive to be the value of possible benefit changes
- What they think about the quality and timeliness of benefits communications and administration
- What they perceive to be the value of existing benefits, compared with those provided by other employers

---

SOURCE: Adapted from Martocchio (2006). *Employee Benefits: A Primer for Human Resource Professionals.* Burr Ridge, IL: McGraw-Hill.

Moreover, the rapidly rising cost of retiree health care benefits has created a tremendous financial strain on companies that choose to offer them. Of course, the various sources of economic uncertainty since 2001 have made it more difficult for companies to support full workforces, as evidenced by sluggish pay increases, reductions in benefits offerings, and layoffs. Many companies have found it more difficult to meet their pension obligations to retirees. There is presently a sobering realization that the soaring costs of retiree health care benefits may be pushing some companies to the limit.

Probationary Period

Another scope issue companies must address is employees' status. In many companies, employees' initial term of employment (usually shorter than 6 months) is deemed a **probationary period**, and companies view such periods as an opportunity to ensure that they have made sound hiring decisions. Many companies choose to withhold discretionary employee benefits for all probationary employees. Companies benefit directly through lower administration-of-benefits costs for these employees during the probationary period; however, probationary employees may experience financial hardships if they require medical attention.

Financing

Human resource managers must consider how to finance benefits. In fact, the available resources and financial goals may influence, to some extent, who will receive coverage. Managers may decide on noncontributory, contributory, and employee-financed programs, or some combination thereof. **Noncontributory financing** implies that the company assumes total costs for each discretionary benefit. Under **contributory financing**, the company and its employees share the costs. Under **employee-financed benefits**, employers do not contribute to the financing of discretionary benefits. The majority of benefit plans today are contributory, largely because the costs of benefits have risen so dramatically.

Employee Choice

Human resource professionals must decide on the degree of choice employees should have in determining the set of benefits they will receive. If employees within a company can choose from among a set of benefits, as opposed to all employees receiving the same set of benefits, the company is using a **flexible benefits plan** or **cafeteria plan**. Companies implement cafeteria plans to meet the challenges of diversity, as discussed earlier. Although there is limited evidence regarding employees' reactions to flexible benefits, the existing information indicates benefit satisfaction, overall job satisfaction, pay satisfaction, and understanding of benefits increased after the implementation of a flexible benefits plan.[32] Many of these outcomes are desirable because they are known to lead to reduced absenteeism and turnover.

Cafeteria plans vary,[33] so only the two most common will be discussed here. As described in this chapter, FSAs permit employees to pay for certain benefits expenses (e.g., child care) with pretax dollars. Prior to each plan year, employees elect the amount of salary-reduction dollars they wish to allocate to this kind of plan. Employers then use this money to reimburse employees for expenses incurred during the plan year that qualify for repayment. Table 12-4 illustrates the features of an FSA for Illinois state employees. These features are typical of FSAs used by private- and public-sector employers.

Core plus option plans extend a preestablished set of such benefits as medical insurance as a program core, which is usually mandatory for all employees. Beyond the core, employees may choose from an array of benefits options that suit their personal

Forms Mailed	31	Children Covered until . . .	413	Accidental Death and Dismemberment Insurance	122
		Filing Claims	4151		
Tax Deferred Plans		*Dental Insurance*		*Medical and/or Dependent Care Assistance Plans*	
403(b) Enrollment	131	Enrollment	112	Enrollment Contribution	14
457 Enrollment	132	Changing Plans	411	Amount	
		Filing Claims	4152	Disability Coverage	123

SUMMARY

This chapter provided a discussion of the legally required benefits concept, the rationale for legally required benefits, varieties of legally required benefits, and the implications of benefits for strategic compensation. Although companies have little choice with regard to the implementation of these benefits, the company management can proactively manage the costs of these legally required benefits to some extent. In the coming years, employees, employers, unions, and the government will pay greater attention to the adequacy of Social Security benefits for the succeeding generations. Likewise, these groups will closely monitor the effectiveness of the FMLA. We also discussed important features for designing benefits programs, particularly with emphasis on explaining the value of benefits to employees and facilitating their access to their employee benefits information.

KEY TERMS

- base period, 292
- supplemental unemployment benefit (SUB), 293
- Federal Unemployment Tax Act (FUTA), 293
- experience rating system, 293
- quarters of coverage, 294
- fully insured, 294
- Medicare Part A, 296
- Medicare Part B, 297
- Medigap, 297
- Medicare Select, 297
- Medicare+Choice, 297
- Medicare Advantage (Part C), 297
- fee-for-service plans, 297
- managed care, 297

- Federal Insurance Contribution Act (FICA), 298
- Self-Employment Contributions Act (SECA), 298
- taxable wage base, 298
- Medicare tax, 298
- hospital insurance tax, 298
- Longshore and Harborworkers' Compensation Act, 299
- Federal Employees' Compensation Act, 299
- injury claims, 300
- occupational disease claims, 300
- death claims, 301
- death benefits, 301
- torts, 302

- deliberate and knowing torts, 302
- violations of an affirmative duty, 302
- dual capacity, 303
- ratemaking service organizations, 304
- rating manuals, 304
- second-injury funds, 304
- probationary period, 309
- noncontributory financing, 309
- contributory financing, 309
- flexible benefits plan, 309
- cafeteria plan, 309
- core plus option plans, 309

DISCUSSION QUESTIONS

1. Except for the Family and Medical Leave Act, the remaining legally required benefits were conceived decades ago. What changes in the business environment and society might affect the relevance or perhaps the viability of any of these benefits? Discuss your ideas.
2. Provide your reaction to the statement, "Employee benefits is seen by employees as an entitlement for their membership in companies." Explain the rationale for your reaction.
3. Conduct some research on the future of the Social Security programs (see the Internet site *www.ssa.gov*). Based on your research, prepare a statement not to exceed 250 words that describes your view of the Social Security programs (e.g., whether they are necessary, their viability, or whether there should be changes in how the programs are funded). Refer to the information obtained from your research efforts, indicating how it influenced your views.

EXERCISES

Compensation Online

For Students

Exercise 1: Find relevant journal articles

You are preparing to debate a legally required benefits topic. Use your school library's online catalog to locate articles pertaining to one of the topics (e.g., Medicare, Social Security benefits, and workers' compensation). Find and read several current articles in these areas. Based on your review, discuss three reasons why the government should provide greater funding to support the selected program.

Exercise 2: Search for federal government information

This chapter dealt in part with the federal government's efforts to help the disabled gain employment. Go to the U.S. Department of Labor's Web site at *www.doleta.gov*. Click on the Research link at the top of the homepage. Look for a site that corresponds to information in this chapter and read it. How does what you read add to or change what you read in the chapter?

Exercise 3: Research current information on Social Security matters

Go to the SSA Web site at *www.ssa.gov/pressoffice/*. Review current information from the SSA Press Office. Select one of the links, read it, and write a brief summary of how the information in this site relates to the textbook chapter.

For Professionals

Exercise 1: Review a professional resource

Though the expense is minimal, your board of directors questions the worth of having membership in the International Foundation of Employee Benefits Plans. Go to the Web page of the International Foundation of Employee Benefit Plans at *www.ifebp.org*. Write a summary of what this group has to offer and how it can be a helpful resource for every HR professional in your corporation.

Exercise 2: Review company Web sites

Visit the Web pages for GE and Southwest Airlines at *www.ge.com* and *www.southwest.com*. View the information on benefits at these companies. What is the purpose of this section of a company's Web site? Explain how descriptions of employee benefits may promote recruitment of talented employees.

Exercise 3: Keep informed of current events related to human resources

Employees turn to the HR department for answers on several issues, even some that do not pertain directly to company policy. It is therefore important to keep abreast of current issues. From Yahoo!, perform an advanced search for "Medicare." Focus on the News section of Yahoo! and review some of the resulting articles. Which two issues do you feel are most pressing? Why?

ENDNOTES

1. U.S. Bureau of Labor Statistics (2007). *Employer costs for employee compensation—March 2007* [online]. Available: *www.bls.gov/ncs/ect/home.htm,* accessed June 30, 2007.
2. The Bureau of National Affairs (1991). *Employee Benefits Law.* Washington, DC: Bureau of National Affairs.
3. Martocchio, J. J. (2008). *Employee Benefits: A Primer for Human Resource Professionals* (3rd ed.). Burr Ridge, IL: Irwin/McGraw-Hill.
4. Social Security Administration. 2007. *Monthly Statistical Snapshot, May 2007.* Online: *www.ssa.gov/policy/docs/quickfacts/stat_snapshot/ index.html,* accessed June 30, 2007.
5. Ibid.
6. 26 U.S.C. §§3101–3125.
7. 26 U.S.C. §§1401–1403.
8. Social Security Commission. 2007. The Future of Social Security. Online: *www.socialsecurity.gov,* accessed February 17, 2007.
9. Dulles, F. R., & Dubofsky, M. (1993). *Labor in America: A History.* Arlington Heights, IL: Harlan Davidson.
10. Rejda, G. E. (1994). *Social Insurance and Economic Security.* Upper Saddle River, NJ: Prentice Hall.
11. U.S. Chamber of Commerce (2004). *2004 Analysis of Workers' Compensation Laws.* Washington, DC: Author.
12. Ibid.
13. Nackley, J. V. (1987). *Primer on Workers' Compensation.* Washington, DC: Bureau of National Affairs.
14. Ibid.
15. Ibid.
16. U.S. Bureau of Labor Statistics. (2006). *Nonfatal occupational injuries and illnesses requiring time away from work, 2005.* USDL 06–1982. Online: *www.bls.gov,* accessed March 26, 2007.
17. U.S. Bureau of Labor Statistics. (2006). *Nonfatal occupational injuries and illnesses requiring time away from work, 2005.* USDL 06–1982. Online: *www.bls.gov,* accessed March 26, 2007.
18. U.S. Bureau of Labor Statistics. (2006). *Census of fatal occupational injuries in 2005.* USDL 06–1364. Online: *www.bls.gov.* Accessed June 30, 2007.
19. U.S. Chamber of Commerce. (2007). *2007 Analysis of Workers' Compensation Laws.* Washington, DC: U.S. Chamber of Commerce.
20. Ibid.
21. Ibid.
22. U.S. Bureau of Labor Statistics (2007). *Employer costs for employee compensation—*March 2007 [online]. Available: *www.bls.gov/ncs/ect/home.htm,* accessed July 1, 2007.
23. U.S. Census Bureau, *Statistical Abstract of the United States: 2007* (126th Edition) Washington, DC, 2006; *www.census.gov/statab/www/.*
24. *Tatrai v. Presbyterian University Hospital,* 439 A.2d 1162 (PA 1982).
25. *Cousins v. Georgia-Pacific Corp.,* 599 A.2d 73 (ME 1991).
26. J. V. Nackley. 1987. *Primer on Workers' Compensation.* Washington, DC: Bureau of National Affairs.
27. I.R.C. §104(a).
28. U.S. Department of Commerce (2004–2005). *Statistical Abstracts of the United States* (124th ed.). Washington, DC: Author.
29. Martocchio, J. J. (2006). *Employee Benefits: A Primer for Human Resource Professionals* (2nd ed.). Burr Ridge, IL: Irwin/McGraw-Hill.
30. Tompkins, N. C. (1992). Around-the-clock medical coverage. *HR Magazine* (June), pp. 66–72.
31. Baker, L. C., & Krueger, A. B. (1993). *Twenty-four-hour coverage and workers' compensation insurance.* Working paper, Princeton University Industrial Relations Section.
32. Barber, A. E., Dunham, R. B., & Formisano, R. (1990). *The impact of flexible benefit plans on employee satisfaction.* Paper presented at the Fiftieth annual meeting of the Academy of Management, San Francisco, CA.
33. Martocchio, J. J. (2006). *Employee Benefits: A Primer for Human Resource Professionals* (2nd ed.). Burr Ridge, IL: Irwin/McGraw-Hill.
34. U.S. Bureau of Labor Statistics (2007). *Employer costs for employee compensation—*March 2007 [online]. Available: *www.bls.gov/ncs/ect/home.htm,* accessed July 1, 2007.
35. Martocchio, J. J. (2006). *Employee Benefits: A Primer for Human Resource Professionals* (2nd ed.). Burr Ridge, IL: Irwin/McGraw-Hill.

CHAPTER 13

Compensating Executives

Chapter Outline

- Contrasting Executive Pay with Pay for Nonexecutive Employees

- Principles of Executive Compensation: Implications for Competitive Strategy

- Defining Executive Status
    Who Are Executives?
    Key Employees
    Highly Compensated Employees

- Executive Compensation Packages
    Components of Current Core Compensation
    Short-Term Incentives
    Components of Deferred Core Compensation
    Employee Benefits: Enhanced Protection Program Benefits and
        Perquisites

- Principles and Processes for Setting Executive Compensation
    The Key Players in Setting Executive Compensation
    Theoretical Explanations for Setting Executive Compensation

- Executive Compensation Disclosure Rules

- Executive Compensation: Are U.S. Executives Paid Too Much?
    Comparison between Executive Compensation and Compensation
        for Other Worker Groups
    Strategic Questions: Is Pay for Performance?
    Ethical Considerations: Is Executive Compensation Fair?
    International Competitiveness

- Summary

- Key Terms

- Discussion Questions

- Exercises

- Endnotes

Learning Objectives

In this chapter, you will learn about

1. Components of executive core compensation

2. Components of executive employee benefits

3. Principles and processes of setting executive compenation

4. Executive compensation disclosure rules

5. The executive compensation controversy: Are U.S. executives paid too much?

Executive compensation practices in U.S. companies have received substantial attention in the press. As we will see in this chapter, executive pay practices have raised concerns that many executives receive lucrative compensation and benefits even when company performance falls below shareholder expectations. Many critics have questioned whether such practices may interfere with some executives' motivation to achieve excellent performance. Moreover, applying such practices to executives contradict the main assumptions of performance-based pay discussed in Chapters 4 and 5 that *successful performance* triggers merit and incentive awards, and the *degree of success* determines the amount of award. After all, pay-for-performance applies to most nonexecutive employees in U.S. companies. In some instances that we will discuss, executives are rewarded after they have not performed well, with multimillion dollar awards contingent on their leaving the company. It is not surprising that instances like these are often referred to as *pay-for-nonperformance* or, more harshly, *pay-for-failure*, and that they have have become increasingly common events in the world of executive compensation.

CONTRASTING EXECUTIVE PAY WITH PAY FOR NONEXECUTIVE EMPLOYEES

From an economic standpoint, the chief executive officer (CEO) is the seller of his or her services, and the compensation committee is the buyer of these services. Under classic economic theory, a reasonable price is obtained through negotiations that are at arm's length between an informed seller and an informed buyer. An awkward situation can result when the CEO hires a professional compensation director or compensation consultant. In this case, the compensation consultant who makes the recommendation to the compensation committee works for the CEO. In theory, the CEO hires the consultant to perform an objective analysis of the company's executive pay package and to make whatever recommendations the consultant feels are appropriate. This relationship has the potential to promote a conflict of interest because of the perceived pressure for the consultant to protect the CEO's financial interests. The irony is that the consultant is often viewed as representing the shareholders' interests. In a sense, the buyers of the CEO's services are the shareholders and their representatives, the compensation committee of the board of directors. They tend to act upon the compensation consultant's recommendation.[1]

This passage illustrates just one of the main differences between compensating executives and compensating other employees. There are many other contrasts. The income disparity between executives and other employees is astounding. We take this issue up in greater detail later in this chapter.

PRINCIPLES OF EXECUTIVE COMPENSATION: IMPLICATIONS FOR COMPETITIVE STRATEGY

Executives are the top leaders in their companies. It intuitively seems reasonable that executives should earn substantial compensation packages. After all, their skills and experience enable them to develop and direct the implementation of competitive strategies. Few dispute the key role executives play in promoting competitive advantage; however, public scrutiny of executive compensation packages intensified during the 1990s because of heightened concerns about global competitiveness, rampant corporate downsizing, and the more recent practice of relocating jobs to countries with lower labor costs (i.e., offshoring) that left hundreds of thousands of employees jobless. The U.S. Bureau of Labor Statistics unfortunately continues to suggest a continuation of the job-loss phenomenon:

> In May 2007, employers took 1,190 mass layoff actions, seasonally adjusted, as measured by new filings for unemployment insurance benefits during the month, the Bureau of Labor Statistics of the U.S. Department of Labor reported today. Each action involved at least 50 persons from a single establishment, and the number of workers involved totaled 119,089, on a seasonally adjusted basis.[2]

We will take up the executive compensation controversy later in this chapter. We will next review fundamental concepts: defining executive status and the components of executive compensation packages.

DEFINING EXECUTIVE STATUS

Who Are Executives?

Virtually all the components of executive compensation plans provide favorable tax treatment for both the executive and the company. Who are executives? From a tax regulation perspective, the Internal Revenue Service (IRS) recognizes two groups of employees who play a major role in a company's policy decisions: highly compensated employees and key employees. The IRS uses "key employees" to determine the necessity of top-heavy provisions in employer-sponsored qualified retirement plans that cover most nonexecutive employees. It uses "highly compensated employees" for nondiscrimination rules in employer-sponsored health insurance benefits (Chapter 11). Although these two designations were created for federal tax rule applications, employees in both groups typically participate in executive compensation and benefits plans.

Key employees and highly compensated employees hold positions of substantial responsibility. Figure 13-1 illustrates the placement of key employees in a typical organizational structure. Although titles vary from company to company and in pay structures, CEOs, presidents, executive vice presidents, vice presidents of functional areas (e.g., human resources), and the directors below them usually meet the criteria for key employees.

Key Employees

The term **key employee** means any employee who at any time during the year is:[3]

- A 5 percent owner of the employer
- A 1 percent owner of the employer having an annual compensation from the employer of more than $150,000
- An officer of the employer having an annual compensation greater than $145,000 in 2007 (indexed for inflation in increments of $5,000 beginning in 2003)

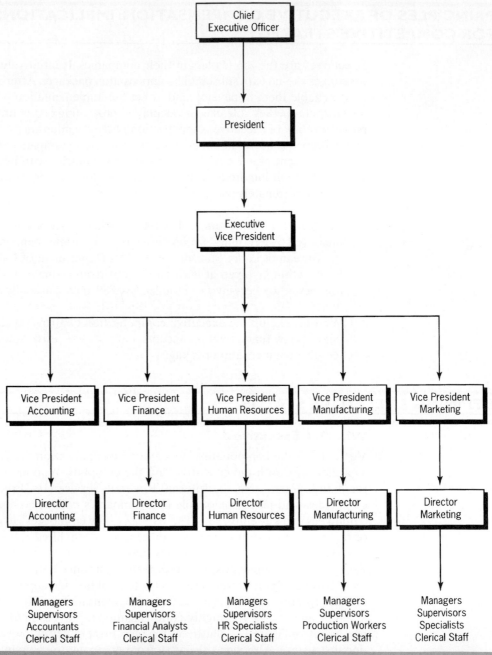

FIGURE 13-1 Examples of Key Employees

U.S. Treasury Regulations define the term *officer* used in this definition of key employees:[4]

> Generally, the term officer means an administrative executive who is in regular and continued service. The term officer implies continuity of service and excludes those employed for a special and single transaction. An employee who merely has the title of an officer but not the authority of an officer is not considered an officer for purposes of the key employee test.

Similarly, an employee who does not have the title of an officer but has the authority of an officer is an officer for purposes of the key employee test.

Highly Compensated Employees

The IRS defines a **highly compensated employee** as one of the following during the current year or preceding year, as[5]

- A 5 percent owner at any time during the year or the preceding year
- For the preceding year had compensation from the employer in excess of $100,000 in 2007
- If the employer elects the application of this clause for a plan year, was in the top-paid group of employees for the preceding year

EXECUTIVE COMPENSATION PACKAGES

Executive compensation has both core and employee benefits elements, much like compensation packages for other employees; however, one noteworthy feature distinguishes executive compensation packages from nonexecutive compensation packages. Executive compensation packages emphasize long-term or deferred rewards over short-term rewards. The main components of executive compensation include:

- Current or annual core compensation
- Deferred core compensation: stock compensation
- Deferred core compensation: golden parachutes
- Employee benefits: enhanced protection program benefits and perquisites

Components of Current Core Compensation

Executive current core compensation packages contain two components: annual base pay and bonuses. Although quite high, current compensation dropped by more than 10 percent in just 1 year.[6]

Base Pay

Base pay is the fixed element of annual cash compensation. Companies that use formal salary structures may have specific pay grades and pay ranges (Chapter 9) for nonexempt employees and exempt employees, including supervisory, management, professional, and executive jobs, with the exception of the CEO.

As discussed in Chapter 9, compensation professionals generally apply different range spreads across pay grades. They most commonly use progressively higher range spreads for pay grades that contain more valuable jobs in terms of a company's competitive strategies. Higher-level jobs afford employees greater promotion opportunities than do entry-level jobs. Employees also tend to remain in higher pay grades longer, and the specialized skills associated with higher-pay-grade jobs are considered valuable. It therefore makes sense to apply larger range spreads to these pay grades.

Chief executive officer (CEO) jobs do not fall within formal pay structures for two reasons. First, CEOs' work is highly complex and unpredictable. It is not possible to specify discrete responsibilities and duties. The choice of competitive strategy by CEOs and other executives, and the influence of external and internal market factors (Chapter 2), make it impossible to describe CEOs' jobs. Second, setting

CEO compensation differs dramatically from the rational processes compensation professionals use to build market-competitive pay structures (Chapter 8). We will discuss agency theory, tournament theory, and social comparison theory later as explanations for setting CEO compensation.

In most cases, annual base pay represents a relatively small part of a CEO's total compensation for two reasons. First, it typically takes years before the fruits of CEOs' strategic initiatives are realized. Second, the IRS limits the amount of annual salary a company may exclude as a business expenses. Only the first $1 million annually for an executive's pay may be excluded from the company's income tax liability. This ruling was put into place to keep companies from boosting CEO annual pay to astronomical levels for the purposes of tax savings.

Bonuses

Bonuses represent single pay-for-performance payments companies use to reward employees for achievement of specific, exceptional goals. As discussed in previous chapters, compensation professionals design bonuses for merit pay programs (Chapter 4), gain sharing plans and referral plans (Chapter 5), and sales incentive compensation programs (Chapter 9). Bonuses also represent a key component of executive compensation packages.

Companies' compensation committees recommend bonus awards to boards of directors for their approval (as we will discuss later in this chapter). Four types of bonuses are common in executive compensation:

- Discretionary bonus
- Performance-contingent bonus
- Predetermined allocation bonus
- Target plan bonus

As the term implies, boards of directors award **discretionary bonuses** to executives on an elective basis. They weigh four factors in determining the amount of discretionary bonus: company profits, the financial condition of the company, business conditions, and prospects for the future. For example, boards of directors may award discretionary bonuses to executives when a company's position in the market is strong.

Executives receive **performance-contingent bonuses** based on the attainment of specific performance criteria. The performance appraisal system for determining bonus awards is often the same appraisal system used for determining merit increases or general performance reviews for salary (Chapter 4).

Unlike the previous executive bonuses, the total bonus pool for the **predetermined allocation bonus** is based on a fixed formula. The central factor in determining the size of the total bonus pool and bonus amounts is company profits.

The **target plan bonus** ties bonuses to executives' performance. The bonus amount increases commensurately with performance. Executives do not receive bonuses when their performance falls below minimally acceptable standards. The target plan bonus differs from the predetermined allocation bonus in an important way: Predetermined allocation bonus amounts are fixed, regardless of how well executives perform.

Short-Term Incentives

Companies award short-term incentive compensation to executives to recognize their progress toward fulfilling competitive strategy goals. Executives may participate in current profit sharing plans and gain sharing plans. Table 13-1 describes these plans. We already discussed the use of current profit sharing plans and gain sharing plans for nonexecutive employees in Chapter 5. Whereas short-term objectives reward

TABLE 13-1 Short-Term Incentive Compensation: Current Profit Sharing Plans and Gain Sharing Plans

Current Profit Sharing Plans

As we discussed in Chapter 5, profit sharing plans pay a portion of company profits to employees, separate from base pay, cost-of-living adjustments, or permanent merit pay increases. Two basic kinds of profit sharing plans are used widely today. First, current profit sharing plans award cash to employees, typically on a quarterly or annual basis. Second, deferred profit sharing plans place cash awards in trust accounts for employees. These trusts are set aside on employees' behalf as a source of retirement income. Current profit sharing plans provide cash to employees as part of their regular core compensation; thus, these payments are subject to IRS taxation when they are earned. Deferred profit sharing plans are not taxed until the employee begins to make withdrawals during retirement.

Gain Sharing Plans

As we discussed in Chapter 5, gain sharing describes group incentive systems that provide participating employees with an incentive payment based on improved company performance such as increased productivity, increased customer satisfaction, lower costs, or better safety records. Gain sharing was developed so that all employees could benefit financially from productivity improvements that result from the suggestion system. Along with serving as a compensation tool, most gain sharing reflects a management philosophy that emphasizes employee involvement.

nonexempt and lower-level management employees for achieving major milestone work objectives, short-term incentives applied to executives are designed to reward them for meeting intermediate performance criteria. The performance criteria relate to the performance of a company as dictated by competitive strategy. Change in the company's earnings per share over a 1-year period, growth in profits, and annual cost savings are criteria that may be used in executives' short-term incentive plans.

Short-term incentive compensation programs usually apply to a group of select executives within a company. The plan applies to more than one executive because the synergy that results from the efforts and expertise of top executives influences corporate performance. The board of directors distributes short-term incentive awards to each executive based on rank and compensation levels. Thus, the CEO will receive a larger performance award than will the executive vice president, whose position is lower in the company's structure than the CEO's position.

For example, let's assume that the CEO and executive vice president of a chain of general merchandise retail stores have agreed to lead the corporation as the lowest-cost chain of stores in the general merchandise retail industry. The CEO and executive vice president establish a 5-year plan to meet this lowest-cost competitive strategy. The vice president of compensation recommends that the company adopt a gain sharing program to reward top executives for contributing to the cost reduction objective. After 1 year, the complementary decisions made by the CEO and executive vice president have enabled the corporation to save $10,000,000. The board of directors agree that the executives' collaborative decisions led to noteworthy progress toward meeting the lowest-cost strategy and award the CEO 2 percent of the annual cost savings ($200,000) and 1 percent to the executive vice president ($100,000).

Components of Deferred Core Compensation

Stock Compensation

Deferred compensation refers to an agreement between an employee and a company to render payments to an employee at a future date. Deferred compensation is a hallmark of executive compensation packages. As an incentive, deferred compensation is supposed to create a sense of ownership, aligning the interests of the executive with those of the owners or shareholders of the company over the long term. The amount of long-term incentive compensation varies tremendously from CEO to CEO. It isn't unusual for CEOs to be awarded $3 million or more each year.

Apart from the incentive value, deferred compensation provides tax advantages to executives. In particular, deferring payment until retirement should lead to lower taxation. Why does deferment create a tax advantage? Executives do not pay taxes on deferred compensation until they receive it. Executives' income tax rates will presumably be substantially lower during retirement, when their total income is lower, than it is while they are employed.

Company stock shares are the main form of executives' deferred compensation. As described in Chapter 5, **company stock** represents total equity of the firm. **Company stock shares** represent equity segments of equal value. Equity interest increases positively with the number of stock shares. Stocks are bought and sold every business day in a public stock exchange. The New York Stock Exchange is among the best-known of the stock exchanges. Table 13-2 lists basic terminology pertaining to stocks.

Companies design executive stock compensation plans to promote an executive's sense of ownership of the company. A sense of ownership should presumably motivate executives to strive for excellent performance. Stock value generally increases with gains in company performance. In particular, a company's stock value rises in response to reports of profit gains; however, factors outside executives' control often influence stock prices despite executives' performance. For example, forecasts of economywide recession, increases in the national unemployment rate, and threats to national security (e.g., the September 11 attacks) often lead to declines in stock value.

Six particular forms of deferred (stock) compensation include:

- Incentive stock option plans
- Nonstatutory stock option plans
- Restricted stock
- Phantom stock plans
- Discount stock option
- Stock appreciation rights

Incentive Stock Options

Incentive stock options entitle executives to purchase their companies' stock in the future at a predetermined price. The predetermined price usually equals the stock price at the time an executive receives the stock option. In effect, executives are purchasing the stocks at a discounted price. Executives generally buy after the price has increased dramatically. An executive receives **capital gains** as the difference

---

TABLE 13-2 Employee Stock Terminology

Stock option. A right granted by a company to an employee to purchase a number of stocks at a designated price within a specified period of time.

Stock grant. A company's offering of stock to an employee.

Exercise of stock grant. An employee's purchase of stock, using stock options.

Disposition. Sale of stock by the stockholder.

Fair market value. The average value between the highest and lowest reported sales price of a stock on the New York Stock Exchange on any given date. The IRS specifies whether an option has a readily ascertainable fair market value at grant. An option has a readily ascertainable fair market value if the option is actively traded on an established stock exchange at the time the option is granted.

between the stock price at the time of purchase and the lower stock price at the time an executive receives the stock option. Executives receive income tax benefits by participating in incentive stock option plans. The federal government does not recognize capital gains until the disposition of the stock.

Nonstatutory Stock Options

Much like incentive stock options, companies award stock options to executives at discounted prices. In contrast to incentive stock options, **nonstatutory stock options** do not qualify for favorable tax treatment. Executives pay income taxes on the difference between the discounted price and the stock's fair market value at the time of the stock grant. They do not pay taxes in the future when they choose to exercise their nonstatutory stock options.

Nonstatutory stock options do provide executives an advantage. Executives' tax liability is ultimately lower over the long term: Stock prices generally increase over time. As a result, the capital gains will probably be much greater in the future when executives exercise their options rather than when their companies grant these options.

Restricted Stock

The term **restricted stock** means that executives do not have any ownership control over the disposition of the stock for a predetermined period, often 5 to 10 years. Executives must sell the stock back to the company for exactly the same discounted price they had at the time of purchase if they terminate their employment before the end of the designated restriction period.[7] In addition, restricted stock grants provide executives tax incentives. They do not pay tax on any income that results from an increase in stock price until after the restriction period ends.[8] Restricted stock is a common type of long-term executive compensation. Boards of directors award restricted stock to executives at considerable discounts.

Phantom Stock

A **phantom stock** plan is a compensation arrangement whereby boards of directors compensate executives with hypothetical company stocks rather than actual shares of company stock. Phantom stock plans are similar to restricted stock plans because executives must meet specific conditions before they can convert these phantom shares into real shares of company stock.[9] There are generally two conditions. First, executives must remain employed for a specified period, anywhere between 5 and 20 years. Second, executives must retire from the company. Upon meeting these conditions, executives receive income equal to the increase in the value of company stock from the date the company granted the phantom stock to the conversion date. Phantom stock plans provide executives with tax advantages. Executives pay taxes on the capital gains after they convert their phantom shares to real shares of company stock during retirement. Executives' retirement incomes will probably be significantly less than their incomes prior to retirement. Thus, the retirees' income tax rates will be lower.

Discount Stock Option Plans

Discount stock option plans[10] are similar to nonstatutory stock option plans with one exception. Companies grant stock options at rates far below the stock's fair market value on the date the option is granted. This means that the participating executive immediately receives a benefit equal to the difference between the exercise price and the fair market value of the employer's stock.

Stock Appreciation Rights

Stock appreciation rights provide executives income at the end of a designated period, much like restricted stock options; however, executives never have to exercise their stock rights to receive income. The company simply awards payment to executives based on the difference in stock price between the time the company granted the stock rights at fair market value to the end of the designated period, permitting the executives to keep the stock. Executives pay tax on any income from gains in stock value when they exercise their stock rights, presumably after retirement when their tax rates are lower.[11]

Golden Parachutes

Most executives' employment agreements contain a golden parachute clause. **Golden parachutes** provide pay and benefits to executives after a termination that results from a change in ownership or corporate takeover. Golden parachutes extend pay and benefits from 1 to 5 years, depending on the agreement. Planned retirement, resignation, or disability does not trigger golden parachute benefits. Boards of directors include golden parachute clauses for two reasons. First, golden parachutes limit executives' risks in the event of these unforeseen events. Second, golden parachutes promote recruitment and retention of talented executives.

Companies benefit from golden parachute payments because they can treat these payments as business expenses. This means that companies can reduce their tax liability by increasing the parachute amount. The total value of golden parachutes came to exceed executives' annual income levels by far. Public outcry led to government-imposed intervention that limited tax benefits to companies. Companies may generally receive tax deductions on golden parachutes that amount to less than several times an executive's average annual compensation for the preceding 5 years.

Platinum Parachutes

In an ideal world, CEOs will perform on an exemplary basis, making decisions to drive up company profits. As you know, we do not live in a perfect world; sometimes, CEOs do not perform their jobs well and companies lose out on profit opportunities. After a period of unsatisfactory performance as determined by shareholders and other company executives, CEOs may often be terminated even before the expiration of their employment contracts. Many companies reach agreements with CEOs to terminate employment, awarding a platinum parachute as an incentive. **Platinum parachutes** are lucrative awards that compensate departing executives with severance pay, continuation of company benefits, and even stock options. Companies use platinum parachutes to avoid long legal battles or critical reports in the press essentially by paying off a CEO to give up their post. For example, Jay S. Sidhu resigned from Sovereign Bancorp amid growing criticism from investors. He left the company with a platinum parachute worth $73.56 million lined with $24.4 million in cash and stock options, 5 years of free health care, and a 3-year, $40,000 per month consulting contract.

Tighter Regulation of Deferred Compensation Plans

Well publicized corporate accounting scandals have recently led to tighter accounting standards. New corporate tax law puts tighter restrictions on deferred compensation payouts to prevent corporate executives from siphoning money out of their corporations. There specifically was a rash of executives withdrawing deferred compensation money before their companies went bankrupt. The most well-known scandal occurred at Enron. In response to corporate accounting scandals, the SEC administered the Sarbanes-Oxley Act of 2002. The Sarbanes-Oxley Act is perhaps the most significant legislation because it imposes rigorous requirements for companies' financial disclosure to limit the chance that covert misuses of corporate funds will occur. In 2002, President George W. Bush strengthened the oversight of the SEC when he signed the **Sarbanes-Oxley Act of 2002** into law. The Act mandated a number of reforms to enhance corporate responsibility, enhance financial disclosures and combat corporate and accounting fraud in response to corporate accounting scandals in Enron, Tyco, and other large U.S. corporations. The Act established **Public Company Accounting Oversight Board (PCAOB)** to oversee the activities of the auditing profession.

Section 103 of the Sarbanes-Oxley Act of 2002 directs the board to establish auditing and related attestation, quality control, ethics, and independence standards and rules to be used by registered public accounting firms in the preparation and issuance of audit reports as required by the Act or the rules of the Securities and Exchange Commission. The board's Office of the Chief Auditor advises the board on the establishment of such auditing and related professional practice standards. The board also seeks advice from its Standing Advisory Group and ad hoc task forces and working groups.

Employee Benefits: Enhanced Protection Program Benefits and Perquisites

Executives receive discretionary benefits like other employees (i.e., protection program benefits, provide paid time off, and employee services); however, executives' discretionary benefits differ in two ways. First, protection programs include supplemental coverage that provides enhanced benefit levels. Second, the services component contains benefits exclusively for executives. These exclusive executive benefits are known as **perquisites** or **perks.** Legally required benefits apply to executives, with the exception of one provision of the Family and Medical Leave Act of 1993.

Enhanced Protection Program Benefits

Supplemental life insurance and supplemental executive retirement plans distinguish protection programs for executive employees from protection programs for other employees. As discussed in Chapter 10, employer-provided life insurance protects employees' families by paying a specified amount to an employee's beneficiaries upon an employee's death. Most policies pay some multiple of the employee's salary (e.g., benefits paid at twice the employee's annual salary). In addition to regular life insurance, executives receive **supplemental life insurance** protection that pays an additional monetary benefit. Companies design executives' supplemental life insurance protection to meet two objectives.[12] First, supplemental life insurance increases the value of executives' estates bequeathed to designated beneficiaries (usually family members) upon their deaths. Life insurance programs may be designed to provide greater benefits than standard plans usually allow. Second, these programs provide executives with favorable tax treatments.

Supplemental retirement plans are designed to restore benefits restricted under qualified plans. As discussed in Chapter 11, qualified plans entitle employers to tax benefits from their contributions to pension plans. In general, this means that employers may take current tax deductions for contributions to fund future retirement income. Employees may also receive some favorable tax treatment (i.e., a lower tax rate). In Chapter 11, we discussed the characteristics of qualified plans. A qualified plan generally entitles employees to favorable tax treatment of the benefits they receive upon their retirement. Any investment income that is generated in the pension program is not taxed until the employee retires.

The IRS limited the annual earnings amount for determining qualified plan benefits to $225,000 in 2007 (indexed for inflation, in increments of $5,000). In general, all annual earnings greater than this level cannot be included in defined benefit plan formulas or the calculation of annual additions to defined contribution plans. In addition, the IRS limits the annual benefit amounts for defined benefit plans to the lesser of $180,000 in 2007, indexed for inflation, or 100 percent of the highest average compensation for three consecutive years.[13] Limits on annual additions to defined contribution plans were the lesser of $45,000 in 2007, indexed for inflation, or 100 percent of the participant's compensation.[14] The annual addition includes employer contributions, employee contributions, and forfeitures allocated to the participant's account. For example, an executive's three highest annual salaries are $690,000, $775,000, and $1,100,000. The average of these three highest salaries is $855,000. Of course, $180,000 is less than $855,000; therefore, an executive's retirement income based on the company's qualified pension plan cannot exceed $180,000 adjusted for inflation.

A supplemental retirement plan can make up this difference. For illustrative purposes, let's assume that the annual benefit under a qualified pension plan is 60 percent of the final average salary for the past 15 years of service, which is $400,000. Based on this formula, the executive should receive an annual retirement benefit of $240,000 ($400,000 × 60 percent). This annual benefit exceeds $180,000 (i.e., the statutory limit for qualified retirement plans). Because of the statutory limit, companies may offer a supplemental executive retirement plan that provides the difference between the value derived from the pension formula ($240,000) and the statutory limit ($180,000). In this example, the executive would receive a supplemental annual retirement benefit of $60,000.

Perquisites

Executive perquisites are an integral part of executive compensation. Perquisites cover a broad range of benefits, from free lunches to the free use of corporate jets. Table 13-3 lists common executive perks. Perquisites serve two purposes. First, these benefits recognize executives' attained status. Membership in an exclusive country club reinforces executives' attained social status. Second, executives use perks for personal comfort or as a business tool. For example, a company may own a well-appointed cabin in Vail, Colorado. Executives may use the cabin for rest and relaxation, or as a place to court new clients or close a lucrative business deal. Arranging relaxing weekends in Vail benefits executives and their families, and provides executives opportunities to develop rapport with prospective clients. It is possible that companies will provide cash in lieu of perquisites because of stricter reporting requirements by the Securities and Exchange Commission. Particularly after the corporate scandals at Enron and other corporations, company shareholders expect management to display greater accountability for the nonbusiness use of such company property as corporate jets. Beginning in 2008, companies will have to report perks valued at $10,000 or more apiece. Prior to 2008, companies were required to report perks valued at more than $50,000 each.

TABLE 13-3 Common Executive Perks

- Company cars
- Financial services
- Legal services (e.g., income tax preparation)
- Recreational facilities (e.g., country club and athletic club memberships)
- Travel perks (e.g., first-class airfare)
- Residential security
- Tickets to sporting events

PRINCIPLES AND PROCESSES FOR SETTING EXECUTIVE COMPENSATION

We discussed the processes compensation professionals use to reward performance (i.e., merit pay and alternative incentive pay methods) and acquisition of job-related knowledge and skills (i.e., pay-for-knowledge and skilled-based pay) in previous chapters. Although pay-for-performance is the public rationale for setting executive compensation, reality is often quite different. Three alternative theories explain the principles and processes for setting executive compensation: agency theory, tournament theory, and social comparison theory. We will begin by discussing the key players in setting executive compensation.

The Key Players in Setting Executive Compensation

Different individuals and groups participate in setting executive compensation. They include compensation consultants, compensation committees, and boards of directors. Each plays a different role in setting executive compensation.

Executive Compensation Consultants

Executive compensation consultants usually propose several recommendations for alternate pay packages. Executive compensation consultants are often employed by large consulting firms that specialize in executive compensation or advise company management on a wide variety of business issues. The regulations involving executive compensation plans are extremely complex. To understanding them fully requires expertise often found in leading executive compensation and benefits consulting firms. Some of the leading and most well-respected firms in this area include the following:

- Buck Consultants (*www.buckconsultants.com*)
- Frederic W. Cook & Company (*www.fwcook.com*)
- The Hay Associates (*www.haygroup.com*)
- Hewitt Associates (*www.hewitt.com*)
- Pearl Meyer & Partners (*www.pearlmeyer.com*)
- Towers Perrin (*www.towersperrin.com*)
- William M. Mercer (*www.mercerhr.com*)
- Watson Wyatt (*www.watsonwyatt.com*)

You will find useful updates about executive compensation and benefits on these firms' Internet sites.

Consultants make recommendations about what and how much to include in executive compensation packages based on strategic analyses, much like the analyses we discussed in Chapter 2. Recall that a **strategic analysis** entails an examination of a company's external market context and internal factors. Examples of external market factors include industry profile, information about competitors, and long-term growth prospects. Financial condition is the most pertinent internal factor regarding executive compensation. Strategic analyses permit compensation consultants to see where their client company stands in the market based on external and internal factors. Strong companies should be able to devote more financial resources to fund lucrative executive compensation programs than weaker companies. More often than not, executive compensation consultants find themselves in conflict of interest situations:

> Ostensibly, compensation consultants were hired by the CEO to perform an objective analysis of the company's executive pay package and to make whatever recommendations the consultant felt were appropriate. In reality, if

those recommendations did not cause the CEO to earn more money than he was earning before the compensation consultant appeared on the scene, the latter was rapidly shown the door.[15]

Executive compensation consultants' professional survival may depend on recommending lucrative compensation packages. Recommending the most lucrative compensation packages will quickly promote a favorable impression of the consultant among CEOs, leading to future consulting engagements.

Starting in 2008 the SEC rulings will require companies to include the identity of the consulting firm in public disclosure statements. This ruling has created concerns about possible conflicts of interest for consulting firms that also provide consulting services in other areas (e.g., performance management, change management) for the same client firms. Executive compensation consulting represents just one of many possible areas of management consulting. The conflict potentially arises when a consultant intentionally recommends a more-lucrative-than-warranted executive compensation package in the hope of gaining management favor and additional other management consulting opportunities. Of course, compensation consulting firms are concerned about the public image of possible conflicts of interest and have considered a variety of tactics to ensure the integrity of their recommendations to client firms. For example, there has been some speculation that executive consulting practices will be spun off into independent businesses. Many companies are concerned about their own public image and have instituted policies to prevent compensation consultants from conducting other work for management.

Board of Directors

A **board of directors** represents shareholders' interests by weighing the pros and cons of top executives' decisions. Boards of directors have approximately 15 members. These members include CEOs and top executives of other successful companies, distinguished community leaders, well-regarded professionals (e.g., physicians and attorneys), and possibly a few top-level executives of the company.

Boards of directors give final approval of the compensation committee's recommendation. Some critics of executive compensation have argued that CEOs use compensation to co-opt board independence.[16] CEOs often nominate candidates for board membership, and their nominations usually lead to candidates' placement on the board. Board members receive compensation for their service to the boards. It's not uncommon for a board member to earn more than $50,000 per year plus a fee ($10,000 or more) for each board meeting attended. Along with monetary and stock compensation, companies are using such benefits as medical insurance, life insurance, and retirement programs to attract top-notch individuals to join boards of directors. In general, board members' failure to cooperate with CEOs may lead either to fewer benefits or their removal.

> The board determines the pay of the CEO. But who determines the pay of the outside directors? Here, a sort of formal Japanese Kabuki has developed. The board of directors determines the pay of the CEO, and for all practical purposes, the CEO determines the pay of the board of directors. Is it any accident, then, that there is a statistical relationship between how highly the CEO is paid and how highly his outside directors are paid?[17]

As we will discuss shortly, recent changes in Securities and Exchange Commission rulings have increased board members' accountability for approving sound executive compensation packages—supportive of shareholders' best interests.

Compensation Committee

Board of directors members within and outside the company make up a company's **compensation committee**. Outside board members serve on compensation committees to minimize conflict of interest. Thus, outside directors usually are the committee's membership majority.

Compensation committees perform three duties. First, compensation committees review consultants' alternate recommendations for compensation packages. Second, compensation committee members discuss the assets and liabilities of the recommendations. The complex tax laws require compensation committees to consult compensation experts, legal counsel, and tax advisers. Third, based on these deliberations, the committee recommends the consultant's best proposal to the board of directors for their consideration.

Theoretical Explanations for Setting Executive Compensation

Three prominent theories describe the processes related to setting executive compensation: agency theory, tournament theory, and social comparison theory. The following discussion provides concrete interpretations of these theories. In addition to the works cited throughout this chapter, several excellent scholarly journal articles provide full explanations of these theoretical frames as applied to executive compensation.[18]

Agency Theory

Ownership is distributed among many thousands of shareholders in such large companies as Ford Motor Company, General Electric, General Motors, and IBM. For example, owning at least one share of stock in Ford Motor Company bestows ownership rights in Ford Motor Company. Each shareholder's ownership is quite small, amounting to less than 1 percent. Inability to communicate frequently or face-to-face to address business concerns is a major disadvantage of thousands of shareholders.

Under **agency theory**, shareholders delegate control to top executives to represent their ownership interests; however, top executives usually do not own majority shares of their companies' stocks. As a result, executives usually do not share the same interests as the collective shareholders. These features make it possible for executives to pursue activities that benefit themselves rather than the shareholders. The actions of executives on behalf of their own self-interest are known as the **agency problem**.[19] Executives may specifically emphasize the attainment of short-term gains (i.e., increasing market share through lower costs) at the expense of long-term objectives (e.g., product differentiation). Boards of directors may be willing to provide executives generous annual bonuses for attaining short-term gains.

Shareholders negotiate executive employment contracts with executives to minimize loss of control. Executive employment contracts define terms of employment pertaining to performance standards and compensation, specifically current and deferred compensation and benefits. The main shareholder objective is to protect the company's competitive interests. Shareholders use compensation to align executives' interests with shareholders' interests. As discussed earlier, boards of directors award company stock to align executives' interests with shareholders' interests.

Tournament Theory

Tournament theory casts lucrative executive compensation as the prize in a series of tournaments or contests among middle- and top-level managers who aspire to become CEOs.[20] Winners of the tournament at one level enter the next tournament level. In other words, an employee's promotion to a higher rank signifies a win, and more lucrative compensation (i.e., higher base pay, incentives, enhanced benefits, and perks) represents the prize. The ultimate prize is promotion to CEO and a lucrative executive compensation package. The chance of winning competitions decreases dramatically as employees rise through the ranks: There are fewer positions at higher levels in

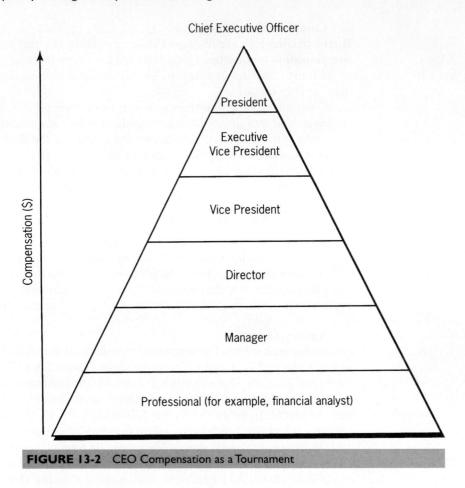

FIGURE 13-2 CEO Compensation as a Tournament

corporate hierarchical structures. Figure 13-2 depicts a visual representation of CEO compensation as a tournament.

Social Comparison Theory

According to **social comparison theory**, individuals need to evaluate their accomplishments, and they do so by comparing themselves to similar individuals.[21] Demographic characteristics (for example, age or race) and occupation are common comparative bases. Individuals tend to select social comparisons who are slightly better than themselves.[22] Researchers have applied social comparison theory to explain the processes for setting executive compensation.[23]

As we discussed earlier, compensation committees play an important role in setting executive compensation, and compensation committees often include CEOs from other companies of equal or greater stature. Based on social comparison theory, compensation committee members probably rely on their own compensation packages and the compensation packages of CEOs in companies of equal or greater stature to determine executive compensation.

EXECUTIVE COMPENSATION DISCLOSURE RULES

Companies that sell and exchange securities (e.g., company stocks and bonds) on public stock exchanges are required to file a wide variety of information with the **Securities and Exchange Commission (SEC)**, including executive compensation

TABLE 13-4 Securities and Exchange Commission Disclosure Requirements for Executive Compensation

- Stock option and stock appreciation right tables
- Long-term incentive plan table
- Pension plan table
- Performance graph comparing the company's stock price performance against a market index and a peer group
- Report from the compensation committee of the board of directors explaining compensation levels and policies
- Description of the directors' compensation, disclosing all amounts paid or payable
- Disclosure of certain employment contracts and golden parachutes

practices. The SEC is a nonpartisan, quasi-judicial federal government agency with responsibility for administering federal securities laws. The **Securities Exchange Act of 1934** applies to the disclosure of executive compensation. In 1992 and 1993, the SEC modified its rules pertaining to the disclosure of executive pay.[24] Table 13-4 lists types of information about executive compensation that companies should disclose. The SEC rulings have two objectives. The first is to clarify the presentation of the compensation paid to the CEO and the four most highly paid executives. The second is to increase the accountability of company boards of directors for executive compensation policies and decisions. Companies' board members may be subject to personal liability for paying excessive compensation. Under securities law, publicly held corporations are required to disclose detailed information on executive compensation to shareholders and the public. Shareholders can bring derivative lawsuits on behalf of a corporation, claiming that executive compensation is excessive.

The courts are thus far generally unwilling to substitute their judgment for the business judgment of a board of directors or compensation committee. Nevertheless, these SEC rulings suggest that directors should exercise more independent judgment in approving executive compensation plans.

The SEC rules are presented in tabular and graphic forms, making information more accessible to the public at large than it was prior to the 1992 and 1993 modifications. These rules indirectly regulate compensation levels through enhanced public access to information by discouraging corporations from granting potentially embarrassing executive pay, especially when corporate performance is weak. There are several tables, but the most important here is the Summary Compensation Table,[25] which discloses compensation information for the CEO and the four most highly paid executives over a 3-year period.

Table 13-5 shows an excerpt of the Summary Compensation Table.

As you can see in Table 13-5, the Summary Compensation Table for General Electric covers the compensation paid to the named executive officers during the last completed fiscal year and the two preceding fiscal years. The table contains two main subheadings: annual compensation and long-term compensation. Annual compensation includes salary (i.e., base pay), bonus, and other annual compensation. Long-term compensation includes restricted stock awards, stock appreciation rights, and long-term incentive payouts. The last column, "All Other Compensation ($)," is a catchall column to record other forms of compensation. Information in this column must be described in a footnote.

In 2006, the U.S. Securities and Exchange Commission (SEC) unveiled additional rules for disclosing executive compensation beginning in 2008. These new

TABLE 13-5 Summary Compensation Table

Name and Principal Position	Year	Salary	Bonus	Stock Awards	Option Awards	Change in Pension Value and Nonqualified Deferred Compensation Earnings	All Other Compensation	Total
Jeffrey R. Immelt, Chairman of the Board and Chief Executive Officer	2006	$3,300,000	$5,000,000	$7,404,2093	$ 574,322	$1,036,908	$548,013	$17,863,452
Keith S. Sherin, Chief Financial Officer	2006	$1,225,000	$2,550,000	$2,808,919	$2,225,749	$1,564,398	$308,222	$10,682,288
Michael A. Neal, Vice Chairman	2006	$1,400,000	$3,300,000	$3,906,929	$1,759,672	$3,032,927	$294,872	$13,694,400
John G. Rice, Vice Chairman	2006	$1,400,000	$2,550,000	$4,122,437	$2,225,749	$2,183,677	$335,866	$12,817,729
Robert C. Wright, Vice Chairman of the Board	2006	$2,500,000	$6,900,000	$2,516,712	$2,473,683	$2,422,714	$1,010,780	$17,823,88

rules require that companies reveal how much executives are paid, making such previously hard-to-find information as pension and estimated severance package totals transparent. Although the new rules represent a substantial improvement in pay disclosure, the SEC made a revision that resulted in a less-meaningful disclosure of stock options.

The SEC disclosure rules will show components of compensation previously hidden as well as provide clarity into elements of compensation already disclosed. The most significant changes follow:

Total. The Summary Compensation Table of a company's proxy will now have a column that adds up and displays the total compensation an executive received for the previous year. In the SEC pay database this year, this is labeled SEC Total.

Change in Pension Value and Nonqualified Deferred Compensation. This column in the Summary Compensation Table shows the increase in actuarial value to the executive officer of all defined-benefit pension plans and earnings on nonqualified deferred compensation plans.

All Other. This column captures compensation that does not fit in any other column of the Summary Compensation Table, including perquisites and other personal items (e.g., aircraft usage, car service, club memberships). Each item of compensation included in All Other that exceeds $10,000 will now be separately identified and quantified in a footnote.

Pension Benefits. The new rules require companies to disclose the present value of accumulated pension benefits, showing the total lump sum amount of money an executive would receive in retirement.

Severance Benefits. Companies must disclose any termination or change-in-control agreements with executives. They must disclose the specific circumstances that will trigger payment and the estimated total payments and benefits provided for each circumstance.

Are U.S. executives paid too much? Popular press and newspaper accounts generally suggest that executives are overpaid. Of course, you should form your own opinion based on the following pertinent information:

- Comparison between executive compensation and other worker groups
- Strategic questions: Is pay for performance?
- Ethical considerations: Is executive compensation fair?
- International competitiveness

The following table describes each component of the All Other Compensation column in the Summary Compensation Table.

Name of Executive	Other Benefits[1]	Tax Payments[2]	Value of Supplemental Life Insurance Premiums[3]	Payments Relating to Employee Savings Plan[4]	Total
Immelt	$296,147	$14,245	$122,121	$115,500	$548,013
Sherin	155,477	9,577	62,518	80,650	308,222
Neal	91,423	0	105,449	98,000	294,872
Rice	161,450	7,525	79,791	87,100	335,866
Wright	294,356	12,968	506,256	197,200	1,010,780

[1] See the Other Benefits Table below for additional information.

[2] This column reports amounts reimbursed for the payment of taxes with respect to financial counseling, tax preparation services and the personal use of NBCU car service. See the Other Benefits Table below for the incremental costs associated with providing these services.

[3] This column reports taxable payments made to the named executives to cover premiums for universal life insurance policies owned by the executives. These policies include: (a) Executive Life, which provides universal life insurance policies for the named executives totaling $3 million in coverage at the time of enrollment, increased 4 percent annually thereafter; and (b) Leadership Life, which provides universal life insurance policies for more than 4,400 of the company's executive-band employees and above with coverage of two times their salary plus 100 percent of their bonus payments. The amount for Mr. Wright also includes Supplemental Life, the predecessor plan to Executive Life.

[4] This column reports (a) company matching contributions to the named executive's 401(k) savings account of 3.5 percent of pay up to the limitations imposed under IRS rules; (b) related matching deferred bonus credits of 3.5 percent of certain pay in excess of amounts eligible for matching under the 401(k) savings plan; and (c) a 3.5 percent one-time credit on the amount of salary deferred for those named executives who participated in the 2006 employee deferral salary plan. See page 30 for a further description of the company contributions related to nonqualified deferred compensation.

OTHER BENEFITS

The following table describes other benefits and the cost to the company of providing them. The total amount of these other benefits is included in the All Other Compensation Table above for each named executive.

Name of Executive	Use of Aircraft [1]	Charitable Contributions [2]	Other [3]	Total
Immelt	$219,533	$0	$76,614	$296,147
Sherin	60,059	50,000	45,418	155,477
Neal	13,555	50,000	27,868	91,423
Rice	60,184	50,000	51,266	161,450
Wright	193,479	50,000	50,877	294,356

[1] The calculation of incremental cost for personal use of company aircraft includes the variable costs incurred as a result of personal flight activity: a portion of ongoing maintenance and repairs, aircraft fuel, satellite communications, and any travel expenses for the flight crew. It excludes nonvariable costs, such as exterior paint, interior refurbishment and regularly scheduled inspections, which would have been incurred regardless of whether there was any personal use of aircraft. Messrs. Immelt and Wright are designated as "security personnel" pursuant to an executive security program established by the MDCC for the protection of the company's senior executive officers, and therefore are required to use company aircraft for all air travel, whether personal or business.

[2] The GE Foundation matches up to $50,000 in contributions a year for all employees, and $100,000 a year in contributions by named executives, to approved charitable organizations. The amount shown represents the additional match on charitable contributions made by the executive above the limit available to all employees.

[3] This column reports the total amount of other benefits provided, none of which individually exceeded the greater of $25,000 or 10 percent of the total amount of these benefits for the named executive. These other benefits include: (a) financial counseling and tax preparation services, (b) a leased car, (c) car service fees, (d) alarm and generator installation, maintenance and monitoring, (e) participation in the Executive Products and Lighting Program, and (f) an annual executive physical examination.

EXECUTIVE COMPENSATION: ARE U.S. EXECUTIVES PAID TOO MUCH?

Comparison between Executive Compensation and Compensation for Other Worker Groups

The median annual earnings for all civilian workers was $39,190 in 2006, up from $37,870 in 2005, and representing a 3.5 percent increase in 1 year.[26] Among the nonexecutive employees, child care workers earned the least (mean annual earnings = $18,820), and anesthesiologists earned the most (mean annual earnings = $184,340).[27] The typical annual salary and bonus for chief executives earned in 2006 was about $2.6 million, representing a 7 percent increase in just 1 year.[28]

Strategic Questions: Is Pay for Performance?

There are several measures of corporate performance (Table 13-6). Are CEOs compensated commensurately with their companies' performance? It is difficult to answer just *yes* or *no* because the evidence is mixed. A study of the relationship between Fortune 500 companies' CEO compensation and corporate performance found:[29]

- CEO annual base pay and annual bonuses showed strong positive relationships with pretax profit margins and return on equity. As company performance (as measured by pretax profit margins and return on equity) increased, so did CEO annual base pay and bonuses.
- All long-term CEO compensation components (e.g., restricted stock and incentive stock options) were not significantly related to company performance (again, as measured by pretax profit margins and return on equity).

Since the publication of this study in 1995, several additional studies have examined the relationship between CEO pay and company performance. The evidence forsubstantiating this relationship continues to be mixed; therefore, a simple statement

TABLE 13-6 Corporate Performance Measures

Size

- Sales
- Assets
- Profits
- Market value
- Number of employees

Growth

- Sales
- Assets
- Profits
- Market value
- Number of employees

Profitability

- Profit margin
- Return on assets (ROA)
- Return on equity (ROE)

Capital Markets

- Dividend yield
- Total return to shareholders
- Price–earnings ratio
- Payout

Liquidity

- Current ratio
- Quick ratio
- Working capital from operations
- Cash flow from operations

Leverage

- Debt-to-equity ratio
- Short-term vs. long-term debt
- Cash flow vs. interest payments

cannot be made about the relationship between CEO pay and company performance. Shareholder returns most often describe company performance. For example, in 2006, L. Patrick Hassey, CEO of Allegheny Technologies, earned $6.3 million based on a shareholder return of nearly 153 percent. On the other hand, Ian J. McCarthy, CEO of Beazer Homes USA, earned $3.2 million, but total shareholder return was 32.9 percent!

Ethical Considerations: Is Executive Compensation Fair?

Is executive compensation fair? Three considerations drive this question: companies' abilities to attract and retain top executives, income disparities between executives and other employees, and layoffs of thousands of nonexecutive employees.

Attract and Retain Top Executives

Many compensation professionals and board of directors members argue that the trends in executive compensation are absolutely necessary for attracting and retaining top executives. Executives' decisions presumably directly promote competitive advantage by positioning companies to achieve lowest-cost and differentiation strategies effectively. In Chapter 3, we indicated that competitive advantage invigorates the economy by increasing business activity, employment levels, and individuals' abilities to participate in the economy as consumers of companies' products and services.

Income Disparities

Table 13-7 illustrates the marked income disparity between annual pay for various nonexecutive jobs and pay for CEOs. The typical annual earnings for the lowest-paid occupation (child care workers) amounted to a mere 0.75 percent (yes, three-quarters of 1 percent) of the average annual CEO salary and bonus. The ratio of highest-paid occupation (anesthesiologist) to the average annual CEO salary and bonus was not much better (i.e., 7 percent). Said differently, the typical CEO's annual salary plus bonus was 138 times greater than the typical child care worker's annual pay and 14 times greater than the typical anesthesiologist's annual pay! The income disparity between executives and nonexecutive employees is increasing. A worker earning $25,000 in 1996 would have earned $94,715 in 2002 (expected to be $177,470 in 2005) if his or her pay rose as quickly as CEO pay for the same period.[30]

Layoffs Borne by Workers but Not Executives

Millions of workers have been laid off since 1990. In 1997 alone, more than 880,000 employees lost their jobs; the number of layoffs increased to nearly 1.5 million workers in 2001. This was expected to settle down in 2007 to about the same number as it was in 1997.[31] Top management typically advances several reasons that necessitate these layoffs (i.e., global competition, reductions in product demand, technological advances that perform many jobs more efficiently than employees, mergers and acquisitions, establishing production operations in foreign countries with lower

TABLE 13-7   Selected Mean Annual Nonexecutive Earnings, 2006

Occupation	Annual Earnings ($)
Anesthesiologists	184,340
Dentist	140,950
Lawyers	113,660
Air traffic controllers	110,270
Computer scientists	96,440
Human resources specialists	54,700
Elementary school teachers	48,700
Cardiovascular technologist	47,174
First-line supervisors	46,530
Firefighters	42,370
Automobile mechanics	32,086
Production workers	28,740
School bus drivers	25,310
Bakers	23,710
Home health aide	20,100
Child care workers	18,820

SOURCE: U.S. Bureau of Labor Statistics (2007). *National Occupational Employment and Wage Estimates, May 2006.* Washington, DC: U.S. Government Printing Office.

labor costs, and the steep economic downturn following the September 11 terrorist attacks). A scant few executives lost their jobs, but millions of workers lost theirs in the years following the attacks.

International Competitiveness

Increased global competition has forced companies in the United States to become more productive. Excessive expenditures on compensation can threaten competitive advantage. Compensation expenditures are excessive when they outpace the quality and quantity of employees' contributions. In addition, compensation expenditures may be excessive when they are substantially higher than competitors' compensation outlays. Concerns about U.S. companies' competitiveness in global markets are common because of the vast differences in compensation levels between the CEOs of U.S. and foreign companies.

International Compensation Comparisons

Comparisons between U.S. executive compensation and foreign executives' compensation can be made on two dimensions: total compensation amount and components.

SEC rules require the disclosure of executive compensation in U.S. companies; however, comparable rules do not exist in foreign countries. As a result, it is difficult to make detailed comparisons between U.S. and foreign executive compensation.

Undermining U.S. Companies' Ability to Compete

At present, there is no evidence showing that U.S. executive compensation pay practices have undermined U.S. companies' ability to compete with other companies in the global marketplace. Might executive compensation practices undermine U.S. companies' competitiveness in the future?

On one hand, it is reasonable to predict that CEO pay will not undermine U.S. companies' ability to compete because CEO pay increased as company profits increased. On the other hand, the current wave of widespread layoffs may hinder U.S. companies' competitiveness. As you recall from Chapter 2, U.S. companies use layoffs to maintain profits and cut costs, heightening workers' job insecurities. The remaining workers may lose their faith in pay-for-performance systems and their trust in their employers as colleagues lose their jobs; yet, CEOs continue to receive higher compensation. Workers may not feel that working hard will lead to higher pay or job security; therefore, they may choose not to work proficiently. As a result, reduced individual performance and destabilized workforces may make it difficult for U.S. companies to compete against foreign companies.

SUMMARY

We reviewed the components and principles of executive compensation. The components include base pay, bonuses, short-term incentives, stock and stock option plans, enhanced benefits, and perquisites. Next, we examined the principles and processes underlying executive compensation. Finally, we addressed whether U.S. executive compensation is excessive. Although popular press accounts suggest that it is, you will have to form your own opinion, particularly as you assume compensation management responsibilities for your employer. As a compensation professional, you are likely to face many difficult questions from employees regarding the rationale for and the fairness of lucrative executive compensation packages.

KEY TERMS

- key employee, 321
- highly compensated employee, 323
- discretionary bonuses, 324
- performance-contingent bonuses, 324
- predetermined allocation bonus, 324
- target plan bonus, 324
- deferred compensation, 325
- company stock, 326
- company stock shares, 326
- incentive stock options, 326
- capital gains, 326

- nonstatutory stock options, 327
- restricted stock, 327
- phantom stock, 327
- discount stock option plans, 327
- stock appreciation rights, 327
- golden parachutes, 328
- Sarbanes-Oxley Act of 2002, 329
- Public Company Accounting Oversight Board (PCAOB), 329
- perquisites, 329
- perks, 329
- supplemental life insurance, 329
- supplemental retirement plans, 329

- executive compensation consultants, 331
- strategic analysis, 331
- board of directors, 331
- compensation committee, 333
- agency theory, 333
- agency problem, 333
- tournament theory, 333
- social comparison theory, 334
- Securities and Exchange Commission, 334
- Securities Exchange Act of 1934, 335

DISCUSSION QUESTIONS

1. What can be done to make the function of compensation committees consistent with shareholders' interests? Explain your answer.
2. Which component of compensation is most essential to motivate executives to lead companies toward competitive advantage? Discuss your rationale.
3. Discuss your position on executive compensation. Is executive compensation excessive or appropriate?
4. Discuss the differences between enhanced benefits and perquisites.
5. Consult the three most recent *BusinessWeek* special reports on executive compensation. These reports appear in the issues published during the third week of April. Pick a company that appears in the survey each year, and note the information about annual and long-term compensation. Next, review some recent materials that describe the industry and future prospects (e.g., consult newspapers, business periodicals, trade magazines, or company information on the Internet, which we discussed in Chapter 2). Finally, write a one-page report summarizing your selected company's current condition and future prospects. Then, comment on whether you believe that the 3-year trend in executive compensation is appropriate. Explain your rationale.

EXERCISES

Compensation Online

For Students

Exercise 1: Find relevant articles

It's debate time again! This time you will be arguing over the fairness of current executive compensation practices. Use your school library's online catalog to locate articles pertaining to the agency theory, deferred compensation, the golden parachute, capital gains, and stock options. Find and read several current articles in these areas.

Exercise 2: Research executive compensation information

Using the Yahoo! search engine, click on advanced search, type in "executive compensation," choose the exact phrase match search method, and click on the *Search* button. Select Business and Economy > Employment and Work > Employee Benefits, and click on Executive Compensation and Employee Benefits—articles and news summaries concerning compensation, pensions, benefits, stock ownership, and other issues. Choose one of the articles, read it, and write a brief summary of what you learned by reading the article.

Select another search engine and conduct an "executive compensation" search. Compare and contrast the results of both searches.

Exercise 3: Review an organization's Web site

On the AFL-CIO Web site, click the "Pay Watch" link. Look up the compensation packages of several executives, and read about organized labor's views regarding executive compensation. Write a short paper outlining points you agree with, what you disagree with, and why.

For Professionals

Exercise 1: Understand stock options

Stock options are a large part of executive compensation packages. To get a better understanding of stock options go to the Chicago Board of Trade Web site at *cbot.com*. Read over this Web site and write a brief summary describing what stock options are and their advantages and disadvantages as compensation benefits.

Exercise 2: Keep up with current events in HR

An executive in your firm has taken issue with his current compensation package. He believes he is worth much more and can find it somewhere else. You have been assigned the task of researching how much of his opinion is actually true. Using Yahoo!, conduct an advanced search for "executive compensation." Click the "News" tab at the top of the resulting page and read some of the articles. Pick out an issue or trend that you notice in the articles and summarize what it is and why you believe it is happening.

Exercise 3: Learn important terms

You will be working with some senior-level analysts from the finance department to develop a stronger stock option plan to aid in recruiting top executive talent. To prepare yourself and make sure you have your proverbial ducks in a row before the first meeting, search for "financial glossary" or "financial terms." Look over some terms that may have been mentioned in this chapter and others, and make sure you understand their meaning.

ENDNOTES

1. Walters, B., Hardin, T., & Schick, J. (1995). Top executive compensation: Equity or excess? Implications for regaining American competitiveness. *Journal of Business Ethics, 14*, pp. 227–234.

2. U.S. Bureau of Labor Statistics (2005). *Mass layoffs in May 2007* (USDL 07–0878). Washington, DC: Government Printing Office [online]. Available: *www.bls.gov,* accessed June 23, 2007.

3. Internal Revenue Code, § 416 (i).

4. Treas. Reg. § 1.416–1, Q13.

5. Internal Revenue Code, § 414 (q).

6. Ibid.

7. Internal Revenue Code 83; *Treasury Regulations* 1.83–1(b)(2), 1.83–1(e), 1.83–2(a).

8. Internal Revenue Code 83; *Treasury Regulations* 1.83–1(b)(1), 1.83–1(c).

9. Internal Revenue Code 61, 83, 162; *Treasury Regulations* 1.83.

10. Ibid.

11. Internal Revenue Code 61, 83, 162, 451; *Treasury Regulations* 1.83.

12. Martocchio, J. J. (2006). *Employee Benefits: A Primer for Human Resource Professionals.* Burr Ridge, IL: McGraw-Hill.

13. I.R.C. § 415 (b)(1)(A).

14. I.R.C. § 415 (c)(1)(A).

15. Crystal, G. S. (1991). Why CEO compensation is so high. *California Management Review, 34*, pp. 9–29.

16. Ibid.

17. Ibid.

18. Agency Theory: Eisenhardt, K. M. (1989). Agency theory: An assessment and review. *Academy of Management Review, 14*, pp. 57–74; Jensen, M., & Meckling, W. H. (1976). Theory of the firm: Managerial behavior, agency costs, and ownership structure. *Journal of Financial Economics, 3*, pp. 305–360; Tosi, H. L., Jr., & Gomez-Mejia, L. R. (1989). The decoupling of CEO pay and performance: An agency theory perspective. *Administrative Science Quarterly, 34*, pp. 169–189; Goodman, P. S. (1974). An examination of referents used in the evaluation of pay. *Organizational Behavior and Human Performance, 12*, pp. 170–195; Lazear, E., & Rosen, S. (1981). Rank-order tournaments as optimum labor contracts. *Journal of Political Economy, 89*, pp. 841–864; O'Reilly, C. A., III, Main, B. G., & Crystal, G. S. (1988). CEO compensation as tournament and social comparison: A tale of two theories. *Administrative Science Quarterly, 33*, pp. 257–274.

19. Jensen, M. C., & Meckling, W. H. (1976). Theory of the firm: Managerial behavior, agency costs, and ownership structure. *Journal of Financial Economics, 3*, pp. 305–360.

20. Lazear, E., & Rosen, S. (1981). Rank-order tournaments as optimum labor contracts. *Journal of Political Economy, 89*, pp. 841–864.

21. Festinger, L. (1954). A theory of social comparison processes. *Human Relations, 7*, pp. 117–140.

22. Tversky, A., & Kahneman, D. (1974). Judgment and uncertainty: Heuristics and biases. *Science, 185*, pp. 1124–1131.

23. O'Reilly, C. A., III, Main, B. G., & Crystal, G. S. (1988). CEO compensation as tournament and social comparison: A tale of two theories. *Administrative Science Quarterly, 33*, pp. 257–274.

24. SEC Release No. 33–6962 (Oct. 16, 1992); SEC Release No. 33–6940 (July 10, 1992); SEC Release No. 34–33229 (Nov. 29, 1993).

25. Summary Compensation Table: 17 C.F.R 229.402(b), as amended Nov. 29, 1993, effective Jan. 1, 1994.

26. U.S. Bureau of Labor Statistics (2007). *National Compensation Survey: Occupational Wages in the United States, May 2006* [online]. Available: *www.bls.gov*, accessed June 23, 2007; U.S. Bureau of Labor Statistics (2006). *National Compensation Survey: Occupational Wages in the United States, May 2005* [online]. Available: *www.bls.gov*, accessed June 24, 2007.

27. Ibid.

28. Lublin, J. S. (2007). The pace of pay gains: A survey overview. *Wall Street Journal*, April 9, p. R1. Dash, E. (2007). Executive pay: A special report; More pieces. Still a puzzle. *New York Times*, April 8 [online]. Available: *www.nytimes.com*, accessed June 22, 2007.

29. Klein, Marc-Andreas (1995). *Top Executive Pay for Performance*. New York: The Conference Board.

30. AFL-CIO. (2002). *Executive paywatch* [online]. Available: *www.aflcio.org/home.htm*, accessed July 18, 2002.

31. U.S. Bureau of Labor Statistics (2006). *Extended mass layoffs in 2005* (Report 997). Washington, DC: Government Printing Office [online]. Available: *www.bls.gov*, accessed June 24, 2007. U.S. Bureau of Labor Statistics (2007). *Mass layoffs in May 2007* (USDL 07–0878). Washington, DC: Government Printing Office [online]. Available: *www.bls.gov*, accessed June 23, 2007.

CHAPTER 14

Compensating the Flexible Workforce
Contingent Employees and Flexible Work Schedules

Chapter Outline

- The Contingent Workforce
  Groups of Contingent Workers
  Reasons for U.S. Employers' Increased Reliance
    on Contingent Workers

- Pay and Employee Benefits for Contingent Workers
  Part-Time Employees
  Temporary Employees
  Leased Workers
  Independent Contractors, Freelancers, and Consultants

- Flexible Work Schedules: Flextime, Compressed Workweeks,
  and Telecommuting
  Flexible Schedules
  Compressed Workweek Schedules
  Telecommuting
  Flexible Work Schedules: Balancing the Demands of Work Life
    and Home Life

- Pay and Employee Benefits for Flexible Employees
  Pay
  Employee Benefits

- Unions' Reactions to Contingent Workers and Flexible Work Schedules

- Strategic Issues and Choices in Using Contingent and Flexible Workers
  Lowest-Cost Competitive Strategy
  Differentiation Competitive Strategy

- Summary

- Key Terms

- Discussion Questions

- Exercises

- Endnotes

Learning Objectives

In this chapter, you will learn about

1. Various groups of contingent workers and the reasons for U.S. employers' increased reliance on them

2. Pay and employee benefits issues for contingent workers

3. Key features of flexible work schedules, compressed workweeks, and telecommuting

4. Pay and employee benefits issues for flexible work schedules, compressed workweeks, and telecommuting

5. Unions' reactions to contingent workers and flexible work schedules

6. Strategic issues and choices in using contingent workers

Changing business conditions and personal preferences for flexibility to accommodate nonwork demands have led to an increase in contingent workers and the use of flexible work schedules in the United States. Companies employed as many as 5.7 million contingent workers in February 2005, representing about 4 percent of total employment.[1] Likewise, the complexities of employees' personal lives (i.e., dependent children and elderly relatives, dual career couples, disabilities) make working standard 8-hour days for five consecutive days every week difficult. About 27 million employees worked flexible work schedules during May 2004.[2] Altogether, contingent and flexible-schedule employees represent about 27.5 percent of the U.S. civilian labor force. (*Author's note:* These statistics represent the most recently available comprehensive data at the time of publication; data on contingent workers and workers on flexible schedules are collected infrequently; that is, once every 3 years.)

This chapter looks at compensation issues for contingent workers and demonstrates that compensating contingent workers is a complex proposition. Human resource (HR) and compensation professionals encounter tremendous challenges in managing both the core and contingent workforces. Many companies employ both types of workers, often in the same jobs. To the casual onlooker, including co-workers, there are no visible differences between these workers; however, HR and compensation professionals must take many factors into consideration.

The previous chapters addressed compensation issues for core employees. **Core employees** have full-time jobs (i.e., they work at least 35 hours per week), and they generally plan long-term or indefinite relationships with their employers. In addition, all core employees were assumed to work standard schedules (i.e., fixed 8-hour work shifts, 5 days per week). Compensation practices differ somewhat for the flexible workforce.

THE CONTINGENT WORKFORCE

According to the U.S. Bureau of Labor Statistics, **contingent workers**[3] are those who do not have an implicit or explicit contract for ongoing employment. Persons who do not expect to continue in their jobs for such personal reasons as retirement or returning to school are not considered contingent workers, provided that they would have the option of continuing in the job were it not for these reasons. The duration of their employment varies according to their convenience and employers' business needs. A slightly larger proportion of contingent workers than noncontingent workers were women (49 versus 47 percent). Contingent workers most commonly hold professional(e.g., accountant), clerical (e.g., secretary), or laborer (e.g., construction worker) positions; they perform jobs in the service and retail trade industries. More and more companies favor contingent employment to control staffing levels and costs.

Groups of Contingent Workers

There are five distinct groups of contingent workers:

- Part-time employees
- Independent contractors, freelancers, and consultants
- On-call employees
- Temporary help agency workers
- Workers provided by contract firms or leased employees

Table 14-1 shows the number of contingent workers in each category.

Part-Time Employees

The Bureau of Labor Statistics distinguishes between two kinds of part-time employees: voluntary and involuntary. A **voluntary part-time employee** chooses to work fewer than 35 hours per regularly scheduled workweek. In some cases, individuals supplement full-time employment with part-time employment to meet financial obligations.

Some workers, including a small but growing number of professionals, elect to work part-time as a lifestyle choice. These part-timers sacrifice pay, and possibly career advancement, in exchange for more free time to devote to family, hobbies, and personal interests. They often have working spouses whose benefits, generally including medical and dental insurance, extend coverage to family members.

Involuntary part-time employees work fewer than 35 hours per week because they are unable to find full-time employment. Involuntary part-time work represents the lion's share of all part-time employment. There is a commonly held but inaccurate stereotype of involuntary part-time workers as being low-skilled and uninterested in career advancement. To the contrary, many involuntary part-time workers hold entry-level career-track jobs.[4] Although we have discussed voluntary and involuntary part-time work as part of the contingent workforce, it is important to emphasize that many core workers negotiate part-time schedules with employers.

Table 14-2 lists the specific reasons for part-time work and the percentage of individuals who work part-time, defined as fewer than 35 hours weekly, for each reason. As previously noted, some individuals who usually work full-time also hold part-time jobs. Others typically work part-time jobs only. Companies may experience advantages and disadvantages from employing part-time workers. Flexibility is the key advantage. Most companies realize a substantial cost savings because they offer few or no discretionary

TABLE 14-1 Number of Contingent Employees, February 2005	
Type of Contingent Workers	*Number*
Part-time employees	2,294,000
On-call employees	2,500,000
Temporary help agency workers	1,200,000
Leased employees	813,000

SOURCE: U.S. Bureau of Labor Statistics (2005). *Contingent and alternative employment arrangements, February 2005* (USDL 05-1433) [online]. Available: *www.bls.gov/ncs/cps/*, accessed June 14, 2007.

TABLE 14-2 Part-Time Workers by Reason: 2006

Persons at work 1 to 34 hours in all and in nonagricultural industries by reason for working less than 35 hours and usual full- or part-time status

(Numbers in thousands)

Reason for working less than 35 hours	All industries			Nonagricultural industries		
	Total	*Usually work full time*	*Usually work part time*	*Total*	*Usually work full time*	*Usually work part time*
Total, 16 years and over..................	32,421	10,223	22,199	31,861	10,057	21,804
Economic reasons............................	4,162	1,554	2,608	4,071	1,504	2,567
Slack work or business conditions.....	2,658	1,294	1,363	2,596	1,259	1,337
Could only find part-time work.........	1,189	–	1,189	1,178	–	1,178
Seasonal work.................................	175	119	56	158	106	52
Job started or ended during week......	141	141	–	139	139	–
Noneconomic reasons.......................	28,259	8,669	19,591	27,790	8,553	19,237
Child-care problems.........................	777	80	697	772	79	693
Other family or personal obligations..	5,492	743	4,749	5,407	731	4,676
Health or medical limitations...........	799	–	799	778	–	778
In school or training........................	6,316	89	6,227	6,247	89	6,158
Retired or Social Security limit on earnings...........	2,096	–	2,096	1,988	–	1,988
Vacation or personal day.................	3,679	3,679	–	3,639	3,639	–
Holiday, legal or religious...............	1,156	1,156	–	1,147	1,147	–
Weather-related curtailment.............	388	388	–	365	365	–
All other reasons............................	7,555	2,533	5,022	7,448	2,504	4,944
Average hours:						
Economic reasons............................	23.1	24.0	22.5	23.1	24.0	22.5
Other reasons.................................	21.5	25.2	19.9	21.6	25.2	20.0

Note: Beginning in January 2006, data reflect revised population controls used in the household survey. Dash indicates no data or data that do not meet publication criteria.

SOURCE: U.S. Bureau of Labor Statistics, *Employment and Earnings*, monthly, January 2007. See Internet site *www.bls.gov/cps/home.htm.*

TABLE 14-3 Employers' Hourly Costs for Full- and Part-Time Employee Benefits, March 2007

Benefit	Full-Time	Part-Time
Paid leave	$2.17	$0.47
Supplemental pay	$0.92	$0.23
Insurance	$2.35	$0.69
Retirement and savings	$1.06	$0.21
Legally required benefits	$2.41	$1.52
Total hourly benefits costs	$8.92	$3.13

SOURCE: U.S. Bureau of Labor Statistics. (2007). *Employer costs for employee compensation*—March 2007 (USDL: 07-0877). Washington, DC: U.S. Government Printing Office.

benefits. In addition, companies realize cost savings for benefits that are linked to hours worked (e.g., retirement plan contributions). Table 14-3 shows employers' costs for providing various discretionary benefits and legally required benefits to full-time and part-time employees. Employers save considerable money in the areas of paid leave, insurance, and legally required benefits.

Companies also save on overtime pay expenses. Hiring part-time workers during peak business periods minimizes overtime pay costs. As we discussed in Chapter 3, the Fair Labor Standards Act of 1938 (FLSA) requires that companies pay nonexempt employees at a rate equaling one and one-half times their regular hourly pay rates. Retail businesses save by employing part-time sales associates during the peak holiday shopping season.

Job sharing is a special kind of part-time employment agreement. Two or more part-time employees perform a single full-time job. These employees may perform all job duties or share the responsibility for particular tasks. Some job sharers meet regularly to coordinate their efforts. Job sharing represents a compromise between employees' needs or desires not to work full-time and employers' needs to staff jobs on a full-time basis. Both employers and employees benefit from the use of job sharing. Table 14-4 lists some of the benefits of job sharing to employers and employees.

Temporary and On-Call Employees
Companies traditionally hire temporary employees for two reasons. First, temporary workers fill in for core employees who are on approved leaves of absence, including sick leave,

TABLE 14-4 Benefits of Job Sharing

Benefits to Employers

- Maintenance of productivity because of higher morale and maintenance of employee skills
- Retention of skilled workers
- Reduction or elimination of the training costs that result from retraining laid-off employees
- Greater flexibility in deploying workers to keep operations going
- Minimization of postrecession costs of hiring and training new workers to replace those who found other jobs during layoff
- Strengthening employees' loyalty to the company

Benefits to Employees

- Continued employee benefits protection
- Continued employment when the likelihood of unemployment is high
- Maintenance of family income
- Continued participation in qualified retirement programs

vacation, bereavement leave, jury duty, and military leave. Second, temporary workers offer extra sets of hands when companies' business activities peak, during such times as the holiday season for retail businesses or summer for amusement parks. Temporary employees perform jobs on a short-term basis usually measured in days, weeks, or months.

Companies have been hiring temporary workers for three additional reasons. First, temporary employment arrangements provide employers the opportunity to evaluate whether legitimate needs exist for creating new positions. Second, temporary employment arrangements give employers the opportunity to decide whether to retain particular workers on an indefinite basis. "The temp job is often what one university placement director calls the '3-month interview'—and a gateway to a full-time job and perhaps a new career."[5] In effect, the temporary arrangement represents a probationary period, when employers observe whether workers are meeting job performance standards. As a corollary, such temporary arrangements provide workers the chance to decide whether to accept employment on a full-time basis after they have had time to "check things out." Third, employing temporary workers is often less costly than employing core workers because temporary workers are less likely to receive costly discretionary benefits (e.g., medical insurance coverage).

Companies hire temporary employees from a variety of sources. The most common source is a **temporary employment agency.** In 2005, companies employed approximately 1.2 million temporary workers.[6] Most temporary employment agencies traditionally placed clerical and administrative workers. Now, some temporary agencies also place workers with specialized skills (e.g., auditors, computer systems analysts, and lawyers). These agencies are becoming more common.

Companies generally establish relationships with temporary employment agencies based on several factors. First, companies consider agencies' reputations as an important factor, judging reputations by how well agencies' placements work out. Some agencies place a wide range of employees, yet others specialize in one type of placement (e.g., financial services professionals). When companies plan to hire a variety of temporary workers, it is often more convenient to work with agencies that do not specialize. Companies should ultimately judge these agencies' placement records for each type of employee.

Second, companies also should consider agencies' fees. Cost is a paramount consideration for companies that are pursuing lowest-cost competitive strategies. Temporary agencies base fees as a percentage of their placements' pay rates. The percentage varies from agency to agency. The competition among temporary agencies fortunately keeps these rates in check.

Although temporary employees work in a variety of companies, their legal employers are the temporary employment agencies. Temporary employment agencies take full responsibility for selecting temporary employee candidates and determine candidates' qualifications through interviews and testing. Many temporary agencies train candidates to use such office equipment as fax machines, electronic mail, and spreadsheet and word processing software programs, particularly for clerical and administrative jobs. Temporary employees receive compensation directly from the agency.

Companies may hire temporary employees through other means. For example, some companies hire individuals directly as temporary workers. Under **direct hire arrangements,** temporary employees typically do not work for more than 1 year. In addition, the hiring companies are the temporary workers' legal employers. Thus, companies take full responsibility for all HR functions that affect temporary employees, including performance evaluation, compensation, and training.

On-call arrangements are another method for employing temporary workers. On-call employees work sporadically throughout the year when companies require their services. Companies can schedule workers for several days or weeks in a row. Some unionized skilled trade workers are available as on-call employees when they are unable to secure permanent, full-time employment. These employees' unions maintain rosters of unemployed members who are available for work. When employed, on-call workers are employees of the hiring companies. Thus, the hiring companies are responsible for managing and implementing HR policies, including compensation.

Leased Employee Arrangements

Lease companies employ qualified individuals and place them in client companies on a long-term basis. Most leasing companies bill the client for the direct costs of employing the workers (e.g., payroll, benefits, and payroll taxes) and then charge a fixed fee. Lease companies base these fees on either a fixed percentage of the client's payroll or a fixed fee per employee.

Leasing arrangements are common in the food service industry. ARAMARK Food Services is an example of a leasing company that provides cafeteria services to client companies. ARAMARK staffs these companies' inhouse cafeterias with cooks, food preparers, and checkout clerks. These cafeteria workers are employees of the leasing company, not the client company. Leasing companies also operate in other industries, including security services, building maintenance, and administrative services. Lease companies and temporary employment agencies are similar because both manage all HR activities. Thus, lease companies provide both wages and benefits to their employees. Lease companies and temporary employment agencies differ in an important respect, however. Lease company placements generally remain in effect for the duration of the lease company's contract with the host company.

Independent Contractors, Freelancers, and Consultants

Independent contractors, freelancers, and **consultants** (the term *independent contractor* will be used in this discussion) establish working relationships with companies on their own rather than through temporary employment agencies or lease companies. Independent contractors typically possess specialized skills that are in short supply in the labor market. Companies select independent contractors to complete particular projects of short-term duration (i.e., usually a year or less). Adjunct faculty members represent a specific example of independent contractors. Colleges and universities hire them to cover for permanent faculty members who are on sabbatical leave or until they hire tenure-track replacements. In addition, some companies staff segments of their workforces with independent contractors to contain discretionary benefits costs.

Reasons for U.S. Employers' Increased Reliance on Contingent Workers

Structural changes in the U.S. economy have contributed to the rise of contingent employment:

- Economic recessions
- International competition
- Shift from manufacturing to a service economy
- Rise in female labor force participation
- Runaway costs to provide employer-sponsored health insurance

Economic Recessions

Many companies lay off segments of their workforces during economic recessions as a cost-control measure. Following economic recessions, some companies restore staffing levels with permanent employees. Many companies are increasingly restoring staffing levels with contingent workers. Since the early 1970s, the U.S. economy experienced several economic recessions. These repeated recessions have shaken employers' confidence about future economic prosperity. Staffing segments of workforces with contingent workers represents a form of risk control because employers save on most discretionary benefits costs. In addition, companies can terminate contingent workers' services more easily: These employment relationships are explicitly tentative. Both the host employer and the workers understand that these engagements are of limited duration.

International Competition

International competition is another pertinent structural change. American companies no longer compete just against each other. Many foreign businesses have demonstrated the ability to manufacture goods at lower costs than their American competitors. As a result, successful American companies have streamlined operations to control costs. These companies are saving costs by reducing the numbers of core employees and using contingent workers as an alternative.

The Shift from Manufacturing to a Service Economy

The service sector refers to six broad divisions of industries: transportation, communication, and public utilities; wholesale trade; retail trade; finance, insurance, and real estate; services; and government. Manufacturing companies' (e.g., automobile makers and textiles) employment declined substantially during the past several years,[7] and economic forecasts predict a loss of jobs in the manufacturing sector through 2012.[8] During this period, a steady decrease in employment in manufacturing industries was offset by a substantial rise in employment in both the retail trade and service sectors.[9] Service sector employment is expected to add nearly 20 million new jobs to the economy by 2012.[10] In addition, contingent workers typically find employment in service businesses, which are more labor intensive than capital intensive (e.g., heavy manufacturing equipment).

A number of trends depict a society that is in some ways increasingly dedicated to future investment by means of both capital and increased effort. Business-oriented services—such as upgrading of software and intelligent machinery, services related to construction, and improvement of business processes with the aid of consultants—may all be interpreted as present investments for a wealthier future. The extension of business operating hours may be interpreted in the same way. Even two rapidly increasing social services, daycare and residential care, enable some people to work outside the home instead of caring for relatives, and to contribute to economic expansion.[11]

Rise in Female Labor Force Participation

The increase in female participation in the labor force has promoted growth in the use of contingent workers. One-income families were commonplace until the early 1970s, and males headed these households. Since then, several economic recessions in the United States left large numbers of individuals unemployed.

Many wives entered the labor force temporarily to supplement family income during their husbands' unemployment spells.[12] The majority took low-paying jobs as clerical or service workers because they did not have sufficient education to attain high-paying jobs. Even educated women could not find high-paying jobs because the recessions limited such opportunities. As a result, many well-educated women also assumed low-paying clerical or service positions.

A large segment of these women remained in the contingent labor force following the end of these economic recessions because their husbands' salaries did not keep up with inflation. Contingent employment enabled women to balance the demands of home and work. Although men have been taking greater responsibility for child rearing, women still bear the brunt of these duties.[13] Thus, contingent employment, compared with core employment, affords women opportunities to balance the demands of home and work. As a result, a substantial portion of contingent workers is female.[14]

The rise in single-parent households also contributed to the rise in contingent employment. Many single female parents possess low levels of education, which limits job opportunities. As a result, single mothers accept such low-paying contingent jobs as domestic work, retail sales, and low-level clerical positions. Apart from low educational attainment, single mothers accept contingent work because it enables them to spend more time with their children. As an aside, these women generally cannot afford to pay for regular day care services.

A large segment of well-educated females enter the contingent workforce because of dual-career pressures. In many areas of the country, employers have the luxury of large pools of educated, skilled workers who have followed as their spouses pursue job opportunities. These areas typically have few large employers such as in Fort Collins, Colorado, and Champaign-Urbana, Illinois, where universities are the main employers. Many spouses with professional credentials take low-paying, part-time jobs because there are few good job opportunities.

Runaway Costs to Provide Employer-Sponsored Health Insurance

Both employees and employers place a great deal of significance on company-sponsored health insurance benefits. Of course, company-sponsored programs provide employees with the means to afford expensive health care services. Companies stand to gain from sponsoring these benefits in at least two ways, as we noted in Chapter 11. First, a healthier workforce should experience a lower incidence of sickness absenteeism. By keeping absenteeism in check, a company's overall productivity and product or service quality should be higher. Second, health insurance offerings should help the recruitment and retention of employees. It's not surprising that a large percentage of companies include health insurance programs as a feature of employee benefits programs, extending coverage to substantial numbers of employees and their dependents. At the same time, the rampant rise in health care prices is putting substantial pressure on cost-conscious companies.

At the time of this edition's publication, the most recent comprehensive national data indicate that just more than approximately 85 percent of all full-time private sector employees had access to employer-sponsored health insurance programs in 2006.[15] In contrast, only 22 percent of part-time employees had access to such plans. Health insurance premiums are quite high, often amounting to as much as one third of annual benefits costs. Most companies choose not to offer health care benefits to part-time workers (and other contingent workers for that matter) because the cost of employers' contributions to provide health insurance coverage is about the same for full- and part-time employees. Part-time employees work far fewer hours than full-time employees, in effect making the hourly cost of benefits substantially higher for part-time employees than for full-time employees. For example, the average monthly health insurance premium in March 2006 was $617.18 per employee.[16] The employer's hourly cost to provide health care insurance is approximately $3.85 for an employee who works 160 hours per month (i.e., 40 hours per week based on 4 weeks per month: $617.18/160). For part-time employees, assuming 80 hours per month (that is, an assumed 20-hour work week based on 4 weeks per month), the hourly cost is $7.71 ($617.18/80).

Health insurance premiums are likely to increase based on the trend in prices for medical services, perhaps increasing the likelihood that companies will rely on contingent employment relationships. For example, the prices for medical care services overall have increased more than 300 percent since 1982 (compared with a 115 percent increase for all goods and services purchased by consumers during the same period).

The substantially higher rate increases for medical services may be explained by several factors, including:

- Longer life expectancies
- Aging baby boom–era individuals who place higher demands on health care
- Advances in medical research that add such diagnostic tests and treatments as substantially more effective (and expensive) treatments to save low-birth-weight babies
- A general tendency for the health profession and family members to treat death as unnatural rather than as a natural ending to life, leading to higher expenditures to prolong the lives of the terminally ill

There is no reason to expect that health care costs will decrease in the foreseeable future. Continuing medical research, more advanced diagnostic tools, and higher demand due to the aging population and for better treatment will contribute to higher costs.

PAY AND EMPLOYEE BENEFITS FOR CONTINGENT WORKERS

Compensation practices for contingent workers vary. We will discuss these practices shortly. Nevertheless, all parties involved in employing contingent workers possess liability under federal and state laws, including:

- Overtime and minimum wages required under the FLSA
- Paying insurance premiums required under state workers' compensation laws
- Nondiscriminatory compensation and employment practices under the Employee Retirement Income Security Act of 1974 (ERISA), National Labor Relations Act (NLRA), Title VII of the Civil Rights Act of 1964, Americans with Disabilities Act of 1990 (ADA), and the Age Discrimination in Employment Act (ADEA)

Temporary employment agencies and leasing companies that place workers in clients' firms are liable under these laws. In addition, the client company may also be liable. "The fact that a worker is somebody else's employee while he or she is on your premises, or performing services for the business, is not necessarily a defense to alleged violations of federal and state labor laws including Title VII of the Civil Rights Act, the Fair Labor Standards Act, and the Americans with Disabilities Act."[17] As we discussed in Chapter 3, each of these laws applies to compensation practice.

Part-Time Employees

Companies that employ part-time workers are the legal employers, as is the case for core employees. Compensating part-time employees poses the following challenges for employers:

- Should companies pay part-time workers on an hourly basis or a salary basis?
- Do equity problems arise between core employees and part-time employees?
- Do companies offer benefits to part-time workers?

Pay

Part-time employees earn less, on average, than core employees. In March 2007, part-time workers in private industry earned an average $11.19 per hour, whereas full-time employees earned $20.49 per hour.[18] Full-time management and professional employees earned $33.52 per hour, whereas their part-time counterparts earned $26.83 per hour. Full-time production workers earned substantially more than their part-time counterparts ($15.44 per hour versus $9.96 per hour). Full-time service employees similarly earned more than part-timers ($10.94 per hour versus $8.13 per hour).

Companies often expect salaried part-time employees to do much more than their fair share of the work because the effective hourly pay rate decreases as the number of hours worked increases. An explicit agreement pertaining to work-hour limits can minimize this problem. An agreement similarly may specify explicit work goals. On the other hand, companies may avoid this problem by paying part-time employees on an hourly basis. Part-time and full-time employees may perceive the situation as inequitable under certain circumstances. For example, equity problems may arise when salaried full-time employees and hourly part-time employees work together. It is possible that highly skilled full-time employees might effectively be underpaid relative to less-skilled part-time employees performing the same work (i.e., full-time employees' "hourly" pay rate will be lower when they perform more and better work in a shorter period than less-skilled part-time workers).

Employee Benefits

Companies generally do not provide discretionary benefits to part-time employees; however, benefits practices for part-time workers vary widely according to company size as well as between the private and public sectors. In 2006, approximately 36 percent of part-time employees earned paid vacation benefits.[19] Fewer received medical insurance coverage (13 percent) or retirement benefits (21 percent).[20]

Employers are not required to offer protective insurance (i.e., medical, dental, vision, or life insurance) to part-time employees; however, part-time employees who do receive health insurance coverage under employer-sponsored plans are entitled to protection under the Consolidated Omnibus Budget Reconciliation Act (COBRA). As discussed in Chapter 3, COBRA provides employees the opportunity to continue receiving employer-sponsored health care insurance coverage temporarily following termination or layoff. Employees who qualify for COBRA protection receive insurance coverage that matches the coverage level during employment.

Employers may be required to provide qualified retirement programs to part-time employees.[21] Part-time employees who meet the following two criteria are eligible to participate in qualified retirement programs:

- Minimum age of 21 years
- Completion of at least 1,000 hours of work in a 12-month period (i.e., "year of service")

Special considerations apply to seasonal employees' eligibilities for qualified retirement benefits because most seasonal employees do not meet the annual service pension eligibility criterion. Maritime industries such as fishing represent seasonal employment, and fishermen are seasonal employees. The Department of Labor defines 125 service days as the "year of service" for maritime workers. Part-time and seasonal employees cannot be excluded from pension plans if they meet the Department of Labor's "year of service" criterion.

Temporary Employees

Temporary employment agencies are the legal employers for temporary employees. Temporary employment agencies are therefore responsible for complying with federal employment legislation with one exception that we will address shortly (i.e., workers' compensation). Compensating temporary employees poses challenges for companies.

- Do equity problems arise between core employees and temporary employees?
- How do the FLSA overtime provisions affect temporary employees?
- Do companies offer temporary workers benefits?
- Who is responsible for providing workers' compensation protection: the temporary agency or the client company?

Pay

Temporary workers who worked full time typically earned $414 per week in February 2005, and those working on a part-time basis earned $224 per week.[22] (Again, the most recently available information.) Pay rates varied widely by occupation and workers' particular qualifications. Equity problems may (or may not) arise where core and temporary employees work together. On one hand, temporary employees may work diligently because they know that their assignments in client companies are explicitly of limited duration. In addition, frequent moves from one company to the next may limit workers' opportunities or desires to build careers with any of these companies. Furthermore, temporary workers may neither take the time nor have the time to scope out pay differences because their engagements are brief (i.e., anywhere from 1 day to a few weeks). These temporary employees are therefore not likely to perceive inequitable pay situations.

On the other hand, some temporary employees may not work diligently because they did not choose temporary employment arrangements. Individuals who lose their jobs because of a sudden layoff and who have few core job alternatives are most susceptible. Pay differences between these temporary employees and core employees are likely to intensify perceptions of inequity.

It is important to distinguish between temporary employees and seasonal employees for determining eligibility under the FLSA minimum wage and overtime pay provisions. Companies hire temporary employees to fill in as needed. This means that companies may hire temporary employees at any time throughout a calendar year; however, seasonal employees work during set regular periods every year. Lifeguards on New England beaches are seasonal employees because they work only during the summer months when people visit beaches to swim. Summer camp counselors are also seasonal employees.

The FLSA extends coverage to temporary employees. Temporary employment agencies must therefore pay temporary workers at least the federal minimum wage rate. In addition, the FLSA requires employers to provide overtime pay at one and one-half times the normal hourly rate for each hour worked beyond 40 hours per week. Host companies are responsible for FLSA compliance if temporary employment agencies are not involved, as in the case of direct hire or on-call arrangements.

Some seasonal employees are exempt from the FLSA's minimum wage and overtime pay provisions.[23] The FLSA itself as drafted does not explicitly address minimum wage and overtime pay practices for seasonal employees; however, professional legal opinions were added as needed to resolve ambiguities and guide practice. The opinions pertain to specific employers' questions about the act's scope of coverage (e.g., the applicability of FLSA overtime and minimum wage provisions to seasonal amusement park workers). Professional opinions do not automatically generalize to all seasonal employees. For example, all amusement or recreational establishment employees are covered by the FLSA's minimum wage and overtime pay provisions when the establishments operate at least 7 months per year; however, youth counselors employed at summer camps are generally exempt from the FLSA minimum wage and overtime pay provisions.

Employee Benefits

Anecdotal evidence indicates that companies typically do not provide discretionary benefits to temporary employees. This information should not be surprising. As we discussed earlier, many companies employ temporary workers to minimize discretionary benefits costs; however, temporary employees (and seasonal workers) are eligible for qualified pension benefits if they meet ERISA's minimum service requirements for seasonal and part-time employees, as discussed earlier.

The **dual employer common law doctrine** establishes temporary workers' rights to receive workers' compensation.[24] According to this doctrine, temporary workers are employees of both temporary employment agencies and the client companies. The written contract between the employment agency and client company specifies which organization's workers' compensation policy applies in the event of injuries.

Leased Workers

Designating leased employees' legal employers is less clear than it is for part-time and temporary employees. Leasing companies are the legal employers regarding wage issues and legally required benefits; however, leasing companies and client companies are the legal employers regarding particular discretionary benefits. Compensating leased employees is therefore complex.

- Do leased employees receive discretionary benefits?
- Who is responsible for providing discretionary benefits: the leasing company or the client company?

Pay

In February 2005, leased employees who worked on a full-time basis typically earned $756 per week; part-time leased workers earned $204.[25] Detailed systematic compensation data for leased employees are currently very limited. It is therefore not possible to compare leased employees' and core employees' wages and salaries.

Employee Benefits

Both pension eligibility and discretionary benefits are key issues. Leased employees are generally entitled to participation in the client companies' qualified retirement programs; however, the leasing company becomes responsible for leased employees' retirement benefits when the **safe harbor rule**[26] requirements are met. Table 14-5 lists the safe harbor rule requirements.

Another section of the IRC influences companies' discretionary benefits policies (excluding retirement benefits) for leased employees.[27] Under this rule, client companies

---

TABLE 14-5 Safe Harbor Rule Requirements

- The leased employee must be covered by the leasing company's pension plan, which must (1) be a money purchase plan with a nonintegrated employer contribution rate for each participant of at least 10 percent of compensation, (2) provide for full and immediate vesting, and (3) allow each employee of the leasing organization to immediately participate in such a plan; and
- Leased employees cannot constitute more than 20 percent of the recipient's "nonhighly compensated workforce." Nonhighly compensated workforce means the total number of (1) nonhighly compensated individuals who are employees of the recipient and who have performed services for the recipient for at least 1 year or (2) individuals who are leased employees of the recipient (determined without regard to the leasing rules).

SOURCE: I.R.C. §414(n)(5).

are responsible for providing leased employees with group medical insurance, group life insurance, educational assistance programs, and continuation coverage requirements for group health plans under COBRA.

Independent Contractors, Freelancers, and Consultants

The Bureau of Labor Statistics does not monitor pay levels for independent contractors. Companies are not obligated to pay the following on behalf of independent contractors, freelancers, and consultants:

- Federal income tax withholding.
- Overtime and minimum wages required under the FLSA; however, employers are obligated to pay financially dependent workers overtime and minimum wages.
- Insurance premiums required under state workers' compensation laws, except where states explicitly require that companies maintain workers' compensation coverage for all workers regardless of whether they are independent contractors.
- Protection under the Employee Retirement Income Security Act of 1974 (ERISA), the Family and Medical Leave Act, the National Labor Relations Act (NLRA), Title VII of the Civil Rights Act of 1964, and the Americans with Disabilities Act (ADA).

To determine whether employees are financially dependent, employers must first apply the **economic reality test**. Table 14-6 lists the criteria. For example, are topless nightclub dancers entitled to minimum wage under FLSA? A nightclub's owners claimed that the dancers were not eligible because they were independent contractors:

- The dancers could perform whenever and wherever they wanted.
- The club had no control over the manner of performance.
- The dancers must furnish their own costumes.

A federal district court ruled that the nightclub's topless dancers were entitled to minimum wage because they were economically dependent on the nightclub.[28] The dancers were economically dependent on the nightclub for the following reasons:

- The club owners set hours in which the dancers could perform.
- The club owners issued guidelines on dancers' behavior at the club.
- The club owners deducted 20 percent from the credit card tips of each dancer to cover administrative costs.

Again, employers' obligations under many federal and state employment laws depend on whether workers are employees or independent contractors. Companies must use the IRC's **right to control test** to determine whether such individuals are employees or independent contractors. Possessing the right to control work

---

TABLE 14-6 Economic Reality Test: Six Criteria to Determine Whether Workers Are Financially Dependent on the Employer

1. The extent to which the worker has the right to control the result of the work and the manner in which the work is performed
2. The degree to which the individual is "economically dependent" on the employer's business or, in other words, the amount of control the employer has over the individual's opportunity to realize a profit or sustain a loss
3. The extent to which the services are an integral part of the employer's business operations
4. The amount of initiative or level of skill required for the worker to perform the job
5. The permanency, exclusivity, or duration of the relationship between the employer and the worker
6. The extent of the worker's investment in equipment or materials required for the job

activities classifies individuals as employees rather than independent contractors. Table 14-7 lists 20 criteria of the right to control test.

TABLE 14-7 Right to Control Test: 20 Factors to Determine Whether an Employer Has the Right to Control a Worker

1. *Instructions.* Requiring a worker to comply with another person's instructions about when, where, and how he or she is to work ordinarily indicates an employer–employee relationship.
2. *Training.* Training a worker indicates that the employer wants the services performed in a particular manner and demonstrates the employer's control over the means by which the result is reached.
3. *Integration.* Integration of the worker's services into the business operations and the dependence of success or continuation of the business on the worker's services generally indicate that the worker is subject to a certain amount of direction and control by the employer.
4. *Services rendered personally.* If the services must be rendered personally, then the employer is presumably interested in the methods used to accomplish the work as well as the result, and control is indicated.
5. *Hiring, supervising, and paying assistants.* The employer's hiring, supervising, and paying the worker's assistants generally indicates control over the worker; however, if it is the worker who hires, supervises, and pays his or her assistants and is ultimately responsible for their work, then the worker has an independent contractor status.
6. *Continuing relationship.* A continuing relationship between the worker and the employer indicates that an employer–employee relationship exists.
7. *Set hours of work.* The establishment of set hours of work by the employer indicates control.
8. *Full-time required.* If the worker must devote full time to the employer's business, the employer has control over the worker's time. An independent contractor, on the other hand, is free to work when and for whom he or she chooses.
9. *Doing work on employer's premises.* If the work is performed on the employer's premises, control is suggested, especially if the work could be performed elsewhere.
10. *Order or sequence set.* If a worker must perform services in the order or sequence set by the employer, control is indicated because the worker is unable to follow his or her own pattern of work.
11. *Oral or written reports.* Requiring the worker to submit regular or written reports to the employer suggests control.
12. *Payment by hour, week, month.* Payment by the hour, week, or month suggests an employer–employee relationship unless it is just a convenient way of paying a lump sum agreed upon as the cost of a job. Payment by the job or on commission generally indicates an independent contractor status.
13. *Payment of business or traveling expenses, or both.* If the employer ordinarily pays the worker's business or traveling expenses, the worker is an employee.
14. *Furnishing of tools and materials.* If the employer furnishes significant tools, materials, and other equipment, an employer–employee relationship usually exists.
15. *Significant investment by worker.* If a worker invests in facilities that he or she uses to perform services and that are not typically maintained by an employee (e.g., rental of office space), an independent contractor status is usually indicated. Lack of investment in facilities tends to indicate that the worker depends on the employer for such facilities.
16. *Realization of profit or loss.* A worker who cannot realize a profit or suffer a loss as a result of his or her services generally is an employee.
17. *Working for more than one firm at a time.* If a worker performs more than *de minimis* services for a multiple of unrelated persons or firms at the same time, independent contractor status is generally indicated.
18. *Making services available to general public.* If a worker makes his or her services available to the general public on a regular and consistent basis, independent contractor status is indicated.
19. *Right to discharge.* The employer's right to discharge a worker indicates employee status.
20. *Right to terminate.* If a worker can terminate his or her relationship with the employer at any time without incurring liability, employee status is indicated.

SOURCE: Rev. Rul. 87-41, 1987-1 C.B. 296.

FLEXIBLE WORK SCHEDULES: FLEXTIME, COMPRESSED WORKWEEKS, AND TELECOMMUTING

Many companies now offer employees flexible work schedules to help them balance work and family demands. Flextime and compressed workweek schedules are the most prominent flexible work schedules used in companies. Flexible work schedule practices apply to both core employees and to contingent employees. Research shows that employees highly value flexibility as a workplace policy.

Flextime Schedules

Flextime schedules allow employees to modify their work schedules within specified limits set by the employer. Employees adjust when they will start work and when they will leave. Flextime, however, generally does not lead to reduced work hours. For instance, an employee may choose to work between 10 A.M. and 6 P.M., 9 A.M. and 5 P.M., or 8 A.M. and 4 P.M.

All workers must be present during certain workday hours when business activity is regularly high. This period is known as **core hours**. The number of core hours may vary from company to company, by departments within companies, or by season. Although employees are relatively free to choose start and completion times that fall outside core hours, management must carefully coordinate these times to avoid understaffing. Some flextime programs incorporate a **banking hours** feature that enables employees to vary the number of work hours daily as long as they maintain the regular number of work hours on a weekly basis.

Employers can expect three possible benefits from using flextime schedules. First, flextime schedules lead to less tardiness and absenteeism. Flexibly defining the workweek better enables employees to schedule medical and other appointments outside work hours. As a result, workers are less likely to be late or miss work altogether.

Second, flexible work schedules should lead to higher work productivity. Employees have more choice about when to work during the day. Individuals who work best during the morning hours may schedule morning hours, and individuals who work best during the afternoons or evenings can choose these times. In addition, possessing the flexibility to attend to personal matters outside work should help employees focus on doing better jobs.

Third, flexible work schedules benefit employers by creating longer business hours and better service. Staggering employees' schedules should enable businesses to stay open longer hours without incurring overtime pay expenses. In addition, customers should perceive better service because of expanded business hours. Companies that conduct business by telephone on national and international bases are more likely to be open during customers' normal operating hours in other time zones.

Two possible limitations of flexible work schedules are increased overhead costs and coordination problems. Maintaining extended operations leads to higher overhead costs, including support staff and utilities. In addition, flexible work schedules may lead to work coordination problems when some employees are not present at the same time.

Compressed Workweek Schedules

Compressed workweek schedules enable employees to perform their work in fewer days than a regular 5-day workweek. As a result, employees may work four 10-hour days or three 12-hour days. These schedules can promote companies' recruitment and retention successes by:

- Reducing the number of times employees must commute between home and work
- Providing more time together for dual-career couples who live apart

Telecommuting

Telecommuting represents an alternative work arrangement in which employees work at home or at some other location besides the office. Telecommuters generally spend part of their time working in the office and the other part working at home. This alternative work arrangement is appropriate for work that does not require regular direct interpersonal interactions with other workers (e.g., accounting, systems analysis, and telephone sales). Telecommuters stay in touch with co-workers and superiors through e-mail, telephone, and faxes. Table 14-8 summarizes the variety of possible telecommuting arrangements.

Potential benefits for employers include increased productivity and lower overhead costs for office space and supplies. Telecommuting also serves as an effective recruiting and retention practice for employees who strongly desire to perform their jobs away from the office. Employers may also increase the retention of valued employees who choose not to move when their companies relocate.

Employees find telecommuting beneficial. Telecommuting enables parents to be near their infants or preschool-age children, and to be home when older children finish their school days. In addition, telecommuting arrangements minimize commuting time and expense, which are exceptional in such congested metropolitan areas as Boston, Los Angeles, and New York City. Travel time may increase threefold during peak "rush hour" traffic periods. Parking and toll costs can be hefty. Monthly parking rates alone often exceed thousands of dollars per car. Finally, employees' involvement in office politics will be reduced, which should promote higher job performance.

Telecommuting programs may also lead to disadvantages for employers and employees. Some employers are concerned about not having direct contact with employees, which makes conducting performance appraisals more difficult. Employees sometimes feel that work-at-home arrangements are disruptive to their personal lives. In addition, some employees feel isolated because they do not personally interact as often with co-workers and superiors.

TABLE 14-8   Alternative Telecommuting Arrangements

- **Satellite work center.** Employees work from a remote extension of the employer's office that includes a clerical staff and a full-time manager.
- **Neighborhood work center.** Employees work from a satellite office shared by several employers.
- **Nomadic executive office.** Executives who travel extensively maintain control over projects through use of telephone, fax, and e-mail.
- **Employees sometimes work entirely outside the office.** Others might work off-site only once a month or 2 to 3 days a week.
- **Telecommuters can be full- or part-time employees.**
- **Telecommuting arrangements can be temporary or permanent.** A temporarily disabled employee may work at home until fully recovered. A permanently disabled employee may work at home exclusively.

SOURCE: Adapted from Bureau of National Affairs, Telecommuting (2005). *Compensation & Benefits* [online]: *www.bna.com,* accessed March 7, 2005.

Flexible Work Schedules: Balancing the Demands of Work Life and Home Life

Some U.S. companies use flexible work schedules to help employees balance the demands of work life and home life. Flextime, compressed workweeks, and telecommuting should provide single parents or dual-career parents the opportunity to spend more time with their children. Flextime gives parents the opportunity to schedule work around special events at their children's schools. Compressed workweeks enable parents on limited incomes to save on day care costs by reducing the number of days at the office. Parents can benefit from telecommuting in a similar fashion. Likewise, dual-career couples living apart also benefit from flexible work schedules. Compressed workweeks and telecommuting reduce the time spouses have to spend away from each other.

PAY AND EMPLOYEE BENEFITS FOR FLEXIBLE EMPLOYEES

The key pay issues for flexible work schedules are overtime pay. The main employee benefits issues are paid time off benefits and working condition fringe benefits.

Pay

In many cases, "flexible" employees work more than 40 hours during some weeks and fewer hours during other weeks. The FLSA requires that companies compensate nonexempt employees at an overtime rate equal to one and one-half times the normal hourly rate for each hour worked in excess of 40 hours per week. The overtime provisions are based on employees working set hours during fixed work periods. How do FLSA overtime provisions apply to flexible work schedules?

Let's assume the following flexible work schedule: An employee works 40 hours during the first week, 30 hours during a second week, and 50 hours during a third week. Although this employee worked 40 hours per week, on average, for the 3-week period ([40 + 30 + 50 hours]/3weeks), is that employee entitled to overtime pay for the additional 10 hours worked during the third week?

Some employees' weekly flexible schedules may fluctuate frequently and unpredictably according to such nonwork demands as chronically ill family members. Unpredictable flexible schedules make overtime pay calculations difficult. It is possible that companies may make inadequate or excessive overtime payments. A Supreme Court ruling (***Walling v. A. H. Belo Corp***).[29] requires employers to guarantee fixed weekly pay for employees whose work hours vary from week to week:

- The employer typically cannot determine the number of hours employees will work each week.
- The workweek period fluctuates both greater and less than 40 hours per week.

This pay provision guarantees employees fixed weekly pay regardless of how many hours they work, and it enables employers to control weekly labor cost expenditures. The use of compressed workweek schedules may lead to differences in overtime practices in some states. Whereas the federal government bases overtime pay on a weekly basis, some states use other time bases to determine overtime pay eligibility. Table 14-9 lists maximum hour provisions for select states. As you can see, there is wide variation in daily overtime practices.

Employee Benefits

Flexible workweek schedules have the greatest impact on paid time off benefits. Many companies determine employees' sick leave benefits and vacation days based

TABLE 14-9 Maximum Hours before Overtime for Selected States

Arkansas
- 10-hour day, 40-hour week for workers with flexible work hour plan if part of collective bargaining agreement or signed employer-employee agreement filed with state Department of Labor.

Connecticut
- 9-hour day, 48-hour week in manufacturing or mechanical establishments for workers under 18 or over 65, handicapped persons, and disabled veterans.
- 10-hour day, 55-hour week during emergencies or peak demand, with commissioner's permission.
- 6-day, 48-hour week for employees under 18 or over 66, handicapped persons, and disabled veterans in public restaurant, café, dining room, barber shop, hairdressing, or manicuring establishment; amusement or recreational establishment; bowling alley, shoe shining establishment; billiard or pool room, or photographic gallery.

Michigan
- 10 hours a day in factories, workshops, salt blocks, sawmills, logging or lumber camps, booms or drivers, mines, or other places used for mechanical or manufacturing purposes.

Nevada
- 8-hour day, 40-hour week, unless mutually agreed 10-hour day, 4-day week.

on the number of hours they work each month. The determination of paid vacation and sick leave for employees on standard work schedules is relatively straightforward; however, flexible employees work fewer hours some months and more hours during other months. This variability complicates companies' calculations of paid time off benefits.

Another issue is the treatment of paid time off for holidays. Under standard work schedules, the vast majority of employees work five 8-hour days from Monday through Friday. For example, all employees take Thanksgiving Day off (a Thursday) with pay. Under flexible schedules, some employees may not be scheduled to work on Thursdays. As a result, standard-schedule employees receive one day off with pay during Thanksgiving week, and some flexible employees work their regular schedules, missing a paid day off from work. Companies must establish policies that provide flexible workers with comparable paid time off benefits or alternative holidays. Such policies are necessary to maintain equity among employees; however, scheduling alternative holidays may lead to coordination problems for small companies: Companies with small staffs may not have enough employees to cover for flexible workers during their alternative holiday time off work.

An employee benefits issue known as **working condition fringe benefits** applies to telecommuters. Employers are likely to provide telecommuters with the necessary equipment to perform their jobs effectively while off-site: computers, modems, printers, photocopy machines, sundry office supplies, and Telex machines. In addition, some employers provide similar equipment to employees who wish to work additional hours outside their regular work schedules during the evenings or weekends. This arrangement does not qualify as telecommuting.

The IRS treats the home use of office equipment and supplies as employees' taxable income when the use falls outside established telecommuting relationships; however, employees are not taxed when the home use of employer-provided equipment falls within established telecommuting relationships. Under this condition, the IRS treats the home use of employer-provided equipment as a working condition fringe benefit.

UNIONS' REACTIONS TO CONTINGENT WORKERS AND FLEXIBLE WORK SCHEDULES

Unions generally do not support companies' use of contingent workers and flexible work schedules. Most union leaders believe that alternative work arrangements threaten members' job security and are prone to unfair and inequitable treatment. The most common concerns include:

- Employers exploit contingent workers by paying them lower wages and benefits than core employees.
- Employers' efforts to get cheap labor will lead to a poorly trained and less-skilled workforce that will hamper competitiveness.
- Part-time employees are difficult to organize because their interests are centered on activities outside the workplace. Part-time workers are therefore probably not good union members.
- Part-time employment erodes labor standards: Part-time workers are often denied fringe benefits, job security, and promotion opportunities. Increasing part-time employment would promote inequitable treatment.
- Temporary employees generally have little concern about improving the productivity of a company for which they will work for only a brief period.
- Unions' bargaining power becomes weak when companies demonstrate their ability to perform effectively with temporaries.
- The long days of compressed workweeks or flextime could endanger workers' safety and health, even if the workers choose these long days themselves.
- Concerns about employee isolation, uncompensated overtime, and company monitoring in the home are among the reasons unions have been reluctant to permit telecommuting by their members.

Unions' positions against contingent employment are unlikely to change because this practice undermines efforts to secure high wages and job security for members; however, some unions, particularly in the public sector, have begun to accept the use of flexible work schedules. The benefits of these arrangements (i.e., increased productivity, lower absence rates, and tardiness) strengthen unions' bargaining power.

STRATEGIC ISSUES AND CHOICES IN USING CONTINGENT AND FLEXIBLE WORKERS

As you will recall, in Chapter 2 we reviewed a framework for selecting particular compensation tactics to match a company's competitive strategy. How do contingent workers and flexible work schedules fit with the two fundamental competitive strategies: lowest-cost and differentiation? These innovations, when properly applied, can ultimately contribute to meeting the goals of lowest-cost and differentiation strategies; however, the rationale for the appropriateness of contingent employment and flexible work schedules differs according to the imperatives of the lowest-cost and differentiation competitive strategies.

Lowest-Cost Competitive Strategy

Lowest-cost strategies require firms to reduce output costs per employee. Contingent employment saves companies considerable amounts of money because they do not give these workers most discretionary benefits. Discretionary benefits represent a significant fiscal cost to companies.

Employers' use of well-trained contingent workers also contributes through reduced training costs; however, not all contingent workers know company-specific work practices and procedures. Company-specific training represents a significant cost to companies. Companies that do not employ contingent workers long enough to realize the productivity benefits from training undermine lowest-cost objectives. Company-sponsored training may seem to contradict the lowest-cost imperative in the short term.

The following factors can increase short-term costs:

- Costs of training materials and instructors' professional fees
- Downtime while employees are participating in training
- Inefficiencies that may result until employees master new skills

A longer-term perspective, however, may lead to the conclusion that contingent work arrangements support the lowest-cost imperatives. Over time, productivity enhancements and increased flexibility should far outweigh the short-run costs if companies establish track records of high productivity, quality, and exemplary customer service.

Flexible schedules should also contribute to lowest-cost imperatives. Limited evidence suggests that flexible employees demonstrate lower absenteeism than employees with fixed work schedules.

Differentiation Competitive Strategy

A differentiation strategy requires creative, open-minded, risk-taking employees. Compared with lowest-cost strategies, companies that pursue differentiation strategies must take a longer-term focus to attain their preestablished objectives. Both arrangements should contribute to innovation; however, systematic studies that demonstrate these relationships are lacking. Contingent employment probably is appropriate because companies will benefit from the influx of "new" employees from time to time who bring fresh ideas with them. Over the long run, contingent employment should minimize problems of **groupthink**, which occurs when all group members agree on mistaken solutions because they share the same mind-set and view issues through the lens of conformity.[30]

Flexible work schedules should also promote differentiation strategies for two reasons. First, flexible work schedules enable employees to work when they are at their physical or mental best. Some individuals are most alert during morning hours, whereas others are most alert during afternoon or evening hours because of differences in biorhythms. Second, flexible work schedules allow employees to work with fewer distractions and worries about personal matters. The inherent flexibility of these schedules allows employees to attend to personal matters as needed.

SUMMARY

This chapter discussed contingent workers and flexible work arrangements, reasons companies rely on contingent employment arrangements and flexible work schedules, special compensation issues, unions' reactions to contingent employment and flexible work schedules, and their fit with competitive strategies. Companies that choose to employ contingent workers must give serious consideration to the possible long-term benefits and consequences. Flexible work schedules seem to accommodate the changing workers' needs well. Given the possible limitations of contingent employment and flexible work schedules, companies should strike a balance between the use of core employment and contingent employment, as well as a balance between standard work schedules and flexible work schedules.

KEY TERMS

- core employees, 346
- contingent workers, 346
- voluntary part-time employees, 347
- involuntary part-time employees, 347
- job sharing, 349
- temporary employment agency, 350
- direct hire arrangements, 350
- on-call arrangements, 350

- lease companies, 351
- independent contractors, 351
- freelancers, 351
- consultants, 351
- dual employer common law doctrine, 357
- safe harbor rule, 357
- economic reality test, 358
- right to control test, 358
- flextime schedules, 360

- core hours, 360
- banking hours, 360
- compressed workweek schedules, 360
- telecommuting, 361
- *Walling v. A. H. Belo Corp.,* 362
- working condition fringe benefits, 363
- groupthink, 365

DISCUSSION QUESTIONS

1. Discuss some of the problems that companies are likely to face when both contingent workers and core employees work in the same location. Does it matter whether contingent workers and core employees are performing the same jobs? Explain your answer.
2. Companies generally pay temporary employees lower wages and offer fewer benefits than they extend to their core counterparts. Nevertheless, what are some of the possible drawbacks for companies that employ temporary workers? Do you believe that these drawbacks outweigh the cost savings? Explain your reasoning.
3. What arguments can be made in favor of using compressed workweek schedules for companies that pursue lowest-cost strategies? What are the arguments against using compressd workweek schedules in such situations?
4. What impact will flexible work schedules have on employees' commitment to their employers? On employee productivity? On company effectiveness?
5. Provide your reactions to the following statement: Contingent workers should be compensated on a pay-for-knowledge system.

EXERCISES

Compensation Online

For Students

Exercise 1: Find relevant journal articles

You have been given a case study regarding a company that attempted to use flexible work arrangements and failed for lack of planning. Use your school library's online catalog to locate articles pertaining to part-time employees, contingent workers, telecommuting, and contingent worker compensation. Find and read several current articles in these areas. Write a paper on what aspects of a flexible system are necessary for success.

Exercise 2: Search for information on flexible work options

The case study you analyzed in class has left you wanting a more in-depth look at alternative work arrangements. To learn more about flexible work options, go to *www.context.org* and click on "Search all the IC Issues." Select one of the articles and write a brief summary about its contents.

Next, use the search engine of your choice and look for sites about "flexible work options." Which search engine was easier to use? Which search engine gave you the most options?

Exercise 3: Research flextime schedules

Your professor has given the class an opportunity for extra credit. You must bring information about or examples of flextime to class and be able to describe and explain the system to the rest of class. Using the Yahoo! search engine, click on the *advanced search* link, type in "flextime schedules," select "an exact phrase match," and search. Scan over a couple of the sites. What did you learn about flextime schedules from these sites? Be prepared to discuss your findings in class.

Next, use the search engine of your choice and search for "flextime schedules." Which search engine was easier to use? Which search engine gave you the most options?

For Professionals

Exercise 1: Research a temporary help company

Your manufacturing firm is cutting back on production, but, rather than lay off workers, you would like to institute an employee leasing program. This way, your employees can continue to earn wages and benefits, and the firm can generate some revenue. To get off on the right foot, you are assigned the task of researching how temporary help companies operate. To gain an understanding of how a temporary help company markets and operates its business, go to Manpower's Web site at *www.manpower.com*. What did you learn about Manpower? Toward what audiences do you think the Web site is geared? How effective do you think it will be in reaching each audience?

Exercise 2: Review worker classification policy and compliance

For tax and benefits purposes, it may suit a company to classify as a temporary worker what is, in essence, a full-time worker. Firms have recently come under government scrutiny for how they classify their workers. To be sure your firm is on the up and up, conduct an advanced search on Yahoo! for the exact phrase match of "worker classification." Review several of the sites and pay specific attention to what implications classifying workers has on their compensation, as well as the financial impact on the employer.

Exercise 3: Keep up with current events in human resources

Visit the Public Policy Association of Senior Human Resource Executives Web site at *www.lpa.org*. Search this site for "contingent workers," "flexible workers," "telecommuting," and any other topics of interest from this chapter. Read news releases and articles published by HR executives, and try to identify trends and significant issues. How would these issues have an impact on your role as an HR professional?

ENDNOTES

1. U.S. Bureau of Labor Statistics (2005). *Contingent and alternative employment arrangements, February 2005* (USDL 05–1433) [online]. Available: *www.bls.gov/ncs/cps/*, accessed June 14, 2007.

2. U.S. Bureau of Labor Statistics (2005). *Workers on flexible and shift schedules in May 2004* (USDL 05–1198) [online]. Available: *www.bls.gov/ncs/cps/*, accessed June 14, 2007.

3. U.S. Bureau of Labor Statistics (2005). *Contingent and alternative employment arrangements, February 2005* (USDL 05–1433) [online]. Available: *www.bls.gov/ncs/cps/*, accessed June 14, 2007.

4. Fallick, B. B. (1999). Part-time work and industry growth. *Monthly Labor Review, 122*, pp. 22–29.

5. Burgess, P. M. (1994). *Making it in America's new economy*. Commencement address, University of Toledo, June 11.

6. U.S. Bureau of Labor Statistics (2005). *Contingent and alternative employment arrangements, February 2005* (USDL 05–1433) [online]. Available: *www.bls.gov/ncs/cps/*, accessed June 14, 2007.

7. U.S. Bureau of Labor Statistics (2007). *Industry at a glance* [online]. Available: *http://www.bls.gov/iag/iaghome.htm*, accessed June 14, 2007.

8. Ibid.

9. Ibid.

10. Ibid.

11. Ibid.

12. England, P. (1992). *Comparable Worth: Theories and Evidence.* New York: Aldine DeGruyler.

13. Hayghe, H. V. (1990). Family members in the workforce. *Monthly Labor Review, 113*, pp. 14–19.

14. U.S. Bureau of Labor Statistics (2001). *Contingent and alternative employment arrangements, February 2001* (USDL 01–153) [online]. Available: *www.bls.gov/bls/newsrels.htm,* accessed March 5, 2005.

15. U.S. Bureau of Labor Statistics (2006). *National Compensation Survey: Employee Benefits in Private Industry, March 2006* (BLS 06–05). Online: *www.bls.gov/ncs/ebs/home.htm,* accessed April 17, 2007.

16. Ibid.

17. Cooper, S. F. (1995). The expanding use of contingent workers in the American economy: New opportunities and dangers for employers. *Employee Relations Law Review, 20*, pp. 525–539.

18. U.S. Department of Labor. (2007). Employer Costs for Employee Compensation–March 2007. USDL: 07–0877. Online: *www.bls.gov/_ecthome.htm,* accessed June 30, 2007.

19. U.S. Department of Labor (2006). *National Compensation Survey: Employee benefits in private industry in the United States, March 2006* (Summary 06–05). [online] Available: *www.bls.gov/ ecthome.htm,* accessed March 5, 2007.

20. Ibid.

21. Internal Revenue Code 410(a)(1).

22. U.S. Bureau of Labor Statistics (2005). *Contingent and alternative employment arrangements, February 2005* (USDL 05–1433) [online]. Available: *www.bls.gov/ncs/cps/,* accessed June 14, 2007.

23. Internal Revenue Code 411(b)(4)(c).

24. Bureau of National Affairs. (1994) *Employee Relations Weekly*, October 24, 1994. Washington, DC: Author.

25. U.S. Bureau of Labor Statistics (2005). *Contingent and alternative employment arrangements, February 2005* (USDL 05–1433) [online]. Available: *www.bls.gov/ncs/cps/,* accessed June 14, 2007.

26. Internal Revenue Code 414(n)(5).

27. Internal Revenue Code 414(n)(1)(2)(3).

28. *Martin v. Priba Corp.,* USDC N. Texas, No. 3:91-CV-278-G (11/6/92).

29. *Walling v. A. H. Belo Corp.,* 316, U.S. 624, 2WH Cases 39 (1942).

30. Sheppard, C. R. (1964). *Small Groups.* San Francisco: Chandler.

CHAPTER 15

Compensating Expatriates

Chapter Outline

■ Competitive Strategies and How International Activities Fit In
    Lowest-Cost Producers' Relocations to Cheaper Production Areas
    Differentiation and the Search for New Global Markets
    How Globalization Is Affecting HR Departments
    Complexity of International Compensation Programs

■ Preliminary Considerations
    Host Country Nationals, Third Country Nationals, and Expatriates
    Definitions and Relevance for Compensation Issues
    Term of International Assignment
    Staff Mobility
    Equity: Pay Referent Groups

■ Components of International Compensation Programs

■ Setting Base Pay for U.S. Expatriates
    Methods for Setting Base Pay
    Purchasing Power

■ Incentive Compensation for U.S. Expatriates
    Foreign Source Premiums
    Hardship Allowances
    Mobility Premiums

■ Establishing Employee Benefits for U.S. Expatriates
    Standard Benefits for U.S. Expatriates
    Enhanced Benefits for U.S. Expatriates

■ Balance Sheet Approach for U.S. Expatriates' Compensation Packages
    Housing and Utilities
    Goods and Services
    Discretionary Income
    Tax Considerations

■ Repatriation Pay Issues

■ Summary

■ Key Terms

■ Discussion Questions

■ Exercises

■ Endnotes

Learning Objectives

In this chapter, you will learn about

1. Competitive strategies and how international activities fit in

2. How globalization affects HR departments

3. Methods for setting expatriates' base pay

4. Incentive compensation for expatriates

5. Employee benefits for expatriates

6. The balance sheet approach

7. Repatriation issues

International compensation programs have strategic value as U.S. businesses continue to establish operations in such foreign locales as Pacific Rim countries, Eastern Europe, and Mexico. The general trend for expanding operations overseas serves as just one indicator of the "globalization" of the economy. U.S. companies place professional and managerial (U.S. citizen) employees overseas to establish and operate satellite plants and offices. Although there are many glamorous aspects about working overseas, the glamor comes at the price of personal and, sometimes, professional sacrifices. Compensation takes on strategic value by providing these employees minimal financial risk associated with working overseas, as well as lifestyles for them and their families comparable to their lifestyles in the United States. Multinational companies (i.e., companies with operations in more than one country) develop special compensation packages to help compensate for the personal sacrifices international assignees and their immediate families make. These sacrifices are associated with cultural variations that affect their lifestyle (i.e., dealing with an unfamiliar culture, enhanced responsibilities, and potentially higher living expenses).

COMPETITIVE STRATEGIES AND HOW INTERNATIONAL ACTIVITIES FIT IN

The presence of U.S. companies in foreign countries is on the rise. You might forget that you are in China while taking a taxi ride through the streets of Beijing: Billboards and establishments for such U.S. companies as McDonald's, Pizza Hut, Pepsi, Coca-Cola, and Motorola are common sights.

Several factors have contributed to the expansion of global markets. These include such free trade agreements as the **North American Free Trade Agreement**, the unification of the European market, and the gradual weakening of Communist influence in Eastern Europe and Asia. Likewise, foreign companies have greater opportunities to invest in the United States.

Lowest-Cost Producers' Relocations to Cheaper Production Areas

Many U.S. businesses have established manufacturing and production facilities in Asian countries and in Mexico because labor is significantly less expensive than it is in the United States. There are two key reasons for the cost difference. First, labor unions generally do not have much bargaining power in developing Asian countries or in Mexico, where the governments possess extensive control over workplace affairs. Second, Asian governments do not value individual employee rights as much as does the U.S. government. As we discussed in Chapter 3, the Fair Labor Standards Act of 1938 (FLSA) provides employees a minimum hourly wage rate, limits exploitation of child labor, and mandates overtime pay.

Differentiation and the Search for New Global Markets

Coca-Cola and Pepsi products are well known worldwide because these companies aggressively introduced their soft drink products throughout numerous countries. Establishing Coke and Pepsi products worldwide does not represent a differentiation strategy, however. Coke and Pepsi could distinguish themselves from competing companies by taking on new business initiatives that depart from "business as usual" and meet specific market needs.

For Coke and Pepsi, "business as usual" means marketing soft drink products (i.e., carbonated water with artificial colors and flavors). Marketing bottled spring water would clearly be a departure from business as usual for them. The People's Republic of China (PRC) possesses a definite need for bottled spring water: The Chinese government is unable to provide its citizens and visitors with drinkable water because the country does not maintain adequate water purification plants. Coke and Pepsi could distinguish themselves from other soft drink companies by marketing spring water along with their regular soft drink products. Coke and Pepsi would be known as companies that serve necessary (bottled water) and recreational (soft drinks) beverage needs.

How Globalization Is Affecting HR Departments

The globalization of business requires that companies send employees overseas to establish and operate satellite plants and offices. Companies naturally must invest in the development of appropriate human resource (HR) practices. International business operations are destined to fail without the "right" people. HR professionals must be certain to identify the selection criteria that are most related to successful international work assignments. For example, do candidates possess adequate cultural sensitivity? Do they believe that U.S. customs are the only appropriate way to approach problems? Are candidates' families willing to adjust to foreign lifestyles?

Another key HR function is training. Expatriates must understand the cultural values that predominate in foreign countries; otherwise, they risk hindering business. For example, one of Procter & Gamble's Camay soap commercials was successful in the United States, but the Japanese perceived the very same commercial that aired in Japan to be rude. The commercial depicted a man barging into the bathroom on his wife while she was using Camay soap. Japanese cultural values led Japanese viewers to judge this commercial as offensive. The Japanese deemed the commercial as acceptable after Procter & Gamble modified the commercial to show a woman using Camay soap in privacy.

Companies' investments in cross-cultural training vary. Some companies provide release time from work to take foreign language courses at local colleges or universities. Highly progressive companies (e.g., Motorola) run corporate universities that offer cross-cultural training courses.

The use of international assignments both is growing and has a changing role, according the 2006 Worldwide Survey of International Assignment Practices and Policies, conducted by ORC Worldwide. In 2006, 56 percent of companies increased expatriate usage. Of particular note is a substantial increase in the use of short-term assignments, defined as fewer than 12 months. In 2006, 78 percent of the companies surveyed acknowledge use of short-term assignments, compared with 75 percent in 2004, and 66 percent and 59 percent in 2002 and 2000, respectively.

"The most sophisticated companies are trying to integrate international programs with talent management programs," said ORC Worldwide Executive Vice President Geoffrey W. Latta. "These companies understand the importance of integrating international experience with local talent, particularly if the company wants to become a true leader among global organizations."[1] The survey indicates that the Middle East is becoming a common destination for expatriates, particularly in the mining and oil industries.

Complexity of International Compensation Programs

The development and implementation of international compensation programs typically pose four challenges to companies that U.S. compensation programs do not have to consider. First, successful international compensation programs further corporate interests abroad and encourage employees to take foreign assignments. Second, well-designed compensation programs minimize financial risk to employees and make their and their families' experiences as pleasant as possible. Third, international compensation programs promote a smooth transition back to life in the United States upon completion of the international assignment. **Repatriation** is the process of making the transition from an international assignment and living abroad to a domestic assignment and living in the home country. Fourth, sound international compensation programs promote U.S. businesses' lowest-cost and differentiation strategies in foreign markets.

PRELIMINARY CONSIDERATIONS

We must take some basic issues under advisement before examining the elements of international compensation programs. Compensation professionals must distinguish among host country nationals (HCNs), third country nationals (TCNs) (to be discussed next), and expatriates as compensation recipients with their own unique issues. In addition, compensation professionals should consider such matters as terms of the international assignment, staff mobility, and equity because these factors pertain directly to the design elements of international compensation programs.

Host Country Nationals, Third Country Nationals, and Expatriates: Definitions and Relevance for Compensation Issues

There are three kinds of recipients of international compensation:

- Host country nationals (HCNs)
- Third country nationals (TCNs)
- Expatriates

We will define these recipients as employees of U.S. companies doing business in foreign countries; however, these definitions also apply to employees of non-U.S. companies doing business in foreign countries.

Host country nationals are foreign national citizens who work in U.S. companies' branch offices or manufacturing plants in their home countries. Japanese citizens working for General Electric in Japan are HCNs.

Third country nationals are foreign national citizens who work in U.S. companies' branch offices or manufacturing plants in foreign countries—excluding the United States and their own home countries. Australian citizens working for General Motors in the People's Republic of China are TCNs.

Expatriates are U.S. citizens employed in U.S. companies with work assignments outside the United States. U.S. citizens employed in CitiBank's London, England, office are expatriates.

Our primary focus is on compensation for expatriates. Following an extensive discussion of expatriate compensation, we will consider some of the challenges compensation professionals face when compensating HCNs and TCNs.

As a reminder, our focus is on U.S. companies, and these definitions reflect this focus. Other countries can be the focus as well. For example, let's define HCN, TCN, and expatriate from the Australian perspective. BHP, an Australian company, conducts business worldwide in such countries as the People's Republic of China and the United States. A Chinese citizen who works for BHP in Shanghai is an HCN. A U.S. citizen who works for BHP in Shanghai is a TCN. An Australian citizen who works for BHP in Shanghai is an expatriate.

HR professionals construct international compensation packages on the basis of three main factors:

- Term of international assignment
- Staff mobility
- Equity: pay referent groups

Term of International Assignment

The term of the international assignment is central in determining compensation policy. Short-term assignments (i.e., usually less than 1 year in duration) generally do not require substantial modifications to domestic compensation packages; however, extended assignments necessitate features that promote a sense of stability and comfort overseas. These features include housing allowances, educational expenses for children, and adjustments to protect expatriates from paying "double" income taxes (i.e., U.S. federal and state taxes as well as applicable foreign taxes).

Staff Mobility

Companies must also consider whether foreign assignments necessitate employees' moving from one foreign location to another (i.e., from Beijing, China, to the Special Economic Zone in China, or from England to Brazil). Such moves within and across foreign cultures can disrupt expatriates' and their families' lives. Staff mobility comes at a price to companies in the form of monetary incentives and measures to make employees' moves as comfortable as possible.

Equity: Pay Referent Groups

Well-designed U.S. compensation programs promote equity among employees: Employees' pay is commensurate with performance or knowledge attainment. Expatriates are likely to evaluate compensation, in part, according to equity considerations. Many U.S. companies use domestic employees as the pay referent groups when developing international compensation packages be cause virtually all expatriate employees eventually return to the United States.

Some companies use local employees as the pay referent groups for long-term assignments because they wish to facilitate expatriates' integration into foreign cultures. As we discuss later, Mexican managerial employees' compensation packages include base pay and such cash allowances as Christmas bonuses. On the other hand, the main components of U.S. managerial employees' compensation packages include base pay and long-term incentives. U.S. expatriates working in Mexico on long-term assignments are likely to have compensation packages that are similar to Mexican managerial employees' compensation packages.

TABLE 15-1 U.S. Expatriates' Compensation Package

Core Compensation
    Base pay
    Incentive compensation
    Foreign service premium
    Hardship allowance
    Mobility premium
Employee Benefits
Standard Benefits
    Protection programs
    Paid time off
Enhanced Benefits
    Relocation assistance
    Educational reimbursement for expatriates' children
    Home leave and travel reimbursement
    Rest and relaxation leave allowance

COMPONENTS OF INTERNATIONAL COMPENSATION PROGRAMS

The basic structure of international compensation programs is similar to the structure of domestic compensation programs. The main components include base pay and fringe compensation. The inclusion of nonperformance-based incentives and allowances distinguishes international compensation packages from domestic compensation packages. Table 15-1 lists the main components of international compensation programs.

SETTING BASE PAY FOR U.S. EXPATRIATES

U.S. companies must determine the method for setting expatriates' base pay. Final determination should come only after companies carefully weigh the strengths and limitations of alternative methods. In addition, the purchasing power of base pay is an important consideration. Purchasing power affects standard of living. The following quote from a U.S. expatriate stationed in Italy captures the essence of purchasing power for expatriates: "Does an Italian lira purchase as much macaroni today as it did yesterday?" Two key factors influence purchasing power: the stability of local currency and inflation.

Methods for Setting Base Pay

U.S. companies use one of three methods to calculate expatriates' base pay:

- Home country-based method
- Host country-based method
- Headquarters-based method

Home Country–Based Method

The **home country–based pay method** compensates expatriates the amount they would receive if they were performing similar work in the United States. Job evaluation procedures enable employers to determine whether jobs at home are equivalent to comparable jobs in foreign locations based on compensable factors. How does location create differences in jobs that are otherwise considered equal? One example may be that foreign language skills are probably essential outside English-speaking countries. Adjustments to expatriates' pay should reflect additional skills.

The home country–based pay method is often most appropriate for expatriates. Equity problems are not very likely to arise because expatriates' assignments are too short to establish local national employees as pay referents. Instead, expatriates will base pay comparisons on their home country standards. In general, the home country–based pay method is most suitable when expatriate assignments are short in duration and local nationals performing comparable jobs receive substantially higher pay. As we discussed earlier, expatriates may rely on local cultural norms over extended periods as the standard for judging the equitableness of their compensation.

Host Country–Based Method

The **host country–based method** compensates expatriates based on the host countries' pay scales. Companies use various standards for determining base pay, including market pricing, job evaluation techniques, and jobholders' past relevant work experience. Other countries use different standards. For instance, the Japanese emphasize seniority. Expatriates' base pay will be competitive with other employees' base pay in the host countries. The host country–based method is most suitable when assignments are of long duration. As we noted previously, expatriates are then more likely to judge the adequacy of their pay relative to their local co-workers rather than to their counterparts at home.

Headquarters-Based Method

The **headquarters-based method** compensates all employees according to the pay scales used at the headquarters. Neither the location of the international work assignment nor home country influences base pay. This method makes the most sense for expatriates who move from one foreign assignment to another and rarely, if ever, work in their home countries. This system is administratively simple because it applies the pay standard of one country to all employees regardless of the location of their foreign assignment or their country of citizenship.

Purchasing Power

Decreases in purchasing power lead to lower standards of living. Expatriates quite simply cannot afford to purchase as many goods and services as they could before, or they must settle for lower quality. Diminished purchasing power undermines the strategic value of expatriates' compensation because top-notch employees are probably not willing to settle for lower standards of living while stationed at foreign posts. In addition, changes in the factors that immediately influence standard of living (i.e., the stability of currency and inflation) are somewhat unpredictable. This unpredictability creates a sense of uncertainty and risk. As we will discuss later in this section, most U.S. companies use the balance sheet approach to minimize this risk.

Currency Stabilization

Most U.S. companies award expatriates' base pay in U.S. currency, not in the local foreign currency; however, foreign countries as a rule do not recognize U.S. currency as legal tender. Expatriates must therefore exchange U.S. currency for local foreign currency based on daily exchange rates. An **exchange rate** is the price at which one country's currency can be swapped for another.[2] Exchange rates are expressed in terms of foreign currency per U.S. dollar or in terms of U.S. dollars per unit of foreign currency. For example, on June 22, 2007, the exchange rate for the Swedish krona was 6.86 KR for each U.S. $1.

Government policies and complex market forces cause exchange rates to fluctuate daily. Exchange rate fluctuations have direct implications for expatriates' purchasing power. For example, let's start with the previous exchange rate of 6.86 KR per U.S. $1. In addition, the exchange rate was 8.50 KR per U.S. $1 on December 31, 1999. This example illustrates a decline in the exchange rate for Swedish money. U.S. expatriates experience lower purchasing power because they receive fewer Swedish KR for every U.S. $1 they exchange.

Inflation

Inflation is the increase in prices for consumer goods and services. Inflation erodes the purchasing power of currency. Let's assume that ABC Corporation did not award pay increases to its expatriates stationed in United Kingdom during 2004. Expatriates' purchasing power remains unaffected as long as there isn't any inflation (and reduced exchange rate) during the same period. These expatriates, however, had lower purchasing power ever since because inflation averaged between 2.4 and 4.8 in the United Kingdom. Table 15-2 shows the annual inflation rates for various countries between 1995 and 2007.

TABLE 15-2 Annual Inflation Rates (%) for Selected Countries, 1995–2007

Period	United States	Canada	Japan	France	Germany	Italy	Sweden	Switzerland	United Kingdom
1995	2.8	2.1	−0.1	1.7	1.7	5.2	2.5	1.8	3.5
1996	3.0	1.6	0.1	2.0	1.5	4.0	0.5	0.8	2.4
1997	2.3	1.6	1.9	1.2	1.9	2.0	0.7	0.5	3.1
1998	1.6	0.9	0.6	0.7	0.9	2.0	−0.3	0.1	3.4
1999	2.2	1.7	−0.3	0.5	0.6	1.7	0.5	0.8	1.5
2000	3.4	2.7	−0.8	1.7	1.4	2.5	0.9	1.5	3.0
2001	2.8	2.6	−0.7	1.7	2.0	2.7	2.4	1.0	1.8
2002	1.6	2.2	−0.9	1.9	1.4	2.5	2.2	0.7	1.7
2003	2.3	2.8	−0.3	2.1	1.1	2.7	1.9	0.6	2.9
2004	2.7	1.9	0.0	2.1	1.6	2.2	0.4	0.8	3.0
2005	3.4	2.2	−0.3	1.8	2.0	2.0	0.5	1.2	2.8
I	3.0	2.1	0.0	1.7	1.7	1.9	0.3	1.3	3.2
II	2.9	1.9	−0.1	1.7	1.7	1.8	0.3	1.1	3.0
III	3.8	2.6	−0.3	1.9	2.1	2.0	0.5	1.2	2.8
IV	3.7	2.3	−0.7	1.6	2.2	2.2	0.7	1.1	2.4
2006	3.2	2.0	0.3	1.6	1.7	2.1	1.4	1.1	3.2
I	3.6	2.4	−0.1	1.8	2.0	2.1	0.8	1.2	2.4
II	4.0	2.6	0.2	1.9	2.0	2.2	1.5	1.3	2.9
III	3.3	1.7	0.6	1.7	1.6	2.2	1.6	1.2	3.4
IV	1.9	1.3	0.3	1.3	1.3	1.8	1.5	0.5	4.0
Nov	2.0	1.4	0.3	1.4	1.5	1.8	1.7	0.5	3.9
Dec	2.5	1.6	0.3	1.5	1.4	1.9	1.6	0.6	4.4
2007									
I	2.4	1.8	−0.1	1.2	1.7	1.7	1.9	0.1	4.5
Jan	2.1	1.2	0.0	1.2	1.6	1.7	1.9	0.1	4.2
Feb	2.4	2.0	−0.2	1.0	1.6	1.8	2.0	0.0	4.6
Mar	2.8	2.3	−0.1	1.2	1.9	1.7	1.9	0.2	4.8
Apr	2.6	2.2	0.0	1.3	1.9	1.5	1.9	0.4	4.5

Note: These annual percent changes are based on national consumer price indexes as published by each country.

SOURCE: Prepared by U.S. Department of Labor, Bureau of Labor Statistics, June 1, 2007.

INCENTIVE COMPENSATION FOR U.S. EXPATRIATES

In the United States, companies offer incentives to promote higher job performance and to minimize dysfunctional turnover, which results when high performers quit their jobs. International compensation plans include a variety of unique incentives to encourage expatriates to accept and remain on international assignments. These incentives also compensate expatriates for their willingness to tolerate less desirable living and working conditions. The main incentives are foreign services premiums, hardship premiums, and mobility premiums.

Foreign service premiums

Foreign service premiums are monetary payments above and beyond regular base pay. Companies offer foreign service premiums to encourage employees to accept expatriate assignments. These premiums generally apply to assignments that extend beyond 1 year. The use of foreign service premiums is widespread.

Companies calculate foreign service premiums as a percentage of base pay, and these premiums range between 10 and 30 percent of base pay. The percentage amount increases with the length of the assignment. Larger amounts are sometimes necessary when there is a shortage of available candidates. Companies disburse payment of the foreign service premium over several installments to manage costs and to "remind" expatriates about the incentive throughout their assignments.

Employers that use foreign service premiums should consider the possible drawbacks. First, employees may misconstrue this premium as a regular permanent increase to base pay, and resentment toward the employer may develop following the last installment. Second, foreign service premiums may not have incentive value when employers make several small installments rather than fewer large installments. Third, employees may feel as if their standard of living has declined when they return to the United States because they no longer receive this extra money.

Hardship Allowances

The **hardship allowance** compensates expatriates for their sacrifices while on assignment. Specifically, these allowances are designed to recognize exceptionally hard living and working conditions at foreign locations. Employers disburse hardship allowances in small amounts throughout the duration of expatriates' assignments. It is easy for expatriates to lose sight of the foreign service premiums and hardship allowances because they appear as relatively small increments to their paychecks. Companies should take care to communicate the role of these payments.

Companies offer hardship allowances at exceptionally severe locations only. The U.S. Department of State has established a list of hardship posts where the living conditions are considered unusually harsh. Most multinational companies award hardship allowances to executive, managerial, and supervisory employees. Hardship allowances range from 5 percent to 25 percent of base pay (i.e., the greater the hardship, the higher the premium). The U.S. Department of State uses three criteria to identify hardship locations:

- Extraordinarily difficult living conditions (e.g., inadequate housing, lack of recreational facilities, isolation, inadequate transportation facilities, and lack of food or consumer services)
- Excessive physical hardship, including severe climates or high altitudes and the presence of dangerous conditions affecting physical and mental well-being

TABLE 15-3   Hardship Locations, Differentials, and Danger Pay, 2007

Country and City	Differential Rate Percentage
Bahrain: Bahrain	10
Belize: Belize City	15
Guatemala: Guatemala City	10
India: Calcutta	25
Macedonia, The Former Yugoslav Republic of: Skopje	20
Mexico: Monterrey	5
Thailand: Udorn	20
Yemen: Sanaa	20

Country and City	Danger Rate Percentage
Afghanistan: Kabul	35
Algeria: Algiers	15
Burundi: Bujumbura	20
Central African Republic: Bangui	20
Colombia: Bogota	15
Cote d'Ivoire: Abidjan	15
Iraq: Baghdad	35
Lebanon: Beirut	30

SOURCE: A complete listing of current locations with hardship differential for federal civilian employees can be found in Section 920 of the Department of State *Standardized Regulations (Government Civilians, Foreign Areas)*, available from the Superintendent of Documents, U.S. Government Printing Office, Washington, DC 20402. [online]. Available: *www.state.gov/m/a/als/920/*, accessed June 24, 2007.

- Notably unhealthy conditions (e.g., diseases and epidemics, lack of public sanitation, and inadequate health facilities)

The U.S. Department of State has deemed more than 150 places as hardship locations. Table 15-3 lists examples of hardship locations and recommended hardship differentials.

Mobility Premiums

Mobility premiums reward employees for moving from one assignment to another. Companies use these premiums to encourage employees to accept, leave, or change assignments—usually between foreign posts or between domestic positions to ones in a foreign country. Expatriates typically receive mobility premiums as single lump-sum payments.

ESTABLISHING EMPLOYEE BENEFITS FOR U.S. EXPATRIATES

Benefits represent an important component of expatriates' compensation packages. Companies design benefits programs to attract and retain the best expatriates. In addition, companies design these programs to promote a sense of security for expatriates and their families. Furthermore, well-designed programs should help expatriates and their families maintain regular contact with other family members and friends in the United States.

Benefits fall into three broad categories: protection programs, paid time off, and services. Protection programs provide family benefits, promote health, and guard against income loss caused by such catastrophic factors as unemployment, disability, or serious illnesses. Paid time off provides employees such paid time off as vacation. Service practices vary widely. Services provide such enhancements as tuition reimbursement and day care assistance to employees and their families.

Just like domestic employee benefits packages, international employee benefits plans include such protection programs as medical insurance and retirement programs.[3] In most cases, U.S. citizens working overseas continue to receive medical insurance and participate in their retirement programs.

International and domestic plans are also similar in that they offer paid time off; however, international packages tend to incorporate more extensive benefits of this kind, which we will discuss later. Moreover, international employee benefits differ from domestic compensation with regard to the types of allowances and reimbursements. For international assignees, these payments are designed to compensate for higher costs of living and housing, relocation allowances, and education allowances for expatriates' children.

Employers should take several considerations into account when designing international benefits programs, including:[4]

- Total remuneration: What is included in the total employee pay structure (e.g., cash wages, benefits, mandated social programs, and other perquisites)? How much can the business afford?
- Benefit adequacy: To what extent must the employer enhance mandated programs to achieve desired staffing levels? Programs already in place and employees' utilization of them should be critically examined before determining what supplementary programs are needed and desirable.
- Tax effectiveness: What is the tax deductibility of these programs for the employer and employee in each country, and how does U.S. tax law treat expenditures in this area?
- Recognition of local customs and practices: Companies often provide benefits and services to employees based on those extended by other businesses in the locality, independent of their own attitude toward these same benefits and services.

International employee benefits packages contain the same components as domestic fringe compensation packages and enhancements. U.S. expatriates receive many of the same standard benefits as their counterparts working in the United States. Expatriates also receive enhanced benefits for taking overseas assignments.

Standard Benefits for U.S. Expatriates

Protection programs and paid time off are the most pertinent standard benefits.

Protection Programs

We previously discussed legally required protection programs (Chapter 12) and discretionary protection programs (Chapters 10 and 11). Let's consider the application of each kind to the international context.

The key legally required protection programs are mandated by the following laws: the Social Security Act of 1935, various state workers' compensation laws, and the Family and Medical Leave Act of 1993. All provide protection programs to employees and their dependents. Expatriates continue to participate in the main Social Security programs (i.e., retirement insurance, benefits for dependents, and Medicare). The Family and Medical Leave Act also applies to expatriates; however, state workers' compensation laws generally do not. Instead, U.S. companies can elect private insurance that provides equivalent protection.

Discretionary protection programs provide family benefits, promote health, and guard against income loss caused by such catastrophic factors as unemployment, disability, or serious illnesses. U.S. companies provide these protection programs to expatriates for the same reasons they do in the United States (i.e., as a strategic response to workforce diversity and to retain the best-performing employees). Withholding these benefits from expatriates would create a disincentive for employees to take international assignments.

Paid Time Off

Standard paid time off benefits include annual vacation, holidays, and emergency leave.

Expatriates typically receive the same annual vacation benefits as do their domestic counterparts. These benefits are particularly common among expatriates with relatively short-term assignments. Companies do not provide expatriates extended regular vacation leave because expatriates are likely to perceive the removal of these benefits on their return to domestic assignments as punitive; however, U.S. companies must comply with foreign laws that govern the amount of vacation.

Expatriates generally receive paid time off for foreign national or local holidays that apply to their foreign locations. Foreign holiday schedules may provide fewer or more holidays than the United States. In addition, some countries require employers to provide all employees paid time off for recognized holidays. In the United States, companies offer paid holidays as a discretionary benefit or as set in collective bargaining agreements.

Paid leave for personal or family emergencies is also a component of most expatriate compensation packages. Such emergencies may include critically ill family members or their deaths in the United States or in the foreign posts. Most companies provide paid emergency leave, but some companies provide unpaid leaves of absence. In either case, companies cover travel expenses between the foreign post and the United States.

Enhanced Benefits for U.S. Expatriates

Enhanced benefits for U.S. expatriates include:

- Relocation assistance
- Education reimbursements for expatriates' children
- Home leave benefits and travel reimbursements
- Rest and relaxation leave and allowance

Relocation Assistance

Relocation assistance payments cover expatriates' expenses to relocate to foreign posts. Table 15-4 lists the items most commonly covered under relocation assistance programs. Relocation assistance is generally large enough to pay for major expenses. Companies usually base these payment amounts on three main factors: distance, length of assignment, and rank in the company.

Education Reimbursements for Expatriates' Children

Expatriates typically place their children in private schools designed for English-speaking students. Tuition in foreign countries is often more expensive than tuition for private U.S. schools. These companies choose to reimburse expatriate children's education for two reasons. First, some foreign public schools are generally not comparable to U.S. public schools. Some are better, and others are below the U.S. standard. Companies make

TABLE 15-4   Relocation Assistance Payments

The relocation allowance or reimbursement provides employees with money for:

- Temporary quarters prior to departure because the expatriate's house has been sold or rented
- Transportation to the foreign post for employees and their families
- Reasonable expenses incurred by the family during travel
- Temporary quarters while waiting for delivery of household goods or while looking for suitable housing
- Moving household goods to the foreign post
- Storing household goods in the United States

generous educational reimbursements where public school quality is low. Second, most U.S. children do not speak foreign languages fluently. Thus, they cannot enroll in foreign public schools.

Home Leave Benefits and Travel Reimbursements

Companies offer home leave benefits to help expatriates manage the adjustment to foreign cultures and to maintain direct personal contact with family and friends. As the name implies, **home leave benefits** enable expatriates to take paid time off in the United States. Home leave benefits vary considerably from company to company. The length and frequency of these leaves usually depends on the expected duration of expatriates' assignments (i.e., longer assignments justify longer home leaves). In addition, expatriates must serve a minimum period at the foreign post before they are eligible for home leave benefits (i.e., anywhere from 6 to 12 months). Companies offer these extended benefits along with the standard paid time off benefits.

Companies compensate expatriates while they are away on home leave. In addition, most companies reimburse expatriates for expenses associated with travel between the foreign post and the United States. These reimbursements apply to expatriates and to family members who live with expatriates at foreign posts. Companies typically reimburse the cost of round-trip airfare, ground transportation, and accommodations while traveling to and from the foreign post.

Rest and Relaxation Leave and Allowance

Expatriates who work in designated hardship foreign locations receive **rest and relaxation leave benefits**. Rest and relaxation leave represents additional paid time off. Progressive employers recognize that expatriates working in hardship locations may need extra time away from the unpleasant conditions to "recharge their batteries." Rest and relaxation leave benefits differ from standard vacation benefits because companies designate where expatriates may spend their time. For example, many U.S. companies with operations in China's Special Economic Zone designate Hong Kong as an acceptable retreat because it is relatively close by, and Hong Kong has many amenities not present in the Special Economic Zone (e.g., diverse ethnic restaurants and Western-style entertainment).

Rest and relaxation leave programs include allowances to cover travel expenses between the foreign post and the retreat location. Companies determine allowance amounts based on such factors as the cost of round-trip transportation, food, and lodging associated with the designated locations. Allowances usually cover the majority of the costs. The U.S. Department of State publishes per diem schedules for various cities. Location and family size determine per diem amounts.

BALANCE SHEET APPROACH FOR U.S. EXPATRIATES' COMPENSATION PACKAGES

Most U.S. multinational companies use the balance sheet approach to determine expatriates' compensation packages. The **balance sheet approach** provides expatriates the standard of living they normally enjoy in the United States. Thus, the United States is the standard for all payments.

The balance sheet approach has strategic value to companies for two important reasons. First, this approach protects expatriates' standards of living. Without it, companies would have a difficult time placing qualified employees in international assignments. Second, the balance sheet approach enables companies to control costs because it relies on objective indexes that measure cost differences between the U.S. and foreign countries. We will discuss these indexes shortly.

The use of the balance sheet approach is most appropriate when:

- The home country is an appropriate reference point for economic comparisons.
- Expatriates are likely to maintain psychological and cultural ties with the home or base country.
- Expatriates prefer not to assimilate into the local foreign culture.
- The assignment is of limited duration.
- The assignment following the international assignment will be in the home country.
- The company promises employees that they will not lose financially while on foreign assignment.[5]

Companies that use the balance sheet approach compare the costs of four major expenditures in the United States and the foreign post:

- Housing and utilities
- Goods and services
- Discretionary income
- Taxes

Employees receive allowances whenever the costs in the foreign country exceed the costs in the United States. Allowance amounts vary according to the lifestyle enjoyed in the United States. In general, individuals with higher incomes tend to live in more expensive homes, and they are in better positions to enjoy more expensive goods and services (e.g., designer labels versus off-brand labels). Higher income also means higher taxes.

Where do U.S. companies obtain pertinent information about costs for foreign countries? U.S. companies may rely on three information sources. First, they can rely on expatriates who have spent considerable time on assignment or foreign government contacts. Second, private consulting companies (e.g., Towers Perrin) or research companies (e.g., Bureau of National Affairs) can conduct custom surveys. Third, most U.S. companies consult the *U.S. Department of State Indexes of Living Costs Abroad, Quarters Allowances, and Hardship Differentials,* which is published quarterly. It is the most cost-effective source because it is available at no charge in libraries with government depositories as well as at *www.state.gov.*

Housing and Utilities

Employers provide expatriate employees with **housing and utilities allowances** to cover the difference between housing and utilities costs in the United States and in the foreign

TABLE 15-5 Quarters Allowances, January 2007

Country and City	*Survey Date*	*Eff. Date*	*Currency*	*Number per U.S. $*	*Family Status*	*Less than $50,470*	*$50,470 to $79,114*	*$79,115 and above*
			Exchange Rate			*Annual allowance by family status and salary range*		
Spain: Madrid	May-04	Aug-06	Euro	0.76	Family	31,100	34,500	36,200
					Single	29,900	31,100	35,500
Rota	Jan-06	Aug-06	Euro	0.76	Family	27,600	31,200	31,200
					Single	23,900	27,600	31,200
Seville	Jan-06	May-06	Euro	0.77	Family	16,100	18,000	19,300
					Single	14,300	16,100	18,700
Switzerland: Bern	Feb-05	Nov-06	Franc	1.24	Family	42,800	49,100	50,500
					Single	42,100	42,800	49,100
Geneva	Sep-06	Dec-06	Franc	1.21	Family	55,100	62,700	70,300
					Single	49,600	55,300	62,700
Thailand: Bangkok	Nov-00	Feb-05	Baht	38.5	Family	28,500	33,900	36,600
					Single	25,800	29,800	32,500
Turkey: Adana-Incirlik	Jan-06	May-06	Lira	1.32	Family	18,200	19,900	20,800
					Single	16,500	18,200	20,300
Ankara	Jan-06	May-06	Lira	1.32	Family	22,200	30,800	31,000
					Single	19,900	30,600	30,500
Izmir-Cigli	Oct-01	Feb-05	Lira	1,345,0007	Family	27,900	29,900	31,600
					Single	24,700	27,900	29,900
United Kingdom: Cheltenham	Dec-05	May-06	Pound	0.5164	Family	25,200	35,500	40,700
					Single	22,300	29,800	40,700
Chicksands	Aug-99	Aug-06	Pound	0.5111	Family	19,800	22,100	24,500
					Single	17,900	19,800	22,100
Harrogate	May-06	Aug-06	Pound	0.5111	Family	34,600	39,500	40,300
					Single	31,300	37,200	39,500
Lakenheath	May-06	Aug-06	Pound	0.5111	Family	41,600	45,100	51,100
					Single	40,000	41,600	45,100
London	May-06	Aug-06	Pound	0.5111	Family	59,200	68,900	72,100
					Single	52,600	63,700	68,900
Oxfordshire	Oct-06	Nov-06	Pound	0.5199	Family	30,700	34,900	35,200
					Single	27,800	34,900	34,900

SOURCE: U.S. Department of State. (2007). *The Department of State indexes of living costs abroad, quarters allowances, and hardship differentials—January 2007*. Washington, DC: U.S. Government Printing Office [online]. Available: *www.state.gov*.

post. The U.S. Department of State uses the term **quarters allowances**. Table 15-5 displays pertinent information from the U.S. Department of State's quarters allowances.

The quarters allowances table contains three main sections: the survey date, exchange rate, and the annual allowance by family status and salary range. The survey date is the month when the Office of Allowances received housing expenditure reports.

The exchange rate section includes three pieces of information: effective date, foreign unit, and number per U.S. dollar. We reviewed the concept of exchange rate earlier. It is expressed as the number of foreign currency units given in exchange for U.S. $1. The U.S. Department of State uses the exchange rate to compute the quarters allowances. In Tokyo City, expatriates receive 113 Japanese yen for every U.S. $1 exchanged. They receive 24,273 Mozambique meticals for every U.S. $1.

As the name implies, the section titled "Annual Allowance by Family Status and Salary Range" contains information on family status and salary range. The table distinguishes between singles and families. The term *single* is self-explanatory. In Stuttgart, the quarters allowance is $24,200 for single expatriates with annual incomes of $79,115 and higher. In Tokyo, the allowance is $35,500!

The term *family* refers to two-or-more-person families. Employees with larger families living with them at the foreign posts receive supplements. Families of three or four persons receive a 10 percent supplement, families of five or six persons receive a 20 percent supplement, and families of seven or more persons receive a 30 percent supplement. In Vicenza, Italy, the quarters allowance is $48,360 for a seven-member expatriate family earning at least $79,115 per year (i.e., $37,200 regular family allowance × 1.30—a 30 percent supplement).

Goods and Services

Expatriates receive **goods and services allowances** when the cost of living is higher in that country than it is in the United States. Employers base these allowances on **indexes of living costs abroad**, which compare the costs (U.S. dollars) of representative goods and services (excluding education) expatriates purchase at the foreign location with the cost of comparable goods and services purchased in the Washington, DC, area. The indexes are place-to-place cost comparisons at specific times and currency exchange rates.

Table 15-6 displays pertinent information from the Department of State's "Indexes of Living Costs Abroad" table. The table contains three pertinent sections: the survey date, the exchange rate, and the local index. The survey date represents the month the Department of State received the cost data. Again, we already reviewed the exchange rate concept. The local index is a measure of the cost of living for expatriates at their foreign posts relative to the cost of living in Washington, DC.

The index for Washington, DC, is 100, which represents the base comparison. The local index for Reykjavik, Iceland, is 132. On average, the costs for goods and services in

TABLE 15-6 Indexes of Living Costs Abroad (Washington, DC = 100)

Country and City	Survey Date	Exchange Rate Foreign Unit	Exchange Rate Number Per US $	Local Relative	Local Index	U.S. Government Relative	U.S. Government Index
Albania: Tirana	5/29/03	Lek	124	105	109	97	101
Angola: Luanda	6/24/02	Kwanza	40.24	139	148	120	126
Argentina: Buenos Aires	12/23/02	Peso	3.53	85	83	84	82
Armenia: Yerevan	3/25/02	Dram	570	109	110	92	90
Australia: Canberra	5/27/06	Dollar	1.35	129	130	126	116
Austria: Vienna	2/10/04	Euro	0.77	186	191	150	159
Azerbaijan: Baku	3/28/05	New Manat	4900	132	134	114	116
Bahamas, The: Nassau	3/20/03	Dollar	1	145	146	136	137
Bahrain: Bahrain	12/8/03	Dinar	0.3763	109	120	104	115
Bangladesh: Dhaka	5/16/04	Taka	58	105	112	93	100
Barbados: Barbados	9/12/03	Dollar	2.02	128	132	122	125
Belarus: Minsk	6/5/03	Ruble	2026	129	128	108	107

SOURCE: U.S. Department of State. (2007). *The Department of State indexes of living costs abroad.* Washington, *DC: U.S. Government Printing Office [online]. Available: www.state.gov.*

Reykjavik are 32 percent higher than they are in Washington, DC: $[(132-100)/100] \times 100$. The local index for La Paz, Bolivia, is 96. On average, the costs for goods and services in La Paz are 4 percent lower than they are in Washington, DC: $[(96-100)/100] \times 100$. Companies should provide allowances to compensate for the higher costs in Reykjavik. Allowances are not needed for La Paz because the cost of living is lower there than it is in the United States.

Discretionary Income

Discretionary income covers a variety of financial obligations in the United States for which expatriates remain responsible. These expenditures are usually of a long-term nature. Companies typically do not provide allowances because expatriates remain responsible for them despite international assignments. Table 15-7 lists examples of discretionary income expenditures.

Tax Considerations

All U.S. citizens working overseas for U.S. corporations are subject to the Federal Unemployment Tax Act (FUTA).[6] Expatriates continue to pay U.S. income taxes and Social Security taxes while on assignment. The Internal Revenue Service (IRS) taxes U.S. citizens' income regardless of whether they earn income in the United States or while on foreign assignment.[7] Expatriates must also pay income taxes to local foreign governments based on the applicable income tax laws. Paying taxes to both the U.S. government and foreign governments is known as "double" taxation.[8] The Internal Revenue Code (IRC) includes two rules that enable expatriates to minimize double taxation by reducing their U.S. federal income tax obligations:

Expatriates can minimize double taxation by claiming a tax credit under IRC Section 901. **IRC Section 901** allows expatriates to credit foreign income taxes against the U.S. income tax liability:

- If the U.S. federal income tax is greater than the foreign tax amount, then expatriates need to pay only the difference to the federal government.
- If the foreign tax exceeds the U.S. federal income tax amount, expatriates can apply the foreign tax excess (i.e., the difference between the foreign income tax and the U.S. federal income tax)—as a deduction from future federal taxable income for up to 5 years.

IRC Section 911 permits "eligible" expatriates to exclude as much as $70,000 of foreign-earned income, plus a housing allowance, from taxation. Let's look at the income exclusion and housing allowance elements separately.

TABLE 15-7 Discretionary Income Expenditures

- Pension contributions
- Savings and investments
- Insurance payments
- Equity portion of mortgage payments
- Alimony payments
- Child support
- Student loan payments
- Car payments
- IRC Section 901
- IRC Section 911

TABLE 15-8   Cash and Noncash Income Exclusions: IRC Section 911

Cash
- Bonuses
- Sales commissions
- Incentives
- Professional fees

Noncash
- Housing
- Meals
- Cars
- Allowances for cost-of-living differentials, education, home leave, tax reimbursements, children's education, and moving expenses

Table 15-8 lists specific types of income that are eligible for exclusion under IRC Section 911, which requires that expatriates pay U.S. federal income taxes only on the income amount greater than $70,000. For example, an expatriate whose foreign-earned income totals $150,000 in 2007 must pay taxes on only $70,000 (i.e., $150,000 – $80,000 exclusion).

Employer Considerations: Tax Protection and Tax Equalization

Although IRC Sections 901 and 911 substantially reduce expatriates' double taxation burdens, neither generally eliminates double taxation. Under the balance sheet approach, companies choose between two approaches to provide expatriates tax allowances:

- Tax protection
- Tax equalization

A key element of both tax protection and tax equalization methods is the **hypothetical tax**. Employers calculate the hypothetical tax as the U.S. income tax based on the same salary level, excluding all foreign allowances. Under **tax protection**, employers reimburse expatriates for the difference between the actual income tax amount and the hypothetical tax when the actual income tax amount—based on tax returns filed with the IRS—is greater. Expatriates simply pay the entire income tax bill when the taxes are less than or equal to the hypothetical tax. Expatriates realize a tax benefit whenever actual taxes amount to less than the hypothetical tax because they will have paid lower income taxes on their overseas assignments than on assignments in the United States.

Under **tax equalization**, employers take the responsibility for paying income taxes to the U.S. and foreign governments on behalf of the expatriates. Tax equalization starts with the calculation of the hypothetical tax. Based on this hypothetical tax amount, employers deduct income from expatriates' paychecks that totals the hypothetical tax amounts at year-end. Employers reimburse expatriates for the difference between the hypothetical tax and actual income tax whenever the actual income tax amount is less. Expatriates reimburse their employers whenever the actual income tax amount exceeds the hypothetical income tax amounts.

Tax equalization offers employers two important advantages over tax protection. First, expatriates receive equitable treatment regardless of their location and do not keep the unexpected tax gain from being posted in countries with income tax rates lower than in the United States. As a result, employers should have an easier time motivating expatriates to move from one foreign post to another. In addition, companies save money by not allowing expatriates to keep tax windfalls.

REPATRIATION PAY ISSUES

Special compensation considerations should not end with the completion of international assignments. Effective expatriate compensation programs promote employees' integration into their companies' domestic workforces. Returnees may initially view their domestic assignments as punishment because their total compensation decreases. Upon return, former expatriates forfeit special pay incentives and extended leave allowances. Although most former expatriates understand the purpose of these incentives and allowances, it often takes time for them to adjust to "normal" compensation practices. Many expatriates may not adjust very well to compensation-as-usual because they feel their international experiences have made them substantially more valuable to their employers. Their heightened sense of value may intensify when former expatriates compare themselves with colleagues who have never taken international assignments. Two consequences are likely. First, former expatriates may find it difficult to work collaboratively with colleagues, which can undermine differentiation objectives. Second, strong resentments may lead former expatriates to find employment with competitors. Adding insult to injury, competitors stand to benefit from former expatriates' international experiences.

Companies can actively prevent many of these problems by the following two measures. First, companies should invest in former expatriates' career development. Career development programs signal that companies value returnees. In addition, former expatriates may view their employers' investments in career development as a form of compensation, reducing the equity problems described earlier. Second, companies should capitalize on expatriates' experiences to gain a better understanding of foreign business environments. In addition, former expatriates can contribute to the quality of international assignments by conveying what did and did not work well during their assignments.

SUMMARY

This chapter provided a discussion of international compensation and its strategic role. The globalization of the economy necessitates U.S. companies' investments overseas. Well-designed expatriate compensation programs support strategic initiatives by attracting and maintaining the best performers. Effective expatriate compensation programs reduce risk and promote expatriate families' comfort while they are stationed at foreign posts. The balance sheet approach minimizes financial risk to expatriates, and various incentives and allowances promote comfort. We also discussed that successful expatriate compensation programs facilitate returnees' transition to domestic assignments.

KEY TERMS

- North American Free Trade Agreement, 370
- repatriation, 372
- host country nationals, 372
- third country nationals, 372
- expatriates, 373
- home country–based pay method, 374
- host country–based method, 375
- headquarters-based method, 375
- exchange rate, 375
- inflation, 376

- foreign service premiums, 377
- hardship allowance, 377
- mobility premiums, 378
- relocation assistance payments, 380
- home leave benefits, 381
- rest and relaxation leave benefits, 381
- balance sheet approach, 382
- housing and utilities allowances, 382

- quarters allowances, 383
- goods and services allowances, 384
- indexes of living costs abroad, 384
- discretionary income, 385
- IRC Section 901, 385
- IRC Section 911, 385
- hypothetical tax, 386
- tax protection, 386
- tax equalization, 386

DISCUSSION QUESTIONS

1. Discuss the strengths and weaknesses of the following methods for establishing base pay in international contexts: home country–based pay, headquarters-based pay, and host country–based pay.
2. For a country of your choice, conduct research into the cultural characteristics that you believe should be important considerations in establishing a core compensation program for a U.S. company that plans to locate there. Discuss these characteristics. Discuss as well whether you feel that pay-for-performance programs are compatible. If compatible in any way, what course of action would you take to promote this compatibility?
3. Discuss your reaction to the following statement: "U.S. companies should increase base pay (beyond the level that would be paid in the United States) to motivate employees to accept foreign assignments."
4. Allowances and reimbursements for international assignments are costly. Should companies avoid international business activities? Explain your answer. If you answer *no*, what can companies do to minimize costs?
5. Of the many reimbursements and allowances that U.S. companies make for employees who take foreign assignments, which one is the most essential? Discuss your reasons.

EXERCISES

Compensation Online

For Students

Exercise 1: Find relevant articles

An HR professional is coming to speak to your class about global HR issues. Your course instructor has asked a few students to do some basic research so that the discussion can be livelier and more productive. He has asked you to research compensation issues specifically. Use your school library's online catalog to locate articles pertaining to expatriates, repatriation, multinational corporations, international compensation, and global competition. Find and read several current articles in these areas.

Exercise 2: Search for latest news on international benefits

While preparing for the speaker to come to your class, you found many interesting articles and wondered what the latest developments were on certain issues. Using the Bureau of Labor Statistics Web site at *www.bls.gov,* click on the News Releases link. Under the International Programs heading, click on one of the links. Read the article and write a brief summary of the information it contained and how it relates to the textbook information.

Exercise 3: Research employee resources

Because you are currently looking for a job, or will be soon enough, use Yahoo! to search for "expat" or "expatriate." Visit resulting sites such as *www.expatexchange.com.* If you had the opportunity to work as an expatriate at some foreign location, how could these sites help you?

For Professionals

Exercise 1: Devise a repatriation package

As a compensation professional, sometimes you need to look at a situation from the employee's point of view. Using the Web site at *www.insiders.com/relocation/,* devise cost-effective ways the company can ease the repatriation shock for an employee and his or her family returning from an assignment.

Exercise 2: Research income tax laws for expatriates

The federal income tax responsibilities for multinational corporations and their American employees who work overseas can be confusing. Your company is about to send some of your colleagues to France, Spain, and Germany. Go the IRS Web site to get a better understanding of the tax laws that pertain to working overseas: *www.irs.gov.* Scroll down the Web page and click on the Individuals link. Click on the Overseas Taxpayers link. Review the information and write a brief summary on what you learned by accessing this site. Did you find this site helpful? What did you learn by reviewing this site that you did not know?

Exercise 3: Research global HR services

Your firm's HR staff is already spread too thin and is not growing fast enough to keep up with the global expansion of the firm as a whole. Expatriate and repatriation issues are not being handled to the satisfaction of either the employees or management. It has been decided to outsource some of these functions to make the experience more worthwhile for everyone involved. Use the Search Yahoo!, Business and Economy, and Business to Business sections to find organizations that provide services such as cross-culture training or repatriation services either to expatriates themselves or to your organization.

ENDNOTES

1. Quotation excerpted from WorldatWork Web site, *Companies are leveraging international assignments to better compete globally* [online]; *www.worldatwork.org,* accessed July 7, 2007.

2. Munn, G. G., Garcia, F. L., & Woelfel, C. J. (1991). *Encyclopedia of Banking and Finance.* Chicago: St. James Press.

3. Bureau of National Affairs (2002). Expatriate pay. *Compensation and benefits* (CD-ROM). Washington, DC: Author.

4. Horn, M. E. (1992). *International Employee Benefits: An Overview.* Brookfield, WI: International Foundation of Employee Benefit Plans.

5. Sheridan, W. R., & Hansen, P. T. (1996). Linking international business and expatriate compensation strategies. *American Compensation Association Journal,* Spring, pp. 66–81.

6. *Internal Revenue Code,* Section 306(c), paragraph 3306(j).

7. Kates, S. M., & Spielman, C. (1995). Reducing the cost of sending employees overseas. *Practical Accountant, 28,* pp. 50–55.

8. Ibid.

CHAPTER 16

*Pay and Benefits Outside the United States**

Chapter Outline

Learning Objectives

In this chapter, you will learn about

1. Differences between pay and benefits in the United States and around the world.

2. Consideration of the regulations that influence pay and benefits.

3. Statutory minimum wage rates and competitive market pay rates.

4. Paid time off benefits in various continents and countries.

5. Protection benefits such as retirement, health care, and social security in various continents and countries.

*Written with the assistance of Ms. Niti Pandey, Institute of Labor and Industrial Relations, University of Illinois at Urbana-Champaign.

6. Legal and regulatory influences on employee benefits practices.

7. Other practices that distinguish countries benefits programs.

> Great companies often are defined by the vibrancy of their leadership, the effectiveness of their organization and their success in motivating their people resources. Keeping these variables on course is a challenge for almost any company, regardless of size and complexity. But for companies that operate across borders, these issues can be more unsettling than a chronic case of jet lag.
>
> Never before in history has the phrase "think globally, act locally" been more appropriate than it is today. Increased global expansion is presenting enormous challenges for the human resources executive. As companies grow geographically, they confront issues beyond the localization of products, managing exchange risks, and politics and culture. Becoming global places demand on HR systems and infrastructure—understanding global capabilities, managing a mobile talent pool and ensuring legal compliance everywhere becomes a critical challenge for which many companies are ill prepared.[1]

The current state of globalization has resulted in a high level of interconnections between the economies of various parts of the world. U.S. employers will increasingly conduct business with entities in a variety of other countries as former underdeveloped parts of the world experience tremendous economic, trade, and standard of living growth. In addition, the move from traditional manufacturing to knowledge- and service-based employment also means that jobs as well as markets are more likely to be dispersed geographically. As the need for employers to interact globally increases, HR management professionals are going to have increased opportunities to develop compensation and benefits programs for U.S. employees in foreign assignments, as well as for indigenous employees in foreign offices of the parent company.

It is essential that compensation professionals know the basic legal employment context and the minimum statutory employment standards of the country where they propose to do business, just as we've discussed throughout this book for U.S. employment (e.g., recall the Fair Labor Standards Act of 1938 and the Employee Retirement Income Security Act of 1974). After that, compensation professionals may consider the norms for competitive pay and benefits needed to attract the desired talent.

In this chapter we will provide a glimpse of the wide variation in compensation and benefits practices across several regions of the world as listed in the chapter outline.

We will start off each review with a brief treatment of governmental structure, norms, and historical events that help shed light on pay and benefits. For each country listed in the chapter outline, we will peruse statutory minimum wage rates. Next, we will consider such basic benefits issues as paid time off, protection programs (including, retirement, health care), and stand-out benefits in particular regions. We will note where such protection programs as retirement and health care are required by the government or offered at the discretion of the employer.

It is important to note that many other governments do not regularly assess pay levels in their economies, which stands in stark contrast to the wealth of data provided regularly on U.S. markets (Chapter 8). The U.S. Bureau of Labor Statistics, however, regularly compares the hourly compensation costs (wage, excluding benefits costs) for production workers in several countries. Tables 16-1 shows the costs expressed in U.S. dollars. For example, in 2005, the hourly cost to pay a production worker expressed in U.S. dollars was $4.07. Table 16-2 shows the relative hourly cost with the United States as the reference point, expressed as 100. For example, in 2005, the Brazil index was 17.

TABLE 16-1 Hourly Compensation Costs for Production Workers in U.S. Dollars

Country or Area	1992	1993	1994	1995	1996	1997	1998	1999	2000	2001	2002	2003	2004	2005
United States	15.95	16.37	16.78	17.17	17.74	18.20	18.52	18.90	19.65	20.52	21.33	22.20	22.82	23.65
Brazil	..	..	..	..	5.76	5.77	5.49	3.39	3.50	2.97	2.57	2.74	3.15	4.09
Canada	17.57	16.97	16.29	16.50	17.04	16.83	15.93	16.10	16.48	16.23	16.72	19.53	21.77	23.82
Mexico	2.16	2.36	2.74	1.70	1.63	1.73	1.65	1.81	2.07	2.34	2.49	2.44	2.44	2.63
Australia	13.23	12.62	14.13	15.36	17.02	16.71	15.11	15.92	14.40	13.32	15.38	19.79	23.38	24.91
Hong Kong Sar (1,2)	3.91	4.28	4.60	4.80	5.12	5.38	5.40	5.37	5.45	5.74	5.66	5.54	5.51	5.65
Israel	8.11	7.86	8.19	9.41	10.11	10.79	10.85	10.57	11.41	12.17	11.00	11.62	12.01	12.42
Japan	16.13	18.86	20.98	23.47	20.44	18.98	17.62	20.44	21.93	19.35	18.60	20.26	21.84	21.76
Korea, Republic of	5.21	5.63	6.38	7.28	8.21	7.85	5.67	7.36	8.23	7.72	8.77	9.69	11.13	13.56
New Zealand	8.05	8.06	9.09	10.35	11.32	11.32	9.38	9.45	8.38	7.97	9.10	11.69	13.65	14.97
Singapore	4.85	5.15	6.16	7.57	8.16	8.02	7.36	6.96	7.18	6.97	6.71	7.18	7.38	7.66
Sri Lanka	0.40	0.42	0.45	0.48	0.48	0.46	0.47	0.46	0.48	0.45	0.49	0.51	0.52	..
Taiwan	5.12	5.16	5.51	5.99	5.98	6.09	5.39	5.78	6.19	6.05	5.64	5.69	5.98	6.38
Austria	20.24	20.11	21.49	25.26	24.75	21.88	22.08	21.63	19.14	19.09	20.71	25.51	28.53	29.42
Belgium	20.51	20.16	21.93	25.67	25.26	22.28	22.62	22.14	20.13	19.84	21.77	26.55	30.01	30.79
Czech Republic	..	..	..	2.63	3.10	2.79	2.99	2.93	2.83	3.13	3.83	4.72	5.45	6.11
Denmark	20.55	19.77	21.12	25.28	25.43	23.48	24.07	24.46	21.87	22.07	24.31	30.22	34.46	35.47
Finland	20.06	16.74	19.21	24.31	23.59	21.47	21.83	21.50	19.44	19.85	21.78	27.10	30.67	31.93
France	17.31	16.46	17.10	19.26	18.99	17.10	17.32	17.00	15.46	15.65	17.13	21.14	23.89	24.63
Germany	..	23.89	25.33	30.10	29.58	25.96	25.17	24.57	22.67	22.47	24.22	29.64	32.50	33.00
Greece	7.66	7.22	7.68	9.07	9.46	9.08	8.80	..	..	..	..	..	..	..
Hungary	..	..	2.71	2.69	2.73	2.73	2.80	2.83	2.79	3.16	3.92	4.76	5.63	6.07
Ireland	13.25	12.02	12.54	13.75	14.11	13.80	13.68	13.77	12.72	13.60	15.26	19.09	21.94	22.76
Italy	18.91	15.38	15.40	15.69	17.10	16.06	15.83	15.55	13.84	13.61	14.75	18.11	20.48	21.05
Luxembourg	18.29	18.16	19.99	23.56	22.56	19.75	19.69	19.61	17.51	17.21	18.71	23.12	26.57	27.68
Netherlands	20.01	19.98	20.88	24.03	23.10	20.73	21.29	21.35	19.33	19.85	22.12	27.47	30.76	31.81
Norway	23.48	20.59	21.40	24.84	25.46	24.12	24.43	24.73	22.56	23.51	27.93	32.73	36.41	39.14
Poland	..	..	..	..	..	2.79	3.00	2.89	2.81	3.19	3.29	3.52	3.85	4.54
Portugal	4.88	4.26	4.36	5.09	5.33	5.13	5.20	5.06	4.49	4.59	5.07	6.24	7.02	7.33
Spain	13.39	11.49	11.39	12.70	13.33	12.07	11.94	11.92	10.65	10.78	11.95	15.01	17.14	17.78
Sweden	24.48	17.52	18.63	21.68	24.35	22.19	22.02	21.62	20.18	18.39	20.23	25.19	28.42	28.73
Switzerland	22.95	22.36	24.61	28.90	27.94	23.85	24.04	23.22	20.95	21.53	23.77	27.78	30.21	30.50
United Kingdom	14.29	12.48	12.97	13.79	14.12	15.68	16.97	17.33	16.84	16.85	18.36	21.33	24.76	25.66

(1) Hong Kong Special Administrative Region of China.
(2) Average of selected manufacturing industries.
SOURCE: U.S. Bureau of Labor Statistcs, April 2007.

TABLE 16-2 Hourly Compensation Costs For Production Workers: Index U.S. = 100

Country or Area	1992	1993	1994	1995	1996	1997	1998	1999	2000	2001	2002	2003	2004	2005
United States...........	100	100	100	100	100	100	100	100	100	100	100	100	100	100
Brazil.................	..	..	..	..	32	32	30	18	18	14	12	12	14	17
Canada.................	110	104	97	96	96	93	86	85	84	79	78	88	95	101
Mexico.................	14	14	16	10	9	10	9	10	11	11	12	11	11	11
Australia..............	83	77	84	89	96	92	82	84	73	65	72	89	102	105
Hong Kong Sar (1, 2)....	25	26	27	28	29	30	29	28	28	28	27	25	24	24
Israel.................	51	48	49	55	57	59	59	56	58	59	52	52	53	53
Japan..................	101	115	125	137	115	104	95	108	112	94	87	91	96	92
Korea, Republic of......	33	34	38	42	46	43	31	39	42	38	41	44	49	57
New Zealand............	50	49	54	60	64	62	51	50	43	39	43	53	60	63
Singapore..............	30	31	37	44	46	44	40	37	37	34	31	32	32	32
Sri Lanka..............	3	3	3	3	3	3	3	2	2	2	2	2	2	..
Taiwan.................	32	32	33	35	34	33	29	31	32	30	26	26	26	27
Austria................	127	123	128	147	139	120	119	114	97	93	97	115	125	124
Belgium................	129	123	131	149	142	122	122	117	102	97	102	120	132	130
Czech Republic.........	..	..	..	15	17	15	16	16	14	15	18	21	24	26
Denmark................	129	121	126	147	143	129	130	129	111	108	114	136	151	150
Finland................	126	102	114	142	133	118	118	114	99	97	102	122	134	135
France.................	109	101	102	112	107	94	94	90	79	76	80	95	105	104
Germany................	..	146	151	175	167	143	136	130	115	109	114	134	142	140
Greece.................	48	44	46	53	53	50	48	..	..	..	..	..	..	..
Hungary................	..	..	16	16	15	15	15	15	14	15	18	21	25	26
Ireland................	83	73	75	80	80	76	74	73	65	66	72	86	96	96
Italy..................	119	94	92	91	96	88	85	82	70	66	69	82	90	89
Luxembourg.............	115	111	119	137	127	109	106	104	89	84	88	104	116	117
Netherlands............	125	122	124	140	130	114	115	113	98	97	104	124	135	135
Norway.................	147	126	128	145	143	133	132	131	115	115	131	147	160	166
Poland.................	..	..	..	..	..	15	16	15	14	16	15	16	17	19
Portugal...............	31	26	26	30	30	28	28	27	23	22	24	28	31	31
Spain..................	84	70	68	74	75	66	64	63	54	53	56	68	75	75
Sweden.................	153	107	111	126	137	122	119	114	103	90	95	113	125	121
Switzerland............	144	137	147	168	157	131	130	123	107	105	111	125	132	129
United Kingdom.........	90	76	77	80	80	86	92	92	86	82	86	96	109	109

(1) Hong Kong Special Administrative Region of China.
(2) Average of selected manufacturing industries.
SOURCE: U.S. Bureau of Labor Statistics, April 2007.

This means that hourly compensation costs in Brazil were 83 percent less than in the United States $(17-100/100) \times 100$ percent. In Canada, the costs were just 1 percent more than in the United States $(101-100/100) \times 100$ percent.

NORTH AMERICA

This section takes a brief glance at the employment relationship and employee benefits in Mexico and Canada. Both countries and the United States are part of a trade bloc known as **NAFTA—the North Atlantic Free Trade Agreement**. According to the Office of the United States Trade Representative, formed as of January 1, 1994, NAFTA called for the elimination of duties and the phasing out of tariffs over a period of 14 years.[2] Trade restrictions were removed under NAFTA from such industries as motor vehicles and automotive parts, computers, textiles, and agriculture. In addition, the treaty also delineated the removal of investment restrictions between the three countries. As a result of supplemental agreements signed in 1993, worker and environmental protection provisions were added.

The labor side of NAFTA is the **North American Agreement on Labor Cooperation (NAALC)**. This was created in order to promote cooperation between trade unions and social organizations in order to champion improved labor conditions.[3] Although there has definitely been a convergence of labor standards in North America as a result of NAALC, there has not been a convergence in employment, productivity, or salary trends.[4] Overall, NAFTA is reported as having been good for Mexico, which saw a fall in poverty rates and a rise in real income as a result of the trade agreement.[5] This section will present a brief overview of the employment relationship in Canada and Mexico and some basic employee benefits required by law in these countries.

Canada

According to the Central Intelligence Agency (CIA) World Factbook, Canada is a constitutional monarchy that is also a parliamentary democracy and a federation consisting of 10 provinces and 3 territories.[6] With a **per capita gross domestic product (GDP)** of $35,200 and 17.59 million labor force, the Canadian economy is very similar to that of the United States' market-based economy. Even though Canada has enjoyed a trade surplus and balanced budgets for many years, recent concern and debate has grown over the increasing cost of the publicly funded health care system, as we noted in Chapter 5.

As an important aside, the gross domestic product describes the size of a country's economy. Size is expressed as the market value of all final goods and services produced within the country over a specified period. The GDP is typically calculated by the country's national statistical agency. GDP per capita generally indicates the standard of living within a country: the larger the per capita GDP, presumably the better is the standard of living. Table 16-3 lists per capital GDP for the countries reviewed in this chapter. The United States clearly shows the largest per capita GDP whereas India reports the lowest amount. These differences are evident in the extent of government-sponsored benefits offered in those countries.

Employment law researchers report that the basic rule of Canadian law holds that labor and employment law fall within the exclusive jurisdiction of the provinces.[7] Thus, both individual and collective employment relationships are controlled at the province level. Federal legislation cannot override provincial laws, even when the industry or employer primarily conducts business overseas (except in the cases where the industries are expressly assigned to federal jurisdiction). The origins of the common law governing individual employment contracts are in the **English Statute of Laboureres** of 1562, which established working hours and wages. This statute was

TABLE 16-3 Per Capita Expenditures by Country

Country	Per Capita GDP ($)	Labor Force Size (millions)
United States of America	43,500	151.4
Canada	35,200	17.59
Mexico	10,600	38.09
Brazil	8,600	96.34
Argentina	15,000	15.35
France	30,100	27.88
Germany	31,400	43.66
Italy	29,700	24.63
Poland	14,100	17.26
Russia	12,100	73.88
People's Republic of China	7,600	798
South Korea	24,200	23.77
India	3,700	509.3

SOURCE: *www.cia.gov* (The Central Intelligence Agency World Factbook) 2006 estimates.

eventually repealed in the early nineteenth century, but it became part of the English common law and later became part of the common law governing all the provinces other than Quebec. Quebec has the **Civil Code of Quebec,** which came into effect in 1866. A modernized version of the Civil Code came into effect on January 1, 1994.

Wage and Salary[8]

Canada does possess a statutory minimum wage law. At the federal level, there is an obligation placed upon provincial governments to establish minimum rates of pay by or under an act of the legislature. The jurisdiction defined by province determines the minimum hourly rate. New Brunswick, Alberta, and Newfoundland currently have the lowest minimum wage rate in Canada (i.e., $7.00). The highest rate (i.e., $8.50) can be found in Nunavut.

Paid Time Off Benefits

Canadian employment law holds that employees are entitled to between 8 and 9 annual paid holidays as well as 2 weeks paid vacation time along with a sum of money as vacation pay (increasing to 3 weeks after 6 years of employment).[9] The amount of vacation pay is equal to 2 percent of an employee's pay for the preceding year per week of vacation. There are slight variations from province to province. Maternity and paternity leave provisions are coordinated under the Federal Employment Insurance Act. Employees are eligible for a total of 17 weeks' benefits during pregnancy and after childbirth. The Canadian government most recently introduced compassionate care leave, which provides 8 weeks of unpaid leave to care for a seriously ill family member. For the purposes of this leave, family members include spouse, common law partner, children, and parents.[10] No laws require the granting of time off for military service.

Protection Benefits

Pensions and Retirement Benefits Canada has two state pension plans: one for Quebec residents only and one for the rest of Canada. Both plans are funded by matching contributions from employers and employees and both are fully portable upon employment changes, much like 401(k) plans in the United States.[11] In addition to the public plans, many employers provide supplementary pension plans that are regulated by provincial or federal legislation that establishes minimum funding standards, specifies the types of investments that the plans may make, and deals with such matters as portability, benefit vesting, and locking-in contributions. Employers frequently have different plans for executive, managerial, and other employees.

Health and Disability Benefits Medical and basic hospital care in Canada is paid for by provincial medical insurance plans with compulsory coverage for all residents and funding revenue derived from both general federal taxation and from provincial taxes.[12] Even though public health plans normally do not provide employed persons with prescription drugs except while they are hospitalized, additional benefits are provided by private supplementary insurance by employers, including dental and vision care. Employers also provide long- and short-term disability benefits for sickness or injury as part of a benefits package.[13] Canada's per capita expenditure on health (the sum of Public Health Expenditure and Private Expenditure on Health) as of 2003 at the international dollar rates was $2,989.[14]

Mexico

Mexico is a federal republic[15] and Mexican labor law is based on the Constitution of the United States of Mexico, adopted in January 1917.[16] The CIA World Factbook reports that Mexico's labor force is about 38 million and its per capita GDP is $10,600.[17] A free-market economy is composed of a mix of new and old industry as well as agriculture, which are both increasingly becoming dominated by the private sector. The "**Labor and Social Security**" article of the constitution is still in effect.[18] Employment relationships in Mexico fall under the Federal Labor Law, which was last revised in January 1997 and clearly defines the terms *worker* and *employer* for the purpose of individual employment. Some of the employee benefits ensured under federal jurisdiction in Mexico will be discussed shortly.

Wage and Salary

The Mexican government requires that two minimum wage rates be applied. The first, general minimum wage, applies to all workers and the amount depends upon the region of the country. For instance, the minimum wage in Geographic area C was 46 pesos per day in 2007. The rate was only slightly higher in Geographic area A.

The second is the occupational minimum wages that are higher than the general minimum wages. Much as it is in the U.S. General Schedule (Chapter 4), occupations that require greater skill, knowledge, and experience are compensated at higher rates.

Paid Time Off Benefits

Mexican employment laws stipulate certain paid time off benefits for all employees, as reported in publications on international employment laws.[19] Workers are entitled to paid time off during public holidays, and workers required to work during a mandatory holiday are entitled to double pay. Female employees are entitled to maternity leave (i.e., 6 weeks' leave prior to giving birth and 6 weeks' leave after birth on full salary). Maternity leave can also be extended with half pay for as long as necessary and does not affect seniority rights. Employees are entitled to six vacation days after being employed for 1 year and to two more days for each subsequent year, up to a maximum of 12 days. As of the fifth year, the worker is entitled to 14 days' vacation and for each additional group of 5 years two more vacation days are added. Employers must pay workers a vacation premium equivalent to 25 percent of the salary earned during scheduled vacation days; vacations must be taken on the date indicated by the employer, within the 6 months following the end of the work year.

Protection Benefits

Social Security Social security programs in Mexico are administered by the Mexican Social Security Institute, which protects employees in the matters of occupational accidents and illnesses, maternity, sicknesses, incapacitation, old age, retirement, and survivor pensions, day care for children of insured workers, and social services.[20] The system is financed by contributions from workers, employers, and the government, with contributions based on salary levels, and with workers earning minimum salary exempt from making contributions, whereas employers bear the bulk of the contributions to the different insurance funds.[21]

The benefits for employees are laid out as follows.[22] Workers with at least 52 weeks' worth of payments into the system who withdraw are entitled to continue making voluntary payments. Should they return to salaried employment again, they may return to the system and maintain all benefits, which may be in cash or in kind. Cash benefits take the form of transfer payments in the early stages of illness or incapacitation, depending on the medical condition and its effects on work and pensions. In-kind benefits take the form of medical attention, including surgery and medicines, hospitalization services, and so forth.

Pensions and Retirement Benefits   The U.S. Social Security Administration (SSA) Office of Policy reports that as of July 1, 1997, all workers must join the mandatory individual account system, slowly replacing the former social insurance system.[23] At retirement, employees covered by the social insurance system before 1997 can choose to receive benefits from either the social insurance system or from the mandatory individual account system.

Health Benefits   Medical services are normally provided directly to patients (including old-age pensioners covered by the 1997 law) through the health facilities of the Mexican Social Security Institute.[24] Benefits include general and specialist care, surgery, maternity care, hospitalization or care in a convalescent home, medicines, laboratory services, dental care, and appliances, and are payable for 52 weeks, but may in some cases be extended to 104 weeks.[25] In addition, the wife of an insured man also receives postnatal benefits in kind, and medical services are provided for dependent children up to age 16 (age 25 if a student, no limit if disabled).[26] Mexico's per capita expenditure on health (sum of Public Health Expenditure and Private Expenditure on Health) at the international dollar rate was $582 as of 2003.[27]

Other Benefits[28]   A national system of worker housing exists paid for by employer contributions in the form of payroll tax fixed at 5 percent and helps workers obtain sufficient credit for the acquisition of housing. Workers not employed after age 50 are entitled to receive the full balance of contributions made in their name to the housing fund.

SOUTH AMERICA

According to the International Monetary Fund's World Economic Outlook Database, Brazil, Argentina, Colombia, and Chile are the largest economies in South America.[29] Venezuela and Peru are experiencing economic development as well. On the other hand, Argentina, Chile, and Uruguay have the best human development index (HDI—a comparative measure of life expectancy, literacy, and standard of living measured by the United Nations),[30] and Venezuela has large oil reserves that have turned the nation into an important player in world trade. The biggest trade bloc in South America used to be Mercosur, or the Southern Common Market, which was composed of Argentina, Brazil, Paraguay, Uruguay, and Venezuela as the main members, and Bolivia, Chile, Colombia, Ecuador, and Peru as associate states.[31] The second-biggest trade bloc was the Andean Community of Nations, made up of Bolivia, Colombia, Ecuador, Peru, Venezuela, and Chile.[32] These two trade blocs merged as of a declaration signed on December 8, 2004, at the Third South American Summit, and they formed one large trade bloc known as the South American Community of Nations, which plans to model itself on the European Union.[33] This section will take a brief look at the two largest economies in the potentially formidable global economic bloc, Brazil and Argentina.

Brazil

The CIA World Factbook reports that Brazil is a federal republic with a 96.34 million strong workforce and a per capita GDP of $8,600, and that Brazil's economy is by far the strongest in South America. This country has a well-developed mining, manufacturing, agricultural, and services sector and is increasingly taking on a larger share of global trade and work.[34] The *Consolidation of Labor Laws (Consolidacao das Leis do Trabalho)* accords many employee benefits the status of fundamental constitutional rights and in general the employment relationship in Brazil is generally highly regulated by statute.[35] For example, Brazilian law states that any and all benefits habitually granted by the employer, whether expressly or tacitly, are considered part of the employee's salary for all legal purposes and cannot be abolished. The status of employment contracts is based on the country's legal principal of continuity. This principal applies to all employment contracts, written and oral; however, in practice, employers discharge employees arbitrarily because there is a substantial supply of readily available workers who are willing to accept lower pay.[36] There simply is not enough incentive provided for employers to engage in good faith labor relations. Job security is also often lacking for most employees.[37]

Wage and Salary

Brazil does impose a minimum wage. In accordance with the Federal Constitution, the minimum wage rate is nationally uniform and set by law. The minimum wage is fixed by a provisional measure, namely an act of the executive having the force of law, in accordance with Article 62 of the Federal Constitution and placed before Congress for conversion into law. In 2005, this wage was 350 R$ (Reais) per month ($US 143.44—2005).

Protection Benefits

Social Security   The social security system that went into effect in 1991 details various benefits for workers in Brazil.[38] Comprehensive social security benefits are provided by law to all workers regarding retirement for illness, old age, or length of service; death benefit pensions; assistance during imprisonment of worker; savings fund; social services; professional rehabilitation assistance; work accident payments; maternity leave payments; family salary support; accident insurance; and sick leave benefits.

Pensions   The U.S. SSA Office of Policy reports that social insurance is provided to employed persons in industry, commerce, and agriculture, domestic servants, some categories of casual workers, elected civil servants, and the self-employed.[39] There is also voluntary coverage for students, housewives, the unemployed and other categories, as well as a special system for public-sector employees and military personnel. The monthly benefit is equal to 70 percent of average earnings plus 1 percent of average earnings for each year of contributions, up to a maximum of 100 percent. Employees contribute between 7.65 percent and 11 percent of gross earnings, and voluntary contributors and members of cooperatives contribute 20 percent of declared earnings. These contributions also finance sickness and maternity benefits and family allowances.

Employers are required to contribute 20 percent of payroll (22.5 percent of payroll for employers in the financial sector), 15 percent of earnings for work cooperatives, 12 percent of payroll on behalf of domestic workers, and 2.7 percent of earnings for rural employers. There are no maximum monthly earnings for contribution purposes. Small-enterprise employers may contribute from 1.2 percent to 4.3 percent of monthly declared earnings, depending on annual earnings declared in the last year.

Health Benefits   In Brazil, medical services are provided directly to patients in rural and urban areas through the Unified Health System, and they include such benefits as general, specialist, maternity, and dental care; hospitalization; medicines (some cost sharing is required), and necessary transportation.[40] Brazil's per capita expenditure on health (sum of Public Health Expenditure and Private Expenditure on Health) as of 2003 at the international dollar rate was $597.[41]

Argentina

The World Factbook of the CIA reports that Argentina, a democratic republic, enjoys an economy that benefits from high education and rich natural resources.[42] With a current per capita GDP of $15,000 and a labor force of 15.35 million, Argentina suffered economic decline and depression in the 1990s, which is a huge fall from being one of the world's wealthiest countries 100 years ago. With various successive governments trying to revive the economy with IMF aid and measures to cut the fiscal deficit it was finally the president in 2002 that devalued the peso compared with the dollar (and froze utility tariffs, curtailed creditors' rights, and imposed high taxes on exports) and helped the economy rebound strongly. Real GDP has been growing at 9 percent annually since 2003. The employment relationship is governed by the Employment Contract Law, and employees in Argentina are entitled to various statutory protections.[43]

Wage and Salary

Among other things, the National Council for Employment, Productivity, and the Adjustable Minimum Living Wage (NCEPAMLW) periodically determines, among other things, the adjustable minimum wage. There is one general minimum wage rate applicable to all workers; however, home workers and domestic workers have specific minimum wage rates. Home workers' pay is determined by the Ministry of Labour and Social Security Resolution, which can set the wage rate lower than the general minimum wage for other workers. In 2007, the general minimum wage was 800.00 pesos per month.

Paid Time Off Benefits[44]

Employees are entitled to 14 days of paid annual vacation when seniority does not exceed 5 years, 21 days when seniority is between 5 and 10 years, 28 days for between 10 and 20 years, and 35 days for more than 20 years. Employees are also entitled to between 3 and 6 months of sick leave based on seniority. Female employees are entitled to maternity leave for 45 days before birth and 45 days after birth and the employee is entitled to cash benefits paid out by the social security funds. All employees are entitled to short leaves of absence for familial events or for examinations. There are 11 national paid holidays, but employers have the discretion to choose whether to grant some of them.

Protection Benefits

Pensions   There is a mandatory retirement and pension system, and all employees must be covered by the social security system.[45] The U.S. SSA Office of Policy reports that both employees and employers are required to pay into the system as a percentage of employee's gross wages (i.e., 11 percent of gross earnings if opting for social insurance only; 7 percent of earnings, including an average 1.27 percent of gross earnings for disability and survivor insurance, and an average 1.25 percent of gross earnings for administrative fees, if opting into the individual account system).[46]

Voluntary contributions are the same as those for the insured person. The employer makes 10.17 percent or 12.71 percent of payroll, according to the type of enterprise. (Additional contributions are made on behalf of workers in hazardous or unhealthy occupations.)

Health Benefits　Employee health insurance is mandated by statute, and the cost of health insurance is financed by a 3 percent employee contribution and a 6 percent employer contribution, based on gross salary. Employers must also hire and pay the premium for collective life insurance in favor of employees.[47] The SSA reports the following about the workers' medical benefits.[48] Benefits include medical, hospital, dental, and palliative care; rehabilitation; prostheses; and transportation. Benefits are defined by the schedule in law issued by the Ministry of Health and Environment. Pharmaceutical products for chronic diseases are either free or require a 30 percent co-payment; 60 percent for other diseases. Pharmaceutical products are free during pregnancy, childbirth, and for postnatal care; for the child until age 1; and in cases of hospitalization. Argentina's per capita expenditure on health (sum of Public Health Expenditure and Private Expenditure on Health) as of 2003 at the international dollar rate was $1,067.[49]

EUROPE

The **European Union (EU)** is a unique international organization that aims at becoming an economic superpower, while still retaining such quintessential European practices as high levels of employment, social welfare protection, and strong trade unions.[50] Even though the EU has its own legal powers and performs executive, legislative, and judicial functions like any other governing body, it has limited authority in the area of labor and employment laws. Although the EU does not attempt to harmonize the employment laws of Member States, under the laws of all **Member States** employers must provide employees with a written document about the terms of the employment contract. The concept of "employment at will" does not exist in the EU as it does in the United States. The EU makes use of Directives and Community Legislations to ensure that some minimum standards are adopted by member states. All member states either have specific legislation or unfair dismissal or general civil code provisions that apply to termination of employment contracts. They all provide employers with a substantive basis for challenging employment dismissal and procedural mechanisms for adjudicating claims.[51]

The EU Web site reports that community labor law was designed with the aim of ensuring that the creation of the single market did not result in a lowering of labor standards or distortions in competition.[52] It has also been increasingly called upon, however, to play a key role in making it easier for the EU to adapt to evolving forms of work organization. On the basis of article 137 of the treaty, the Community shall support and complement the activities of the Member States in the area of social policy. In particular, it defines minimum requirements at the EU level in the fields of working and employment conditions, and with regard to the information and consultation of workers. Improving living and working conditions in Member States depends on national legislation, but also to a large extent on agreements concluded by the social partners at all levels (i.e., country, sector, and company). This section will briefly present some of the basic employee benefits practices in the EU Member States of France, Germany, and Italy. In addition, the practices in Russia will also be examined even though Russia is not a member of the EU.

France

According to the CIA World Factbook, France, a democratic republic, is currently transitioning to greater reliance on market mechanism from the traditional model in which government ownership and intervention were strongly featured.[53] France's per capita GDP is $30,100 and labor force is 27.88 million. The government has recently given up stakes in such large companies as Air France, Renault, and Thales, while still maintaining a strong presence in public transport and defense. The population, however, has resisted reforms targeted at labor market flexibility. In addition, with the highest tax burden in Europe at nearly half the GDP, the French economy is slacking off.

A compendium on international labor and employment laws reports that with a 35-hour-long workweek and 5 weeks of paid vacations, French workers typically get better benefits than do their U.S. counterparts.[54] Employment laws are incorporated in the **French Labor Code (*Code du Travail*)** and reflect the social-democratic ideology that has guided the employment relationship. Such features as mandatory profit sharing and greater employee participation in management, as well as **"just cause dismissal"** (as opposed to **"employment at will"**), make French employment relationships different from the United States.

Wage and Salary

France does have a minimum wage. The minimum wage applies to all salaried workers, including those working in both the public and private businesses of an industrial or commercial nature. The minimum wage applies to workers in commercial and industrial professions, agricultural professions utilizing salaried workers as defined in the Rural Code, liberal professions, home workers, domestic workers, doormen, nursery school assistants, union personnel, personnel in insurance companies and social security companies that are not public bodies, and personnel in associations or organizations governed by private law regardless of their make up or objectives. In 2005, the wage was set at EUR 8.03 per hour ($US 9.96).

Paid Time Off Benefits[55]

French law grants every employee the right to minimum 5 weeks paid leave after 1 year of employment. Employees are paid during statutory holidays. The only mandatory public holiday in France is Labor Day (May 1) and employees who work on this day must be paid double time. Paid vacation cannot exceed 24 working days; the period of vacation is decided by the employer after consultation with employee representatives or based on mutual agreement. Paid leave cannot be replaced by a cash payment. Employees between the ages of 18 and 21 receive an additional benefit of a 30-day annual leave regardless of the time they have served in a company. Maternity leave is provided to female employees at a minimum of 16 weeks, at least 10 weeks of which should be after a child is born. The employer has no legal obligation to pay an employee during maternity leave. Following a mother's return to work, the employer will grant the employee an interview to help place her in equivalent activity. Companies must provide employees with at least 24 months' employment, half of which is with the current employer, to pursue training opportunities not included in the company's training program.

Protection Benefits

Retirement[56]   Effective August 21, 2003, the government mandated that employees must work longer before they may receive full government pension. The increase from 40 to 41 years will take effect by 2012. Retirees will also be prohibited from receiving their pensions while working on a part-time basis because the pension amount is set at a generous level (i.e., 85 percent of annual earnings prior to retirement).

Social Security[57]   Social security benefits granted to employees contain three components: health insurance, unemployment insurance, and retirement insurance. There is a base regime of social insurance that applies equally to all employees with rules on reimbursement rates for medical expenses, rules on calculation of unemployment allowance, or the right to a retirement allowance are all the same for all employees. In addition, private employers can provide such company benefits as additional medical coverage and additional retirement benefits. In addition, French law provides for mandatory profit sharing for employers with more than 50 employees. Employers and employees may also enter into a variety of voluntary profit sharing programs. The use of either voluntary or mandatory schemes is encouraged by the government.

Health Insurance   Organization of medical services for employees is the responsibility of the employer, and the employer must bear the costs, A doctor selected by the employer conducts medical examinations, but has no power to prescribe treatment or sick leave.[58] France's per capita expenditure on health (sum of Public Health Expenditure and Private Expenditure on Health) as of 2003 at the international dollar rate was $2,902.[59] The SSA Office of Policy reports that workers' medical benefits include general and specialist care, hospitalization, laboratory services, medicines, optical and dental care, maternity care, appliances, and transportation.[60] The insured normally pays for services and is reimbursed by the local sickness fund. A €1 flat-rate contribution is paid for each medical service up to an annual ceiling. Note that pregnant women or women on maternity leave, hospitalized persons, and persons with low income are exempt. After the deduction of the flat-rate contribution, the sickness insurance reimburses fully or in part the cost incurred by the insured. The amount reimbursed depends on the type of service: 100 percent of the medical service cost for certain severe illnesses, for work injury beneficiaries who are assessed as 66.6 percent or more disabled, and for pregnant women from the sixth month of pregnancy up to the twelfth day after childbirth, regardless of whether the costs are related to the pregnancy or not; 70 percent for medical services; 60 percent for paramedic services; 35 percent or 65 percent for pharmaceuticals; 60 percent or 70 percent for laboratory services; 65 percent for optical and appliance fees up to an annual ceiling; and 80 percent for hospitalization after the deduction of a flat-rate daily contribution of €15 (€16 in 2007) (1 USD = .744€).

Other Benefits[61]

As an exception to the general rules, French law provides more flexible rules for management-level employees. Executive managers (*cadres dirigeants*) or top executives are not subject to French regulation; integrated managers (*cadres integers*) (e.g., office managers or foremen) are subject to regulations similar to regular employees; autonomous managers (*cadres autonomes*) or managers whose work schedules cannot be determined in advance can enter into individual agreements with the employer.

Germany

Germany is a federal republic with the fifth largest economy in the world as indicated by a per capita GDP of $31,400, according to the World Factbook.[62] The German labor force has about 43.66 million workers. The integration of the former East German economy is a strain on the overall economy of unified Germany and unemployment rates have been very high. Germany has recently been pushing such labor market reforms as increasing the retirement age and increasing female workforce participation. There have been increasing concerns about the aging workforce and high unemployment bankrupting the social security system, but for now Germany has managed to bring the deficit to within the EU debt limit. Germany's employment laws provide considerable voice to labor and job security to employees and the **German Civil Code** provides numerous statutes that deal with individual employment as well as collective agreements.[63]

Wage and Salary

Minimum wage in Germany is established through the collective bargaining process. In Germany, there are two types of collective agreements. First, association agreements are made between trade unions and employers' associations. Second, company agreements are made between trade unions and individual employers. An extension of either type of agreement to other sectors or employers may be granted upon request of at least one party to the collective agreement.

As an example, the agreement for the metalworking industry in Baden-Württemberg has been selected because it concluded a new pay framework agreement (ERA-Eckentgelt) in 2003 and in February 2004 concluded a collective agreement fixing the projected percentage increases in the minimum wage for the next 26 months. In 2007, the German? In 2007, the German minimum wage was €8.27 per hour.

Different Minimum Wage by Sector   Minimum wage rates are determined by sectoral collective agreements. The collective agreement for the metalworking industry in Baden-Württemberg has been taken as an example because it concluded a new pay framework agreement (ERA-Eckentgelt) in 2003 that will run.

Different Minimum Wage by Region as Determined by Collective Agreement   The collective agreement for the metalworking industry in Baden-Württemberg determines minimum wage rates for the regions of Nordwürttemberg and Nordbaden, Südwürttemberg-Hohenzollern, and Südbaden. As there are numerous collective agreements, the agreement for the metalworking industry in Baden-Württemberg is just one example of a minimum pay framework agreement. In March 2005, the minimum wage was at €1,371.98 for first step (K1) commercial agents (Kaufmännische Angestellte) in the metalworking industry in Südwürttemberg-Hohenzollern.

Paid Time Off Benefits[64]

Employees cannot be required to work on official holidays, which range from 10 holidays per year in northern Germany to 13 in southern Germany. The statutory minimum vacation has been set at 24 working days (or 4 weeks because Saturdays are counted). Younger workers have a right to a vacation of 25 to 30 working days; disabled workers have an additional 5 days of vacation. There is minimum 6-month employment eligibility for vacation. Under the terms of the **Maternity Leave Law**, time away from work as a result of maternity leave or other limits on work by pregnant women and mothers must be counted as time worked for the purpose of determining entitlement to vacation time. Employees may take 5 days annually or 10 days every 2 years (under individual state level statutes) as paid holidays for continuing education purposes at only state-approved institutions. The employee retains a job if he is drafted for military or called for military exercises with a suspended employment relationship. The employee should receive regular pay during illness for a period of 6 weeks.

Expectant mothers can take 6 weeks' leave before the due date and 8 weeks after giving birth. During this time the employee must be paid at least average salary or wages calculated on the basis of the last 13 weeks before commencement of leave. An employee can request up to 3 years of child-rearing leave. Employers must guarantee return to the same job following completion of this leave. Any payments for child-rearing leave are made solely by the national health authority.

Protection Benefits

Pensions[65]   Germany has a statutory pension system analogous to the Social Security system in the United States. In addition, employers offer the company pension plan and a tax-favored investment plan. Employees have three different sources for their pension benefits: statutory pension insurance, company pension plans, and private life insurance.

Health Insurance   German laws stipulate guidelines for minimal health welfare of worker.[66] For blue-collar workers (and some white-collar workers) mandatory state health insurance premiums are borne 50 percent by the insured and 50 percent by the employer. The employer is required to collect the employees' contributions and to pay the entire amount to the appropriate collector. Employees whose income exceeds a certain amount can opt out of the state plan and purchase private health insurance. In such cases, employees may request that the employer's health insurance contribution be included in their salary. Germany's per capita expenditure on health (sum of Public Health Expenditure and Private Expenditure on Health) as of 2003 at the international dollar rate was $3,001.[67]

Italy

The republic of Italy has a diversified industrial economy, with a well-developed and industrial north, and a less well-developed agricultural south dependent on welfare, according to the World Factbook.[68] With a 24.63 million people in the labor force and a per capital GDP of $29,700, Italy's total and per capita output equals that of France and the United Kingdom. Italy has moved slowly with regard to reforming its high tax burden and overgenerous pension system, mainly because of the current economic slowdown and opposition from labor unions. The **Civil Code**, enacted in 1942, and a legislatively implemented EU directive cover the employment relationship.[69]

Wage and Salary

There is no national minimum wage rate in Italy. Minimum wage rates are set in binding sectoral collective agreements. The Constitution provides that all workers are entitled to receive wages that are fair and just, and sufficient to provide workers and their families with freedom and dignity. In accordance with this principle, the judiciary has passed down decisions concerning workers not covered by a collective agreement, stating that they should receive wages that are equal to those established in collective agreements for workers in the same category and industry. As a result, even workers who are not covered should receive wages at least equal to the minimum rates determined in collective agreements. The collective agreement made in the metal-working sector established a minimum wage of €995.60 per month for unskilled workers.

Paid Time Off Benefits[70]

Depending on the category of the worker and seniority within the business, employees are entitled to between 3 and 5 weeks of paid vacation, which should, if possible, be taken consecutively. There are approximately 11 public holidays in Italy, and an additional 4 days that used to be public holidays but are now working days on which employees are paid double time. In the event of illness or accident, employees are entitled to full compensation for the first month, and one half thereof for the next 2 months, when they have less than 10 years' seniority. With more than 10 years' seniority workers get full pay for the first 2 months and one half thereof for the next 4 months. Blue collar workers receive a percentage of their compensation for a period established by the collective bargaining agreement.

Pregnant employees have the right to time off during working hours for medical appointments. Maternity leave with salary is allowed during: mandatory 2 months before birth and 3 months after birth; optional 6 months with reduced salary until child is 8 years old; if there is only one parent, for a maximum of 10 days a working mother is entitled to 2 hours' paid leave per day until child is 1 year old in order to feed the baby. Fathers are allowed to take leave for 3 months if they possess sole custody of the child, or if the child's mother dies or is seriously ill. Employers are obligated to preserve the worker's position during the entire time of conscription and for 30 days after discharge; no payment is required.

Protection Benefits

Pensions[71] There are two types of pension plans: compulsory and complementary. Compulsory pensions are granted to all workers (including the self-employed) by the Institute for Social Security or other government entities. Complementary pension plans, which are also granted to all workers and the self-employed, ensure that retirees maintain approximately the same standard of living that they had prior to retirement. Over time, complementary plans increase payments to retirees to adjust for cost-of-living increases. There are two different types of complementary pension schemes: collective pension schemes and individual pension schemes and life insurance.

Health Benefits Italy's per capita expenditure on health (sum of Public Health Expenditure and Private Expenditure on Health) as of 2003 at the international dollar rate was $2,266.[72] The SSA Office of Policy reports on workers' medical benefits that healthcare is provided to patients by doctors, hospitals, and pharmacists under contract with sickness funds.[73] Benefits include comprehensive medical and dental care, preventive examinations and treatment, laboratory tests, maternity care with a midwife or doctor, hospitalization, surgery, appliances, and prescribed medicines. Individuals are responsible for cost sharing in the form of co-payment for certain benefits (e.g., medicines, medical equipment, ambulatory care, hospitalization, and transportation). Financial hardship exempts individuals from the copayment requirement.

Russia

The Federation of Russia has been experiencing a 6.7 percent annual growth rate since the economic crisis of 1998, with a labor force of 73.88 million, a per capita GDP of $12,100, and has been slowly building rule of law that seems to be poised on the brink of a return to greater state control over the economy.[74] Labor relations have been established in the **Labor Code of the Russian Federation**, which came into force on February 1, 2002.[75] The Constitution of the Russian Federation, which was approved on December 12, 1993, contains articles that deal with various aspects of the employment relationship.[76]

Wage and Salary

The Russian government determines the minimum subsistence income. States within the Russan Federation may establish regional minimum wage rates that are higher than the national minimum wage following consideration of the opinion of a tripartite commission for the regulation of social and labor relations. Nonetheless, regional minimum wage rates are subject to the consent of the federal government. The federal minimum wage was set at 1,100 rubles per month in 2006.

Paid Time Off Benefits[77]

Eleven nonworking days corresponding with nine national holidays are provided to employees and holidays that coincide with the weekend roll over during the week. Workers are entitled to 28 days' annual paid leave, during which they are paid their average wages. A paid annual leave must be granted at least every 2 years and may accumulate and carry over into the second year. Federal law also provides partially paid leave for various reasons, including education, maternity, childcare, and adoption.

Protection Benefits

Pensions   The SSA Office of Policy reports that everyone in Russia is guaranteed social insurance adequate for their age in the event of disease or disability[78] (i.e., 20 percent of payroll; agricultural enterprises contribute 10.3 percent of payroll; pension fund administrators may charge up to a maximum of 1.1 percent of accumulated funds per year for administrative fees for the individual account). If each employee's annual earnings are less than 280,000 rubles, the total contribution is 26 percent of payroll. If each employee's annual earnings are greater than 280,000 rubles up to 600,000 rubles, the contribution is equal to 72,800 rubles plus 10 percent of annual earnings exceeding 280,000 rubles; if each employee's annual earnings exceed 600,000 rubles, the contributions are equal to 104,800 rubles plus 2 percent of annual earnings exceeding 600,000 rubles. The employer's contributions also finance sickness and maternity benefits, medical benefits, and family allowances. Employers may finance supplementary benefits out of their own budgets. Government pensions are paid out of a federal budget (1 USD = 25.86 rubles).

Health Insurance Benefits[79]

Compulsory medical insurance covers medical services provided directly to patients by public and private health providers. Benefits include general, preventive, and emergency care; hospitalization; laboratory services; dental care; maternity care; vaccination; and transportation.

Cost Sharing   Medicines prescribed during hospitalization are provided free or at reduced rates to persons with certain categories of illness, the disabled, and war veterans. Voluntary medical insurance covers specialized care, expensive medicines, and appliances. In accordance with legislative reform where special in-kind social benefits were replaced by cash compensation, some categories of the population, including the elderly, persons with disabilities, and war veterans, may receive cash compensation for some medicines in 2006. Russia's per capita expenditure on health (sum of Public Health Expenditure and Private Expenditure on Health) as of 2003 at the international dollar rate was $551.[80]

ASIA

As of 2007, China is the largest economy in Asia, followed by India and Japan.[81] Although the Japanese economy in the 1980s and 1990s used to be larger than that of the entire continent combined, since then the Chinese currency has grown and become the second-largest and is expected to surpass Japan's.[82] Asia has several trade blocs, including **Asia-Pacific Economic Cooperation, Asia-Europe Economic Meeting, Association of Southeast Asian Nations**, and **South Asian Association for Regional Cooperation**. Given the wide variation and diversity in the world's largest and most populous continent, however, there is no unifying economic body like the EU or NAFTA that represents all the countries of Asia. This section will examine a representative sample of the relatively more developed and developing economies in Asia: India, China, and South Korea. A bloc of countries that is not examined here, but that nonetheless deserves mention because considerable jobs are being outsourced there, are those in southeast Asia: Thailand, Vietnam, Singapore, Malaysia, Philippines, Cambodia, and Laos. These economies are seeing a current influx of foreign investment, although they are not close to the countries discussed here in terms of annual growth rates.

India

According to the CIA World Handbook, India is a democratic federal republic with a diverse economy ranging from traditional farming to high technology industries.[83] India's labor force is quite large with 509.3 million individuals with a per capita GDP of only $3,700. The Indian economy, though steadily growing at a close to 8 percent annual rate, is plagued with income disparity and developmental challenges similar to China. More than half of India's output is created with less than one quarter of its labor force, and services are the major source of economic growth. Strong economic growth combined with easy consumer credit and a real estate boom is fueling inflation concerns and the huge and growing population poses fundamental social, economic, and environmental problems. Basic constitutional legislation governs the employment relationship for all employees, ensuring equality of opportunity to public employment and prohibition of child labor.

The Directive Principle of State Policy has statutes that affect various aspects of the employment relationship (e.g., working conditions and participation in management).[84] Some of the key employee benefits provided by employers in India are provident fund, gratuity (bonus), pension (i.e., either defined benefit or defined contribution), housing, car, loans, life insurance protection for dependents, health and disability benefits, medical benefits for employees and their families, and leave encashment.[85] The Employees' Provident Fund Organization is one of the world's largest social security programs with more than 35 million members. Gratuities apply to most employees in India, and these are funded through employer contributions totaling 4.5 percent of payroll.

There are wide variations between the public and private sectors, with the Ministry of Labour and labor laws governing employment relationships in the public sector, with more employer discretion allowed in the private sector. In addition, all blue-collar employees and factory workers are governed under existing labor laws.

Wage and Salary Minimum wage is fixed by an authority dual system. Minimum wage rates are determined by the government for certain sectors, and a collective agreement determines others. Minimum wage rates for occupations that are largely nonunionized or have little bargaining power may be set in accordance with the Minimum Wages Act, 1948. This Act applies throughout India, including the provinces of Jammu and Kashmir. Schedules 1 and 2 of the Act set forth the occupations for which applicable central and regional governments may set minimum wage rates. The central government sets minimum wages for 45 different occupations, including agricultural work construction and road maintenance workers, workers in mines, railway works and stone breaking or crushing work. In addition, states have set minimum wages for 1,232 different occupations in their respective regions. Minimum wage rates set apply only to those scheduled occupations that have more than 1,000 employees working in the applicable state. For example, in Arunachal Pradesh the minimum wage rate was 39.87 rupees per day in 2005.

Paid Time Off Benefits[86]

Leave is usually calculated for each year based on the number of days worked in the previous year. If a worker does not take all of the accumulated leave she or he is allowed to roll over to the succeeding calendar year up to a maximum of 30 days. There is no statutory provision of paternity leave but maternity leave is allowed in the form of paid time off and possible medical bonus. All employees get paid time off for various public and national holidays.

Protection Benefits

Pensions[87] First and current laws regarding pensions were passed in 1952 (i.e., employees' provident funds), with amendments in 1972 (i.e., payment of gratuity), 1976 (i.e., employees' deposit-linked insurance), 1995 (i.e., employees' pension scheme), and 1995 (i.e., national social assistance program). Pension benefits include provident fund with survivor (i.e., deposit-linked) insurance and a pension fund, a gratuity schemes for industrial workers, and a social assistance system. In 2004, a voluntary old-age, disability, and survivors' benefits scheme was enacted. This program is part of the Unorganized Sector Social Security Scheme for employees and self-employed persons aged 36 to 50 with monthly earnings of 6,500 rupees or less but without mandatory coverage, was introduced as a pilot program in 50 districts. Contributions are income related and flat rate. Coverage includes employees, including casual, part-time, and daily wage workers, and those employed through contractors, with monthly earnings of 6,500 rupees or less working in establishments with a minimum of 20 employees in one of the 182 categories of covered industry (the establishment remains covered even if the number of employees falls below 20).

Employees covered by equivalent occupational private plans may contract out. Voluntary coverage exists for employees of covered establishments with monthly earnings of more than 6,500 rupees, with the agreement of the employer and for establishments with less than 20 employees if the employer and a majority of the employees agree to contribute. Provident fund contributions include 12 percent of basic wages (10 percent of basic wages in five specified categories of industry) in covered establishments with less than 20 employees and some other specific cases. The maximum monthly earnings for contribution purposes are 6,500 rupees (1 USD = 42.67 rupees).

Health Benefits SSA reports that state governments arrange for the provision of medical care on behalf of the Employees' State Insurance Corporation.[88] Services are provided in different states through social insurance dispensaries and hospitals, state government services, or private doctors under contract. Benefits include outpatient treatment, specialist consultations, hospitalization, surgery and obstetric care, imaging and laboratory services, transportation, and the free supply of medications, dressings, artificial limbs, aids, and appliances. The duration of benefits is from 3 months to 1 year, according to the insured's contribution record. India's per capita expenditure on health (sum of Public Health Expenditure and Private Expenditure on Health) as of 2003 at the international dollar rate was $82.[89]

People's Republic of China

The People's Republic of China (PRC), as reported by the World Factbook, is a communist state characterized by a fast-growing economy that has shifted over the past couple of decades from a centrally planned system to a more market-oriented one.[90] With a massive labor force of 798 million and a per capita GDP of $7,600, PRC has been experiencing continuously high annual GDP growth at around 10 percent. Even though the purchasing power parity of PRC has become one of the top in the world, the lower per capita GDP is an indication of income disparity within various strata of society. One of the key challenges for the government has been to sustain adequate job growth for tens of millions of workers laid off from state-owned enterprises, migrants, and new entrants to the workforce.

The PRC Labor Law was established in 1995, resulting in a break from the traditional "iron rice bowl" system of employment, with a shift from state-owned enterprises to private ones, a move which has given rise to new employment relationship issues.[91] Under the older welfare system the workforce was considered the property of the state, and such benefits as housing, medical, and retirement schemes were payable directly by the state-owned enterprises to the employees. Since the introduction of the PRC Labor Law the employment relationship is now defined by individual contracts.[92]

Wage and Salary

According to China's Labor Act, 1994, the State possesses the responsibility to implement a system of guaranteed minimum wages. There is no national minimum wage rate in China; instead, minimum wage rates are set by region. Separate standards are stipulated by provincial, regional, and municipal peoples' governments for their respective region and reported to the State Council for consent. The provisions concerning minimum wages apply to enterprises, private nonenterprise entities, individual industrial and commercial households with employees (the employing entities), and the laborers who have formed a labor relationship with them. The minimum wage rate was 270 yuan per month in the Province of Jiangxi in 2005.

Paid Time-Off Benefits[93]

The length of an employer-approved medical treatment period generally depends on employee age and period of service, and can range from 3 to 24 months. During this period the salary paid to the employee may not be less than 80 percent of the local minimum wage. Employees who have worked for 1 or more years are entitled to paid annual leave, but there are no binding laws about this; national policy guidelines recommend 7 to 14 days. Employees who have worked for more than 1 year are entitled to "home leave" if they do not live in the same place as their spouse or parents. Employees earn normal wages during this period and employers are obligated to pay all travel expenses for employees visiting their spouse and for unmarried employees visiting their parents. Women are entitled to no less than 90 days of maternity leave starting 15 days prior to birth.

Protection Benefits

Pensions   The Office of Policy of the SSA reports that there has been a new law to decouple the employment relationship from the social insurance system, setting up a unified basic pension system.[94] The system now has social insurance and mandatory individual accounts (i.e., provincial and city or county social insurance agencies and employers do adapt central government guidelines to local conditions). Coverage includes employees in urban enterprises and urban institutions managed as enterprises and the urban self-employed. In some provinces, coverage for the urban self-employed is voluntary. (Urban enterprises comprise all state-owned enterprises, regardless of their location.) Old-age provision in rural areas is based mainly on family support and through community and state financial support. Pilot schemes in the form of individual accounts, supported at the town and village level and subject to preferential support by the state, operate in some rural areas. Employees of government and communist party organizations, and of cultural, educational, and scientific institutions (except for institutions financed off-budget), are covered under a government-funded, employer-administered system. Enterprise-based pension systems cover some employees (including the self-employed) in cities.

An employee contribution to mandatory individual accounts is 8 percent of gross insured earnings. (The contribution rate is higher in some provinces.) The minimum earnings for employee contribution and benefit purposes are equal to 60 percent of the local average wage for the previous year. The maximum earnings for employee contribution and benefit purposes vary, but they may be as much as 300 percent of the local average wage for the previous year. Employer contribution to mandatory individual accounts is 3 percent of insured payroll. The contribution is taken from the total contribution made to basic pension insurance. Central and local government subsidies are provided to city and council retirement pension pools as needed.

Health Insurance[95] There is a unified medical insurance system with all employers and workers participating in this system. Employers contribute 6 percent of payroll to the system, whereas employees contribute 2 percent of their salary. Health insurance is based on **Basic Medical Insurance Fund** consisting of a **Pooled Fund** and **Personal Accounts**. Employees' contributions go directly to their personal accounts and 30 percent of employer contributions are paid into this account. Covered workers receive medical benefits at a chosen accredited hospital or clinic on a fee-for-service basis. The individual account is used to finance medical benefits only, up to a maximum equal to 10 percent of the local average annual wage. The social insurance fund reimburses the cost of the medical benefit from 10 percent up to 400 percent of the local average annual wage, according to the schedule. Medical treatment in high-grade hospitals results in lower percentage reimbursements, and vice versa. Reimbursement for payments beyond 400 percent of the local average annual wage must be covered by private insurance or public supplementary schemes. Contract workers receive the same benefits as permanent workers. Per capita expenditure on health (per capita amount of the sum of Public Health Expenditure and Private Expenditure on Health) as of 2003 at the international dollar rate was $278.[96]

South Korea

South Korea is a republic which, since the 1960s, has achieved considerable economic growth and become a member of the high technology global economy, according to the World Handbook.[97] With a labor force of 23.77 million and a per capita GDP of $24,200, the South Korean economy achieved its current developed status by pursuing a system of close government and business ties, including directed credit, import restrictions, sponsorship of specific industries, and a strong labor effort, and it continues to be a strong and stable economy in current times. Most aspects of employment in South Korea are governed by laws and violations of mandatory provision as a criminal offense and a free enterprise economic system allows for the existence of individual, collective, and collaborative systems of employment law designed to protect employees and regulate working conditions.[98]

Wage and Salary The minister of labor sets the national minimum wage each year, following the Minimum Wage Council's wage proposal. If the minister of labor does not agree with the wage proposal, but a two-thirds majority of the Minimum Wage Council supports it, the minister must adopt the proposal. The minister of labor publishes the minimum wage rate proposals submitted by the Council so that representatives of workers or employers may raise any objections within 10 days of the proposal's publication. Any seaman who comes within the scope of the Seaman Act is subject to a separate mechanism when minimum wage rates are being determined. The administrator of the Korean Maritime and Port Administration may set minimum wages for seamen, following a period of deliberation by the Seaman Policy Council. In 2006, the minimum wage was 100 South Korean won per hour and 24,800 won per day as of December 2006.

Paid Time Off Benefits[99] Employees are entitled to paid holidays designated by the company and are also entitled to 10 days' paid leave for those who have worked 1 year without absence and 8 days off for employees who worked 90 percent or more. Female employees are entitled to 90 days' paid maternity leave, of which 45 days must be used after childbirth, with the final 30 days compensated by the **Unemployment Insurance Fund**. Sick leave is statutorily required only in connection with occupational injuries or diseases. Males spend 26 months on active duty in the military and are called back after that for training. Employers cannot penalize any employee for being away on military training. Special leave might be granted to perform civic duties. There is no specific legal provision for paternity leave.

Protection Benefits

Pensions[100] Peoples' Pension covers most workers, whereas **Local Pension** covers public workers, military personnel, and private schoolteachers. Participants must contribute for at least 20 years to be entitled to retirement benefits. Employers and employees each contribute 4.5 percent of an employee's monthly salary. Expatriate employees are not required to contribute to the pension program.

Health Benefits All employers are required to subscribe to the national health insurance plan, pursuant to the National Health Insurance Act as of July 1, 2001. As of 2004, a premium rate of 4.21 percent of the subscriber's standard monthly salary has been fixed with employer and employee making equal contributions.[101] SSA reports that workers' medical benefits include medical treatment, surgery, hospitalization, and mediciations.[102] Medical services are provided by doctors, clinics, hospitals, and pharmacists under contract to the **National Health Insurance Corporation (NHIC)**. Benefits are payable for up to 365 treatment days per year, with each individual medical service used being counted as a day of treatment. If the treatment days exceed 365, the patient pays all subsequent costs. If the total amount paid by the NHIC for 365 days does not exceed 1,500,000 won per patient per year, the NHIC may continue to pay benefits up to that limit. Maternity care is provided, with no limit on the number of children. There are no cash maternity benefits. The insured pays 20 percent of hospitalization costs and between 30 percent and 50 percent of outpatient care (e.g., 50 percent if provided by a specialized general hospital, 50 percent if provided by a general hospital, 35 percent to 40 percent if provided by a hospital, or 30 percent if provided by a clinic). The NHIC refunds 50 percent of the patient's costs exceeding 1,200,000 won in 30 days. The overall limit paid by each patient is 3,000,000 won every 6 months. (1 USD = 933 wons)

SUMMARY

We reviewed minimum wage and benefits offerings mandated by the governments of several countries across the world. There is extensive variation in minimum standards. A striking difference between the United States and other countries are the less-generous family leave benefits in the United States and the relatively fewer paid days off. The governments in other countries mandate paid time off, reflecting the importance of family and religion. Most countries offer social security pensions and, in many cases, these benefits are not lucrative. We also noticed that health care costs are a concern in all countries. Various health care delivery systems, single-payer, and multiple-payer, struggle with rising health care costs and adequate coverage.

KEY TERMS

- NAFTA—the North Atlantic Free Trade Agreement, 394
- North American Agreement on Labor Cooperation (NAALC), 394
- per capita gross domestic product (GDP), 394

- English Statue of Labourers, 294
- Civil Code of Quebec, 295
- Labor and Social Security, 396
- European Union (EU), 400
- Member States, 400
- French Labor Code (*Code du Travail*), 401

- just cause dismissal, 401
- employment-at-will, 401
- German Civil Code, 403
- Maternity Leave Law, 403
- Civil Code, 404
- Labor Code of the Russian Federation, 405

ENDNOTES

1. Gandossy, R., & Varghese, E. (2005). Global HR. In *Global Rewards: A Collection of Articles from WorldatWork* (edited by WorldatWork). Quote located on page 3.
2. *www.ustr.gov/Trade_Agreements/Regional/NAFTA/Section_Index.html*
3. *www.worldtradelaw.net/nafta/*
4. Floudas, D. A., & Rojas, L. F. (2000). Some Thoughts on NAFTA and Trade Integration in the American Continent, International Problems, 4. *www.diplomacy.bg.ac.yu/mpro_sa00_4.htm*
5. Ibid.
6. *www.cia.gov/cia/publications/factbook/geos/ ca.html*
7. Heenan, R. L., & Brady, T. E. F. (2003). In Keller, W. L., & Darby. T. J. (Eds.), *International Labor and Employment Laws,* Second Edition, Volume I, 21-2–21-6.
8. Information in this chapter about minimum wage policy was found on the International Labour Organization Web site (2007). *Wages and Income. www.ilo.org/travaildatabase/servlet/minimumwages.* Accessed June 29, 2007.
9. Id. at 21-54–21-56.
10. Heenan, R. L., & Brady, T. E. F., 21-9.
11. Id. at 21-66–21-67.
12. Id. at 21-67.
13. Id. at 21-68.
14. *www.who.int/countries/can/en/*
15. *www.cia.gov/cia/publications/factbook/geos/ mx.html*
16. de Buen Lozano, N., & de Buen Unna, C. (2003). In Keller, W. L., & Darby, T. J. (Eds.), *International Labor and Employment Laws,* Second Edition, Volume I, 22-1.
17. *www.cia.gov/cia/publications/factbook/geos/ mx.html*
18. de Buen Lozano, N., & de Buen Unna, C. (2003). In Keller, W. L., & Darby, T. J. (Eds.), *International Labor and Employment Laws,* Second Edition, Volume I, 22-1.
19. Id. at 22-60.
20. Id. at 22-67.
21. Id. at 22-68.
22. Ibid.
23. *www.ssa.gov/policy/docs/progdesc/ssptw/2004–2005/americas/mexico.html*
24. Ibid.
25. Ibid.
26. Ibid.
27. *www.who.int/countries/mex/en/*
28. de Buen Lozano, N., & de Buen Unna, C. (2003). In Keller, W. L., & Darby, T. J. (Eds.), *International Labor and Employment Laws,* Second Edition, Volume I, 22-69–22-70.
29. *www.imf.org/external/pubs/ft/weo/2006/02/data/index.aspx*
30. *hdr.undp.org/hdr2006/*
31. *www.bilaterals.org/rubrique.php3? id_rubrique=165*
32. *www.comunidadandina.org/endex.htm*
33. *news.bbc.co.uk/2/hi/business/4079505.stm*
34. *www.cia.gov/cia/publications/factbook/geos/ br.html*
35. Pires, P. R. F., & Gomes, L. C. M. (2003). In Keller, W. L., & Darby, T. J. (Eds.), *International Labor and Employment Laws,* Second Edition, Volume I, 30-2–30-19.
36. Id. at 30-3.
37. Id. at 30-3.
38. Id. at 30-57.
39. *www.ssa.gov/policy/docs/progdesc/ssptw/2004-2005/americas/brazil.html*
40. Ibid.
41. *www.who.int/countries/bra/en/*
42. *www.cia.gov/cia/publications/factbook/geos/ ar.html*
43. Cowman, J. W., Dodds, C. A., & Orlansky, J. D. (2003). In Keller, W. L., & Darby, T. J. (Eds.), *International Labor and Employment Laws,* Second Edition, Volume II, 37-8.
44. Id. at 37-47–37-50
45. Id. at 37-55
46. *www.ssa.gov/policy/docs/progdesc/ssptw/2004–2005/americas/argentina.html*
47. Cowman, J. W., Dodds, C. A., & Orlansky, J. D. (2003). In Keller, W. L., & Darby T. J. (Eds.), *International Labor and Employment Laws,* Second Edition, Volume II, 37-58.
48. *www.ssa.gov/policy/docs/progdesc/ssptw/2004–2005/americas/argentina.html*
49. *www.who.int/countries/arg/en/*
50. Kenner, J. (2003). In Keller, W. L., & Darby, T. J. (Eds.), *International Labor and Employment Laws,* Second Edition, Volume I, 1-1–1-2.
51. Id. at 1-68.
52. *www.europa.eu/scadplus/leg/en/s02300.htm*

53. *www.cia.gov/cia/publications/factbook/ geos/fr.html*

54. Tallent, S. E., Grinspan, B., & Sauvage, F. (2003). In Keller, W. L., & Darby T. J. (Eds.), *International Labor and Employment Laws,* Second Edition, Volume I, 3-1–3-3.

55. Id. at 3-64–3-68

56. Grinspan, B., & Sauvage, F. (2005). In Keller, W. L., & Darby, T. J. (Eds.), *International Labor and Employment Laws, Cumulative Supplement,* Volume I, 3-10.

57. Id. at 3-75–3-76

58. Ibid.

59. *www.who.int/countries/fra/en/*

60. *www.ssa.gov/policy/docs/progdesc/ssptw/ 2006–2007/europe/france.html*

61. Tallent, S. E., Grinspan, B., & Sauvage, F. (2003). In Keller, W. L., & Darby, T. J. (Eds.), *International Labor and Employment Laws,* Second Edition, Volume I, 3-65.

62. *www.cia.gov/cia/publications/factbook/geos/ gm.html*

63. Lutringer, R., & Dichter, M. S. (2003). In Keller, W. L., & Darby, T. J. (Eds.), *International Labor and Employment Laws,* Second Edition, Volume I, 4-4–4-5.

64. Id. at 4-86–4-91

65. Id. at 4-99

66. Id. at 4-103

67. *www.who.int/countries/deu/en/*

68. *www.cia.gov/cia/publications/factbook/geos/ it.html*

69. Mandruzzato, P. (2003). In Keller, W. L., & Darby, T. J. (Eds.), *International Labor and Employment Laws,* Second Edition, Volume I, 5–6.

70. Id. at 5-73–5-77

71. Id. at 5-86–5-87

72. *www.who.int/countries/ita/en/*

73. *www.ssa.gov/policy/docs/progdesc/ssptw/ 2006–2007/europe/italy.html*

74. *www.cia.gov/cia/publications/factbook/geos/ rs.html*

75. Danilov, E. A., & Adams, S. T. (2003). In Keller, W. L. & Darby, T. J. (Eds.), *International Labor and Employment Laws,* Second Edition, Volume II, 28-4.

76. Id. at 28-1

77. Id. at 28-47–28-49

78. *www.ssa.gov/policy/docs/progdesc/ssptw/ 2006–2007/europe/russia.html*

79. Ibid.

80. *www.who.int/countries/rus/en/*

81. *www.imf.org/external/pubs/ft/weo/2006/02/ data/index.aspx*

82. *www.britannica.com/eb/article-48208/Asia*

83. *www.cia.gov/cia/publications/factbook/geos/ in.html*

84. Singhania, R. (2003). In Keller, W. L., & Darby, T. J. (Eds.), *International Labor and Employment Laws,* Second Edition, Volume II, 24-10–24-13.

85. *www.watsonwyatt.com/asia-pacific/localsites/india/services/ebcas.asp*

86. Singhania, R.. (2003). In Keller, W. L., & Darby, T. J. (Eds.), *International Labor and Employment Laws,* Second Edition, Volume II, 24-56–24-57.

87. *www.ssa.gov/policy/docs/progdesc/ssptw/ 2006–2007/asia/india.html*

88. Ibid.

89. *www.who.int/countries/ind/en/*

90. *www.cia.gov/cia/publications/factbook/geos/ ch.html*

91. Lauffs, A. W., et al. (2003). In Keller, W. L., & Darby, T. J. (Eds.), *International Labor and Employment Laws,* Second Edition, Volume I, 31-5.

92. Ibid.

93. Id. at 31-38–31-39

94. *www.ssa.gov/policy/docs/progdesc/ssptw/ 2006–2007/asia/china.html*

95. Lauffs, A. W., et al. (2003). In Keller, W. L., & Darby, T. J. (Eds.), *International Labor and Employment Laws,* Second Edition, Volume I, 31-47–31-48.

96. *www.who.int/countries/chn/en/*

97. *www.cia.gov/cia/publications/factbook/geos/ ks.html*

98. Hyun, C. W., Jung. J. C., & Yu, H. C. (2003). In Keller, W. L., & Darby, T. J. (Eds.), *International Labor and Employment Laws,* Second Edition, Volume II, 26-4–26-5.

99. Id. at 26-61–26-64

100. Id. at 26–75

101. Id. at 26-77–26-78

102. *www.ssa.gov/policy/docs/progdesc/ssptw/ 2006–2007/asia/southkorea.html*

Glossary

360-degree performance appraisals incorporate several sources of pertinent information to give a more complete (and presumably) less-biased assessment of job performance. Examples of pertinent sources include supervisor, co-workers, and clients.

Aaron v. City of Wichita, Kansas, a court ruling, offered several criteria to determine whether City of Wichita fire chiefs are exempt employees, including the relative importance of management as opposed to other duties, frequency with which they exercise discretionary powers, relative freedom from supervision, and the relationship between their salaries and wages paid to other employees for similar nonexempt work.

Ability, based on Equal Employment Opportunity Commission guidelines, refers to a present competence to perform an observable behavior or a behavior that results in an observable product.

Abilities are enduring attributes of the individual that influence performance. Accrual rules specify the rate at which participants accumulate (or earn) retirement benefits.

Affirmative action refers to a written document that state's a company's goals to recruit and hire under-represented minorities.

Age Discrimination in Employment Act of 1967 (ADEA) protects older workers age 40 and over from illegal discrimination.

Agency problem describes an executive's behavior that promotes his or her self-interests rather than the interests of the company owners or shareholders.

Agency theory provides an explanation of executive compensation determination based on the relationship between company owners (shareholders) and agents (executives).

Alternation ranking, a variation of simple ranking job evaluation plans, orders all jobs from lowest to highest, based on alternately identifying the jobs of lowest and highest worth.

Americans with Disabilities Act of 1990 (ADA) prohibits discrimination against individuals with mental or physical disabilities within and outside employment settings, including public services and transportation, public accommodations, and employment.

Andrews v. DuBois, a district court ruling, determined that the following activities at employees' home associated with the care of dogs used for law enforcement are compensable under the Fair Labor Standards Act of 1938 (FLSA): feeding, grooming, and walking the dogs. The court reasoned that these activities were indispensable to maintaining dogs as a critical law enforcement tool, they are part of officers' principal activities, and they benefit the employer.

Annuities are a series of payments for the life of the participant and beneficiary. Annuity contracts are usually purchased from insurance companies, which make payments according to the contract.

Atonio v. Wards Cove Packing Company, a Supreme Court case, ruled that plaintiffs (i.e., employees) in employment discrimination suits must indicate which employment practice created disparate impact and demonstrate how the employment practice created disparate impact (intentional discrimination).

Baby boom generation refers to the generation of people born between 1946 and 1964.

Balance sheet approach provides expatriates the standard of living they normally enjoy in the United States.

Banking hours refers to a feature of flextime scheduling that allows employees to vary the number of hours they work each day as long as they work a set number of hours each week.

Base pay represents the monetary compensation employees earn on a regular basis for performing their jobs. Hourly pay and salary are the main forms of base pay.

Base period is the minimum period of time an individual must be employed before becoming eligible to receive unemployment insurance under the Social Security Act of 1935.

Basic skills information describes developed capacities that facilitate learning or the more rapid acquisition of knowledge.

Behavioral encouragement plans are individual incentive pay plans that reward employees for specific such behavioral accomplishments as good attendance or safety records.

Behavioral observation scale (BOS), a specific kind of behavioral system, displays illustrations of positive incidents (or behaviors) of job performance for various job dimensions. The evaluator rates the employee on each behavior according to the extent to which the employee performs in a manner consistent with each behavioral description.

Behavioral systems, a type of performance appraisal method, requires that raters (e.g., supervisors) judge the extent to which employees display successful job performance behaviors.

Behaviorally anchored rating scale (BARS), a specific kind of behavioral system, is based on the critical incident technique (CIT), and these scales are developed in the same fashion with one exception. For the CIT, a critical incident would be written as, "the incumbent completed the task in a timely fashion." For the BARS format, this incident would be written as, "the incumbent is expected to complete the task in a timely fashion."

Benchmark jobs, found outside the company, provide reference points against which the values of jobs within the company are judged.

Bennett Amendment allows employees to charge employers with Title VII violations regarding pay only when the employer has violated the Equal Pay Act of 1963.

Bias errors happen in the performance evaluation process when the rater evaluates the employee based on the rater's negative or positive opinion of the employee rather than on the employee's actual performance.

Board of directors represents shareholders' interests by weighing the pros and cons of top executives' decisions. Members include chief executive officers and top executives of other successful companies, distinguished community leaders, well-regarded professionals (e.g., physicians and attorneys), and a few of the company's top-level executives.

Boureslan v. Aramco, a Supreme Court case in which the Supreme Court ruled that federal job discrimination laws do not apply to U.S. citizens working for U.S. companies in foreign countries.

Brito v. Zia Company, a Supreme Court ruling, deemed that the Zia Company violated Title VII of the Civil Rights Act of 1964 when a disproportionate number of protected-class individuals were laid off on the basis of low performance appraisal scores. Zia Company's action was a violation of Title VII because the use of the performance appraisal system in determining layoffs was indeed an employment test. In addition, the court ruled that the Zia Company had not demonstrated that its performance appraisal instrument was valid.

Broadbanding is a pay structure form that leads to the consolidation of existing pay grades and pay ranges into fewer wider pay grades.

Buy-back provision in Improshare plans, sets a maximum productivity improvement payout level on productivity gains. Any bonus money that is generated because of improvements above the maximum is placed in a reserve. If productivity improves to the point where the maximum is repeatedly exceeded, the firm buys back the amount of the productivity improvement over the maximum with a one-time payment to employees.

Cafeteria plan (see flexible benefits plan).

Capital gains is the difference between the company stock price at the time of purchase and the lower stock price at the time an executive receives the stock options.

Capital requirements include automated manufacturing technology and office and plant facilities.

Capital-intensity refers to the extent to which companies' operations are based on the use of large-scale equipment. On average, capital-intensive industries (e.g., manufacturing) pay more than less capital-intensive industries (e.g., service industries).

Cash balance plans represent a cross between traditional defined benefits and defined contributions retirement plans. The rate of monetary accumulation slows as the employee's years of service increase.

Central tendency represents the fact that a set of data clusters around or centers on a central point. Central tendency is a number that represents the typical numerical value in a data set.

Certification ensures that employees possess at least a minimally acceptable level of skill proficiency upon completion of a training unit. Certification methods can include work samples, oral questioning, and written tests.

Civil Rights Act of 1964 is a major piece of federal legislation designed to protect the rights of underrepresented minorities.

Civil Rights Act of 1991 shifted the burden of proof of disparate impact from employees to employers, overturning several 1989 Supreme Court rulings.

Classification plans, particular methods of job evaluation, place jobs into categories based on compensable factors.

Cliff vesting enables employees to earn 100 percent vesting rights after no more than 3 years of service.

Coinsurance refers to the percentage of covered expenses paid by the insured. Most commercial plans stipulate 20 percent coinsurance. This means that the insured will pay 20 percent of covered expenses, whereas the insurance company pays the remaining 80 percent.

Collective bargaining agreements are written documents that describe the terms of employment reached between management and unions.

Commercial dental insurance provides cash benefits by reimbursing patients for out-of-pocket costs for particular dental care procedures or by paying dentists directly for patient costs.

Commission is a form of incentive compensation, based on a percentage of the product or service selling price and the number of units sold.

Commission-only plans are specific kinds of sales compensation plans. Salespeople derive their entire income through commissions.

Commission-plus-draw plans award sales professionals commissions and draws.

Common review date is the designated date when all employees receive performance appraisals.

Common review period is the designated period (e.g., the month of June) when all employees receive performance appraisals.

Company stock represents the total equity or worth of the company.

Company stock shares represent equity segments of equal value. Equity interest increases with the number of stock shares held.

Comparable worth represents an ongoing debate in society regarding pay differentials between men and women who perform similar but not identical work.

Compa-ratios index, the relative competitiveness of internal pay rates based on pay range midpoints.

Comparison systems, a type of performance appraisal method, require that raters (e.g., supervisors) evaluate a given employee's performance against other employees' performance attainments. Employees are ranked from the best performer to the poorest performer.

Compensable factors are job attributes (e.g., skill, effort, responsibility, and working conditions) that compensation professionals use to determine the value of jobs.

Compensation budgets are blueprints that describe the allocation of monetary resources to fund pay structures.

Compensation committees contain board of directors members within and outside a company. Compensation committees review executive compensation consultants' alternate recommendations for compensation packages, discuss the assets and liabilities of the recommendations, and recommend the consultant's best proposal to the board of directors for their consideration.

Compensation strategies describe the use of compensation practices that support HR and competitive strategies.

Compensation surveys involve the collection and subsequent analysis of competitors' compensation data.

Competency-based pay refers to two specific types of pay programs: pay-for-knowledge and skill-based pay.

Competitive advantage describes a company's success based on employees' efforts to maintain market share and profitability over several years.

Competitive strategy refers to the planned use of company resources—technology, capital, and human resources—to promote and sustain competitive advantage.

Compressed workweek schedules enable employees to perform their full-time weekly work obligations in fewer days than a regular 5-day workweek.

Concessionary bargaining focuses on unions promoting job security over large wage increases in negotiations with management.

Consolidated Omnibus Budget Reconciliation Act of 1985 (COBRA) was enacted to provide employees with the opportunity to continue receiving their employer-sponsored medical care insurance temporarily under their employer's plan if their coverage would otherwise cease due to termination, layoff, or other change in employment status.

Consultants (see independent contractors).

Consumer-driven health care refers to employer-sponsored programs that shift a greater amount of the responsibility to employees for selecting health care providers.

Consumer Price Index (CPI) indexes monthly price changes of goods and services that people buy for day-to-day living.

Contingent workers engage in explicitly tentative employment relationships with companies.

Contractors for the purposes of compensation-related laws, are businesses that provide services to the government (e.g., repair of public buildings).

Contrast errors occur when a rater (e.g., a supervisor) compares an employee to other employees rather than to specific explicit performance standards.

Contributory financing implies that the company and its employees share the costs for discretionary benefits.

Contributory pension plans require monetary contributions by the employee, who will benefit from the income upon retirement.

Copayments represent nominal payments individuals make for office visits to their doctors or for prescription drugs.

Core compensation describes the monetary rewards employees receive. There are six types of core compensation: base pay, seniority pay, merit pay, incentive pay, cost-of-living adjustments (COLAs), and pay-for-knowledge and skill-based pay.

Core employees possess full-time jobs, and they generally plan long-term or indefinite relationships with their employers.

Core hours, as applied to flextime schedule, are the hours when all workers must be present.

Core plus option plans establish a set of benefits (e.g., medical insurance), as mandatory for all employees who participate in flexible benefits plans.

Cost leadership strategy focuses on gaining competitive advantage by being the lowest-cost producer of a good or service within the marketplace, while selling the good or service at a price advantage relative to the industry average.

Cost-of-living adjustments (COLAs) represent periodic base pay increases that are based on changes in prices, as indexed by the Consumer Price Index (CPI). COLAs enable workers to maintain their purchasing power and standard of living by adjusting base pay for inflation.

coverage requirements limit an employer's freedom to exclude employees from qualified plans. Tests to determine whether coverage requirements are met include the ratio percentage test and the average benefit tests.

Critical incident technique (CIT), a specific kind of behavioral system, requires job incumbents and their supervisors to identify performance incidents—on-the-job behaviors and behavioral outcomes—that distinguish successful performance from unsuccessful performance. The supervisor then observes the employees and records their performance on these critical job aspects.

Cross-departmental models, a kind of pay-for-knowledge program, promote staffing flexibility by training employees in one department with some of the critical skills they would need to perform effectively in other departments.

Cross-functional skills information indicates developed capacities that facilitate performance of activities that occur across jobs.

Current profit sharing plans award cash to employees, typically on a quarterly or annual basis.

Davis–Bacon Act of 1931 established employment standards for construction contractors holding federal government contracts valued at more than $2,000. Such contractors must pay laborers and mechanics at least the prevailing wage in their local area.

Day care refers to programs that supervise and care for young children and elderly relatives when their regular caretakers are at work.

Death claims under workers' compensation are claims for deaths that occur in the course of employment or that are caused by compensable injuries or occupational diseases.

Deductible is the out-of-pocket expense that employees must pay before dental, medical, or vision insurance benefits become active.

Deferred compensation refers to an agreement between an employee and a company to render payments to an employee at a future date. Deferred compensation is a hallmark of executive compensation packages.

Deferred profit sharing plans place cash awards in trust accounts for employees. These trusts are set aside on employees' behalf as a source of retirement income.

Defined benefit plans guarantee retirement benefits specified in the plan document. This benefit usually is expressed in terms of a monthly sum equal to a percentage of a participant's preretirement pay multiplied by the number of years he or she has worked for the employer.

Defined contribution plans require that employers and employees make annual contributions to separate retirement fund accounts established for each participating employee, based on a formula contained in the plan document.

Dental insurance provides reimbursement for routine dental check-ups and particular corrective procedures.

Dental maintenance organizations deliver dental services through the comprehensive health care plans of many health maintenance organizations (HMOs) and preferred provider organizations (PPOs).

Dental service corporations owned and administered by state dental associations are nonprofit corporations of dentists.

Depth of knowledge refers to the level of specialization, based on job-related knowledge, an employee brings to a particular job.

Depth of skills refers to the level of specialization, based on skills, an employee brings to a particular job.

Dictionary of Occupational Titles (DOT) includes more than 20,000 private and public sector job descriptions. It has been replaced by the Standard Occupational Classification system.

Differentiation strategies focus on product or service development that is unique from those of its competitors. Differentiation can take many forms, including design or brand image, technology, features, customer service, or price.

Direct hire arrangements refer to companies' recruitment and selection of temporary workers without assistance from employment agencies.

Disability insured refers to an employee's eligibility to receive disability benefits under the Social Security Act of 1935. Eligibility depends on the worker's age and the type of disability.

Discount stock options, a kind of executive deferred compensation, entitle executives to purchase their companies' stock in the future at a predetermined price. Discount stock options are similar to nonstatutory stock options with one exception. Companies grant stock options at rates far below the stock's fair market value on the date the option is granted.

Discretionary benefits are benefits that employers offer at their own choice. These benefits fall into three broad categories: protection programs, pay for time not worked, and services.

Discretionary bonuses are awarded to executives on an elective basis by boards of directors. Boards of directors weigh four factors in determining discretionary bonus amounts: company profits, the financial condition of the company, business conditions, and prospects for the future.

Discretionary income covers a variety of financial obligations in the United States for which expatriates remain responsible.

Disparate impact represents unintentional employment discrimination. It occurs whenever an employer applies an employment practice to all employees, but the practice leads to unequal treatment of protected employee groups.

Disparate treatment represents intentional employment discrimination, occurring whenever employers intentionally treat some workers less favorably than others because of their race, color, sex, national origin, or religion.

Draw is a subsistence pay component (i.e., to cover basic living expenses) in sales compensation plans. Companies usually charge draws against commissions that sales professionals are expected to earn.

Dual employer common law doctrine establishes temporary workers' rights to receive workers' compensation. According to this doctrine, temporary workers are employees of both temporary employment agencies and the client companies. The written contract between the employment agency and the client company specifies which organization's workers' compensation policy applies in the event of injuries.

Early retirement programs contain incentives designed to encourage highly paid employees with substantial seniority to retire earlier than they planned. These incentives expedite senior employees' retirement eligibility and increase retirement income. In addition, many companies include continuation of medical benefits.

Economic Growth and Tax Relief Reconciliation Act of 2001 created tax benefits to individuals and companies in various ways (e.g., increasing the amount companies and employees can contribute to qualified retirement plans on a pretax basis).

Economic reality test helps companies determine whether employees are financially dependent on them.

Education, based on Equal Employment Opportunity Commission guidelines, refers to formal training.

Education information details prior educational experience required to perform in a job.

EEOC v. Chrysler, a district court ruling, deemed that early retirement programs are permissible when companies offer them to employees on a voluntary basis. Forcing early retirement upon older workers represents age discrimination.

EEOC v. Madison Community Unit School District No. 12 a circuit court ruling, shed light on judging whether jobs are equal based on four compensable factors: skill, effort, responsibility, and working conditions.

Employee assistance programs (EAPs) help employees cope with personal problems that may impair their job performance (e.g., alcohol or drug abuse, domestic violence, the emotional impact of AIDS and other diseases, clinical depression, and eating disorders).

Employee benefits include any variety of programs that provide paid time-off (e.g., vacation), employee services (e.g., transportation services), and protection programs (e.g., life insurance).

Employee Retirement Income Security Act of 1974 (ERISA) was established to regulate the establishment and implementation of various fringe compensation programs. These include medical, life, and disability insurance programs, as well as pension programs. The essence of ERISA is the protection of employee benefits rights.

Employee stock option plans represent one type of companywide incentives. Companies grant employees the right to purchase shares of company stock.

Employee stock ownership plans (ESOPs) may be the basis for a company's Section 401(k) plan, and these plans invest in company securities, making them similar to profit sharing plans and stock bonus plans, presumably when the value of stock has increased.

Employee-financed benefits mean that employers do not contribute to the financing of discretionary benefits.

Employee's anniversary date represents the date an employee began working for his or her present employer. Employees often receive performance appraisals on their anniversary dates.

Equal benefit or equal cost principle contained within the Older Workers Benefit Protection Act (OWBPA) requires employers to offer benefits to older workers of equal to or of greater value than the benefits offered to younger workers.

Equal Employment Opportunity Commission, a federal government agency, oversees and enforces various employment laws that guard against illegal discrimination including Title VII of the Civil Rights Act of 1964.

Equal Pay Act of 1963 requires that men and women should receive equal pay for performing equal work.

Equity theory suggests that an employee must regard his or her own ratio of merit increase pay to performance as similar to the ratio for other comparably performing people in the company.

Errors of central tendency occur when raters (e.g., supervisors) judge all employees as average or close to average.

Exchange rate is the price at which one country's currency can be swapped for another.

Executive branch enforces the laws of various quasi-legislative and judicial agencies and executive orders.

Executive compensation consultants propose recommendations to chief executive officers and board of director members for alternate executive compensation packages.

Executive Order 11141 prohibits companies holding contracts with the federal government from discriminating against employees on the basis of age.

Executive Order 11246 requires companies holding contracts (worth more than $50,000 per year and employing 50 or more employees) with the federal government to develop written affirmative action plans each year.

Executive Order 11478 prohibits employment discrimination on the basis of race, color, religion, sex, national origin, handicap, and age (401 FEP Manual 4061).

Executive Order 11935 prohibits employment of nonresidents in U.S. civil service jobs (401 FEP Manual 4121).

Executive orders influence the operation of the federal government and companies that are engaged in business relationships with the federal government.

Exempt refers to an employee's status regarding the overtime pay provision of the Fair Labor Standards Act of 1938 (FLSA). Administrative, professional, and executive employees are generally exempt from the FLSA overtime and minimum wage provisions.

Expatriates are U.S. citizens employed in U.S. companies with work assignments outside the United States.

Experience and training information describes specific preparation required for entry into a job plus past work experience contributing to qualifications for an occupation.

Experience rating system establishes higher contributions (to fund unemployment insurance programs) for employers with higher incidences of unemployment.

Extrinsic compensation includes both monetary and nonmonetary rewards.

Fair Labor Standards Act of 1938 (FLSA) addresses major abuses that intensified during the Great Depression and the transition from agricultural to industrial enterprises. These include substandard pay, excessive work hours, and the employment of children in oppressive working conditions.

Family and Medical Leave Act of 1993 (FMLA) requires employers to provide employees 12 weeks of unpaid leave per year in cases of family or medical emergency.

Family assistance programs help employees provide elder care and child care. Elder care provides physical, emotional, or financial assistance for aging parents, spouses, or other relatives who are not fully self-sufficient because they are too frail or disabled. Child care programs focus on supervising preschool-age–dependent children whose parents work outside the home.

Federal Employees' Compensation Act mandates workers' compensation insurance protection for federal civilian employees.

Federal government oversees the entire United States and its territories. The vast majority of laws that influence compensation were established at the federal level.

Federal Unemployment Tax Act (FUTA) specifies employees' and employers' tax or contribution to unemployment insurance programs required by the Social Security Act of 1935.

Fee-for-service plans provide protection for three types of medical expenses: hospital expenses, surgical expenses, and physician's charges.

Financial condition is an important consideration in the strategic analysis of a company's compensation program.

First-impression effect occurs when a rater (e.g., a supervisor) makes an initial favorable or unfavorable judgment about an employee and then ignores or distorts the employee's actual performance based on this impression.

Fiduciaries are individuals who manage employee benefits plans and pension plan funds.

Fiduciary responsibilities pertain to the management of employee benefits programs and pension plan funds.

Flat benefit formula in retirement plans designates either a flat dollar amount per employee (flat amount formula) or dollar amount based on an employee's compensation (flat percentage formula). Annual benefits are usually expressed as a percentage of final average wage or salary.

Flexible benefits plan allows employees to choose a portion of their discretionary benefits based on a company's discretionary benefits options.

Flexible scheduling and leave allows employees to take time off during work hours to care for relatives or react to emergencies.

Flextime schedules allow employees to modify work schedules within specified limits set by the employer.

Flexible spending accounts permit employees to pay for certain benefits expenses (e.g., childcare) with pretax dollars.

Forced distribution is a specific kind of comparison performance appraisal system in which raters (i.e., supervisors) assign employees to groups that represent the entire range of performance.

Foreign service premium is a monetary payment awarded to expatriates above their regular base pay.

Forfeitures are amounts from the accounts of employees who terminated their employment prior to earning vesting rights.

Formularies are lists of drugs proven to be clinically appropriate and cost effective. The basis for setting formularies varies for each insurance plan.

Freelancers (see independent contractors).

Free rider effect occurs when employees of lower ability, skill, and effort benefit equally as employees of higher ability, skill, and effort in group incentive plans. The free rider effect can lead to resentment and turnover of stronger contributors because weaker contributors are getting a "free ride."

Fully insured refers to an employee's status in the retirement income program under the Social Security

Act of 1935. Forty quarters of coverage lead to fully insured status.

Gain sharing describes group incentive systems that provide participating employees an incentive payment based on improved company performance, whether for increased productivity, increased customer satisfaction, lower costs, or better safety records.

General educational development (GED) refers to education of a general nature that contributes to reasoning development and to the acquisition of mathematical and language skills. The GED has three components: reasoning development, mathematical development, and language development.

Generalized work activities information describes general types of job behaviors occurring on multiple jobs.

General Schedule (GS) classifies federal government jobs into 15 classifications (GS-1 through GS-15), based on such factors as skill, education, and experience levels. In addition, jobs that require high levels of specialized education (e.g., a physicist), significantly influence public policy (e.g., law judges), or require executive decision making are classified in three additional categories: Senior level (SL), Scientific & Professional (SP) positions, and the Senior Executive Service (SES).

Golden parachutes, a kind of executive deferred compensation, provide pay and benefits to executives following their termination resulting from a change in ownership or corporate takeover.

Goods and services allowances compensate expatriates for the difference between goods and services costs in the United States and in the foreign post.

Government Employee Rights Act of 1991 protects U.S. Senate employees from employment discrimination on the basis of race, color, religion, sex, national origin, age, and disability (401 FEP Manual 851).

Graduated commissions increase percentage pay rates for progressively higher sales volume in a given period.

Great Depression refers to the period during the 1930s when many businesses failed and many workers became chronically unemployed.

Green circle rates represent pay rates for jobs that fall below the designated pay minimums.

Group incentive programs reward employees for their collective performance, rather than for each employee's individual performance.

Groupthink occurs when all group members agree on mistaken solutions because they share the same mindset and view issues through the lens of conformity.

Hardship allowance compensates expatriates for their sacrifices while on assignment.

Headquarters-based method compensates all employees according to the pay scales used at the headquarters.

Health Maintenance Organization Act of 1973 encouraged the use of HMOs as an alternative approach to delivering health care services.

Health maintenance organizations (HMOs) are sometimes described as providing "prepaid medical services" because fixed periodic enrollment fees cover HMO members for all medically necessary services, as long as the services are delivered or approved by the HMO. HMOs represent an alternative to commercial and self-funded insurance plans.

Health savings accounts (HSAs) are established by employers for employees as a source to cover eligible health care costs. Employees, employers, or both, may make contributions to fund these accounts.

High-deductible health insurance plans require substantial deductibles and low out-of-pocket maximums.

Home country–based pay method compensates expatriates the amount they would receive if they were performing similar work in the United States.

Home leave benefits enable expatriates to take paid time off in the United States.

Horizontal knowledge refers to similar knowledge (e.g., record keeping applied to payroll applications and record keeping applied to employee benefits).

Horizontal skills refer to similar skills (e.g., assembly skills applied to lawn mowers and assembly skills applied to snow blowers).

Host country-based methods compensate expatriates based on the host countries' pay scales.

Host country nationals (HCNs) are foreign national citizens who work in U.S. companies' branch offices or manufacturing plants in their home countries.

Hourly pay is one type of base pay. Employees earn hourly pay for each hour worked.

Housing and utilities allowances compensate expatriates for the difference between housing and utilities costs in the United States and in the foreign post.

Human capital refers to employees' knowledge and skills, enabling them to be productive (see also human capital theory).

Human capital theory states that employees' knowledge and skills generate productive capital known as human capital. Employees can develop knowledge and skills from formal education or on-the-job experiences.

Human resource strategies specify the particular use of HR practices to be consistent with competitive strategy.

Hypothetical tax is the U.S. income tax based on the same salary level, excluding all foreign allowances.

Illegal discriminatory bias occurs when a supervisor rates members of his or her race, gender, nationality, or religion more favorably than members of other classes.

Improshare is a specific kind of gain sharing program that rewards employees based on a labor hour ratio formula. A standard is determined by analyzing historical accounting data to find the number of labor hours needed to complete a product. Productivity is then measured as a ratio of standard labor hours and actual labor hours.

Incentive pay or variable pay is defined as compensation, other than base wages or salaries, that fluctuates according to employees' attainment of some standard (e.g., a preestablished formula, individual or group goals, or company earnings).

Incentive stock options entitle executives to purchase their companies' stock in the future at a predetermined price. The predetermined price usually equals the stock price at the time an executive receives the stock options. Incentive stock options entitle executives to favorable tax treatment.

Income annuities distribute income to retirees based on retirement savings paid to insurance companies in exchange for guaranteed monthly checks for life.

Indemnity dental insurance plans provide dental benefits, operating on the same basis as indemnity plans do for health insurance coverage.

Indemnity plans refer to traditional health insurance plans in which the insurance company agrees to pay a designated percentage of the costs for health insurance procedures and the insured (i.e., recipient of the insurance benefit) agrees to pay a designated percentage.

Independent contractors are contingent workers who typically possess specialized skills that are in short supply in the labor market. Companies select independent contractors to complete particular projects of short-term duration—usually a year or less.

Indexes of living costs abroad compare the costs (U.S. dollars) of representative goods and services (excluding education) expatriates purchase at the foreign location and the cost of comparable goods and services purchased in the Washington, DC, area. Companies use these indexes to determine appropriate goods and service allowances.

Individual incentive plans reward employees for meeting work-related performance standards (e.g., quality, productivity, customer satisfaction, safety, and attendance). Any one or a combination of these standards may be used.

Individual practice associations, a particular kind of HMO, are partnerships or other legal entities that arrange health care services by entering into service agreements with independent physicians, health professionals, and group practices.

Individualism–collectivism a dimension of national culture, is the extent to which individuals value personal independence versus group membership.

Industry represents the narrowest (i.e., the most specific) classification of an industry within the North American Industry Classification System.

Industry group is the fourth broadest classification of industries within the North American Industry Classification System.

Industry profiles describe such basic industry characteristics as sales volume, the impact of relevant government regulation on competitive strategies, and the impact of recent technological advances on business activity.

Inflation is the increase in prices for consumer goods and services. Inflation erodes the purchasing power of currency.

Injury claims, under workers' compensation, are claims for disabilities that have resulted from accidents (e.g., falls, injuries from equipment use, or physical strains from heavy lifting).

Interests represent individuals' liking or preference for performing specific jobs.

Inpatient benefits are covered expenses associated with hospital stays.

Interindustry wage differentials represent the pattern of pay and benefits associated with characteristics of industries. Interindustry wage differentials can be attributed to a number of factors, including the industry's product market, the degree of capital intensity, and the profitability of the industry.

Internally consistent compensation systems clearly define the relative value of each job among all jobs within a company. This ordered set of jobs represents the job structure or hierarchy. Companies rely on a simple, yet fundamental, principle for building internally consistent compensation systems: Jobs that require greater qualifications, more responsibilities, and more complex duties should be paid more highly than jobs that require lesser qualifications, fewer responsibilities, and less complex job duties.

Intrinsic compensation reflects employees' psychological mind-sets that result from performing their jobs.

Involuntary part-time employees work fewer than 35 hours per week because they are unable to find full-time employment.

Involuntary terminations are initiated by companies for a variety of reasons, including poor job performance, insubordination, violation of work rules, reduced business activity due to sluggish economic conditions, or plant closings.

IRC Section 901 allows expatriates to credit foreign income taxes against their U.S. income liability.

IRC Section 911 permits eligible expatriates to exclude as much as $70,000 of foreign-earned income from taxation, plus a housing allowance.

Job analysis is a systematic process for gathering, documenting, and analyzing information in order to describe jobs.

Job-based pay compensates employees for jobs they currently perform.

Job characteristics theory describes the critical psychological states that employees experience when they perform their jobs (i.e., intrinsic compensation). According to job characteristics theory, employees experience enhanced psychological states when their jobs rate high on five core job dimensions: skill variety, task identity, task significance, autonomy, and feedback.

Job content refers to the actual activities that employees must perform in the job. Job content descriptions may be broad, general statements of job activities or detailed descriptions of duties and tasks performed in the job.

Job control unionism refers to a union's success in negotiating formal contracts with employees and establishing quasi-judicial grievance procedures to adjudicate disputes between union members and employers.

Job descriptions summarize a job's purpose and list its tasks, duties, and responsibilities, as well as the skills, knowledge, and abilities necessary to perform the job at a minimum level.

Job duties, a section in job descriptions, describes the major work activities and, if pertinent, supervisory responsibilities.

Job evaluation systematically recognizes differences in the relative worth among a set of jobs and establishes pay differentials accordingly.

Job sharing is a special kind of part-time employment agreement. Two or more part-time employees perform a single full-time job.

Job summary a statement contained in job descriptions, summarizes the job based on two to four descriptive statements.

Job titles, listed in job descriptions, indicate job designations.

Job-content evaluation, an approach to evaluating job worth, takes skill, effort, responsibility, and working conditions into account.

Job-point accrual model, a type of pay-for-knowledge program, provides employees opportunities to develop skills and learn to perform jobs from different job families.

Judicial branch refers to the organization of the federal government that interprets laws.

Just-meaningful pay increase refers to the minimum pay increase that employees will see as making a substantial change in compensation.

Key employees, as defined by the Internal Revenue Service, includes any employee who is an officer of the employer during the current year that has an annual compensation greater than $135,000 (indexed for inflation in increments of $5,000), a 5 percent owner of the employer, or a 1 percent owner of the employer with an annual compensation from the employer of more than $150,000.

Knowledge based on Equal Employment Opportunity Commission guidelines, refers to a body of information applied directly to the performance of a function.

Knowledge information describes organized sets of principles and facts applying in general domains.

Labor hour ratio formula, used in determining the payouts in Improshare plans, refers to a standard determined by analyzing historical accounting data to find the number of labor hours needed to complete a product. Productivity is then measured as a ratio of standard labor hours and actual labor hours.

Labor market assessments are part of the strategic analysis and focus on describing the current and anticipated supply and demand of workers.

Lease companies employ qualified individuals and place them in client companies on a long-term, presumably "permanent" basis. Lease companies place employees within client companies in exchange for fees.

Legally required benefits are protection programs that attempt to promote worker safety and health, maintain family income streams, and assist families in crisis. The key legally required benefits are mandated by the following laws: the Social Security Act of 1935, various state workers' compensation laws, and the Family and Medical Leave Act of 1993.

Legislative branch refers to the organization of the federal government in which Congress passes and enacts laws.

Leniency errors occur when raters (e.g., supervisors) appraise an employee's performance more highly than it really rates, compared with objective criteria.

Licensing information describes licenses, certificates, or registrations that are used to identify levels of skill or performance relevant to occupations.

Life insurance protects employees' families by paying a specified amount to employees' beneficiaries upon employees' deaths. Most policies pay some multiple of the employees' salaries.

Line employees are directly involved in producing companies' goods or service delivery. Assembler, production worker, and sales employee are examples of line jobs.

Local governments refer to municipal or county-level organizations that provide public services and ensure that the rights of citizens and employees are upheld in accordance with pertinent laws and regulations.

Longevity pay systems reward with permanent additions to base pay those employees who have reached pay grade maximums and who are not likely to move into higher pay grades.

Longshore and Harborworkers' Compensation Act mandates workers' compensation insurance protection for maritime workers.

Long-term disability insurance provides income benefits for extended periods of time, between 6 months and life.

Lorance v. AT&T Technologies, a Supreme Court case, limited employees' rights to challenge the use of seniority systems to only 180 days from the system's implementation date.

Lowest-cost strategy (see cost leadership strategy).

Managed care plans emphasize cost control by limiting an employee's choice of doctors and hospitals. These plans also provide protection against health care expenses in the form of prepayment to health care providers.

Management by objectives (MBO), a goal-oriented performance appraisal method, requires that supervisors and employees determine objectives for employees to meet during the rating period, and then employees appraise how well they have achieved their objectives.

Management incentive plans award bonuses to managers who meet or exceed objectives based on sales, profit, production, or other measures for their division, department, or unit.

Mandatory bargaining subjects are issues that employers and unions must bargain on if either constituent makes proposals about them.

Mail order prescription drug programs dispense expensive medications used to treat chronic health conditions.

Major occupational groups refer to the 23 broad classifications of similar jobs in the Standard Occupational Classification system.

Market lag policy distinguishes companies from the competition by compensating employees less than most competitors. Lagging the market indicates that pay levels fall below the market pay line.

Market lead policy distinguishes companies from the competition by compensating employees more highly than most competitors. Leading the market denotes pay levels above the market pay line.

Market match policy most closely follows the typical market pay rates because companies pay according to the market pay line. Thus, pay rates fall along the market pay line.

Market pay line is representative of typical market pay rates relative to a company's job structure.

Market-based evaluation an approach to job evaluation, uses market data to determine differences in job worth.

Market-competitive pay systems represent companies' compensation policies that fit the imperatives of competitive advantage.

Masculinity–femininity, a dimension of national culture, refers to whether masculine or feminine values are dominant in society. Masculinity favors material possessions. Femininity encourages caring and nurturing behavior.

McNamara–O'Hara Service Contract Act of 1965 requires that all federal contractors employing service workers must pay at least the minimum wage as specified in the FLSA. In addition, contractors holding contracts with the federal government that exceed $2,500 in value must pay the local prevailing wages and offer fringe compensation equal to the local prevailing benefits.

Mean is a measure of central tendency calculated as the sum of numbers (e.g., annual salaries in the marketing department) divided by the number of salaries.

Median is the middle value in an ordered sequence of numerical data.

Medical reimbursement plans reimburse employees for some or all of the cost of prescription drugs. These plans pay benefits after an employee has met an annual deductible for the plan.

Medicare serves nearly all U.S. citizens aged 65 or older by providing insurance coverage for hospitalization, convalescent care, and major doctor bills. The Medicare program includes four separate features: Medicare Part A or compulsory hospitalization insurance; Medicare Part B, or voluntary supplementary medical insurance; Medigap, voluntary supplemental insurance to fill in the gaps for Parts A and B, Medicare Advantage, new choices in health care providers; and Medicare Prescription Drug Benefit, coverage for prescription drug medication.

Medicare Advantage refers to a variety of health insurance coverage options for individuals eligible for Medicare protection who choose not to participate in Parts A and B. It is informally referred to as Medicare Part C.

Medicare Prescription Drug Improvement and Modernization Act of 2003 led to changes in the Medicare program by adding prescription drug coverage and recognizing health savings accounts (HSAs).

Medicare Select plans are Medigap policies that offer lower premiums in exchange for limiting the choice of health care providers.

Medigap insurance supplements Medicare Part A and Part B coverage and is available to Medicare recipients in most states from private insurance companies for an extra fee.

Merit pay increase budget limits the amount of pay raises that can be awarded to employees for a specified time period. A merit pay increase budget is expressed as a percentage of the sum of employees' current base pay.

Merit pay programs reward employees with permanent increases to base pay according to differences in job performance.

Midpoint pay value is the halfway mark between the range minimum and maximum rates. Midpoints represent the competitive market rate determined by the analysis of compensation survey data.

Mobility premiums reward employees for moving from one assignment to another.

Morbidity tables express annual probabilities of the occurrence of health problems. Insurance companies generally set insurance rates higher as the probability of death or the occurrence of health problems increases.

Mortality tables indicate yearly probabilities of death based on such factors such age and sex established by the Society of Actuaries. Insurance companies rely on these tables in the underwriting process.

Multiple payer system refers to a system in which there is more than one party responsible for covering the cost of health care, including the government, employers, labor unions, employees, or individuals not currently employed (e.g., retirees, the unemployed, and employees whose employer does not pay for health care coverage).

Multiple tiers specify copayment amounts an individual will pay for a specific prescription.

Multiple-tiered commissions increase percentage pay rates for progressively higher sales volume in a given period only if sales exceed a predetermined level.

National Compensation Survey is a U.S. Bureau of Labor Statistics program that comprehensively describes pay and benefits information in U.S. companies.

National culture refers to the set of shared norms and beliefs among individuals within national boundaries who are indigenous to that area.

National industry, in the NAICS system, refers to the national level detail necessary for economic statistics in an industry classification.

National Labor Relations Act of 1935 (NLRA) establishes employees' rights to bargain collectively with employers on such issues as wages, work hours, and working conditions.

Negative halo effect occurs when a rater (e.g., a supervisor) generalizes an employee's negative behavior on one aspect of the job to all aspects of the job.

Noncash incentives complement monetary sales compensation components. Such noncash incentives as contests, recognition programs, expense reimbursements, and benefits policies can encourage sales performance and attract sales talent.

Noncontributory financing implies that the company assumes total costs for discretionary benefits.

Noncontributory pension plans do not require employee contributions to fund retirement income.

Nonexempt refers to an employee's status regarding the overtime pay provision of the Fair Labor Standards Act of 1938 (FLSA). Employees whose jobs do not fall into particular categories (i.e., administrative, professional, and executive employees) are generally covered by overtime and minimum wage provisions.

Nonqualified plans are welfare and pension plans that do not meet various requirements set forth by the Employee Retirement Income Security Act of 1974 (ERISA), disallowing favorable tax treatment for employee and employer contributions.

Nonrecoverable draws act as salary because sales employees are not obligated to repay the loans if they do not sell enough.

Nonrecurring merit increases or merit bonuses are lump sum monetary awards based on employees' past job performances. Employees do not continue to receive nonrecurring merit increases every year. Employees must instead earn them each time.

Nonstatutory stock options, a kind of executive deferred compensation, entitles executives to purchase their companies' stock in the future at a predetermined price. The predetermined price usually equals the stock price at the time an executive receives the stock options. Nonstatutory stock options do not entitle executives to favorable tax treatment.

North American Free Trade Agreement (NAFTA) became effective on January 1, 1994. NAFTA has two main goals. First, NAFTA was designed to reduce trade barriers among Mexico, Canada, and the United States. Second, NAFTA also set out to remove barriers to investment among these three countries.

North American Industry Classification System (NAICS), codes represent keys to pertinent information for strategic analyses. The NAICS codes generally contain five digits, representing the sector (first two digits), subsector (the first three digits), industry group (first four digits), and the industry (all five digits).

North American Industry Classification System Manual classifies industries based on the NAICS.

Occupational disease claims are workers' compensation claims for disabilities caused by ailments associated with particular industrial trades or processes.

Occupational Information Network (O*NET) is a database designed to describe jobs in the relatively new service sector of the economy and to more accurately describe jobs that evolved as the result of technological advances. O*NET replaces the *Revised Handbook for Analyzing Jobs*.

Occupation characteristics information describes labor market information, occupational outlook, and wages.

Occupation-specific requirements information describes the characteristics of a particular occupation. These particular requirements are occupational skills, knowledge, tasks, duties, machines, tools, and equipment.

Older Workers Benefit Protection Act (OWBPA), the 1990 amendment to the ADEA, indicates that employers can require older employees to pay more than younger employees for health care insurance coverage. This practice is permissible when older workers collectively do not make proportionately larger contributions than the younger workers.

On-call arrangements are a method for employing temporary workers.

O*NET database (see Occupational Information Network [O*NET]).

Operating requirements encompass all HR programs.

Organizational and product life cycles describe the evolution of company and product change using human life cycle stages. Much like people are born, grow, mature, decline, and die, so do companies, products, and services. Business priorities, including human resources, vary with life cycles.

Organizational context information indicates the characteristics of the organization that influence how people do their work.

Out-of-pocket maximum provisions in medical insurance plans limit the total dollar expenditure a beneficiary must pay during any plan year. This provision is most common in commercial medical insurance plans.

Outplacement assistance refers to company-sponsored technical and emotional support to employees who are being laid off or terminated.

Paid time off represents discretionary employee benefits (e.g., vacation time) that provide employees time off with pay.

Paired comparison, a variation of simple ranking job evaluation plans, orders all jobs from lowest to highest based on comparing the worth of each job in all possible job pairs. Paired comparison also refers to a specific kind of comparison method for appraising job performance. Supervisors compare each employee to every other employee, identifying the better performer in each pair.

Part A refers to compulsory hospitalization insurance under Medicare.

Part B refers to voluntary supplementary medical insurance under Medicare.

Part C refers to a broad variety of health care choices under Medicare.

Pay compression occurs whenever a company's pay spread between newly hired or less-qualified employees and more-qualified job incumbents is small.

Pay grades group jobs for pay policy application. Human resource professionals typically group jobs into pay grades based on similar compensable factors and value.

Pay ranges represent the span of possible pay rates for each pay grade. Pay ranges include midpoint, minimum, and maximum pay rates. The minimum and maximum values denote the acceptable lower and upper bounds of pay for the jobs within particular pay grades.

Pay structures represent pay rate differences for jobs of unequal worth and the framework for recognizing differences in employee contributions.

Pay-for-knowledge plans reward managerial, service, or professional workers for successfully learning specific curricula.

Pension programs provide income to individuals throughout their retirement. Companies sometimes use early retirement programs to reduce workforce size and trim compensation expenditures.

Percentiles describe dispersion by indicating the percentage of figures that fall below certain points. There are 100 percentiles ranging from the first percentile to the one-hundredth percentile.

Performance appraisal describes an employee's past performance and serves as a basis to recommend how to improve future performance.

Performance-contingent bonuses, awarded to executives, are based on the attainment of such specific performance criteria as market share.

Perks (see perquisites).

Permissive bargaining subjects are those subjects on which neither the employer nor the union is obligated to bargain.

Perquisites are benefits offered exclusively to executives (e.g., country club memberships).

Person-focused pay plans generally reward employees for acquiring job-related competencies, knowledge, or skills rather than for demonstrating successful job performances.

Phantom stock, a type of executive deferred compensation, is an arrangement whereby boards of directors compensate executives with hypothetical company stock rather than actual shares of company stock. Phantom stock plans are similar to restricted stock plans because executives must meet specific conditions before they can convert these phantom shares into real shares of company stock.

Piecework plan, an individual incentive pay program, rewards employees based on their individual hourly production against an objective output standard, determined by the pace at which manufacturing equipment operates. For each hour, workers receive piecework incentives for every item produced over the designated production standard. Workers also receive a guaranteed hourly pay rate regardless of whether they meet the designated production standard.

Plan termination rules are specifications set forth by the Pension Benefit & Guaranty Corporation regarding the discontinuation of an employer's defined benefit pension plan.

Point method represents a job-content evaluation technique that uses quantitative methodology. Quantitative methods assign numerical values to compensable factors that describe jobs, and these values are summed as an indicator of the overall value for the job.

Portal-to-Portal Act of 1947 defines the term hours worked that appears in the FLSA.

Positive halo effect occurs when a rater (e.g., a supervisor) generalizes employees' positive behavior on one aspect of the job to all aspects of the job.

Poverty threshold represents the minimum annual earnings needed to afford housing and other basic necessities. The federal government determines these levels each year for families of different sizes.

Power distance, a dimension of national culture, is the extent to which people accept a hierarchical system or power structure in companies.

Predetermined allocation bonuses, awarded to executives, are based on a fixed formula. Company profits are often the main determinant of the bonus amounts.

Pre-existing conditions apply to all health insurance plans. These are conditions for which medical advice, diagnosis, care, or treatment was received or recommended during the 6-month period preceding the beginning of coverage.

Preferred provider organizations (PPOs) are select groups of health care providers that provide health care services to a given population at a higher level of reimbursement than under commercial insurance plans.

Pregnancy Discrimination Act of 1978 (PDA) is an amendment to Title VII of the Civil Rights Act of 1964. The PDA prohibits disparate impact discrimination against pregnant women for all employment practices.

Premium is the amount of money an individual or company pays to maintain insurance coverage.

Prepaid group practices, a specific type of HMO, provide medical care for a set premium, rather than a fee-for-service basis.

Prescription card programs operate like HMOs by providing prepaid benefits with nominal copayments for prescription drugs.

Prescription drug plans cover the costs of drugs that state or federal laws require be dispensed by licensed pharmacists.

Probationary period is the initial term of employment (usually less than 6 months) during which companies attempt to ensure that they have made sound hiring decisions. Employees are often not entitled to participate in discretionary benefits programs during their probationary periods.

Production plan (see piecework plan).

Profit sharing plans pay a portion of company profits to employees, separate from base pay, cost-of-living adjustments, or permanent merit pay increases. Two basic kinds of profit sharing plans are used widely today: current profit sharing and deferred profit sharing.

Protection programs are either legally required or discretionary employee benefits that provide family benefits, promote health, and guard against income loss caused by such catastrophic factors as unemployment, disability, or serious illnesses.

Qualified pension plans entitle employers to tax benefits from their contributions to pension plans. This gen-erally means that employers may take current tax deductions for contributions to fund future retirement income.

Quarters allowance is the U.S. Department of State term for housing and utilities allowances.

Quarters of coverage refers to each 3-month period of employment during which an employee contributes to the retirement income program under the Social Security Act of 1935.

Quartiles allow compensation professionals to describe the distribution of data, usually annual base pay amount, based on four groupings.

Range spread is the difference between the maximum and the minimum pay rates of a given pay grade.

Rating errors in performance appraisals reflect differences between human judgment processes versus objective, accurate assessments uncolored by bias, prejudice, or other subjective, extraneous influences.

Recertification ensures that employees periodically demonstrate mastery of all the jobs they have learned.

Recoverable draws act as company loans to employees that are carried forward indefinitely until employees sell enough (i.e., earn a sufficient amount in commissions) to repay their draws.

Red circle rates represent pay rates that are higher than the designated pay range maximums.

Referral plans are individual incentive pay plans that reward employees for referring new customers or recruiting successful job applicants.

Regression analysis describes the linear relationship between two variables (i.e., simple regression) or between the linear composite of multiple variables and one other variable (i.e., multiple regression).

Rehabilitation Act mandates that federal government agencies take affirmative action in providing jobs for individuals with disabilities (401 FEP Manual 325).

Relevant labor markets represent the fields of potentially qualified candidates for particular jobs.

Reliable job analysis yields consistent results under similar conditions.

Relocation assistance payments cover expatriates' expenses to relocate to foreign posts.

Repatriation is the process of making the transition from an international assignment and living abroad to a domestic assignment and living in the home country.

Rest and relaxation benefits provide expatriates assigned to hardship locations with paid time off. Rest and relaxation leave benefits differ from standard vacation benefits because companies designate where expatriates may spend their time.

Restricted stock, a type of executive deferred compensation, requires that executives do not have any ownership control over the disposition of the stock for a predetermined period, often 5 to 10 years.

Right to control test helps companies determine whether their workers are employees or independent contractors.

Risk-of-loss rules (alternatively, **uniform coverage requirement**) require that employers make the full amount of benefits and coverage elected under a flexible spending account (FSA) plan available to employees from the first day the plan becomes effective regardless of how much money an employee has actually contributed.

Rucker Plan is a particular type of gain sharing program that emphasizes employee involvement. Gain sharing awards are based on the ratio between value added (less the costs of materials, supplies, and services rendered) and the total cost of employment.

Salary is one type of base pay. Employees earn salaries for performing their jobs, regardless of the actual number of hours worked. Companies generally measure salary on an annual basis.

Salary-only plans are specific types of sales compensation plans. Sales professionals receive fixed-base compensation, which does not vary with the level of units sold, increase in market share, or any other indicator of sales performance.

Salary-plus-bonus plans are specific types of sales compensation plans. Sales professionals receive fixed base compensation, coupled with a bonus. Bonuses are usually single payments that reward employees for achievement of specific, exceptional goals.

Salary-plus-commission plans are particular types of sales compensation plans. Sales professionals receive fixed base compensation and commission.

Sales value of production (SVOP) is the sum of sales revenue plus the value of goods in inventory. This is part of the equation to determine payout amounts in Scanlon gain sharing plans.

Scanlon Plan is a specific type of gain sharing program that emphasizes employee involvement. Gain sharing awards are based on the ratio between labor costs and sales value of production.

Scientific management practices promote labor cost control by replacing inefficient production methods with efficient production methods.

Sector is the broadest classification of industries within the North American Industry Classification System (NAICS).

Securities and Exchange Commission (SEC) is a non-partisan, quasi-judicial federal government agency with responsibility for administering federal securities laws.

Securities Exchange Act of 1934 applies to the disclosure of executive compensation.

Selection is the process HR professionals employ to hire qualified candidates for job openings.

Self-funded insurance plans are similar to commercial insurance plans with one key difference: Companies typically draw from their own assets to fund claims when self-funded.

Self-insured dental plans are similar to fee-for-service dental plans, except companies fund payment for dental procedures themselves.

Seniority pay systems reward employees with permanent additions to base pay periodically, according to employees' length of service performing their jobs.

Services represent discretionary employee benefits that provide enhancements to employees and their families (e.g., tuition reimbursement and day care assistance).

Severance pay usually includes several months of pay following involuntary termination and, in some cases, continued coverage under the employer's medical insurance plan. Employees often rely on severance pay to meet financial obligations while searching for employment.

Short-term disability insurance provides income benefits for limited periods of time, usually less than 6 months.

Similar-to-me effect refers to the tendency on the part of raters (e.g., supervisors) to judge employees favorably that they perceive as similar to themselves.

Simple ranking plans specific methods of job evaluation, order all jobs from lowest to highest according to a single criterion (e.g., job complexity or the centrality of the job to the company's competitive strategy).

Single-payer system refers to health care system in which the government regulates the health care and uses taxpayer dollars to fund health care such as in Canada and some other economically developed countries. Single-payer systems are often referred to as universal health care systems because the government ensures that all of its citizens have access to quality health care regardless of ability to pay.

6-year graduated schedule allows workers to become 20 percent vested after 2 years and to vest at a rate of 20 percent each year thereafter until they are 100 percent vested after 6 years of service.

Skill, based on Equal Employment Opportunity Commission guidelines, refers to an observable competence to perform a learned psychomotor act.

Skill (knowledge) blocks are sets of skills (knowledge) necessary to perform a specific job (e.g., typing skills versus analytical reasoning) or group of similar jobs (e.g., junior accounting clerk, intermediate accounting clerk, and senior accounting clerk).

Skill-based pay, used mostly for employees who do physical work, increases these workers' pay as they master new skills.

Skills blocks model, a kind of pay-for-knowledge program, applies to jobs from within the same job family. Just as in the stair-step model, employees progress to increasingly complex jobs; however, skills do not necessarily build on each other in a skill blocks program.

Small group incentive plans reward groups of individuals with financial awards when a specific objective is met.

Smoking cessation plans are particular types of wellness programs that stress the negative aspects of smoking and can include intensive programs directed at helping individuals to stop smoking.

Social comparison theory provides an explanation for executive compensation determination based on the tendency for the board of directors to offer executive compensation packages that are similar to those in peer companies.

Social Security Act of 1935 established three main types of legally required benefits: unemployment insurance, retirement income and benefits for dependents, and medical insurance (Medicare).

Spillover effect refers to nonunion companies' offer of similar compensation to similar compensation as offered by union companies to their employees. The goal is to reduce the likelihood that nonunion workforces will seek union representation.

Staff employees support the functions performed by line employees. Human resources and accounting are examples of staff functions.

Stair-step model, a type of pay-for-knowledge program, resembles a flight of stairs. The steps represent jobs from a particular job family that differs in terms of complexity. Skills at higher levels build upon previous lower-level skills.

Standard deviation refers to the mean distance of each salary figure from the mean (i.e., how larger observations fluctuate above the mean and how small observations fluctuate below the mean).

Standard Occupational Classification System (SOC) describes 23 major occupational groups. It replaces the *Dictionary of Occupational Titles*.

State governments enact and enforce laws that pertain exclusively to their respective regions (e.g., Illinois and Michigan).

Stock appreciation rights, a type of executive deferred compensation, provides executives income at the end of a designated period, much like restricted stock options; however, executives never have to exercise their stock rights to receive income. The company simply awards payment to executives based on the difference in stock price between the time the company granted the stock rights at fair market value to the end of the designated period, permitting the executives to keep the stock.

Stock compensation plans are companywide incentive plans that grant employees the right to purchase shares of company stock.

Stock options describe an employee's right to purchase company stock.

Straight commission is based on a fixed percentage of the sales price of the produce or service.

Strategic analysis entails an examination of a company's external market context and internal factors. Examples of external market factors include industry profile, information about competitors, and long-term growth prospects. Internal factors encompass financial condition and functional capabilities (e.g., marketing and human resources).

Strategic decisions support business objectives.

Strategic management entails a series of judgments, under uncertainty, that companies direct toward achieving specific goals.

Stress management is a specific kind of wellness program designed to help employees cope with many factors inside and outside their work that contribute to stress.

Strictness errors occur when raters (e.g., supervisors) judge employee performance to be less than what it is when compared against objective criteria.

Subsector is the second broadest classification of industries within the North American Industry Classification System (NAICS).

Summary Compensation Table discloses compensation information for CEOs and the four most highly paid executives during a 3-year period employed by companies whose stock is traded on public stock exchanges. The information in this table is presented in tabular and graphic forms to make information more accessible to the public.

Supplemental life insurance protection represents additional life insurance offered exclusively to executives. Companies design executives' supplemental life insurance protection to increase the value of executives' estates, bequeathed to designated beneficiaries (usually family members) upon their death and to provide greater benefits than standard plans usually allow.

Supplemental retirement plans, offered to executives, are designed to restore benefits restricted under qualified plans.

Supplemental unemployment benefit (SUB) refers to unemployment insurance that is usually awarded to individuals who were employed in cyclical industries. This benefit supplements unemployment insurance that is required by the Social Security Act of 1935.

Tactical decisions support competitive strategy.

Target plan bonuses, awarded to executives, are based on executives' performance. Executives do not receive bonuses unless their performance exceeds minimally acceptable standards.

Tax equalization is one of two approaches (the other is tax protection) to provide expatriates tax allowances. Employers take the responsibility for paying income taxes to the U.S. and foreign governments on behalf of the expatriates.

Tax protection is one of two approaches (the other is tax equalization) to provide expatriates tax allowances.

Employers reimburse expatriates for the difference between the actual income tax amount and the hypothetical tax when the actual income tax amount—based on tax returns filed with the Internal Revenue Service—is greater.

Team-based incentives (see small group incentive plans).

Telecommuting represents alternative work arrangements in which employees perform work at home or some other location besides the office.

Temporary employment agencies place individuals in client companies as employees on a temporary basis.

Term coverage is a type of life insurance that provides protection to an employee's beneficiaries only during the insured person's employment.

Third country nationals (TCNs) are foreign national citizens who work in U.S. companies' branch offices or manufacturing plants in foreign countries—excluding the United States and their home countries.

Time-and-motion studies analyzed the time it took employees to complete their jobs. Factory owners used time-and-motion studies and job analysis to meet this objective.

Title I of the Americans with Disabilities Act of 1990 (ADA) requires that employers provide "reasonable accommodation" to disabled employees. Reasonable accommodation may include such efforts as making existing facilities readily accessible, job restructuring, and modifying work schedules.

Title VII of the Civil Rights Act of 1964 indicates that it shall be an unlawful employment practice for an employer to discriminate against any individual with respect to compensation, terms, conditions, or privileges of employment because of such individual's race, color, religion, sex, or national origin.

Top-heavy provisions apply to minimum benefits accrual and vesting rights. Plans are said to be top-heavy if the accrued benefits or account balances for key employees exceed 60 percent of the accrued benefits or account balances for all employees.

Tournament theory provides an explanation for executive compensation determination based on substantially greater competition for high-ranking jobs. Lucrative chief executive compensation packages represent the prize to those who win the competition by becoming chief executives.

Trait systems, a type of performance appraisal method, requires raters (e.g., supervisors or customers) to evaluate each employee's traits or characteristics (e.g., quality of work, quantity of work, appearance, dependability, cooperation, initiative, judgment, leadership responsibility, decision-making ability, and creativity).

Transportation services represent energy-efficient ways to transport employees to and from the workplace. Employers cover part or all of the transportation costs.

Tuition reimbursement programs promote employees' education. Under a tuition reimbursement program, an employer fully or partially reimburses an employee for expenses incurred for education or training.

Two-tier pay structures reward newly hired employees less than established employees on either a temporary or permanent basis.

Uncertainty avoidance, a dimension of national culture, represents the method by which society deals with risk and instability for its members.

Unit benefit formulas recognize length of service in retirement plans. Employers typically decide to contribute a specified dollar amount per years worked by an employee. They may also choose to contribute a specified percentage amount per years of service.

Universal compensable factors, based on the Equal Pay Act of 1963, include skill, effort, responsibility, and working conditions.

Usual, customary, and reasonable charges are defined as being not more than the physician's usual charge, within the customary range of fees charged in the locality, and reasonable, based on the medical circumstances. Commercial insurance plans generally do not pay more than this amount.

Value added is the difference between the value of the sales price of a product and the value of materials purchased to make the product. This is part of the equation to determine payout amounts in Rucker gain sharing plans.

Variable pay (see incentive pay).

Variation represents the amount of spread or dispersion in a set of data.

Vertical knowledge refers to knowledge traditionally associated with supervisory activities (e.g., performance appraisal and grievance review procedures).

Vertical skills are those skills traditionally considered supervisory skills (e.g., scheduling, coordinating, training, and leading others).

Vesting refers to employees' acquisition of nonforfeitable rights to pension benefits.

Vietnam Era Veterans Readjustment Assistance Act applies the principles of the Rehabilitation Act to veterans with disabilities and veterans of the Vietnam War (401 FEP Manual 379).

Vision insurance provides reimbursement for routine optical check-ups and particular corrective procedures.

Voluntary part-time employees choose to work fewer than 35 hours per regularly scheduled workweek.

Wage (see hourly pay).

Wagner–Peyser Act established a federal–state employment service system.

Walling v. A. H. Belo Corp., a Supreme Court ruling, requires that employers guarantee fixed weekly pay when the following conditions prevail: The employer typically cannot determine the number of hours employees will work each week, and the workweek period fluctuates both above and below 40 hours per week.

Walsh–Healey Public Contracts Act of 1936 mandates that contractors with federal contracts meet guidelines regarding wages and hours, child labor, convict labor, and hazardous working conditions. Contractors must observe the minimum wage and overtime provisions of the FLSA. In addition, this act prohibits the employment of individuals younger than 16 and convicted criminals. Furthermore, it prohibits contractors from exposing workers to any conditions that violate the Occupational Safety and Health Act.

Wearaway occurs when some (usually older) employees do not accrue benefits for a period of time following conversion of a defined benefit plan to a cash balance plan, whereas other (usually younger) employees do not experience an interruption in accruing benefits.

Weight control and nutrition programs, a particular type of wellness program, are designed to educate employees about proper nutrition and weight loss, both of which are critical to good health.

Welfare practices were generous endeavors undertaken by some employers, motivated to minimize employees' desire to seek union representation, to promote good management, and to enhance worker productivity.

Wellness programs promote employees' physical and psychological health.

Whole life insurance is a type of life insurance that provides protection to employees' beneficiaries during employees' employment and into the retirement years.

Work context information describes physical and social factors that influence the nature of work.

Work Hours and Safety Standards Act of 1962 requires that all contractors pay employees one-and-one-half times their regular hourly rate for each hour worked in excess of 40 hours per week.

Worker requirements represent the minimum qualifications and skills that people must have to perform a particular job. Such requirements usually include education, experience, licenses, permits, and specific abilities such as typing, drafting, or editing.

Worker specification a section in job descriptions, lists the education, skills, abilities, knowledge, and other qualifications individuals must possess to perform the job adequately.

Workers' compensation refers to state-run insurance programs that are designed to cover medical, rehabilitation, and disability income expenses resulting from employees' work-related accidents.

Working conditions are the social context or physical environment where work will be performed.

Working condition fringe benefits refer to the work equipment (e.g., computer) and services (e.g., an additional telephone line) employers purchase for telecommuters' use at home.

Work styles are personal characteristics that describe important interpersonal and work style requirements in jobs and occupations.

Author Index

Subject Index